The Dark Past

The US Supreme Court and African Americans, 1800–2015

WILLIAM M. WIECEK

OXFORD
UNIVERSITY PRESS

Oxford University Press is a department of the University of Oxford.
It furthers the University's objective of excellence in research, scholarship,
and education by publishing worldwide. Oxford is a registered trade mark of
Oxford University Press in the UK and in certain other countries.

Published in the United States of America by Oxford University Press
198 Madison Avenue, New York, NY 10016, United States of America.

© Oxford University Press 2024

All rights reserved. No part of this publication may be reproduced,
stored in a retrieval system, or transmitted, in any form or by any means,
without the prior permission in writing of Oxford University Press,
or as expressly permitted by law, by license or under terms agreed with
the appropriate reprographics rights organization. Inquiries concerning
reproduction outside the scope of the above should be sent to
the Rights Department, Oxford University Press, at the address above.

You must not circulate this work in any other form
and you must impose this same condition on any acquirer

Library of Congress Cataloging-in-Publication Data
Names: Wiecek, William M., author.
Title: The dark past : the US Supreme Court and African Americans,
1800–2015 / William M. Wiecek.
Description: New York : Oxford University Press, [2024] |
Includes bibliographical references and index.
Identifiers: LCCN 2024026009 (print) | LCCN 2024026010 (ebook) |
ISBN 9780197654439 (hardback) | ISBN 9780197654453 (epub)
Subjects: LCSH: African Americans—Legal status, laws, etc.—History. |
African Americans—Legal status, laws, etc.—History—Cases. |
African Americans—Civil rights—History. | African Americans—Civil rights—Cases |
Race discrimination—Law and legislation—United States—History. |
Segregation—Law and legislation—United States—History. |
Affirmative action programs—Law and legislation—United States—History. |
United States. Supreme Court—History.
Classification: LCC KF4757 .W49 2024 (print) | LCC KF4757 (ebook) |
DDC 342.7308/73—dc23/eng/20240614
LC record available at https://lccn.loc.gov/2024026009
LC ebook record available at https://lccn.loc.gov/2024026010

DOI: 10.1093/9780197654460.001.0001

Sheridan Books, Inc., United States of America

For Judy, always

Contents

Acknowledgments   ix
Prologue: The Supreme Court and Racial Inequality in American History   xi

1. The Supreme Court and Slavery, 1800–1860   1
2. Reconstruction and the Supreme Court, 1862–1880   45
3. Redemption, 1880–1900   87
4. The Nadir and the Blue Hour, 1900–1920   121
5. Civil Rights and Civil Liberties between the Wars, 1920–1940   148
6. War and Cold War, 1941–1953   180
7. The Second Reconstruction, 1954–1971   210
8. Right Turn, 1960–1980   259
9. The Resegregation of America's Schools   295
10. The Death of Affirmative Action   343
11. Redemption Redux, 1972–2015   370
    Epilogue: "The Gloomy Past"   426

Notes   435
Suggested Reading   519
Index   523

Acknowledgments

This book has been a long time in the making. Throughout its lengthy gestation, I have accumulated debts, and now I can finally express my gratitude.

Since taking emeritus status at my academic home, Syracuse University College of Law, I have enjoyed the opportunity to teach at other law schools: the University of California, Davis; the University of Kentucky; Arizona State University; Pacific McGeorge, as well as Syracuse. The deans at these schools (particularly Kevin Johnson and Vikram Amar at Davis, David Brennen at Kentucky, Doug Sylvester at ASU) and their colleagues have warmly welcomed me as a temporary colleague. In particular I thank Dean Brennen and Associate Dean Mary Davis at Kentucky for the extraordinary amount of time and resources they committed to hosting the symposium "Structural Racism: Inequality in America Today," in February 2011, which Dr. Judy Hamilton and I organized as part of my responsibilities as the inaugural Lassiter Distinguished Visiting Professor there. I was also privileged to serve as the inaugural presenter at Transylvania University in Lexington, Kentucky, for the John Marshall Harlan Lecture Series, named after one of Transy's most distinguished alumni, the first Justice Harlan, who figures so prominently in this book. Thanks to the generous support of Dr. Owen Williams, then President of the University, and his colleagues, I was able to explore Harlan's role in the legal world of the nineteenth century in the warm ambience of his alma mater.

I twice participated in the summer workshops on slavery hosted by Sterling Professor of History David W. Blight of Yale in 2007 and 2008. These extraordinary conclaves enabled luminaries in slavery scholarship to exchange ideas in the congenial atmosphere of Yale's Department of History under the auspices of the Gilder Lehrman Institute of American History. This book is to some extent a product of my interactions with the participants at those seminars. We are all in David's debt. I similarly benefited from the opportunity to join Dr. James Oakes, Distinguished Professor at the Graduate Center of the City University of New York, in leading a summer research seminar on the Fourteenth Amendment for junior historians under the joint auspices of the Institute for Constitutional History and the

x ACKNOWLEDGMENTS

Stanford Constitutional Law Center, offered in the summer of 2016 at the Stanford Law School. Earlier, I partnered with Professor Dennis Hutchinson of the University of Chicago to direct a predecessor Institute for Constitutional Studies seminar in 2000 at the Federal Judicial Center in Washington, DC. The world of constitutional scholarship owes an incalculable debt to Dr. Maeva Marcus, Director of the Institute, for her tireless work over the past three decades in promoting the study and teaching of American constitutional history. She is the guiding spirit behind these wonderful scholarly and pedagogical gatherings. I thank the Supreme Court Historical Society for the opportunity to reevaluate conservative constitutionalism as part of a lecture series in 2007–2008 on the Supreme Court in the Gilded Age.

I salute public libraries throughout the United States as institutions vital to our future as a democratic republic. Beginning with the Fleet Branch of the Cleveland, Ohio Public Library, the place where as a child I encountered the world opened up by books, I have throughout my life benefited from the resources at these centers of our democratic communities. Parts of this book were written in the public libraries of La Grange, Kentucky, Salina, Kansas, and Scottsdale, Arizona. I gratefully recall their welcoming hospitality to an out-of-town stranger.

My greatest debt is to Dr. Judy Hamilton, who has spent countless hours discussing structural racism and other kinds of inequality in America with me. She has generously shared her own research on structural racism. This book would not have been written without her support. We are partners in life as well as in scholarship.

Prologue

The Supreme Court and Racial Inequality in American History

Racial injustice has been an enduring constant of Americans' historical experience. Considered historically, racial inequality is a defining feature of American national character, and one of its most important. It has been there since the beginning in 1619, and it remains powerful today. To ignore it, deny it, or wish it away only perpetuates it. Slavery, the most extreme form of racial inequality, remains at the center of the American national narrative. The inequality that derives from slavery has been confirmed by the US Supreme Court in hundreds of decisions over two centuries. Occasionally the Court's judgments have affirmed the rights and dignity of African Americans, but more often the Court has disappointed their hopes.

The story told here of Black Americans and the Court unfolds within historical frameworks that lend coherence to what could otherwise be a disjointed chronicle of cases. This historical overview offers an interpretive guide that helps us make sense of the whole of our past. It confirms the pattern aptly described by the legal scholar Michelle Alexander: "a cycle of racial reform, backlash and re-formation of systems of racial and social control." A long view of racial inequality in America reveals what Alexander calls "predictable cycles of racial progress, retrenchment and rebirth of caste-like systems that have defined our racial history since slavery."[1]

Over the past four centuries, the relationship of inequality between white and Black Americans evolved through three major phases. From the first encounter of English people with Africans in North America in 1619 until 1865, the dominant legal structure of white-Black relations was slavery, a system of total racial inequality. Then from the end of slavery in 1865 to the mid-twentieth century, a regime of what this study labels "servitude" replaced the formal structure of slavery. Servitude was a racial order that preserved the two principal features of the earlier slave society, race control and forced labor, but without the claim to own human beings. The dictionary definitions of the word confirm the popular senses of subjection to a master and lack of personal freedom.[2] It provides a useful one-word designation for the twilight state that lies between the totality of slavery before it, and the end of de jure inequality that began in 1954. As servitude deteriorated in the twentieth century, it segued into a third racial regime, referred to here as "structural racism," which describes our present moment. In this latest iteration of inequality, the formal legal codes of racial subordination have been replaced by a structure of de facto inequality based on the systemic duality of white advantage and Black subordination.

For America's first two centuries, slavery determined all racial relations. At some indistinct time a generation after the first appearance of Africans, Virginia legal records began to reflect the civil status of most Blacks as lifelong unfreedom passed on by mothers to their children.[3] Until 1865, when the legal regime of slavery came to a cataclysmic end, the relationship between the two races was one of near-absolute inequality. African Americans, as Chief Justice Roger B. Taney declared in the *Dred Scott* case of 1857, were "so inferior . . . that they had no rights which the white man was bound to respect."[4] If equality had a temperature, it would have been near zero Kelvin.

The two-century run of slavery was succeeded by a brief interlude that lasted about fifteen years, in which the American nation attempted to make some progress toward racial equality. We know this era as Reconstruction. It lasted from 1863 through 1877. Republican Congresses in that period, frustrated by southern white racial intransigence, progressed from abolishing slavery (1862–1865), to creating a civic status for the freedpeople[5] (in the 1866 Civil Rights Act), to mandating a constitutional guarantee of citizenship and equality (by the Fourteenth Amendment, ratified in 1868), to ensuring the right to vote free of racial discrimination (by the Fifteenth Amendment, ratified in 1870), to policing the political restoration of government in the seceded states (by the Military Reconstruction[6] and Enforcement Acts of 1870–71[7]), to ensuring access to public accommodations (in the 1875 Civil Rights Act). As the southern states returned to the Union, they adopted similar measures. But Reconstruction died a premature political death after 1877, strangled in its cradle, and was interred by the US Supreme Court during the next two decades.

The nation then entered a successor phase of unfreedom, referred to here as "servitude." From the end of Reconstruction until 1954, white Americans imposed on their Black fellow-citizens a legal, political, social, and economic status that reinstated the core functions of slavery, race control and labor coercion. Historians, borrowing a term current in the 1870s, refer to this era of inequality as "Redemption."[8] The prevailing constitutional motif of the time was nominal equality, a system of white supremacy and Black oppression that functioned behind a mask of pretended equality. Its principal features were Jim Crow segregation and political disfranchisement. In this seventy-five-year period, southern whites stripped African Americans of all political power, imposed residential apartheid (the foundation of all other forms of inequality in America today), and confined Blacks to menial labor that kept most of them an impoverished rural peasantry. The equal protection clause was a dead letter, and the ideal of equal justice under law a mockery, as southern courts assured a steady supply of unfree workers to provide convict labor and to man chain gangs. Jim Crow reigned supreme. Black Americans touched the nadir of their historical experience at the turn of the twentieth century.

By the 1920s, the frozen hell of Servitude began to thaw, imperceptibly at first, then accelerating in the 1930s and 1940s, as the Supreme Court cautiously edged back toward an earlier aspirational ideal of equality. When the Court handed down its epochal decision in *Brown v. Board of Education I* in 1954, the Civil Rights Era dawned. Historians refer to this period as the second Reconstruction,[9] since the nation again attempted to realize the ideal of equality before the law. Congress enacted far-reaching measures banning racial discrimination in the Civil Rights Acts of 1964 (public accommodations, employment), 1965 (voting), and 1968 (housing). In the fifteen-year period that ended around 1970, the Supreme Court moved in tandem with Congress's initiatives, groping intuitively toward resolving the impacts by which race distorted American life.

But the second Reconstruction ended as did the first, after only a decade and a half, ushering in the third era of inequality, which some liken to a second Redemption.[10] The constitutional aspirations of the civil rights era were overridden by a third racial regime, referred to here as "structural racism," in which the formal, explicit legal structures of racial discrimination are being discarded, but the underlying social and economic realities of dominance and subordination endure for many African Americans. In this period, structural racism took the place of overt racism to again frustrate Black equality and opportunity. It preserves the kinder, gentler form of white supremacy that sociologists refer to as white privilege.[11] In this latest period, the Supreme Court has disavowed the integrationist ideal of *Brown v. Board of Education I* (1954) and strangled affirmative action programs.

White advantage endures, while a large part of the African American population continues to languish in poverty and systemic inequality. To be sure, the justices of the US Supreme Court ritualistically deplore overt forms of racism today, but those have been receding until recently. While the Court piously beats the dying horse of explicit Jim Crow racism, it shores up protections for the dominant forms of non-intent-based racism and limits the ability of other agencies—Congress, the states, and non-governmental entities—to eradicate the social structures of inequality.

A timeline may be helpful to follow the narrative of this study. It identifies distinct periods that characterize the Supreme Court's encounter with African Americans over the past two centuries. Each of these periods had a defining quality that captures the Court's reaction to prevalent forms of racial inequality at that time.

1801–1850: Avoidance. Through the first half of the nineteenth century, the Court managed to avoid involvement with the slavery controversies of the era.[12] Few cases came before it that required it to resolve some burning issue posed by slavery. There were such issues aplenty, of course, but those were resolved legislatively by Congress or the state legislatures. Slavery as the era's dominant expression of racial inequality went unquestioned, except by African Americans and their white abolitionist allies. The Supreme Court managed to settle specific controversies that came before it by circumspect avoidance without deranging the political dynamics or temporary equilibriums of the slavery controversies.

1850–1860: the slaveholders' constitution. In this fatal decade, the Supreme Court upheld and implemented what may be called "the slaveholders' constitution."[13] Abandoning their earlier discretion, a majority of the justices interpreted the Constitution in ways meant to assure slavery's absolute security where it existed and to support its expansion into the western territories and into the free states themselves. This cemented the domination of what contemporaries called the Slave Power. Racial inequality was overt, absolute, and sanctioned by law. The Court's recklessness produced the constitutional disaster of *Dred Scott* (1857).

1861–1877: Reconstruction. In the period we know as Reconstruction, Congress and the American people revised the Constitution substantively, abolishing slavery and laying the foundations for a new social order based on equality among citizens. Congress overthrew the antebellum state-centered constitutional order and assumed broad new powers for itself and the federal courts to assure equality. For the first time, African Americans, now free and citizens, could claim the privileges and immunities derived from that citizenship, as well as the equal protection of the laws. But in the *Slaughterhouse Cases* (1873), the Supreme Court nullified those changes, falling back on a pre-war understanding of the federal system.

1877–1890: Redemption. By a reactionary counterrevolution that some southerners called Redemption, southern whites stymied, then reversed, the egalitarian gains of Reconstruction. They began to impose a social regime of Jim Crow segregation and racial inequality throughout the South. The Supreme Court crushed the egalitarian potential of Reconstruction and approved all segregationist innovations. To take the place of slavery, the Justices affirmed a regime of racial inequality based on segregation and racial discrimination. In the *Civil Rights Cases* (1883), the Court minimized Congress's power to assure equality under the Reconstruction Amendments.

1890–1910: the Nadir. Redemption crushed racial equality in a culmination of Jim Crow that is known as the nadir of Black experience. In this period, the Supreme Court upheld the program of separate-but-equal and ratified the disfranchisement of Black voters. Racial segregation became pervasive and absolute. White terrorist violence enforced legal inequality. *Plessy v. Ferguson* (1896) confirmed this regressive regime of inequality.

1910–1954: Jim Crow wobbles. After World War I, the Supreme Court began to relent in its support for segregation and discrimination. It curbed a few of the worst excesses of the Redemption legal order and began challenging some aspects of segregation. Glacial social change throughout the nation began to thaw the ice-bound inequality of Jim Crow. *United States v. Carolene Products* (1938) foretold a much different constitutional order, marked by greater protections for the rights of African Americans.

1954–1972: the second Reconstruction. The Civil Rights Era, inaugurated by *Brown v. Board of Education I* (1954), began the overthrow of segregation imposed by law and state action. Americans saw this period as a second Reconstruction. Congress enacted expansive legislation to realize the potential of the Civil War Amendments, while the Supreme Court approved a broad agenda of equality.

1972–present: the second Redemption. But then the Court abandoned its support for racial justice, bringing the civil rights era to a close. Regressive judicial doctrines halted further progress in dismantling discrimination in housing and employment. *Washington v. Davis* (1976) injected the destructive purpose/impact distinction into civil rights doctrine, and *Shelby County v. Holder* (2015) hobbled the Voting Rights Act. The Court ratified, and even imposed, educational inequality in the nation's public schools. Critics have labelled this period as the second Redemption, where the Court again acts behind a thin veneer of formal equality to sustain racially disparate outcomes throughout American society. Judicial doctrine assures that structural racism preserves white advantage and Black inequality.

* * * * *

The titles of this book and of the Epilogue are taken from "Lift Every Voice and Sing," written by James Weldon Johnson and known as the Black National Anthem:

> Lift every voice and sing,
> till earth and heaven ring,
> Ring with the harmonies of liberty;
> Let our rejoicing rise, high as the listening skies,
> Let it resound loud as the rolling sea.
> Sing a song full of faith that the dark past has taught us,
> Sing a song full of hope that the present has brought us;
> Facing the rising sun of our new day begun,
> Let us march on till victory won.
>
> Stony the road we trod, bitter the chastening rod,
> Felt in the days when hope unborn had died;
> Yet with a steady beat,
> have not our weary feet,
> Come to the place for which our fathers sighed?
> We have come over a way that with tears has been watered,
> We have come, treading our path through the blood of the
>   slaughtered;
> Out from the gloomy past, till now we stand at last
> Where the white gleam of our star is cast.[14] [third stanza
>   omitted]

I am uncomfortably aware that this book considers the experiences only of African Americans. A complete study of the Court's confrontation with racism would take into account all people of color—Native Americans, Asians, Latino/as.[15] And it would have to include that other racial group, Americans of European descent, and their experience of the advantages that come with being white.[16] All these racial groups have their own histories in the United States, and their own distinctive experiences of oppression. But to incorporate those histories would result in a book more than twice the size of this one, and tell a story, or rather, stories, so complex that the narrative would become confusing, and analysis dissipated.

The experience of African Americans has been unique. True, the native peoples were despoiled of their lands and culture and marked for extermination or at least extinction as a matter of deliberate government policy. The Chinese were brutalized; Japanese Americans were herded into concentration camps. Latino people experienced forced labor and treatment no less violent. But only Black Americans suffered the ultimate degradation of slavery and its successive surrogates. This book takes note of Supreme Court decisions involving other people of color where those cases spawned doctrines that impacted African Americans. But this remains a history of Black Americans' encounter with the US Constitution, as mediated through the opinions of the Supreme Court.

I must acknowledge a second constraint: except for a part of chapter 5, this study does not survey the vast domains of substantive criminal law and procedure, and of the carceral state that that criminal process has produced.[17] Again, this omission is necessary because the topic is so sprawling that its inclusion would double the size of this book. Constitutional criminal procedure is a world unto itself, and I must leave it to others to explore its historical dimensions.

1
The Supreme Court and Slavery, 1800–1860

When the American people, in the name of liberty, proclaimed their independence from Great Britain, one in five of them was an enslaved African American.[1] Only one in a hundred Black people was free ("Free colored," the census of 1790 called them); the rest were held in slavery. Nearly all of them lived in the states south of Pennsylvania. But slavery as a legal institution existed in all the new states except the republic of Vermont, which became a state in 1791. Massachusetts, along with its daughter-colony Maine, rid itself of slavery as a result of freedom suits and other legal actions throughout the 1790s that were brought under the Massachusetts Constitution of 1780.[2] Within a generation, gradual emancipation was underway in all the states north of Maryland.[3] Congress excluded slavery from the broad domains of the Northwest Territory by the Northwest Ordinance of 1787.[4] But otherwise, the United States was a "slaveholding republic,"[5] a "slaveholders' union."[6]

Before 1865, slavery was the legal institution that defined the status of most African Americans. It obliterated almost every civil right that they might claim. Slavery was not created by law, either in the British mainland colonies or in the states after Independence. It evolved out of indefinite forms of unfreedom, under which some people were compelled to labor for others and were not free to walk away. By 1690, the mainland British colonies had begun codifying their scattered enactments regulating these unfree people. South Carolina took the lead, adopting as its 1690 slave code earlier codifications from the British island colony of Barbados. By a century later, slavery existed under the sanction of law everywhere in the new republics unless and until it was abolished by a particular state.[7] Though law did not create the system of slavery, by the antebellum period an extensive body of common and statutory law in the states regulated it pervasively.[8]

Because slavery permeated the new nation, the federal Constitution of 1787 protected slavery directly in three provisions that confirmed its existence, but without referring to it by its proper name. Instead, the framers resorted to euphemisms or circumlocutions: "three fifths of all other Persons";[9] "Person held to Service or Labour";[10] and "Migration or Importation of such Persons."[11] A dozen other provisions of the Constitution protected slavery indirectly in various ways, by, for example, prohibiting taxes on exports or providing for federal assistance in putting down insurrections.[12]

This led the nineteenth-century abolitionist William Lloyd Garrison to denounce the US Constitution in 1845 as a "covenant with death" and "an agreement with hell."[13] His colleague Wendell Phillips elaborated on that critique in the same year in his influential polemic *The Constitution a Proslavery Compact* (1845).[14] In the twentieth century, some historians picked up this theme and amplified the Garrison/Phillips critique, providing a neo-Garrisonian interpretation of slavery's role in the constitutional order.[15] Other scholars have emphatically rejected the neo-Garrisonian view of the Constitution as a pro-slavery document,[16] insisting that the framers took "every step possible to make certain that the Constitution excluded property in man, [and] rendered slavery a wholly local institution, the creature entirely of state laws." They "left room for the new federal government to hinder slavery's expansion."[17] In this view, the framers had made regrettable but necessary concessions to the existence of slavery in the southern states. But the authentic spirit of the Constitution, its "genius," as contemporaries would have called it,[18] anticipated that slavery would eventually disappear, somehow. Both sides of this scholarly debate concur that slavery was, in the words of one of the debate's participants, "the nemesis of the Constitution,"[19] exacting inexorable retribution for the crime of enslavement. Or, to change the simile, slavery was the witch at the christening in European fairy tales, blighting by its curse the auspices of the new republic.[20]

John Marshall and the Supreme Court over which he presided from 1801 to 1835 had a profound impact on so many issues and doctrines of constitutional law: federalism, the separation of powers, the authority of Congress, the scope of the commerce clause, judicial power, the place of the states in the Union, the balance of governmental regulatory power versus individual liberty.[21] So we might have assumed that the Marshall Court would have a comparable impact on slavery, race, and African American people, especially when the institution of slavery underwent an explosive growth phase after 1815 when cotton culture expanded into the fertile southwest.

But the decisions of the Marshall Court involving race and slavery were relatively inconsequential, compared to what came after: they were few, sporadic, and of little political resonance. Their principal significance two centuries later is that they serve as a foil for comparisons with the Taney Court (1836–1864). In contrast to its successor, the Marshall Court moved cautiously and circumspectly in this area, avoiding momentous decisions involving slavery, sensitive to the consequences of its holdings, constrained by a heightened sense of the limits on its power. With due regard for the political touchiness of the subject, Marshall and his colleagues took care to steer clear of the constitutional Scylla lurking abeam. When constitutional issues involving slavery had to be confronted before 1835 at the federal level, it was Congress, not the Court, that resolved them.

Marshall and his colleagues shared beliefs about slavery, race, and the place of African Americans in American society like those of most of their white fellow citizens.[22] By 1815 a consensus had formed among white Americans that comprised some basic beliefs.

Slavery in the United States might be regrettable, but it was a necessary evil that had to be endured, at least for the time being, simply because no one could come up with a feasible, realistic way of getting rid of it altogether.[23] There were two principal obstacles to abolishing slavery: first, it was an essential element in the economies of the southern states, more in some (slave societies like Georgia and the Carolinas),[24] less in others (Maryland, Delaware); and second, what was to be done with the people held in slavery if they were all suddenly—or even gradually—freed? This early consensus faded in the slave states by 1820 as the cotton gin opened up the interior South to cultivation of short-staple cotton and international demand for the region's monoculture export boomed. The enslavement of African Americans became essential to American economic growth and the development of a mature capitalist economy. The export of monoculture staples—sugar, tobacco, cotton, and later rice—drove capitalist development.[25] Slavery was the necessary form of labor organization for each of those staples. So, after 1830 the necessary-evil apology ceded place to the "positive good" thesis propounded by southern radicals like John C. Calhoun: far from being an evil, slavery was a benefit to both races, a positive good, not a regrettable necessity.

The international slave trade, on the other hand, was an evil to be extirpated. Congress outlawed it at the earliest possible moment,[26] but subsequent enforcement by the navy's Africa Squadron was sporadic at best, and always underfunded.[27] Smuggling brought in a regular infusion of new Black bodies from the Caribbean, and to a far lesser extent from Africa. The interstate slave trade (including the waterborne riverine and coastal trade), however, was protected and even encouraged. It was essential for regional economies to move the growing surplus of enslaved people[28] in the upper South to the new lands of Alabama and Mississippi, where their labor was urgently in demand.[29]

Slavery and the enslaved population were becoming more regionalized after 1800. As Black population growth stabilized in the upper South, African American people become concentrated south of the Potomac and the Ohio Rivers. Meanwhile the northern states were implementing programs of gradual abolition. Slavery died out abruptly in Massachusetts, was banned from the outset in Vermont and the Northwest Territory, and was gradually eliminated by apprenticeship schemes for postnati elsewhere.[30] Black populations were small in most of the free or becoming-free states. These trends led to the potentially dangerous situation where the white population of the North could enjoy the luxury of condemning slavery at no cost to themselves since it was someone else's problem, while sustaining racial discrimination in their own backyard with a clear conscience.[31]

Despite its pervasive global importance,[32] slavery appeared more and more anomalous to northerners as the nineteenth century wore on. Status, in Henry Sumner Maine's influential aperçu, was ceding place to contract: "the movement of the progressive societies has been a movement from status to contract."[33] Unfree labor systems were giving way to free-labor regimes. Indentured servitude for whites was nearly extinct by 1800, while apprenticeship became voluntaristic, rather than being the servile status of unlucky youths in the colonial period.[34] The Married Women's Property Acts accorded legal agency to married women beginning in the 1840s. But at the same time, many whites came to regard people of African descent in their midst as a foreign element in the population, visibly distinct, unassimilable. Thus, just as Blacks were a people apart because of their skin color, so they also appeared to be egregious in their status: mostly unfree and subject to discrimination even where free.

Race seemed to be an obvious and visible characteristic in American society. The people of African descent (and Native Americans as well) were visibly distinct from people of European descent by physiognomy, skin color, and culture (language, accent, dialect). Until recently, white Americans assumed that race was natural, a function of biology and genetics. Biological destiny assigned not only physiognomy (skin pigmentation, hair, facial features) but probably intelligence as well, plus other emotional and cultural characteristics. Because it was natural, race was innate in all people and immutable. Race, in a word, was real. This was not just a matter of observable scientific fact. No less an authority than God himself (or at least Moses, Joshua, and the prophet Jeremiah) testified to this. "Can the Ethiopian change his skin, or the leopard his spots?"[35] Enslavement and degradation followed from race: "And [Noah] said, Cursed be Canaan [the son of Ham]; a servant of servants shall he be unto his brethren."[36] "Now therefore ye are cursed, and there shall none of you be freed from being bondmen, and hewers of wood and drawers of water for the house of my God."[37] In the Protestant society of the nineteenth-century United States, this was a powerful validation.

Race was a signifier of merit and a determinant of a person's proper place in society. Whites believed that the relation between them on one hand and Blacks and Indians on the other was properly one of dominance and subordination. The ideal of equality must remain the exclusive prerogative of white males only. Most whites believed that African Americans, whatever their individual capabilities, civic status (free vs. enslaved), or potential, were at that time collectively a backward people, lacking the skills necessary to function as independent, self-reliant members of civil society.[38]

Slavery might have been theoretically incompatible with the foundational premises of the American Republic, as they were expressed in the Declaration of Independence and most of the state constitutions. But at the same time, it was an existing reality. Later, in the 1840s, two small but influential abolitionist sects would reach diametrically opposite conclusions about this incompatible presence. One, those aligned with the views of abolition's patriarch, William Lloyd Garrison, agreed that the Constitution coddled slavery. Garrison accordingly renounced allegiance to it, refused to vote or hold office, advocated secession by the free states, and in one dramatic incident in 1854, burned a copy of the Constitution in Boston Common to demonstrate his repudiation.[39] Another utopian group of politically oriented abolitionists insisted, on the contrary, that because the word "slavery" did not appear in the document, the Constitution did not recognize slavery and in fact assumed its universal illegitimacy. Both these views were outliers and attracted the support of no more than a handful of committed citizens in the North.[40] Americans almost unanimously accepted the fact that for better or worse the Constitution recognized and protected slavery in at least three particulars: the three-fifths clause, the slave trade (until 1807), and fugitives.

Some small steps might be taken to ameliorate slavery's harsher aspects for enslaved people, but its stubborn and expanding presence could not be wished away by magical thinking, no matter how offensive it was to the purity of American ideals. As North Carolina's chief judge, Thomas Ruffin, unforgettably put it in his despairing lament in *State v. Mann* (1829),[41] "the power of the master must be absolute, to render the submission of the slave perfect. I most freely confess my sense of the harshness of this proposition, I feel it as deeply as any man can. And as a principle of moral right, every person in his retirement must repudiate it. But in the actual condition of things, it must be so. There is no remedy. This discipline belongs to the state of slavery."

When white Americans did give some thought to the problem of what to do about Black people as they became individually emancipated, a widely favored solution was colonization. The American Colonization Society, founded in 1816, promoted voluntary resettlement of free Blacks in Africa, specifically, in the Afro-American colony of Liberia.[42] The society enjoyed support in Virginia and throughout the North, because anxious whites saw it as a way of "draining off," as Henry Clay put it, a segment of the Black population that could not be integrated into white society and that posed a danger to the security of slavery. Colonization's would-be beneficiaries, African American people, adamantly opposed it, insisting that America was their true and only homeland.[43]

Finally, Americans after 1787 shared a consensus on the place of slavery in the American constitutional order. In line with the general early understanding of American federalism, they believed that Congress lacked power to do anything about slavery, except in the one explicitly specified matter of the international slave trade (Art. I § 9), and inferentially in the matter of fugitive slaves (Art. IV, § 3).[44] Aside from those two issues, slavery was exclusively within the constitutional power of the states. (I have elsewhere referred to this understanding as the "federal consensus.")[45] Any other congressional action respecting slavery would violate the basic compact that lay at the foundation of the union. This consensus began to fray after 1830.

The Marshall Court, 1801–1835: Prudent Avoidance

It might be possible to explain Supreme Court adjudication, both doctrine and social consequences, by extensive study of the public and private writings of all the justices, plus those who influenced them, integrated into a history of their times. This is not that study. Rather, this book focuses on judicial doctrines that emerged from the major cases that affected the status, rights, and opportunities of African American people since the nation's founding. Given that emphasis, biographies of individual justices become less important than the cases themselves. Yet we cannot ignore entirely the men (and in the last few decades, the women) who wrote those opinions. The justices were not equally important for the development of doctrine. Nearly half were obscure or unimportant, or for whatever reason contributed little besides their vote to the outcome of the decisions. A few, on the other hand, were influential in shaping doctrine, for better or worse. This study will note the contributions of those few judges and evaluate their influence. The vignettes of individual justices that appear throughout this study reflect either of those characteristics. For the others, biographic encyclopedias provide mostly factual information about the judges.[46]

Chief Justice John Marshall came to the Court in 1801 with a distinguished record of public service. He had no formal schooling when he enlisted in the Continental Army in 1776. He served for four years, then studied law with Chancellor George Wythe at the College of William and Mary. He practiced law and served in the Virginia legislature and in its 1788 ratifying convention. His army service had left him a convinced nationalist, a supporter of the federal Constitution, and a Federalist. He represented the United States in a diplomatic mission to France, served briefly in Congress and as secretary of state, and was nominated by President John Adams to be chief justice in 1801.

As both a "southern paternalist" (in his role as urban slaveowner) and "conservative nationalist" in his views of the Union, Marshall as a jurist was tugged in inconsistent directions when confronted with slavery or race questions.[47] Prudence always won out, though: he studiously avoided wading into the political controversies attendant on all slavery litigation. He was himself a slaveholder who bought and sold enslaved men and women throughout his life.[48] He did not sell them off to the Deep South, as his colleague Bushrod Washington did,[49] nor was he known to order them whipped or to advertise for runaways, as Thomas Jefferson had. (And he did not father children with one of his female chattels, as Jefferson likewise did.)[50] He did not free any of the men and women he "owned," even by will.[51] He never condemned slavery itself, but he did worry about its potential for disrupting the Union. When slavery was not directly at issue, Marshall occasionally went so far as to affirm the humanity of an enslaved person. For example, in *Boyce v. Anderson* (1829)[52] the question presented was whether an enslaved man who was drowned in a steamboat accident should be considered a passenger or as cargo for purposes of the common carrier's liability (if a passenger, the carrier would be liable only for gross negligence; if cargo, ordinary negligence). Holding that enslaved people were "intelligent beings" and "living men," Marshall declared that he was a passenger, not the equivalent of a bale of cotton. But this small concession to the humanity of the victim carried little weight when Marshall and his colleagues thought that the security of the slave system might be imperiled.

Throughout his service on the Court, Marshall feared the divisive potential of slavery and its threat to the Union.[53] Writing of the abolition of slavery in the French island colonies during the French Revolution, which led to what southerners invariably referred to as "the horrors of Santo Domingo," Marshall condemned abolition as a "malignant philosophy" and an "abstract system" that pursued "some fancied untried good." "The revolutionists of France formed the mad and wicked project of spreading their doctrines of equality among persons, between whom distinctions and prejudices exist to be subdued only by the grave."[54] Paul Finkelman concludes that "Marshall always supported slavery and consistently opposed liberty. [He] shaped the law in favor of human bondage."[55] In addition, Marshall and his colleagues tried to erect a facade of "judicial objectivity" around their slavery-related decisions to forestall partisan attacks by President Thomas Jefferson and Congress.[56]

As a Virginian, Marshall also worried about the difficulties that would follow widespread emancipation. He supported colonization as a practical but only partial solution to the problem of slavery. Both he and Bushrod Washington were active members of the American Colonization Society from its founding in 1816, Washington long serving as its national president, and Marshall as president of a local chapter. For him, colonization was a partial and ambiguous solution to what he saw as several of the problems posed by slavery, chiefly a growing free Black population. "Voluntary emigration will reliève [sic] us from our free coloured people." "The whole union would be strengthened by it."[57] But he was not optimistic: deportation "is attended with such difficulties as to impress despair rather than hope on the minds of those who take a near view of the subject."[58]

William Johnson of South Carolina, who served as associate justice from 1804 to 1834, almost conterminously with Marshall, was a special case.[59] Himself a slaveholder, Johnson had no sympathy for abolition, which he denounced as fanatical. Like his contemporaries, he considered slavery a national evil, but one that could not be abolished unless an economically superior labor system could replace it. South Carolinians, in reaction to the abortive 1822 Denmark Vesey rebellion, enacted the first Negro Seamen's Act, which required that any free Black seaman coming into a South Carolina harbor be imprisoned while his ship remained in port. If his ship left without him, he was to be sold into slavery.[60] In *Elkison v. Deliesseline* (1823), Johnson on circuit held the statute unconstitutional as an interference with the federal commerce power and with treaty obligations.[61] A fierce newspaper debate ensued because Johnson's position seemed to threaten the police powers of the states and the federal consensus. Charlestonians condemned him as a traitor to the state, while he only grew more obdurate in his defense of national power. Later, he was forced to self-exile from the state because of his nationalist position in the Nullification controversy of 1832.

John Marshall's contrasting reaction to a similar challenge is instructive. An 1819 Virginia statute that prohibited any ship's master from bringing into the commonwealth any "free negro or mulatto" was challenged as conflicting with a federal statute that regulated importation of "negroes, mulattoes, or other persons of color."[62] Marshall on circuit in *The Brig Wilson* (1820) held that there was no proof that the seamen in question were "negroes or mulattoes" and thus the Virginia statute did not apply to them.[63] This reading was strained, but not implausible: American seafarers of the time included numerous non-African "persons of color," especially Malaysians and, on whalers, Native Americans.[64]

Marshall explained in private correspondence with Justice Joseph Story that "fuel is continually adding to the fire at which the exaltees are about to roast the judicial department." (He was referring to the political controversy following *McCulloch v. Maryland* (1819),[65] which had reignited Jeffersonian hostility to federal judicial power.) "Our brother Johnson, I perceive, has hung himself on a democratic snag in a hedge composed entirely of thorny state rights in South Carolina.... The subject is one of much feeling in the South. Of this I was apprized, but did not think it would have shown itself in such strength as it has.... the sentiment has been avowed that if this be the constitution, it is better to break that instrument than submit to the principle." Marshall then contrasted his own, more prudent, response to the same problem: "a case has been brought before me [*Brig Wilson*] in which I might have considered [the act's] unconstitutionality had I chosen to do so, but it was not absolutely necessary, and, as I am not fond of butting against a wall in sport, I escaped on the construction of the act."[66] This epitomizes the Marshall Court's approach to the contentious issues posed by slavery and race in the young American republic: a prudential avoidance of constitutional questions where the background political controversies were explosive. Marshall's successor would spurn such caution, with disastrous results.

A few of Marshall's other colleagues entertained weak antislavery sympathies, chiefly Joseph Story. Story was originally that New England anomaly, a Jeffersonian Republican, but later in his career gravitated to a conservative outlook more consonant with the Whig nationalism of Daniel Webster. His *Commentaries on the Constitution of the United States* (3 vols., 1833) became the classic statement of a nationalist constitutionalism at odds with the emerging state-sovereignty particularism that was the constitutional foundation of the Slave Power.[67] But Story's contributions to resolving the place of slavery in the American constitutional order were ambivalent: he would be found, equivocal, on all sides of the issue in his thirty-three-year tenure on the Supreme Court.[68]

Smith Thompson, a New Yorker, condemned the slave trade, though that was hardly a radical view (even Thomas Jefferson, who otherwise was notoriously solicitous of slavery, condemned slave traders as the "faeculum of society").[69] John McLean of Ohio thought that "principles of natural justice" entitled all people to claim their freedom.[70] But of the rest the justices, we know little. Five of them were obscure nonentities, short-termers, or jurists whose presence had no apparent effect on the Court's work.[71]

Somerset in America: *La Jeune Eugenie* (1822) and *The Antelope* (1825)

For the antebellum Supreme Court, cases coming before it involving slavery also posed questions of race, even if only implicitly. This forced the justices to consider the connection between human nature and freedom. What was the relationship between slavery and race? Are all human beings by nature free? Was slavery therefore some sort of aberrant anomaly in the eyes of the law? Did slavery exist independently of and prior to law, or was it the creature of law? Did English law recognize slavery as a legitimate status? If slavery did not exist in England after the demise of villeinage, could colonial slave law reinstate it there? These momentous issues were addressed by English courts before and during John Marshall's tenure as chief justice. Those English decisions cast a long shadow over American law, in ways unforeseen by the jurists who handed them down. *Somerset's Case* was the most influential.

Charles Stewart, a royal customs official, bought the enslaved boy who was to be baptized as James Somerset in Virginia in 1757, took him first to Boston, and then to London. Somerset there tried to liberate himself by disappearing into the teeming mass of Africans in the great metropolis, but Stewart recaptured him and consigned him to a ship captain to be transported to Jamaica and there sold back into slavery. Hearing of his plight, the great English emancipationist Granville Sharp helped procure a writ of habeas corpus on Somerset's behalf. In 1772, William Murray, Baron Mansfield, chief justice of King's Bench, rendered an oral decision granting the writ. Mansfield there said:

> So high an act of dominion [i.e., slavery and its incidents] must be recognized by the law of the country where it is used. The power of a master over his slave has been extremely different, in different countries. The state of slavery is of such a nature, that it is incapable of being introduced on any reasons, moral or political; but only positive law, which preserves its force long after the reasons, occasion and time itself from whence it was created, is erased from memory: It's so odious, that nothing can be suffered to support it but positive law.[72]

Somerset's Case had vast and lasting repercussions in America because, as a common-law decision, its doctrines passed into American law with the reception of English law in the British colonies and new states.[73] This history calls to mind Frederic William Maitland's evocative closing sentence of his magisterial treatise known as "Pollock and Maitland": "Those few men who were gathered round Pateshull and Raleigh and Bracton were penning writs that would run in the name of the kingless commonwealths on the other shore of the Atlantic Ocean; they were making right and wrong for us and for our children."[74]

If slavery was "so odious, that nothing can be suffered to support it but positive law," did that mean that it was illegitimate under natural law? If it was, could it be rendered legitimate anywhere, even by positive law? If it could be, what kinds of positive law (written constitution, statute, common law, codified custom) were necessary or adequate to do the job? Was slavery universally illegitimate, incapable of being imposed anywhere? Or was slavery the universal norm or default condition for people of color, with freedom being possible only by positive law?

Mansfield had definitely not held that slavery was illegitimate in England itself, though some abolitionists thought that he had, or that his opinion at least implied that slavery was illegitimate. Assuming for sake of argument that *Somerset v. Stewart* had called into question slavery's legitimacy under English law, did the repugnancy or conformity clauses of the colonial charters mean that slavery was of questionable legitimacy in those colonies as well?[75] By the mid-eighteenth century, most of the colonial charters mandated that colonial laws not be repugnant to the laws of England or that they conform to the law of the metropolis.[76] If *Somerset* were read as holding that slavery could not exist in the metropolis (Great Britain), did that imply that it was somehow illegitimate in the colonies as well? The repugnancy/conformity clauses notwithstanding, could the colonial governments or the settlers themselves establish slavery in the colonies?

Somerset's assumptions about international law also influenced American thinking about interstate relations, especially as those involved slavery. For example, if a person was later held in slavery in, say, Missouri (a slave state), and became free when he passed into a free state (Illinois) and into a territory made free under the Northwest Ordinance (Wisconsin), and then returned to Missouri, did his original enslaved status reattach, or did he remain free because of his sojourn in a free state and territory? That was the situation of Dred Scott, and the original litigation of his case in the Missouri state courts treated the issue entirely in a *Somerset* framework.

Joseph Story, who served as an associate justice of the Supreme Court from 1811 to 1845, was a firm opponent of the slave trade and of slavery itself, rhetorically at least. During the controversy over the admission of Missouri as a slave state in 1819–1821, he called for slavery to be excluded from all territories and from the new state seeking admission. "The principles of our free government, the tenor of the Declaration of Independence, and the dictates of humanity and sound policy, were all directly opposed to the extension of slavery."[77] A year later, in charges to federal grand juries in Providence, Rhode Island; Boston; and Portland, Maine, he lectured the jurymen that "the existence of slavery, under any shape, is so repugnant to the natural rights of man and the dictates of justice, that it seems difficult to find for it any adequate justification." He twice endorsed its "gradual abolition."[78] (Later though, Story backpedaled considerably on the subject.)

Acting on his antislavery and anti-slave-trade enthusiasms of the time, Story, sitting as the circuit justice of the federal Circuit Court of Massachusetts in 1822, seized the opportunity to condemn the trade and, implicitly, slavery itself. An American navy schooner seized a French slaver off the west coast of Africa and brought it to Boston, where it was libeled in his court for violating federal statutes banning the slave trade.[79] Story used the occasion to condemn the slave trade as universally illegitimate under public international law. If his opinion had been sustained, then any American court, federal or state,[80] could hold any aspect of the international slave trade illegitimate (but not, it must be emphasized, the domestic slave trade), thereby rendering participants in the trade subject to prosecution.

In an opinion resolving this admiralty dispute, known as *La Jeune Eugenie* (1822),[81] Story identified the sources of public international law as threefold: (1) natural law ("the general principles of right and justice"); (2) custom (which he referred to as the "usages" of nations); and (3) positive law (statutory law or treaties.) He relied on the first, natural law, to uphold the power of Congress to criminalize the slave trade and federal courts to enforce those statutes. Public international law included "every doctrine, that may be deduced by correct reasoning from the rights and duties of nations, and the nature of moral obligation," including "the general principles of justice and humanity." Story condemned the slave trade as piracy (at the time, a capital offense). It was "repugnant to the great principles of Christian duty, the dictates of natural religion, the obligations of good faith and morality, and the eternal maxims of social justice." Story left unstated, but implied, the suggestion that slavery itself could not be legitimate if it originated in such corrupt beginnings.[82] Story's fervent condemnation of the trade would make no sense unless its primary victims were entitled to rights common to all humanity. The implications of *Somerset* were beginning to cast a long shadow over the American law of slavery.

Chief Justice Marshall would soon repudiate Story's reliance on natural law, both secular and divine. In the US Supreme Court, republican natural rights did not apply to Blacks, whether enslaved or free. The justices did not permit their personal moral opinions to override the mandates of law. This was succinctly expressed by Justice John McLean, who rejected Story's position: "Judges are sworn to support the Constitution and laws. They cannot consider slavery in the abstract. If they disregard what they conscientiously believe to be the written law in any case, they act corruptly and are traitors to their country."[83] That in turn pointed to the later reinterpretation of the Declaration of Independence as having an implied exception for Black Americans from its principles of liberty and equality, which in turn led to *Dred Scott*. Marshall's distinction between the urgings of conscience and the obligations of law became critical not only for emergent positivism later in the century but also for the law's approach to race and enslavement before 1865, and Jim Crow discrimination afterward.

The Marshall Court's slavery opinions break chronologically around 1817, with opinions of the earlier period almost always resolving cases that might have resulted in either freedom or continued enslavement in favor of the slaveowner and against the freedom claim.[84] After 1817, more decisions resulted in favor of the enslaved petitioners. This might be attributed to a heightened respect for property rights in the earlier period, and the influence of colonization sentiments shared by Marshall and Washington afterward. Personnel changes mattered, and the later cases often involved issues concerning the slave trade, where congressional determination to delegitimize the traffic may have influenced the Court's outlook.

But John Marshall refused to interpret law, on the rare occasions when he had a chance to do so, *in favorem libertatis*, "in favor of liberty."[85] *Mima Queen v. Hepburn* (1813) provides us a brief glimpse into Marshall's, and the Court's, attitudes toward freedom for Black people. Mima Queen sought freedom for herself and her daughter on the grounds that she was descended from a free woman, Mary Queen. But Mary Queen's status could be proved only by hearsay (which, under the laws of Maryland that governed in this case, was admissible). On appeal, Marshall rejected the Maryland rule on admissibility of hearsay evidence in cases of personal status, thus damning the petitioners to continued enslavement. If such evidence were admitted, he warned, "no man could feel safe in any property."[86] Marshall's preference for a white man's property claim over a Black woman's plea for freedom was all the starker in light of Justice Gabriel Duvall's dissent in that case. Duvall, himself a Marylander, insisted that "the right to freedom is more important than the right of property." "People of color, from their helpless condition,...are entitled to all reasonable protection." Marshall shrugged that off: "however the feelings of the individual may be interested on the part of a person claiming freedom, the court cannot perceive any legal distinction between the assertion of this, and of any other right."

Conservative jurists like Marshall believed that the implications of Story's *Jeune Eugenie* speculations about natural law were too dangerous to be left unaddressed, and they pushed back by exalting positive law, at least where it protected the interests of the slaveowner. Marshall's opportunity to repudiate Story's inconvenient appeal to the natural law of freedom came in another admiralty case involving a slaver. In *The Antelope* (1825),[87] he rejected Story's humanitarian sympathies and upheld the legitimacy of both slavery and the slave trade. A Uruguayan privateer captured a Spanish slaver off the coast of Africa and brought it, after various mishaps, to American waters, where it was seized by a cutter of the US Revenue Cutter Service.[88] Both Spanish and Portuguese consular officials libeled the vessel, claiming the enslaved people on board on behalf of their nationals.[89] Complicating matters, the US attorney filed another libel claiming that the Africans were free because they had been captured in Africa by persons intending to sell them in the United States, a violation of federal statutes.

Marshall sorted out the various complicated and conflicting claims. A peculiarity in the disposition of the case in the US circuit court had been that, of the dwindling number of the approximately 280 people on board the *Antelope* at the time of its seizure by the revenue cutter, only those deemed to be owned by Spanish claimants continued to be enslaved. Because the Portuguese claimant failed to prove ownership, the remainder were free. But how to determine who was which among the survivors? William Johnson, the presiding circuit justice in the trial, unlike Story in *La Jeune Eugenie*, upheld the legitimacy of the international slave trade in his *Antelope* opinion. He resolved the insoluble problem of sorting out the captives by decreeing that their fate—some to be freed, some to be enslaved—was be decided by lottery. Under federal law,[90] all should have been freed and returned to Africa. As it was, all were effectively enslaved and forced to do involuntary labor while in federal custody for eight years as the litigation dragged on, and thirty-seven of them were eventually consigned to permanent enslavement under Justice Johnson's lottery expedient. One hundred and twenty were deemed free and transported to Liberia in 1828.

Marshall conceded at the outset of his opinion that in this case "the sacred rights of liberty and of property come in conflict with each other."[91] But he framed the issues of the case as involving exclusively the question of who the owners of the enslaved people were, not whether the captured Africans were entitled to their freedom. He resolved the conflict between the "sacred rights" of human liberty and property in favor of property. The *Antelope* Africans may have been humans entitled to freedom in the abstract as a natural right, but their claims were subordinated to the property interests of other (white) humans.

Marshall admitted "that [the slave trade] is contrary to the law of nature will scarcely be denied." Thus, in the spirit of *Somerset*, both slavery and the trade in slaves could be established only by positive law. But Marshall warned that "this court must not yield to feelings which might seduce it from the path of duty, and must obey the mandate of the law." He upheld both slavery and the slave trade based on "usage," that is, custom, one variety of positive law. Marshall thereby rejected abstract natural law or rights as a source of substantive rights. Slavery was sanctioned by a traditional, indeed ancient, justification: captivity in war. "The victor might enslave the vanquished" as a humane alternative to simply killing the defeated enemy. "Slavery, then, has its origin in force; but as the world has agreed that it is a legitimate result of force, [it] cannot be pronounced to be unlawful." By accepting custom as the basis of both slavery and the slave trade, Marshall repudiated Story's proto-abolitionist sentiments in *La Jeune Eugenie*. The maritime nations not only established the slave trade by customary practice (i.e., simply by engaging in it over time) but also regulated it by treaties and domestic legislation (referred to at the time as "municipal law"), thus providing the positive law that Mansfield had demanded.

Marshall implicitly rebuked Story's humanitarian zeal in favor of a cautious conservatism that recoiled from destabilizing settled institutions, no matter how much those institutions (like slavery) might have troubled an individual judge's conscience. He adverted to this conflict at several points in his opinion, contrasting "public feeling" with "strict law," pitting the role of "a moralist" against that of "a jurist." Story remained unbowed two decades later, though. Writing to a friend in 1842, he insisted that "I always thought I was right [in *La Jeune Eugenie*], and continue to think so."[92]

The Taney-era justices continued the Marshall tradition of expanding federal power to promote the nation's economic development while at the same time respecting state sovereignty, especially over issues like slavery that were central to the states' economies and society. The Court advanced development of a capitalist market economy but had to balance that against a respect for democratic governance at the state level.[93] As judges, the justices protected federal judicial authority yet allowed ample room for Jacksonian democracy in policymaking at the state level. Partisan politics intruded, and sectional concerns weighed heavily, but the justices had to balance those partisan and sectional goals against other ideological demands and professional commitments.[94] The Taney Court blended concern for the security of slavery, a racist worldview, and a dedication to state sovereignty with support for capitalism and the market economy, respect for national power (especially where it would advance the interests of a slave economy), and an appreciation for the opportunities that technology was opening up for the expanding nation.

When Roger B. Taney succeeded Marshall as chief justice in 1835, the Court at first continued along the path of reticence that marked the earlier Court. With one important exception, *Prigg v. Pennsylvania* (1842), the early Jacksonian Justices produced only modest opinions in potentially controversial slavery cases. That changed dramatically after 1846, though, when the Taney Court became ever more activist in confining legislative discretion on substantive issues concerning slavery. When faced with a choice between democracy and the slavocracy after 1850, the Taney Court justices grimly embraced slavery and the slaveholders' constitution.[95]

Two explanations, one internal and the other external, account for this constitutional degeneration. Within the Court itself, new justices came onto the bench in the 1830s and brought with them a different outlook on issues related to slavery. Outside the Court, momentous political events were altering the sectional balance and threatening the security of slavery.

Roger B. Taney, who served as chief justice from 1836 until his death in 1864, was descended from one of Maryland's early Catholic families.[96] A Jacksonian in politics, Taney served successively in both houses of the Maryland legislature, and as state attorney general. He manumitted nearly all the enslaved people he owned in his lifetime, but nevertheless remained throughout his life profoundly racist in his views of the place and future of African Americans in American society. As the US attorney general he prepared an unpublished opinion in 1832 that upheld the power of South Carolina to enact the Negro Seamen's Act. In it, he declared that

> The African race in the United States even when free, are everywhere a degraded class....They are the only class of persons who can be held as mere property, as slaves....[They] are permitted to be citizens by the

sufferance of the white population and hold whatever rights they enjoy at their mercy. They were never regarded as a constituent portion of the sovereignty of any state, but as a separate and degraded people.... They were evidently not supposed to be included in the term citizens. And were not intended to be embraced in any provisions of that Constitution but those which point to them in terms not to be mistaken.[97]

Thus, a quarter century before *Dred Scott*, Taney anticipated opinions expressed there about African Americans as well as an irrepressible tendency to go beyond the issue at hand to deliver gratuitous asides on controversial political issues. As the leader of the Court for more than twenty-eight years, he was not the most extreme pro-slavery voice (that distinction belongs to Peter V. Daniel), but he was a dogged defender of slavery as the fundamental ordering structure of southern society.

Daniel, who served on the Court from 1841 to 1860, was the most extreme proponent of a states'-rights, pro-slavery outlook on the Court. A disciple of Thomas Jefferson and an agrarian follower of John Taylor of Caroline, Daniel was grim, humorless, uncompromising, inflexible, and given to extremes in both substance and expression. He dissented more than any other member of the Court.[98] Daniel went even further than Taney in his defense of southern and slaveholding interests.[99] Passionately committed to slavery, he saw no role for African Americans but as slaves.[100] Daniel supported secession in 1812 and again after 1848. His sectionalism degenerated into fanaticism, a seething hatred of the free states and a determination to protect slavery at all costs. The remaining seven justices who sat on the Court while Taney was chief justice were for the most part judicial nonentities. John Archibald Campbell of Alabama (associate justice, 1853–1861) was so dedicated to slavery that he resigned his judicial commission in 1861 to throw in his lot with the Confederacy, which he served as assistant secretary of war. He re-emerged after the war as a prominent opponent of Republican Reconstruction.[101] Some justices were what were called at the time "Doughfaces": "northern men with southern principles," as zealous in their condemnation of abolitionists as Daniel. One of them, Robert C. Grier of Pennsylvania (served 1846–1879), decried abolitionists from the bench as "infuriated fanatics and unprincipled demagogues...[who] denounce the constitution, the laws, and the Bible, [and] who promulgate doctrines subversive of all morality and all government."[102]

The Taney Court Accommodates Slavery, 1835–1850

In its first seventy-one years, the federal Union was buffeted by six successive crises brought on by slavery, each more severe than the preceding, and the final one proving fatal.[103] Five of these were fueled by the problem of slavery's expansion into the western territories.[104] These were the crises:

- The formation of the new nation, 1787–1789, provoked the first crisis and was resolved by the slavery compromises built into the Constitution, plus the Northwest Ordinance of 1787 and the lesser-known Southwest Ordinance of 1790, which sorted the territories into free (north of the Ohio River) and slave (south). But the continual expansion of the Union after 1787 upset these complex constitutional settlements.[105]
- The admission of Missouri erupted in two successive crises between 1819 and 1821, the first involving Missouri's future as a slave or free state, and the second the entry into the state of free African Americans after statehood.[106]
- The South Carolina Nullification crisis of 1832, the only one of the eruptions not caused by slavery's territorial expansion, was nominally a dispute over the tariff, but in reality was an outburst of the slave South's mounting anxiety over the emergence of immediatist antislavery.[107]
- The fourth crisis of the Union was precipitated by the admission of the slaveholding republic of Texas as a state in 1845, the ensuing Mexican War of 1846–1848, the Mexican cession of the modern Southwest by the Treaty of Guadalupe Hidalgo (1848), and the simultaneous acquisition of Oregon Territory from Great Britain in 1848. The focus of this fourth crisis was the Wilmot Proviso of 1846, which would have excluded slavery from any territories acquired as a result of the Mexican War. The Compromise of 1850 attempted to resolve this fourth crisis by an expedient package of political measures that its proponents hoped would settle all outstanding slavery-related questions with finality.
- But then the fifth crisis struck. The Kansas-Nebraska Act of 1854 would have opened up the remainder of the Louisiana Purchase territory to slavery by repeal of the Missouri Compromise. In rapid succession, the Whig Party dissolved; the Democratic Party split into northern and southern factions; antislavery northern Democrats, Free-Soilers, and rootless Whigs coalesced to form the Republican

Party; freelancing abolitionists and pro-slavery forces organized competing militias that fought the localized skirmishes and atrocities that are known as Bleeding Kansas (1854–1861), until it was subsumed in the larger Civil War. The *Dred Scott* case of 1857 confirmed the pro-slavery outcome of the Kansas-Nebraska clash. A severe economic downturn that began in 1857 only made matters worse.
- The terminal crisis of the Union, the sixth, came with the election of 1860 and the ensuing secession of South Carolina and ten other slave states. The Union finally succumbed.

The political resolution each of these crises was based on a bedrock constitutional understanding that has become known as the "federal consensus": the states, not the federal government, had complete and exclusive control over slavery as a domestic institution. The federal government had no authority over slavery except what was explicitly delegated to it by the Constitution. The federal consensus in turn rested on the underlying nature of the American Union: the federal government is a government of limited and delegated powers. The states exercise residuary sovereignty over all matters not explicitly denied to them by their constitutions or by the federal Constitution.

Abolitionists began thinking in constitutional terms in the early 1830s, and their theorizing first appeared in arguments before state supreme and lower courts. While the results of this litigation were mixed at best, marked by repeated disappointments to the antislavery cause, the constitutional ideas broached in these tribunals formed the nucleus of later, more matured antislavery thought.[108] When antislavery lawyers defended a Connecticut schoolmistress, Prudence Crandall, in 1833 against a state prosecution for running a school for nonresident African American girls without permission of the town's selectmen, they explored the potential of the privileges and immunities clause of Article IV[109] as a protection for the rights of free Blacks.[110] That in turn precipitated the formation of the American Anti-Slavery Society in 1833. Its constitution and Declaration of Sentiments set forth a rudimentary body of constitutional ideas emphasizing egalitarianism, the federal consensus, and a program of action that included abolition of slavery in the District of Columbia and the federal territories,[111] abolition of the interstate slave trade, and banning the spread of slavery into new states.[112]

Commonwealth v. Aves (Massachusetts, 1837),[113] popularly known as *Med's Case*, gave abolitionists their first great legal triumph when Chief

Justice Lemuel Shaw of the Massachusetts Supreme Judicial Court held that under the constitution of the commonwealth, enslaved persons brought into the state, including mere sojourners, could not be forced to return to slavery in their home state. The law of a slave state could not extend into a free state. *Med's Case* constituted the almost complete absorption of *Somerset* into Massachusetts law.[114] New Jersey disappointed antislavery lawyers who tried to get the state's supreme court to proclaim total abolition under a similar constitutional provision.[115] A contemporary Pennsylvania case, *Hobbs v. Fogg* (1837), held that African Americans were not entitled to vote in the Keystone State because they were not "freemen" as that term was used in the commonwealth's constitution.[116]

The earliest cases to come before the Taney Court involving slavery were resolved in the relaxed atmosphere of an approach that Earl Maltz describes as "accommodationist."[117] At first the Taney Court tried to maintain sectional harmony and avoid conflict among the states.[118] The justices managed to detach their beliefs about slavery from their inclination to resolve issues on purely legal, nonpolitical grounds such as common-law pleading and practice, standing, stare decisis, and federalism.

In 1787, the issue of congressional control over the interstate slave trade had been merely theoretical, since the interstate movement of enslaved people was both inconsequential compared to a generation later and not essential to the profitability of the slave economy at that time. Thus, the commerce clause[119] did not provoke explosive slavery-related controversies when it was adopted. But the slave trade clause[120] had a different resonance. It spoke of "Migration or Importation." If we may impose on the clause Chief Justice John Marshall's later canon of interpretation that no word or clause of the Constitution is without meaning,[121] we must assume that "migration" meant something different from "importation," and that the two terms were not synonymous or redundant. Giving words their obvious meaning, "importation" would refer to the international slave trade, but "migration" would refer to interstate movement, and thus might support the inference that after 1808, Congress could regulate the interstate movement of enslaved people.[122]

The cotton boom in the fertile lands of the southwest created an insatiable demand for unfree labor after 1815, while the depleted soils of the seaboard slave states produced a labor surplus. Both the pull of demand and the push of a growing Black population in the East that had diminishing economic value ensured that the interstate slave trade would be essential, both as a safety value for the eastern states and a guarantee of enslaved labor for the southwest. Slavery's antagonists early on recognized the latent potential of the commerce clause to disrupt this Black population flow and demanded that Congress ban the interstate trade.[123]

Pro-slavery politicians took this threat seriously. A Virginia Jeffersonian, John Randolph of Roanoke, declaimed in 1807 that congressional authority over the interstate trade would "blow up the Constitution in ruins" because it "might be made the pretext for universal emancipation."[124] He thereby identified the issue that lurked within all debates over congressional power to regulate interstate commerce. Abolitionists made restriction of the interstate slave trade a major weapon in their arsenal. They reinforced the point by demanding that Congress abolish at least the slave trade (and better yet, slavery itself) in the District of Columbia, a subject over which Congress had a separate, distinct, and equally plenary authority given by the federal district clause of Article I, section 8 "to exercise exclusive Legislation in all Cases whatsoever" over the district.[125]

The issues presented by the commerce clause were not limited to interstate trafficking in enslaved people. Abolitionists challenged other state powers as well under the clause, such as the power to exclude free Blacks (the focus of the second Missouri crisis of 1821), the Negro Seamen's Acts, the status of sojourners or other enslaved people coming into the jurisdiction by mischance (as by shipwreck), and enslaved people in transit and only temporarily passing through the state. Those issues might also include state control of white people as well: abolitionists from the free states, slave catchers from the South.

At first, the justices were not stampeded into extreme positions on these topics. In 1837 the Court had stated in dictum in *Mayor of New York v. Miln* that humans could not be considered objects of trade or commerce,[126] but there the justices had in mind white ship passengers. *Miln* did not foreclose the question of enslaved people's humanity in the context of the interstate trade. The trade itself was unquestionably commerce, so the issue became whether the interstate slave trade was somehow sui generis. Did the clause either subject the trade to complete authority of Congress or deny it altogether? Abolitionists seized on this potential, assuming (probably correctly) that if Congress could shut down the interstate slave trade, that would strangle slavery itself, since a human surplus would accumulate and reach dangerous levels in the upper South, while the cotton South was starved of needed manpower.

Groves v. Slaughter (1841) posed the question not addressed in *Miln*: whether enslaved people could be the subjects of commerce.[127] *Groves* challenged the power of Mississippi to regulate the interstate slave trade into the state, even to the point of shutting it off entirely. In *Groves*, the Court, speaking thorough Justice Smith Thompson, avoided taking a position on that potentially explosive issue, merely holding that the state constitutional provision was not self-enforcing and therefore did not of its own force void the notes. The remaining justices each expressed an opinion in dicta on the underlying constitutional issue, but carefully avoided blowing up the Constitution, as Randolph had put it a generation earlier.[128] Nevertheless, the issue had been broached: did the US Constitution recognize the humanity of men and women held in slavery and, if so, with what consequences?

That issue was raised that same year by *United States v. The Amistad* (1841). The case came to the US Supreme Court against a background of vivid political drama, diligently popularized by the dynamic abolitionist movement.[129] A Spanish-flagged schooner, *La Amistad*, was transporting fifty-three Africans who had been captured and enslaved in Africa,[130] then brought to Cuba in violation of Spanish laws abolishing the high-seas slave trade. While sailing in Cuban coastal waters, the captives revolted and killed all but two of their captors, whom they ordered to sail back to Africa. The captors sailed east during the day but veered to a northerly course at night in hopes of landing at a friendly port in an American slave state. They made it to American waters near Long Island Sound, where the ship and its occupants were seized by a US survey brig and brought to port to resolve the legal status of ship and passengers. Complex litigation and diplomatic maneuvering followed as multiple claimants sought to reclaim the ship and its occupants. Abolitionists who heard of these events intervened on behalf of the Africans, insisting that they were all free men entitled to return to their African homes. The litigation came to the US Supreme Court when the putative Spanish owners appealed a federal district court ruling holding the Africans to be free under an 1819 federal statute requiring return of persons kidnapped for enslavement back to Africa.

In a brief opinion, Justice Joseph Story for a six-justice majority held all but one of the Africans to be free because the documents purporting to prove their ownership were fraudulent and thus insufficient to sustain the claims of the Spaniards.[131] Because the Africans were free, "the United States are bound to respect their rights as much as those of Spanish subjects. The conflict of rights between the parties [the Spanish claimants vs. the Africans] under such circumstances, becomes positive and inevitable, and must be decided upon the eternal principles of justice and international law." This was an extraordinary statement for the time: enslaved Africans who had rebelled and killed the crew of the slaver were nonetheless accorded rights equal to those of white Spanish subjects, and those rights were protected "under the eternal principles of justice" (another echo of *Somerset*). And as a practical matter, the specific holding of the case, that a slaver's papers could be impugned for fraud, was a valuable concession to abolitionists combating the slave trade.

The dicta and specific holdings of Story's opinion appear even more significant because the most pro-slavery justices on the Court at the time, Taney, James M. Wayne of Georgia, and John Catron of Tennessee, chose not to dissent. The Court was not yet so polarized that an outcome that was favorable to enslaved men and that rejected the claims of their supposed owners could antagonize the defenders of slavery into dissent. These three southern Democratic jurists went along with an opinion that not only declared fifty of the captives free but did so based on universalistic claims under natural law. National tensions over slavery were rising, but for the time being, sensitivity over such questions remained confined to the South. (That would soon change with Texas annexation and the Mexican War.) Thus, it was possible for the Court to avoid plunging into the controversy over slavery, and the justices appeared willing to let that particular sleeping dog lie.

As sectional tensions intensified in the 1840s because of white southerners' deepening insecurity over slavery, inflamed by growing abolition sentiment in the North, each region developed mirror-image fears of encirclement and penetration by the other. These twinned anxieties drove all slavery-related constitutional controversies from 1845 through the destruction of the Union.

From white southerners' point of view, after the admission of Arkansas as a slave state in 1836, almost nothing was left of American territory for slavery's expansion under the first Missouri Compromise (1820) except Indian Territory (roughly, modern Oklahoma), a thin slice of what is now north Texas, and a small piece of today's northeast New Mexico. Unless slavery could somehow expand into Mexico (where it had been abolished in 1829) or into the Caribbean, the slave South would be effectively hemmed in by the free states and territories, twice the size of the slave South in area and greatly outstripping it in population and wealth—thus, southern fears of encirclement. As for penetration, the spread of antislavery propaganda, in the form of newspapers, pamphlets, and handbills through the abolitionist mails campaign of 1835, was of serious enough concern to whites that the Jackson administration banned their delivery by the post office. A growing free Black population, Black seamen, itinerant abolitionists, and "inflammatory, incendiary, and insurrectionist" mailings, as Postmaster General Amos Kendall called them in the mails controversy, convinced whites that the slave states were barraged by an unwelcome influx of dangerous ideas and people.

Residents of the North were dogged by corresponding fears. If the Missouri Compromise prohibition of slavery north of 36°30′ could somehow be evaded, ignored, or repealed—just what happened by the Kansas-Nebraska Act of 1854—the free North would find itself surrounded by slave domains, and all hope of expansion westward by free white settlers extinguished. Penetration came in the form of enslaved men and women liberating themselves by escaping slavery and migrating to the North, and by slave catchers pursuing them.[132] Despite prevalent racial prejudice among northern whites,[133] it was increasingly the slave catchers who were less welcome. The free states enacted personal liberty laws to provide some limited measure of procedural protection for captured individuals claimed to be runaways.[134] The potential for constitutional conflict grew as the dramatis personae multiplied in rescues and recaptures: fugitives, those who succored them, slave catchers, sheriffs and constables, federal officials, bystanders, abolitionists.

But it was not only fugitives who were implicated. Free people, both Black and white, were ensnared in the nets of slave catchers.[135] Free Blacks were arguably citizens of the states where they resided and possibly of the United States as well, though the question of citizenship was confused and unresolved before the Fourteenth Amendment's citizenship clause cut that Gordian knot.[136] Thus in fugitive cases the Court could not avoid implicit questions of how race affected rights and status. Moreover, fugitive cases were theaters of ever-more-contentious conflicts between slave and free states. The free states sought to protect their citizens from kidnapping and other kinds of abuse,[137] and to prevent their citizens from being forced to participate in the distasteful role of slave-catching auxiliaries. The slave states were trying to enforce both property rights and what they considered to be the constitutional obligations of sister states in a federal union that required interstate comity.[138] The property rights of the slaveholder were protected by the common-law right of recaption: the power of a property owner to retrieve property that had escaped from him.[139] In the Alice-in-Wonderland logic of the laws of slavery, a fugitive was considered to have wrongfully taken his master's property—that is, himself—by escaping.

The common-law right was reinforced by the federal Fugitive Slave Act of 1793.[140] The statute permitted a slaveowner or his agent "to seize or arrest" the "fugitive from labour" and bring him before a federal judge or local magistrate. The captor could prove slave status by affidavit or oral testimony. The judicial officer was then obliged to issue a certificate permitting the owner to remove the fugitive. State supreme courts were divided on the constitutionality of the statute.[141] Northern state anti-kidnapping statutes prohibited the capture of free people and provided some procedural protections for persons seized by slave catchers, including the right to jury trial, habeas corpus, and some exotic writs like personal replevin or the antique *homine replegiando*. Some also prohibited local officials (judges and sheriffs) from participating in recaptures or banned use of local jails as barracoons.[142] Slaveowners loudly denounced such measures.

These issues came before the US Supreme Court in the collusive case of *Prigg v. Pennsylvania* in 1842.[143] Edward Prigg, a slave catcher from Maryland, was prosecuted under the Pennsylvania Personal Liberty of 1826, which prohibited kidnapping free Blacks for transport out of state to be sold as slaves. He was indicted for seizing Margaret Morgan, a supposedly free woman, her husband, and her children, hauling them off to Maryland, and selling them there. Her husband had been born free in Pennsylvania; Margaret had lived there as a free woman; and one or more of her children had been born in Pennsylvania and were therefore free under that state's gradual-emancipation act. Prigg formed a slave-catching posse, seized Margaret and her family, and sought a certificate of rendition from a state justice of the peace. The justice of the peace refused, whereupon Prigg hustled Margaret and her children off to Maryland, where they were sold into slavery and passed into obscurity. Pennsylvanians were outraged at this affront to their recently enacted personal liberty law. Prigg was convicted of violating the Pennsylvania statute in a pro forma trial after the two states had agreed to create a test case to go to the US Supreme Court to determine the validity of the Pennsylvania statute.

In *Prigg*, the Court was faced with urgent issues of federalism, the place of slavery in the American legal order, and the conflict between human liberty and property claims, against a backdrop of simmering sectional tensions that would erupt in a few years. Once again, the justices tried to avoid blowing up the Constitution in a majority opinion by Justice Story that Maltz considers a "delicately crafted compromise,"[144] but that others have condemned as a capitulation to slaveholding interests.[145] Given the high stakes and political pressures, the Court split, producing seven opinions, but managed to coalesce, by bare and shifting majorities, on seven or eight holdings or dicta in Story's majority opinion.

Story affirmed that slavery existed as a "mere municipal regulation" established by the positive law of some jurisdiction, which in theory no other jurisdiction was bound to recognize or enforce. Once again, *Somerset* had reappeared in American jurisprudence, casting a shadow over slavery's legitimacy. But the fugitive slave clause changed that for the federal Union, imposing restraints and obligations on the states respecting fugitives. Story insisted that the clause was essential to the formation of the Union, "a fundamental article without the adoption of which the Union could not have been formed." (Historians reject this historical-necessity thesis.) He held that the clause empowered the federal government to enforce its commands. Under it, the Fugitive Slave Act was constitutional, and state personal liberty laws interfering with its operation or the master's rights recognized by it were unconstitutional on underlying principles of federalism and national supremacy. The master's claims, like slavery itself, were secured as "a positive and absolute right." Here Story seemed to abandon his earlier natural-rights view in favor of a stark positivism. Story also affirmed the common-law right of recaption and its operation even in states that had abolished slavery (thus giving constitutional sanction to slavery's penetration of the free states). The effect of these various holdings or dicta was to make it impossible for the states to prevent kidnaping of African Americans. The claimant's authority was absolute and constitutionally protected: "under the Constitution, the owner of a slave is clothed with entire authority, in every state in the Union, to seize and recapture his slave, whenever he can do it, without any breach of the peace or any illegal violence."[146] In that sense, the fugitive slave clause was self-executing.

But Story also stated that the states lacked power to enforce the federal fugitive statute, and opined, in a view unique to him, that states were not compelled to enforce it or require their officers to participate in recaptures. The last point—states need not participate in enforcement of the federal act—led some northern states to adopt second-generation personal liberty laws that refused the aid of state officers in enforcement of the statute.[147]

Accompanying this formal legislative resistance, residents of the free states began to frustrate capture attempts in the streets by mobbing. White southerners, in turn, saw such behavior, both legislative and popular, as proof of northern bad faith and demanded more effective enforcement of the Fugitive Slave Act.

Story's *Prigg* opinion, and the result of the decision itself, sought to strike a balance between valid free state concerns that their free Black citizens not be kidnapped and that their white citizens not be conscripted into slave-catching posses, on the one hand, and slave state demands for extraterritorial, indeed nationwide, enforcement of slavery. Not one of the seven *Prigg* opinions mentioned the rights of Blacks, free or enslaved; apparently it did not occur to any of the justices that African Americans might even have rights. All the justices, including the soi-disant antislavery Story, emphasized the rights of white men—slaveowners and slave catchers—but Black people were simply not in the viewfinder of American judges and lawyers in the 1840s. The only people who did think of African Americans as rights-bearing human beings were African Americans themselves and their white abolitionist allies.

Story supposedly claimed that his opinion was a "Triumph of Freedom."[148] But in private correspondence he suggested to Senator John Berrien of Georgia that Congress find ways to make the federal statute more effective in returning fugitives to slavery, by empowering federal commissioners to return fugitives, a suggestion that bore fruit in the 1850 Fugitive Slave Act. He suggested that Berrien pursue the matter quietly, so as not to provoke debate.[149]

Prigg's seven opinions made it the first in a line of cases where the pressures of slavery fractured the Court and produced a sprawl of dangerously discordant views. Taney's and Daniel's concurring/dissenting opinions in *Prigg* showed that the pro-slavery wing of the Court was growing restive with northern attacks on the South's chief domestic institution and source of wealth. They began to explore the potential of pro-slavery nationalism, using national authority to force the free states to subordinate their laws and public policy to the demands of what was coming to be seen as the Slave Power.[150]

Though the fugitive slave clause continued to be an irritant in American politics, it did not present the lethal potential that the territorial question did. Thus, issues involving runaways could recur before the Supreme Court without threatening disruption of the constitutional order. In *Jones v. Van*

Zandt (1847),[151] the Court unanimously sustained an award for damages against a conductor of the Underground Railroad who had attempted to help fugitives escape by conveying them in a wagon near Cincinnati, Ohio. The defendant was represented by Salmon P. Chase, the abolitionist lawyer from southern Ohio who by now had earned his sobriquet "Attorney General for Runaway Slaves" and who in twenty years would be the chief justice of the United States. Chase urged the Court to adopt a *Somerset* understanding of slavery in the American Union. Under this theory, the moment an enslaved person reaches a free jurisdiction, his slave status disappears, "because he continues to be a man, and leaves behind him the law of force."[152] Because slavery was contrary to "natural right," it could be maintained only by "local and municipal" law, which had no force outside the slave jurisdiction that enacted it. Chase's argument accepted the federal consensus, leaving slavery to be regulated by the states, but he tried to lop off any federal effort to sustain it.

Writing for the Court, Justice Levi Woodbury, a New Hampshire Doughface, would have none of that. Instead, he fell back on familiar themes. The fugitive slave clause was "one of [the Constitution's] sacred compromises, and which we possess no authority as a judicial body to modify or overrule." Woodbury explicitly addressed Chase's appeal to a judge's conscience and spurned it: "Whatever may be the theoretical opinions of any as to the expediency of some of those compromises, or of the right of property in persons which they recognize," he went on, "this court has no alternative, while they exist, but to stand by the constitution and laws with fidelity to their duties and their oaths. Their path is a strait and narrow one, to go where that constitution and the laws lead, and not to break both, by travelling without or beyond them." Hiding behind this formalist posture enabled judges to anesthetize the promptings of conscience by invoking positive law.[153] A disappointed Chase wrote to Massachusetts senator Charles Sumner that the Supreme Court "cannot be trusted at all when that great corporate interest [i.e., slavery] is in question."[154]

Dred Scott and the Slaveholders' Constitution, 1850–1860

Slaveholding Americans had been migrating into Mexican Texas since the 1820s. Restive over the Mexican Republic's prohibition of slavery and incredulous that its second president, Vicente Guerrero, was the son of

African and Mestizo parents, the American immigrants revolted and established the Texas Republic in 1836. Their petition to be annexed to the United States as a slave state set off a decade-long debate over the future of slavery in the beckoning West. Arkansas's admission in 1836 followed by Michigan's in 1837 reaffirmed the unwritten but iron-clad constitutional understanding that free and slave territories would be admitted to statehood in pairs to preserve the sectional political balance. The prospect of the huge territory of Texas, whose boundaries were undefined, being cloned into as many as six slave states was unsettling, to say the least, to northerners. When their resistance stymied an annexation treaty in the Senate, Presidents John Tyler and James K. Polk hit on the expedient of admitting Texas by joint resolution. (The resolution provided that as many as five states might be carved out of it.) Negotiations with Great Britain over the boundaries of Oregon Country only complicated the issue.[155]

These controversies were eclipsed by the outbreak of the Mexican War in 1846 and the introduction of the Wilmot Proviso that year, which would have banned slavery in all territories acquired because of the war.[156] Drawing on the Northwest Ordinance of 1787, the Proviso stated that "neither slavery nor involuntary servitude shall ever exist in said territory, except for crime, whereof the party shall first be duly convicted." Both North and South proved intransigent on the issue, southerners unanimously rejecting it, and a large bloc of northern Whigs and Democrats just as vociferously opposed to opening the vast lands of the Southwest to slavery. Extension of the Missouri Compromise line of 36°30' to the Pacific repeatedly proved to be a nonstarter, while "popular sovereignty"—the idea that the settlers of a territory should decide the future of slavery there, not people in the rest of the United States—had a pseudo-democratic appeal to northern Democrats for over a decade.

In this political context in 1848 Whig senator John M. Clayton of Delaware first suggested the lethal idea that became part of the package known as the "Clayton Compromise": let the US Supreme Court resolve all constitutional questions surrounding slavery, which was proving to be insoluble by normal political processes. More specifically, Clayton's proposal would have organized California and New Mexico Territories (roughly encompassing all of modern California, Nevada, and Utah, nearly all of Arizona, and large chunks of New Mexico, Colorado, and Wyoming) but forbidden them to take any action one way or another on slavery. Instead, the Clayton bill provided that any person being held in slavery in the territories would be permitted to bring a freedom suit in the territorial courts, with a direct appeal to the US Supreme Court. Clayton and others hoped thereby to get a definitive ruling on all constitutional issues surrounding slavery in the territories.

The Clayton bill never got out of the Senate, but it provided one of the pillars of the Compromise of 1850.[157] That omnibus series of measures admitted California as a free state, organized Utah and New Mexico Territories (modern Nevada, Utah, New Mexico, most of Arizona, and parts of Colorado and Wyoming) on the basis of popular sovereignty, abolished the slave trade in the District of Columbia, settled Texas's boundaries, and enacted a drastic new Fugitive Slave Act.[158] Congress did not explicitly adopt Clayton's judicial proposal, but political leaders anticipated that slavery questions of one sort or another were certain to emerge from the Utah / New Mexico territorial settlements and eventually make their way to the US Supreme Court for definitive resolution.

Americans at the time breathed a collective sigh of relief, concluding that the slavery controversy, which was proving to be as alarming as it was intractable, had been finally and definitively resolved. The fourth crisis of the Union seemed to have passed. But the Compromise of 1850 proved to be illusory and far more fragile than anyone had imagined. It was an armistice, not a peace treaty. Salmon P. Chase, then in the US Senate, wrote presciently: "the question of slavery in the territories has been avoided. It has not been settled."[159] The nation emerged from it into a more threatening and volatile environment, where controversies that might have been elided, temporized, or compromised a decade earlier became explosive.

The judicial sang froid on display in *Prigg* would not last once the political climate heated up over the other lethal irritant, slavery into the territories. *Prigg* indicated that the Court's cohesion on slavery issues was fraying dangerously, and that the most pro-slavery members of the Court would not brook constitutional arguments much longer that challenged slavery's grip on the constitutional order. The Constitution had not blown up yet, but explosives lay about everywhere, and fuses were ready to be lit. All that was needed was some major disruption of the constitutional order, and that was occurring out on the plains of Texas.

In his *Prigg* concurrence/dissent, Chief Justice Taney displayed one of his most destructive traits as a judge: his inclination to reach out for issues not before him to provide an advisory opinion on something not necessary to the decision. (In *Prigg* it was his claim that the states were obliged to enact legislation to supplement the federal Fugitive Slave Act's protection for slaveowners' claims.) This tendency resurfaced in the first important slavery-related case to come before the Court in the post-1850 environment, *Strader v. Graham* (1851),[160] which imposed liability on a riverboat owner for damages when he took enslaved people out of a slave state without the owner's permission. Three young men enslaved in Kentucky had spent time in Indiana and Ohio, both free states under the Northwest Ordinance, with their master's permission, then returned to Kentucky. They escaped enslavement by later traveling again to Ohio on Strader's boat, and then going on to Upper Canada. Strader defended on the ground that the three were not slaves at the time they boarded his boat because of their sojourn in free states. He was not alone in invoking the implied *Somerset* principle "once free, always free," the basis of hundreds of freedom suits brought in the antebellum period, demonstrating that the potential of Mansfield's opinion had penetrated deeply into the crevices of American law.[161]

The case turned on another reverberation of *Somerset* doctrine in America, though: the reattachment principle. Mansfield had held that an enslaved person brought into England may seek a writ of habeas corpus to prevent his return to a slave jurisdiction. But what if that person does in fact return from a free jurisdiction (England) to a slave society (Antigua)? This was the case of *The Slave, Grace* (1827), decided by William Stowell of the English High Court of Admiralty.[162] *Grace* was in a way the anti-*Somerset*: Stowell tried to correct what he saw as antislavery misinterpretations of what Mansfield had said. When a mistress brought an enslaved woman from a slave society (Antigua) to England and then took her back, her slave status reattached there. Her stay in England conferred only a "sort of limited liberty" that vanished once she was back in a slave society. Stowell expressed it as a metaphor: English law "put [enslaved people's] liberty, as it were, into a sort of parenthesis." Just as *Somerset* appealed to abolitionists in the antebellum era, *Grace* became a favorite of slave-state jurists.

Thus, the question in *Strader* was whether, assuming the three men were free in Ohio and Indiana, they became re-enslaved upon their return to Kentucky. The Kentucky Court of Appeals (the highest court of the commonwealth at the time) twice held that they remained enslaved there because of the reattachment principle. In the US Supreme Court, Taney held that the case should be dismissed, relying on the controlling principle that a state court interpretation of its own laws was binding on federal courts.

Had he stopped there, this disposition of the case would have been unexceptionable. But driven by his compulsion to speak out on issues unnecessarily, Taney stated in a sinister dictum that "every state has an undoubted right to determine the status, or domestic and social condition, of the persons domiciled within its territory; except in so far as the powers of the states in this respect are restrained, or duties and obligations imposed upon them, by the Constitution of the United States." This may have been a careless but empty truism. But the qualification after the semicolon might also suggest that the federal Constitution imposed limits on the powers of the states to declare people free, as in the case of sojourners' slaves, or conceivably, even limit their ability to abolish slavery.

Taney could not stop with that. He recklessly went on to declare in dicta that the Northwest Ordinance, a document of constitutional stature coeval with the Constitution (they were drafted in the same year, 1787) was superseded by the US Constitution and the state constitutions. Not content with that, he then went on to opine gratuitously that the Ordinance's ban on slavery might have been per se unconstitutional because it placed the states carved out of the Northwest Territory "in an inferior condition as compared with the other states, and subject[ed] their domestic institutions [i.e., slavery] and municipal regulations to the constant supervision and control of this court."[163] These dicta did no harm at the time, but they evinced a tendency that Taney carried to fatal extremes six years later.

Abolitionists feared the broader implications of Taney's loose dicta. James G. Birney charged that "in order to reach our colored people—especially the free portion of them—our Supreme Court are willing to trample down & disregard the constitutional safeguards of all our rights."[164] *Strader* implied a power of the slave states to seize and enslave any free Black within its borders. This would facilitate kidnaping under the relaxed machinery of the 1850 Act. *Strader* validated northern fears of slavery's intrusion into the free states.

Meanwhile, momentous events were rushing forward on the national scene. Entrepreneurs, investors, and local boosters were eager to begin building a transcontinental railroad to connect the settled United States with the vast territories lately wrested from Mexico. A major geopolitical conflict turned on which city was to become its eastern terminus: Chicago, St. Louis, or New Orleans. Senator Stephen A. Douglas, Democrat of Illinois, promoted Chicago. But to build along this northerly route, he would first have to provide for government in the territory west of Missouri and Iowa. His bill to organize Nebraska Territory went nowhere because southerners refused to carve new states out of Missouri Compromise lands where slavery was forbidden. So when Douglas, the preeminent exponent of the "popular sovereignty" doctrine at the time,[165] reintroduced the Nebraska bill in the next session, he provided that the Missouri Compromise was "inoperative and void" and that the territory be split in half, assuming that Kansas would eventually be admitted slave and Nebraska free.

Enactment of the Kansas-Nebraska Act in 1854 ignited the fifth crisis of the Union. Northern fears of encirclement seemed about to be become a nightmarish reality. The Whig Party disintegrated. The Democratic Party split into northern and southern halves, the northern wing clinging to "popular sovereignty" and the southerners pushing ever-more-drastic schemes for promoting slavery in the territories. They backed up their ideas with action, as Missouri "Border Ruffians," as they were called, streamed across the Missouri River into Kansas to create a slave territory. Resistance by antislavery counterparts from the North led to Bleeding Kansas, a localized civil war marked by bushwhacking and atrocities. In retrospect, Bleeding Kansas bore the same relationship to the Civil War as the Spanish Civil War bore to World War II: the prelude to a catastrophe.

In these fraught political circumstances, the justices decided to take up the invitation originally tendered by Congress in 1848 and resolve the otherwise-insoluble constitutional questions concerning slavery, particularly those concerning its advance into the western territories. Dred Scott was enslaved to an army physician named Emerson who was resident in Missouri. Dr. Emerson was posted to duty stations at Fort Armstrong in the state of Illinois (1833) and Fort Snelling (1836), in what was Wisconsin Territory (now a part of Minnesota) and therefore was a part of the Louisiana Purchase lands north of 36°30' where slavery had been excluded by the Missouri Compromise. Scott accompanied him, then returned to Missouri.[166] In 1846, Scott and his wife brought a routine freedom suit, based on *Somerset* principles, in Missouri state courts alleging that they had become free by reason of their extended residence in a free state (Illinois) and a free territory (Louisiana Purchase lands). The Missouri Supreme Court reversed the trial court's opinion finding in favor of Scott, trumpeting in dicta that

> times are not now as they were when the former decisions on this subject were made. Since then not only individuals but States have been possessed

with a dark and fell spirit in relation to slavery [i.e., antislavery], whose gratification is sought in the pursuit of measures, whose inevitable consequences must be the overthrow and destruction of our government. Under such circumstances it does not behoove the State of Missouri to show the least countenance to any measure which might gratify this spirit. She is willing to assume her full responsibility for the existence of slavery within her limits, nor does she seek to share or divide it with others."[167]

The case then made its way to the US Supreme Court because the nominal defendant, John F. A. Sanford, executor of Emerson's will and brother of his widow, was a resident of New York and Scott a resident of Missouri, thus providing the diversity of citizenship necessary for the diversity jurisdiction of the federal courts.[168] But that in turn posed the question of whether Scott was, or could be, a citizen of Missouri. That raised the question, as Taney presented it, of whether Blacks, enslaved or free, ever had been or could ever claim to be part of the American people.

The case was first argued before the US Supreme Court on February 11, 1856. At conference, the justices agreed on a noncontroversial disposition, upholding the decision of the federal circuit court, which in turn had affirmed the holding of the Missouri Supreme Court that Scott's travels did not liberate him and that he remained enslaved under Missouri law. But some of the justices were uneasy about the larger implications that that result left unaddressed. Violence was erupting throughout the nation: Congressman Preston Brooks of South Carolina bludgeoned Massachusetts senator Charles Sumner, while in Bleeding Kansas, both sides continued to bushwhack. In the national elections that fall, the new Republican Party, with its central plank the Wilmot Proviso, showed surprising electoral strength throughout the North, while the Whig Party disintegrated. These political developments combined with Taney's and Daniel's churning resentments to lead the Court to schedule reargument, opening up the broader potentials of the case. They and the other pro-slavery justices were determined to elevate the extreme southern political program to untouchable constitutional status. The case was reargued on December 15, 1856, and the lethal result announced four months later.

Dred Scott is remembered today chiefly for its two principal holdings, plus one utterance in Taney's opinion that is quasi-dictum.[169] First, Taney held that African Americans could not be citizens of the United States because they were Black and descended from enslaved people. Second, he held that the Missouri Compromise was unconstitutional as being beyond Congress's legitimate powers to regulate the territories.[170] Finally, in what reads almost as a throwaway line toward the end of his opinion, he announced for the first time in the US Supreme Court the principle of substantive due process.[171]

Beyond those two specific holdings and its numerous dicta, Taney's opinion resonates with modern concerns for three broad reasons. First, it provides a window into the racial thinking of mid-nineteenth-century justices. Second, it is the Court's most notorious attempt to suppress democratic self-governance. In his conclusion, Taney held unconstitutional not only the Missouri Compromise but also the core constitutional positions of the northern Democratic Party (the principle of "popular sovereignty"), and of the Republican Party (Free Soil: the exclusion of slavery from the territories). That left standing as the only constitutionally legitimate option the platform of the extremist and minority southern Democratic Party, namely, that all territories must be open to slavery and Congress must enact legislation to protect it there.

Third, it rested on an originalist approach to constitutional interpretation expressed in its starkest form:

> No one, we presume, supposes that any change in public opinion or feeling, in relation to this unfortunate race, in the civilized nations of Europe or in this country, should induce the court to give to the words of the Constitution a more liberal construction in their favor than they were intended to bear when the instrument was framed and adopted. Such an argument would be altogether inadmissible in any tribunal called on to interpret it. If any of its provisions are deemed unjust, there is a mode prescribed in the instrument itself by which it may be amended; but while it remains unaltered, it must be construed now as it was understood at the time of its adoption. It is not only the same in words, but the same in meaning, and delegates the same powers to the Government, and reserves and secures the same rights and privileges to the citizen; and as long as it continues to exist in its present form, it speaks not only in the same words, but with the same meaning and intent with which it spoke when it came from the hands of its framers, and was voted on and adopted by the people of the United States. Any other rule of construction would abrogate the judicial character of this court, and make it the mere reflex of the popular opinion or passion of the day.[172]

Significant as the latter two topics (substantive due process and originalism) are, they are beyond the scope of this book. But Taney's and his colleagues' comments speak more directly to the question of race than any other utterance of the Court until *Plessy v. Ferguson* (1896). The race passages are urgent, candid, and heartfelt: the justices were directly addressing their most pressing concerns. They speak to us across the decades with a power that no paraphrase can match. Taney's *Dred Scott* opinion is the Supreme Court's most explicit—and most infamous—discussion of race in the *United States Reports*. Ironically, it was also unnecessary, the most extreme and damaging example of Taney's inclination to attempt to resolve issues not before the Court and to impose a judicial solution on momentous issues better left to the political process and the American people.

"The question before us," Taney began his discourse,

> is whether [enslaved African Americans[173]] compose a portion of this people, and are constituent members of this sovereignty? We think they are not, and that they are not included, and were not intended to be included, under the word "citizens" in the Constitution, and can therefore claim none of the rights and privileges which that instrument provides for and secures to citizens of the United States. On the contrary, they were at that time considered as a subordinate and inferior class of beings, who had been subjugated by the dominant race, and, whether emancipated or not, yet remained subject to their authority, and had no rights or privileges but such as those who held the power and the Government might choose to grant them.[174]

In this and the following passages, Taney was determined, in Don Fehrenbacher's words, to "separate the Negro race absolutely from the federal Constitution and all the rights that it bestowed."[175] As Fehrenbacher meticulously demonstrated,[176] most of his assertions were as error-ridden as they were malicious, but what matters for us today are the sentiments themselves, whether factually accurate or not.

To support his conclusions, Taney invoked what he deemed to be "the state of public opinion in relation to that unfortunate race, which prevailed in the civilized and enlightened portions of the world" in the late eighteenth century. Without citation or attribution, he confidently claimed that African Americans had for more than a century before been regarded as beings of an inferior order, and altogether unfit to associate with the white race, either in social or political relations; and so far inferior, that they had no rights which the white man was bound to respect; and that the negro might justly and lawfully be reduced to slavery for his benefit. He was bought and sold, and treated as an ordinary article of merchandise and traffic, whenever a profit could be made by it. This opinion was at that time fixed and universal in the civilized portion of the white race. It was regarded as an axiom in morals as well as in politics.[177]

But what of Thomas Jefferson's proclamation in the Declaration of Independence "that all men are created equal, that they are endowed by their Creator with certain unalienable Rights, that among these are Life, Liberty and the pursuit of Happiness"? The chief justice had a ready answer:

the enslaved African race were not intended to be included, and formed no part of the people who framed and adopted this declaration; for if the language, as understood in that day, would embrace them, the conduct of the distinguished men who framed the Declaration of Independence would have been utterly and flagrantly inconsistent with the principles they asserted.[178]

Taney excluded African Americans rigidly and comprehensively from any possibility that they might be citizens under the US Constitution. He contemptuously dismissed the possibility that some state might be misguided enough to confer rights upon them by its own constitution; but even if they tried to do so, the effects would be confined within that state and could not be projected into sister states. Taney's vision denied Blacks, free or enslaved, not only the protections accorded to citizens but even those accorded to "persons" as that word was used in the Fifth Amendment.[179] Fehrenbacher observed that "the effect of Taney's statement was to place Negroes of the 1780s—even free Negroes—on the same level, legally, as domestic animals."[180]

Appalling as Taney's opinion was because of its racism, it should have been conclusive as a jurisdictional matter, and its racist asides could have been dismissed as dicta. But Taney recklessly determined to take up the other major question presented by the case, the constitutionality of the Missouri Compromise. Did Congress have the power to exclude slavery from the territories formed out of the Louisiana Purchase? Taney held that it did not. His reasoning here became convoluted, distorted by his determination to advance slavery everywhere in America. He claimed that the correct basis of Congress's power over the territories was not the obvious one, the territories clause of Article IV, section 3,[181] but rather from its power to admit new states, found in the preceding paragraph of section 3. In exercising its power to admit new states, Congress was bound by the Fifth Amendment's due process clause: "nor shall any person...be deprived of life, liberty, or property, without due process of law."

Taney's claim had two momentous consequences. First, it implicitly held unconstitutional three of the contemporary views of slavery in the territories: (1) all versions of antislavery constitutionalism; (2) the popular-sovereignty position of the northern Democrats; and (3) the Republican plank of excluding slavery from the territories. This left as legitimate only the extremist pro-slavery stance of the southern Democrats, that Congress must protect and promote slavery in all the territories. This was rigidly antidemocratic: it imposed the views of a sectional minority on the rest of the nation.

Second, for the first time, the US Supreme Court embraced the doctrine of substantive due process. Taney held that "an act of Congress which deprives a citizen of the United States of his property, merely because he came himself or brought his property into a particular Territory of the United States, and who committed no offence against the laws, could hardly be dignified with the name of due process of law."[182]

Finally, in yet another dictum, Taney insisted that slavery was a form of super-property. Congress could not provide less protection for it than for any other form of property, such as horses or wagons. "The only power conferred is the power coupled with the duty of guarding and protecting the owner in his rights."[183] This strongly implied that Congress had an obligation to extend slavery into all territories and to protect it there, an advanced pro-slavery view not asserted in Congress until 1860.

What made *Dred Scott* the foul disaster that it was, unique in its malignancy, was the lethal combination of its racism, its hostility to democracy, and its dogmatic originalism. In the view of two leading constitutional historians, "Taney's opinion is one of the worst he wrote: he ignored precedent, distorted history, imposed a static construction on the Constitution, ignored specific grants of power in the document, and tortured meanings out of other, more obscure clauses....The South could not have asked for more."[184]

It is painful to read Taney's words today, and the emotionally easy way out for Americans would be to dismiss them either as aberrations, not the sort of things most decent Americans of the antebellum era would believe, or as an unfortunate moral lapse that is now behind us, something to be noted with regret and then consigned to the past. But Taney's ideas were not aberrational—only a handful of the most egalitarian abolitionists of the time took notice of them to critique on moral grounds. As for their obsolescence, William Faulkner's aperçu remains pertinent: "The past is never dead. It's not even past."[185] Further comment would be superfluous: Taney's words speak for themselves with a starkness that no commentary can enhance.

After *Dred Scott*, any subsequent Supreme Court pronouncements on slavery might seem anticlimactic, especially in view of what happened after 1860. But two other major slavery-related issues were in the judicial pipeline, and the Court could not ignore them. The first arose out of the Wisconsin Supreme Court's defiance of federal authority under the 1850 Fugitive Slave Act. In 1854 a Wisconsin abolitionist, Sherman Booth, helped rescue of a man who had escaped slavery. While in the custody of a federal commissioner pending charges for violation of the 1850 Fugitive Slave Act, Booth sought a writ of habeas corpus from a state supreme court judge, who, being an abolitionist himself, gladly granted it and pronounced the 1850 act unconstitutional. The full bench affirmed, though it split two to one on the constitutionality issue.[186] Alarmed by this challenge to federal authority, the US attorney general sought a writ of error from the US Supreme Court. Meanwhile, Booth was indicted for violation of the 1850 act by a federal grand jury. He was tried in a federal court and convicted under the 1850 act of aiding and abetting a fugitive escape, but the jury took the extraordinary step on its own volition of composing a formal statement regretting the necessity of conviction under "a most cruel and odious law," and commending the defendant for performing "a most noble, benevolent and humane act." It too denounced the 1850 act.[187]

Booth petitioned yet again for a writ of habeas corpus from the state supreme court, which it granted on the grounds of what amounted to a pleading technicality.[188] The Pierce administration could not ignore this challenge to federal authority, and it appealed the last decision to the US Supreme Court. The Wisconsin Supreme Court then carried its defiance of the odious federal act and federal authority a radical step further by instructing its Clerk to ignore the writ of error sent down by the US Supreme Court and then refusing to enter the writ in the records of the court.[189] This was overt judicial nullification, flouting the authority of both a federal statute, the venerable Judiciary Act of 1789 (which provided for writs of error), and the Supreme Court's equally venerable decision in *Martin v. Hunter's Lessee* (1816) upholding the constitutionality of that act.[190]

The US Supreme Court nevertheless forged ahead on the basis of an authenticated record of the Wisconsin Supreme Court's decision and, in *Ableman v. Booth* (1858),[191] held that the actions of the Wisconsin judges were unconstitutional. In a ringing nationalistic opinion for a unanimous Court, Chief Justice Taney denounced the obstructive behavior of the Wisconsin court in ignoring the writ of error. He insisted on the necessity of federal judicial power for the existence of the Union. In this respect, the opinion justifies Charles Warren's encomium as "the most powerful" of all of Taney's oeuvre.[192] But again, Taney would not leave good enough alone. He could not suppress his urge to speak on issues not before the Court, and in dictum insisted that "the fugitive slave law is, in all of its provisions, fully authorized by the Constitution of the United States." Thus, one of the greatest of all Taney's opinions, enduring today as a bedrock of American federalism, is marred by the pestilent intrusion of slavery and his gratuitous subservience to it. In the end, slavery was an ultra-nationalizing force in American politics. Looking back from the end of the century, Henry Adams identified this nationalizing tendency: "The slave power, when in control, was a centralizing influence.... Whenever a question arose of extending or protecting slavery, the slaveholders became friends of centralized power, and used that dangerous weapon with a kind of frenzy. Slavery in fact required centralization in order to maintain and protect itself, but it required to control the centralized machine."[193]

Ableman was not the last challenge to the power of the northern states to protect freedom within their borders. *Dred Scott* had alarmed people of the free states with its unsettling hints that there were limits on the power of the free states to protect their free citizens within and outside their borders. Samuel Nelson's concurring opinion in *Dred Scott* had repeated Taney's troubling *Strader* dictum about the power of states over the status of their residents: "except in cases where the power is restrained by the Constitution of the United States, the law of the State is supreme over the subject of slavery within its jurisdiction."[194] What did that exception mean? Was it meant to suggest that free states could not declare enslaved people who had come into their jurisdiction free—thwarting an American *Somerset*? In a leading antebellum precedent, *Med's Case* (1836), Chief Justice Shaw of the Massachusetts Supreme Judicial Court had declared an enslaved girl claimed by a sojourner free under *Somerset* principles.[195] Could the free states no longer protect their residents against kidnaping, the issue raised in *Prigg*? Most ominously of all, was there something in the federal Constitution (or Taney's reading of it) that might imply a limit on the power of the free states to abolish slavery itself? In Congress, southern radicals were hinting at just such a possibility. Sometime around 1856, Georgia senator Robert Toombs supposedly boasted in Congress that he "would call the roll of his slaves on Bunker Hill."[196] Might the US Supreme Court be inching toward such a possibility?

Abraham Lincoln thought so. In the Lincoln-Douglas debates of 1858, he warned: "put this and that together, and we have another nice little niche, which we may, ere long, see filled with another Supreme Court decision, declaring that the Constitution of the United States does not permit a State to exclude slavery from its limits.... We shall lie down pleasantly dreaming that the people of Missouri are on the verge of making their State free, and we shall awake to the reality instead, that the Supreme Court has made Illinois a slave State."[197] In his 1858 "House Divided" speech, Lincoln warned that the Taney Court could hold "that the Constitution of the United States does not permit a state to exclude slavery from its limits."[198] This was not paranoid or a groundless conspiracy theory; it was an alarm widely shared in the North. Figures as disparate as an Ohio Democratic senator and the Vermont legislature warned that the trajectory from *Strader* to *Dred Scott* pointed in the direction of converting the North into slave states.[199] New York judge Samuel A. Foot warned that the Supreme Court had perverted the US Constitution "so fundamentally, as to nationalize slavery, and turn this nation into a great slaveholding republic."[200] Massachusetts Republican senator Charles Sumner warned that the "Slave Oligarchy...contemplates not merely the political subjugation of the National Government, but the actual introduction of Slavery into the Free States."[201] Southerners concurred, reversing the abolitionist slogan of "Freedom National" and developing instead the doctrine of "Slavery National." Turning *Somerset* on its head, they argued that slavery is the universal default condition of human society, and freedom the localized, anomalous exception.[202]

Today we might dismiss all of this as hysteria or hyperbole, were it not for the fact that a case was on its way to the Supreme Court that might have provided just the vehicle for nationalizing slavery. In 1852, a Virginia slaveholder named Jonathan Lemon attempted to move to Texas by steamship with his family and eight enslaved young people.[203] A delay in connections forced the entourage to detour through New York City, where a state judge issued a writ of habeas corpus on behalf of the youngsters at the behest of local abolitionists and activists in the Underground Railroad. He subsequently held them to be free under New York law on *Somerset* principles.[204] Virginians appealed the case to the state supreme court, anticipating an unfavorable ruling there and planning to appeal thence to the New York Court of Appeals,[205] and then to the US Supreme Court. A combination of the due process, full faith and credit, and privileges and immunities clauses of the federal Constitution could provide the bases for a holding that the rights of property in enslaved people must be respected everywhere in the United States, not just the territories.[206]

After the New York Supreme Court affirmed the decision below in 1857,[207] *Lemmon* attracted attention throughout the nation. The *Washington Union*, organ of the Buchanan administration, proclaimed that property in enslaved people is "recognized as property by the Constitution of the United States, by a provision which applies equally to all the States, [and] has an inalienable right to be protected in all the States."[208] The New York legislature responded with resolutions declaring "that this state will now allow slavery within her borders, in any form, or under any pretence, or for any time however short" and that "the supreme court of the United States [in *Dred Scott*], by reason of a majority of the judges thereof having identified it with a sectional and aggressive party, has impaired the confidence and respect of the people of this state."[209] The New York Court of Appeals affirmed the results below in March 1860.[210]

We can only speculate about what might have happened had Lemon pursued an appeal up to the US Supreme Court. The case itself was soon eclipsed by the excitements of the 1860 presidential contest and then secession. But given the trajectory of cases after 1850, it is at least possible that the Taney Court would continue on its fatal course, prostituting the US Constitution to subservience to slavery.

The Taney Court cases on slavery and race continue to speak to us today, but they do so equivocally. Justice Antonin Scalia, dissenting in *Planned Parenthood v. Casey* (1992) drew an arresting image of Taney. Describing an actual portrait, Scalia wrote:

> He is all in black, sitting in a shadowed red armchair, left hand resting upon a pad of paper in his lap, right hand hanging limply, almost lifelessly, beside the inner arm of the chair. He sits facing the viewer and staring straight out. There seems to be on his face, and in his deep-set eyes, an expression of profound sadness and disillusionment. Perhaps he always

looked that way, even when dwelling upon the happiest of thoughts. But those of us who know how the lustre of his great Chief Justiceship came to be eclipsed by *Dred Scott* cannot help believing that he had that case—its already apparent consequences for the Court and its soon-to-be-played-out consequences for the Nation—burning on his mind.[211]

If Scalia imagined that Taney had any regrets about his decision, he knew little about the chief justice in his last years. Concerned that his *Dred Scott* holding might be misinterpreted to be based on status (slavery) rather than race (negritude), in 1860 Taney drafted a supplement to his opinion insisting that it applied to all African Americans, not just to those whose ancestors had been brought to America enslaved.[212] Defiant to the end, he wrote anticipatory opinions on conscription and the Legal Tender Acts, pronouncing both to be unconstitutional.[213] Taney certainly had neither second thoughts nor regrets about his determination to settle all constitutional questions about slavery and race definitively, imposing them not only on the states and the political branches of the national government but on the American people as well. Scalia was right to detect hubris in this, but it was the willfulness of a man who exalted race to a constitutional dimension.

The US Supreme Court was in existence for only seventy-five years of slavery's two centuries' ascendance in America. For all but a decade of those years, the justices managed to avoid making catastrophic errors that involved slavery. They did not veer from the common racial consensus shared by nearly all white Americans, and their decisions reflected that. Slavery and the racism that underlay it were pervasive in antebellum society, and the Court found no reason to disturb that status quo. But if the Court did not meliorate racial relations before 1850, it did not severely worsen them either.

In its last decade before the war, though, the Court increasingly intruded in Americans' debates over the future of slavery, especially in the trans-Mississippi West, entirely to disastrous effect. A Court dominated by strong-willed slaveholders and pliant Doughfaces determined to force American constitutional development in a direction that confirmed the extremist views of the slave South, and in the end, seemed to threaten freedom everywhere in the nation.

The Dark Past: The US Supreme Court and African Americans, 1800–2015. William M. Wiecek, Oxford University Press. © Oxford University Press 2024. DOI: 10.1093/9780197654460.003.0001

2

Reconstruction and the Supreme Court, 1862–1880

By 1865, slavery came to a cataclysmic end.[1] It was succeeded by a tragically brief period—a mere fifteen years or so—when the American people tried to create a society based on some measure of racial equality. We know this moment as Reconstruction, a time when the constitutions of nation and states began to realize the promise of the Declaration of Independence: "that all men are created equal, that they are endowed by their creator with certain unalienable rights, that among these are life, liberty and the pursuit of happiness."[2]

So revolutionary a change in the social order required a revised constitutional framework, something necessarily much different from one where African Americans had no rights that the white man need respect. This did not entail change on the order of the French Revolution, where all of society's institutions were overthrown. The background structures of federalism, separation of powers, limited government, written constitutions, judicial review, and other fundamentals endured. But when an organizing social system as pervasive as slavery was abolished, something comparable had to fill the vacuum. Abolition was not the work of a day. Rather it was what Ira Berlin, the premier historian of slavery and its abolition, called "the long emancipation."[3] The people held in slavery assumed the primary role in their own emancipation, first by resistance and escape, then by forcing all Americans to confront the question of what succeeds enslavement. Freedom, obviously, but what exactly did "freedom" mean? To the freedpeople, freedom meant citizenship and equality, their rightful heritage under the Declaration of Independence.

Americans of differing views, north and south, Republicans and ex-Confederates, all vied to create the new constitutional order that was to succeed the regime of slavery and the slaveholders' constitution. At first, white ex-Confederates tried to reinstate something like slavery throughout the south through a series of laws known as the Black Codes, which reimposed unfree labor discipline through vagrancy laws and other legal structures of unfree labor. That in turn drove a reluctant but indignant Congress and Republican Party to devise their own alternative. With some hesitancy, Republicans and their party leader, Abraham Lincoln, embraced antebellum antislavery constitutional ideas that outlined the contours of freedom and equality.[4] They affirmed the basic idea derived from *Somerset* and captured in the slogan "freedom national": liberty is the normal condition of all humans. Slavery was nothing more than a local and temporary aberration from that normal status, an anomaly that first had to be confined, then eventually destroyed.

Republicans then endowed the freedpeople with a basic civic status that enabled them to function as free individuals in a market economy. The freedpeople assumed rights necessary to act as citizens and could invoke the protection of law to secure those rights. Congressional Republicans empowered Congress and, most importantly, the federal courts, to protect the fundamental rights of all American citizens, including those newly enfranchised, against infringement not only by state actors but by private persons, under section 2 of the Thirteenth Amendment. This latest regime, centered on the Thirteenth, Fourteenth, and Fifteenth Amendments, embodied a new constitution of equality.

But the egalitarian values that animated those Amendments were anathema to many whites in all sections of the country. They determined to reject those values and replace the egalitarian constitution after 1876, leaving nominal guarantees of equality in the parchment document, but imposing a much different reality on the ground. Though the rights of the freedpeople became nugatory for eighty years, they survived in the constitutional order, dormant but awaiting revival.

As the guns of the Civil War armies fell silent in 1865, the US Supreme Court was confronted with a profoundly important question: Had the war and the resulting abolition of slavery effected a revolution in the American constitutional order, or were those momentous events merely a passing disruption of the normal routine of governance?[5] The answer to this question would be worked out along three axes: federalism, the status of the freedpeople, and the role that federal courts would play in the new order.

The Reconstruction Amendments

The image of Abraham Lincoln as the Great Emancipator has a tenacious hold on the popular imagination, but it is misleading in important ways.

In a legal sense, the effective emancipation of most enslaved people—their transition under law from slavery to freedom—was achieved by the Thirteenth Amendment. More importantly, the image overlooks the fact that Black Americans played an active role in their own liberation, serving as soldiers and sailors, military laborers, teamsters, drovers, cooks, washerwomen.[6] They decamped, sought refuge behind federal lines, joined Union forces, simply stopped working, or negotiated new arrangements for themselves with their former masters.[7] Steven Hahn calls this collective action "the greatest slave rebellion in modern history."[8]

We are only now beginning to recognize the extent to which African American thought and action before the Civil War shaped the Reconstruction constitution afterward. African Americans in the free states energetically advocated for their own conceptions of citizenship, privileges and immunities, rights, and status throughout the antebellum period.[9] They spread their ideas through petitions to Congress and the state legislatures. They published pamphlets and newspapers exploring constitutional ideas. They organized colored conventions beginning in 1830 to debate laws, tactics, and constitutional issues.[10] They protested laws in the northern states that restricted their mobility, excluded them altogether, or deprived them of rights enjoyed by whites.[11] The Ohio black laws throughout the antebellum period were a favorite target of Black activists.[12] They demanded equality and all rights of citizenship. To challenge discriminatory northern laws and customs, they elaborated ideas centered on the privileges and immunities clause of the original Constitution (Art. IV, sec. 2, cl. 1).[13] From that source they claimed rights as citizens of the states, rights founded on natural law, that must be respected throughout the Union. In this trove of ideas, the framers of the Fourteenth Amendment would later derive their understanding of citizenship as well as privileges and immunities.[14]

Lincoln at first proceeded cautiously in refusing to proclaim all enslaved people within Union lines free. He rebuked the enthusiasm of some Union officers for encouraging them, but he let the contraband policy continue as a practical matter. In doing so, he implemented a policy of what his contemporaries called "military emancipation." Drawing on antebellum abolitionist arguments, Lincoln endorsed the idea that the federal government could abolish slavery as a necessary step for successfully prosecuting the war. As the president admitted in another context, "I claim not to have controlled events, but confess plainly that events have controlled me."[15]

Congress then stepped in with emancipation by legislative action, passing a series of measures beginning with the first Confiscation Act in 1862 and the second the year following. This began the statutory process of freeing all persons claimed by Confederate military and civilian personnel.[16] Like the president, Congress justified this on the rationale of military necessity. It followed up by abolishing slavery, first in the District of Columbia in April 1862[17] and then in all the territories two months later.[18] Thus at a stroke, Congress finally resolved the issues that had destroyed the Union. In a supreme irony, these abolition measures aroused little controversy, nearly the entire southern delegation having withdrawn from Congress a year earlier. Their enactment was almost uneventful, compared to the turmoil surrounding the same issues in the preceding decade. Though more symbolic than practical in significance, the statutes marked Congress's first steps toward ultimate abolition.

In January 1863, President Lincoln issued the Emancipation Proclamation, which accelerated the pace of self-liberation and held out the promise of emancipation for everyone.[19] The president justified it as a war measure. Under pressure from the federal government, six states achieved abolition either by constitutional amendment or through ordinary legislation.[20] But that left slavery legally intact in nine states, with 85 percent of the enslaved population still nominally or actually unfree.

Capping the process at war's end, Congress adopted the Thirteenth Amendment, which swept away the remaining slavery in the United States as of December 1865.[21] Abolition was absolute and universal: "neither slavery nor involuntary servitude...shall exist within the United States." State action was not required or relevant. The Thirteenth Amendment created a substantive individual right to freedom (except for the crypto-slavery that emerged under the punishment clause, a problem discussed below in this chapter). "Freedom" in turn meant more than the minimum recognized in the antebellum laws of the slave states, which was no more than the liberty of an individual to go where he wanted, and not to have to obey the commands of a master.[22] The substantive heart of the freedom assured by emancipation was individual autonomy and dignity. The amendment culminated the abolitionist movement, with its insistence on equality, dignity, and rights. It was the first step in the progression from emancipation and the abolition of slavery to restoring the freed people to full "civil equality" (Fourteenth Amendment), to protection for political rights (Fifteenth Amendment).[23] The sponsors of the Thirteenth Amendment believed that it did more than merely abolish the legal institution of slavery. It implied positive liberties (individual autonomy, agency, and dignity) and a new enfranchised civil status. The amendment established "equality before the law [as] the great cornerstone" of American government. It protected "those great natural rights to which every man is entitled." Its section 2 empowered Congress to protect the freedpeople in all their basic civil rights and liberties.[24]

The Thirteenth Amendment was never color-blind: it is racially coded, abolishing a system of racial slavery where "whites dominated an entire race of subordinated black people."[25] Though it prohibits enslavement of any racial group, including whites,[26] the amendment was meant to abolish African enslavement, along with what the Supreme Court later called its "badges and incidents."[27] However, the scope and content of "badges and incidents" has been contested from the beginning. Democrats insisted the amendment reached only physical enslavement and labor enforced by law. Republicans saw a much broader scope, which they immediately defined in section 1 of the 1866 Civil Rights Act. In the twentieth century, judicial interpretation has tended toward the defective Democratic view, while academic understanding has embraced the broader Republican vision.[28]

The Thirteenth Amendment provides a constitutional foundation for racial equality and for broad judicial as well as congressional power to sweep away invidious racial discrimination.[29] In this sense, it realized the abolitionists' basic aim of bringing the freedpeople under the protection of law and vindicating their innate rights as human beings.[30] "Abolitionists forged the critical ethical arguments through which the revolutionary constitutionalism of the Reconstruction amendments conceived and framed the mission of constitutional Reconstruction."[31] The Thirteenth Amendment filtered abolitionist egalitarianism through the political mesh of the Republican Party, reaching into the states to create a direct link between individual people and the federal government. It marked an unprecedented expansion of federal authority, displacing the states as the source of individual rights and status.[32]

But the sweep of the Thirteenth Amendment contained a dangerous carve-out: slavery was abolished "except as a punishment for crime whereof the party shall have been duly convicted." The punishment clause[33] later provided justification for forms of crypto-slavery that lasted into the twentieth century. In 1867, John Kasson, a Republican congressman from Iowa, introduced a resolution that might have defanged the punishment exemption of the amendment, but it went nowhere.[34]

With slavery abolished, all Americans, white and Black, Union and Confederate, had to resolve the question of what was to be the legal and civic status of the freedpeople. What were the rights and status of the freedpeople vis-à-vis whites? The legal systems of the free and slave states provided radically different answers to that question. Free-state citizens assumed that after slave status was dissolved, formerly enslaved people would emerge as rights-bearing individuals, entitled to claim natural and civil rights, as those concepts were understood at the time. If perhaps not fully equal in political status to whites, they were nevertheless persons who could demand the full and equal protection of the laws. White residents of the slave states, on the other hand, believed that an emancipated person had no rights or status whatsoever beyond the power of locomotion: the ability to go where he wished (and even that right was severely curtailed legally and practically in the antebellum South). As Chief Justice Joseph Lumpkin of Georgia held in an 1853 case, "the African in Georgia [free or enslaved]...has no civil, social or political rights or capacity."[35] Neither the Confederacy's defeat nor emancipation altered that. The ex-Confederates who remained in control of the southern state governments imposed the slave state view immediately in the summer and autumn of 1865.

In late 1865, the governments in the former seceded states adopted statutes known collectively as the "Black Codes." These provisions included vagrancy laws that mandated employment and criminalized unemployment. They authorized convict labor and convict leasing, including the form of neo-slavery known as "hiring out," by which a court could order someone convicted of vagrancy, invariably a Black man, to work for anyone willing to pay his fine. Judges were empowered to take Black children from their parents and place them in "apprenticeships." Contract enforcement laws, including those permitting recapture of "fugitive" workers, policed Black labor. Other laws restricted Black mobility or prohibited owning or renting real property in towns. The codes criminalized certain behaviors that would not be criminal for white people, such as "impudence" and "disobedience."[36] A Freedmen's Bureau official testified before Congress in 1866 that "these [black] codes were simply the old black code of the state, with the word 'slave' expunged, and 'negro' substituted. The most odious features of slavery were preserved in them."[37] It took a century before the US Supreme Court would belatedly hold such vagrancy and loitering statutes to be unconstitutional because they were vague and arbitrary.[38]

The North, speaking through Congress, indignantly repudiated the Black Codes as well as the governments that had enacted them. In their place, Congress enacted the Civil Rights Act of 1866, a measure almost as significant for Black freedom and empowerment as its constitutional foundation, the Thirteenth Amendment. The formal title of the statute proclaimed its dual significance: it was "An Act to Protect All Persons in the United States in Their Civil Rights, and Furnish the Means of Their Vindication."[39] Thus it both identified the substance of rights and conferred power on the federal courts to enforce those rights.

The civil rights bill's Senate sponsor, Lyman Trumbull of Illinois, insisted that the freedpeople "being now free and citizens of the United States, as citizens they are entitled… to the great fundamental rights belonging to free citizens, and we have a right to protect them in the enjoyment of them."[40] Rep. Martin Thayer, a Pennsylvania Republican, lauded "the fundamental rights of citizenship; those rights which constitute the essence of freedom, and which are common to the citizens of all civilized states; those rights which secure life, liberty, and property and which make all men equal before the law."[41] The substantive rights conferred by the act included most of the powers necessary to function in civil society and in a market economy as an autonomous rights-bearing citizen, beginning with national citizenship itself:

> all persons born in the united states and not subject to any foreign power, excluding Indians not taxed, are hereby declared to be citizens of the United States; and such citizens, of every race and color, without regard to any previous condition of slavery or involuntary servitude, except as a punishment for crime whereof the party shall have been duly convicted, shall have the same right, in every state and territory in the United States, to make and enforce contracts, to sue, be parties, and give evidence, to inherit, purchase, lease, sell, hold, and convey real and personal property, and to full and equal benefit of all laws and proceedings for the security of person and property, as is enjoyed by white citizens, and shall be subject to like punishment, pains, and penalties, and to none other, any law, statute, ordinance, regulation, or custom, to the contrary notwithstanding.[42]

The newly empowered citizens could make contracts; access all courts, federal as well as state, as parties and witnesses; exercise full property-owning capacity; and in general, claim the benefit of the same rights "as is enjoyed by white citizens." The effect of the citizenship and ensuing property/contracts provisions, read in tandem, was to create a privilege and right of equal protection for, or access to, basic common-law empowerments: the power to enter into contractual relations, or to own property. George Rutherglen refers to these as a "common law understanding of civil rights." Congress first identified "the rights among citizens at common law—and gave them a new meaning based on racial equality—basic rights protected against racial discrimination."[43] This marked a progression from the minimalist conception of emancipation, which would have been nothing more than the "physical liberty" of not being "owned" by someone, not having to obey another's commands, and being free to go where you wish. Freedom, as Rep. James A. Garfield (R.-OH) insisted, was more than "the bare privilege of not being chained."[44] The next step in this progression was "civil rights" in the common-law sense—contract, property, juridical capacity. The Thirteenth Amendment, by restoring submerged human autonomy, created the conditions where law could endow the freedpeople with full affirmative contractual agency.[45] The final step was political empowerment. Section 2, the vital enforcement provision, made it a federal felony for any person acting under color of state law or custom to deprive anyone of the substantive rights enumerated in section 1.[46]

The 1866 Civil Rights Act and the ensuing Fourteenth Amendment were momentous. Before 1866, responsibility for protecting individual rights lay with the states, not the federal government, both in defining the content of those rights and in enforcing them. But because the southern states obviously could not be depended upon to protect the rights of their new Black citizens, the federal government had to step in lest those rights lapse in abeyance. Lot Morrell, a Maine Republican and Senate supporter of the civil rights bill, conceded in this respect that "this species of legislation is absolutely revolutionary." But, he went on, "are we not in the midst of a revolution?"[47] Indeed, they were. Congressional Republicans were creating a new constitutional order for the United States, self-aware and deliberately.

So-called radical Republicans embraced the fundamentally revolutionary changes in federalism that were entailed by racial egalitarianism.[48] Since African Americans were now free people, they were to be subsumed into this scope of protection.[49] Their conservative Republican colleagues were more solicitous for traditional structures of federalism.[50] But even they conceded that some institution of government would have to take responsibility for enforcing the rights of the freedpeople. The antebellum constitutional order, as it evolved under the pressures of the slavery controversies, was premised on the assumption that the purpose of the Constitution was to impose limits on federal power (except when that power was to be used to protect and promote slavery). The postwar order was radically different: the Constitution became "a source of sovereign, positive, regulatory government able to establish and enforce national rights."[51]

Democrats and a few Republican conservatives entertained lingering doubts about Congress's constitutional authority to enact such sweeping legislation.[52] So one of the doubters (though by no means a conservative), Congressman John A. Bingham of Ohio, introduced the elements of what was to become the Fourteenth Amendment.[53] These joined numerous other proposals for constitutional amendment—more than seventy in all—being considered by the Thirty-Ninth Congress. All were referred to the Joint Committee on Reconstruction, which in June 1867 reported out a measure that became the Fourteenth Amendment. Though the amendment's framers disagreed among themselves on its meanings and impact, they adopted general principles that courts would later translate into specific legal doctrines.[54]

Five of its provisions bore directly on the status, rights, and prospects of African Americans.[55] Section 1 first confers citizenship, both federal and state, on "all persons born or naturalized in the United States."[56] This is known today as birthright citizenship: someone born in the United States is a citizen of the nation, irrespective of the citizenship or other status markers of her parents, and a citizen as well "of the state wherein they reside." This provision finally settled the basic contours of citizenship in the American federation. Before the Civil War, no authoritative definition of citizenship existed. In 1862, US attorney general Edward Bates observed that citizenship was "now as little understood in its details and elements, and the question as open to argument and speculative criticism as it was at the founding of the government." There was no general agreement about "either the exact meaning of the word, or the constituent elements of the thing."[57] The possibility of citizenship for free African Americans was particularly contested.[58] The Fourteenth Amendment finally began resolving that problem. It "reversed" *Dred Scott*, only the second time the American people overturned a decision of the Supreme Court by constitutional amendment.[59] People formerly enslaved were now incorporated into the American polity as citizens, a status that provided a basis for other rights that the law acknowledged.

The citizenship clause embodied abolitionist and Republican understandings of the meaning and content of national citizenship.[60] Emancipation meant more than merely the negative state of not-slavery. As slave status disintegrated into nothing, it revealed the freedperson as a full member of the polity, endowed with full citizenship rights. Those rights had to be the same as—no more, no less—the rights possessed by all other citizens. This idea of birthright citizenship was in large measure a result of unceasing bottom-up grassroots organizing by African Americans themselves, who in their everyday lives assumed that they *were* citizens who had a broad panoply of rights. They not only demanded these rights but exercised them, whether the law permitted them to do so or not. They organized, carried on petition drives, litigated, debated, propagandized, pushed both for grand objectives like freedom and equality and for mundane issues affecting their individual situation in what the historian Martha Jones calls "vernacular legal cultures." They contended that birth in the United States made them citizens, endowed with all the rights and powers of citizenship, even when those rights were denied by the states.[61] This popular activism played a major role in constitutionalizing the principle of birthright citizenship embodied in the citizenship clause.[62]

This equality of status and rights was reinforced by the sibling equal protection clause of section 1. The grant or recognition of full and equal citizenship carried with it a federal power to protect that status and those rights.[63] In part this was because rights and status that could not be enforced were no rights at all, merely an empty gesture. Bingham and the other framers believed that the states could not be trusted to protect that status and rights, and they feared that in time the federal courts, on which they placed so much faith, might not be reliable either. Thus, the grant of citizenship status had to be plenary (conveying the full panoply of rights and status). It had as well to confer on the federal government in all its branches, including Congress, the power to identify and protect those rights. As the first Justice Harlan stressed in his *Civil Rights Cases* dissent of 1883, the citizenship clause is of "an affirmative character," conferring enforcement power and not merely inert status. He elaborated, spelling out the implications:

> the citizenship thus acquired by that race, in virtue of an affirmative grant by the nation, may be protected, not alone by the judicial branch of the government, but by congressional legislation of a primary direct character; this, because the power of Congress is not restricted to the enforcement of prohibitions upon state laws or state action. It is, in terms distinct and positive, to enforce "the *provisions* of *this article*" of amendment; not

simply those of a prohibitive character, but the provisions,—*all* of the provisions,—affirmative and prohibitive, of the amendment.[64]

The citizenship clause, unlike its three following siblings, does not contain a state action limitation. Thus, Congress may act directly on private individuals and groups who interfere with any rights of citizenship, national or state.[65]

But this new national citizenship eventually became riddled with exceptions based on what the political scientist Rogers Smith calls "ascriptive hierarchies" or characteristics, principally race, gender, and ethnicity.[66] Such ascriptive principles of social ordering partially displaced Lockean liberal ideals of individual rights and republican communitarian ideals of civic status within a polity. Ascriptive citizenship stunted the possibilities for all African Americans (and, for a time, all women) to participate fully in civic life and to exercise political power to protect that participation. Within a generation of the Civil War, white society had reaffirmed its identity "as a white nation, a Protestant nation, a nation in which true Americans were native-born men of Anglo-Saxon ancestors."[67]

The citizenship clause implies an affirmative power to protect that national citizenship, particularly the requirement of equality among all citizens.[68] Because the wording of the amendment's section 5—"the Congress shall have power to . . ." is identical to the grant of power to Congress in the original Constitution,[69] it should be measured by the standard Chief Justice Marshall identified in *McCulloch v. Maryland* (1819):[70] "let the end be legitimate, let it be within the scope of the constitution, and all means which are appropriate, which are plainly adapted to that end, which are not prohibited, but consist with the letter and spirit of the constitution, are constitutional."[71] This includes the right to be protected in the exercise of citizenship rights, such as voting, assembly, and so on, a right also identified by John Marshall, this time in *Marbury v. Madison* (1803): "the very essence of civil liberty consists of the right of every individual to claim the protection of the laws, whenever he receives an injury. One of the first duties of government is to afford that protection."[72] This right is not limited only to protection against positive wrongdoing by the state or one of its officers. It also encompasses a right to be protected against the state's failure to protect.[73] Justice Bushrod Washington reaffirmed that in *Corfield v. Coryell* (1823) as one of "those privileges and immunities which are, in their nature, fundamental; which belong, of right, to the citizens of all free governments.... what these fundamental principles are [may] be all comprehended under the following general heads: protection by the government..."[74]

The privileges or immunities clause differed from the original privileges and immunities clause of the Constitution's Article IV, section 2 (commonly referred to as the "comity clause").[75] The original clause was the "interstate" privileges and immunities clause, because it required that a citizen of state A going into state B would be entitled to all the privileges and immunities that state B extended to its own citizens. It was meant to bar discrimination against out-of-staters. In that character, Alexander Hamilton thought it was "the basis of the union."[76] The new Fourteenth Amendment's privileges or immunities clause is an "intrastate" provision in that it bars any state from enacting or enforcing legislation that would limit the rights of national citizens, that is, "the privileges and immunities of citizens of the United States."[77] Congress intended it to prohibit states from limiting the rights of their new Black citizens. Rep. Bingham asserted that the amendment would authorize Congress to "protect by national law the privileges and immunities of all the citizens of the republic and the inborn rights of every person within its jurisdiction, whenever the same shall be abridged or denied by the unconstitutional acts of any state."[78] A modern reading of the clause suggests that it may ban either discrimination among individuals within a state or denial by a state of civil liberties that are generally recognized elsewhere or some combination of these two approaches.[79]

Bingham's remarks raise the possibility that the Fourteenth Amendment's privileges or immunities clause, rather than its sibling the due process clause, was meant to incorporate the various rights guaranteed in the Bill of Rights. Multiple scholars across the ideological spectrum contend that it was.[80] If this interpretation were to be widely accepted (most importantly, by the justices themselves), the implications would be sprawling. Would the privileges or immunities clause displace the due process clause as the basis of a substantive reading of the sources of constitutional rights, not only for African Americans but for everyone? If it did, would that erase or negate a century of substantive due process? Would we begin to construct from scratch a wholly new interpretation of privileges and immunities? The potential for such unimaginable change exists, and it occasionally erupts, only to subside again, perhaps because those who entertain it glimpse the uncontrolled potential for such a drastic revision.

The third of section 1's sibling provisions, the due process clause,[81] was derived from its Fifth Amendment counterpart, but it was now made explicitly applicable as a limitation on state power. A decade earlier, Justice Benjamin R. Curtis stated for the Court that "the words 'due process of law,' were undoubtedly intended to convey the same meaning as the words 'by the law of the land' in Magna Carta."[82] He thereby anchored the due process clause and its meaning for African Americans to a venerable legal tradition then more than six centuries old.

A major question spawned by the new due process clause is whether it "incorporated" the Bill of Rights as a limitation on state regulatory power.[83] That is, were the first eight amendments to the constitution now somehow by the operation of the due process clause made a limit on state power to the same extent that they were limits on federal power?[84] The Supreme Court had held in 1833 that those amendments limited only the powers of the federal government, not the states.[85] The framers of the Fourteenth Amendment, led by Bingham and Senator Jacob Howard of Michigan, meant to overturn this and oblige the states to respect the guarantees for personal liberties embodied in those Amendments, but they probably were in a minority on that question in the Thirty-Ninth Congress.

Suppose, though, that the Amendment as a whole, or any one of the constituent clauses of section 1, did in fact make some parts of the Bill of Rights, or all of it, applicable against the states. That possibility raises conceptual and practical problems. To begin with, what *were* those rights? As of 1868, they were sparse and poorly defined, nothing like the panoply of rights we refer to today as "the Bill of Rights." Were they the natural rights that Justice Samuel Chase referred to in *Calder v. Bull* (1798)[86] as "the fundamental principle[s that] flow from the very nature of our free republican governments," including "security for personal liberty or private property"? If so, were they protected by the guarantee clause of Article IV, section 4, which confirms that "every state in this union" must have "a republican form of government"? Were they the "general principles of right and justice" that Story had alluded to in *Jeune Eugenie* (1822)? Were they rights derived from citizenship? If so, they could not have been based on national citizenship, a vague and undefined concept until 1868. Were they the rights derived from *state* citizenship, "those privileges and immunities which are in their nature fundamental, which belong of right to the citizens of all free governments"? Justice Bushrod Washington enumerated these in 1823: "the enjoyment of life and liberty, with the right to acquire and possess property of every kind, and to pursue and obtain happiness and safety,...the right of every citizen...to claim the benefit of habeas corpus; to institute and maintain actions of any kind in the courts of the state; to take, hold, and dispose of property, real or personal; and an exemption from higher taxes and impositions than are paid by the other citizens of the state," and possibly "the elective franchise."[87] Were they the rights of subjects and citizens at common law? Debates over incorporation continued into the twenty-first century and continue today, after the US Supreme Court began incorporating rights piecemeal, beginning with the takings clause of the Fifth Amendment in 1896.[88] The repercussions for African Americans were vast.

Unlike the due process clause, with its ancestry tracing back to the Middle Ages, the ideal of racial equality affirmed by the equal protection clause[89] was entirely new. Nothing like it had appeared in any previous American constitutional regime.[90] Interpersonal equality as a value was unknown to the Constitution before 1868. Senator Jacob Howard declared in 1864 that the idea of equality before the law "was not known at all."[91] The novelty of the equal protection clause has an important consequence: its meaning is not dictated by centuries-old traditions. To the extent that it had any meaning contemporary with its drafting, that meaning was derived from the values and ideals promoted by antebellum abolitionists. Equality does not exist in some Platonic realm in a pure or definitive state. It is a human construct; it means what we say it means.[92] The framers of the Fourteenth Amendment's section 1 adapted antislavery constitutional theories to create new rights, principally equality before the law, and extend old ones, such as the rights and privileges of citizenship, to the newly freed African Americans.[93]

The other component of the equal protection clause, the "protection of the laws," on the other hand, was well established in constitutional theory at the time of the American Revolution. In exchange for allegiance and support by its citizens, the nation was obliged to extend to them the protection of law. William Blackstone put it pithily: "allegiance is the tie...which binds the subject to the king in return for that protection which the king affords the subject."[94] Chief Justice Marshall adopted that view in *Marbury v. Madison* (1803): "the very essence of civil liberty consists in the right of every individual to claim the protection of the laws, whenever he receives an injury. One of the first duties of government is to afford that protection."[95]

To the degree that this protection had to be "equal," before 1868 that equality did not extend to the African race, as Chief Justice Taney made abundantly clear. The enslaved African was the ever-present exception.

Though few members of the Thirty-Ninth Congress, or the state legislatures that ratified the amendment, had been abolitionists themselves, Republicans in both houses were driven to embrace those values by white southern racism and intransigence. For some of them, the embrace may have been reluctant, but where the choice was between the neo-slavery imposed by the Black Codes and the abolitionist vision of equality before the law, they chose equality. The framers embraced uncertainty, with all the possibilities that might lie in an unknown future. But the clause and its innate value of racial justice and equality lay moribund for almost a century after its appearance. Americans did not take up the task of defining its values and scope until after World War II. Thus, its meaning, far from being apparent, fixed, or inherent, is an artifact of our times. It means what the American people want it to mean.

The congressional Republicans who drafted the Thirteenth and Fourteenth Amendments and the Civil Rights Act of 1866 achieved a revolutionary revision of American constitutionalism and the federal system. Under it, the federal government was to have plenary authority to protect the fundamental rights of American citizens, shared with the states concurrently, but ultimately supreme. The national citizenship bestowed by section 1 of both the Civil Rights Act and the Fourteenth Amendment embraced all the natural rights of a free people. Fundamental rights became nationalized, in the sense that the federal government assumed authority to define and enforce them.[96] Beyond that, the citizenship clauses embodied a vision of participation in political and civic life that included much more than merely voting, though voting is the indispensable sine qua non of full citizenship.[97] The African Americans seeking full and equal citizenship since the American Revolution demanded full legal and political rights, acceptance, inclusion, and respect across the color line.[98] The Reconstruction Amendments were transformative: they both democratized and centralized personal rights in America. African Americans and their abolitionist supporters linked their demands for rights to larger conceptions of social justice, which in turn became universal legal principles, embedded in the Constitution. These became operative at the federal level by 1866. The Union was itself transformed by African American freedom.[99] But freedom alone was not enough. Of itself, freedom did not confer political power, much less true equality. The next phase of the Reconstruction struggle centered on the right to vote.[100]

Americans in the Reconstruction era thought of "civil rights" in a way much different from modern understandings. To them, the rights that pertained to free individuals were layered in three tiers or strata: civil, political, and social.[101] Civil rights in the nineteenth-century sense of the term were precisely those rights affirmed by the Civil Rights Act of 1866: the basic abilities that enabled a person to function as a member of society. These included the right to go where one pleased and to be exempt from having to obey the commands of others; the right to enter into legally protected economic relationships involving contracts and property; the right of access to courts as both party and witness; the right to form stable, legally protected family relationships (husband and wife, parent and child); and finally, a generalized right to be treated more or less equally by the law. That "more or less" qualification left plenty of room to discriminate on various grounds: sex, citizenship, race, wealth. Of these civil rights, only the first was conceded by southern whites to Blacks, and that reluctantly and with numerous exceptions and qualifications, as the Black Codes attested. But in the free states, the assumption prevailed that when a person shook off the unnatural status of slavery, he emerged as a person recognized by law as bearing the basic range of civil rights just enumerated.[102]

"Political rights" were another matter. These embraced the power to vote, to hold office, and to serve on juries. In the exercise of these rights, a man[103] played a political role in society more exalted than merely someone who is trying to get by economically. He assumed a political station, functioning as one who was empowered to participate in governance of the state, and be entrusted with the lives, liberty, and property of his fellow citizens. Such power was not to be conferred lightly. But it was not as obvious to people of the nineteenth century as it is to us that that such civic enfranchisement is a precondition of full citizenship status. Thus, men in the northeastern states were reluctant to enfranchise Irish immigrants, and in California to concede such powers to Chinese. Political rights were readily encumbered by racial and ethnic barriers.

"Social rights" embraced various interpersonal matters that were fundamentally a matter of physical proximity: the power to enter into social relationships ranging from the most intimate and lasting—marriage—to the most casual and fleeting, like riding in a train car. Here the preferences and biases of whites had much freer play. Whites in all regions cherished their ability to exclude others from being close to them and saw no merit in claims that such exclusion deprived anyone of something that rose to the dignity of a "right." Thus, northern Republicans had little trouble in extending civil rights, in the nineteenth-century sense of the term, to Blacks, but sharing political power was far touchier, and according full access to white society and opportunity at the social level was out of the question.

Had the Supreme Court been inclined to deal comprehensively with the problem of African Americans' rights at that time, it would have found only ambiguous constitutional text to guide its deliberations. In 1867, Republicans in the Thirty-Ninth Congress faced several dilemmas as they contemplated restoration of the seceded states. Elections held in 1865 and 1866 returned numerous former Confederate military and civilian officials to Congress. Could men who had committed treason for the previous four years and who were responsible for the deaths of countless Union soldiers be entrusted with governance of the nation they had betrayed and waged war against? Worse: because of the operation of the three-fifths clause of Article I, section 2, the southern delegation would perversely be rewarded with an *increase* in its congressional delegation.[104] Southern whites had emphatically signaled their determination that African Americans would be completely excluded from political power, so the enlarged southern congressional delegation would represent only racist, secessionist white Democrats. Further complicating this picture was the fact that section 1 of the emergent Fourteenth Amendment would create a new constitutional order, with the old slavocracy destroyed and a new regime replacing the old, based on federal citizenship, a nationalized inventory of privileges and immunities, and a guarantee of the equal protection of the laws. Formerly enslaved people would now be full citizens of the nation and their states.

But in the spring of 1866, for a variety of reasons, not least of which was their own racist attitudes, congressional Republicans evinced little appetite for enfranchising African Americans en masse.[105] So they came up with a clumsy compromise, section 2 of the Fourteenth Amendment, which perpetuated control of the franchise by the states themselves, with the risk that they would continue to confine the vote to white men.[106] But if they did so, they would proportionately lose representation in the House of Representatives. That might have seemed to Republicans like an elegant and conservative compromise: it solved the dilemma of the three-fifths clause, yet it did not radically destabilize the antebellum structure of federalism.[107] It would not alienate northern constituents by forcing increased

Black suffrage on the North to any significant degree. The North was in effect saying to the South: you may cling to the white man's government if you wish, but you will suffer a proportional loss of power in the House of Representatives if you do; or you may accept the results of the war, including full Black citizenship as the price of restoration. Justice Thurgood Marshall put it more succinctly: "it put Southern States to a choice—enfranchise Negro voters or lose congressional representation."[108]

Section 2 prohibited the states from denying or abridging "the right to vote" in federal and state elections, "except for participation in rebellion, or other crime." It might be argued[109] that the phrase "or other crime" is textually bounded by "rebellion" and thus refers only to criminal acts committed in the course of rebellion, but most modern authority interprets it to refer to felonies of all sorts. Read in this way, Section 2 might provide a constitutional affirmation of the idea that felon disenfranchisement is legitimate, recognized by the supreme law. But whatever the expectations of its framers, Section 2 was a dead letter from the outset. Congress never enacted enforcement legislation of any sort, and no court has ever entertained litigation seeking its implementation.

Enfranchising African American citizens was not a straightforward matter, though. Republican enthusiasm for sustaining military Reconstruction dwindled exponentially after 1868. Northerners wanted to shed the expense of maintaining an army of occupation in the South, which, after all, seemed somehow un-American, aside from its financial costs. Ideally, northern whites thought, the freedpeople should assume responsibility for looking after themselves as soon and as fully as possible. Political power seemed to be the fast, cheap, and easy solution to the vexing political burden of Reconstruction. Extend political power to African Americans and they could protect their own interests at the ballot box, or so Republicans hoped.

But that was not an easy sell in 1868. This was reflected in the awkward and ultimately futile compromise over Black voting incorporated in section 2 of the Fourteenth Amendment. Prodded by fears that returning southern states would actually increase their power in the House or Representatives because of abrogation of the three-fifths clause,[110] Republicans provided that if a state disfranchised any of its male inhabitants, it would suffer a proportionate reduction in their representation in the House. This was a nonstarter: Congress never even attempted to enforce it.

Republicans soon realized that the suffrage provisions contained in section 2 of the Fourteenth Amendment were an unwieldy makeshift, with no likelihood that they would produce or protect a single Black voter. Besides, by 1869 the party had no stomach for the sort of draconian enforcement section 2 authorized. The party's electoral prospects were darkening; continuing Republican dominance of Congress was doubtful. So, ensuring Black suffrage was necessary for the survival of the party, in the North no less than in the South. All these pressures spurred the Republicans in the lame-duck session of the Fortieth Congress to propose a constitutional amendment securing the vote. This was easier said than done, though, because of conflicting demands from differing constituencies of the GOP.[111] Women, represented by the American Equal Rights Association, were demanding the vote. Northern Republicans were determined to exclude noncitizen immigrants; westerners likewise wanted to exclude the Chinese. All Republicans were insistent that the guarantee of the vote must not be broad enough to enfranchise ex-Confederates stripped of the vote by sections 2 and 3 of the Fourteenth Amendment.

Republicans cobbled together section 1 of the Fifteenth Amendment in its present form, stripping away proposed specific bans on poll taxes or literacy tests.[112] The amendment, as the Supreme Court was soon to point out, recognized "the right of citizens of the United States to vote," but did not guarantee that right to anyone. Instead, it only prohibited denial of that right "on account of race, color, or previous condition of servitude." By 1869, Republicans wanted to firm up the support of northern African American voters, since the southern Black vote was secure (for the time being, anyway) because of military Reconstruction and amended southern state constitutions. Women were not included, which split the feminist movement for the next two decades between those who supported the amendment and those who rejected it.[113] Ratification was as contentious as the congressional debate had been; Congress forced the four states still undergoing Reconstruction to ratify it as a condition of readmission. But by 1870 the amendment was ratified and launched on its checkered career.

Apart from the amendments' substantive provisions, their enforcement clauses took on an independent significance. They all provided, in nearly verbatim terms, that "The Congress shall have power to enforce, by appropriate legislation, the provisions of this article" (Fourteenth Amendment, section 5). To a modern lay reader, this might seem truistic; when the Constitution created or affirmed a right, did that not necessarily imply power in the federal government to enforce that right and protect against its violation? But that obvious point was contested by antebellum states' rights dogma where the rights of African Americans were concerned. To forestall any resurrection of such a rights-denying resistance after the war, Congress prudently added the sibling enforcement clauses to make plain beyond quibble that Congress could enforce the rights identified in the new constitutional order.[114]

All the enforcement clauses begin with the formulation "Congress shall have power..." That choice of phraseology confirmed two obvious but crucial ideas: (1) Congress was bestowing power upon *itself*, as well as upon the federal courts and the executive branch and (2) the four words were identical to, and copied from, Article I, section 8 of the Constitution.[115] Under the legal canon of construction known as *in pari materia*,[116] statutes using identical language are to be construed as meaning the same thing and to be interpreted the same way. One may serve as a conclusive guide to the meaning of the other. Chief Justice John Marshall provided the definitive construction of implied congressional powers under the necessary and proper clause[117] in *McCulloch v. Maryland* (1819):[118] "Let the end be legitimate, let it be within the scope of the constitution, and all means which are appropriate, which are plainly adapted to that end, which are not prohibited, but consist with the letter and spirit of the constitution, are constitutional."

Justice William Strong elaborated on this point in one of the 1879–1880 jury cases, *Ex parte Virginia* (1879):

> Some legislation is contemplated to make the amendments fully effective. Whatever legislation is appropriate, that is, adapted to carry out the objects the [Reconstruction] amendments have in view, whatever tends to enforce submission to the prohibitions they contain, and to secure to all persons the enjoyment of perfect equality of civil rights and the equal protection of the laws against State denial or invasion, if not prohibited, is brought within the domain of congressional power.
>
> Nor does it make any difference that such legislation is restrictive of what the State might have done before the constitutional amendment was adopted. The prohibitions of the Fourteenth Amendment are directed to the States, and they are to a degree restrictions of State power. It is these which Congress is empowered to enforce, and to enforce against State action, however put forth, whether that action be executive, legislative, or judicial. Such enforcement is no invasion of State sovereignty. No law can be, which the people of the States have, by the Constitution of the United States, empowered Congress to enact.

Justice Strong viewed this as a zero-sum game: "every addition of power to the general government involves a corresponding diminution of the governmental powers of the States. It is carved out of them."[119]

Earlier, the Court had held that "it must be taken then as finally settled, so far as judicial decisions can settle anything, that the words of the Necessary and Proper Clause were 'equivalent' to the word 'appropriate.'"[120] Thus, the word "appropriate" in the enforcement clauses imports into the Constitution itself *McCulloch*'s expansive vision of congressional power, not confined to merely enforcing rights and remedies previously defined by the Supreme Court. Though the framers of the Reconstruction Amendments intended to empower the federal courts and endow them with primary responsibility for protecting the rights of the freedpeople, they were prudently dubious about the willingness or reliability of future courts, and thus reserved to Congress the power to enforce the guarantees of equality and citizenship if the courts defaulted.

The framers who sat in the Reconstruction Congresses intended the new constitutional order to protect African American citizens. The three amendments and their enforcement statutes were race-explicit, either by their terms or by their obvious context. The framers had no illusions of the sort cherished by the Roberts Court today that they were creating a color-blind constitutional order—"color-blind" in the sense that governments (federal, state, and local) could neither take race into account nor fashion race-conscious remedies to protect Blacks' rights and overcome two centuries of the degradation imposed by slavery. The framers were acutely aware that they were legislating for a society where African American people had been beaten down by law and custom to a state of rightslessness, as Taney had so emphatically confirmed. In that frame of mind, the framers meant to protect African Americans both as a racial group—people who had been oppressed collectively because of their race—and as individuals. They extended this protection based on both race and status: as the Fifteenth Amendment puts it, "on account of race, color, or previous condition of servitude." While this restates the obvious, the Court's recent interpretations of the Reconstruction Amendments seem to ignore it.

The framers understood that threats to the rights of the newly enfranchised citizens (and to their white supporters) would come from three sources: the state and local governments (legislature, executive, local law enforcement); private groups, such as the Ku Klux Klan and its ilk; and individuals. They meant to protect those rights against all three sources of threat, private as well as public. They knew that the southern states and the white people of those states, left to themselves, could not be relied on to adequately define the rights of Black people or to enforce them impartially. Nor could they be counted on to treat both races equally. The southern states had already given ample proof of that in the Black Codes. The reports coming in from the field to the Joint Committee on Reconstruction in 1866 provided massive confirmation of continuing counterrevolutionary violence against Blacks and Unionists from the states, local governments, terrorist bands, and individuals.[121] The most influential of these field reports came from General (later Senator) Carl Schurz, who toured the South in the summer of 1865 and reported on the intransigence of white southerners, who were determined in restore slavery or some equivalent.[122] Republicans intended to empower the federal government to protect African Americans in the enjoyment of their rights against all sources of threats to them.

As of 1875, some of the major questions hovering over Reconstruction had been settled: slavery as a legal institution was dead, beyond any hope of full restoration. The state-sovereignty understanding of the Constitution that had animated the Slave Power and secession was discredited, though powerful strains lingered on in the southern legal mentality and would later re-emerge like some ineradicable, lethal virus. The freedpeople had now been raised to the rank of citizens and had scaled at least the first two tiers of civil rights—on paper. The federal courts were more powerful than ever, but would they use these powers as the framers of Reconstruction legislation had intended, to protect the newly enfranchised African Americans and federal supremacy? The seceded states had been readmitted and their representatives in Congress seated. Increasingly the southern states recovered what southern whites called "home rule," which, tragically, meant power over their Black fellow citizens. A new constitutional framework was in place, within which these issues would be resolved. The fate of Reconstruction as far as the freedpeople were concerned now lay in hands of the justices of the Supreme Court.

The Supreme Court and Reconstruction, 1865–1880

A new constitutional order was now emerging. What would the US Supreme Court make of it?

As of 1865, what was to succeed slavery as the determinant of white-Black legal relations? A range of possibilities presented themselves.

At one extreme, white Americans might have imposed a new legal status on Blacks resembling slavery as much as possible. The white South tried to achieve this through the Black Codes. At the opposite extreme, white Americans might have conferred full civic status and complete equality with themselves upon African Americans. Viewed realistically, given the prevalent racism of the time, the new status for the freedpeople was probably going to fall somewhere between these extremes, short of full equality and closer to the neo-slavery extreme. But how short and how close?

By 1900, the answer had jelled: African Americans were subordinated in a regime that approached the neo-slavery extreme, referred to here as servitude. This second phase of inequality in America, lasting three-quarters of a century, from 1875 to 1950, was marked by a regime of apartheid. In every domain—social, political, economic—African American citizens were stripped of power, denigrated, excluded, and reduced to the status of a landless proletariat in the countryside, but without the customary protections that other peasant societies afforded their rural poor. At the social level, the mass of laws, customs, practices, and illegalities that achieved this is known as Jim Crow. The white South called this form of apartheid "segregation." But for purposes of describing the legal regime that prevailed after the end of Reconstruction, a better term is "servitude," a state of subjection to those having authority over a person or an entire class of people, coupled with a loss of personal freedom, autonomy, and agency. Servitude denied the dignity and humanity that should be accorded all members of a society.

Servitude began with the demise of Reconstruction in the ex-slave states and lasted until the civil rights era began in 1954.[123] Seen through the lens of the Supreme Court's reaction to legislation of the period, it evolved through two phases, a "crescendo" phase lasting from the war years until 1910, followed by a "diminuendo" period from 1910 to *Brown* in 1954. From the late nineteenth century through the Progressive Era, the Court was indifferent to the lot of African Americans as they were suppressed into Jim Crow servitude. The Court, with the notable (but inconsistent) exception of the first John Marshall Harlan, supported the southern program of subordinating Blacks and confirming white supremacy. By the Nadir, in the first decade of the twentieth century, the Supreme Court had followed the lead of Congress in abandoning African Americans to the violence of Redemption and its lingering aftermath. Beginning with the appointment of Justice Charles Evans Hughes to the Court in 1910, however, the justices grew increasingly skeptical of the pretense-and-pretext form of equality that then prevailed. In hindsight, we can see that they were beginning to repudiate Redemption.

The Court dealt with the triad of constitutional issues presented by Reconstruction—federalism, African Americans' rights, federal judicial power—in a pattern that it would later repeat in the second Reconstruction of the 1960s. At first it confronted the realities that newly freed Black citizens faced, recognized the need for federal power to protect their rights, and accepted the role of federal courts in doing so. The justices were momentarily disenthralled from their antebellum proslavery outlook. It seemed for a time that they could contemplate a constitutional order based on freedom and equality. But the Court then wavered weakly and uncertainly. Its openness shut down all too soon, giving way to a conservative resolution of these issues, and a stinting, formalistic approach to interpreting both the substance of rights and their enforcement. In both Reconstruction eras, the Court was never out of step with popular sentiment[124]—meaning, in both instances, the political attitudes of white people.

In the summer of 1865, with the fate of secession and slavery settled at the cannons' mouth, the Court took on the momentous responsibility of giving shape and direction to the new constitutional order inaugurated by the Reconstruction Amendments. Out of the welter of debates on the framing and ratification of the amendments and statutes, the state and federal courts had to fashion a coherent, judicially applicable body of doctrine that would effectively implement and protect the rights they guaranteed. Those judges reflected the cacophony of different interpretations offered by the framers and commentators. They came down on both sides of the questions whether the Fourteenth Amendment banned racial segregation in schools, or forbade anti-miscegenation statutes, or protected the right to vote.[125]

At first, the Supreme Court seemed to embrace Reconstruction policies in the spirit that congressional Republicans had intended. Their earliest opinions involving African Americans displayed two characteristics that soon evaporated: they respected congressional authority to determine policy and evinced a concern for the rights of the freedpeople. Early decisions by justices of the US Supreme Court sitting on circuit seemed promising for the cause of racial justice. They suggested that the Court might read the amendments and statutes expansively, in the breadth intended by their Republican sponsors.

In *United States v. Rhodes* (1866),[126] Justice Noah Swayne, sitting as a judge of the federal Circuit Court for Kentucky, upheld removal to a federal court of a criminal prosecution of three white men for burglarizing the home of a freedwoman. The prosecution sought removal because under Kentucky law, Blacks could not testify against whites. Swayne upheld the removal provisions of the 1866 Civil Rights Act, as well as the act itself, in sweeping terms. He insisted that "the second section of the [Thirteenth] amendment was framed...to give expressly to congress the requisite authority [to abolish "the badges of the bondman's degradation"], and to leave no room for doubt or cavil upon the subject." "Who will say it [the Civil Rights Act] is not an 'appropriate' means of carrying out the object of the first section of the amendment, and a necessary and proper execution of the power conferred by the second? Blot out this act and deny the constitutional power to pass it, and the worst effects of slavery might speedily follow." He was soon proved prescient.

Chief Justice Chase echoed his colleague's expansive view of congressional power in *In re Turner* (1867). After abolishing slavery, Maryland enacted an apprenticeship statute, a part of its version of the Black Codes, which authorized putting young people out to apprenticeships that resembled eighteenth-century indentured servitude. Elizabeth Turner, a previously enslaved teenager, was apprenticed to her former owner by a contract that did not contain the customary provisions for education and maintenance of the apprentice. She was held in service under conditions resembling slavery.[127] She sought a writ of habeas corpus to recover her liberty, and, on circuit, Chase granted it. In a brief opinion, he held that Turner was being held in the kind of involuntary servitude forbidden by the Thirteenth Amendment, in contravention of the amendment itself, which "establishes freedom as the constitutional right of all persons in the United States."[128] That statement is not as truistic as it may sound to a twenty-first-century ear: Chase was saying that the Thirteenth Amendment went beyond merely abolishing slavery and leaving its victims to fend for themselves. It had a positive effect, confirming freedom as the natural condition of all people, with the rights, privileges, immunities, and opportunities that that status entailed. He held the statute itself constitutional as an exercise of the power conferred on Congress in section 2. *Turner* presaged a generous reception of Reconstruction policy, where federal judges operated in tandem with Congress to secure the rights of the freedpeople.

Potentially the most significant circuit court decision involving Reconstruction came from a judge who seemed to be involved in all the major cases of the era, William B. Woods.[129] In *United States v. Hall* (1871)[130] two white men were prosecuted under the 1870 Enforcement Act for breaking up a Black political assembly before an election. They were charged with interfering with the victims' First Amendment rights of speech and assembly. State and local law enforcement authorities did nothing to prevent or punish the defendants' actions. Judge Woods sustained the conviction, the first time that federal power was used to enforce federal constitutional rights against aggressions by private individuals. This introduced the problem of state action, which later developed into a major impediment to protection of African Americans' rights.[131]

The state action problem derives from the words of the Fourteenth Amendment itself, which reads in part: "No State shall make or enforce any law which shall abridge the privileges or immunities of citizens of the United States; nor shall any State deprive any person of life, liberty, or property, without due process of law; nor deny to any person within its jurisdiction the equal protection of the laws." Since 1883, the Supreme Court has read those provisions to require some active state involvement in the defendant's wrongful act. The actions of purely private individuals having no connection with the state are beyond the reach of federal authority under the due process and equal protection clauses. But in *Hall*, Judge Woods, in consultation with Justice Bradley (who presided over Woods's circuit, the Fifth), had no difficulty reaching private actors: "Congress has the power, by appropriate legislation, to protect the fundamental rights of citizens of the United States against unfriendly or insufficient legislation.... Denying includes inaction as well as action, and denying the equal protection of the laws includes omission to protect, as well as the omission to pass laws for protection." Had the Supreme Court adopted Judge Woods's insight, Fourteenth Amendment law would be radically different today, and we would be much further along the path of racial justice than we find ourselves because of the roadblock of the state action doctrine. Woods also held that the Fourteenth Amendment's privileges or immunities clause incorporated the entire Bill of Rights against the states as privileges and immunities of the national citizenship conferred by the preceding citizenship clause.[132]

The full Court did not hear appeals in the *Rhodes, Turner,* or *Hall* cases, but other issues involving Reconstruction policy came before it. In *Texas v. White* (1869)[133] the Court finally and fully endorsed congressional Reconstruction. As part of the 1850 Compromise, the federal government had given Texas $10 million in federal bonds. The state still held some of these at the time of secession, and the state government sold them to help pay for costs of waging war against the United States. After the war, the Reconstruction state government sued to recover these bonds. When this suit came before the Supreme Court, Chase framed the issue procedurally as whether the petitioner state was still a "State" in the Union entitled to sue as a state in the original jurisdiction of the Supreme Court conferred by Article III, section 2.[134]

Structuring the issue this way gave Chase the opportunity to finally address most of the important constitutional structural issues of Reconstruction, either forthrightly or implicitly. He held that secession and all acts in furtherance of it were nullities: Texas never forfeited its status as a state, and its people remained American citizens. "The Constitution, in all its provisions, looks to an indestructible Union, composed of indestructible States." He spurned the compact theory that underlay secession, as well as the entire body of state sovereignty theory that southern political leaders had advanced to protect slavery. Chase, the only member of his Court who could be considered an abolitionist, enjoyed the satisfaction of seeing antislavery constitutional theories vindicated by the High Court.

But the status of the state had been deranged by secession and war, and its relationship to the Union "impaired." The rights of both state and its people were "suspended." Congress had to reintegrate it by organizing a permanent state government under its Article IV, section 4 power to "guarantee to every State in this Union a Republican Form of Government."[135] Though Chase declined to address the constitutionality of the Military Reconstruction Acts explicitly, he implicitly upheld Congress's actions by recognizing the legitimacy of the governments organized under them.

Chase based his reasoning on the definition of a state as being identified with and by its people, including its new Black citizens. "The new freemen necessarily became part of the people, and the people still constituted the State." He thus affirmed the indissoluble status of African Americans as a constituent part of the state's sovereign people. Blacks were thus doubly beneficiaries of Chase's *Texas v. White* opinion: it upheld all the acts of Congress enacted to create legitimate postwar state governments, which were essential for their new status as citizens; and it confirmed that African Americans themselves were themselves members of this reconstituted political society. The Court seemed to understand the imperatives of the postwar constitutional order.

That would not last much longer, though. Chase had been weakened by strokes and he presided over a Court of forceful individuals, including three who aspired to his place who shared little of his abolitionist commitment. Nathan Clifford and Stephen J. Field, the only Democrats on the Court, were at best indifferent to the freedpeople's plight. Miller, an instinctive centrist, had been a strong supporter of Lincoln's war efforts and acknowledged the need for vigorous federal authority, but he was immovably conservative on the nature of the federal balance. The postwar Court became ever more concerned with interests of business and corporations than the antebellum Court had been. By 1873, the animating spirit of Reconstruction was a fading memory for the justices.

The *Slaughterhouse Cases* of 1873[136] were the pivot on which the constitutional impact of Reconstruction turned. Could a Constitution that had hitherto been construed to protect slavery reverse course and protect the freedom, liberties, and rights of all Americans, irrespective of race? Until 1873, the Reconstruction Amendments had the potential for radically transforming the constitutional regime from the white supremacist world of Taney's morbid *Dred Scott* vision to a transformative egalitarian order where the authority of the national government would promote the states' efforts to create societies dedicated to equality and racial justice under their new Reconstruction constitutions. At the critical moment where the Court stood poised to choose between two radically different ways of understanding the constitutional changes wrought by war and Reconstruction, it chose the wrong one, with incalculable results for Black Americans. In the *Slaughterhouse Cases* (1873), the Court abandoned the freedpeople to their fate at the hands of southern Democrats.[137]

The problem was not that the Court misunderstood the significance of the case or underestimated it. At the outset of his majority opinion, Justice Miller laid out that significance explicitly, and all his colleagues concurred:

> This court is thus called upon for the first time to give construction to these articles [the Reconstruction Amendments]. We do not conceal from ourselves the great responsibility which this duty devolves upon us. No questions so far-reaching and pervading in their consequences,

so profoundly interesting to the people of this country, and so important in their bearing upon the relations of the United States, and of the several States to each other and to the citizens of the States and of the United States, have been before this court during the official life of any of its present members.

The justices were about to do nothing less than determine whether the United States entered a new, egalitarian constitutional system premised on racial equality or would relapse into the antebellum world where whites dominated African Americans and the federal government's enforcement power was neutered. As Michael Kent Curtis framed the issue: "was the Constitution a system designed to protect slavery or guarantee liberty? While it recognized the inevitable death of slavery, the *Slaughterhouse Cases* left the protection of liberty much as it had been under a Constitution construed to protect slavery."[138] Tragically, *Slaughterhouse* shunted American constitutional development back into that dark world of racial domination, which was to persist into the twentieth century. It was the foundation of servitude and Jim Crow.

Miller began with some basic assumptions that at first seemed to bode well for the cause of equality. "Undoubtedly the overshadowing and efficient cause [of the Civil War] was African slavery." Therefore "the one pervading purpose found in them all [was] the freedom of the slave race, the security and firm establishment of that freedom, and the protection of the newly-made freeman and citizen from the oppressions of those who had formerly exercised unlimited dominion over him."[139] Without going further, a contemporary reader might have assumed that Miller would go on to construe the amendments in a way that robustly expanded Blacks' liberties.

But the facts of the *Slaughterhouse* case were mischievous and wreaked havoc on Miller's sound premises. Those factual circumstances diverted the majority justices' understanding of the amendments and resulted in a warped, defective construction of their promise. The case was brought by white butchers who were obliged by a state statute to do their slaughtering outside the city of New Orleans at a single location, the Crescent City Live-Stock Landing and Slaughter-House Company. The plaintiffs hoped to drive African Americans out of the skilled trade of butchering altogether. They challenged the statute as a violation of the Thirteenth Amendment and section 1 of the Fourteenth, as imposing involuntary servitude on them (by forcing them to labor in only one site and pay a fee for doing so), and as depriving them of privileges and immunities, due process, and equal protection of the laws. They were represented by former US Supreme Court justice John Archibald Campbell, who, after his treasonous service as Confederate assistant secretary of war, had relocated to New Orleans and embarked on a quarter century of successful legal practice. He was a leading opponent of Reconstruction and did more than any other single individual to frustrate its objectives by legal arguments.[140]

Miller readily resolved the core legal question presented, holding that the state had ample authority to regulate noxious uses of property, abattoirs being a classic example of the noxious-use doctrine at common law. These regulatory requirements were legitimate and well-established means of exercising what jurists of the time called "the police power": the power of the state to regulate for the health, safety, welfare, and morals of its people.[141] By 1873, this authority was well established in American law,[142] and Miller's invocation of it was unexceptionable. Regulating the places and methods of slaughtering was a typical exercise of the police power, so there was nothing untoward about the substance of the Louisiana statute. This holding was dispositive, and if Miller had stopped at that point, the *Slaughterhouse Cases* would have merited no more than a footnote in studies of the nineteenth-century regulatory state.

But he forged on to rebut the butchers' arguments. Miller rejected out of hand the claim that the monopoly imposed "involuntary servitude" on the white butchers. He scorned the idea that it might refer to common-law servitudes imposed on property. The Thirteenth Amendment was meant to "forbid all shades and conditions of African slavery," nothing more, nothing less.[143] But this view of slavery was encased in a narrow conception of what emancipation meant as a matter of common law. Miller thought that emancipation conferred nothing more than self-ownership. This understanding of slavery conformed to northern Democratic white-supremacist views rather than the beliefs of congressional Republicans, with long-term harmful consequences for Black citizens.[144] This restrictive view of slavery became central to the Court's interpretation of the Reconstruction Amendments. It did not admit of a broader understanding that would see emancipation as endowing the newly freed person with the civic status and rights of all other free people in a republic. In this narrow view, the only rights the freedpeople might claim were those given them by white society. This conformed to the Black Codes, which Miller condemned without apparently realizing that he was unwittingly trapped in their underlying assumptions about freedom.

Turning to the Fourteenth Amendment, Miller emphasized the distinction between the national and state citizenships conferred by section 1.[145] He sorted out and identified the privileges and immunities derived from these two different sources, federal and state. In doing so, Miller worked within contemporary understandings of the sources and nature of these rights.[146] Some were "natural" or "secured": they were derived from state citizenship and were antecedent to the federal Constitution.[147] As preexisting, they could only be "secured" or recognized by the federal Constitution, not bestowed by it. The other category of rights was "conferred": they were created by the federal Constitution. The secured/conferred distinction matters because the federal government may act directly upon individuals to enforce conferred rights and is not bound by the state action limitation, as it is in the case of secured rights. Only in that secured/conferred context does Miller's opinion make sense. Miller may have deliberately misquoted the Article IV privileges and immunities clause to create this artificial distinction between state (secured) and national (conferred) rights, insulating state rights from federal oversight and enforcement.[148]

Though Miller did not further elaborate on the significance of the distinction, it re-emerged as he segued into his next topic, the privileges or immunities clause of the Fourteenth Amendment. Miller might have construed the privileges or immunities clause as securing not only equality among citizens but fundamental substantive liberties as well to individuals.[149] "Text, context, history, ethical aspirations, precedent and constitutional structure suggest that the...Clause was designed to make the Constitution what its preamble promised—a guarantee of liberty."[150]

Instead, Miller insisted that only the privileges and immunities of national citizenship could be enforced by the federal government. He enumerated a few, a "miserable bundle of bromides and irrelevancies," as they have been called:[151] the right to come to Washington, DC, to hold federal office or do business with the government, to access seaports, federal courts, land offices, to demand protection while on the high seas and navigable waters, and to claim treaty rights. To these few rights secured by national citizenship, Miller added the assembly-and-petition right guaranteed by the First Amendment, habeas corpus (a right of potentially considerable consequence) and, intriguingly, "the rights secured by the thirteenth and fifteenth articles of amendment, and by the other clause of the fourteenth," the due process clause.[152] Conceivably, by developing the due process clause as a source of African Americans' rights, Miller might have retrieved most of the privileges-and-immunities potential that he was about to squander. But nothing ever came of this casual and overlooked aside.

Otherwise, only the states, not the federal government, could protect the rights deriving from state citizenship, which were

> those privileges and immunities which are *fundamental*; which belong of right to the citizens of all free governments, and which have at all times been enjoyed by citizens of the several States which compose this Union, from the time of their becoming free, independent, and sovereign. What these fundamental principles are, it would be more tedious than difficult to enumerate. They may all, however, be comprehended under the following general heads: protection by the government, with the right to acquire and possess property of every kind, and to pursue and obtain happiness and safety...[153]

These included "nearly every civil right for the establishment and protection of which organized government is instituted."

The tragic irony here is that Miller was thereby consigning the freedpeople to precisely those governments that, at that time, were most hostile to their interests, most determined to drive them back into a state of near-slavery. Miller privileged state control over individuals' rights, rather than preserving ultimate federal authority and the liberty of free people. He rejected the Republican view of the revolution in federalism wrought by the war. The result was African Americans' "marginalization by law,"[154] whereby they were subjected to control by local white legislative majorities. It was cold comfort to an Alabama freedman to be told that for protection against a county sheriff who was terrorizing him that he must look to the state of Alabama for protect him from its own sheriff. Miller thereby cast the privileges and immunities clause into a deep coma that has lasted for over a century. It is stirring restlessly in the present,[155] but nothing portends that it will be revived in ways that will be of particular benefit to its intended beneficiaries, people of color.

Having dispatched the privileges or immunities clause as a source of protecting African Americans' rights, Miller moved on to the due process clause of the Fourteenth Amendment. He dealt with it summarily: "under no construction of that provision that we have ever seen, or any that we deem admissible, can the restraint imposed by the State of Louisiana upon the exercise of their trade by the butchers of New Orleans be held to be a deprivation of property within the meaning of that provision."[156] That was an odd observation, given that Taney's substantive due process claim for the rights of slaveowners in *Dred Scott* lay only sixteen years in the past, and that state supreme courts had been interpreting state due process or law-of-the-land clauses substantively for the previous half-century.

The equal protection clause got similar short shrift. "We doubt very much whether any action of a State not directed by way of discrimination against the negroes as a class, or on account of their race, will ever be held to come within the purview of this provision. It is so clearly a provision for that race and that emergency, that a strong case would be necessary for its application to any other."[157] Since the plaintiffs in the present case were all white, the clause was irrelevant to their complaints. Another irony of *Slaughterhouse* was that in time the equal protection clause, shrunk by Miller, became the basis for vindicating civil rights, while the privileges or immunities clause remains vestigial today.

Why did Miller impose on the four components of section 1 such a constrictive reading, which became so lethal to the hopes of Black Americans? The answer lies in his conservative vision of federalism, his refusal to accept the possibility that Congress actually did intend vast, far-reaching changes to the prewar federal balance. The Republican-dominated Thirty-Ninth Congress was determined to repudiate the states' rights constitutional outlook of the antebellum Democratic Congresses because they saw that it produced state oppression of individuals, particularly new Black citizens. In its place, Congress substituted a constitutional vision that exalted the national government as the primary guarantor of individual liberty against state aggressions.

But Miller could not fathom that Congress did in fact intend "to transfer the security and protection of all the civil rights which we have mentioned, from the States to the Federal government." By section 5 of the Fourteenth Amendment, "was it intended to bring within the power of Congress the entire domain of civil rights heretofore belonging exclusively to the States?" Surely not, he thought. Otherwise, individual rights would be "subject to the control of Congress whenever in its discretion any of them are supposed to be abridged by State legislation, but that body may also pass laws in advance, limiting and restricting the exercise of legislative power by the States." Even worse, such a construction "would constitute this court a perpetual censor upon all legislation of the States, on the civil rights of their own citizens." He thought this was inconceivable:

when, as in the case before us, these consequences are so serious, so far-reaching and pervading, so great a departure from the structure and spirit of our institutions; when the effect is to fetter and degrade the State governments by subjecting them to the control of Congress, in the exercise of powers heretofore universally conceded to them of the most ordinary and fundamental character; when in fact it radically changes the whole theory of the relations of the State and Federal governments to each other and of both these governments to the people; the argument has a force that is irresistible, in the absence of language which expresses such a purpose too clearly to admit of doubt. We are convinced that no such results were intended by the Congress which proposed these amendments, nor by the legislatures of the States which ratified them.[158]

Nor could the revolutionary changes wrought by the war have such an effect:

we do not see in those amendments any purpose to destroy the main features of the general system. Under the pressure of all the excited feeling growing out of the war, our statesmen have still believed that the existence of the State with powers for domestic and local government, including the regulation of civil rights—the rights of person and of property—was essential to the perfect working of our complex form of government, though they have thought proper to impose additional limitations on the States, and to confer additional power on that of the Nation.[159]

In Robert Kaczorowski's judgment, the opinion "annulled a revolution in American constitutionalism."[160]

If most Reconstruction-era Republicans could not be considered reactionary, neither were they willing to countenance a revolutionary disruption of the federal system.[161] As the foremost proponent of this view of Republican conservatism expresses it, "Republicans opted to expand national power to protect rights whenever events forced them to. But they did so reluctantly and still attempted to preserve the traditional constitutional order of federalism as much as possible."[162] Miller feared that the war had unleashed nationalizing forces so powerful that they would breach foundational bounds of federalism, creating an all-powerful national government that would override state powers. He did not want to see the triumph over secessionist disintegration come at the cost of creating a new unitary sovereignty that obliterated the states.[163]

In fairness to Miller, it may be that his conservatism on the question of federalism was in part strategic, to protect the biracial Reconstruction state governments from potential assault by their enemies and their police powers from being overridden by conservative federal judges.[164] In his *Slaughterhouse* arguments for the butchers, one of the most formidable of these enemies, John Archibald Campbell, propounded expansive readings of the due process, equal protection, and privileges or immunities clauses of the Fourteenth Amendment, as well as the Thirteenth Amendment, as the proper bases for federal judicial restriction of the power of state legislatures. Had Campbell and his supporters had their way, a conservative Supreme Court, hostile to the equal-rights goals of Reconstruction, could have throttled state legislative experimentation in protecting the civil rights of its citizens. Miller despised Campbell, considering him a dangerous and unrepentant traitor,[165] and rightly suspected him of orchestrating a judicial assault on the power of Republican governments in the South. He may have also feared that an expansive reading of the Second Amendment, a possibility implicit in Campbell's arguments, could have been used to protect the crypto-military operations of the Klan, the White League, and other white-supremacist terrorist organizations.[166]

There are other positive things to be said for Miller's opinion, disappointing though its results may have been for Black citizens.[167] His enumerated privileges and rights of national citizenship were not entirely trivial, and later developments built on them to protect civil rights in the twentieth century. These included the right to be free of racial discrimination in interstate travel,[168] protection for voting and other forms of political participation in federal elections,[169] protection of the right to assemble,[170] and the right of habeas corpus.[171] In place of the now-comatose privileges or immunities clause, Miller's opinion left open broad possibilities for enforcement of civil rights through the commerce clause, the Thirteenth Amendment, the due process and equal protection clauses of the Fourteenth Amendment, and the guarantee clause of Article IV. Though a forlorn hope at the time, most of these possibilities were realized in the second Reconstruction.

Slaughterhouse was nevertheless a disaster for Black Americans, immediately and in the long term. Reconstruction was a three-legged stool: it revolutionized the federal system, the status of African Americans, and the role of federal courts. Miller's opinion sawed off one of those legs, that involving the status of Blacks. That missing leg would soon be replaced by a substituted concern for the economic liberties of white people, as expressed in the Court's substantive-due-process jurisprudence of the *Lochner* era. But for the succeeding eighty years, Black Americans were thrown to the wolves of Redemption, at that time already taking place throughout the South.

Most historians today are agreed that *Slaughterhouse* was wrongly decided, even if Justice Samuel Alito and seven of his colleagues do not agree.[172] As early as 1908, Justice William Moody could remark that "criticism [of *Slaughterhouse*] has never entirely ceased, nor has it ever received universal assent by members of this Court."[173] We stagger under its weight today. For the ensuing eighty years, the US Supreme Court obstructed the path forward to full freedom, equality, and justice for America's Black citizens.

After *Slaughterhouse*, the reactionary terror known as Redemption metastasized through the South. "Redeemers" and "Redemption" were terms adopted by elements of the southern Democratic Party who were determined to overthrow the Republican regimes that briefly came to power in the southern states during the first Reconstruction. Redeemers formed a loose coalition that shared the following characteristics: they were determined to assert white control over African Americans, and to that end supported the policy of the Black Codes and subsequent racially repressive laws. They had been secessionists and mostly Democrats. Many had served the Confederacy in a civilian or military capacity. They demanded state self-government, which meant their return to power by ousting the governments organized under military Reconstruction and the revised 1867–1868 state constitutions. Drawing on implicit but powerful Christian imagery,[174] they sought the "redemption" of the South from rule by African Americans and their white Republican colleagues, whom they portrayed as corrupt and incompetent. The political alignments and coalitions of the postwar South were fluid and mercurial, but this cluster of characteristics remained a constant among what was probably a consistent, large majority of the white southern population.[175]

If *Slaughterhouse* sawed off one leg of the Reconstruction stool, a case decided the previous year, *Blyew v. United States* (1872)[176] sawed another, the power of federal courts to enforce freedpeople's rights. In 1868, two white men, hoping to detonate a racial conflict that would restart the Civil War, brutally ax-murdered four members of an African American family in their home. They were tried and convicted of homicide in a federal district court in Kentucky, which had jurisdiction under section 3 of the 1866 Civil Rights Act. Section 3 conferred jurisdiction over causes "affecting persons who are denied, or cannot enforce in the courts or judicial tribunals of the

State, or locality, where they may be, any of the rights secured to them by" section 1 of the act. The problem posed by *Blyew* was that crucial testimony was provided by two of the victims who, under Kentucky law at that time, could not testify against white people. Could section 3 jurisdiction extend to persons disqualified as witnesses because of race? Were they the "affected persons" the sponsors of the 1866 Civil Rights Act had in mind? The Court, in a five-to-two decision written by Justice William Strong, held that they were not.

Strong's *Blyew* majority opinion, interpreted charitably, was a compromise: it upheld the constitutionality of the Civil Rights Act, a victory for African Americans, since the commonwealth of Kentucky had argued for the unconstitutionality of the entire act on antebellum federalism grounds.[177] But by confining the "affecting persons" language to persons who were defendants in criminal prosecutions,[178] Strong gutted the enforcement provisions of the act, leaving it weakened by rejecting the broad interpretive reach its sponsors had intended. Justice Bradley countered in dissent that the majority promoted "a view of the law too narrow, too technical, and too forgetful of the liberal objects it had in view."[179] The effect of the majority holding "is to leave [freedpeople's] lives, their families, and their property unprotected by law. It gives unrestricted license and impunity to vindictive outlaws and felons to rush upon these helpless people and kill and slay them at will." Bradley's dire prediction was soon borne out as Klan and White League violence against Blacks grew worse. *Blyew* became the constitutional shield of the Klan. It marked "a full-fledged retreat" from congressional policy and "occurred so early in Reconstruction that the case surely contributed in some small measure to Reconstruction's demise" and continues to "deform" our understanding of civil rights law today. *Blyew* was a harbinger of worse to come. The Court for the first time emerged as an "ideological and political leader in the reaction to Reconstruction."[180]

In 1876, the Court decided two companion cases that further weakened Congress's power to protect African Americans in the South. The traditional account of *United States v. Reese* and *United States v. Cruikshank* holds that these cases respectively disabled Congress's power to enforce African Americans' voting rights under the Fifteenth Amendment and limited its ability to protect Black Americans against Klan violence.[181] They began an era when the Supreme Court repeatedly struck down legislation that enforced the Reconstruction Amendments. Together they constitute a key part of the "death of Reconstruction" narrative, in which Republican

Reconstruction was killed by a combination of growing indifference in the North, white terrorism in the South, and a Supreme Court that abetted that counterrevolutionary violence. By invalidating vital portions of enforcement statutes, the Court supposedly withdrew federal protection of Blacks and enabled the Redeemers' disfranchisement efforts. This account remains substantially valid, but the complete story and its aftermath are more nuanced.

United States v. Cruikshank[182] arose from the prosecution of the men who perpetrated the horrific Colfax massacre of 1873. In the political turmoil that followed the riotous 1872 Louisiana gubernatorial election, white Democrats surrounded a courthouse in Colfax, Louisiana, where a Black political gathering was taking place, and in the ensuing melee slaughtered between one hundred and two hundred men.[183] Three of the mob were convicted of a mélange of offenses including interference with the First Amendment right to assemble to petition for a redress of grievances, the Second Amendment right to bear arms, the Fourteenth Amendment right not to be deprived of life or liberty without due process, the right to the equal benefit of the laws, and the right to vote under the Fifteenth Amendment. Trial was before the US Circuit Court for Louisiana, and the judges divided, with Justice Bradley, riding circuit, voting to acquit. Though he sat for only a few days of the trial, Bradley wrote an extensive opinion in an effort to formulate the questions for the Supreme Court, which heard the case because of the division in the lower court.

Cruikshank and its companion *Reese* were grievous setbacks for the cause of racial equality and for federal authority. In part, this may be attributed to the weakness of their author, Chief Justice Morrison Waite. After the death of Chief Justice Chase in 1873, President Ulysses S. Grant offered the position to six successive political figures, each of whom declined or for one reason or another was unable to accept. Grant then turned to the obscure Waite, who was speedily confirmed by a Senate apparently relieved that the president had at last found someone who was (*a*) not obviously unqualified and (*b*) willing to take the job. Waite was little more than a provincial lawyer who had served a term in the Ohio House as an antislavery Whig and then migrated with most other northern Whigs to the Republican Party. Political observers were underwhelmed by the selection. *The Nation* spoke for Grant's critics when it editorialized: "Mr. Waite stands in the front-rank of second-rank lawyers."[184] His future colleagues, the disappointed Miller and Stephen J. Field, concurred, deeming him "mediocre," "of modest abilities."[185] He served as chief justice until his death in 1888. His tenure, like that of his successor, Melville Weston Fuller, was a disaster for African Americans, as the Court ratified the entire program of Redemption.

In an obfuscated opinion, Waite toggled back and forth between sweeping disquisitions on post-*Slaughterhouse* federalism and fussily precise criticisms of the indictments. Read narrowly, the opinion did nothing more than dismiss the indictments as defective. But Waite's opinion was understood—correctly—by contemporaries and later critics to weaken federal enforcement power and thereby immunize Redemption from federal oversight.[186] Drawing on the *Slaughterhouse* concept of dual citizenship, Waite insisted that "the duty of [the federal] government to afford protection is limited always by the power it possesses," which did not extend to "natural rights" protected by state law, such as the right not to be murdered. The Fourteenth Amendment "adds nothing to the rights of one citizen as against another. It simply furnishes an additional guaranty against any encroachment by the States upon the fundamental rights of citizens." Thus, the Court simultaneously anticipated the state action doctrine, rejected incorporation of the Bill of Rights, and retained the antiquated federalism understanding of *Barron v. Baltimore*. Waite concluded that individual violation of rights like assembly, petition, speech, and bearing arms could be punished only by the states, not the federal government.

Cruikshank is a strangely underappreciated precedent, missing entirely from our constitutional canon today. James Gray Pope considers it to be "the single most important civil rights ruling ever issued by the United States Supreme Court."[187] It precociously announced or anticipated four major constitutional doctrines that have inhibited effective enforcement of the rights of African Americans. These are the state action doctrine, usually attributed to the *Civil Rights Cases* (1883); the neutering of the privileges or immunities clause of the Fourteenth Amendment by holding that it did not incorporate the Bill of Rights against the states; the requirement that actions under the equal protection clause or the Fifteenth Amendment prove intentional discrimination, not just disparate impact, foreshadowing *Washington v. Davis* (1976); and a narrowed congressional discretion in choosing the means to implement its powers exercised under section 5 of the Fourteenth Amendment, anticipating *Boerne v. Flores* (1997).[188]

Doctrine aside, *Cruikshank* had the practical effect of restraining federal power to cope with white terrorism and subversion of state governments. Bradley's circuit court opinion "unleashed the second and decisive phase of Reconstruction-era white terrorism, while the ruling of the full Court ensured its successful culmination in the white supremacist 'redemption' of the majority-black states."[189] All in all, quite a remarkable impact for a case little known outside the small circle of constitutional historians. Justice Clarence Thomas, alone among modern conservatives, most clearly understands *Cruikshank*'s deficiencies: its "holding that blacks could look only to state governments for protection of their right to keep and bear arms enabled private forces, often with the assistance of local governments, to subjugate the newly freed slaves and their descendants through a wave of private violence designed to drive blacks from the voting booth and force them into peonage, an effective return to slavery."[190]

March 27, 1876, was not a good day for African Americans. On that date the Court handed down both *Cruikshank* and its companion, *United States v. Reese*, the Court's first case interpreting the Fifteenth Amendment.[191] Kentucky election officials had refused to receive and count the ballot of a Black citizen and were prosecuted under the 1870 Enforcement Act. The Court, again speaking through Waite, reversed the convictions, holding two sections of the act unconstitutional by narrow and formalistic reasoning. The justices shut their eyes to the obvious, namely, the blatant racial discrimination in voting occurring not only in Kentucky but throughout the South. Waite began on a negative note, constricting the potential of the amendment: "The Fifteenth Amendment does not confer the right of suffrage upon any one."[192] He went on to construe the Enforcement Act in the context of that view. The substantive section 1 explicitly prohibited refusals or interferences "on account of race, color, or previous condition of servitude," as did the first enforcement provision, section 2. But the later enforcement provisions, sections 3 and 4, did not repeat this constitutional phrase, instead employing the backward-referencing term "required...as aforesaid." This was not good enough for Waite, who seemed to dote on excruciating technicalities when it came to protecting African Americans' rights. A penal statute "should be explicit in its terms."[193] It was thus not the "appropriate legislation" required by section 2 of the Fifteenth Amendment. Seventy-four years later, the Supreme Court recognized the fatuousness of Waite's opinion and abrogated *Reese*: "to the extent Reese did depend on an approach inconsistent with what we think the better one and the one established by the weightiest of the subsequent cases, we cannot follow it here."[194]

In dissent, Justice Ward Hunt abandoned the usual decorum that prevails among the justices to deliver a pointed critique of Waite's finicky formalism. Hunt lamented that "the particularity required in an indictment...has at times been extreme, the distinctions almost ridiculous. I cannot but think that in some cases good sense is sacrificed to technical nicety, and a sound principle carried to an extravagant extent."[195] He went at length into Congress's intent in enacting the statute to demonstrate that it clearly had in mind the required racial qualification. He then discussed the purposes of the Fifteenth Amendment and the constitutionality of the act, both of which he read generously for the cause of racial justice.

Cruikshank and *Reese* closed the first chapter of a story that will repeat through this study: the US Supreme Court failed to protect Black American citizens' right to participate in the civic polity by voting and office-holding. Congress had created the constitutional and statutory structure in which this empowerment could take place. But real progress toward racial justice comes only when at least two of the branches of the federal government (executive, legislative, and judicial) cooperate. In the first voting-rights cases that it considered, the Supreme Court did not condemn congressional efforts, but it did little to promote them, and instead adopted a formalistic, exquisitely technical attitude toward statutory drafting.

The justices at first seemed to understand and endorse Congress's expanding goals for Reconstruction, especially the need to protect the safety and status of the nation's newly enfranchised Black citizens. But when confronted with a treacherously deceptive case (it involved whites backed by lawyers who hoped to defeat Reconstruction who invoked the new amendments), the Court lost its bearings. Justice Miller for the *Slaughterhouse* majority may have meant to endorse the congressional objectives of protecting Blacks' rights, but he construed the Reconstruction Amendments in ways that effectively excluded African Americans from their benefits. The privileges or immunities clause was thereafter a dead letter, the potential of the citizenship clause left unrealized, the due process clause diverted to other agendas, and the equal protection clause left to wither in the drought of Redemption. The result was an empty, lifeless residue of protection for the civic status and civil rights of African Americans. Summarizing the Court's impact, George Rutherglen concluded that it was "not a stable equilibrium with full enforcement of enacted laws, but retrenchment through repeal of some laws, invalidation of others, and restrictive interpretations of many that remained. What was left more closely resembled formal statements of equal rights rather than a practical program for achieving racial equality."[196] Eric Foner concludes that the Court "retreated from an expansive definition of federal power, and moved a long way toward emasculating the postwar amendments—a crucial development in view of the fact that Congress had placed so much of the burden for enforcing Blacks' civil and political rights on the federal judiciary."[197] After 1876, the Republican Party and the Supreme Court abandoned Black Americans to white supremacist Democratic legislatures in the South. As African Americans slid toward the Nadir of their experience, the US Supreme Court turned away, indifferent.

3

Redemption, 1880–1900

In 1954, the African American historian Rayford Logan published a history of Redemption, *The Negro in American Life and Thought: The Nadir, 1877–1901*.[1] He there introduced what has become the dominant metaphor for thinking about Black experience after Reconstruction. Other historians have modified his periodization, locating the Nadir in the 1890s or, as in this study, to the first decade of the twentieth century. But exact dating is less important than his basic idea, which now commands universal assent: at some point between the political demise of Reconstruction and the Great War, the experience of African Americans in the United States sunk to its lowest point, worse in some ways than during slavery times. Blacks were systematically stripped of all political power in the southern states, losing the ability to vote, to hold office, and to serve on juries. The white North, Congress, and the Republican Party gave up on them, abandoning any commitment that Black people should be incorporated into the polity. The prewar southern view of Blacks' post-emancipation legal status prevailed, enjoying a postmortem triumph: they had no inherent rights except locomotion, plus whatever else whites might choose to give them. White supremacy became the official policy of governments and parties in all the southern states.[2]

The historian Ulrich Bonnell Phillips confidently proclaimed in 1925 that "the central theme of Southern history" was "a common resolve indomitably maintained—that [the South] shall be and remain a white man's country."[3] "Reconciliation" between the sections came at a terrible cost, and not just in the mawkish sentimentality of Blue-and-Gray reunions or the myth of the Lost Cause.[4] Three dominant themes emerged from the haze of historical memory after the war: reconciliation and reunion; white supremacy; and emancipation. By 1913, the semi-centennial of the Emancipation Proclamation and Gettysburg, the first two had smothered the third, emancipation. National reunification was accomplished by abandoning Black folk to the malevolence of southern whites. Jim Crow apartheid prevailed everywhere in the South, and in less overt ways in the rest of the nation. The Supreme Court under Chief Justice Melville Weston Fuller—the Fuller Court—sanctioned all of this.[5]

It might be unfair to characterize the Fuller Court as the Redeemers' Court, as if they were appointed by southern racists or were themselves Redeemers. Only six of the twenty men who served at one time or another with Fuller were native southerners, and none of them was active in Redeemer politics. But if it was not a Court *of* Redeemers, it was certainly a Court *for* Redeemers, a judiciary solicitous for their interests and responsive to their demands. The Fuller Court consistently struck down federal and state efforts to secure Blacks' rights; was overtly hostile to desegregation while consistently supporting segregation; turned a blind eye to white electoral fraud; and shrugged with indifference at terrorist violence. Collectively, with the standout but inconsistent exception of the first John Marshall Harlan, they ratified Jim Crow.[6]

The Triumph of Pretense and Pretext

After Reconstruction gave way to Redemption, southern Democrats stripped African Americans of rights, power, and agency. In every domain—political, social, economic—they imposed segregation and vaunted white supremacy. By 1900, the segregationist drive had triumphed. Apartheid was imposed everywhere and strictly policed. It was reinforced by both illegal and legal violence (the latter administered by the southern court systems) and by the development of a full-blown intellectual justification of racism.[7] Some of these matters came before the Supreme Court, and throughout Redemption the Court sustained segregationist innovations.[8]

The challenge to the historian is to explain how this could have happened in a political order whose ideals were defined by the Declaration of Independence and whose Constitution protected life, liberty, and property, and guaranteed the equal protection of the laws. How was the egalitarian foundation of Reconstruction so quickly overthrown and a regime of inequality imposed that blatantly flouted those ideals? The answer is found in the related ideas of pretense and pretextuality. Pretense occurs when a legal regime adopts egalitarian trappings as a cover for a discriminatory social reality. Pretextuality refers to a way to achieve something forbidden by enacting a seemingly innocent policy that nevertheless serves as a proxy for the prohibited end. Chief Justice John Marshall had warned against pretextuality in *McCulloch v. Maryland* (1819): "should congress, under the pretext of executing its powers, pass laws for the accomplishment of objects not intrusted to the government; it would become the painful duty of this tribunal, should a case requiring such a decision come before it, to say, that such an act was not the law of the land."[9] He cautioned: "the judiciary may, indeed, and must, see that what has been done is not a mere evasive pretext." But that "mere evasive pretext" has proved too useful a lawyer's device to be ignored for getting around inconvenient barriers to a desired, though illegitimate, goal. An ostensibly race-neutral law might provide a vehicle or surrogate for an overtly discriminatory provision that would otherwise run afoul of the Fourteenth or Fifteenth Amendments. Racial inequality, prohibited by the equal protection clause, became legitimated by validating *non*racial inequality. Pretense and pretextuality became the heart of Jim Crow America, and they lingered on after the demise of Jim Crow itself. In the modern era, they are the legal foundations that enable the Supreme Court to sustain structural racism.

The justices are sometimes uneasy about looking for pretext behind legislative or executive policy decisions. As recently as 2019, Justice Clarence Thomas warned that "pretext is virtually never an appropriate or relevant inquiry for a reviewing court to undertake."[10] The Court has disabled itself from looking behind pretextual claims, thus providing cover for countless instances of structural racism. For example, pretext has justified racial profiling in traffic stops, upheld recently by the Supreme Court in the 1996 case of *Whren v. United States*.[11] Despite the Fourth Amendment's ban on unlawful searches and seizures, Justice Antonin Scalia for a unanimous Court there held that a police officer's motive for making a traffic stop, even if illegitimate as it presumably would be in racial profiling, was irrelevant if there was some plausible reason, no matter how thin or specious, for making the stop.[12] (It was no coincidence that the two defendants in *Whren* were African American men.) A pretext thus provides cover for illegal and unconstitutional behavior. Pretextuality continues to uphold racially differential application of laws to African Americans today.[13]

Another way of understanding the role that pretense and pretextuality play is to see them as the legal profession's way of managing societal cognitive dissonance.[14] Even to the racist mind of the late nineteenth century, it was obvious that there was a conflict between the egalitarian and democratic ideals of the Reconstruction Amendments, on one hand, and the intensifying reality of racial oppression occurring in the 1880s. The two could not continue to coexist without some way of rationalizing and reconciling them. This could have been accomplished by abandoning Jim Crow and striving to attain a truly egalitarian society. But that was unthinkable, so lawyers and courts reversed the process, forcing egalitarian ideas to conform to the discordant sordid social reality.[15]

In four decisions commonly known as the Jury Cases, handed down between March 1 and October 1, 1880—*Strauder v. West Virginia*, *Virginia v. Rives*, *Ex parte Virginia*, and *Neal v. Delaware*—the US Supreme Court confirmed pretextual ways of legitimating racial discrimination that sustained the white South's determination to subordinate Black fellow citizens despite the ideals of equality enshrined in the federal Constitution. The Court accomplished this by establishing parameters for racial discrimination in jury selection. The resulting doctrine would last a half century and enable the perversion of justice in criminal trials of Black men in southern state courts.[16]

In *Strauder v. West Virginia*,[17] a Black defendant appealed his conviction for murder on the grounds that West Virginia statutes confined service on juries to "all white male persons." He alleged that such racial discrimination deprived him of a Fourteenth Amendment–based right of due process.[18] The Court, speaking through Justice William Strong in a six-to-two decision,[19] held the statutes unconstitutional. He could scarcely have done otherwise, since the discrimination was so blatant and explicit.[20] But he justified this result defending the status of African Americans in remarkably strong terms, given that the politics of the moment were decidedly inhospitable to Blacks' civil rights. The Fourteenth Amendment "was designed to assure to the colored race the enjoyment of all the civil rights that under the law are enjoyed by white persons, and to give to that race the protection of the general government, in that enjoyment, whenever it should be denied by the States." The amendment "is to be construed liberally, to carry out the purposes of its framers."

Strong concluded expansively:

What is this but declaring that the law in the States shall be the same for the black as for the white; that all persons, whether colored or white, shall stand equal before the laws of the States, and, in regard to the colored race, for whose protection the amendment was primarily designed, that no discrimination shall be made against them by law because of their color? The words of the amendment, it is true, are prohibitory, but they contain a necessary implication of a positive immunity, or right, most valuable to the colored race,—the right to exemption from unfriendly legislation against them distinctively as colored,—exemption from legal discriminations, implying inferiority in civil society, lessening the security of their enjoyment of the rights which others enjoy, and discriminations which are steps towards reducing them to the condition of a subject race.[21]

Such discrimination was "practically a brand upon them, affixed by the law, an assertion of their inferiority, and a stimulant to that race prejudice which is an impediment to securing to individuals of the race that equal justice which the law aims to secure to all others."

In light of developments a century later, Strong's emphasis on invidious racial discrimination, enforced by an explicitly race-based criterion of equal treatment, stands out. The modern Court has given the equal protection clause an individualistic reading, emphasizing the right of the individual to be free from disadvantage caused by racial classification. But that is only one possible reading of the clause, and one not supported by its legislative history. Strong referred to "the colored race," not the colored individual. His emphasis on explicit racial discrimination supports an alternative reading of the clause, one that focuses on racially discriminatory intent, directed at an entire race of people.[22] Strong went on to point out that the language of the amendment "is prohibitory; but every prohibition implies the existence of rights and immunities, prominent among which is an immunity from inequality of legal protection." That implied that states have a duty to act and not remain impassive in the face of private racial discrimination. Unfortunately, however, his egalitarian dicta were not Justice Strong's last word on the subject.

The grand rhetoric of Strong's dicta belies the narrowness of the Court's actual holding, which struck down the state statute only because it was an explicit, blanket exclusion of all racial minorities. It did not require inclusion, in the sense of affirmatively assuring that Blacks were included in the venire (the jury panel), nor did it require proportionality. A segregationist seeking to salvage something from the opinion could take some comfort from the fact that, as long as a state did not explicitly bar nonwhites, it had no obligation to assure Blacks of some representation, even nominal, on jury rolls. Moreover, after *Strauder*, the US Supreme Court never overturned a conviction of a Black defendant on the grounds that Blacks had been excluded from a grand or petit jury.[23] The Fuller Court was determined not to implement *Strauder* in any meaningful way. Chief Justice Fuller wrote in one of his last opinions that "whether such [jury] discrimination was practised in this case was a question of fact, and the determination of that question adversely to plaintiff in error by the trial court and by the court of criminal appeals was decisive, so far as this court is concerned, unless it could be held that these decisions constitute such abuse as amounted to an infraction of the Federal Constitution, which cannot be presumed."[24]

In *Ex parte Virginia*,[25] Strong again upheld the indictment of a Virginia state judge who was prosecuted under the 1875 Civil Rights Act's ban on discrimination in jury selection for excluding Blacks altogether. As in *Strauder*, Strong read the Fourteenth Amendment and supportive legislation like the 1875 act generously with respect to congressional power, finding in both an ample source of federal authority to act against race prejudice in the administration of justice. *Strauder* and *Virginia* together validated the Reconstruction motifs of change and individual rights.

But *Virginia v. Rives*[26] endorsed the other side of Reconstruction's dualism: continuity and states' sovereignty. The constitutional issue in *Rives* was not as straightforward as it had been in *Strauder*. *Rives* centered on the removal provisions of section 3 of the 1866 Civil Rights Act.[27] Two Black defendants convicted of murder in a Virginia state court alleged that though Virginia had no statute confining jury service to whites or excluding Blacks, no Black had ever served on a petit jury in their county. They asked that a new jury be impaneled on which one-third of the jurors should be Black.

Strong, again speaking for the Court, rejected the petition. Strong read the 1866 removal statute narrowly, holding that it applied only to a denial of rights that occurred *before* trial commenced. Though he claimed that Congress had power to enact a more comprehensive statute, the practical effect of this narrow reading was to confine the kinds of state action under the 1866 act's removal provisions to positive law, that is, to state constitutional provisions and statutes that explicitly discriminate on their face.[28] This eliminated from judicial ken the whole range of sub-legislative forms of discrimination, including every kind perpetrated by executive officers of the state, like sheriffs or other officials who had responsibility for forming venires. This provided another component of pretextuality: it did not matter much, from a segregationist's viewpoint, if laws mandated nominal equality or required Blacks to have some opportunity, like jury service, as long as the administration of the law could be freely discriminatory. The Court concluded the quartet of jury cases with *Neal v. Delaware* in 1881.[29]

Neal reaffirmed *Rives* on the removal point, leaving the removal option for Black defendants in southern state criminal trials so weakened as to be nearly useless. Thus by 1881, two of the four jury cases had offered some support for the elements of change and support for protecting the rights of Black Americans, while two had attempted to preserve the continuity of antebellum federalism conceptions of state authority over the rights of individual citizens. The consequence, however, was that for a half century, the southern criminal justice system remained effectively immunized from federal judicial oversight.

Even worse was the problem of pretextuality. Toward the end of his *Strauder* opinion, Justice Strong made this fatal concession:

> We do not say that...a State may not prescribe the qualifications of its jurors, and in so doing make discriminations. It may confine the selection to males, to freeholders, to citizens, to persons within certain ages, or to persons having educational qualifications. We do not believe the Fourteenth Amendment was ever intended to prohibit this.[30]

This notion was not new: southern political leaders had often made such a claim since the end of the war. But Strong's dicta marked the first time that the Supreme Court officially endorsed it. The justices had previously read the text of the Reconstruction Amendments narrowly, as in *Slaughterhouse* and *Cruikshank*. But here the Court went further, providing a hint, if not an invitation, to southern lawyers and legislators to use their ingenuity to come up with electoral qualifications that, while nominally not racial, nevertheless had the effect of excluding Blacks from jury service by denying them the vote. (Venire lists were compiled from voter rolls.) Within a decade, the white South would realize that potential to the fullest. But the effects of Strong's concession were not limited to disfranchisement. Pretextuality has afforded a basis stretching into the present that has enabled the southern states to evade the substance of constitutional guarantees of the rights of Black citizens. It has legitimized superficially nonracial facades covering institutionalized racial discrimination that enjoy the sanction of law because they were not on their face explicitly racial. The Supreme Court sustains the pretense by blessing such legislation as facially neutral.

The 1880 jury cases mark the last time that the Court seriously considered the conflict of fundamental principles presented by Reconstruction. Foremost on one hand was the right to be free from invidious discrimination based on race, affirmed by the Civil Rights Act of 1866 and the Reconstruction Amendments. On the other hand was respect for the continuing validity of the federalism established by the Constitution of 1787. Antebellum understandings of federalism mandated that it was the states, not the federal government, that bore primary, perhaps exclusive, responsibility for protecting the rights of their citizens. Conservatives considered that responsibility to be essential to the states' sovereignty and autonomy. The *Slaughterhouse Cases* resolved that conflict by tipping the balance in favor of state-sovereignty federalism, and the jury cases confirmed that.

Confining Congressional Power: The State Action Doctrine

The federalism component of Reconstruction's constitutional triad[31] presented two questions to the Court: First, could the states implement social policy free of constraints or supervision by the federal government? This was a question of state power, usually clothed in the language of "states' rights" or "state sovereignty." Second: What powers did Congress have, particularly under the new amendments, to impose its own social policies in the states or revise state-imposed policies? These were often intertwined because they were correlative: the greater the congressional supervisory power was, the more constrained were the states, and vice versa. If not a zero-sum game, the contest over federalism sometimes resembled a tug-of-war, in which Democrats strove to insulate state (read: white) autonomy from federal constraints, while Republicans promoted greater national power.

The single most potent impediment to congressional power under the Reconstruction Amendments has been the state action doctrine.[32] Its effects, stretching into the present, are incalculable. It limits federal power to enforce federal laws that promote racial equality. The state action doctrine also reinforces other limiting structural principles, including the de jure / de facto distinction and the public-private distinction. When individual liberty and racial equality collide, the state action doctrine tilts the scale in favor of individual liberty, which in fact is one of its two principal modern justifications (the other being state sovereignty).[33]

The Supreme Court hobbled Reconstruction at the outset first by its *Slaughterhouse* opinion, which enervated the four operative provisions of section 1 of the 1866 Civil Rights Act. Justice Miller's *Slaughterhouse* majority opinion implied a state action principle but did not make the requirement of state involvement explicit. Chief Justice Waite filled that gap in *Cruikshank*, where he observed that "sovereignty, for this purpose [protecting individual's rights], rests alone with the States." He went on to declare that the Fourteenth Amendment does not

> add any thing to the rights which one citizen has under the Constitution against another. The equality of the rights of citizens is a principle of republicanism. Every republican government is in duty bound to protect all its citizens in the enjoyment of this principle, if within its power. That duty was originally assumed by the States; and it still remains there. The only obligation resting upon the United States is to see that the States do not deny the right. This the amendment guarantees, but no more. The power of the national government is limited to the enforcement of this guaranty.[34]

Justice Strong in turn affirmed that point in *Virginia v. Rives*: "the provisions of the Fourteenth Amendment of the Constitution we have quoted all have reference to State action exclusively, and not to any action of private individuals."[35] These anticipations of the state action doctrine were not essential to the results in any of these cases and so technically were dicta. But when the Court had to consider a direct challenge to the constitutionality of the public accommodations provisions of the Civil Rights Act of 1875, the issue moved to center stage.

Section 1 of the 1875 statute created a right of "full and equal enjoyment of the accommodations, advantages, facilities, and privileges of inns, public conveyances on land or water, theaters, and other places of public amusement."[36] Five appeals were consolidated as the *Civil Rights Cases* (1883)[37] involving prosecutions of proprietors of hotels, theaters, and a railroad for refusing access to African American patrons. In an eight-to-one decision, Justice Joseph Bradley overturned the convictions, holding sections 1 and 2 of the act unconstitutional. He explained that "it is State action of a particular character that is prohibited. Individual invasion of individual rights is not the subject-matter of the amendment." The Fourteenth Amendment is "prohibitory upon the States," not on individuals. Superficially, this seems reasonable: the language of its section 1 states that "No State shall . . ." Under the powers conferred by section 5 of the Fourteenth Amendment,[38] Congress could reach only public, not private, action. This reified the public-private distinction that was later to figure prominently in cases implicating African Americans' rights.[39]

Bradley went on to declare that "civil rights, such as are guarantied by the Constitution against State aggression, cannot be impaired by the wrongful acts of individuals, unsupported by State authority in the shape of laws, customs, or judicial or executive proceedings." In that passage, he transformed the nineteenth-century concept of "civil rights" into something enforceable only by the state. He explained: "the wrongful act of an individual, unsupported by [state] authority, is simply a private wrong, or a crime of that individual;...but if not sanctioned in some way by the State, or not done under State authority, [the victim's] rights remain in full force, and may presumably be vindicated by resort to the laws of the State for redress." That is where the doctrine exploded in its contemporary setting. Bradley was telling Black complainants that in order to force unwilling whites to serve them at a hotel or restaurant, they must resort to state law enforcement, state courts, and state legislatures to vindicate their rights. This was the height, if not of folly, then certainly of formalism. The Supreme Court scholar Eugene Gressman mourned: "seldom if ever, have the power and purposes of legislation been rendered so impotent."[40]

Defenders of the 1875 Civil Rights Act also relied on the Thirteenth Amendment, contending that racial discrimination in access to public accommodations was one of the "badges and incidents of slavery" that Congress had power to prohibit.[41] The words "badges" and "incidents" had identifiable meanings in the mid-nineteenth century.[42] "Incidents" referred to specific legal consequences of the slavery relationship as they pertained to enslaved people, to those who claimed to own them, and to the legal institution itself. Thus, for example, it might refer to the inability to own firearms, the claim to offspring of an enslaved mother, and the status of an enslaved person as a chattel in the eyes of the law, respectively. Before the war, "badges" was more metaphorical and looser in its connotations, but after the war in legal parlance it took on the legalistic meanings associated with the more lawyerlike term "incident." In debates on the 1866 Civil Rights Act, Republicans identified badges of slavery with the various disabilities imposed by the Black Codes.

Bradley conceded that "Congress has a right to enact all necessary and proper laws for the obliteration and prevention of slavery, with all its badges and incidents" under its Thirteenth Amendment section 2 enforcement power.[43] But he denied that racial discrimination in accommodations could be a badge or incident of slavery. This produced the passages of his opinion that are most execrated today. Displaying impatience with the argument itself,

Bradley harrumphed that "it would be running the slavery argument into the ground to make it apply to every act of discrimination which a person may see fit to make as to the guests he will entertain." He concluded that "when a man has emerged from slavery, and by the aid of beneficent legislation has shaken off the inseparable concomitants of that state, there must be some stage in the progress of his elevation when he takes the rank of a mere citizen, and ceases to be the special favorite of the laws."[44] That passage was a bitter irony for the survivors of the Colfax Massacre and other incidents of white terror.

Justice John Marshall Harlan's lone dissent in the *Civil Rights Cases* remains astonishing in its modernity and comprehensive sweep. It was unusually long—nearly fourteen thousand words—and constituted a veritable treatise on the meaning of the Reconstruction Amendments. Harlan's unusual background offers some suggestive hints about the formative influences that shaped the outlook that produced this opinion. Harlan was a remarkable judge by any measure.[45] Scion of a slaveholding Kentucky family and himself for a time a slaveowner, Harlan nevertheless served with distinction as a colonel of the Tenth Kentucky (Union) Infantry. He was nominated to the Supreme Court in 1877 and promptly confirmed. He served there for thirty-three years, during which he wrote some of its most enduring opinions. He was sometimes called "the Great Dissenter," an apt sobriquet for a judge who was not always captive to contemporary conventional wisdom. Yet Harlan's record on race-related issues before his appointment to the Court was not promising: he opposed emancipation, the Thirteenth Amendment, the Civil Rights Act of 1866, and the Civil Rights Act of 1875. Ironically, though, it was he who proved to be the lone voice for racial justice on the Gilded Age Court.

In his dissent, Harlan dismissed Bradley's opinion as "too narrow and artificial."[46] He denied that the Thirteenth Amendment was limited to merely ending the legal institution of slavery, leaving the freedpeople to the states for the determination of their status. Rather, its purpose was "to establish universal freedom," a positive grant of status and rights, enforceable "by [federal] legislation of a direct and primary character, for the eradication, not simply of the institution [of slavery], but of its badges and incidents," operating directly on individuals. Harlan insisted that racial discrimination in access to civil rights was a badge or incident of slavery that Congress had power to suppress.

Harlan argued that railroads and all other common carriers or "public conveyances" were a "governmental agency, created primarily for public purposes," and on that account subject to extensive regulatory constraints. An innkeeper is "in the exercise of a *quasi*-public employment." Places of public amusement were subject to regulation because they were licensed by the state. "A license from the public to establish a place of public amusement, imports, in law, equality of right, at such places, among all the members of that public." "In every material sense applicable to the practical enforcement of the Fourteenth Amendment, railroad corporations, keepers of inns, and managers of places of public amusement are agents of the State, because they are charged with duties to the public, and are amenable, in respect of their public duties and functions, to governmental regulation."

Moving on to the Fourteenth Amendment, Harlan insisted that the citizenship clause was "of a distinctly affirmative character." The clause said nothing about action by the states, so Congress can protect the rights of citizens directly against infringement by individuals. A privilege or immunity of national citizenship was "exemption from race discrimination in respect of any civil right belonging to citizens of the white race in the same State." Since the nation conferred that right, it may protect it as well. (It was a conferred, not a natural, right, in the parlance of the time.) However, the Court has not subsequently expanded on Harlan's insight that the citizenship clause does not contain a state action limitation. For good measure, Harlan also contended that Congress had power to prevent discrimination on interstate carriers under the commerce clause.

Finally, Harlan addressed Bradley's conclusion: it was "scarcely just to say that the colored race has been the special favorite of the laws." When attempting to secure the privileges and immunities of state citizenship, "at every step in this direction, the nation has been confronted with class tyranny." "There cannot be, in this republic, any class of human beings in practical subjection to another class, with power in the latter to dole out to the former just such privileges as they may choose to grant." Here Harlan articulated the caste principle, insisting that the Reconstruction Amendments were drafted in class terms.

Though Harlan was unheeded in his time, his thoughts had a prophetic quality, more attuned than the majority to the intentions of the framers of the Reconstruction Amendments and more alive to the possibilities for equality than his more cautious colleagues could imagine. But for the moment and for seventy years thereafter, Bradley's view prevailed.[47] Not only was the scope of the Thirteenth and Fourteenth Amendments curtailed, but Congress's enforcement powers were limited just at the time they were most needed, as the southern states sunk into the quicksand of Redemption. Later, the modern Court repeatedly reaffirmed the state action doctrine as a limitation on federal civil rights enforcement authority, and on the scope of the Fourteenth Amendment.[48]

The Court further gutted federal enforcement power that same year in *United States v. Harris* (1883),[49] which struck down section 2 of the 1871 Enforcement Act,[50] popularly and appropriately known as the "Ku Klux Klan Act," a provision that made it a felony to go in disguise on the highway to deprive another of equal protection of the law or privileges or immunities of citizenship. The defendant led a mob that broke into a county jail, abducted four Black detainees, beat them, and lynched one of them. Justice William B. Woods, forsaking the broad vision of federal power he had affirmed in *United States v. Hall* twelve years earlier,[51] held section 2 unconstitutional under the state action doctrine. He found no warrant for it under the Fourteenth Amendment because the indictment did not allege any action by the state, citing *Slaughterhouse*, *Cruikshank*, and *Rives*.

Eighty-eight years later, the Court recognized how strained Woods's construction was, and abrogated *Harris* in *Griffin v. Breckinridge* (1971).[52] But in its time, the harm was done,[53] and *Harris* disabled federal enforcement authority. As a result, lynching began to proliferate in part because the federal government had no power to punish them. With Congress sidelined, the North and the Republican Party indifferent, and the white South determined to assert its supremacy, Black Americans had no recourse against the discrimination and terror being visited upon them. In the face of all this, the justices remained supine.

In the early phase of Redemption, nearly all of the Court's decisions affecting Black Americans were setbacks to the cause of racial justice, but there were two anomalous exceptions, *Ex parte Siebold* (1880)[54] and *Ex parte Yarbrough* (1884).[55] *Siebold* upheld a conviction for ballot tampering (ballot-box stuffing and destruction of ballots) in a federal election, while *Yarbrough* sustained a conviction for beating an African American to deter him and other Blacks from voting in a congressional election. Both cases sustained the convictions and affirmed a sturdy federal power to protect the integrity of federal elections. In *Siebold*, Bradley for the Court insisted that federal power is "paramount" to state authority even when state officials supervise elections. Justice Miller writing in *Yarbrough* held that the Fifteenth Amendment "may operate as the immediate source of a right to vote." It "does, proprio vigore, substantially confer on the negro the right to vote, and congress has the power to protect and enforce that right."[56] This temporarily exempted the Fifteenth Amendment from the state-action limitation, thereby protecting Black citizens' voting power until the final political collapse of the Reconstruction project in 1890. The anomalous character of the *Siebold* and *Yarbrough* cases is difficult to explain. They seem to be to be legal unicorns, inconsistent with other cases of the era. Perhaps their outcome was determined by the fact that the right was conferred, not natural, and/or that there is something uniquely compelling about the federal government's power to police the conduct of federal elections.

Miscegenation

Whites had regulated interracial intimacy[57] since the earliest years of English settlement in North America.[58] In 1630, the governor and Council in Court of Virginia "ordered Hugh Davis [a white man] to be soundly whipped before an assembly of Negroes and others for abusing himself to the dishonor of God and shame of a Christian by defiling his body in lying with a Negro."[59] Anti-miscegenation statutes soon followed in most of the colonies, and were carried forward in the states following Independence. Thus, if a criterion of legitimacy and constitutionality is long-sanctioned custom, then the legal prohibition of interracial unions must be acknowledged as one of the hoariest principles of the American public order.

Reconstruction disrupted that understanding, as it did so much else in postbellum America. Rushing to shore up the racial system, the Alabama legislature included a ban on interracial marriage in its 1865 Black Code. The Alabama Supreme Court declared that statute unconstitutional in 1872,[60] finding that it violated the Fourteenth Amendment and the 1866 Civil Rights Act. The judges of that Court were Republicans, appointed by the post-1867 Reconstruction state government. When that government was overthrown, a Democratic Supreme Court promptly reversed that decision in *Green v. State* (1878).[61] "It is for the peace and happiness of the Black race, as well as of the white," wrote the judges, that such [anti-miscegenation] laws should exist. And surely there can not be any tyranny or injustice in requiring both alike, to form this union with those of their own race only, whom God hath joined together by indelible peculiarities, which declare that He has made the two races distinct."

The *Green* decision was part of a long-term project of establishing white supremacy as the foundational principle of social organization and government throughout the South. Once assured by the Wormley Compromise of 1877 that there would be no intervention forthcoming from the federal government that would interfere with their program, Redeemer Democrats in Alabama and elsewhere throughout the South established the white nuclear family as the basic and normative component of society. Interracial marriage posed a potentially fatal danger to the integrity of the white state itself, threatening to undermine that core component of the state.[62] White supremacy evolved from being a taken-for-granted emotional response to the shocks of defeat and emancipation, to being an ideological support for state social policies, to being *the* foundational constitutional principle ensconced in the 1901 Alabama state constitution. The anti-miscegenation statutes were at the heart of that project.

Against this background, Tony Pace and Mary Jane Cox were prosecuted for violation of the anti-miscegenation law, and their conviction was affirmed by the Alabama Supreme Court.[63] (Technically, the couple were charged with adultery or fornication rather than interracial marriage because under Alabama law, such marriages were absolutely void and therefore of no legal effect.) The Court explained why state policy forbade interracial intimacy: interracial cohabitation may result in "the amalgamation of the two races, producing a mongrel population and a degraded civilization, the prevention of which is dictated by a sound public policy affecting the highest interests of society and government."

Before the US Supreme Court, the couple contended that the anti-miscegenation statute discriminated on a racial basis: *intra*racial cohabitation (between persons of the same race, whether fornication or adultery) was merely a misdemeanor, whereas *inter*racial cohabitation was a felony. In *Pace v. Alabama* (1883),[64] Justice Stephen J. Field for a unanimous Court rejected the distinction, relying instead on formalist symmetry: both parties to an interracial union were punished similarly. Whether Field and his colleagues intended it or not, the effect of *Pace*'s principle of formal equality implicitly assured Alabama and its sister states that the Supreme Court would not pose any roadblocks to the larger project of validating white supremacy as the cornerstone of southern state government. When Chief Justice Earl Warren invalidated Virginia's miscegenation statute in *Loving v. Virginia* in 1967[65] on the grounds that such laws were "measures designed to maintain White Supremacy," he was historically right on the mark.

The Supreme Court's approval of anti-miscegenation statutes in *Pace* ensured that such laws were unassailable well into the 1960s. The US Supreme Court twice ducked the issue in *Naim v. Naim* (1955),[66] before it finally faced up to it in *McLaughlin v. Florida* (1964),[67] striking down an interracial cohabitation statute as a violation of the equal protection clause and abrogating *Pace*. The Court finally interred *Pace* in *Loving v. Virginia* (1967), holding that a Virginia statue banning interracial marriage violated both the due process and the equal protection clauses.[68] But before the Court overruled *Pace*, the miscegenation statutes had a long and effective career,[69] first providing the cornerstone of white supremacy in the South, then spreading throughout the nation.

Jim Crow on the Move: Segregated Transportation and the Commerce Clause

When the problem of racial control shifted from intimate interpersonal relations to public spaces like railroads, steam vessels, and streetcars, the social and legal environments became more complicated. For that reason, the railroad segregation that produced *Plessy v. Ferguson* did not come about quickly or easily. In the generation after the Civil War, legal and social developments affecting transportation in the southern states were fluid, reflecting rapidly changing ideas about race, class, and gender.[70] More parties promoted their own interests, and these sometimes proved incompatible. The governing law derived from multiple sources, some of them conflicting. Amid this confusion, though, the US Supreme Court hewed to a policy that consistently pointed in only one direction: Jim Crow. The Court first supported racial discrimination by invalidating anti-discrimination statutes, and then affirmed segregation when the states began to impose it around 1890.[71]

At common law, common carriers and innkeepers had a duty to accept all customers who could pay and who were not a threat to the business. Proprietors could impose regulations governing the conduct of their customers, but these regulations had to be reasonable, and it was courts that determined what was reasonable. As common law, this body of legal regulation was received in the new states at Independence, subject to subsequent modification by statute. By the mid-nineteenth century, a large body of common and statutory law governed common carriers and innkeepers.[72]

The earliest forms of segregation on railroads were concerned more with divisions of class and gender than of race.[73] Carriers were permitted to segregate passengers racially if they provided equal accommodations. The controlling legal formula was "if separate, then equal." "Equal" did not mean identical or the same, but merely substantially equivalent, whatever that might mean.[74] Under these circumstances, middle-class Black passengers, both male and female, often found themselves relegated either to the smoking car, where smoke from cigars sometimes blended with smoke from the engine and fumes from whiskey, or to separate cars maintained for Black passengers. Such Jim Crow cars were frequently dirty, uncomfortable, and poorly maintained. Until the 1890s, both races mingled indiscriminately in the dingy second-class cars.

Layered atop this social practice was the structure of constitutional law that defined Congress's regulatory power over interstate commerce under the commerce clause of the US Constitution.[75] Chief Justice John Marshall's opinion in *Gibbons v. Ogden* (1824)[76] recognized a broad scope for Congress's power to regulate interstate commerce:

> It is the power to regulate; that is, to prescribe the rule by which commerce is to be governed. This power, like all others vested in Congress, is complete in itself, may be exercised to its utmost extent, and acknowledges no limitations, other than are prescribed in the constitution.... If, as has always been understood, the sovereignty of Congress, though limited to specified objects, is plenary as to those objects, the power over commerce with foreign nations, and among the several States, is vested in Congress as absolutely as it would be in a single government.

Willson v. Black Bird Creek Marsh Co. (1829)[77] acknowledged a residuum of state power to regulate economic activities in the absence of congressional regulation even if such regulation had an impact on interstate commerce. The innately interstate character of many railroad and steam vessel operations meant that Congress's authority, whether exercised or not, would be implicated when states began to regulate land or water transportation. The revolution in commerce and society wrought by steam propulsion assured that such regulatory conflicts would occur sooner rather than later.

After the Civil War, three southern states mandated segregation in railroad seating as part of their Black Codes. Congress squelched that in the Civil Rights Acts of 1866 and 1875. The Supreme Court at first upheld

Congress's determination to ban segregation. In *Railroad Co. v. Brown* (1873), it sustained a claim for damages against a street railroad that tried to segregate a line running between Alexandria, Virginia, and Washington, DC.[78] The railroad's congressional charter specified that "no person shall be excluded from the cars on account of color." Even before ratification of the Fourteenth Amendment, the Court readily found a source of power in Congress to impose this condition, presumably from the federal district clause of Article I, section 8.[79]

Meanwhile, different interests jostled to assert control over racial seating practices. Between 1868 and 1875, Reconstruction state governments legislated to prevent racial discrimination on railroads and other modalities of transportation. Segregationists pushed a program of Jim Crow subordination. Given this welter of conflicting ambitions, conflicts over segregated seating came to the federal courts, and their judges had to wade into the complex of common, statutory, and constitutional legal issues presented in such litigation.[80]

Hall v. DeCuir (1878)[81] involved a Reconstruction-era Louisiana statute that prohibited "discrimination on account of race or color" in access to accommodations on railroads and steamboats. On a steamboat engaged in interstate transportation between New Orleans, Louisiana, and Vicksburg, Mississippi, Josephine DeCuir, "a person of color" on an intrastate trip, was denied seating in a section reserved for whites. The master of the vessel was fined under the statute, and after his death, his executrix appealed. Chief Justice Waite for a unanimous Court held the Louisiana statute unconstitutional because it conflicted with Congress's "exclusive" power to regulate interstate commerce.[82] Louisiana had attempted to regulate only in-state commerce, under its police powers. But Waite contended that shipowners would be inconvenienced by having to move their passengers about from segregated to unsegregated seating as they crossed state lines. This, Waite insisted, imposed a "direct burden" on interstate commerce.

Waite disingenuously implied that Congress had not spoken to the issue. It had not, in fact, at the time that DeCuir began her suit, but in 1875 it did explicitly address the issue in the 1875 Civil Rights Act, a statute that Waite studiously ignored. The silence that Waite imputed to Congress meant that it left the shipowner free to segregate. "Congressional inaction left [the carrier] at liberty to adopt such reasonable rules and regulations for the disposition of passengers upon his boat, while pursuing her voyage within Louisiana or without, as seemed to him most for the interest of all concerned."[83]

By supposedly remaining silent, Congress accepted by implication the customs of the locality, which included segregation.

But the Court did not display a similar hostility to state authority when it was deployed to impose segregation. In 1887, the spread of Jim Crow was much further along than when Josephine DeCuir challenged separate seating. Southern states led by Florida and Mississippi began adopting "separate coach" statutes, which were true Jim Crow segregation laws, mandating that all Black passengers, whatever their gender or social condition, ride in cars reserved exclusively for them. A contemporary observer might have thought that *Hall v. DeCuir* would invalidate these innovations, since the core of Waite's reasoning there—the disruption of interstate commerce caused by state statutes prohibiting segregation—would be equally implicated by state statutes *requiring* it. If nothing else were influencing the outcome, logical symmetry alone, which had a powerful hold on judges of that era, would void both types of statutes, since their disruptive effect would be identical.[84]

But that was not how the US Supreme Court responded when the Mississippi statute came before it in 1890. In *Louisville, New Orleans and Texas Railway Co. v. Mississippi*,[85] the statute required railroads to provide "equal, but separate, accommodations for the white and colored races." Justice David J. Brewer saw no problem with that requirement, seeing it solely as a regulation of intrastate commerce. "If it be a matter respecting wholly commerce within a state, and not interfering with commerce between the states, then, obviously, there is no violation of the commerce clause of the federal constitution." But what of interstate trains forced to stop at the Mississippi state line to add the "colored" car? "This may cause an extra expense to the railroad company," Brewer breezily replied, "but not more so than state statutes requiring certain accommodations at depots, compelling trains to stop at crossings of other railroads, and a multitude of other matters confessedly within the power of the state." Harlan, joined by Bradley, dissented, pointing out the obvious: "It is difficult to understand how a state enactment requiring the separation of the white and black races on interstate carriers of passengers is a regulation of commerce among the states, while a similar enactment forbidding such separation is not a regulation of that character."

Plessy v. Ferguson is more notorious, but it was the *Louisville Railway* case of 1890 that first sustained separate-coach laws, and thus full Jim Crow segregation, in interstate railroad and steamboat travel. The other southern states quickly adopted similar measures, bringing to a decisive end the fluid evolution of social practices that had taken place since the end of the war. Jim Crow now rode the rails. But his dominance was not constitutionally secure. The Court soon took seriously the "equal" part of the separate-but-equal formula. Then, in the run-up to the second Reconstruction after World War II, the Court flipped the *DeCuir / Louisville Railway* dichotomy, striking down a state segregation ordinance as it affected a boat traveling in international waters, while sustaining federal power to ban Jim Crow in interstate bus transportation.[86] But for half a century, African Americans were compelled to endure the demeaning inconveniences of segregated interstate travel.

The Triumph of Jim Crow

The railroad experience demonstrates that consistent racial segregation under the separate-but-equal formula was not imposed overnight. It evolved out of uncertainty, experimentation, opportunism, resistance, changing social practices, conflicting pressures from different interest groups, and a growing commitment to white supremacy. Segregation was a response to the Reconstruction ideal of equality before the law, including the anti-caste principle that the state could not favor or disfavor a class of people based on an arbitrary criterion like race. But this ideal clashed with another belief firmly held by whites, that nothing in the constitutional order ordained social equality, understood as the mingling of people in physical proximity, like seating in public accommodations. Nor did the ideal of civic equality necessarily imply political equality: merely because African Americans could now contract or own property did not mean that they could or should exercise political power by voting or holding office. Resolving this clash of ideals and assumptions took time, but by 1890, that conflict was settled. To protect white supremacy, with its rejection of social equality, whites had to be able to monopolize access to every kind of opportunity, not limited to public accommodations. Segregation became the essential social structure of Gilded Age America.

The Court confirmed Jim Crow's triumph in three cases decided just before the turn of the century: *Plessy v. Ferguson* (1896), *Williams v. Mississippi* (1898), and *Cumming v. Richmond County Board of Education* (1899).[87] *Plessy* endorsed segregation and approved several rationales for the states' power to mandate it. *Williams* approved disfranchisement, stripping political power from the African American community. *Cumming* went beyond separation to exclusion, validating total denial of public high school education to Black youth in a Georgia county.

When the southern states began to adopt separate-coach laws in the late 1880s, African Americans resisted, seeing physical separation as white people's symbolic and practical way of imputing inferiority to them. They endorsed instead the principle of "equal public dignity" and respect among citizens, which they saw enshrined in the 1868 Louisiana Reconstruction constitution in its guarantee of "civil, political, and public rights and privileges." (Unfortunately for their cause, that constitution had been overturned by the 1879 Louisiana Redeemers constitution.) In a deliberate effort to assert white supremacy and impose a status of public degradation on African Americans, white Louisiana lawmakers in 1890 required that all railways "provide equal but separate accommodations for the white and colored races," and prohibited all persons from occupying seats in a car or section designated for people of the other race.[88] A group of activists, the Comité des Citoyens, carefully structured test litigation to challenge the act and reclaim rights guaranteed them under the Thirteenth and Fourteenth Amendments. They selected a plaintiff of predominantly European ancestry, Homer Plessy, arranged for a private detective to challenge him when he chose a seat in a car reserved for whites, and had him arrested by New Orleans police for violation of the act. (They were forced to take these elaborate steps because they feared that otherwise white passengers either would not recognize Plessy as colored or, if they did, would simply rough him up and throw him off the train, thereby aborting a legal challenge.) The committee brought an aging abolitionist, Union officer, and Republican advocate for equal rights, Albion Tourgee, out of semi-retirement to lead the legal challenge to the act.[89] It was Tourgee who in argument before the Court proffered the concept of "color-blindness."

The Court by a seven-to-one decision sustained the Jim Crow statute in a decision, *Plessy v. Ferguson* (1896),[90] that ranks second only to *Dred Scott* in infamy.[91] Justice Henry B. Brown, writing for the majority, dismissed the Thirteenth Amendment challenge to segregation by assuming a difference between discrimination and a legislative "distinction" between the races. He relied on a judicial understanding of equal protection common at the time, which assumed that absolute exclusion or clearly inferior accommodations would run afoul of the amendment, but that mere separation would not. He did not acknowledge the badges-of-slavery argument, but he did make the first of his several assertions about the reality of race: the "distinction" that he relied on "is founded in the color of the two races, and which must always exists as long as white men are distinguished from the other race by color."[92] For Brown and other white Americans of the time, racial differences were real, and were based entirely on "color," as opposed to genetics or culture. These cultural assumptions were essential to his doctrinal points. "In the nature of things," he insisted, the Fourteenth Amendment could not "abolish distinctions based upon color."[93]

When Brown turned to the more substantial Fourteenth Amendment challenge, he relied largely on the concept of the police power, which is the power of any sovereign government to regulate for the health, safety, welfare, or morals of its people. In keeping with contemporary understandings of the concept, Brown held that any exercise of the police power by a state legislature must be reasonable, but "there must necessarily be a large discretion on the part of the legislature."[94] In this, he was following the precedent set by Chief Justice Lemuel Shaw of the Massachusetts Supreme Judicial Court in the landmark case of *Roberts v. City of Boston* (1850),[95] which upheld racial segregation in Boston's public schools. There Shaw affirmed that legislative bodies may classify, but that all classifications must be reasonable. Extending this precedent, Brown in *Plessy* held that in their exercise of the police power, legislators may consider "the established usages, customs, and traditions of the people," a concession that would be fatal to challengers' case, given the racism of the time. Though the legislature could not enact a statute "for the annoyance or oppression of a particular class," Brown did not see the relevance of that to racial segregation, because emergent forms of racial separation seemed so reasonable and appropriate to most whites at the time.

Brown insisted that "legislation is powerless to eradicate racial instincts, or to abolish distinctions based upon physical differences." "Social prejudices may [not] be overcome by legislation."[96] This made the equal protection clause something of a constitutional butterfly valve in the Gilded Age, permitting the flow of legislative power in one direction (segregation), but blocking it in the opposite (equality). That paralleled the Court's application of the commerce clause in *Hall v. DeCuir*, which stymied integration, and *Louisville Railway v. Mississippi*, which permitted segregation. (Brown cited both cases approvingly.) He concluded expansively: segregation "neither abridges the privileges or immunities of the colored man, deprives him of his property without due process of law, nor denies him the equal protection of the laws."[97]

Brown invoked the distinction among civil, political, and social rights. The Fourteenth Amendment could not "enforce social, as distinguished from political, equality." "If the civil and political rights of both races be equal," by definition, equality has been achieved. But "if one race be inferior to the other socially, the constitution" cannot change that. Segregation laws do "not necessarily imply the inferiority of either race to the other."[98] The "underlying fallacy" of the challengers' argument was that segregation "stamps the colored race with a badge of inferiority." Ignoring the social reality around him, Brown instead blamed the victim: "if this be so," it is "solely because the colored race chooses to put that construction upon it."[99] Rebecca Scott has demonstrated how segregationist thought had captured the judicial mentality in these passages: "the language of the majority decision thus incorporated a key tenet of white supremacist ideology—the sleight of hand through which public rights were re-characterized as importunate social claims. These, in turn, were associated with 'social equality,' with all the blurring of boundaries between public and private, the phantasms of 'miscegenation,' and the dangers of social transgression that phrase could evoke."[100]

Brown's opinion imposed a formalist account of race and equality. It overlooked the actual racial hierarchy and white hegemony of American society in favor of an abstract, formal approach that made it impossible for courts to confront racial subordination. The air of unreality that permeates Brown's opinion, coupled with the fact that it attracted scant attention at the time, testifies to the pervasiveness of such racial thinking among whites. It ignored the reality of de facto unequal treatment in a way that African Americans dared not. *Plessy* made racial hierarchy and hegemony irremediable as beyond judicial remedy or even notice.[101] The decision legalized white supremacy and Black subordination.

Justice Harlan in his solitary dissent presented a radically different understanding of the Reconstruction Amendments. He saw that the thenconventional hierarchy of civil, political, and social rights led the majority to cut off social equality from basic civil rights, thereby weakening both. Instead, Harlan invoked an "equality of right which pertains to citizenship, national and state, [and] with the personal liberty enjoyed by every one within the United States."[102] This embraced "every right that inheres in civil freedom, and the equality before the law of all citizens of the United

States."[103] This conception of rights was based on Harlan's vision of what the Reconstruction Amendments had accomplished, a view derived from his unique experience as a slaveholder converted first to a nationalist outlook through his political involvements and battlefield service as a Union officer, then to a commitment to African Americans' status as rights-bearing citizens through postwar political struggles. In his vision, emancipation led necessarily to full rights and equality for the freedpeople, a status that was being denied by Redeemers' creation of a state of neo-servitude masked by a merely notional equality. Harlan rejected the pretense-and-pretext core of Jim Crow servitude.

It is in this context that we encounter his celebrated paean to the color-blind constitution: "in the eye of the law, there is in this country no superior, dominant, ruling class of citizens. There is no caste here. Our constitution is color-blind, and neither knows nor tolerates classes among citizens."[104] This statement can be understood and interpreted only in its context.[105] The color-blindness that Harlan invoked is appropriate only in a society like his in which a dominant caste imposes separation and degradation on a disfavored racial group.[106] "Everyone knows," Harlan explained, pointing out the obvious to a Court determined to ignore it or pretend otherwise, "that the statute in question had its origin in the purpose, not so much to exclude white persons from railroad cars occupied by Blacks, as to exclude colored people from coaches" occupied by whites.[107]

But Harlan's opinion also had a dark underside, usually overlooked by his admirers. He extolled white supremacy: "the white race deems itself to be the dominant race in this country. And so it is, in prestige, in achievements, in education, in wealth, and in power. So, I doubt not, it will continue to be for all time."[108] This passage precedes the color-blind constitution sentence,[109] but it seldom gets the attention it deserves as a gloss on the meaning of color-blind constitutionalism.

Harlan's arguments supporting his condemnation of separate but equal focused on two doctrines: badges-of-slavery and what later came to be known as the "public function doctrine." "Any burdens or disabilities that constitute badges of slavery" are forbidden by the Thirteenth Amendment, he insisted, and the kind of racial discrimination embedded in segregation was just such a badge. "No one would be so wanting in candor as to assert the contrary," he thought, ignoring the fact that Brown's majority opinion did just that.[110] While this may be obvious to us today, the climate of formalism and pretextuality that characterized the Court's race-related cases in the period of the Nadir enabled the justices and most of their white fellow Americans to pretend that segregation delivered bilateral equality. In the tug-of-war between candor and pretense, pretense won out, clothed in the vestments of formalist legal reasoning.

Harlan also anticipated the public function doctrine that emerged after World War II.[111] If an instrumentality of commerce, such as a railroad, particularly one that was incorporated by the state, performs a public function, it may not discriminate in the delivery of service. For Harlan, common carriers like railroads were archetypes of private entities analogous to public highways that performed public functions and accordingly were prohibited from discriminating at common law. The public function doctrine flowered in the mid-twentieth century, beginning with *Marsh v. Alabama* (1946),[112] and performed yeoman service in striking down the white primaries of the southern states.[113] But in the second Redemption, the Supreme Court shut down this doctrinal potential, limiting the public function doctrine to company towns and the white primary, foreclosing an avenue of redress for civil rights plaintiffs.[114]

The most passionate passages in Harlan's opinion condemned the sham equality of separate but equal. "Every one knows," he wrote, that the real purpose of segregation statutes was to force Blacks "to keep to themselves" and not mingle among whites. It was in reality an assertion that "colored citizens are so inferior and degraded that they cannot be allowed to sit in public coaches occupied by white citizens."[115] Pretextuality and formalism did their work here, legitimating a nominal equality—whites were banned from Black company as much as Blacks were banned from white company—in a classic example of the logical fallacy of false symmetry. But "the thin disguise of 'equal' accommodations...will not mislead any one, nor atone for the wrong this day done." Segregation statutes were in reality "conceived in hostility to, and enacted for the purpose of humiliating, citizens of the United States of a particular race."[116]

Harlan's *Plessy* dissent was prophetic. He called the majority opinion the *Dred Scott* of its era, empowering "a dominant race a superior class of citizens—which assumes to regulate the enjoyment of civil rights, common to all citizens, upon the basis of race."[117] This would grant "a power in the states, by sinister legislation,...to place in a condition of legal inferiority a large body of American citizens."[118] Aside from the inherent wrong to human dignity, this would imperil republican government itself. It "will not only stimulate aggressions, more or less brutal and irritating, upon the admitted rights of colored citizens, but will encourage the belief that it is possible, by means of state enactments, to defeat the beneficent purposes" of the Reconstruction Amendments themselves.[119]

Plessy canonized a concept of equality that reconciled the Fourteenth Amendment and Jim Crow, creating the foundation for the pretextual equality that dominated American constitutional thought for the next half century. The British historian J. R. Pole described this innovation: "what the Court did in 1896 was to give constitutional sanction to a policy which regarded the rights of individuals as determined by their status as members of designated [racial] blocs, as opposed to regarding their rights as Americans as equal individuals."[120] This effectively legitimized a bi-level structure of equality: "the equal protection of the laws" meant one thing for whites, and something void of meaning for African Americans.

Disfranchisement

The Jim Crow segregation that *Plessy* affirmed might not have been possible if African Americans had retained the political power they enjoyed in the years 1875–1880. Then they were able to elect members of Congress, state legislatures, and constitutional conventions. They seemed to be realizing the framers' hopes that under the Fourteenth and Fifteenth Amendments, they could protect their own interests through normal political processes. But by 1915, a half century after emancipation, they were again reduced to the powerlessness they had experienced as newly freed citizens in 1865. African American voters did not return to 1880 levels of political empowerment until around 1970, a century after ratification of the Fifteenth Amendment. The Redeemer states of the South ignored the Fifteenth Amendment and stripped Black citizens of all political power. The Supreme Court acquiesced, embracing the pretext that voter qualifications that did not mention race were racially innocent.

In 1865, congressional Republicans had been reluctant to grant freedmen the vote, in part because their northern constituencies had little desire to share political power with their new Black fellow citizens, or more to the point, with the immigrant Irish. But ex-Confederates showed themselves determined to seize power not just in the South but in the nation as a whole. This forced Republicans to seek a self-effectuating way of protecting Black and Republican interests in the South at minimal cost. Black enfranchisement seemed to be the answer. From a combination of principle and opportunism, the Thirty-Ninth and Fortieth Congresses adopted two constitutional amendments (section 2 of the Fourteenth and the Fifteenth) to provide, first, a disincentive for denying Black men the vote, and then an outright prohibition of such behavior. They strengthened the general guarantees of access to civil rights contained in the 1866 Civil Rights Act with three statutes specifically aimed at securing Black men access to the ballot and protecting them against interference with that right.[121]

The initial response of ex-Confederates and segregationists to Black enfranchisement was fraud and violence directed at Black voters, their white allies, and Republicans generally.[122] After the Grant administration forcefully repressed the most overt outbreaks in South Carolina, violence subsided, and whites turned to nonviolent modes of obstructing Black voting. The Supreme Court's initial response to these struggles over political power was disappointing. In *United States v. Reese* (1876),[123] the Court struck down the vital enforcement provisions of the 1870 act in a case involving nonviolent interference with the right to vote. *Cruikshank v. United States* (1876),[124] decided at the same time as *Reese*, weakened the federal government's power to protect Black political actors in the exercise of their First and Fifteenth Amendment rights, among others, against murderous assault.

Encouraged by these setbacks to Black political power, southern whites began a persistent campaign of administrative nullification of the Fifteenth Amendment. Even as the amendment was being debated on the floor of Congress, its supporters warned that it could be evaded "for want of education or for want of intelligence...or by property or educational tests."[125] Southern Democrats used these devices with increasing frequency beginning in the 1880s.[126] They began with complex registration requirements, which stymied many illiterate would-be Black voters. This diminished, but did not eliminate, Black political power in the South. The federal Department of Justice strove to enforce Black voting rights throughout the 1880s, sometimes against insuperable odds.[127]

Redeemer governments then levied poll taxes, sited polling places distant from Black neighborhoods, sometimes arbitrarily changed them at the last minute, created complex and confusing ballots, adopted onerous registration procedures, devised literacy and understanding tests (to be administered by hostile white registrars), adopted the secret ballot (another impediment to illiterate voters), imposed disqualifications based on misdemeanor convictions, enacted grandfather clauses, and required extended periods of residency.[128] Each of these schemes could be made to seem facially neutral, and that was good enough for the Court. At the same time, as social and political conditions throughout the South deteriorated, whites resorted to economic pressure on sharecroppers, terrorist tactics like night-riding, and other forms of violence to discourage voting.

After Republicans were returned to political power in the 1888 national elections, they responded by one last hurrah with the Lodge Force Bill of 1890, named after its sponsor, Republican representative Henry Cabot Lodge of Massachusetts.[129] It would have enabled federal circuit court judges to appoint elections supervisors who would oversee congressional elections to prevent fraud and other electoral irregularities on the rise throughout the South.[130] It failed due to determined Democratic opposition, supported by Republican defectors who were lured away by the politics of the tariff and silver.[131] The Lodge Bill was the dying gasp of the Reconstruction impulse of a quarter century earlier. Seeing Black suffrage as a lost cause, sharing in whites' general intellectual and emotional abandonment of African Americans in the Gilded Age, misled and disillusioned about the supposed misdeeds of integrated southern legislatures, distracted by emergent imperialism, perturbed by the rise of Populism, worried about the influx of eastern and southern European immigrants, and above all seduced by the racism of the era,[132] Republicans wrote off their one-time wards and redirected their energies to economic matters. Southern whites were free to pursue disfranchisement unimpeded by northern Republican concern for African Americans.

The Mississippi constitutional convention of 1890 led the parade, and its scheme for eliminating the Black vote has been known since as the Mississippi Plan. Under it, a poll tax, early registration, a requirement that the would-be voter present a certificate of his registration, residency requirements, criminal disabilities, literacy and interpretation mandates, and redistricting promoted an ambitious program of disfranchisement.[133] In 1900, James Vardaman, later governor and US senator from Mississippi, boasted: "There is no use to equivocate or lie about the matter....Mississippi's constitutional convention [of 1890] was held for no other purpose than to eliminate the nigger from politics. Not the 'ignorant and vicious,' as some of the apologists would have you believe, but the nigger....In Mississippi we have in our constitution legislated against the racial peculiarities of the Negro....When that device fails, we will resort to something else."[134]

The remaining ex-slave states adopted all or parts of the Mississippi Plan by World War I, adding their own refinements.

Mississippians, unabashed, did not even try to hide the racial motive behind the Mississippi Plan. In an 1896 case, *Ratliffe v. Beale*, the Mississippi Supreme Court boasted about its pretextuality:

> Within the field of permissible action under the limitations imposed by the federal constitution, the convention swept the circle of expedients to obstruct the exercise of the franchise by the negro race. By reason of its previous condition of servitude and dependence, this race had acquired or accentuated certain peculiarities of habit, of temperament, and of character, which clearly distinguished it as a race from that of the whites,—a patient, docile people, but careless, landless, and migratory within narrow limits, without forethought, and its criminal members given rather to furtive offenses than to the robust crimes of the whites. Restrained by the federal constitution from discriminating against the negro race, the convention discriminated against its characteristics and the offenses to which its weaker members were prone.[135]

Not to be outdone, Senator Carter Glass exclaimed at the 1901 Virginia constitutional convention: "Discrimination! Why that is precisely what we propose, that, exactly, is what this convention was elected for." The delegates were to "discriminate to the very extremity of permissible action under the limitations of the Federal Constitution, with a view to the elimination of every negro voter who can be gotten rid of, legally, without materially impairing the white electorate."[136]

Seeing that they now had a free hand, segregationists turned with zest to the task of total disfranchisement. In three states, numerical white minorities, not majorities, pulled this off.[137] The Mississippi court admitted this in *Ratliffe*: "the anomaly was then presented of a government whose distinctive characteristic was that it rested upon the will of the majority, being controlled and administered by a minority of those entitled under its organic law to exercise the electoral franchise."[138] Only a mop-up operation remained to assure an all-white electorate in the South. Democrats seized the opportunity after they returned to power in Congress after 1892 by repealing all the remaining statutory structure for enforcing voting rights that had survived the US Supreme Court's slash-and-burn foray of 1875.[139]

Williams v. Mississippi (1898)[140] mounted a forlorn challenge to the Mississippi Plan. A Black defendant seeking removal of his homicide trial to federal court alleged discrimination in grand jury selection, which was limited to qualified voters. He claimed that the 1890 constitution eliminated potential Black jurors, alleging two flaws in the juror/voter selection process: the literacy requirement left excessive discretion in registrars to reject Black voters; and adoption of the plan was motivated by a determination to disfranchise Blacks. On the latter point, ample evidence backed up his claim. S. S. Calhoon, the president of the 1890 constitutional convention, addressed the delegates, exhorting them that "Negro suffrage is an evil and an evil to both races.... Repeal of the constitutional clause conferring the ballot if of course the only sweeping and certain remedy."[141] The impact of the resulting Mississippi Plan was staggering. In 1890, before the convention convened, 189,884 Black Mississippians were registered to vote, as compared with 118,890 whites. Two years later, both those numbers dwindled: Blacks now amounted to 8,615 registered voters, whites 68,127.[142]

The petitioner challenging his conviction and disfranchisement itself relied on the equal protection clause of the Fourteenth Amendment, not on the Fifteenth Amendment. It did him no good. Justice Joseph McKenna, for a unanimous Court, rejected his challenge. His opinion, dizzying in the repeated circularity of its reasoning, addressed two issues: facial unconstitutionality and discriminatory administration. As to the first, McKenna quoted the Mississippi's court's reasoning in *Ratliffe v. Beale* at length, accepting its characterization of Blacks as "a patient, docile people, but careless, landless, migratory within narrow limits, without forethought," but concluded that "nothing tangible can be deduced from this." McKenna agreed that if white Mississippians took advantage of Blacks' supposed docility and lack of forethought, that was permissible under the federal Constitution. He then fell back on the usual resort of false equivalence: the constitutional provisions applied to "weak and vicious white men as well as weak and vicious black men." (It seemingly did not occur to him or his colleagues to question whether illiteracy proved that an individual was vicious.) He concluded smarmily that "both races" can avoid disfranchisement "by the exertion of that duty which voluntarily pays taxes and refrains from crime."

McKenna's lapse in logic was unintentionally accurate, though. The disfranchisers at southern state constitutional conventions sometimes did acknowledge that a literacy or poll tax clause would strike from the polls many poor whites as well as Blacks. But some of these disfranchisers welcomed the prospect. As Morgan Kousser has shown, the intent as well as the effect of disfranchisement was to secure the power of the Black Belt planter, commercial, and industrial oligarchy over the lower orders, white as well as Black. Putting down white Populists was no less urgent than suppressing Blacks. In this "reactionary revolution," as he terms it, "segregation, single-party hegemony, [and] a concentration of power in the hands of upper-class whites" destroyed democracy in southern politics "by sterilizing the political system against the disease of conflict over real issues."[143]

Responding to the second claim of excessive discretion in *Williams*, McKenna quoted at length from the most relevant precedent, *Yick Wo v. Hopkins* (1886),[144] a case voiding a facially neutral ordinance because it was invidiously administered against Chinese launderers in San Francisco. Justice Stanley Matthews there wrote that "though the law itself be fair on its face and impartial in appearance, yet, if it is applied and administered by public authority with an evil eye and an unequal hand, so as practically to make unjust an illegal discrimination between persons in similar circumstances," the equal protection clause was violated. But the defendant in *Williams* had not shown that there was actual discriminatory administration, only that it was possible. Without that showing, the facial neutrality of the constitutional provision rendered it immune from challenge. The Mississippi Constitution and statutes "do not on their face discriminate between the races, and it has not been shown that their actual administration was evil; only that evil was possible under them."[145] Pretext triumphed again.

The last case of the Jim Crow triad decided by the Supreme Court as the century drew to a close permitted southern lawmakers to deny high school education altogether to Black youth. In *Cumming v. Richmond County Board of Education* (1899),[146] Harlan wrote for a unanimous Court approving the decision of a county school board to provide a high school for whites while eliminating a high school for Blacks. *Cumming* has perplexed Harlan's admirers ever since: how could the clarion voice of the *Plessy* dissent sustain such an overt act of discrimination? The outcome can be rationalized doctrinally, but it takes fancy logical footwork to do so.

The facts of the case were more complex than the simple formulation of the question would suggest, and provide a partial answer.[147] Under Georgia law, school boards were obliged to establish elementary schools, but it was discretionary with them whether to create high schools. Segregation was mandatory in all public schools. Ware High School in Augusta (Richmond

County) Georgia, founded in 1880, was the only public high school for Black students in the state, and only one of four in the entire South. In 1897, the all-white school board voted to discontinue the school and redirect the funds that had supported it to hire more teachers for the segregated Black elementary schools, at a time when the extant Black schools could not accommodate all the children wishing to attend, estimated to number between three hundred and four hundred. There were then three private high schools in Richmond County that Blacks might attend. They would have had to pay tuition there, but then they as well as whites had to pay tuition at the public high schools too.

Black Augustans brought two suits, one seeking injunctive relief to prevent the school board from continuing the white high school unless it also provided a Black high school, and another for a mandamus ordering the board to reopen Ware. In both cases, they claimed violation of the equal protection clause. The petitioners did not challenge segregation per se, but only the decision to close Ware. From reversal of a favorable lower court decision by the Georgia Supreme Court, they appealed to the High Court, where they were again disappointed. The petitioners unwisely chose to appeal only the injunction suit, where their position was weaker because of the discretion allowed to the school board under state law. Moreover, they failed to prove that the board acted out of a discriminatory animus. They seemed to be merely demanding that the white high school be closed.

Harlan and the rest of the Court were unsympathetic to that position. It would do no good to the petitioners' interests, he pointed out, to deny whites a high school education. The board's decision was reasonable: it "was in the interest of the greater number of colored children, leaving the smaller number [sixty] to obtain a high-school education in existing private institutions at an expense not beyond that incurred in the high school discontinued by the board." Had the unappealed mandamus action proven that the board acted "in hostility to the colored population because of their race, different questions might have arisen in the state court."[148]

For Harlan and his colleagues, federalism considerations dictated that federal courts not interfere with traditional state functions such as educational funding, especially where state law provided unlimited discretion to an administrative body. "Any interference on the part of Federal authority with the management of such schools cannot be justified except in the case of a clear and unmistakable disregard of rights secured by the supreme law of the land," Harlan wrote.[149] Harlan's conservative understanding of federalism, close to Miller's *Slaughterhouse* position, respected state authority. He was loath to second-guess state policy decisions in the absence of clear proof of racially discriminatory intent.[150] To an extent, they explain the difference between the Harlan of *Plessy* and the Harlan of *Cumming*. There was no proof of discriminatory intent in the latter, however much we might be willing to infer it a century later. Harlan's nationalism still left considerable leeway for state autonomy in matters traditionally left to the states that did not appear to challenge federal authority, absent a clear showing of discriminatory intent. In these respects, he anticipated the attitudes of his successors a century later.

Reconstruction had been undone by the turn of the twentieth century. The Thirteenth Amendment seemed defunct. Having served its function of bringing the legal existence of slavery to an end, it seemed sapped of all vitality or relevance. It went into a comatose state for two generations, until its miraculous-seeming revival in 1968—a reawakening that, sadly, marked the end of the second Reconstruction.

The Fifteenth Amendment likewise seemed to be a dead letter. African Americans in the South never quit the struggle, though, and their efforts to overturn disfranchisement began to bear fruit by World War II. But it was not until the second Reconstruction that they finally succeeded in affirming their place in the political sun—though there too the struggle goes on today.

As for the Fourteenth Amendment, *Slaughterhouse* treated the citizenship clause of section 1 as little more than an ancillary to the privileges or immunities clause, and it has never since realized its potential. Miller's decision seemingly interred the privileges or immunities clause too, or at least left it in a stupor from which it has yet to awaken. The due process clause was diverted to succor the economic interests of white property owners when the Court invented the doctrines of liberty of contract and substantive due process. The justices left Blacks behind, shut out from benefiting from the remarkable growth of substantive due process. Finally, the Court drained the equal protection clause of any significance for African Americans, rendering it the empty and hopeless promise that Holmes sneered at, the "usual last resort of constitutional argument."[151]

The US Supreme Court did not impose Jim Crow on America on its own. For that matter, neither did law or legal institutions like state courts. At most, the law and its institutions ratified a social reality already in place. The decisions that affirmed the triumph of Jim Crow did not overthrow Reconstruction; that had already been accomplished by 1890. The Court merely acquiesced in the social changes they observed around them. The Supreme Court seldom moves out in front of dominant social opinion. At times it may give voice to an inchoate opinion about to cohere and emerge, but most of the time it merely affirms what is already a social reality. The Court's turn-of-the-century race decisions confirmed an extant status quo. In the next decade, though, the Court began to move in a different direction.

4

The Nadir and the Blue Hour, 1900–1920

Between the dead of night and sunrise, a "blue hour" intervenes. The blue hour is the period before dawn when the sun is still below the horizon and the short blue wavelengths of its light are diffused through the sky, creating an ethereal effect, captured so well in the paintings of Maxfield Parrish. It has become an artistic metaphor for the passage from the dark night of despair to the dawning of hope. The blue hour for African Americans came in the years between the Nadir and the 1920s. In this decade, the Supreme Court invoked the Thirteenth Amendment's ban on involuntary servitude for the first time and revisited some of its regrettable holdings of the prior period involving transportation, suffrage, and segregation. This judicial awakening did not suddenly usher in a new day of racial justice, but it did signal an approaching turnaround in the Court's thinking. The justices left behind the Fuller Court's dead indifference of the *Plessy* era and began to reconsider the promise of the Reconstruction Amendments.

The Nadir

In the decade of the Nadir (1900–1910), the Supreme Court slammed the doors of the federal courts shut to African Americans struggling against the disfranchisement inaugurated by the Mississippi Plan; enfeebled the protections for civic status contained in the 1866 Civil Rights Act and the Enforcement Acts; and permitted the states to impose segregation in private colleges. The Court's abandonment of African Americans seemed complete and final.[1] The Constitution appeared impotent, lifeless, unable to prevent their oppression or protect their rights. It was as if *Dred Scott* had risen from its grave: African Americans again had no rights the white man need respect.

Despite the disappointment of *Williams v. Mississippi*, determined Black voters in Alabama doggedly continued to fight disfranchisement. The Alabama constitutional convention of 1901 was convened to implement the Mississippi Plan. In his opening address, the president of the convention, John Knox, rallied the delegates to the cause like a cheerleader: "What is it that we want to do? Why it is within the limits imposed by the Federal Constitution, to establish white supremacy in this State."[2] The convention did just that, adopting a panoply of disfranchising clauses to screen out Black voters: a poll tax, residency, good character, literacy, understanding, ownership of real property, and, to salvage some of the white vote, a grandfather clause. The effect was drastic: before the convention, 181,471 Black Alabamians were registered to vote; after the convention had done its work, only 3,000 remained on the rolls. An African American voter and activist sued in equity to enjoin enforcement of those provisions, and to have his name restored to the voting rolls, alleging both the discriminatory intent and the disparate effect of the new provisions.

In a terse opinion that typified his style, *Giles v. Harris* (1903),[3] Justice Oliver Wendell Holmes leapt over several important jurisdictional barriers (political question, Eleventh Amendment) to reach the substantive issues presented. He refused to grant relief on two grounds. First, he thought the petitioner's position was logically self-contradictory. The petitioner had alleged that the registration scheme was unconstitutional. But if it was, how could he sue to enforce it? Why should the Court implicitly sustain it by "adding another voter to its fraudulent lists?" Second, the Court would be impotent to enforce any decree it might issue in the face of determined white opposition. The Supreme Court "has as little practical power to deal with the people of the state in a body. The bill imports that the great mass of the white population intends to keep the Blacks from voting. To meet such an intent something more than ordering the plaintiff's name to be inscribed upon the lists of 1902 will be needed. If the conspiracy and the intent exist, a name on a piece of paper will not defeat them. Unless we are prepared to supervise the voting in that state by officers of the court, it seems to us that all that the plaintiff could get from equity would be an empty form." "Relief from a great political wrong," Holmes intoned, "if done, as alleged, by the people of a state and the state itself, must be given by them or by the legislative and political department of the government of the United States." This implicitly conceded that it would be useless to petition those who had perpetrated the wrong to correct themselves.

In his thirty-year tenure on the Court, Holmes displayed a startling indifference, amounting almost to hostility, to the plight of African Americans in the Nadir. His *Giles* opinion is typical. Though sharing the antislavery sentiments of his class and city, the young Holmes who eagerly enlisted in the Twentieth Massachusetts in 1861 seems to have had something burned out of him by his experiences in war. This may have reflected post-traumatic stress disorder.[4] One consequence was a loss of empathy for enslaved people,[5] another a conviction that the white South could not, and would not, be defeated.[6] It also reflected his generally bleak, nihilistic view of the human condition.[7] Seeing human existence in starkly social-Darwinian terms as an unending struggle for survival and domination, Holmes displayed no empathy for the losers in that struggle.[8] Because he thought that majorities inevitably would and should have their way, it seemed to him pointless to try to protect Blacks in the South from the imperatives of white supremacy.[9] Whatever the psychological causes, Holmes was strikingly unsympathetic to Black petitioners.

The Court repeated Holmes's points the next year when the petitioner returned, this time seeking relief in law (for monetary damages) rather than in equity. In *Giles v. Teasley* (1904),[10] Justice William Day held that if the plaintiff's allegations of unconstitutionality were correct, then the registration board was not legally constituted, and its actions could therefore not have any legal effect in denying Blacks the right to vote. Day explained that the state supreme court had ruled that if the 1902 state constitution was adopted with a purpose "to prevent negroes from voting and to exclude them from registration for that purpose, no damage has been suffered by the plaintiff, because no refusal to register by a board thus constituted in defiance of the Federal Constitution could have the effect to disqualify a legal voter." This was another illogical catch-22 that enabled the US Supreme Court to refuse relief.

Modern commentators condemn *Giles v. Harris* as "particularly poorly reasoned," "probably the most momentous ignored decision in the history of the Supreme Court,"[11] and more spaciously, "one of the worst decisions about race in the Court's history."[12] In *Giles*, the Court locked in white supremacy and the Democratic domination of what quickly became the one-party South. The Court's message seemed to be that the Fifteenth Amendment was a dead letter. African Americans could no longer look to the federal courts for relief.

To close out the Nadir voting rights cases, in *James v. Bowman* (1903) the Court imposed the state action requirement on the Fifteenth Amendment, throwing out a conviction for bribing African American men not to vote in a congressional election.[13] It held unconstitutional a federal statute, derived from the Enforcement Acts, that criminalized bribery or threats directed at one "exercising the right of suffrage, to whom that right is guaranteed by the Fifteenth Amendment," on the grounds that it was not limited to actions by the state's agents, or to federal elections, or to discrimination on the basis of race. This was superficially reasonable, given that the Fifteenth Amendment speaks of the franchise being "denied or abridged…by any State." But both opinions in *Cruikshank* had intimated that there was no state action requirement for Fifteenth Amendment violations, and *Yarbrough* and *Siebold* had displayed a concern for voting rights clearly absent here. Not until the white primary cases after World War I would the Court again show any concern at all for the problem of Black disfranchisement.

If any single case can be said to mark the low point of African Americans' legal fortunes at the turn of the twentieth century, the absolute nadir, it should be *Hodges v. United States* (1906),[14] a relatively unknown decision of the White Court that demonstrates how indifferent the US Supreme Court had become to the plight of Black citizens in the heyday of Jim Crow.[15] *Hodges* involved the social phenomenon known as "whitecapping," an outburst of vigilantism that bridged the first era of Ku Klux Klan power in the 1860–1870s, and the Klan's second coming in the 1920s. Beginning in the 1870s with goals and tactics anticipating the second Klan, poor whites throughout the upper South resorted to nighttime violence to police deviant social behavior. After the onset of the depression of 1893, whitecappers redirected their malevolence to Blacks and the white merchants and landowners who hired them, seeking to drive the former away and intimidate the latter.[16]

Hodges originated in two incidents in Arkansas in 1903, where whites attempted to drive Black sharecroppers off the land and force Black millworkers to quit their jobs. The whitecappers were prosecuted for violation of the 1866 Civil Rights Act, which guaranteed the right to make contracts, and the 1870 Enforcement Act prohibiting conspiracies to interfere with rights guaranteed by the federal Constitution or laws.[17] The trial court convicted, holding that the Thirteenth Amendment protected African Americans' rights to contract, including labor contracts, as a "fundamental or natural" right.[18] The United States on appeal to the Supreme Court reinforced this argument, arguing that the essence of slavery was denial of contractual liberty, being denied the opportunity to choose whether to work and for whom. The federal government's power to protect such contractual freedom was plenary, especially in view of the southern states' refusal to protect it.

But in his opinion for the Court, Justice David J. Brewer rejected the ambitious arguments of the attorney general and threw out the indictment. He held that federal courts had no jurisdiction over the activities of the defendants, which were prosecutable, if at all, only by the states, and no power to prosecute them for denying victims the opportunity to work. Relying exclusively on *Slaughterhouse*, Brewer claimed that the Reconstruction Amendments had achieved only an extremely limited shift in federalism. The Thirteenth Amendment did not "denounce every act done to an individual which was wrong if done to a free man." Had it done so, the "protection of individual rights which, prior to the 13th Amendment, was unquestionably within the jurisdiction solely of the states, would, by virtue of that Amendment, be transferred to the nation, and subject to the legislation of Congress."[19] The Thirteenth Amendment was "not a declaration in favor of a particular people," African Americans, but had reference only to a condition—a strange and tortured construction.

The Court interpreted the Constitution to be color-blind, indifferent to the race of oppression's victims, concerned only with abstract categories of status. In reaching this conclusion, Brewer ignored the dicta in Bradley's *Civil Rights Cases* that federal "legislation may be necessary and proper to meet all the various cases and circumstances.... And such legislation may be primary and direct in its character; for the amendment is not a mere prohibition of State laws."[20] Bradley had further argued there that "[the] disability...to make contracts...and such like burdens and incapacities...were the inseparable incidents of the institution," that is, slavery. By ignoring this argument Brewer shrunk the concept of badges and incidents of slavery to vanishing. The Court squeezed the Thirteenth Amendment into its narrowest possible meaning, as accomplishing little more than the simple abolition of slavery. With that, the amendment became a practical dead letter. Brewer concluded that Congress "gave [the freedpeople] citizenship, doubtless believing that thereby in the long run their best interests would be subserved, they taking their chances with other citizens in the states where they should make their homes." And that was that: Congress had no further appropriate role in securing freedom.

Justice Harlan in a futile dissent maintained that the right to contract was a fundamental liberty protected by the Thirteenth Amendment that had given practical effect by the 1866 Civil Rights Act. "I cannot assent to an interpretation of the Constitution which denies national protection to vast numbers of our people in respect of rights derived by them from the nation. The interpretation now placed on the 13th Amendment is, I think, entirely too narrow, and is hostile to the freedom established by the Supreme Law of the land."[21] In the second Reconstruction, the Court came around to this view, and overruled *Hodges* in 1968: "the conclusion of the majority in Hodges rested upon a concept of congressional power under the Thirteenth Amendment irreconcilable with the position taken by every member of this Court in the Civil Rights Cases and incompatible with the history and purpose of the Amendment itself. Insofar as Hodges is inconsistent with our holding today, it is hereby overruled."[22]

The incongruity of *Hodges* can be appreciated by contrasting it with its contemporary, *Lochner v. New York* (1905).[23] In *Lochner*, the majority went to extreme lengths to protect the liberty of contract of white workers (bakery employees in Utica, New York) by confining the states' police powers to protect workingmen[24] from being exploited by long hours and unhealthy working conditions. But when the employees in question were Black sharecroppers and lumber mill laborers, the charms of liberty of contract evaporated. As Pamela Karlan observed, "only a year after Lochner, in Hodges v. United States, the Court that had so recently extolled 'the right of free contract' as an aspect of personal liberty refused to protect Black workers' ability to carry out their employment contracts as an aspect of the liberty that the Thirteenth Amendment protects."[25] The Court's expansive notion of white men's Fourteenth Amendment liberty stands in sharp contrast with its shriveled concept of liberty for Black men under the Thirteenth Amendment. The Court's conclusions rested on unstated assumptions about racial inferiority and the role of federal courts in policing racial intimidation.

The "apotheosis of Jim Crow," as Benno Schmidt called it,[26] came in *Berea College v. Kentucky* (1908).[27] The Commonwealth of Kentucky enacted legislation in 1904 that barred any person, corporation, or association from operating schools that admitted both Blacks and whites. The statute was directed at pioneering Berea College, the only institution in the commonwealth and one of only two in the entire South that was racially integrated. The statute was a product of the segregationist mania sweeping the South at the turn of the century. The Kentucky Court of Appeals upheld the legislation.[28] Its reasoning conveys an idea of the mélange of religion and pseudoscience that justified segregation in the era of the Nadir:

> The separation of the human family into races, distinguished no less by color than by temperament and other qualities, is as certain as anything in nature. Those of us who believe that all of this was divinely ordered have no doubt that there was wisdom in the provision; albeit we are unable to say with assurance why it is so. Those who see in it only nature's work must also concede that in this order, as in all others in nature, there is an unerring justification. There exists in each race a homogenesis by which it will perpetually reproduce itself, if unadulterated. Its instinct is gregarious. As a check there is another, an antipathy to other races, which some call race prejudice. This is nature's guard to prevent amalgamation of the races.

The Kentucky judges were concerned that a libertarian substantive due process argument might appeal to the nation's highest court, as it had in *Allgeyer v. Louisiana* (1897) and *Lochner v. New York* (1905).[29] Unbridled statist legislation such as the Kentucky statute might have offended justices like Fuller and Rufus Peckham who were hostile to state interference with voluntary private arrangements. The challenge of *Berea College* is to explain why they did not do so in this case.

A divided US Supreme Court[30] upheld the statute, but only on the narrow grounds that a state had broad powers to regulate corporations that it had created. Brewer, writing for the majority, held that "the granting of such right or privilege [the ability to incorporate] rests entirely in the discretion of the state, and, when granted, may be accompanied with such conditions as its legislature may judge most befitting to its interests and policy."[31] He conspicuously ignored the Kentucky court's grandiloquent disquisition on social (pseudo)science and its police power justification for racial segregation. The result of the case was harsh: states could now impose racial segregation on all their corporate creatures, including educational institutions. Inferentially, this might have implied that the Court would sustain segregation in all levels of education. Curiously, though, the Court never so held explicitly, and *Berea College* could not be read to hold that states could ban integration in all private schools, such as, for example, parochial schools. Brewer did add as a casual afterthought that "the right to teach white and negro children in a private school at the same time and place is not a property right. Besides, appellant, as a corporation created by this state, has no natural right to teach at all. Its right to teach is such as the state sees fit to give to it. The state may withhold it altogether, or qualify it." But that rationale was weak and evasive. Andrew Kull considered it a "transparent and undignified evasion" of the real issue, which was prohibiting miscegenation.[32]

Harlan delivered his last great dissent on racial issues in *Berea College*. He spent most of his effort shredding the majority's distinction between individuals and corporations, easily demonstrating that its artificiality belied the Court's reliance on the corporate rationale. But in prose unusually confrontational for the good-natured Harlan, he insisted that "the statute is an arbitrary invasion of the rights of liberty and property guaranteed by the 14th Amendment against hostile state action,"[33] a due process rather than an equal protection violation. To reach this surprising doctrinal claim, which anticipated two major cases of the 1920s affirming the right to teach as a liberty and property interest protected by the due process clause,[34] Harlan diverted to a subject that held a strong lifelong interest for him as an active Presbyterian layman, religious liberty.[35] He was especially outraged that the state might ban interracial Sunday school or religious observances. "The right to enjoy one's religious belief, unmolested by any human power, is no more sacred nor more fully or distinctly recognized than is the right to impart and receive instruction not harmful to the public. The denial of either right would be an infringement of the liberty inherent in the freedom secured by the fundamental law."[36] Such "cruel" legislation would be "inconsistent...with the great principle of the equality of citizens before the law."

The contrast between the Kentucky Court of Appeals and the US Supreme Court's handling of the segregation issue in *Berea College* was striking. Where the Kentucky judges' opinion and Harlan's dissent were confident, resounding, and expansive, Brewer's majority opinion seemed halfhearted and evasive, skirting the real issue of segregation, and relying on a technical point only indirectly related to the racial implications of the case. What might account for this difference? By 1908, the US Supreme Court had touched its own nadir of unconcern for racial equality and had begun, however haltingly, to breathe some life into the Reconstruction Amendments. The day of a full-throated justification for racial segregation in the US Supreme Court like *Plessy* had passed, and the feeble *Berea College* majority opinion signaled that transit. Jim Crow had enjoyed its last triumph in the Supreme Court. Its power was waning, and it began its slow retreat.

Peonage and Involuntary Servitude

At first glance, the peonage cases that came before the US Supreme Court between 1905 and 1914 seem anomalous. Against the background of the justices' Nadir-era apathy toward the injustices visited daily on African Americans in voting, jury service, criminal justice, and the ordinary interactions of everyday life, the Court's willingness to treat peonage as actionable involuntary servitude, and to support vigorous federal law enforcement that produced convictions of white peon-masters, requires explanation.

Several things account for the rights-friendly outcomes of the peonage cases.[37] Doctrinally, the justices did not treat these as being essentially cases about the rights and liberties of Black people. Indeed, the justices seldom alluded to the race of the victims, and discussed the prosecutions in color-blind terms, ignoring their racial context and impact. Read superficially, then, the peonage cases were only incidentally about African Americans. Instead, in a framework more congenial to the laissez-faire mentality of the *Lochner* era, the justices thought of involuntary servitude not as racial oppression, but as an affront to the ideal of liberty of contract. (But if so, how account for *Hodges*?) This would explain their unreal, or at least extremely abstract, treatment of the crypto-slavery of the twentieth century. To deal candidly with the reality of Black peonage would have forced the Court to challenge illegitimate purpose, and burst through pretextuality, something it had resolutely refused to do since at least *Plessy* and *Williams*. Nor could the Court dare to probe discriminatory administration of criminal statutes, *Yick Wo* notwithstanding, because that would challenge the entire basis of civil and criminal justice throughout the South. The White Court was hardly about to undertake that social revolution.

In addition, the justices had the advantage of vigorous executive investigation and prosecution of peonage conditions in the South, at least in the Roosevelt and Taft administrations. (The segregationist Wilson administration had no interest at all in the matter.) Roosevelt's Justice Department appointed a special assistant attorney general, Charles W. Russell, to head up this effort, and his 1908 *Report on Peonage* laid the basis for the vigorous enforcement that in turn provided cover for the Court.[38]

Third, the attack on peonage comported with the values of white Progressives of the time, both North and South. It did not challenge racial hierarchy and did not affront white supremacy, except for the lowlifes who were involved as latter-day slave-catchers and overseers. Nothing in the peonage cases threatened the benchmarks of the previous decade that legitimized segregation, disfranchisement, and exclusion from jury service. It enabled middle-class Progressives to congratulate themselves on their paternalistic concern for the most helpless and brutalized of workers (who happened to be Black). Therefore, the reaction of the white South to these cases was surprisingly muted: almost no one complained of threats to state sovereignty or the social order.

At the end of the Civil War, the ex-slave states enacted the Black Codes to force involuntary labor, but Congress immediately quashed the resulting servitude that they imposed. That did not stymie whites' determination to force Blacks into unfree labor in the South, though. Against the background of the postwar emergence of sharecropping, tenant farming, the crop-lien system, and illegal exploitation and cheating of landless workers both Black and white,[39] the southern states enacted an interlocking web of statutes that restricted where and when African Americans could work and forced them to labor against their will.[40] These statutes included vagrancy laws and ordinances derived from Elizabethan-era English precedents that sometimes retained their quaint terminology; criminal surety statutes, by which a defendant convicted of a minor offense, usually vagrancy, could be bound out to anyone willing to pay his fine to work off the indebtedness; enticement statutes, which forbade luring a laborer away from his extant employment; contract enforcement laws, which provided both civil and criminal penalties for breaching a labor contract (these were often supplemented by fraud or false pretenses provisions); and emigrant agent laws, which prohibited or regulated efforts of persons to recruit workers for opportunities elsewhere. These unfree labor laws created a class of racially identified helots who were subject to being rounded up at any time by local police and sheriffs to work in the fields when hands were needed for planting or harvest. They produced what the economist Robert Higgs called "the legacy of landless emancipation."[41]

This web of labor laws was enforced by the judicial systems of the southern states. Charles Russell, the assistant US attorney general who exposed peonage, wrote that positive law and custom "result[s] in making the petty officers of the law—deputy sheriffs, constables, justices of the peace, and the like—an outer cordon of guards to hold the peons in slavery, and also cause[s] the neighbors to acquiesce in what they would otherwise regard as outrages."[42] The foremost authority on this system, Douglas Blackmon, concludes that "by 1900, the South's judicial system had been wholly reconfigured to make one of its primary purposes the coercion of African Americans to comply with the social custom and labor demands of whites."[43]

Even worse was the system of chain gangs, convict labor, and convict lease, the capstone of neo-slavery during and after Redemption. When the states leased out Black convicts to industrial, mining, lumber, and agricultural employers, it created a horrifying system of industrial slavery that recapitulated the antebellum original in most respects except hereditability.[44] Because, unlike slaves, convict labor could not be monetized, prisoners had no cash value. They were literally worked to death. "One dies, get another," was the mantra of the industrial masters.[45] But no cases came before the US Supreme Court that directly challenged this new and lethal form of enslavement.

The Peonage Act of 1867 originally was not related to this web of unfree labor laws. Peonage as a system of debt servitude took root in Mexico during the eighteenth century. It persisted in the territories ceded to the United States in 1848, particularly New Mexico. Under peonage laws, a debtor could bind himself to serve the creditor until the debt was repaid, but manipulation of interest rates could prolong the period of unfree labor, often for the lifetime of the debtor. Worse, the condition was hereditary: children inherited the unfree status of peon parents. Contemporaries traveling through the Southwest invariably compared peonage with slavery. According to one, "the creditor has as much command over the labor of the debtor, as the Southern slaveholder has over that of the negro." Thaddeus Stevens, scourge of the slavocracy, put it epigrammatically: peonage "saves the poor man's cow to furnish milk for his children, by selling the father instead of the cow."[46] Clearly, such a system could not survive the Thirteenth Amendment's ban on "involuntary servitude."

Justice Miller stated in a *Slaughterhouse* dictum that the words of the amendment "include something more than slavery in the strict sense of the term; they include also serfage, vassalage, villenage, peonage, and all other forms of compulsory service for the mere benefit or pleasure of others."[47] Therefore "while negro slavery alone was in the mind of the Congress which proposed the thirteenth article, it forbids any other kind of slavery, now or hereafter. If Mexican peonage or the Chinese coolie labor system shall develop slavery of the Mexican or Chinese race within our territory," it would be void under the amendment. So, when Congress declared in 1867 that "the holding of any person to service or labor under the system known as peonage is hereby declared to be unlawful," its abolition was uncontroversial.[48] Peonage soon died out in New Mexico, but the statute remains in the US Code.[49]

Against the backdrop of coerced Black labor, a prosecution under the Peonage Act first came before the US Supreme Court in *Clyatt v. United States* (1905).[50] Operators of lumber camps, sawmills, and turpentine plantations believed that unless they "were permitted to control their labor as they saw fit, without any interference from the federal authorities, they would be unable to carry on the sawmill business."[51] A local sheriff testified that "it has been the universal custom and practice of the turpentine men in Georgia and Florida to go and take negroes whenever they wanted to in this way."[52] A proprietor of a Georgia turpentine still seized two African Americans in Florida and dragged them back to Georgia, accusing them of having left his employ while still indebted to him. He was convicted of violating the Peonage Act and appealed his conviction to the Supreme Court. Justice Brewer, for a unanimous Court, upheld both the conviction and the statute itself. "We entertain no doubt of the validity of this legislation, or its applicability to the case of any person holding" another in debt bondage.[53] This decision was a major victory in the struggle against unfree labor, and for Congress's power under section 2 of the Thirteenth Amendment. The Court rejected a state action limitation on section 2, a triumph for freedom and Congress's authority. But at the same time Brewer narrowed the scope of the statute: he defined peonage "as a status or condition of compulsory service, based upon the indebtedness of the peon to the master. The basal fact is indebtedness."[54] This requirement of preexisting indebtedness prevented the statute from being more liberally enforced to strike at other forms of unfree labor.

Nevertheless, *Clyatt* authorized numerous prosecutions for virtual enslavement of Black workers throughout the South. Defendants usually got off lightly, but the weight of both federal authority and public opinion slowly turned against abusive labor practices involving nominally free men.[55] (Convict labor was another story.) *Clyatt* sustained not only the Peonage Act itself (not a trivial achievement, given the pervasive racism of the era) but also its vigorous enforcement. Moreover, it provided the foundation for later peonage prosecutions extending into the present. A century of federal efforts to suppress unfree labor is no mean accomplishment.

Some Progressives hoped to build on *Clyatt* to shred the whole net of unfree-labor laws that enmeshed Black men in the South. Their opportunity came in *Bailey v. Alabama* (1910),[56] a case contesting a state statute that criminalized entering a labor contract with intent to defraud the employer by accepting an advance and then quitting without repayment. The legislature later added to this a presumption that breach alone was prima facie evidence of the necessary fraudulent intent. Alabama evidence law made the effect of the presumption watertight because it banned testimony by a party about his motives. The effect of these statutes read in tandem was to make it a crime to quit a job if the employer had paid an advance. Conviction would then inevitably entail either further enforced labor under a criminal surety statute or the more dreaded alternative of the chain gang. Needless to say, only Black men were prosecuted under these statutes. When Alonzo Bailey was charged under the Alabama act, his case provided a vehicle for challenging the employment fraud statutes as a form of debt bondage under the Peonage Act.

The Court first rejected an appeal from denial of habeas corpus on ripeness grounds.[57] Then, after conviction and at a time when the Court was shorthanded because of the deaths of Rufus Peckham, David Brewer, and Melville Fuller within nine months of each other, it agreed to take the appeal on the merits. President William Howard Taft had just appointed the Charles Evans Hughes to the Court but had not yet nominated Justice White for the center seat. Harlan, presiding as the senior justice in lieu of the deceased chief, assigned the opinion to Hughes.

Hughes's maiden opinion in *Bailey v. Alabama*,[58] which held the Alabama statutes unconstitutional, treated the issue as a matter of both constitutional and statutory interpretation. Reading the state statutes together, he concluded that the effect of the later prima facie evidence statute was to make the mere act of quitting a criminal offense, which violated both the Peonage Acts ban on debt bondage and the Thirteenth Amendment's prohibition of involuntary servitude. (State and lower federal courts had repeatedly held that a state could not criminalize mere breach of contract without running afoul of the Thirteenth Amendment.) Calling the Thirteenth Amendment "a charter of universal civil freedom for all persons, of whatever race, color, or estate,"[59] Hughes emphasized that its section 2 was ample authority for the Peonage Act, which he interpreted to condemn the type of involuntary labor to which Bailey had been condemned under the operation of Alabama's laws. The state "may not compel one man to labor for another in payment of a debt, by punishing him as a criminal if he does not perform the service or pay the debt." The statute "furnishes a convenient instrument for the coercion which the Constitution and [the Peonage Act] forbid; an instrument of compulsion peculiarly effective as against the poor and the ignorant, its most likely victims."[60]

The oddest feature of Hughes's opinion appeared in its opening lines: "We at once dismiss from consideration the fact that the plaintiff in error is a Black man." "No question of a sectional character is presented, and we may view the legislation in the same manner as if it had been enacted in New York or in Idaho. Opportunities for coercion and oppression, in varying circumstances, exist in all parts of the Union."[61] Hughes might simply have ignored the subject altogether, not mentioning race, but his deliberate injection of the topic imposed an incongruous otherworldly air onto the opinion. There may have been both tactical and jurisprudential reasons for this unforced pretense, though. Tactically, he may have been trying to assuage the resentments of white supremacists who would feel threatened by any Supreme Court decision that threatened white domination of Black labor. Or perhaps he was trying to make the result palatable to whites by suggesting that it would protect white workers as well as Black.

Had Hughes and his colleagues tried to base the decision on racial discrimination, they would have had to inquire into legislative intent, something the Court is usually reluctant to do. Nor was the *Yick Wo* option of discriminatory administration of facially neutral statutes available because that would threaten the delicate facade of pretextuality needed to preserve Jim Crow and separate but equal. Jurisprudentially and tactically, Hughes may have been trying to divert the discussion from a focus on racial injustice (at that time, a losing approach) and in the direction of emphasizing a right available even to the most abject Black farmworker in the South: the right to liberty of contract as a universal human right.[62] (Hughes twice emphasized the "freedom of labor" as the animating force of the opinion.) Substantive due process may have trumped white supremacy, or at least made the result easier to accept in the South. Or, if this seems strained, perhaps Hughes was trying to put the best face he could on a decision that could be explained only by the revulsion of five members of the Court[63] to the white South's barbaric labor practices in the service of white supremacy. Whatever the explanation, in *Bailey* the Court deployed liberty-of-contract reasoning to protect Black workers against the rapacity of their employers, even if it had to pretend that it was doing so in a color-blind fashion. It suggested that the sociological and jurisprudential assumptions that underlay *Hodges* only five years earlier no longer held.

As our own times amply demonstrate, involuntary servitude in one form or another seems impossible to eradicate. Merely because *Bailey* had condemned modern peonage did not guarantee that the practice would disappear. Without vigilant enforcement efforts by civil rights groups and labor unions, employers will enslave vulnerable workers when they can, especially when those workers are African American or female. Thus, it should be no surprise that unfree Black labor survived *Bailey* and persisted long after.

This problem soon reappeared on the Court's docket in 1914 when the Justice Department and a US attorney determined to challenge the constitutionality of the Alabama criminal-surety statute. Under such statutes, if an individual convicted of a criminal offense was fined and could not pay the fine, a third party could post surety. The convicted defendant would then be obliged to work for his benefactor to pay off the fine and costs. This system invited abuse: employers and law enforcement officials colluded to manufacture Black offenders through vagrancy laws or other petty criminal offenses. The accused usually was unable to pay the fine, and would-be white employers readily seized this opportunity to acquire cheap labor compelled to work under the threat of an indefinite series of such convictions for infraction of the surety statute.

In *United States v. Reynolds* (1914),[64] a unanimous Court, speaking through Justice William Day, held the statute unconstitutional based on the same logic Hughes had articulated in *Bailey*: both the Thirteenth Amendment and the Peonage Act condemned involuntary labor performed to pay off a debt. The fine paid on behalf of the defendant was a debt owed to the surety, and the threat of further prosecutions for walking off the job provided the element of compulsion that made the labor unfree. (Day did not mention it, but the real compulsion was the alternative of the chain gang or convict lease, both more horrific than the milder system of the criminal surety.) "Compulsion of such service by the constant fear of imprisonment under the criminal laws renders the work compulsory" and thus offends both the federal statute and the amendment.

Holmes concurred in an opinion that provides a chilling glimpse into the mentality of white elites at that time. In a typically terse opinion, he insisted that a state may criminally punish breach of contract. "But impulsive people with little intelligence or foresight may be expected to lay hold of anything that affords a relief from present pain, even though it will cause greater trouble by and by."[65] He claimed that the state enacted the statutes with this progression in mind, and thus in effect imposed involuntary labor. To him, as to so many of his contemporaries (including Presidents Roosevelt, Taft, and Wilson), it was axiomatic that Blacks were "impulsive people with little intelligence." Even in its benign moments, American public law rested on the bedrock of unquestioning racism.

Did the trio of peonage cases, *Clyatt*, *Bailey*, and *Reynolds*, matter at all? Michael Klarman thinks that they had no practical significance.[66] The southern states continued their formal and informal systems of compelling unfree Black labor. During the great Mississippi River flood of 1927, white sheriffs freely raided Black refugee camps to round up Black men and women as conscripted labor to maintain the levees.[67] During World War II, the Court had to revisit the question of Black peonage, only to reaffirm its conclusions of a generation earlier, hinting at its annoyance that the South would continue to flout its opinions so insouciantly. First Georgia and then Florida enacted contract-labor statutes that contained the presumption-of-fraud provisions rejected in *Bailey*. The Court condemned that statute in *Taylor v. Georgia* (1942) as a violation of the Peonage Act.[68] It returned to the same issue in *Pollock v. Williams* (1944),[69] when Florida seemed to deliberately flout the Court's rulings by enacting a statute with the feature that the Court had condemned, the prima facie evidence provision. Yet like Hughes, Justice Robert H. Jackson could not bring himself to acknowledge the racist basis of Florida's action. He found it necessary to cloak his holding in pretense. "This is not to intimate," he wrote, that the South "more than others was sympathetic with peonage...[which is] neither sectional nor racial." Jackson was no fool, and like any other sentient observer of America in 1944 he must have seen southern peonage for what it was. But out of a misplaced desire to palliate white southern sensitivities on the matter—nothing else can explain such a willfully blind pose by an otherwise candid judge—he found it expedient to dissemble on the matter of lingering involuntary servitude in the states of the old Confederacy.

In a cynical view, only the Great Migration and the mid-century invention of the mechanical cotton picker finally put an end to the lingering pestilence of unfree Black labor in the South, not Supreme Court rulings. But there is more to be said for the peonage cases than that. They were a step, however disguised, toward the complete eradication of the lingering vestiges of slavery itself.[70] That the struggle continues today testifies not to the failure of constitutional principle, but to the resiliency of human evil and its ingenuity in finding new victims for forced labor (including sexual exploitation). Meanwhile, the principle of free labor endures, as well as its embodiment in the Peonage Act, and in the readiness of the Supreme Court to uphold its enforcement. More importantly, these cases were an early crack in the edifice of the Supreme Court's complicity in Redemption. For almost the first time since the days of the Chase Court, the justices acted affirmatively to enforce one of the Reconstruction Amendments and their statutory apparatus on behalf of African Americans. Pretextuality no longer held absolute sway. The Waite and Fuller Courts had immured the great constitutional achievements of Reconstruction in a judicially erected mausoleum, but now the amendments were stirring to life, and the door of the charnel house began to creak open.

The justices did not create the Jim Crow world of segregation and disfranchisement. That was the work of Redemption in the states. At most, the judges contrived doctrines that acknowledged Jim Crow, then affirmed it, even protected it. Judges follow the development of public policy in the states; they do not lead it. Thus, when they began to rethink their doctrinal assumptions, the resulting doctrinal changes did not by themselves change the course of public policy. The tail does not wag the dog. We may condemn the turn-of-the-century judges for being obtuse or disingenuous, but not for failing to change a public policy that they had little effective power to direct.

The Blue Hour

The peonage cases were the first sign that the edifice of Jim Crow was not as sturdy as its supporters thought. Two months after *Reynolds*, in *McCabe v. Atchison, Topeka, & Santa Fe Ry.* (1914),[71] the Supreme Court offered a more forceful hint that Jim Crow might be perched on an unstable throne. Oklahoma enacted a separate-coach law like those of all the other southern states,[72] but it had a proviso tacked on that permitted railroads to offer luxury accommodations (sleepers and dining cars) for either race, "separately but not jointly." The effect of the proviso was to permit trains running in Oklahoma to provide luxury cars for whites, but not for Blacks if there was insufficient Black demand. African American activists sought to enjoin the statute from going into operation shortly after its passage.

The Court might have rejected their petition entirely on noncontroversial constitutional and equitable principles unrelated to race: petitioners lacked standing because they did not show personal injury to themselves (none had been denied a Pullman berth or seating in a dining car); the case was not ripe for adjudication (because the statute had not yet gone into effect); and petitioners had an adequate remedy at law (damages).[73] And in fact that is how the Court did dispose of the case. But before getting there, Justice Hughes delivered some forceful dicta that contemporaries mistook to be the holding of the case. "If facilities are provided, substantial equality of treatment of persons traveling under like conditions cannot be refused," he wrote. He emphasized that "the essence of the constitutional right is that it is a personal one [and not a group right].... It is the individual who is entitled to the equal protection of the laws."[74]

In recent times, this individualist emphasis has proved pernicious to the cause of civil rights. But in the shorter run, through the second Reconstruction, the individual-rights theme emphasized by Hughes lay at the heart of modern understandings of equal protection. His dicta did not work any immediate change in substantive equal protection doctrine. But they betokened a much different attitude toward the Fourteenth Amendment, separate but equal, and the cause of African Americans than had prevailed on the Court for the previous generation. The center of gravity of *Plessy*, which Hughes acknowledged but pointedly did not endorse, was *separate*; in *McCabe*, the center of gravity shifted to the *equal* side of the equation. The Court's majority was displaying a new—and to segregationists, unwelcome—interest in ensuring Black access to opportunity and imposing limits on the states' power to deny such access outright. Segregation itself remained unchallenged: railroads were free to partition luxury cars, which they did. But separate but equal was proving to be another matter. For the first time, it looked vulnerable, simply by being taken seriously.

These hints of change are backed by several details surrounding the opinion. First, White, Holmes, Lamar, and McReynolds did not join Hughes's opinion, but concurred without opinion. Three of them were men of the South, while Holmes was arguably the justice most antagonistic to African Americans' interests at that point. He would soon be eclipsed in that distinction by the overtly racist James McReynolds. McReynolds was one of the judicial quartet that contemporary journalists dubbed "the Four Horsemen" of the Apocalypse. (The others were Willis Van Devanter, George Sutherland, and Pierce Butler. The unflattering biblical reference suggested that they were harbingers of their eponyms in the book of

Revelation,[75] bringing war, famine, plague, and death to the American constitutional order.) Of them, only McReynolds may be justly considered an explicit racist, but as a group they opposed all reform and progressive measures that might have alleviated Jim Crow servitude. They constituted a formidable barrier to racial justice.

The Court's more conservative justices surely had no objection to dismissal of the McCabe appeal on procedural grounds, so we must infer that they dissociated themselves from the substantive dicta of Hughes's opinion because they disapproved of its ideas or sensed in them a remote danger to white southern values. Second, in private correspondence with Holmes, Hughes wrote, "I don't see that it is a case calling for 'logical exactness' in enforcing equal rights, but rather as it seems to me it is a bald, wholly unjustified, discrimination against a passenger on account of race."[76] This more unbuttoned statement of the underlying issues suggests that Hughes, the son of an abolitionist New York Baptist minister, was motivated by the underlying reality of discrimination and was rebutting criticism that he was being unrealistically finicky in his sense of equality. Third, when Hughes, speaking in 1938 as chief justice in his second period of service on the Court, condemned a comparable denial of access in the 1938 case of *Missouri ex rel. Gaines v. Canada*,[77] he cited his *McCabe* dicta as authority. A few contemporary observers recognized the significance of these implications. A note in the *Harvard Law Review* hailed *McCabe* as heralding a "new phase of Jim Crow," while *The Nation* saw the opinion as repudiating "Jim Crow government."[78] These claims may have been premature, but they expressed a presentiment that Jim Crow had passed its zenith and was in decline.

From transportation, the Court turned its attention to the festering problem of Black disfranchisement under the Mississippi Plan.[79] By the outbreak of the Great War, disfranchisement throughout the South was complete.[80] Few African Americans were registered to vote in the former Confederacy, and even fewer of those who were dared to exercise their right in a meaningful way.[81] White conservatives achieved this disfranchisement through a complex of provisions regulating elections that included the following components: complicated registration requirements, coupled with broad discretion in election officials to administer the laws in a discriminatory fashion; residency requirements, which fell with particular force on a mobile Black population; "good character" requirements; the secret ballot, which functioned as a de facto literacy test excluding voters who could not read the ballot; disfranchisement for the kind of criminal offenses that whites ascribed to Blacks, like petty theft; the poll tax, sometimes cumulative in its operation, which fell with particular force on poor voters; the white primary; and literacy requirements.

The problem with the literacy test, though, was that it might bar illiterate whites as well as illiterate Blacks. Some conservative Democrats admitted openly that this would not be regrettable, but that was not a generally viable political posture as long as poor whites still had the ballot at the turn of the century. So, to preserve the literacy requirement lawmakers and convention delegates crafted two exceptions that would restore the vote to illiterate whites. First, "understanding clauses" enabled illiterates to vote if they could demonstrate an understanding of the state's constitution and laws. Administrative discretion ensured that registrars would wave in white illiterates based on minimal compliance, while excluding even well-educated Blacks. Second, a half-dozen southern states adopted "grandfather clauses" that admitted illiterates if they voted before 1867 or were descendants of such voters. A variant on the 1867 provision admitted illiterates if they had served in the military in the Civil War or were descended from such veterans.[82] And reinforcing these above-board disfranchisement measures were the constants of southern electoral fraud and violence. A particularly egregious example of electoral violence was the Wilmington, North Carolina, massacre and coup d'état of 1898, where Democrats drove out a biracial fusion city government, killing an unknown number, possibly in the hundreds, of African Americans in the accompanying violence.[83]

By 1915, prospects for the cause of Black suffrage were discouraging, to say the least. The US Supreme Court had drastically trimmed Congress's power to protect Black voting in *United States v. Reese* (1876)[84] by limiting it to racially motivated actions, holding most of the voting-rights provisions of the 1870 Enforcement Act unconstitutional. At the same time, in *United States v. Cruikshank* (1876),[85] the Court denied Congress power to protect Black voters from private violence not sponsored by the state. Congress ratified these setbacks by the Posse Comitatus Act of 1878, which banned use of the army to police elections in the South in 1878,[86] by failing to enact the Lodge elections bill in 1890, and by repealing most of the remaining substantive provisions of the 1870 and 1871 Enforcement Acts in 1894. The spirit of the times (or at least the Democratic outlook) was captured in an 1893 House report recommending repeal: "Let every trace of the reconstruction measures be wiped from the statute books, let the States of this great Union understand that the elections are in their own hands," so as to "eliminate the judiciary from the political arena."[87] Congress never displayed any interest in enforcing the provisions of section 2 of the Fourteenth Amendment, which has been a dead letter throughout its entire existence.

At the same time the states were taking matters into their own hands by enacting Mississippi Plan elements into their constitutions and codes. Carter Glass assured Virginia's 1901 constitutional convention that "discrimination within the letter of the law...to the very extremity of permissible action under the limitations of the Federal Constitution with a view to the elimination of every Negro voter who can be gotten rid of legally" was the whole point of the electoral revisions.[88] The US Supreme Court benignly approved this disfranchisement in *Williams v. Mississippi* (1898) and twice confessed its impotence to do anything about it, even had it wished to, in 1903–1904.[89] All of this conformed to the temper of the times, where Progressives abandoned their earlier support for Black suffrage, blaming the victim on the grounds that Black political power fomented corruption and violence. Contemporary imperialist adventures abroad reinforced racist outlooks by the prevalent assumption that nonwhite, Catholic, or Muslim Filipinos could not be entrusted with Anglo-Saxon practices like the vote or self-government. Scientific racism enjoyed a vogue among American intellectuals, who denounced the Fifteenth Amendment as a pernicious mistake. The outlook for protecting African Americans' voting rights seemed dismal.

But a peculiar combination of circumstances converged to permit a challenge to the grandfather clauses. Oklahoma Republicans prodded the local US attorney and successively the Taft and Wilson administrations to challenge the combined literacy and grandfather clauses adopted there in 1910. When the Justice Department attacked the clauses before the Supreme Court, it won a surprisingly sweeping victory in *Guinn v. Oklahoma* (1915).[90] Chief Justice White, writing for a unanimous bench, thought the unconstitutionality of the grandfather clause was "beyond doubt," "beyond the possibility of question," with no "room for any serious dispute." The core of White's holding was obscured by his characteristically impenetrable prose:

> there seems no escape from the conclusion that to hold that there was even possibility for dispute on the subject would be but to declare that the Fifteenth Amendment not only had not the self-executing power which it has been recognized to have from the beginning, but that its provisions

were wholly inoperative because susceptible of being rendered inapplicable by mere forms of expression embodying no exercise of judgment and resting upon no discernible reason other than the purpose to disregard the prohibitions of the Amendment by creating a standard of voting which on its face was in substance but a revitalization of conditions which when they prevailed in the past had been destroyed by the self-operative force of the Amendment.[91]

What White seems to have been trying to say in this word salad was that the self-executing force of the Fifteenth Amendment could not be nullified by a transparent subterfuge that revived the pre-1868 world where African Americans were deprived of the vote. He gratuitously insisted that the Court was not holding the clauses unconstitutional either because they were motivated by wrongful administration (the *Yick Wo* standard) or by targeted effects. (White apparently did not notice that he was contradicting himself.) He seems to have been offended simply by Oklahoma's blatant attempt to ignore the Fifteenth Amendment and exclude African Americans from the electorate as if the amendment had no force or even existence.[92] In a companion case, *United States v. Mosley* (1915),[93] Holmes held that a surviving remnant of the 1870 Enforcement Act did not require a showing of violence by the defendants. In dicta of surprising force, he wrote, "It is not open to question that this statute is constitutional, and constitutionally extends some protection, at least, to the right to vote for members of Congress. We regard it as equally unquestionable that the right to have one's vote counted is as open to protection by Congress as the right to put a ballot in a box."

But as with all cases of this period that seemed to hold promise for African Americans, we must ask: did it matter? In the short run, not much. Far from being abashed by having its disfranchisement scheme declared unconstitutional, Oklahoma then audaciously grandfathered in its grandfather clause. That is, it enacted legislation registering all those who had voted in the 1914 election, when the original grandfather clause had produced an all-white electorate. All others had to register in a narrow six-week window of time in 1916, which winnowed Black voters. Eventually, the Supreme Court struck down that scheme in *Lane v. Wilson* (1939),[94] where Justice Felix Frankfurter memorably observed that "the Amendment nullifies sophisticated as well as simple-minded modes of discrimination." But until then, Oklahoma succeeded in suppressing most of the Black vote. Moreover, even if *Guinn* had stricken the grandfather clause at the outset, the holding left intact all the other Mississippi Plan devices, and Blacks remained just as disfranchised after the decision as before it. Michael Klarman accordingly dismissed *Guinn* and the other blue-hour cases as "minimalist and inconsequential."[95]

But more can be said of them than that. They marked the point in time when the Court halted its trajectory of indifference and collusion in the spread of Jim Crow. However slight, the line it drew *was* a line, frustrating for almost the first time the southern states' determination to go to any lengths to subordinate their Black citizens. Had the Court reverted to its *Plessy-Williams-Giles* mentality after 1916, we might dismiss *Guinn* its companions as an aberration of no consequence. But it did not. Fuller, Brewer, and Peckham were gone; Hughes replaced them in one of those rare moments when the appointment of a single justice marks a pivot in the Court's history. The Court after 1915 would reflect his view rather than theirs. It was a beginning; modest perhaps, even timid. But the Court had begun to change its heading.

The most consequential of the blue-hour cases involved an attempt to impose residential apartheid throughout the South by local ordinances. Had this succeeded, the consequences would have been ineradicable: cities, towns, and even rural areas would have evolved into a checkerboard of lily white and all Black. The past century has demonstrated how tenacious housing segregation is, but if the drive for "Black ghetto ordinances" had succeeded, segregation would have been even more deeply entrenched. For that reason, *Buchanan v. Warley* (1917) was, in Moorfield Storey's opinion, "the most important decision that has been made since the Dred Scott case."[96] The cities of the border states and the upper South, beginning with Baltimore, began adopting segregation ordinances in 1910.[97] These prohibited persons of one race from purchasing or occupying a house in a block where the majority of the residents were of the other race. Exceptions for servants demonstrated that the objection was not physical proximity per se, but rather maintenance of a system of racial domination. Richmond, St. Louis, Oklahoma City, and Louisville adopted copycat ordinances by 1916.[98]

Louisville's ordinance prohibited Blacks from occupying residences in majority-white blocks, and with scrupulous evenhandedness, likewise prohibited whites from occupying residences in majority-Black blocks. The ordinance excepted occupancy "by white or colored servants or employés of occupants of such residences."[99] The local chapter of the NAACP organized a test case, blatantly collusive,[100] to challenge the ordinance. The head of the local NAACP chapter, William Warley (who was Black), arranged for a local real estate broker, George Buchanan (who was white), to sell him a lot in a white block, with a proviso in the contract that let him get out of the deal if the transaction was not legal under Kentucky law. They then performed their collusive dance: Buchanan offered to sell, Warley refused to buy because the ordinance made the transaction illegal, and Buchanan sought specific performance. The Kentucky Court of Appeals (the highest court of the commonwealth at that time) upheld the ordinance on a combination of Progressive respect for social engineering[101] and paternalistic racism: "Much is being done to-day, by the white people of the nation for the uplift of the colored race."[102]

State supreme courts split on the question of the constitutionality of such legislation, with the courts of Maryland, North Carolina, and Georgia striking down comparable ordinances as interferences with property rights, while Virginia, Kentucky, and Georgia (after it reversed itself) upholding them under the police power. This teed up the question for the US Supreme Court, which, in *Buchanan v. Warley* (1917),[103] held the segregation ordinance unconstitutional. Justice William Day's opinion for a unanimous Court is usually treated as being ambivalent, resting in equal parts on a due-process-based hostility to state interference with property rights and an equal-protection-based condemnation of unequal treatment of African Americans.[104]

In reality, though, the opinion relied more on the property claim, particularly the ability of the white property owner to alienate to whom he pleased. Day repeatedly identified the right involved as "the constitutional right of the white man to sell his property to a colored man" and "the right which the ordinance annulled was the civil right of a white man to dispose of his property if he saw fit to do so to a person of color and of a colored person to make such disposition to a white person."[105] He asked rhetorically, "can a white man be denied, consistently with due process of law, the right to dispose of his property[?]" and concluded that "this attempt to prevent the alienation of the property in question to a person of color was not a legitimate exercise of the police power of the state, and is in direct violation of the fundamental law enacted in the Fourteenth Amendment of the Constitution preventing state interference with property rights except by due process of law."[106] He mentioned the equal protection clause only when quoting the Fourteenth Amendment or in direct quotations from another case. Nowhere in the opinion is there a suggestion that when Day thought about whose rights were being protected, he had in his mind's eye a

Black buyer. There was no ambiguity in this opinion: it was cast in the language of protecting the property interests of white people.

Yet that does not support the cynical conclusion that this most important of the blue-hour decisions was driven solely by concerns for the interests of whites, with Blacks being at most incidental beneficiaries of a constitutional order premised on the supreme sanctity of white interests. It is misleading to envision the case as if it were a seesaw, with due process protection of whites' property interests on one end and equal protection for Blacks' civil rights on the other, and the Court coming down decisively on the side of whites' interests. The true long-term significance of the case lies in its meld of protection for the property interests of all people through the due process clause with an understated but nevertheless evident concern for endowing the equal protection clause with some real significance for its intended beneficiaries, the freedpeople and their descendants.[107]

To make this meld more obvious, consider two counterfactuals. First, had the seats occupied by Day and Hughes gone instead to judges who thought like Fuller and Peckham, and had the southerners Lamar and Lurton lingered on a bit longer, it is easy, indeed compelling, to imagine that the Court would have accepted the meticulous bridges-of-Paris evenhandedness of the ordinance as the true measure of formal equality, and called it a day. (Recall that the *Plessy* Court did just that.) Pretextuality, around ever since *Strauder*, could claim with a straight face that the equal protection clause demanded no more than that whites and Blacks be treated exactly alike, and the Louisville ordinance did just that with scrupulous care for (false) symmetry. (It would have notionally permitted white servants of Black masters to reside in blocks otherwise closed to them, offsetting comparable permission for Black servants.) Formal equality might thus have become the canonical understanding for equal protection. There was nothing foreordained about the *Buchanan* outcome, however compelling it may seem to us today. The Court rejected formalism in favor of going directly to the substance, but to do that on a due process rationale protecting the rights of property, it had to subsume the equal protection clause and the interests of African Americans, at least implicitly.

Second, consider potential alternative outcomes of the case in light of principles of property law, which were underutilized here. For centuries, the common law had affirmed legislative power to abate nuisances and noxious uses.[108] Promoters of the segregation ordinances insisted that Black residence in a white neighborhood was a nuisance comparable to maintaining a pigsty or a brothel.[109] Two years earlier, in a major precedent in property law, the Court had endorsed the use of local legislative power to ban a use deemed noxious by neighbors (a brickyard in a residential area),[110] and it might have just as easily seen the Louisville ordinance as comparable. The Court's ready acceptance of analogous police power reasoning in upholding zoning nine years later[111] shows that the judges of this period readily acceded to Progressives' demand for regulation of incompatible uses, and to a segregationist, having Black neighbors was the epitome of incompatible use. Most white Progressives would have agreed.

Instead, Day's opinion stressed the core purposes of the Fourteenth Amendment, which established "certain fundamental rights which all are bound to respect." He quoted the grandiloquent dicta of *Strauder*: the Fourteenth Amendment "speaks in general terms, and those are as comprehensive as possible. Its language is prohibitory; but every prohibition implies the existence of rights and immunities, prominent among which is an immunity from inequality of legal protection, either for life, liberty, or property. Any state action that denies this immunity to a colored man is in conflict with the Constitution." He referred respectfully to the Civil Rights Act of 1866 and the Enforcement Act of 1870, quoting liberally from both. They "did not deal with the social rights of men, but with those fundamental rights in property" protected by the amendment.[112] This respect for Fourteenth Amendment rights of all people was not a fluke for Day. All the opinions he wrote affecting African Americans came out strongly affirming their rights,[113] and *Buchanan* was of a piece with them. Seeing the outcome of the *Buchanan* opinion as its author did, as a question of fundamental rights, resolves the seeming conflict between a property rights decision and a civil rights decision. It was both, but only if we understand civil rights in its Reconstruction-era sense as expressed in the 1866 Civil Rights Act. Understood in that light, *Buchanan* becomes a bridge between the first and second Reconstructions.[114]

Buchanan v. Warley was the first Supreme Court opinion after *Plessy* to restrict the separate-but-equal doctrine. The potential spread of that noxious formula now had limits imposed on it. In Benno Schmidt's judgment, it "introduced elements of principle into the trackless mush of judicial deference, self-induced blindness to social and doctrinal realities, and avoidance of decision that made up the constitutional law of race relations by 1910."[115]

But as with other cases of the era, the benign potential of *Buchanan* had little immediate practical effect. Despite its interdict, municipalities continued to enact segregation ordinances anyway. When they were challenged, the Court struck them down per curiam.[116] But residential segregation grew apace, throughout the nation and not just the South, secured by custom, real estate practices, and local violence, especially after the war. Nevertheless, segregation by positive law eventually withered. It came to be replaced by the racially restrictive covenant.

The first two decades of the twentieth century were momentous for the constitutional rights of African Americans, though that becomes apparent only in hindsight. At first, the justices seemed to reinforce the worst potential of Jim Crow on issues of segregation and disfranchisement. Justice Holmes's cold indifference and insensitivity were if anything worse than the complacent willingness of Fuller and other conservatives to normalize racial discrimination.

But in the depths of gloom, the justices began to take note of at least the most severe forms of racial oppression, especially the involuntary servitude rampant in the Deep South, and for almost the first time since the Grant administration, find that the Constitution authorized federal remedies where the violations were most blatant and violent. Pretense and pretext seemed inadequate to bridge the gap between constitutional ideals and sordid reality.

The peonage cases began invoking the protections of the Reconstruction Amendments and treated African Americans as rights-bearing citizens (or at least as human beings). After that, the justices seemed to find it easier to recognize that the Fourteenth and Fifteenth Amendments might meaningfully protect Blacks' rights against overt exclusion. The Court did not at once overthrow the regime of servitude that had replaced slavery, but it took the necessary first steps toward identifying constitutional principles that in time would dismantle the tomb in which the amendments had been buried. The years before the Great War marked the beginning of a long, difficult struggle to make the rights of America's Black citizens a reality.

5
Civil Rights and Civil Liberties between the Wars, 1920–1940

After 1918, the Supreme Court struck out in new directions. That occurred partly because the Taft and Hughes Courts consisted of new members.[1] In the period between 1914 and 1941, no fewer than sixteen new justices took their seats. Though a majority of them were stolid conservatives, they nevertheless brought with them a twentieth-century outlook that was sometimes responsive to changed postwar conditions.

The justices tried their hand several times at articulating an authoritative legal construction of race, only to come up with something no better than "we know it when we see it." They continued to flounder on the subject, sure that there was such a thing and that it did have a legal valence, even if every attempt to define it legally failed. Race continued to display its quicksilver quality, eluding all efforts to identify its constitutional quiddity.

Even if the Court had maintained its Nadir-era sodden indifference to racial oppression, it probably could not have continued to overlook the kangaroo-court reality of southern state courts when they tried African American defendants for criminal offenses. Though the Court declined to overturn most convictions of Black defendants that were brought to it between the wars, in a half-dozen prominent cases it insisted that southern judges and juries not flout the express mandates of the Bill of Rights in criminal trials.

Black disfranchisement similarly was too blatant to ignore. The Court was not ready to challenge pretextuality yet; once begun, that process could not be contained, and neither Court nor nation was ready to ignite a social justice revolution in the twenties. But explicit exclusion from voting was another matter: the justices were not about to repudiate *Strauder*'s minimalist position. They were determined to exact at least that minimum of compliance with the words and spirit of the Fifteenth Amendment.

The Court also took up two substantive issues in the period: African Americans' First Amendment liberties of speech and association, and segregation in higher education. Capping this at the end of the interwar era, the justices announced a new direction for judicial activism, one that in time would be of incalculable benefit to people of color.

When William Howard Taft replaced Edward D. White as chief justice in 1921, every one of the justices who sat in the *Plessy* case of 1896 was gone. It was now a wholly new Court. Yet despite this complete turnover, few of the new justices individually had much impact on issues affecting African Americans. The Taft Court was consistently sympathetic to business interests, hostile to labor unions, but sometimes willing to expand the reach of the Constitution's protections for civil liberties and civil rights. Its record was mixed, but it did continue the tentative steps toward protecting the rights of Black Americans that had begun before the war.

The Legal Construction of Race

For almost a century and a half after the founding, the US Supreme Court resolved cases involving African Americans and their place in American society without directly interrogating the idea of race itself. Except for a bit of amateur anthropology by Chief Justice John Marshall in *Johnson v. M'Intosh* (1823),[2] the justices took race for granted. Taney's and Daniel's *Dred Scott* opinions assumed racial inferiority without re-examining the bases of that assumption. For over a century, the justices never thought to explore such basic questions as what, exactly, *was* "race"? What basis did it have in reality, if any? More specifically, what did it mean to be "white" or any other racial designation? What legal consequences followed for people when they were determined not to be white? Was it even possible for lawyers and judges to come up with rational, sensible, scientifically grounded answers to such questions?[3]

When the justices did take up the challenge in the 1920s, they failed to answer these questions in any satisfactory way, but they seemed neither embarrassed by that failure nor even aware of it. Like nearly all other white Americans of the time, they simply assumed that race was real, natural, and scientifically validated. It followed that the consequences that law ascribed to race were legitimate. We are still dealing with the effects of that failure of a century ago. The Supreme Court continues to operate on unexamined assumptions that, if interrogated, might prove to be embarrassingly racist.

Law—meaning legal actors and the rules they apply—creates racial categories and assigns significance to them.[4] Law constructs race in three ways: it invests physical features like skin color with legal significance; by reifying such apparent differences, these meanings shape social processes like slavery or discrimination; and then these meanings determine the material conditions of people in society. Judges are not passive spectators of a racial game being played in front of them; they are active participants on the field.

The consequences of judicial activism in questions of race are strikingly illustrated in a case involving the legal status of Armenian immigrants. As a matter of simple geography, Armenia is located in western Asia, and thus its people ought to have been classified as Asians ("Asiatics," in the terminology of the day, a term now fallen into disrepute and considered derogatory). But a federal circuit court in 1909 held that they were white,[5] with striking consequences for those who moved to California. As whites, or at least not "Asiatics," immigrant Armenians were not under the disabilities imposed by the California Alien Land Laws,[6] and thus could acquire landholdings, particularly in Fresno County. Thus settled, they were able to build up a flourishing ethnic community that retains its cohesion and vitality to this day (it produced, among others, William Saroyan and California governor George Deukmejian).

In contrast, other Asians, the Japanese, were inhibited from owning land and thus did not have access to the same opportunities for community building that landownership would have provided. Judges constituted Armenians "white" through the processes of law and thereby gave them access to one of the most valuable resources that American society had to bestow on its racially correct newcomers: the ability to own land.[7] Armenians were not unique in this respect; Irish immigrants were beneficiaries of a comparable process in the nineteenth century.[8] Racial categories and identities have always been fluid in the United States, but especially after the massive migration from eastern and southern Europe between 1870 and 1920. New racial groupings appeared, mutated, and dissolved. As the Armenian experience demonstrated, a group once considered nonwhite can become "white" by judicial or administrative fiat, or by evolving social acceptance. Jews, Slavs, Italians, Greeks all became "white" over time.[9] Race is not innate; it is ascribed to individuals and groups by dominant groups in society. It is, in other words, socially constructed.[10]

The justices of the US Supreme Court took up the challenge of defining race in the 1920s at a particularly active period in the development of beliefs about racial identity. At least three developments explain why the Court felt willing to address the issue at that time. First, a large body of purportedly scientific literature had accumulated that defined race and classified humankind into different racial groups. Since the sixteenth century, the concept of race had been linked to skin color, producing the simplistic color-coding that is conventional today: black, white, brown, yellow, red. Judges could draw on these writings to demonstrate that legislative and judicial decisions ascribing racial status had some basis in objectively determined reality. (Or so it seemed, for a time.) Second, by 1920, the simple Black/white binary was being complicated by the expanding legal presence of other races: Asian, Native American, and ethnicities that seemed racially ambiguous (like Armenians, Italians, or Greeks).[11] Third, the NAACP's rights-conscious pursuit of racial justice forced the debate over race on to new terrain, or at least territory that had not been trodden since Reconstruction. If disadvantaging racial distinctions were to be upheld, it became increasingly necessary to explain why. It was one thing to acknowledge that social prejudices were ineluctable, as the Court had done, most conspicuously in *Plessy*. But it was something else to claim that those prejudices justified an inequality that could no longer be denied. Pretextuality was wearing thin.

Since the eighteenth century, Europeans and white Americans had believed that races actually existed among humans as natural attributes, that those races could be rationally identified and scientifically classified, that these classifications could be arranged in a hierarchy of merit, and that the white race(s) of Europe was (were) superior to the colored races in terms of intelligence, capacity, and achievements. ("Beauty" was often a fourth criterion.)[12] Carl Linnaeus's taxonomy in *Systema Naturae* (1767) provided the basis for subsequent racial classification schemes as well as a scientific legitimation for the effort. Philosophers and scientists enthusiastically took up the task of identifying races and attributing characteristics to them. The German physician Johann Blumenbach pioneered ideas like craniometry (measuring skulls), five global races ("Caucasian," "Mongolian," etc.), and the "degenerative hypothesis" (colored races were degenerate versions of the original white race).

In his *Notes on the State of Virginia* (1785), Thomas Jefferson, America's foremost early scientific racist and Blumenbach's contemporary, relied on both physical and cultural anthropology to support his speculations that Africans were congenitally inferior. In the nineteenth century, Europeans like Arthur de Gobineau and Houston Stuart Chamberlain, plus Americans like Josiah Nott, maintained that Africans were biologically inferior and warned that race mixing threatened the accomplishments of white civilization.[13] These intellectual developments came to a head in the early twentieth century when three prominent members of America's social and educational elite, Madison Grant, Lothrop Stoddard, and Henry Fairfield Osborne, popularized these themes, captured in the title of Grant's influential book *The Passing of the Great Race* (1916).

In 1790 Congress had restricted naturalization to "a free white person."[14] After the Civil War, it extended the privilege to "free white persons, and to aliens of African nativity, and to persons of African descent."[15] After the need for plentiful cheap male labor in the West was filled by others by around 1870, the Chinese Exclusion Act of 1882[16] made explicit what had always been an implicit understanding that Chinese (and by extension, all Asians) would be ineligible to become citizens. The Supreme Court upheld the constitutionality of that statute in 1889.[17] In 1917, on the eve of American entry into World War I, Congress created an "Asiatic barred zone" that excluded all Asians.[18] The Immigration Act of 1924[19] attempted to freeze the racial and ethnic composition of the nation at then-current levels. Based on such racial designations, law distributed racial advantage and disability. In countless ways, federal, state, and local laws determined what opportunities lay open to which racial groupings, and which were foreclosed to them. The most important was eligibility for citizenship.

In this environment, the pseudoscience of eugenics flourished, with lethal consequences.[20] The US Army's intelligence testing during World War I provided data for scientific racists to prove the mental inferiority of the colored races. The nation's experience with imperialism, together with anti-immigrant agitation, led to enactment of the restrictive Immigration Acts of 1921 and 1924, which severely restricted European immigration and shut off Asian immigration entirely. Progressives in the early twentieth century applauded these efforts, convinced that the colored races were permanently inferior and congenitally incapable of evolutionary development toward something better.[21] This provided the context in which the Court took on the task of making sense out of racial classifications, a "fluctuating, decentered complex of social meanings that are formed and transformed under the constant pressures of political struggle."[22]

Law, both statutory and common, has always been constitutive in the social construction of race. When the US Supreme Court decided to address issues of racial identity head-on in the 1920s, it had a half century's worth of lower-court precedent to guide its deliberations.[23] Juristic development produced two approaches to the problem of defining race: either by "common parlance," based primarily on perceptions of color and other physiognomic features,[24] or by contemporary scientific understanding.[25] Opinions based on science rather than popular understanding demoted color as such as a criterion, relying instead on other various pseudoscientific criteria on offer at the time. The debate became more confused when the scientific approach gained ascendancy and conflated the common-parlance and statutory term "white" with the "scientific" designation "Caucasian." The latter term was first propounded by Blumenbach in the eighteenth century,[26] and was then validated in the emergence of scientific racism of the early twentieth century.

With only such crude junk-science materials to guide its deliberations, the Court took up the task of imposing legal coherence on legislative classifications of color. In *Ozawa v. United States* (1922),[27] the justices determined that a Japanese native who had become thoroughly Americanized after twenty years of domicile in the United States was ineligible to become an American citizen under the statutory language restricting naturalization to "aliens, being free white persons and to aliens of African nativity and to persons of African descent." The question was whether someone like Ozawa could be considered a "free white person," and Justice George Sutherland, writing for a unanimous Court, held that he could not be. To reach that conclusion, Sutherland had to determine what "white" signified as a racial classification. He stumbled through an aimless discourse on race, at one point seemingly endorsing reliance on popular understanding ("only a person of what is popularly known as the Caucasian race"), yet in the end affirming "ethnological knowledge," "the science of ethnology," as the correct touchstone.[28] But that did not help much: to resolve the case, all he could do was assert by ipse dixit[29] that whatever the word might mean in popular or scientific discourse, it did not include Japanese, "the black or African race," and Indians.

Along the way to this conclusion, Sutherland insisted that skin color alone would be an unreliable determinant of race, because it would admit into the privileged class of whites "the swarthy brunette" and "result in a confused overlapping of races and a gradual merging of one into the other," the dreaded miscegenation.[30] Ozawa had asserted in argument that he was light-skinned, "showing the transparent pink tint which whites assume as their own privilege." In this claim, he was backed by the authority of John Henry Wigmore, dean of the Northwestern Law School and the twentieth century's leading authority on evidence. Based on his three years' residence

154   THE DARK PAST

in Japan, Wigmore had earlier argued that Japanese were white.[31] But Sutherland's rejection of color raised a troubling point: if color, the most obvious physiognomic test, could not reliably identify races, what could? Was it possible that there was no physical or scientific basis for race differentiation? Could it be that racial distinctions were all chimerical, mere social constructs designed to preserve privilege and impose degradation? The Supreme Court in 1922 was not about to open *that* question.

Sutherland also affirmed the equivalence of the terms "white" and "Caucasian," thereby importing into legal discourse all the confusion that the latter pseudoscientific term generated.[32] (The designation "Caucasian" was based on nothing more substantial than that one human skull out of Blumenbach's collection of sixty came from the Caucasus. Blumenbach thought it resembled German skulls and concluded that this identified the Caucasus Mountains as the ancestral homeland of European whites.) Sutherland felt compelled to conclude his opinion with a lame disclaimer: "Of course there is not implied...any suggestion of individual unworthiness or racial inferiority."[33] The ethereal realm of scientific discourse could not be contaminated by any such taint. (This would return to vex him a few months later.) But that fig leaf did not deflect the wave of anti-Japanese discrimination validated by the *Ozawa* opinion, beginning with congressional enactment of the Immigration Act of 1924 (which was a direct response to the permission for Japanese exclusion signaled in *Ozawa*), continuing with the going Alien Land Law discrimination in California and Washington State, and culminating with Japanese internment two decades later.[34]

The *Ozawa* decision was muddled and proved to be short-lived. Sutherland and his brethren abandoned their embrace of the scientific definition of race in a mere three months, a surprising turnabout that requires explanation. Again writing for a unanimous Court, in *United States v. Thind* (1923) Sutherland rejected an appeal from a denial of naturalization by Bhagat Singh Thind, described as "a high-caste Hindu, of full Indian blood" and a veteran of the US Army in World War I.[35] Without explicitly overruling *Ozawa*, Sutherland gutted its substance, reinstating the common-parlance (rather than scientific) understanding of race, in an emphatic passage: "the word [Caucasian] by common usage has acquired a popular meaning, not clearly defined to be sure, but sufficiently so to enable us to say that its popular as distinguished from its scientific application is of appreciably narrower scope. It is in the popular sense of the word, therefore, that we employ is as an aid to the construction of the statute.... The words of the statute are to be interpreted in accordance with the understanding of the common man from whose vocabulary they were taken." He dismissed "the speculative processes of ethnological reasoning" as a key to interpreting "written in the words of common speech, for common understanding, by unscientific men."[36] (Cue Aaron Copland's "Fanfare for the Common Man.") In view of that common understanding, "a review of [ethnographers'] contentions would serve no useful purpose." So he gave up: the Court need not "pursue the matter of scientific classification further." Instead, "familiar observation and knowledge" would readily reveal that "Hindus" (as Sutherland called them)[37] could not be included in the groups of Americans "commonly recognized as white."[38]

In *Thind*, Sutherland found himself hoist by his own logical petard. *Ozawa* mandated the following doctrinal syllogism:

All Caucasians are white.
Thind is Caucasian.
Therefore, Thind is white.

But that result was a priori unacceptable to Sutherland and his colleagues. Given the racial predilections of white Americans of that era, Sutherland had to abandon the scientific standard, repudiate his own thinking in *Ozawa*, and embrace the popular understanding of race. Both cases were decided unanimously, so Sutherland carried all the Brethren with him in his volte-face. What explains this remarkable reversal?

The clue explaining why Sutherland repudiated *Ozawa* is found in a passage in *Thind* where he asserted that "children born in this country of Hindu parents would retain indefinitely the clear evidence of their ancestry.... The great body of our people instinctively recognize it and reject the thought of assimilation."[39] To promiscuously admit dark-skinned people from the Asian subcontinent, no matter how Caucasian or Aryan they might be, would lead to miscegenation, the pollution of fair, blond, northwestern European "blood" by the darker races of the southern hemisphere. Underlying the *Thind* opinion was an unstated sense that whiteness as a racial category was unstable and vulnerable, and if disrupted might be unable to sustain white supremacy. Therefore, readily observable "physical characteristics" must trump all scientific "speculations," lest white supremacy be undermined. Race had to be treated as natural, self-evident, and above all, real. Science must not be allowed to undermine the stable and enduring sense of racial self that whites required to preserve their dominance.

Sutherland's rejection of science for purposes of racial classification, and his exaltation of common understanding and visible physical characteristics, have proved enduring. A decade later, even as sensitive a jurist as Benjamin N. Cardozo could write that "the race of a Japanese or a Chinaman will be known to any one who looks at him.... The triers of the facts will look upon the defendant sitting in the courtroom and will draw their own conclusions" about his racial identity.[40]

Adopting the popular-understanding approach to defining race and discarding purportedly scientific classifications meant that the prejudices of the white community would be determinative in assigning society's benefits and burdens. This was borne out in the third of the Taft Court's racial construction cases, *Gong Lum v. Rice* (1927).[41] A Mississippi school board excluded a nine-year old American of Chinese descent from attending a white school in the Delta. The state supreme court upheld the exclusion, stating that "the dominant purpose of the two sections of the Constitution of our state [dealing with education and intermarriage] was to preserve the integrity and purity of the white race." It construed the term "white" to be exclusively limited to Caucasians, while the correlative "colored" included all others.[42] Chief Justice William Howard Taft, writing for a unanimous Court in *Gong Lum v. Rice* (1927), upheld the Mississippi decision, holding that the equal protection clause of the Fourteenth Amendment did not bar the Mississippi arrangements. He confirmed that states have the power to maintain racially segregated school systems (the first and only time the Court explicitly so held), citing as authority *Plessy, Cumming v. Richmond County Board of Education,* and *Roberts v. City of Boston*.[43] Thus school authorities had power to exclude an Asian ("Mongolian," in the racial terminology of the time) from white schools and shunt her to the nearest "colored" school. *Gong Lum* demonstrated that the underlying purpose of racial classification was to preserve the advantages of whites and exclude all others. The Black/white binary was extended to take others into account by lumping them on the colored side of the line. The concept of race now shed all pretensions to be a neutral and impartial scientific classification, and appeared in its true character, a social artifact that protected white advantage.

It was just as well that the Court abandoned the claims of the scientific account of race at that time. Anthropologists began to question, then to reject entirely, the very concept of race itself: first, Franz Boas at Columbia, then Melville Herskovits, Ruth Benedict, Margaret Mead, and Bronislaw Malinowski attacked the racism of Madison Grant and his predecessors.[44] They popularized their views in bestsellers like Mead's *Coming of Age in Samoa* (1928).[45] Within two decades, the edifice of scientific racism collapsed. Sutherland's fumbling efforts to ground the legal significance of race in popular prejudice was exposed as the judicial endorsement of racism that it inherently was.

Unfortunately, despite its near-universal repudiation, scientific racism would stage a comeback after World War II. Paradoxically, racism's irrationality and quicksilver quality proved to be the source of its enduring strength.

The modern Court has managed to free itself from these racial coils by sidestepping the Taft's Court's doomed efforts to make sense out of something that does not exist (race). In companion 1987 cases construing the modern avatars of section 1 of the 1866 Civil Rights Act,[46] Justice Byron White deftly avoided determining whether Jews and Arabs constituted races so as to be able to claim the protection of the acts.[47] The relevant query was whether the members of the Thirty-Ninth Congress who drafted the legislation thought they were distinct races. The issue is therefore whether "Jews [and Arabs] constituted a group of people that Congress intended to protect." White revealed the distance the Court had come since Sutherland's labored efforts: "There is a common popular understanding that there are three major human races—Caucasoid, Mongoloid, and Negroid. Many modern biologists and anthropologists, however, criticize racial classifications as arbitrary and of little use in understanding the variability of human beings.... Clear-cut categories do not exist. The particular traits which have generally been chosen to characterize races have been criticized as having little biological significance.... Racial classifications are for the most part sociopolitical, rather than biological, in nature."[48] With that, the modern Court seems to have buried scientific racism, though like so much else involving racism, the zombie somehow manages to shamble on.[49]

Procedural Due Process in State Criminal Trials

Between 1920 and 1940, the Supreme Court handed down a half-dozen major decisions mandating minimal standards of procedural due process in cases involving Black defendants tried for crimes in southern state courts.[50]

The justices condemned mob domination of trials, ineffective assistance of counsel, exclusion of African Americans from grand and petit juries, and confessions coerced by torture. In the context of the times, this was a remarkable achievement.[51] Previously, the Court, like the nation, ignored such routine travesties of justice perpetrated daily on African Americans in southern courts.

Trials of Black men for criminal offenses in southern courts, especially capital offenses and alleged rapes or assaults on white women, were parodies of criminal justice.[52] Little better than legal lynchings, such trials moved relentlessly to foreordained results, often fatal.[53] Before trial began, white mobs surged outside the courthouse, demanding that they be allowed to lynch the accused. In response, lawyers, editorialists, and sometimes even judges assured the rabble that if they let the trial proceed, speedy and condign punishment would be certain. The African American educator William Holtzclaw observed that in 1915 "it is somewhat difficult to draw at this time a sharp line marking off distinctly the point where the lynching spirit stops and the spirit of legal procedure commences."[54]

Sheriffs and private citizens tortured accused African Americans before trial to extort confessions from them, and all too often succeeded when the men's resistance was broken by exhaustion, pain, and terror. Trials were a travesty: only whites served on grand and petit juries. Legal representation was nonexistent, nominal, or indifferent, and in most cases involuntary. (Atticus Finch, it must be remembered, was fictional, a fantasy.)[55] Lawyers had no time to prepare for trial even if they had wanted to do so. They did not or could not consult with their clients, seldom called witnesses, did not cross-examine the prosecution's witnesses or move to strike testimony. Prosecutors made overtly racist and demagogic appeals to the prejudices of the jurymen without rebuke. Trials were speedy and perfunctory. Testimony from the defendants was coerced. Appeals were rare, procedurally constricted, and invariably unsuccessful. Throughout the process, "negro law," "an important branch of the law here in Mississippi," according to a local judge, Sidney Fant Davis, "was unwritten, learned only through experience and observation, and fully understood...only by the native-born. In a society in which race mattered above all else, 'negro law' determined who was punished for what."[56]

It took sixty years after the end of the Civil War for the federal courts to assert their supervisory responsibilities in the realm of criminal procedure. The emergence of federal oversight of state courts in criminal cases lay in changing understandings of federalism. Criminal law had always been the exclusive province of the states, save for a small body of federal crimes like piracy or counterfeiting. It was the states that defined the substance of criminal offenses and that prescribed the procedures by which violators would be tried. After 1865, this changed because of the revolution in federalism that resulted from the war. Though substantive criminal law still remained the responsibility of the states, in the twentieth century some provisions of the federal Bill of Rights began to be "incorporated" against the states, that is, imposed as restraints on state legislative or judicial processes, a process that is sometimes called nationalizing civil liberties.[57] Once the Court began incorporating substantive liberties in 1896–1897,[58] it was inevitable that it should incorporate procedural liberties as well. As Justice Felix Frankfurter insisted in 1943, "the history of liberty has largely been the history of the observance of procedural safeguards."[59]

As the Supreme Court was developing doctrines of substantive due process and liberty of contract beginning in 1890,[60] it concurrently began to enforce the criminal procedural rights secured by the due process clauses. Thus, for example, in *Weeks v. United States* (1914),[61] the Court adopted the exclusionary rule, prohibiting use of evidence illegally obtained from being used in a criminal trial. *Twining v. New Jersey* (1908)[62] held that some of the liberties protected in the federal Bill of Rights might limit state authority because state procedures did not constitute due process of law. The rise of rights consciousness throughout the twentieth century encouraged all Americans to think in terms of liberties under the federal and state constitutions as protecting them from abusive state power. The awakening sense of procedural protection for the rights of those accused of crime soon extended to the plight of African Americans being tried in southern courts.

Before the Civil War, southern state courts often accorded enslaved people accused of major crimes a surprising degree of procedural justice.[63] But one of their incentives for doing so, the monetary value of an enslaved person, vanished after emancipation, and the counterrevolution of Redemption led white southerners to seek summary justice in the judicial system, with no concern for the wasteful niceties of procedural justice where Blacks were concerned.[64]

Criminal trials in southern courts had to be sorted out on a racial matrix of perpetrator/victim: white on white, Black on Black, white on Black, Black on white. In the first category, white on white, southern courts most closely aspired to justice and procedural regularity. But Black-on-Black and white-on-Black crimes, where an African American was the victim, were less urgent, sometimes not even being worth the bother and expense of prosecution unless the local community saw some need to discipline a particular Black defendant. For Black-victim crimes, administrative efficiency, in the form of speedy process and cost control, became the top priority. As for white-on-Black crimes, many went overlooked by common consent among the white population, and for those that did go to trial, the defendant could be assured of sympathetic triers of fact. Black-on-white crimes, though, had a high priority because of the need to protect whites and to forestall lynchings when the mob felt that the mills of justice ground too slowly.

Criminal prosecutions in southern state courts took place against a background of extralegal violence dating from the Civil War and continuing into the twentieth century. The 1920s were a particularly violent decade. Lynchings increased, nightriding and vigilantism erupted when whites feared some threat to social order, and police brutality was a quotidian reality throughout the nation, but particularly in the South. Post–World War I "race riots"—a misnomer: these were usually mobs of whites assaulting Blacks—made the racial background of generalized violence explicit. The Klan re-emerged in its second avatar in the 1920s, though this time its principal energies were directed at immigrants, Catholics, and Jews. It was urban, northern, and modern, with strongholds in such unlikely places as Oregon, Indiana, and Long Island, New York.[65] In 1931, the congressionally appointed Wickersham Commission's report showed through extensive graphic detail that police violence in law enforcement was pervasive. It concluded that "'the inflicting of pain, physical or mental, to extract confessions or statements' was widespread throughout the United States."[66] Against this backdrop, regular criminal proceedings in duly constituted southern courts provided an alternative to vigilantism and anarchy. But they could do so only if the mob was assured that African American defendants would be brutally subdued, by law if possible, outside the law if necessary.

In *Hurtado v. California* (1884),[67] the Supreme Court had stated in dictum that in their criminal proceedings the states were constrained by "those fundamental principles of liberty and justice which lie at the base of all our civil and political institutions," and suggested that these principles were mandated by the due process clause of the Fourteenth Amendment. A generation later, in *Twining v. New Jersey* (1908),[68] the Court stated that some of the liberties specified in the federal Bill of Rights might be applicable to the states because "they are of such a nature that they are included in the conception of due process of law." With those general principles in place, the Court after 1920 began to hear appeals from some of the most blatant miscarriages of justice in the southern courts.

Its first opportunity came in the aftermath of the Elaine, Arkansas, massacre of 1919. In a year marred by racial violence in Chicago, Washington, DC, Charleston, Omaha, Knoxville, and countless other cities and towns (contemporaries referred to this period as the "Red Summer"),[69] a particularly lethal outbreak occurred near Elaine, a small town in the Mississippi River Delta when two white men approached a meeting of Black sharecroppers who were forming a tenant farmers union.[70] Gunshots were fired; no one has ever determined who was responsible. One of the whites was killed, the other wounded. The state erupted into an orgy of violence, nearly all of it directed at innocent Blacks, stimulated by lurid headlines in local newspapers: "Vicious Blacks Were Planning Great Uprising," "Planned Massacre of Whites Today," "Negroes Plan to Kill All Whites." In two days of unrestrained white violence, over a hundred African Americans were killed, along with five whites.

After a month of unrelenting torture that included whipping, threats, near-suffocation, and electrical shock, Arkansas charged 122 African American men with murder or intent to commit murder. The ensuing trials were prompt, hasty, and perfunctory. African Americans were excluded from the petit jury. Appointed defense counsel did not meet with their clients, did not call any witnesses, did not have their clients testify, did not make any objections or motions, and did not make any opening or closing statements. A white mob milled around the Elaine courthouse, but their lust to lynch the defendants was assuaged by assurances from local white community leaders that the seething throng needn't trouble themselves, since the Black defendants would be sentenced to death anyway.[71] As Justice Holmes put it in summarizing the facts of the case, "if the mob would refrain,... they would execute those found guilty in the form of law."

To appreciate the significance of *Moore v. Dempsey* (1923),[72] the Supreme Court decision that reversed these proceedings, we must trace the procedural route by which it came to the Court.[73] After a pro forma trial, twelve of the defendants were condemned to death, and the rest sentenced to long prison terms. (No whites were indicted for the deaths of over one hundred Black citizens.) On appeal, the Arkansas Supreme Court held that despite the howling mob, jury discrimination, and testimony coerced by torture, the defendants had not been denied due process.[74] Defendants then sought a writ of habeas corpus from a federal district court in Arkansas, which dismissed the petition on the authority of *Frank v. Mangum* (1915).[75]

In that earlier case, a white man[76] had been convicted of the murder of a young woman in a trial overborne by threats of violence by an attendant mob. In *Frank*, a majority of the US Supreme Court speaking through Justice Mahlon Pitney denied habeas relief. The majority justices were sensitive to the issues of federalism and indifferent to claims of mob disorder. They held that a trial "conducted according to the settled course of judicial proceedings as established by the law of the state, so long as it includes notice and a hearing, or an opportunity to be heard, before a court of competent jurisdiction, according to established modes of procedure, is 'due process' in the constitutional sense." Holmes and Hughes in dissent condemned such formalism, contending that "although every form may have been preserved, [federal habeas corpus] opens the inquiry whether they have been more than an empty shell." "This is not a matter for polite presumptions; we must look facts in the face," they warned.

Holmes vindicated his position in *Frank* in *Moore v. Dempsey* (1923), vacating the convictions and remanding for trial before the federal district court on the claims that the original trial proceedings were dominated by a threatening mob and were mere empty formal proceedings that provided only the nominal pretense of a trial. The challenge for Holmes was to bring around the *Frank* majority to a more realistic approach, overriding their federalism concerns for the prerogatives of state judicial systems in favor of mandating minima of civilized procedure in criminal trials of African American men.[77] If "the whole proceeding is a mask—that counsel, jury and judge were swept to the fatal end by an irresistible wave of public passion" and appeals to the state supreme court did not correct the situation, the threat of mob violence "cannot prevent this Court from securing to the petitioners their constitutional rights." Under such circumstances, the trial was "absolutely void." A federal court hearing a habeas petition had to review the facts de novo to evaluate the fairness of the trial, rather than dismissing the petition if the forms had been met.

Holmes's opinion was, as was his wont, succinct and dispassionate, but its tone provided a striking contrast to his opinion of twenty years earlier in *Giles v. Harris*. There he was dismissive of the claims of the Black petitioners; here he was willing to concede implicitly that they might be correct, at least for purposes of giving them a chance to make their case before a federal court. Gone was his earlier scarcely concealed disdain for African

Americans seeking to have federal courts protect their rights. In its place was a new openness to the possibility that the US Constitution actually did endow African Americans with rights that judges must honor. Hitherto, federal judges regarded criminal law and most matters pertaining to the civil rights of African Americans as matters exclusively for the states, except where the federal Constitution or laws explicitly provided otherwise. *Moore v. Dempsey* relaxed that attitude and signaled that if the states failed to ensure procedural due process, federal courts stood by to provide relief. No longer would criminal trials in state courts in the South be merely a more polite version of lynching. *Moore* began to vindicate the decision of the Thirty-Ninth Congress to make the federal courts the ultimate guarantors of justice and federal constitutional rights where the states had failed to ensure them.

Moore constituted a monumental extension of federal habeas corpus and, more to the point here, a clear sign that the US Supreme Court was beginning to hold the southern states to an unprecedented accountability in what had been until then unfettered discretion in using their criminal justice systems as an ersatz substitute for slavery and a more genteel alternative to lynching. It merits Michael Klarman's praise as "a progenitor of modern American criminal procedure."[78]

The issue of criminal trials in the South returned to the Court dramatically a decade later in the cases of the Scottsboro Boys, nine Black teenagers ranging in age from twelve to nineteen who were accused of raping two white women while all were hoboes riding the rails in Tennessee.[79] When a white posse pulled the youths off the train in Scottsboro, Alabama, and word spread of the women's allegations, a mob gathered and the governor of Alabama had to send in the state's National Guard to prevent a lynching. The young men were tried two weeks later. Their legal representation was nominal, the trials hurried, and the small county seat mobbed by threatening locals.

Though the presiding judge appointed all the members of the local bar as counsel to the defendants, nearly all withdrew, leaving only two lawyers, one of them an alcoholic who was not a member of the Alabama bar, the other an elderly man unkindly described as "doddering, extremely unreliable, senile,"[80] to do what they could. Neither had experience in cases of this magnitude. They had only a half hour to confer with their clients and could not conduct an independent investigation or summon witnesses. Eight of the youths were promptly convicted and sentenced to death in hasty, perfunctory trials. The International Labor Defense (ILD), the legal defense arm of the Communist Party USA, then elbowed out the NAACP for the opportunity to represent the defendants in their subsequent appeals and retrials.[81] On appeal, the Alabama Supreme Court affirmed over the forceful dissent of its chief justice, John C. Anderson, who cited the intimidating presence of the National Guard and the "pro forma" performance of counsel as denying the defendants a fair and impartial trial.[82]

The ILD appealed the Alabama court's decision to the US Supreme Court and retained the eminent civil libertarian Walter Pollak to argue the case. He challenged the convictions on three grounds: denial of a fair trial, inadequate representation by counsel, and exclusion of African Americans from grand and petit juries, but the Court took up only the second, inadequate counsel. Chief Justice Hughes assigned the majority opinion in the first of the Scottsboro Boys cases, *Powell v. Alabama* (1932),[83] to Justice Sutherland, who devoted his lengthy opinion to reviewing the minima necessary for adequate representation in capital trials. He framed the issue as "whether the defendants were in substance denied the right of counsel" in violation of the Fourteenth Amendment. The Sixth Amendment's guarantee of the right of "the assistance of counsel for his defence," plus the related rights of speedy trial, impartial jury, to be informed of the charges, to confront witnesses, and to have compulsory process to subpoena witnesses were not mandatory in state courts, because they had not yet been incorporated via the Fourteenth Amendment.[84] So Sutherland instead turned to the capacious possibilities of the Fourteenth Amendment's due process clause. This in itself was remarkable because the Court for almost a half century had rejected the due process clause as a basis for protecting various civil liberties.[85]

Drawing on Chief Justice Anderson's dissent, Sutherland engaged in a detailed review of the facts and circumstances of the trial to demonstrate the patent inadequacy of representation afforded the Scottsboro youths. They "did not have the aid of counsel in any real sense," he concluded.[86] The Alabama Supreme Court had relied on pretextuality, the nominal appearance of counsel, as sufficient. Sutherland's opinion indicated that would no longer suffice as the unspoken mode of interpreting the Constitution when capital trials for Black defendants were involved.

Having shown how insufficient representation was, Sutherland then turned to the due process clause as the source of the right. He relied on the formula the Court had coined in *Hurtado v. California* (1884):[87] whether the right claimed is one of the "fundamental principles of liberty and justice which lie at the base of all our civil and political institutions." He concluded that "the ignorance and illiteracy of the defendants, their youth, the circumstances of public hostility, the imprisonment and the close surveillance of the defendants by the military forces, the fact that their friends and families were all in other states and communication with them necessarily difficult, and above all that they stood in deadly peril of their lives—we think the failure of the trial court to give them reasonable time and opportunity to secure counsel was a clear denial of due process."[88] The Supreme Court reversed and remanded the case for a new trial. Felix Frankfurter, then a professor at the Harvard Law School, noted in a *New York Times* op-ed that the Court was clearly signaling that it would no longer condone "judicial murder." "Here lies the deepest significance of the case."[89] *Powell* was the first instance where the Supreme Court reversed a conviction on the grounds of inadequate assistance of counsel. As such, it was the forerunner of *Gideon v. Wainwright* (1963).[90] Together with *Moore*, it marked the birth of modern criminal procedure.[91]

On retrial, this time of another of the defendants, Clarence Norris, the dramatis personae changed: a new trial judge, James E. Horton, displayed a determination to do justice, reflected both in his stern control of mob unruliness and in his skepticism about the state's evidence.[92] Leading the defense was a man regarded as the nation's premier criminal defense attorney, Samuel Leibowitz. In the second round of trials, Leibowitz emphasized a point not heavily argued the first time, exclusion of African Americans from the grand and petit juries. This provoked a series of snide anti-Semitic comments from the prosecuting attorney, who in the interim had been elected lieutenant governor of the state largely on the strength of his role in prosecuting the case originally. Ruby Bates, one of the two prosecutrices,[93] dramatically recanted her charges, while the other, Victoria Price, repeatedly contradicted both herself and Bates. Despite that, the jury again convicted, and the Alabama Supreme Court predictably affirmed.[94]

So the Scottsboro Boys cases went back to the US Supreme Court, this time as *Norris v. Alabama* (1935),[95] but now on the issue of exclusion of African Americans from jury service. Alabama contended that it was not so much excluding Blacks from jury duty as it was being scrupulously selective in choosing only the best men from its venires. Chief Justice Hughes treated that claim as beneath contempt and did not dignify it with a rebuttal. When Leibowitz alleged that jury commissioners had tampered with the jury rolls to add five Black names during the trial, Hughes challenged him to prove his claim. Anticipating that, Leibowitz produced the rolls, and, in an unprecedented move, the justices examined the jury lists for themselves on the spot, some of them using a magnifying glass.

Perhaps influenced by that demonstration of the state's duplicity, the Court unanimously held that exclusion of African Americans from juries deprived criminal defendants of equal protection, citing the Jury Cases of 1880.[96] That in itself was significant: though the principle had been established in theory, Hughes was now invoking it, almost for the first time, to protect Black rights in practice. He held that the Court had the duty to re-examine the facts of the alleged exclusion. Doing so now, it readily confirmed the obvious: Alabama had systematically excluded all Blacks from juries for half a century. The Court reversed and sent the cases back for trial yet again.[97] The Court extended its supervision of southern juries in *Smith v. Texas* (1940),[98] where it unanimously reversed a conviction for rape in a Texas court where only a handful of African Americans had been selected for grand jury service, re-evaluating the facts de novo and finding per se discrimination where jury commissioners did not select Blacks because they did not know any personally.

First *Moore*, then *Powell* and *Norris*, began a new era in Supreme Court oversight of state-court criminal proceedings. Though the Court had long held that state criminal prosecutions had to provide fair trials according to the traditional modes of proceeding under the common law, it had not imposed any realistic oversight on the state courts except for the problem of racial discrimination in jury selection—and even there it had not actually intervened until *Norris*. But the climate had changed by the 1930s, and the Court became increasingly activist, especially where the violation of civil liberties was particularly egregious, the costs of intervention were not high, and the climate of opinion was supportive. *Moore* and *Powell* signaled that the justices would no longer wink at plain violations of African American defendants' rights in the southern state courts.

Brown v. Mississippi (1936)[99] continued this trend. After a white farmer was found dying of a brutal ax assault in his rural Mississippi home, a sheriff's deputy arrested a Black neighbor and sharecropper, Yank Ellington. A mob seized him, hanged him twice but let him down before he died, then whipped him. The next day, another deputy whipped him again. Deputies also arrested Ed Brown and Henry Shields, and together with a mob whipped them in jail with a leather strap. All three confessed to the murder under the threat of further whippings. At trial, the deputy admitted the whippings, and other witnesses confirmed them. When asked at trial about how severely the defendants were whipped, the deputy laconically replied, "Not too much for a negro; not as much as I would have done if it were left to me."[100] The defendants were convicted anyway based on nothing more than their torture-extorted confessions. The defendants were sentenced to be hanged, only seven days after the murder itself. The Mississippi Supreme Court affirmed, upholding the convictions, torture notwithstanding, on the grounds that a motion to exclude the evidence was not timely made. As for the torture itself, the majority piously intoned that "all litigants, of every race or color, are equal at the bar of this court, and we would feel deeply humiliated if the contrary could be justly said. Nothing herein said is intended to even remotely sanction the method by which these confessions were obtained."[101]

The US Supreme Court unanimously reversed in *Brown v. Mississippi*. Chief Justice Hughes recurred to the conception of due process quoted in *Powell*: if a state proceeding "offends some principle of justice so rooted in the traditions and conscience of our people as to be ranked as fundamental" (the *Hurtado* standard), it had to be overturned. Conviction based on confessions extracted under torture met that standard. State trial procedures must "be consistent with the fundamental principles of liberty and justice which lie at the base of all our civil and political institutions." "The rack and torture chamber may not be substituted for the witness stand. The state may not permit an accused to be hurried to conviction under mob domination—where the whole proceeding is but a mask—without supplying corrective process." Hughes concluded that "it would be difficult to conceive of methods more revolting to the sense of justice than those taken to procure the confessions of these petitioners, and the use of the confessions thus obtained as the basis for conviction and sentence was a clear denial of due process."

In 1940, the Court heard another dramatic case that raised due process issues in the trial of African American men in southern state courts. *Chambers v. Florida* (1940)[102] extended *Powell*'s ban on torture to forms of coercion that did not involve physical violence, but rather to what at the time was known as "the third degree": coercive interrogation that did not include physical violence like beating. When a white man was robbed and murdered in Pompano Beach, Florida, in 1933, police conducted a dragnet that rounded up forty local Black men. The police began a series of unremitting interrogations of all of them, winnowing the group down to four. Then they subjected the unlucky quartet to intense questioning for five days, without physical torture. This marathon interrogation culminated in what the Florida Supreme Court characterized as "an all night vigil" that lasted fifteen hours and finally produced the confessions that the prosecutor was seeking. The suspects were held incommunicado and were not permitted to consult friends, family members, or an attorney at any time.[103] After the Florida Supreme Court twice reversed and then finally affirmed, the US Supreme Court granted certiorari and, in a unanimous opinion by Justice Hugo Black, reversed. *Chambers* marked a double debut: the first major decision involving civil rights issues written by Justice Hugo Black after the controversy over his membership in the Ku Klux Klan, and the first appearance before the Supreme Court of thirty-two-year-old attorney Thurgood Marshall.

Black extolled due process as essential to free government. He indulged himself in the sort of grandiloquent rhetoric that was to become his hallmark:

> the rights and liberties of people accused of crime [can] not be safely entrusted to secret inquisitorial processes.... The rack, the thumbscrew, the wheel, solitary confinement, protracted questioning and cross questioning, and other ingenious forms of entrapment of the helpless or unpopular had left their wake of mutilated bodies and shattered minds along the way to the cross, the guillotine, the stake and the hangman's noose. And they who have suffered most from secret and dictatorial proceedings have almost always been the poor, the ignorant, the numerically weak, the friendless, and the powerless.[104]

He concluded his opinion with another grand rhetorical flourish:

> Under our constitutional system, courts stand against any winds that blow as havens of refuge for those who might otherwise suffer because they are helpless, weak, outnumbered, or because they are non-conforming victims of prejudice and public excitement.... No higher duty, no more solemn responsibility, rests upon this Court, than that of translating into living law and maintaining this constitutional shield deliberately planned and inscribed for the benefit of every human being subject to our Constitution—of whatever race, creed or persuasion.[105]

The Court was putting the South on notice that Black criminal defendants were entitled to the same minimal standards of procedural due process that white defendants might claim.

Michael Klarman is skeptical that *Chambers* and the other criminal justice decisions discussed here made any difference at all in the day-to-day experiences of African Americans. In his magisterial study *From Jim Crow to Civil Rights* (2004), he contends that the sonorous and self-congratulatory rhetoric of Black's opinion may have had the perverse effect of placing authentic justice further out of reach of African American defendants.[106] This "insidious" effect occurred because censuring the most egregious abuses, such as those of *Moore* and *Brown*, misled Americans into thinking that reality conformed to rhetoric, whereas the quotidian administration of law in the Deep South remained substantively unchanged, albeit a little cleaned up in outward appearances. Klarman is unsparing: "the rhetoric of *Chambers* suggests that the justices had convinced themselves, and perhaps others, that they had already taken enormous strides toward eliminating race discrimination from southern criminal justice. They had not. Their accomplishments were actually fairly trivial—more a change in form than in substance."

But this undervalues the momentous change underway in the Court's impact on African American life. Granted, this change took place in the realm of doctrine, not on the streets; a new day did not suddenly dawn on a nation now bathed in racial harmony. But that doctrinal shift was nevertheless important. Without it, the Court would have remained mired in the pretense of the previous seventy years. American law would have continued to accept and affirm Jim Crow and judicial lynchings. Though change did not come overnight, it had at least begun, giving hope to advocates like Thurgood Marshall and millions of African Americans that, as Martin Luther King prophesied, "the arc of the moral universe is long, but it bends toward justice."

Voting Rights

The Reconstruction-era Republicans who drafted the Fourteenth Amendment's section 2 and the Fifteenth Amendment considered the ballot to be the ultimate guarantor of all other rights. Ominously, so did their Democratic opponents. After two decades of intimidating voters by extralegal violence, Redeemers legally eliminated African Americans from political power after 1890 by a broad catalog of exclusionary devices: the poll tax (which was often made cumulative), residency requirements, literacy tests, good-character requirements, educational minima, felon disfranchisement, and, after 1900, the white primary.[107] The Supreme Court benignly gave the process its blessing in *Williams v. Mississippi* (1898) and *Giles v. Harris* (1903).[108]

By 1900, the states of the old Confederacy were well on their way to becoming the one-party Democratic "Solid South" that played such an outsize role in American politics for the first half of the twentieth century.[109] In that political environment, with the Republican Party marginalized, the critical election in the states became the primary, with the general election being merely the ritualized ratification of the primary results. Hence an easy way to eliminate African Americans from political power was to exclude them from voting in primary elections. The Democratic Party in all the ex-slave states managed to accomplish this by custom and internal regulation. But in 1923, the state of Texas intervened in a ham-handed way, excluding Blacks from Democratic Party primaries by statute. For a unanimous Court in *Nixon v. Herndon* (1927),[110] Justice Holmes summarily held the statue unconstitutional in three brief paragraphs. Holmes cited *Strauder*, *Yick Wo*, and *Buchanan v. Warley* as authority for the proposition that the equal protection clause of the Fourteenth Amendment was meant to protect African Americans against racially based discrimination. He considered it too obvious to merit discussion that the statute was a "direct and obvious infringement of the Fourteenth [Amendment]."[111] (He explicitly bypassed the Fifteenth Amendment.) "States may do a good deal of classifying that it is difficult to believe rational, but there are limits," he concluded, and those limits were plainly transgressed here. Something had gotten to Holmes in the years since his *Giles v. Harris* opinion in 1903. His unwonted sensitivity to issues of race, plus his openness to equal protection arguments in *Nixon*, suggest that, in Brad Snyder's surmise, "he had not completely abandoned his abolitionist roots."[112]

The impact of *Nixon v. Herndon* was amplified by the fact that the Court had held only six years earlier that Congress could not regulate primary elections under the time-place-manner provisions of Article I, section 4.[113] This decision, *Newberry v. United States* (1921), had implicitly suggested that states were free to discriminate in the primaries, or at least would not be subjected to federal oversight if they did. Yet *Nixon* brusquely interposed the equal protection clause and the federal courts as a shield against Texas-style disfranchisement, *Newberry* notwithstanding.

Texas, undaunted, returned to the legislative drawing board and came up with a fix: a statute that authorized the executive committee of political parties to control their membership. The Texas Democrats promptly did so, reinstating the white primary. Lawrence Nixon, an El Paso physician who was the original petitioner in *Herndon*, stepped up once again to challenge the legislation, and again won, though this time only by a five-to-four margin. In *Nixon v. Condon* (1932),[114] Justice Benjamin Cardozo held that the executive committee acted not under the authority of the party (which arguably might have placed its doings outside the bounds of state action), but rather under authority delegated to it by the state. He concluded with what (for him, anyway) was a blaze of rhetoric: "The Fourteenth Amendment, adopted as it was with special solicitude for the equal protection of members of the Negro race, lays a duty upon the court to level by its judgment these barriers of color."

But *Condon* only postponed the inevitable. Sooner or later the Court would have to confront the problem of state action that it dodged there. Texas obligingly set the stage by repealing the statute targeted in *Condon*. The Democratic Party, acting now without the state's official imprimatur, authorized its executive committee to adopt the racial bar. Now there was no formal state involvement, and the Court again confronted the challenge of pretextuality: can a private organization (a political party in a one-party state) exclude African Americans from participation in primaries, thereby denying them a voice in the only meaningful elections, leaving them the empty privilege of voting in a rubber-stamp ceremony that did no more than affirm what white voters had already decided?

Framed that way, the question could have only one answer in the 1930s. So, it came as no surprise when the Court unanimously held in *Grovey v. Townsend* (1935)[115] that no state action was involved when the Texas Democratic Party excluded Blacks from voting in its primary elections. This was a triumph of form over substance. Nominally aloof, Texas, like all other states, regulated political parties and their primaries in numerous ways, so that finding no state action in the white primary so long as the state did not expressly mandate it was effectively a choice among competing views of state action, none of which was obviously compelling. *Grovey* extended the regime of pretextuality for another nine years in the realm of electoral politics,[116] allowing the baneful state-action doctrine to insulate racial discrimination at the polls a bit longer.

Grovey v. Townsend was an unstable precedent. Though its result seemed compelling in 1935, Justice Roberts's opinion was weakly reasoned. Moreover, the opinion was adrift in crosscurrents of racial bias and constitutional doctrine. Three contemporary cases demonstrated how turbid those doctrinal waters were.

In *Breedlove v. Suttles* (1937),[117] the Court unanimously sustained the Georgia poll tax against a challenge presented by a would-be white voter who argued that the age and sex limits (it fell only on males aged twenty-one to sixty) violated the equal protection clause. Justice Pierce Butler brushed off the claim. He did not mention the role of the poll tax after 1890 as a device to limit Black voting. But because the tax was sometimes cumulative, and because would-be voters had to present a receipt for payment, with the tax date sometimes occurring as much as six months before the election, registrars could easily reject Black voters. In 1966, the Court did eventually get around to holding the tax unconstitutional as applied to state elections,[118] after the American people had ratified the Twenty-Fourth Amendment annulling it for federal elections. But when the justices did strike it down, they condemned the tax as a wealth classification, not even nodding to its historic role in Black voter suppression.

Despite *Breedlove*, though, the Court's willingness to overlook racial subterfuges was ebbing. In 1939, the Court recalled *Guinn v. United States* (1915)[119] from its honorable retirement to strike down another patent evasion of the Fifteenth Amendment. After *Guinn* buried the grandfather clause, Oklahoma immediately disinterred the clause in lightly disguised form in a transparent attempt to disfranchise most Blacks. The state confirmed the franchise for all who had been eligible under the now-discredited clause and gave all others (read: African Americans) a narrow twelve-day window to re-register. The Court, speaking thorough Justice Felix Frankfurter in *Lane v. Wilson* (1939),[120] struck down the measure. Delivering the first of the memorable aphorisms that characterized his opinions, Frankfurter wrote that "the [Fifteenth] Amendment nullifies sophisticated as well as simple-minded modes of discrimination." He then went conspicuously beyond earlier holdings to condemn pretextuality as "onerous procedural requirements which effectively handicap exercise of the franchise by the colored race although the abstract right to vote may remain unrestricted as to race." When ideas like that were openly avowed on the Court, pretextuality appeared moribund.[121] Frankfurter distinguished the Nadir-era voting case *Giles v. Harris* so sharply that its days as viable precedent appeared to be numbered.[122] *Lane* identified the Fifteenth Amendment as the source for protecting Blacks' ability to participate in the political process. That amendment, somnolent for so long, was stirring to life.

The last case in the prewar voting-rights series did not on its face involve the Fifteenth Amendment. Yet *United States v. Classic* (1941)[123] had momentous implications for Black suffrage. It suggested that restrictions on Black suffrage were constitutionally suspect and likely invalid. The Mississippi Plan now seemed vulnerable. Defendants were convicted of violating latter-day descendants of the Reconstruction-era Enforcement Acts by ballot tampering in a congressional primary election. Justice Harlan Fiske Stone, writing for the majority,[124] sustained Congress's regulatory power over primary elections under the "Times, Places and Manner" clause of Article I, section 4,[125] not the Fourteenth or Fifteenth Amendments.[126] He wrote: "where in fact the primary effectively controls the choice [of a candidate for Congress], the right of the elector to have his ballot counted at the primary, is likewise included in the right."[127] He explained: "we think that the authority of Congress, given by sec. 4, includes the authority to regulate primary elections when, as in this case, they are a step in the exercise by the people of their choice of representatives in Congress." Even though the Fifteenth Amendment counterpart of the time-place-manner clause was still hobbled by the state action requirement, *Classic* seemed obviously pertinent, at least as an indicator of which way the wind was blowing. Stone, for one, considered *Grovey* defunct after his *Classic* opinion.[128] The Court in the interwar period had not quite killed off the white primary, but its end was inevitable, and soon.

Substantive Liberties

The few cases involving the substantive rights of African Americans that came before the Court between the wars left behind the dead indifference of the Fuller Court, replacing it with an openness to understanding the conditions of Black Americans' lived experience in a nation where servitude and Jim Crow still held sway. The Hughes Court was now more receptive to claims of racial discrimination.

In June 1932, Angelo Herndon, an idealistic nineteen-year-old Black Communist, organized a peaceful demonstration by unemployed Black and white citizens in Atlanta demanding that the city government do more to relieve poverty and hunger.[129] He was charged with violating the state's antiquated insurrection statute, a capital offense, on the basis of having Communist literature in his possession. The law had its origins in a 1829 Georgia statute imposing the death penalty for "exciting to insurrections, conspiracy, or resistance among the slaves, negroes, or free persons of color, or revolt of slaves," a measure aimed at suppressing abolitionist propaganda.[130] In 1866, the legislature had to drop the reference to slaves, but the remainder of the statute was too useful to discard at a time when the freedpeople were challenging laws like the Black Codes. The updated postwar statute condemned "exciting insurrections, riot, conspiracy, or resistance against the lawful authority of the State," still a capital offense.[131]

Unlike most other states, Georgia never got around to adopting a criminal anarchy, criminal syndicalism, or sedition act in the decades before the Great War, so it dusted off the old Civil War–era insurrection act to put down the Black Communist. An all-white jury convicted him, responding the prosecution's plea that they "send this damnable anarchistic Bolsheviki to his death by electrocution, and God will be satisfied that justice has been done and the daughters of state officials can walk the streets safely."[132] The Georgia Supreme Court affirmed, relying on a bad-tendency interpretation of *Gitlow v. New York* (1925), the US Supreme Court's most recent and pertinent First Amendment speech precedent.[133] In a near-contemporaneous comment, the constitutional authority Zechariah Chafee noted that Georgia "was afraid, not that the Constitution would be overthrown, but that it might be enforced."[134]

Though the Communist International Labor Defense took charge of the trial, Herndon was represented in his appeal to the US Supreme Court by establishment pillars of the bar: Whitney North Seymour, Walter Gellhorn, Herbert Wechsler, and Elbert Tuttle.[135] After a false start,[136] the Court finally decided *Herndon v. Lowry* (1937)[137] by a five-to-four margin, holding that the Georgia insurrection statute was unconstitutionally vague and did not have an adequate relationship to legitimate legislative ends. Justice Owen Roberts's majority opinion was not significant for the lucidity of its reasoning (his opinions seldom were), but rather was an assertion of First Amendment liberties of speech and assembly in dramatic circumstances. At a time of rising international tensions, for the Supreme Court to defend the rights of a young African American Communist was extraordinary. It signaled an openness on the part of the Court to the liberties of all Black citizens.[138]

The Court had been cautiously inching toward an expansion of speech and press freedoms since *Gitlow* (1925).[139] *Herndon*, together with *DeJonge v. Oregon*, decided a few months earlier, extended protections for speech freedom in more challenging conditions, as Communists stirred up crowds in the depths of the Great Depression. In *Herndon* and *De Jonge* the Supreme Court for the first time explicitly recognized assembly as a distinct liberty protected by the First Amendment and incorporated by the Fourteenth.[140] *Herndon v. Lowry* affirmed the right of an African American to speak freely, pushing ideas obnoxious to many whites in a time and place marked by social unrest. This impression was reinforced the next year when in *New Negro Alliance v. Sanitary Grocery Co.* (1938)[141] the Court construed the Norris-LaGuardia Act of 1932 broadly to permit labor picketing by African American activists who were not employees of their target but who merely wanted it to open up employment opportunities to them at a newly opened store. This new access to expressive liberties heralded a time when Black citizens could claim opportunities previously available only to whites.

Herndon invites comparison to a contemporaneous case, *De Jonge v. Oregon* (1937), which raised identical issues.[142] Dirk De Jonge was convicted under a state criminal syndicalism statute for organizing a political rally in Portland, Oregon, in the context of a longshoreman's strike. The Court overturned the conviction on grounds identical to those of Angelo Herndon's case, with a strong emphasis on the right of assembly ("peaceable assembly for lawful discussion cannot be made a crime"). But the Court was unanimous in *De Jonge*,[143] while split five to four in *Herndon*. Why this difference if the cases raised identical doctrinal issues? Why did January's *De Jonge* unanimity dissolve into a five-to-four split by the time the Court heard Herndon's case in April? There is nothing in the record to indicate Dirk De Jonge's race (though his name suggests Dutch descent). But he was phenotypically white.[144] Justice Roberts's *Herndon* opinion, on the other hand, was replete with references to Angelo Herndon's race, and Van Devanter's dissent repeated the emphasis. The cases were identical in every respect: facts, state of the law, doctrine. There was only one apparent variable: race. Apparently, the Court's conservative bloc retained reservations about freedom to speak and assemble for Black citizens even when the context of their activism was not specifically racial.

Advocates for racial justice achieved their most salient pre–World War II victory in the field of higher education. African Americans had been chipping away at segregated education after World War I. A frontal assault on segregation in public elementary schools would have been foredoomed at the time, but higher education, particularly law schools, offered a more promising target for the NAACP because it shifted the focus to exclusion and inequality among adults.[145] Ironically, though, the first major foray of the Court into this area challenged a state effort to provide at least some modicum of higher educational opportunity for Blacks.

Few African Americans sought graduate or professional degrees in the interwar years, in part because so few had gotten undergraduate degrees. But some did, and to fend them off while preserving segregation under the separate-but-equal formula, the border states instituted out-of-state tuition programs. Under these, if an in-state HBCU[146] did not offer the desired graduate or professional program, the state offered to pay the applicant's tuition at a public university of any contiguous state that would accept him. This was a clever way of preserving segregation, sustaining the pretense of separate but equal, and ridding the state at least temporarily of dangerously ambitious and capable Black citizens. In 1936, the Maryland Court of Appeals struck down an out-of-state tuition scheme on equal protection grounds, setting a precedent for the US Supreme Court to follow.[147] (It marked Thurgood Marshall's first major victory as a civil rights attorney.)[148] In *Missouri ex rel. Gaines v. Canada* (1938),[149] the Court nipped off this segregationist bud as soon as it appeared.[150] Chief Justice Hughes, speaking for a seven-justice majority,[151] condemned the Missouri scheme. Repeating a theme from his *McCabe* opinion of a quarter century earlier, Hughes insisted that separate opportunities offered to Black citizens must be "substantially equal," and educational exile was not. The Missouri program constituted a "denial of the equality of legal right to the enjoyment of the privilege which the State has set up," and that alone condemned it.

The *Gaines* case marked the beginning of the end of segregation.[152] It was the first in a succession of decisions that brought down segregation in public schools. World War II forced a hiatus in this development, but a dozen years after the Missouri program was stricken, the Court handed down a trio of decisions ending segregation in graduate and professional education, and then struck down segregation itself four years after that in *Brown v. Board of Education*.

"Discrete and Insular Minorities": The *Carolene Products* Case

The Court's decisions affecting African Americans in the interwar period coincided with one of the most momentous changes in the Court's doctrinal orientation in its entire history. The justices abandoned *Lochner*-era jurisprudence and pivoted to judicial activism in the interests of civil liberties and civil rights. Not since the Taney-to-Chase transition during the Civil War had the Court changed course so abruptly and decisively. It discarded the paradigm of public law that had been dominant since the Gilded Age, something that various authors have labeled "classical legal thought."[153] In its place, the Court redirected its activist impulses to protecting the non-economic interests of individuals and groups hitherto marginalized in American society. There was an obvious but indirect connection between these two momentous developments. That link, and the transition itself, was announced with deceptive modesty in a case little noted at the time, *United States v. Carolene Products Co.* (1938).[154]

Carolene Products is paradoxical yet pivotal. Relatively unimportant among the blockbuster opinions of 1937–1938, it nevertheless set the Court's agenda for the remainder of the twentieth century.[155] Yet it did so in a mere footnote, in dicta that seemed on a first reading like speculative ruminations, rather than a bold proclamation of a new era in the Court's history—which is what it really was. Two of its three components heralded a new day for Black Americans. Even Justice Lewis Powell, no friend to the possibilities opened by the case, called it "the most celebrated footnote in constitutional law."[156]

The "substantive due process" decisions of the *Lochner* era struck down federal and state legislation that regulated economic activities on the grounds that such laws deprived individuals of their liberty or property without due process of law.[157] In 1937, the Supreme Court began to dismantle *Lochner*-era substantive due process. In its place, the Court announced that henceforward it would subject state and federal economic legislation to merely deferential scrutiny and would not impose the justices' own ideas of what is wise or desirable policy on legislatures.

Carolene Products rejected a substantive due process challenge to a federal statute that banned interstate shipment of a dairy product known as "filled milk."[158] Justice Stone spurned the challenge, imposing a highly deferential standard of review for "legislation affecting ordinary commercial transactions." The Court held that judges should not overturn a legislative policy determination unless they could not find that it "rests upon some rational basis within the knowledge and experience of the legislators."[159] In a later re-argument, the Court repeated that only a "clear and convincing showing that there is no rational basis for the legislation; that it is an arbitrary fiat" could serve as the basis of a judicial decision invalidating an economic regulatory statute.[160]

Justice Stone and his law clerk Louis Lusky[161] crafted *Carolene Products'* celebrated footnote 4, projecting a new role for judicial activism in the post-1937 era. Attached to the "rational basis" sentence they dropped a footnote consisting of three paragraphs.[162] The first (paragraph 1) suggested that the Court would relax its presumption that legislation is constitutional when such "legislation appears on its face to be within a specific prohibition of the Constitution, such as those of the first ten Amendments." This first component had little direct impact on cases implicating African Americans' rights. It forecast the Court's postwar role in protecting civil liberties.

Second, paragraph 2 reoriented judicial review to scrutinize "legislation which restricts those political processes which can ordinarily be expected to bring about repeal of undesirable legislation," citing the two *Nixon* white primary cases and *Herndon v. Lowry*, among others. This sent an unmistakable signal that prominent among issues affecting the purity of the democratic process (the concern of paragraph 2) would be Black disfranchisement. Third, paragraph 3 targeted "statutes directed at particular...racial minorities," again citing the *Nixon* cases. "Prejudice against discrete and insular minorities may be a special condition, which tends seriously to curtail the operation of those political processes ordinarily to be relied upon to protect minorities," and thus be subject to heightened scrutiny.

Carolene Products justified and legitimated judicial review as the Court has exercised it since 1938. The power of courts to overturn the policy judgments of democratically elected legislatures and executives has always been controversial, even before *Marbury v. Madison* (1803). Its use by the Court became far more disputed in times of intense sectional or social conflict, after *Dred Scott* and during the Depression. To be legitimate—to be accepted and respected by the American people—the justices and their defenders had to identify a set of criteria or guidelines that offered credible assurance that the judges were not simply imposing their political or ideological preferences, behaving like a third legislative chamber with veto authority. Judicial review was most vulnerable when it was seen as threatening democratic governance (as in *Dred Scott*), and contrariwise, most defensible when it strengthened democratic processes.

That was precisely the justification that *Carolene Products* provided. In its second and third paragraphs, it withdrew the judges from making overt substantive policy judgments on the merits of legislation, and instead redirected their role to clearing clogged channels of democratic information flows and legislative responsibility. Thus reconceived, judicial review reformed and thereby strengthened the democratic process.[163]

Before 1938, American democracy had excluded African Americans from its ambit, except in the brief period of Reconstruction and its rapidly dimming afterglow. To that extent, democratic government in the southern states lacked legitimacy. No one could pretend that, as to Blacks, southern state legislatures were democratic or even legitimate. But if the Court refereed the democratic process, opening self-government to Black Americans and incorporating their involvement as one part of the hodgepodge that made up legislative decision-making, the deformed governance structures of the American South might finally evolve into something authentically democratic. Anything else would continue the Herrenvolk democracy that more resembled ancient Sparta than the Lincolnian republic of the Gettysburg Address.

The Dark Past: The US Supreme Court and African Americans, 1800–2015. William M. Wiecek,
Oxford University Press. © Oxford University Press 2024. DOI: 10.1093/9780197654460.003.0005

6
War and Cold War, 1941–1953

The constitutional experiences of African Americans during World War II and the early Cold War were paradoxical. Wartime is not a propitious environment for social reform. War and international tension impede reform movements, breed hostility to minorities, and create a climate of anxiety in which advocates for social justice swim against the current. That was partially true of the 1940s, too: witness the internment of Japanese Americans, the Los Angeles "zoot suit riots" of 1943, the political annihilation of the American Left by 1955. Yet in retrospect, the constitutional advances made by Black Americans during and after World War II were momentous. The equal protection clause emerged from its *Slaughterhouse* exile and finally resumed its long-postponed development.[1] The Court unanimously embraced a robust strict-scrutiny metric for evaluating violations of that clause. The Stone and Vinson Courts energetically promoted egalitarian doctrinal developments in residential segregation, education, transportation, and access to the ballot.[2] They even began to protect the economic dimensions of the civil rights movement.[3]

This produced a remarkable though underappreciated surge of protection for the rights of African Americans between 1941 and 1953. The Court struck down racial segregation in interstate commerce and sustained state bans on discrimination in intrastate transportation. It halted judicial enforcement of racial covenants, which was at the time the most important private law means of imposing residential segregation in American cities. It finally swept away the white primary. The Court began to ensure Black access to the labor market, in part by restraining the exclusionary practices of labor unions. Most significantly, it condemned exclusion and segregation in the topmost strata of public higher education, law and graduate school. This unmistakably presaged the coming assault on segregation in public schools.[4]

The Roosevelt Court

All this came about because the justices who were attuned to the interests of African Americans in the 1930s—Stone and Hughes—were augmented by

FDR's nominees Hugo Black, Felix Frankfurter, William O. Douglas, Frank Murphy, Robert H. Jackson, and Wiley Rutledge.[5] These six displayed an openness to claims of social justice broad enough to include African Americans. After his frustrations in the 1930s with the intransigent Four Horsemen and the enigmatic Owen Roberts, FDR was determined to avoid conservative obstruction of his social and economic policies. He chose his nominees by one overriding criterion: the likelihood that they would support the policies of the New Deal. Because he was indifferent to the travails of African Americans, the president gave no thought to how his nominees might resolve questions affecting them. As a result, those nominees ranged along a wide spectrum defined by the overt racist James F. Byrnes of South Carolina at one end and the fervent opponent of racism Frank Murphy of Michigan at the other.

Franklin D. Roosevelt completely reconstituted the Supreme Court. Not since George Washington has one president been able to (re)shape the Court so thoroughly. Of the nine justices sitting in 1937, the final year of the constitutional revolution that brought an end to the *Lochner* era, only two, Stone and Owen Roberts, remained on the Court five years later. FDR's appointees expanded the momentum of the post–World War I cases that had begun to protect the rights and dignity of African Americans. All of them (except James F. Byrnes, a short-term anomaly on the Court) were open to expanding the constitutional prospects of Black Americans. Some— Frank Murphy and Wiley Rutledge—were more willing to do so than others; Frankfurter and Jackson were less so, despite their disdain for discrimination. But all of them shared an outlook much different from the one that had prevailed on the Taft and Hughes Courts.

The dynamic of the Vinson and Warren Courts was largely driven by the collaborations of three pairs of justices: William O. Douglas and Hugo Black, Felix Frankfurter and Robert H. Jackson, Frank Murphy and Wiley Rutledge. Each of these pairs influenced racially inflected cases in differing ways. The longest-lived of these partnerships was between justices Black and Douglas. Until Black's death in 1971, the two men formed the enduring liberal pole in the ideological polarity of the postwar Court, consistently siding with minorities of all sorts—ideological, racial, political, religious—in defense of individual liberty against government constraint. Though neither man was particularly stirred by systemic racial injustice, both regularly voted to support the rights of African Americans from a more generalized ideological commitment to personal freedom and an aversion to discrimination by government.

The Frankfurter-Jackson duo offset the influence of Black and Douglas. It derived much of its negative energy from the intense personal dislike of both men for Douglas. But the division transcended mere interpersonal animosity. Both Jackson and Frankfurter advocated judicial self-restraint, though Frankfurter was the more opportunistic of the two in sometimes advancing a results-driven agenda unconvincingly masked by his pretensions of judicial impartiality and objectivity. Frankfurter would pursue some particular goal, such as school desegregation, and rationalize his means of getting there as being compatible with the image of judicial objectivity projected in his vision of the ideal jurist in the common-law tradition. Jackson was more honest (or less self-deceiving) in confronting the conflict between his desire for the just outcome versus his view of the role of the judge in promoting that outcome. Together, Jackson and Frankfurter constituted the opposing pole of judicial self-restraint that offset Black-Douglas activist liberalism.

Justices Murphy and Rutledge were by far the most liberal and rights-conscious of the justices in the six years they served together on the Court. Both, but particularly Murphy, were fervent foes of racism, Murphy being the first justice to use the word "racism" in the text of a Supreme Court opinion.[6] Paired with the more generalized and less fervid liberalism of the Black/Douglas duo, the anti-racism of Murphy and Rutledge swept all before it in cases involving the rights of racial minorities after 1945. But the death of both men in the summer of 1949 drained much of the activism of the Court in racial cases, which submerged and did not reappear until the civil rights era a half-dozen years later.

The New Paradigm: Strict Scrutiny for Racial Classifications

The momentum toward racial justice that was building in the justices' thinking in the 1930s stalled for the duration of the war. The nation's energies diverted from domestic economic recovery into an unprecedented unity focused on the war against Nazi aggression and Japanese expansion. Consequently, the Court decided only two major cases affecting racial justice during the war years: *Korematsu v. United States* and *Smith v. Allwright*, both in 1944.

But in this fallow period, the justices' understanding of racial issues underwent a shift in unexamined assumptions and social context. Before mid-century, they, like other white Americans, took it as a given that Jim Crow, segregation, and the pretense of separate but equal were normal and constitutionally unobjectionable. The Court shared the assumption that the racial regime imposed by southern whites was compatible with the equal protection clause. But the wartime cases revealed that this complacent understanding of the Constitution had become passé. It was replaced by new and different ways of thinking about the Constitution and race. The constitutional equivalent of a paradigm shift was underway, though it was little noticed at the time.[7]

Korematsu v. United States (1944) foreshadowed *Brown v. Board of Education I* for its impact on racial justice. Though its result implicitly sanctioning Japanese internment was a short-term disappointment, *Korematsu* replaced the dominant paradigm for judging government actions that are based on racial classifications. It ended the regime of pretextuality and launched American public law into the modern era. *Korematsu*'s strict-scrutiny test doomed official racial discrimination, though few foresaw that possibility at the time. It set a new standard of judicial review so high that few later racial classifications survived.

West Coast whites' fear and dislike of Japanese immigrants had been building throughout the twentieth century. Anti-Asian racism based on Yellow Peril fears stoked by rising Japanese economic power[8] reinforced West Coast growers' resentment of economic competition by Japanese truck farmers. The California and Washington Alien Land Laws were the states' legal reaction,[9] but that was not enough to soothe whites' anxieties. Pearl Harbor detonated their built-up fears and produced a spasm of anti-Japanese reaction, which was shared by FDR. His Executive Order 9066, promulgated in February 1942, authorized a three-step program of curfew, exclusion, and "relocation" (the euphemism of the day for internment in concentration camps) of all persons of Japanese descent, citizens as well as aliens.[10] Congress backed up the president's executive decision with a law criminalizing refusal to obey curfew and evacuation orders.[11]

Four Japanese American citizens challenged all three components of the internment package. Two of their cases laid the groundwork for modern interpretations of the equal protection clause. *Hirabayashi v. United States* (1943)[12] sustained the first step of the internment process, curfew, but on as narrow a basis as possible. Relying on race-based generalizations that were a part of the anti-Japanese sentiment of the time ("solidarity" with the ancestral homeland, doubtful loyalty, and lack of "assimilation"), Chief Justice Stone upheld the power of military authorities to impose a curfew. But he warned that "distinctions between citizens solely because of their ancestry are by their very nature odious to a free people whose institutions are founded upon the doctrine of equality." Justice Frank Murphy agreed in a reluctant concurrence, contending that the result "goes to the very brink of constitutional power."

Stone's dictum was a prelude to the themes of *Korematsu v. United States* (1944), which created the template by which we interpret the equal protection clause today. After Fred Korematsu refused to leave an exclusion zone in San Leandro, California, he was convicted for disobeying the evacuation order and appealed to the Supreme Court. Lawyers for the federal government suppressed evidence showing that there was no basis for the War Department's claim that many of the Japanese trundled off to concentration camps were disloyal or posed a security threat. Presented with this incomplete and distorted justification for internment, the Court upheld it by a six-to-three vote. Justice Black, speaking for the majority, accepted the plea of military necessity and carefully avoided affirming detention, confining his opinion to the issue of exclusion alone. He lamely denied that the Court was permitting "imprisonment in a concentration camp solely because of his ancestry."[13] The decision was denounced almost immediately as a disaster,[14] and it has been reviled ever since as one of the Court's greatest errors. It was effectively overruled in *Trump v. Hawaii* (2018).[15] It now leads the anti-canon along with *Dred Scott* and *Plessy v. Ferguson*.

Black could not ignore the uncomfortable fact that an entire population of people were cast out of their homes and despoiled of their property, solely because of their race. Perhaps with that in mind, he announced a new basic principle of equal protection law: "all legal restrictions which curtail the civil rights of a single racial group are immediately suspect. That is not to say that all such restrictions are unconstitutional. It is to say that courts must subject them to the most rigid scrutiny. Pressing public necessity may sometimes justify the existence of such restrictions; racial antagonism never can." In that momentous passage, the Court for the first time devised the scrutiny-level test that has since dominated interpretation of the equal protection clause: courts must subject challenges to government actions to one of two (later, three) levels of scrutiny, strict or deferential. All racial classifications must undergo strict scrutiny of "the most rigid" degree. But, as Black later insisted, sometimes (though rarely) a racial classification can survive even that stern test.

Justices Jackson, Roberts, and Murphy dissented, and their disagreements with the majority reinforced Black's "most rigid scrutiny" dictum. Murphy condemned the decision outright: Japanese exclusion "exclusion goes over 'the very brink of constitutional power' and falls into the ugly abyss of racism." In Murphy's eyes the decision amounted to a "legalization of racism." "Racial discrimination in any form and in any degree has no justifiable part whatever in our democratic way of life."[16] Not since the first Harlan had a justice of the US Supreme Court spoken in such blunt terms on racial issues. And yet, strangely, it remains one of the few times that the word "racism" appears in an opinion of any justice.[17] Seventy years later, only about thirty times has a justice in an opinion referred by name to one of the most conspicuous features of American society. It is as if the Court has been unable to bring itself to admit that racism permeates the nation. Frank Murphy was one of the few justices willing to confront racism and call it out forthrightly.

In dissent, Justice Jackson lamented that the "Court for all time has validated the principle of racial discrimination in criminal procedure." He went on: "Every repetition imbeds that principle more deeply in our law and thinking and expands it to new purposes." It "becomes the doctrine of the Constitution. There it has a generative power of its own, and all that it creates will be in its own image."[18] But Jackson proved to be prophetic in a way that he did not anticipate: strict scrutiny has indeed become the doctrine of the Constitution.

This was borne out almost immediately in other cases involving Japanese Americans. After the war, Japanese Americans continued to serve as bellwethers for advancing the rights of their Black fellow citizens. Throughout the twentieth century, Japanese had been the targets of discriminatory legislation by West Coast whites. In the World War I era, California and some ten other states first enacted Alien Land Laws, statutes that prohibited landownership by "aliens ineligible to citizenship," a category that included only Japanese, and then closed loopholes by which affected landowners were able to evade the strictures of the ban.[19] As white Americans slowly began to recover from their spasms of wartime prejudice that produced internment, judges were able to view such overt anti-Japanese discrimination in a broader perspective. In *Oyama v. California* (1948),[20] the Court struck down the later California act by relying on the equal protection clause and the holdings of *Korematsu*. Chief Justice Fred Vinson's majority opinion held that the discriminatory effect of voiding the transfer of real property to a minor based on a racial classification constituted discrimination prohibited by the equal protection clause. Murphy in a concurrence denounced the Alien Land Laws as "racism in one of its most malignant forms" and an affront to "the dignity of each individual." The California Supreme Court then followed in a mopping-up operation by striking down the original statutes themselves on equal protection grounds.[21] In that same year the Court in *Takahashi v. Fish and Game Commission* relied on the clause to overturn a related California statute that denied commercial fishing licenses to aliens ineligible for citizenship, that is, Japanese.[22] Justice Black condemned the measure because it relied on racial grounds to deny an opportunity to seek employment. This suggested a potential substantive interpretation of the equal protection clause. *Oyama* and *Takahashi* marked the formal debut of the clause as the revived source of protection for African Americans' rights.

The Near Death of Reconstruction-Era Civil Rights Legislation

At war's end, the Court resumed the trajectory of its decisions that had begun to protect the constitutional liberties of African Americans in the 1930s. But it promptly ran into a stumbling block that almost derailed the entire project: the case of *Screws v. United States* (1945).[23] *Screws* impaled the justices on the horns of a logical dilemma and exposed their shallow understanding of the history of Reconstruction, which was freighted with unacknowledged racial stereotypes and Lost Cause clichés. It nearly destroyed two major components of Reconstruction-era legislation. Only tactical maneuvering by Justice Rutledge avoided a disaster.

In 1870, Congress had supplemented the Fourteenth Amendment with a legislative program that went as far as constitutional understandings of the era would permit in implementing its section 5 empowerment of Congress to enforce the substantive guarantees. Two provisions of that enforcement regime were challenged in *Screws*: section 2 of the 1866 Civil Rights Act, which made it a federal felony to deprive any person of "rights... secured or protected by the Constitution" "under color of any [state] law, statute, ordinance, regulation, or custom"; and section 6 of the 1870 Enforcement Act, which criminalized conspiracies to deprive any person of rights guaranteed by the federal Constitution.²⁴

These provisions came before the Court in a federal prosecution of a Georgia sheriff for beating to death an African American man in his custody. The state declined to prosecute for homicide, so it was left to the US Department of Justice to undertake prosecution. The prosecution confronted a logical dilemma: if Screws was to be prosecuted under 18 U.S.C. sec. 242, the modern descendant of section 2 of the 1866 Civil Rights Act, it would have to be for an act done under color of state law. But by definition, if Screws was to be convicted of an action that consisted of murdering the victim, it had to be in violation of a state law prohibiting homicide and could not logically be "under color" of that law. This conundrum provided grounds for Justices Frankfurter and Jackson to vent their distaste for Reconstruction policy.

Justices like Frankfurter and Jackson were captives of the then-dominant white narrative of Reconstruction, derived from Lost Cause mythmaking. In this understanding, Reconstruction-era legislation securing the rights of the freedpeople was hasty, ill-advised, and vindictive.²⁵ The Black beneficiaries themselves were not prepared for freedom, much less full civic participation as voters and office holders. The violence of Redemption was perhaps regrettable but was a necessary expedient to put the top rail back on top, to return competence and stability to state and local government. Any federal interference with this wise restoration threatened to derange the federal system and deprive the white people of the South of self-government in a foolish effort to confer political capacity on a people not ready or even fit for it. Trapped in those assumptions, the nation and its highest Court left the 1866 Civil Rights Act and the Thirteenth Amendment itself to molder for seventy years.

Though Frankfurter shared to some extent the social biases and stereotypes held by white elites of his time, he was offended by racial discrimination. He deplored racism for its effect on its victims and he shared liberal ideals of toleration, social harmony, and equal opportunity. But his personal disdain for racism and discrimination ran up against his dedication to judicial self-restraint and deference to legislative judgment. He resolved the conflict between these commitments opportunistically and with little regard for consistency. Thus, he promoted desegregation of public schools and condemned overt racial disfranchisement, while resisting appeals for judicial intervention in anti-miscegenation laws and malapportionment.²⁶

In *Screws*, his historical myopia nearly led to disaster. Like Frankfurter, the justice with whom he was most closely aligned, Jackson's disdain for racial discrimination was effectively offset by his commitment to judicial restraint. In tandem, they functioned like a sea anchor to the Court in cases involving civil rights issues: they provided stability but at the cost of slowing progress.

It was the second difficulty in the case that fractured the liberal wing of the Court. The applicable statutory language was broad to the point of vagueness: "injure, oppress, threaten, or intimidate" anyone in the "free exercise or enjoyment of any right" protected by the federal Constitution. The generality of this phrasing set up a potential conflict between protecting civil *rights* of Black victims and respecting the civil *liberties* of the white perpetrator, that is, the right not to be prosecuted under a statute that was too vague to provide a clear guide to behavior or that was so broad that it could take on concrete meaning only as an ex post facto law. The statute might have been too vague to clearly identify the prohibited action, and thus would be held void for vagueness. Defining that action subsequently through criminal prosecution could in effect be criminalizing something that was not illegal at the time it was performed and thus fall afoul of the ex post facto bar in Article I, section 9. If this thinking seems strained to us, it did not appear so to the fastidious Frankfurter and the scrupulous Jackson, both in their own ways dedicated civil libertarians.

These complications fragmented the Court. Douglas for the plurality cut the Gordian knot of the logical conundrum by holding that the sheriff was acting in his capacity as a state officer at the time he committed the murder. He narrowed the section 242 ancestral provision by construing the statue to require that the defendant have "a specific intent to deprive a person of a federal right made definite by decision or other rule of law." Mere homicidal intent would not suffice. This posed an impossibly high standard of scienter and criminal intent.[27] It was sharply criticized at the time for potentially weakening civil rights enforcement.[28]

Rutledge voted tactically, against his true convictions, to remand the case for retrial to conform to Douglas's new standard of willfulness and intent. He would have preferred to join Murphy's simpler conclusion that Screws the sheriff deprived the victim of his life, a right explicitly secured by the due process clause. But that would have left the case unresolved. Better to join the Douglas plurality to remand for retrial with the faint hope (which predictably was disappointed by a white Georgia jury) that a conviction might be secured under the tighter standard. Rutledge and Murphy were determined to avoid at all costs the Frankfurter/Jackson dissenting position, which condemned section 242 as a "shapeless...statute [that] can serve as a dangerous instrument of political intimidation and coercion." In Frankfurter's abstract and formalistic world, apparently the true danger to liberty was coercion and intimidation of white people. But section 242 survived through Douglas's casuistry and Rutledge's artful maneuvering to enable federal prosecutions in the future for police violations of African Americans' liberties.[29]

Residential Segregation

Residential racial segregation has been the matrix of all social ills afflicting people of color in the United States.[30] It shut them out from the benefits of the good life that poured out of the cornucopia of economic growth after World War II: housing, food, education, healthcare, employment, transportation, wealth accumulation. Neighborhoods segregated by race and poverty provide poor public schools, joblessness, inadequate medical services, food deserts, drugs, crime and routine violence, restricted access to social capital. All this flows from racial segregation and discrimination in access to shelter. Segregated housing enables whites to monopolize the benefits of privilege, with all the blessings that derive from safe neighborhoods, while excluding African Americans. Urban ghettoes confine their residents, making escape difficult, while restricted white neighborhoods deny them a place to escape to. The web of oppression bound all forms of racial inequality into a mutually supportive, interlocking system of racial disparities in housing, education, healthcare, employment, and residential security, where each disparity reinforced all the others.[31] Residential segregation is the foundation of structural racism in modern American life.

Racial segregation was created by law, by legal stratagems and legal processes.[32] It did not "just happen" by chance, nor did it "reflect voluntary housing choices or other private decisions," notwithstanding Justice Clarence Thomas's imaginings.[33] People did not spontaneously and voluntarily sort themselves out in racially exclusive patterns. Because it was enabled and protected by law, segregation's constitutional dimensions inevitably came before the Supreme Court.

Segregation by law developed through four overlapping phases that constituted whites' response to the Great Migration:[34]

Phase 1: from *about* 1890 to 1925, municipal governments imposed neighborhood residential segregation by positive law, that is, by ordinances. In top-down lawmaking, a legislative body adopts commands and imposes them on the polity. These segregation ordinances derived from the Progressive innovation of zoning, which provided a legislative petri dish for legal experimentation seeking an effective way of confining African Americans to urban ghettoes.[35]

Phase 2: then from about 1920 to 1970, after segregation by positive law was nullified by *Buchanan*, segregation was imposed by voluntary cooperation among sellers and buyers of real property and their neighbors, abetted by real estate brokers, lawyers, and lenders. This was achieved by racial covenants. In this half century, white residents supplemented legal action with violence directed at Black newcomers to their neighborhoods. The federal government demanded racial covenants for loans that it insured.

Phase 3: from 1934 through about 1970, the federal government, acting through newly created housing agencies, forced segregation on cities. Again, this was top-down, but the mandates were imposed by administrative agencies, not legislatures. Once established, such racial sorting persisted even after active federal involvement ceased. In the postwar period, federal segregation was complemented by an aggressive program of displacing African Americans from their neighborhoods through highway construction and what was called urban renewal.

Phase 4: from about 1960 to the present, local suburban governments segregated their jurisdictions by exclusionary zoning. Suburban municipalities discovered that they could achieve segregationist goals by non-facially discriminatory means such as banning mobile homes and multifamily dwellings, and by mandating large lot sizes or generous setbacks. Unlike the previous phases, this form of segregation was nominally neutral: it did not refer to race at all, and in most instances did not even refer to people. Segregation became a matter of class, not geography. It realized zoning's implicit potential for segregation by the simple expedient of mandating more expensive kinds of housing. Based on the assumption that keeping poor people out would keep people of color out as well, exclusionary zoning merged race and class to form caste.

Around the turn of the twentieth century, border state cities attempted to impose segregation explicitly and directly by positive law. They were thwarted by the US Supreme Court's ambiguous holding in *Buchanan v. Warley* (1917)[36] that such ordinances violated the due process clause of the Fourteenth Amendment by interfering with the rights of property owners to dispose of their property as they wished. But Justice William Day also claimed that the equal protection clause and the Civil Rights Act of 1866 protected the "fundamental rights" of all people to acquire property. This ruling seemed to hint that the Court might be open to protecting the rights of African Americans in some meaningful way. Segregation ordinances did not disappear overnight because of *Buchanan*, but the Court consistently swatted them down.[37]

At the same time, would-be segregationists also resorted to illegal violence to supplement more acceptable ways of excluding people of color. Whites reacted violently to what they saw as Black "infiltration" after World War I. "Race riots"—in reality, white pogroms waged against Black newcomers—broke out throughout the North. Western cities proclaimed themselves "sundown towns," warning away any African Americans who might be foolhardy enough to remain after dark.[38] Nighttime vandalism and cross-burnings terrorized newly arrived migrants of color.[39]

Supplementing such urban, northern, middle-class nightriding, the National Association of Real Estate Boards[40] (a realtors' trade-industry group, the predecessor of the current National Association of Realtors), its local affiliates, homeowners' associations, and neighborhood improvement groups enthusiastically turned to voluntarism among white homeowners in place of compulsion by local government as a way to exclude African Americans from white neighborhoods. Their most effective weapon was the restrictive covenant. If ordinances could not be used for racist public land-use planning, perhaps private land-use controls like covenants might work better.[41] In contrast to segregation ordinances, imposed by positive law, the racial covenant depended for its effect on the voluntary acts of private individuals, enforced if need be by the coercive power of the state through its courts.

A racial covenant is an agreement between a seller and a buyer of residential property that the buyer would not sell or lease the property to a member of specified racial, religious, or ethnic groups. It was usually incorporated into the deed, which is recorded and thus is a matter of public record. But enforcement of the covenant proved problematic. If the buyer later chose to renege and convey to a member of the prohibited race, who could seek to enforce the covenant? Should the covenant be enforceable at all, as a matter of public policy? The common law traditionally frowned on what were called restraints on alienation, which clogged the real estate market and invited litigation. Would the due process or equal protection clauses pose a problem?

Racially restrictive covenants originally appeared in the late nineteenth century in the western states as a means of excluding Chinese and Japanese people. At first, racial covenants met a hostile reception in federal and state courts,[42] but after the Great War, state courts warmed to them[43] and they proliferated.[44] The NAACP became alarmed when it saw its *Buchanan* victory slipping through its fingers by this shift from public to private discrimination, and challenged them, only to meet with a discouraging defeat in the High Court.

A claque of white Washington, DC, homeowners agreed among themselves that they would not sell or lease their properties to "any person of the negro race or blood." District of Columbia courts spurned the claim that such a covenant violated the due process clause of the Fifth Amendment and the 1866 Civil Rights Act.[45] On appeal to the US Supreme Court, in *Corrigan v. Buckley* (1926)[46] Justice Edward Sanford brusquely dismissed the suit because it presented questions "so unsubstantial as to be plainly without color of merit and frivolous." He explained that the Fifth Amendment, like the Fourteenth, was a limitation only on government, not on individual behavior. He further held that the 1866 Civil Rights Act did not inhibit actions of private individuals when contracting for the use and transfer of their property. The fact that a potential African American buyer might have a right did not impose a corresponding duty or constraint on a reluctant seller. Construed in this way, the contractual liberty affirmed in the 1866 Civil Rights Act might become an empty or notional right, existing in theory but meaningless in practice.

For the time being, private arrangements imposing racial discrimination, like racial covenants or segregated hotels, remained legitimate. The first *Restatement of Property* (1944), bearing the imprimatur of the prestigious American Law Institute, spoke for the (white) American bar in endorsing racial covenants as a means of "avoidance of unpleasant racial and social relations and stabilization of the value of the land."[47]

The role of the state was not yet as apparent as it would become a quarter century later after public understanding of the social context of discrimination evolved. Until this shift occurred, the Court could operate within the public/private paradigm, untroubled by the state's non-apparent impact on private racial behavior, unchallenged because unseen. An understanding of public law current at the time drew a line between the realm of private relationships, where individuals dealt with each other without interference by the state, and the public realm, governed by the constitutional order, where considerations of public policy could more freely limit individual liberty. In the private realm, individual agents like property owners were free to act without the restraints imposed by consequentialist considerations of their impact on others. To the extent that there was any moral constraint at all on individual or group behavior, it lay outside the reach of law, even to those jurists like Hughes or Stone who accepted African Americans as fully rights-bearing civic equals to whites.

Later, after the doctrinal barrier between the public and private realms became destabilized, judges became open to imagining a truly (as opposed to a pretextually) egalitarian society. That time had not yet come in the 1920s, but the Depression and the New Deal undermined the assumptions about the social order that produced the *Corrigan* outcome. In that changed climate, African Americans were able to assert claims to First Amendment freedoms and access to equal opportunities that would have been unthinkable in the previous decade. In a mere two decades, *Corrigan v. Buckley* became a bit of jetsam in a social order in flux.

Meanwhile, restrictive covenants got a further boost when federal agencies began imposing a national policy of underwriting urban housing for whites and excluding Blacks from its benefits and from white neighborhoods generally.[48] This third wave of segregation by law laid the foundations for the structural racism of the present. Once the federal government mandated segregation, and neighborhood residential patterns gelled accordingly, the overt role of federal agencies could recede, and segregation would continue autonomously, its deliberate origins forgotten, hidden, or ignored.

The Home Owners Loan Corporation (HOLC), founded in 1933 and thus one of the earliest New Deal agencies, played an important role in protecting widespread homeownership in the wake of foreclosures following the crash of 1929 by refinancing existing mortgages.[49] The HOLC prepared "Residential Security Maps" with accompanying neighborhood descriptions.

These identified and color-coded urban neighborhoods, downgrading those "infiltrated" or "invaded" by "undesirable elements," meaning "the colored element." The Federal Housing Administration (FHA), formed in 1934, insured mortgages. It also popularized the long-term self-amortizing mortgage. This resulted in a transformation in the forms and financing of homeownership, but the benefits of that change accrued only to white American homebuyers.[50] Ninety-eight percent of FHA-insured mortgages went to white mortgagors. The FHA adopted HOLC's appraisal methods, including its maps, as did all the banks under the supervision of the Federal Home Loan Bank Board. The FHA implemented the segregation program in its *Underwriting Manuals* published throughout the 1930s that promoted a model racial covenant, urged explicitly racial zoning, and either refused to insure properties that were not segregated or offered to insure them only at exorbitant rates. The FHA disguised its proactive leadership role of promoting racial covenants and deflected blame for its policies on the supposedly private housing market. It "accepted the ghettoization of African Americans as the cost of insuring the American dream for white citizens."[51] The Veterans Administration, founded in 1944, adopted programs and methods similar to HOLC's and the FHA's. By refusing to extend insurance benefits to Black homeowners, these agencies denied African Americans access to the housing credit market, and by endorsing racial covenants, it provided an even more explicit means of excluding them.

After World War II, the federal program of promoting segregation through restrictive covenants came under attack. California Supreme Court justice Roger Traynor[52] condemned racial covenants as incompatible with public policy.[53] He was seconded by legal academics who identified enforcement of such covenants as state action and thus actionable under the equal protection clause.[54] Thus when the Supreme Court in 1948 held such covenants unenforceable, it was in a sense returning to the original turn-of-the-century understanding that such covenants offended constitutional securities for liberty and equality.

In *Shelley v. Kraemer* (1948),[55] Chief Justice Vinson, writing for a unanimous Court, held that restrictive covenants could not be enforced by state courts in Missouri and Michigan.[56] He opened with a concession that racial covenants were not per se violative of either Constitution or statute, as long as the parties to the covenant voluntarily complied. This proved to be a tactical error. It may have encouraged transactional attorneys to continue using racial covenants in real estate transfers. Racial covenants continued to proliferate in post-1948 deeds and only gradually dwindled.[57] Even if technically unenforceable in state courts, racial covenants could still deter laypeople who did not know any better from selling to a member of the proscribed race or ethnicity. It was in a legal document, witnessed, with an imposing gold seal bearing a notary's impress. It may have *seemed* legally effective from appearances, and that would be enough.

But Vinson went on to hold that when state courts enforced those covenants against a recalcitrant party, state action was implicated. The courts were themselves state actors enforcing policies permitted, legitimated, or mandated by the common law of the states. "The action of state courts and judicial officers in their official capacities must be regarded as action of the State...supported by the full panoply of state power." The states "have made available to such individuals the full coercive power of government."[58]

Vinson insisted that the authority of the state could not be used to deny African Americans access to property as ensured by the 1866 Civil Rights Act. He maintained that "primary concern" of the framers of the Fourteenth Amendment was "the establishment of equality in the enjoyment of basic civil and political rights and the preservation of those rights from discriminatory action on the part of the States based on considerations of race or color."[59] Though that reads like a bland truism today, in its time such a statement was almost inflammatory. Vinson also brushed aside the faux-parity argument that whites were potentially discomfited by racial covenants as well as Blacks. In a memorable aphorism, he drily noted that "Equal protection of the laws is not achieved through indiscriminate imposition of inequalities."[60]

An alternative rationale, not considered by the Court, also sustains *Shelley*'s holding.[61] Acting under the authority of section 2 of the Thirteenth Amendment[62] (not under the Fourteenth Amendment, which had not yet been ratified), Congress enacted the Civil Rights Act of 1866, with its section 1 guarantees of a right to contract and to own property. The Thirteenth Amendment, as the Court conceded in the *Civil Rights Cases* (1883), applies directly to the actions of individuals and does not need to satisfy the state action requirement, which was potentially the Achilles heel of *Shelley*. Both the law of slavery and some of the 1865–1866 Black Codes prohibited enslaved and freed people from owning real property. Thus, the racial covenant could have been held illegitimate and unenforceable under the 1866 Civil Rights Act as one of the badges and incidents of slavery proscribed implicitly by the amendment and explicitly by the statute.

In a companion case, *Hurd v. Hodge* (1948),[63] Vinson held that federal courts could not enforce racial covenants either. (*Shelley* had applied only to state courts.) State action was not at issue here: if racial segregation was to be enforced in the District of Columbia, the setting of *Hurd*, it would have to be by federal authority. But that was precluded, Vinson held, by the Civil Rights Act of 1866 and because racial covenants violated the "public policy of the United States."[64] Segregationists nevertheless doggedly resisted the *Shelley/Hurd* outcomes and tried to get around them by stipulating for damages for violation of a racial covenant,[65] but the Court batted away that attempt in 1953, holding in *Barrows v. Jackson* that damages suits were also unenforceable in federal courts.[66] *Shelley* and *Hurd* were suits in equity; *Barrows* was a suit at law, and thus stopped up an important loophole that might have permitted enforcement of racial covenants.

Despite the significance of *Shelley*, Vinson gets little credit for it. He suffers from a pervasive but undeserved perception that he was a mediocre jurist and an ineffectual leader of the Court.[67] In part this was because he presided over a fractious bench of contentious rivals (Black, Douglas, Frankfurter, Jackson, two of them disappointed in their ambitions for his job);[68] in part because by temperament he was easygoing, affable, and tolerant of divergent views; and in part because of Frankfurter's scorn for his pragmatic, non-ideological approach to judging, which was amplified and disseminated by Frankfurter's acolytes. Though dismissed as inconsequential, if not downright hostile to civil rights causes,[69] Vinson was in fact the author of several of the most significant opinions of the postwar years, all of them advancing the cause of African Americans' rights, including those involving discrimination in housing and higher education. He was not in the avant-garde of racial thinking in the 1940s and 1950s. But his fundamental decency and New Deal–inflected liberalism pointed him inerrantly in the right direction on racial causes. That is more than can be said of later justices who enjoy a more favorable reputation than he.

Vinson's opinion in *Shelley v. Kraemer* has been the butt of ceaseless criticism since it was handed down. Eminent academic commentators, among them Herbert Wechsler, Louis Henkin, and Laurence Tribe, have lambasted its reasoning.[70] Justice Antonin Scalia later sneered at its weakened authority: "any argument driven to reliance upon an extension of that volatile case is obviously in serious trouble."[71] But such criticisms fail to appreciate the merits of Vinson's neorealist reasoning.[72]

The state action doctrine as originally announced in the 1883 *Civil Rights Cases* requires that before federal judicial authority is invoked to suppress a discriminatory act, the party invoking it must show that the state by its personnel or its subdivisions, like cities or school boards, was somehow involved in that act. So the issue raised by *Shelley* is whether the state was involved in making a racial covenant possible or giving it effect. Stated that way, the answer becomes obvious. The state and the force of its authority are present in three ways. First, the state has provided a body of law, statutory and common, that created the property regime in the first place. That regime includes such things as real covenants and equitable servitudes that run with the land. Without that body of substantive law, property relations and restrictions would be impossible. A racial covenant can exist and work only if the state's law authorizes and enforces it.

Second, the state is twice involved in enforcing a racial covenant against a recalcitrant party. Its courts construe the meaning of the covenant and then issue a decree or order that imposes that meaning on the parties. Then if one of the parties refuses to comply, the state's law enforcement agencies deploy the force of the state to compel that compliance. This is just what occurred in Shelley's companion case from Michigan, *McGhee v. Sipes*. The trial court issued an order commanding the McGhees, an African American couple, to vacate the home they had bought within ninety days. Had they refused to do so, Detroit police would have come by to eject them forcibly, and the court could have punished their resistance by a finding of contempt. When a state judge and a city police officer combine to compel someone to do something, how can it be said that the state is not involved? If neither court nor law enforcement played their roles, the covenant would have no effect. It would have merely been what is known in legal terms as precatory.[73] Without such state intervention, the "private" discrimination would have no power.

Third, Vinson and his colleagues were confronted with a choice that they could not evade once they accepted jurisdiction of the case. If they found for the respondents (the parties seeking to enforce the covenant), they would be privileging a private preference to discriminate, a desire to perform a hate-driven and hate-expressive action that would harm the petitioners. But if the Court found for petitioners instead, they would be protecting a personal liberty that Congress in the 1866 Civil Rights Act had determined was essential for the civic status constitutive of civil society, the power to acquire property, at the trivial cost of denying respondents an opportunity to express their bigotry.

Justice Harold H. Burton identified the larger consequence at stake in this litigation over covenants. In a note to Vinson, he predicted that *Shelley* would be "a major contribution to the vitality of the 14th Amendment, the Civil Rights Act, the general subject of interracial justice and the strength of the Court as the 'living voice of the Constitution.'"[74]

The Ballot

The long struggle to enfranchise African Americans, enabling their full participation in the self-governance mandated by a republican form of government, foundered on the shoals of pretextuality and state action in 1935 when the Court in *Grovey v. Townsend* acquiesced in the Texas white primary because it was the Democratic Party, not the state, that excluded voters.[75] Exclusionary white political domination in the South hung on a while longer because of a conceptual dilemma. Under the First Amendment, individuals have a constitutionally protected right to advocate political ideas like white supremacy and perhaps also some kinds of political exclusion, and they have a derivative right to band together to do so. But somewhere a line must be drawn between a group of like-minded people advocating a political cause like white supremacy (constitutionally protected), and an entire political party in a one-party state like Texas excluding African Americans (constitutionally suspect). Where to draw that line on a principled basis gave some of the justices pause for a decade. The difficulty arose because any concession to the First Amendment associational rights of segregationists threatened the 1930s cases that had begun dismantling the white primary.

This impasse could not last. *Carolene Products'* footnote 4 had promised "more exacting judicial scrutiny" for "legislation which restricts those political processes which can ordinarily be expected to bring about repeal of undesirable legislation," and had suggested that "prejudice against discrete and insular minorities may be a special condition, which tends seriously to curtail the operation of those political processes ordinarily to be relied upon to protect minorities." As if to underscore the relevance of those observations for the 1940s, in *Carolene Products* Stone cited the pre-*Grovey* white primary cases for both those propositions.[76]

The solution to the dilemma came from an unexpected quarter, Article I of the Constitution, rather than the First, Fourteenth, or Fifteenth Amendment. The framers of the original Constitution had given Congress power to regulate "the Times, Places and Manner of holding Elections" for Congress, and Reconstruction-era legislation (the 1866 Civil Rights Act and the 1870 Enforcement Act) might be construed as having done so. When Louisiana ballot commissioners tampered with primary ballots in 1940 to discount Black voters' influence, the Court held in *United States v. Classic* (1941) that the Reconstruction-era statutes reached primaries as "a step in the exercise by the people in their choice of representatives in Congress."[77] *Classic* indicated that the Court was now thinking of the place of minorities in society in distinctly racial terms.[78] (Ironically, though, neither majority nor dissent adverted to the fact that the criminal activity in the case was directed at the ballots of Black voters.) By indirection, the Court was mounting a final assault on the white primary and Black disfranchisement.

The citadel finally fell in *Smith v. Allwright* (1944).[79] Building on the obvious fact that in the one-party South, primary elections determined the final outcome and thus were an integral part of the states' electoral machinery, the Court concluded that Texas had cast "its electoral processes in a form which permits a private organization to practice racial discrimination in the election." The Democratic Party had become a "state agency" by performing the public function of regulating elections. The Court's Article I rationale in *Classic* for the role of primaries transferred readily to the Fourteenth and Fifteenth Amendments, and thereby doomed the white primary. *Grovey v. Townsend* was unceremoniously overruled.

In *Schnell v. Davis* (1949),[80] the Court per curiam upheld a lower-court decision that invalidated an amendment to the Alabama Constitution that had been adopted to evade the holding of *Smith v. Allwright*. It required voters to explain a provision of the federal Constitution. Sponsors of the measure had boasted that its purpose was "to make the Democratic Party in Alabama the 'White Man's Party'" to "continue to fight for white supremacy in our State."[81] The trial court merely affirmed the obvious: "while it is true that there is no mention of race or color in the Boswell Amendment, this does not save it." Facial neutrality could no longer be relied on to save a discriminatory law. Jim Crow pretextuality was near death.

But diehard Texas white supremacists and their supporters refused to give up. A local subset of the Democratic Party, the Jaybird Political Association, organized a whites-only pre-primary election in Fort Bend County.

The victors in that election then went on to win the primary and then the general. This presented the First Amendment dilemma in unavoidable form: the Jaybirds claimed to be a private group, no different from the Rotary or a garden club, who simply believed in white dominance and acted together to promote it by recommending candidates for office. In *Terry v. Adams* (1953),[82] a deeply divided Court[83] relied on the public-function rationale and extended it to "any election in which public issues are decided or public officials selected," which begged the question as far as the Jaybirds were concerned. But the white primary was at last formally and finally slain. Racial disfranchisement hung on, largely as a matter of norms, practice, and the threat of terror, but one major prop of white political supremacy had been removed.

No one foresaw it at the time, but a minor player in the Jaybird drama stepped briefly onto the stage to which he would later return in a starring role. One of Justice Jackson's law clerks, William H. Rehnquist, advised his boss that "I take a dim view of this pathological search for discrimination.... it is about time the Court faced the fact that the white people on [sic] the South don't like the colored people." The Constitution "most assuredly [sic again] did not appoint the Court as a sociological watchdog to rear up every time private discrimination raises its admittedly ugly head." A ruling against the Jaybirds would threaten "freedom of association and majority rule."[84] Jackson, divided within himself on the issue, nevertheless ignored his clerk's hectoring and concurred in the holding. Rehnquist's actions at the time provided a preview of the role he would later play in cases implicating racial discrimination.

Direct disfranchisement schemes did not exhaust the repertoire of those who would deny African Americans participation in civic life. Indirect methods like redistricting and reapportionment could also reduce, if not eliminate, Black political power. The Court encountered both shortly after the war. In *Colegrove v. Green* (1946),[85] the justices by a narrow plurality[86] rejected a challenge to the malapportionment of Illinois congressional districts. Frankfurter insisted that federal courts had no power to resolve political controversies like those presented by widely divergent populations in political districts. Both he and the dissenting and concurring justices ignored the reality that the rural-urban split prevalent at the time in many states, especially in the South, masked a racial disadvantage: the outsize political power of rural white districts suppressed the political influence of African American city dwellers. Frankfurter insisted that all "political questions," including apportionment, were non-justiciable. For the time being, until overturned in 1962 by *Baker v. Carr*,[87] Frankfurter's ambiguous generalizations shunted Black challenges to apportionment schemes to white state legislatures, which complacently smothered them.

The result was repeated in *South v. Peters*, a 1950 challenge to Georgia's "county unit" voting system where rural counties were given disproportionate numerical weight compared to urban and "town" counties, assuring that the white outstate areas of Georgia maintained control of the state's politics.[88] The Court's majority saw nothing wrong with this apportionment of political power. Black and Douglas dissented and placed the racial issue center stage. Georgia's unique voting structure created "a system of discrimination in primary voting...by a device as deeply rooted in discrimination as the practice which keeps a man from the voting booth because of his race, creed, or color." For the moment, only they perceived the feint, but the structure of racial disfranchisement under the Mississippi Plan was beginning to disintegrate.

Interstate Travel

Segregation's weakening constitutional hold appeared in a quartet of 1940s cases that involved interstate travel.[89] Civilian and military wartime traffic had alerted Americans to the importance of travel among the states on public transportation while exposing African American passengers to the discomforts and petty annoyances of Jim Crow seating and all the other inconveniences of racial discrimination in travel.[90] But by 1950, interstate Jim Crow transportation was in tatters, though segregation in local transportation persisted a few years longer, until Rosa Parks brought it down as well after 1955.

Segregation in bus, rail, and water traffic was constitutionally vulnerable on two grounds: the equal protection clause and the commerce clause. The Court first explored the equal protection approach in a 1941 decision, *Mitchell v. United States*,[91] construing the Interstate Commerce Act of 1887[92] to forbid private (as opposed to state-mandated) denial of access to accommodations in all modes of travel. The statute made it illegal for common carriers "to subject any particular person...to any undue or unreasonable prejudice or disadvantage in any respect whatsoever." The Court held that this statute guaranteed "a fundamental right to equality of treatment."

Railroads could no longer deny African American passengers access to luxury services like dining cars. This ruling did not challenge racial segregation as such, but it did align statutory construction (the Interstate Commerce Act) with the Court's earlier constitutional holding in *McCabe v. Atchison, Topeka & Santa Fe Railway* (1914), which had struck down a state statute that permitted carriers to deny Pullman accommodations to African Americans if low demand did not justify the expense.

The equality principle now began to influence the Court's interpretation of Congress's handiwork, a result even more remarkable for the fact that under no plausible reading of legislative intent could the 1887 Congress have been thought to intend to ban racial discrimination in travel. The result in *Mitchell* would have been inevitable whatever the Court's rationale, though, since the appellant, Rep. Arthur Mitchell, was an African American congressman from Illinois traveling on official business. Even in 1941, it would have been unthinkable for the justices to accept the degradation of Arkansas's Jim Crow customs discomfiting a member of Congress.

After the war, the Court returned to the issue of racial discrimination in interstate travel as a problem of equal protection in *Henderson v. United States* (1950).[93] The Interstate Commerce Commission authorized a railroad to set aside a portion of the dining car by a "Colored" partition for the use of Black passengers. A federal district court upheld the Commission's rulings.[94] When a federal employee, Elmer Henderson, challenged this practice before the Supreme Court, the US Justice Department faced a momentous decision. If it defended the ICC's actions, the federal government would endorse *Plessy* and Jim Crow for the modern era. Instead, Solicitor General Philip Perlman chose to confess error, a procedure whereby the federal government argues that the decision of the lower court was erroneous.[95] For the first time, the US government had attacked *Plessy* head-on, with no equivocation. "Separate but equal is a plain contradiction in terms," the government's brief contended, "intended to signify [African American] inequality."[96] Perlman argued that Justice Harlan's dissent in *Plessy* expressed the correct interpretation of the equal protection clause. The justices were not prepared to go that far, though. Justice Harold Burton, writing for a unanimous Court, evaded the constitutional issue. Rather, he merely reaffirmed *Mitchell*'s construction of the Interstate Commerce Act to ban discrimination in interstate rail service. The Court hovered, uncertainly, on the brink of holding that segregation violated the Constitution, but in 1950, it was not yet ready to take the leap.

When the Court found an opportunity to invalidate segregation on constitutional grounds that did not raise issues of racial equal protection, it readily did so. A constitutional doctrine known as the "dormant commerce clause"[97] holds that the commerce clause of Article I, section 8 not only authorizes Congress to regulate international, interstate, and Indian commerce but also contains an implied restraint on state regulations that burden such commerce. The Marshall Court announced the existence of such a constraint as early as 1829.[98] The Taney Court recognized a distinction between subjects of regulation that are national and require a uniform rule versus other subjects that are innately local, "imperatively demanding that diversity which alone can meet the local necessities."[99] Under the doctrinal understanding that has evolved from these distinctions, states may exercise their police power over transportation, but not in ways that interfere with or burden interstate commerce, or that discriminate against out-of-state trade. There is no clear, universal, objective criterion that determines what constitutes such a burden or instructs judges where to draw the line. So the Court's interpretations of the dormant commerce clause oscillate between conflicting considerations of national interests as against state policymaking authority. This oscillation is seen in two pairs of cases that demonstrate the pliability of the doctrine as the Court conforms to the dominant racial imperatives of the time.

During Redemption, the Court accommodated white southern determination to repeal egalitarian laws and to impose segregation in their stead. In *Hall v. De Cuir* (1877),[100] the Court struck down Louisiana public accommodations measure as applied to interstate steamboat travel on the grounds that the statute imposed a burden on interstate commerce (the burden apparently being the need to permit passengers to move from segregated to integrated seating as the boat crossed a state line). But in *Louisville, New Orleans & Texas Ry. Co v. Mississippi* (1890),[101] the justices with seeming inconsistency sustained a state segregation requirement impacting interstate railroad travel by holding that it applied only to intrastate travel. With a disingenuousness remarkable even for the Court of that era, the justices reasoned that the burden of shuffling passengers around from integrated to segregated seating posed only a trivial inconvenience on interstate commerce, whereas in *Hall v. De Cuir*, the burden of permitting passengers to shuffle around from segregated to integrated seating was intolerable.

The commonality reconciling these inconsistent outcomes was a judicial willingness to accept the racial policies of Redeemer regimes intent on imposing Jim Crow. That imperative readily overrode apparent doctrinal incompatibilities between the two cases. An alternative reading of these two cases might disclose some doctrinal consistency, though: courts condemned those state statutes that enabled state authority to intrude on interstate commerce, whether it be to segregate or to ban segregation. In this view, the eventual triumph of Jim Crow in interstate railroad travel was accomplished by the carriers themselves mandating segregation without being compelled to do so by state legislation.[102]

Two 1940s cases reversed both these outcomes. *Morgan v. Virginia* (1946)[103] limited a Virginia segregation statute as it applied to bus transportation, prohibiting its application in interstate travel but implicitly permitting it for purely intrastate runs. The Court reasoned that state-mandated Jim Crow seating on buses burdened interstate commerce. Yet it remained reluctant to challenge local segregationist mores when that might bring the judiciary into direct conflict with local practices. Desegregating immobile local facilities like buildings, with their toilets and drinking fountains, would have proved too incendiary in 1946. Not until desegregation was underway in other venues after 1954 was the Court willing to antagonize segregationist preferences about public buildings. Sometimes prudence is a necessary auxiliary to justice, even though it seems temporizing to those who enjoy the luxury of viewing it at a historical remove. The Court did not get around to banning segregation in bus terminals until 1960. But when it did, in *Boynton v. Virginia* (1960),[104] its holding spurred the civil rights movement. The Freedom Riders responded by challenging segregation in buses and terminals throughout the Deep South, igniting the dramatic, activist phase of the civil rights struggle.[105]

Just as *Morgan* flipped its 1877 predecessor, two years later *Bob-Lo Excursion Co. v. Michigan* (1948)[106] flipped its 1890 antecedent. In *Bob-Lo*, the Court sustained a Michigan public accommodations statute's ban on racial discrimination (which in this case took the form of outright exclusion, not just segregated seating) as applied to the peculiar facts of an excursion boat that plied nominally international waters. Thus international, not interstate, commerce was involved, though that made no difference to the doctrinal outcome. Bob-Lo, a popular amusement park that served the Detroit metropolitan area, was located on an island in the Detroit River that was actually in the Canadian province of Ontario and was accessible only by ferry from the American side. The justices upheld the power of the state to prohibit racial exclusion in the international commerce that was involved in the shuttle from Detroit to its Canadian recreational island. The Court saw no undue burden on international commerce. Once again, any seeming inconsistency between these nearly contemporaneous decisions can be explained by the justices' determination to respect the dominant racial movements of their times. In the 1940s that was an emergent hostility to racial segregation.

The justices encountered the problem of racial discrimination in transportation in one other sector as well: labor unions. The railway brotherhoods[107] throughout their existence were notoriously racist, often refusing to admit African Americans as members and pressuring railroad employers to refuse to hire Black workers and fire those already employed.[108] Black firemen who were members of the Brotherhood of Locomotive Firemen and Enginemen sued both the union and employers to stop their gradual expulsion and employer/union collusion in refusing to hire Black firemen. In *Steele v. Louisville & Nashville Railroad* (1944),[109] Chief Justice Stone construed the Railway Labor Act of 1934 to require unions to represent the interests of all their members in bargaining with employers, and not to discriminate based on color. The Court extended this holding in *Brotherhood of Railway Trainmen v. Howard* (1952)[110] to prohibit a union that had no African American members from trying to exclude Black brakemen and porters from employment so that the jobs could be held by white workers. But union racism has proven to be intractable, and small victories like *Steele* and *Howard* did little to advance the cause of Black workers.

Higher Education

Gunnar Myrdal's *An American Dilemma*, published in 1944, provided the NAACP and its Legal Defense Fund with a massive compilation of data showing the pervasive destructiveness of racial discrimination in the United States. This came at a propitious time, as the Fund and its principal litigators, Thurgood Marshall, Charles Hamilton Houston, and Robert Carter, were preparing to challenge racial segregation throughout America's public schools.

The *Gaines* case of 1938 had begun the assault on *Plessy*-sanctioned Jim Crow in education,[111] but it had not repudiated the doctrine of separate but equal. Rather, it seemed to hold out to southern political leaders and educators an uncomfortable choice: if you maintain separate schools, they must be equal, and they must be provided in state, not somewhere else. Hoping to slide along on the pretextuality that had sustained Jim Crow for over half a century, southern legislatures responded either by doing nothing (hoping that the problem would just somehow go away), by evasive temporizing, or by creating nominal institutions for Black students that might appease their demand for educational opportunities. Marshall and his colleagues were determined to challenge all these responses, but they were uncertain about how comprehensively to do so. Danger lurked in all options.

They faced a wide spectrum of possibilities.[112] At one extreme, the least likely in 1945, the Supreme Court might reject *Plessy*'s extrapolation to education[113] and hold racial segregation unconstitutional in public education as a violation of the Fourteenth Amendment's guarantee of equal protection. Or it might insist on absolute and authentic equality as the price of acquiescing in segregation. This would have been impossible to achieve in any meaningful way and would have amounted to nothing more than a face-saving fig-leaf that justified continuation of the status quo, inviting endless evasion. At the opposite extreme, the all-too-possible prospect of disaster loomed: the Court might reaffirm *Plessy* and go along with the pretense necessary to sustain it, prolonging it into the indefinite future. In between these extremes lay a third possibility: continued evasion of the challenge to *Plessy*, consisting of innumerable variations involving segregation, discrimination, inequality, and denial, the only certainty being that whites would try to monopolize opportunity for themselves and deny it to African Americans.

When Ada Sipuel applied for admission to the law school of the University of Oklahoma in 1945, she was rejected, with the empty assurance that the university would create a separate law school for Black applicants when enough of them applied. In his appeal to the US Supreme Court, Marshall rejected that possibility, arguing ambiguously that "there can be no separate equality."[114] The Court in a per curiam opinion responded with its own ambiguity in *Sipuel v. Oklahoma Board of Regents* (1948): Oklahoma had to provide Sipuel with a legal education "as soon as it does for applicants of any other group."[115] Seizing the opportunity opened up by that ambiguity, the regents of the state university created a nominal, ephemeral, ad hoc law school in some unused space in the state capitol. When Sipuel (since wed and now known by her married name, Fisher) appealed, the Court sustained the state's action, limply explaining that it had not previously held that segregated education of the sort provided by Oklahoma violated the equal protection clause.[116] For the time being, the Court seemed content to go along with the last of the alternatives (affirming forms of discrimination in education and implicitly accepting *Plessy*), which would produce an unstable and unsatisfactory compromise that resolved nothing and satisfied nobody. Sipuel/Fisher refused to attend the one-off Black law school (which soon dissolved) and eventually graduated from the real law school in Norman. In time she was appointed to the board of regents of the university that had rejected her in 1946. The outcome of *Sipuel* seemed to offer two lessons. First, the hold of separate but equal in public higher education appeared to be weakening. But second, the Court was not inclined to hurry to that development along, particularly as white southern resolve to maintain segregation appeared to be as hardened as ever. A decade after *Gaines v. Canada*, little seemed to have changed.

Two years later, though, the Court lurched forward toward desegregation, a surprising result considering that in the interim its two most committed advocates for racial equality, Justices Murphy and Rutledge, died, their places taken by two unpromising replacements, Tom Clark and Sherman Minton. Nevertheless, in 1950 the Court decided three cases on the same day that rejected Jim Crow in graduate and professional education, and in interstate rail transportation.[117]

Sweatt v. Painter (1950)[118] began as a replay of *Sipuel*. Heman Sweatt applied for admission to the University of Texas Law School in 1945. After he was rebuffed, state courts ordered Texas to create a Black law school, consisting of a few rooms in a Houston basement. Challenging this arrangement, Thurgood Marshall continued his cautious approach: his brief argued both that any form of discrimination or inferiority resulted in constitutionally prohibited inequality, and that *Plessy* should be overruled. But unlike Ada Sipuel's situation, here the state had provided an actual, though inferior, law school that had enough authenticity and vitality to survive.[119] This forced the Court to confront the issues that it had so far managed to duck: segregation and pretextuality. A group of 187 law faculty nationwide helped matters along by submitting an amicus brief arguing that in the context of legal education, separate could never be equal because of the differences in quality between established and minimally funded upstart institutions. They urged that *Plessy* be overruled.[120]

These arguments were addressed to a deeply divided Court.[121] Reed and maybe Vinson did not think segregation was prohibited. Burton and Clark on the other hand both indicated a willingness to overrule *Plessy*. Black and

Frankfurter, from different premises, cautioned against overruling but were willing to exempt graduate and professional education. Frankfurter fastidiously insisted that the Court not condemn segregation, while somehow prohibiting it in these particular cases. Jackson was hopelessly ambivalent and undecided, reluctant to endorse segregation but certain that the Constitution did not prohibit it. "I don't know the answer," he plaintively said in conference; "my views are fluid enough to join any theory."[122] It was the law professors' brief, plus a lengthy memorandum from Clark, coincident with the arguments and results in *Sweatt*'s companion cases *Henderson* and *McLaurin*, that enabled the surprising unanimity of holdings in all three cases. Clark, an alumnus of the University of Texas Law School and the justice most familiar with the facts and environment of the case, argued that segregation was wrong at the graduate and professional level, and categorically rejected pretextuality. "My question," he wrote in a draft of his memorandum, "is 'how' to reverse [*Plessy*], not 'whether' or 'why.'" "If some say this undermines Plessy, then let it fall."[123]

In *Sweatt*, the Court speaking through Vinson ordered the petitioner admitted to the University of Texas Law School at Austin. The law professors' brief was determinative, as the chief justice enumerated multiple criteria that demonstrated the hopeless inequality between the two institutions: "In terms of number of the faculty, variety of courses and opportunity for specialization, size of the student body, scope of the library, availability of law review and similar activities, the University of Texas Law School is superior. What is more important, the University of Texas Law School possesses to a far greater degree those qualities which are incapable of objective measurement but which make for greatness in a law school. Such qualities, to name but a few, include reputation of the faculty, experience of the administration, position and influence of the alumni, standing in the community, traditions and prestige."[124] Clark's emphasis on such intangible qualities carried the day, and the Court ordered Sweatt admitted.

Sweatt was decided on the same day as *Henderson* and the third of the 1950 triad, *McLaurin v. Oklahoma State Regents* (1950).[125] George McLaurin sought a doctoral degree in education at the University of Oklahoma. When forced to admit him by judicial decree, the university at first segregated him physically, seating him in separate spaces in classroom, library, and dining hall. When forced to abandon this separate seating, the school then permitted him to sit in the same room as his white classmates, but behind a cordon marked "Reserved for Colored." (His classmates immediately tore it down.)

McLaurin forced on the justices the now-inescapable issue of segregation per se: George McLaurin was getting exactly the same education as his white classmates—same lectures, same physical environment, no pretextuality— but separated by a symbolic line that designated him as "Colored." As Richard Kluger memorably put it: "the state was punishing George McLaurin for requiring it to honor his rights as a citizen. In so doing, it had resolved to shame him as a man."[126] Vinson again writing for the Court swept away all of the university's stigmatic gestures: "The removal of the state restrictions will not necessarily abate individual and group predilections, prejudices and choices. But at the very least, the state will not be depriving appellant of the opportunity to secure acceptance by his fellow students on his own merits."[127]

The three 1950 opinions, *Henderson, Sweatt,* and *McLaurin,* marked the first time that the Court clearly and explicitly rebuffed *Plessy's* arguments for separate but equal. Each struck down state-imposed racial segregation and denial of equal opportunity, though in carefully confined contexts: passenger railroad travel, law schools, graduate study. Though divided among themselves, ambivalent, uncertain, and fluctuating, the justices were moving inexorably toward the confrontation that would become the Armageddon of de jure segregation in twentieth-century America.

7

The Second Reconstruction, 1954–1971

During the civil rights era, from 1954 until 1971, the American people tried once again, for the second time in their three and a half centuries' history, to achieve some measure of equality between whites and African Americans through constitutional and legal change.[1]

Historians refer to this period as the second Reconstruction. Both Reconstructions lasted approximately fifteen years. Both followed major wars that were the source of unforeseeable social change in American society. Both overthrew the legal and social system of race relations that had previously prevailed: slavery was ended by the first Reconstruction, the regime of servitude based on de jure discrimination by the second. Neither era succeeded in establishing comprehensive racial equality. Both Reconstructions came to a premature end and were followed by a time of racial reaction. After each, the Supreme Court contributed to rolling back egalitarian advances.

The debut of the second Reconstruction was *Brown v. Board of Education*. Like a dynamite charge blasting apart a logjam, it liberated pent-up forces seeking greater equality of life for African Americans. It began the systematic dismantling of Jim Crow and its pervasive, demeaning discriminations that were part of everyday life for Black citizens.[2] Like its 1866 predecessor, the Civil Rights Act of 1964 attempted to protect African Americans in major aspects of civic life: work, education, citizenship. Together, those two great measures vindicated the right of Black Americans to access property, whether to buy, rent, or occupy. The Supreme Court protected Black Americans' rights to communicate and to engage in concerted political action. Congress and the Court in tandem finally began to realize the promise of the Fifteenth Amendment, protecting the right of political participation. The Court struck down hoary laws that imposed penalties on people of both races for marrying or having interracial sex. The second Reconstruction was as ambitious as the first, seeking to achieve equality in all spheres of American life. For a tragically short period, the justices did better the second time around in advancing that ambitious goal, but then they too faltered.

The Warren Court

The US Supreme Court was the godparent of the civil rights era. Without the Warren Court, the second Reconstruction would not have happened. Congress might have enacted a few pieces of limited voting rights legislation along the lines of the 1957 and 1960 Civil Rights Acts, and the executive branch under President Dwight D. Eisenhower might have backed them up with unenthusiastic enforcement. But the real force behind the drive for equality after 1954 at first came from the federal judiciary. The Warren Court fully realized the promise of *Carolene Products*' footnote 4, advancing the liberties identified in the Bill of Rights, protecting speech and religious freedoms under the First Amendment, clearing the channels of democratic political change, and vindicating the rights of minorities. Its decisions in matters of racial equality; voting, redistricting, and malapportionment; the rights of persons accused of a crime; religion clause issues of free exercise and establishment; and privacy, especially in reproductive rights, established its enduring reputation as a paladin of liberty and individual rights.[3]

As the second Reconstruction was unthinkable without the Warren Court, so the Court itself would have been unthinkable without Earl Warren.[4] Though he was not the intellectual leader of the Court, Warren was the catalyst for its leading decisions. His uncomplicated vision of justice and equality, combined with his political and interpersonal skills, harmonized the activist impulses of the fractious Vinson Court to forge the remarkable unity that drove the agenda of the Warren Court. The irony and paradox of the Warren Court is how these liberal accomplishments could have been anticipated from someone who before his appointment to the Court in 1953 had compiled so illiberal a record as a politician.

After graduation from the University of California Berkeley (both undergraduate and law), and stateside army service in World War I, Warren was successively city attorney for Oakland, district attorney for Alameda County, and then attorney general of California. In each of these positions, though he was a liberal, an admirer of Progressive governor Hiram Johnson, and by repute a moderate Republican, Warren pushed a conservative agenda. He supported the prosecution of Anita Whitney under the state's Criminal Syndicalism Act for her role in organizing the Communist Party of California;[5] helped suppress the 1934 San Francisco General Strike; earned a reputation as a tough-on-crime prosecutor; defended eugenic sterilization; and aggressively confiscated Japanese-owned farmland under the

Alien Land Laws until *Oyama v. California* (1948)[6] put an end to the practice. He enthusiastically backed Japanese relocation and confinement in concentration camps throughout the war.[7]

Warren was elected governor of California as a Republican for three terms, beginning in 1942. In 1948, he was chosen as the Republican Party's vice presidential candidate and running mate of Tom Dewey. Four years later he was a GOP favorite-son candidate for the presidency, only to have his ambitions dashed by behind-the-scenes intrigues of congressman Richard M. Nixon. From that experience, Warren nursed an abiding dislike of Nixon, though Nixon supported President Dwight D. Eisenhower's decision to nominate Warren to the chief justiceship of the United States. As always, Nixon's motives were not disinterested: he simply wanted to kick a potential rival upstairs. (Nixon would later rue his support for Warren's appointment.) The relationship between Warren and Ike, the president who nominated him, was never cordial, and their disagreements intensified over the years.[8]

Warren's leadership of the Court was transformative. Proceeding from uncomplicated intuitions of fairness and justice, rather than from a comprehensive theory of judging, Warren strove to achieve results that were just, sensible, and acceptable in a democratic society. He was the epitome of liberal pragmatism. He subordinated precedent, tradition, history, and stare decisis in the service of decency and a sense of justice that could readily be comprehended by ordinary people. Together with William J. Brennan, he skillfully formed coalitions, wheedled and cajoled the Brethren, cobbled together majorities, strove for consensus, and projected both a personal and a collective gravitas that helped gain acceptance for controversial outcomes.

A year after his confirmation, Warren was joined on the Court by his jurisprudential opposite, John Marshall Harlan II. Grandson of his namesake, the first Justice Harlan, Harlan II was the archetype of a judicial conservative, resistant to judicial activism and skeptical of the Court's ability to correct social ills. But he was not a reactionary in the mold of Melville Fuller or James McReynolds. He appreciated as clearly as his liberal brethren the need for the Constitution to respond to modern conditions. He was called "the great dissenter of the Warren Court,"[9] the natural ally of Felix Frankfurter as an apostle of judicial self-restraint. For seven years, the Frankfurter/Harlan duo would provide an effective counterweight to the emergent liberal activist bloc of Black and Douglas, who were augmented by Warren and William Brennan. On the Supreme Court, Harlan enjoyed a reputation for unfailing courtesy and respect for the views of others—"Frankfurter without the mustard," as some Court observers noted. Though they agreed on matters of substance, the often-abrasive Frankfurter contrasted conspicuously with the courtly Harlan.

Harlan's jurisprudential legacy was a mixture of judicial self-restraint somehow yoked with a willingness to read certain provisions of the Constitution broadly. In this, he shared Frankfurter's confidence that judges could be trusted to inerrantly discern which liberties are fundamental, and thus binding on the states, and which were merely desirable. But Harlan's overriding value was a skepticism about the proper role of the courts in identifying constitutional limits on legislative power. Harlan's stringent view of judicial self-restraint did not prevent him from becoming a proponent of the equal protection clause, though. Harlan consistently voted to recognize constitutional protections for African Americans' claims of belonging that underlie modern civil rights issues.[10] His career demonstrates that principled judicial conservatism could be consistent with support for the rights and opportunities of African Americans. In this, unfortunately, Harlan was a rarity among conservatives.

When Justice Sherman Minton announced his retirement in September 1956, Eisenhower decided that his nomination for a replacement should be a Catholic Democrat from the Northeast with plausible judicial experience. William J. Brennan fit the bill.[11] Brennan expanded the liberal trio of Black-Douglas-Warren, forming a cohesive and effective bloc determined to realize the promise of *Carolene Product*'s footnote 4. With the accession of Brennan, the liberal bloc came to predominate on the Court, to the displeasure of Frankfurter and Harlan, who often found themselves relegated to critiquing the ascendant preoccupation with issues of civil liberties and civil rights. Brennan and Warren soon became close friends and partners in strategizing the direction of the Warren Court in the second Reconstruction. They were the core of the liberal bloc, skilled tacticians, persuasive in one-on-one dealings, warm and personable. They above all, more than the mercurial Douglas and the later Black, defined the liberal moment of the second Reconstruction. With the confirmation of Arthur Goldberg in 1962, the dominance of the "Brennan Court" as some have called it, was ensured, at least for a decade. Brennan was the personification of Warren Court liberal activism. He merited Antonin Scalia's grudging evaluation: "probably the most influential justice of the [twentieth] century."[12]

As a justice, Byron White, President John F. Kennedy's first appointment, defies categorization.[13] A major part of his judicial legacy was a conservatism grounded on a powerful sense of judicial self-restraint. He was "a jurist who facilitated, and was reluctant to override, the policy judgments made by democratically accountable branches of government."[14] He extolled this value on several occasions, as in *Moore v. East Cleveland* (1977), where he rejected an expansive interpretation of the due process clause:

> this Court is the most vulnerable and comes nearest to illegitimacy when it deals with judge-made constitutional law having little or no cognizable roots in the language or even the design of the Constitution.... The Court should be extremely reluctant to breathe still further substantive content into the Due Process clause so as to strike down legislation adopted by a State or city to promote its welfare. Whenever the Judiciary does so, it unavoidably pre-empts for itself another part of the governance of the country without express constitutional authority.[15]

Such reluctance to intrude judicial review into the domain of legislative discretion runs throughout the conservative resistance to expansive interpretations of the equal protection clause during the Warren years and after. Yet White did not adhere to a consistent judicial conservatism. He dutifully supported desegregation and racial justice cases coming before the Court throughout the second Reconstruction, including his dissent in *Milliken v. Bradley* (1974).[16]

But as the Court veered in a direction less supportive of African Americans' rights after 1972, White followed. He wrote the majority opinion in *Washington v. Davis* (1976),[17] disabling effective judicial response to structural racism; supported the majority in *Richmond v. J. A. Croson* (1989),[18] setting back affirmative action at the state level; and dissented in *Runyon v. McCrary* (1976),[19] insisting that purely private racial discrimination in education did not run afoul of the Constitution or federal statutes. In all these instances, his distrust of judicial activism and his respect for stare decisis led him to accept results that he might regret as a matter of social policy but that he believed were not forbidden by the Constitution.

The appointment of Thurgood Marshall to the Court in 1977 was the coda of the second Reconstruction.[20] When he applied to the law school of the University of Maryland in 1930 and was rejected because of his race, he went instead to Howard University, where he finished at the top of his class. He immediately became active in the local chapter of the NAACP and with his mentor Charles Hamilton Houston won a gratifying victory in *Murray v. Pearson* (Md. 1936) that overturned the racial exclusion that had kept him out of the state's law school.[21] *Murray* marked the start of Marshall's stellar career in civil rights litigation. His crowning litigation achievement was *Brown v. Board of Education*. But Marshall was a litigator, and he traveled throughout the South, often at terrifying risk to his life, to defend countless Black men in capital trials.

Marshall himself provided the most effective summation of his judicial outlook in his constitutional "Bicentennial Address" of 1987, which shocked many Americans in a time of unthinking patriotism. He rejected the "complacent view" that Americans now enjoy the "Blessings of Liberty" promised in the Preamble:

> I cannot accept this invitation, for I do not believe that the meaning of the Constitution was forever "fixed" at the Philadelphia Convention. Nor do I find the wisdom, foresight, and sense of justice exhibited by the Framers particularly profound. To the contrary, the government they devised was defective from the start, requiring several amendments, a civil war, and momentous social transformation to attain the system of constitutional government, and its respect for the individual freedoms and human rights, we hold as fundamental today. When contemporary Americans cite "The Constitution," they invoke a concept that is vastly different from what the Framers barely began to construct two centuries ago.
>
> "We the People" no longer enslave, but the credit does not belong to the Framers. It belongs to those who refused to acquiesce in outdated notions of "liberty," "justice," and "equality," and who strived to better them.
>
> Thus, in this bicentennial year, we may not all participate in the festivities with flagwaving fervor. Some may more quietly commemorate the suffering, struggle, and sacrifice that has triumphed over much of what was wrong with the original document, and observe the anniversary with hopes not realized and promises not fulfilled. I plan to celebrate the bicentennial of the Constitution as a living document, including the Bill of Rights and the other amendments protecting individual freedoms and human rights.[22]

No Court has before or since so effectively promoted the cause of racial equality in America as the justices who sat during the tenure of Earl Warren. The second Reconstruction owes most of its lingering vitality today to them.

Brown v. Board of Education and Its Impact

Local challenges to segregation were spontaneously cropping up throughout the South by 1952, and the NAACP could no longer temporize on litigation strategy. Thurgood Marshall and the NAACP's Legal Defense Fund had previously tried an equalization argument that did not challenge *Plessy* and separate but equal head-on, but rather insisted that if white southern society wanted separation, it would have to provide truly equal facilities in all spheres of life. Since this was obviously impractical, the South would be forced to accept desegregation as the only available alternative.[23] But after 1952 they abandoned that alternative and argued that separate but equal was per se unconstitutional, not only in public schools but throughout American society.

Five cases challenging segregation under the head-on approach were consolidated for hearing before the US Supreme Court as *Brown v. Board of Education*, and the Court heard argument in December 1952. Briefs for the NAACP, the American Civil Liberties Union, and the federal government as amicus all called for *Plessy* to be overruled, but they proposed differing reasons for doing so. These included the Fourteenth Amendment itself prohibited segregation; or if it did not, segregation could not survive the strict scrutiny mandated by *Korematsu* in equal protection cases; or social science evidence demonstrated that segregation was harmful to the Black children who were its primary victims.

These arguments were addressed to nine men who were of various minds about those issues in 1952.[24] Justice William O. Douglas's headcount,[25] which scholars agree was probably accurate, identified four who at that time were then prepared to overrule *Plessy* and declare segregation unconstitutional: Black, Douglas, Burton, and Minton.[26] Two seemed willing to accept segregation: Vinson and Stanley Reed. The remaining three were deeply conflicted within themselves, ambivalent, and reluctant to reach a result at that time: Frankfurter, Jackson, and Clark (who leaned toward affirmance). Partly to buy time and partly to clarify the justices' positions, Frankfurter proposed re-argument, which was scheduled for December 1953.

But then, in Frankfurter's telling, a divine intervention occurred.[27] Chief Justice Fred Vinson unexpectedly died in September 1953, and President Eisenhower appointed Earl Warren, a much different individual, to replace him. By that time, it had become clear that much had changed: one way or another, segregation was doomed. The question was how to ease it out with minimal disruption of the social order in the South. Signaling the importance of the case, the Court scheduled ten hours, rather than the customary one, for re-arguments.

In conference after re-argument, the justices again decided, as they had after the first argument, to postpone the vote until after discussion, a procedure that enabled a fuller airing of views and did not lock any of them into a position from which he would find it difficult to retreat. Warren, as is the Court's custom, spoke first as chief justice, and he firmly came out in favor of overruling *Plessy*. The ambivalent justices had to be brought around, though. Frankfurter and Jackson both disdained segregation, but they also believed that a decision to overrule *Plessy* could not be justified by the usual judicial criteria that guided their thinking as judges: constitutional text, Framers' intent, precedent, judicial norms.[28] They thought that a vote to overrule would be for them not law but politics or "sociology," as Jackson scornfully put it.[29] But all recognized that the vote in *Brown* had to be unanimous, so they subordinated their scruples and voted to hold de jure school segregation a violation of the equal protection clause.[30]

The new chief justice wisely took the opinion for himself, and crafted a politic resolution of issues, particularly the framers' intent, that would have stymied a more irresolute justice like Vinson or Jackson. In the end, Warren simply dismissed the issue of framers' intent in *Brown v. Board of Education* (1954) (*Brown I*).[31] "Consideration of the [Fourteenth] Amendment in Congress, ratification by the states, then existing practices in racial segregation, and the views of proponents and opponents...cast some light [but] not enough....At best they are inconclusive." With that masterstroke, Warren moved beyond the irresolvable question of framers' intent that threatened to paralyze the Court and took up the real issue: "the effect of segregation itself on public education."

Warren brushed aside the problem of *Plessy* as if it were inconsequential: "we cannot turn the clock back to 1868 when the Amendment was adopted, or even to 1896 when *Plessy v. Ferguson* was written." Instead, he wrote, "we must consider public education in the light of its full development and its present place in American life." [It] "is perhaps the most important function of state and local governments." and a "principal instrument in awakening the child to cultural values."

With that paean to the place of education in American society, Warren turned to the conclusions of social scientists on the impact of segregation, which "generates a feeling of inferiority as to their status in the community that may affect their hearts and minds in a way unlikely ever to be undone." He buttressed this with the problematic footnote 11, citing social psychological research of Kenneth and Mamie Clark and a half-dozen other social scientists on the deleterious effects of segregation on childhood development.[32] He concluded that footnote with a "see generally" cite to Gunnar Myrdal's enormously influential *An American Dilemma* (1944).[33] While that particular reference was apt, it left the *Brown* opinion vulnerable to charges that its outcome was driven by the views of a Swedish socialist, which in the McCarthyite climate of the era was tantamount to claiming that desegregation was "Communist inspired." Warren concluded by endorsing the NAACP's basic point: "separate educational facilities are inherently unequal." Segregation violated the equal protection clause because separate was not, and could never be, equal. The decision was unanimous. De jure segregation under the doctrine of separate but equal had been dealt a mortal blow. The second Reconstruction had begun.

In a companion case, *Bolling v. Sharpe* (1954),[34] the Court held racial segregation in the public schools of the District of Columbia unconstitutional, but it could not rely directly on the equal protection clause, which applied only to the states,[35] to reach that result. Warren achieved the same outcome by interpreting the Fifth Amendment's due process clause (which does apply to the District) to incorporate the principle of equal protection as a restraint on the powers of the federal government. Constitutional scholars label this "reverse incorporation," referring to the doctrine of incorporation, which holds that most of the provisions of the Bill of Rights of the federal Constitution are restraints on the states as well. Warren held that segregation constituted an "arbitrary deprivation of liberty," thereby adding another arrow to the constitutional quiver being used to destroy Jim Crow, with due process reinforcing its equal protection sibling.

Warren's opinion implicitly overruled *Plessy* and repudiated its doctrine of separate but equal. But Warren did not disentangle two issues that Harlan's *Plessy* dissent had conjoined. Harlan had written: "in view of the Constitution, in the eye of the law, there is in this country no superior, dominant, ruling class of citizens. There is no caste here. Our Constitution is color-blind, and neither knows nor tolerates classes among citizens."[36] Harlan there smoothly linked "caste" and race, treating them as closely related, if not identical.[37] But do they have differing constitutional significance? The passage of time revealed this to be a latent ambiguity in *Brown*'s holding that derived from its failure to distinguish caste from race.[38]

One reading of *Brown*, known as the anticlassification principle, holds that the equal protection clause prohibits the states from making any legally significant classifications by race at all, whether for malignant or for benign purposes. This is the interpretation adopted by Justice Clarence Thomas and other conservatives, including a majority of the Roberts Court. It would prohibit the state from identifying individuals by race in such matters as affirmative action. Justice Thomas insists on the moral and practical equivalence of racially conscious decisions meant to subordinate a race of people and decisions meant to correct inequalities derived from past racial discrimination. It would prohibit group-based remedies, demanding instead that government treat all people only as individuals, not as members of a race. Thomas claims that "government must treat citizens as individuals, and not as members of racial, ethnic, or religious groups."[39] This interpretation, which relies exclusively on the color-blindness half of the Harlan equation, would prohibit the states from addressing problems of structural racism. The result is a caste system in which the dominant group (in the United States, white people) valorizes race, converting it to a form of property interest that, along with its entitlements, must be protected by law.

The emphasis on individuals (as opposed to groups) as the basis of rights claims reinforces whiteness as property.[40] White people and the institutions they dominate have claimed the power to define norms for those who are subordinate to them—people of color—and to assign benefits and privilege accordingly. This "reified privilege of power…reconstitutes the property interest in whiteness." Robert Carter, who participated in the *Brown I* briefs and argument, identified the fatal flaw of this view. He believed that the Court, like the rest of the country, mistook the real nature of racial inequality: "segregation was merely a symptom, not the disease; that the real sickness in our society in all of its manifestations is geared to the maintenance of white superiority."[41]

The caste component of the Harlan *Plessy* dissent points in another direction: the state may not take any actions that subordinate or impose disadvantages on any racial group.[42] States may not adopt policies that reduce opportunities for racially defined groups of people or diminish their status in society by tolerating invidious discrimination.[43] This is known as the "antisubordination" reading of *Brown*. It emphasizes the *effects* of state actions, not formal classifications. It would prohibit any treatment of groups or individuals by the state that would reproduce inequality. This ambiguity in *Brown*'s core meaning remained latent for two decades. When the Court did begin to explore its implications in the 1970s, the struggle over racial stratification intensified.

Brown v. Board of Education I is a beacon of interpretive wisdom. As a human artifact, it has its failings, as does any human endeavor.[44] But not before or since has the Supreme Court risen so magnificently to the occasion, announcing a vision of our public law based on freedom and equality. Its understanding of rights applied not only to individuals but also to all African American people, indeed all peoples that make up the rainbow of races and ethnicities that is America. *Brown*'s strengths lay in its openness to growth, its inclusiveness, its understanding of the vision of the framers, and most fundamentally, its respect for the humanity and rights of those previously outside the pale of We the People. Where *Dred Scott* imposed stultification, a constitutionalism of, by, and for slaveholders, *Brown* opened the constitutional order to all Americans, further ridding the nation of its rotting legacies of slavery and Jim Crow servitude.

Even as the substantive issue of segregation was being resolved, the problem of remedies loomed large throughout the *Brown I* arguments, for two reasons. The first was practical: how to prevent violence erupting from white backlash to the decision. The justices were agreed that immediate desegregation was utopian, impractical, and fraught with dangers for those it was primarily meant to benefit, the African American communities of the South. Lynching was an ever-looming reality: Emmett Till was murdered in Mississippi in 1955. They also hoped that a tactful approach might cajole white southerners into compliance. But this hopeful attitude underestimated white southern determination to resist. The Court's tact perversely emboldened white resolve. Southern whites mistook a gesture of goodwill as a sign of weakness.

The second consideration on the justices' minds was less threatening but of greater moment for the long-term future of the federal courts. They observed the emerging role of the branch of law known as equity in American courts generally, and in the federal courts in particular. After the systems of common law and equity were merged in the federal courts when the Federal Rules of Civil Procedure were adopted in 1938, the flexible modes of procedure and remedies provided by traditional equity courts came to prevail in practice after World War II.[45] *Brown* was a major event in this development, being the single most important moment in the emergence of what lawyers refer to as "structural litigation," the strategic use of litigation, usually against government agencies, to advance reform causes like school desegregation, prison reform, and treatment of mental illness.[46] Structural litigation has become a major source of institutional reform in the United States, with *Brown* as the flagship decision. The result in *Brown I* was achieved only by deferring the question of remedies to what became known as *Brown II*: *Brown v. Board of Education* (1955). The justices turned to the remedies issue with a sense of unacknowledged relief for the option of handing the problem over to the federal district courts to devise remedies, relying on the broad scope of discretion of courts sitting in equity. Frankfurter and Black, who disagreed on so much else, were of one mind on this. "These are equity suits," Frankfurter insisted at the first *Brown* conference in 1952. "They involve imagination in shaping decrees." Black elaborated: the federal district courts would have to assume responsibility for day-to-day implementation. They "would then be in the firing line for enforcement through injunctions and contempt."[47] After the first argument in 1952, the Court ordered re-argument on five questions, three of them going to the framers' intentions, and the latter two requesting guidance on formulating remedies.[48] The remedies questions were structured around the polarity of desegregation "forthwith" versus "gradual adjustment." The latter phrase reflected Frankfurter's insistence on a gradualist approach to the problem of imposing desegregation in the real world of the South.

Brown II was unanimous, with Warren again writing the opinion.[49] In it, equity came into its own: the federal district courts "will be guided by equitable principles. Traditionally, equity has been characterized by a practical flexibility in shaping its remedies and by a facility for adjusting and reconciling public and private needs. These cases call for the exercise of these traditional attributes of equity power." That cemented the triumph of equity in the federal courts. But the justices overestimated the willingness of the white South to comply with district court orders. In a tragic expression of misplaced confidence, Warren adopted a phrase at Frankfurter's urging stating that students must be admitted to "public schools on a racially nondiscriminatory basis," but "with all deliberate speed." Frankfurter's gradualist approach prevailed and dominated not only *Brown II* but the entire subsequent course of litigation over desegregation. The resistant white South read that phrase as license for foot-dragging, defiance, and obstruction. "All deliberate speed" undercut the substantive triumph of *Brown I*.

Desegregation to Integration

The two decades that followed *Brown* were momentous, as both Court and nation moved from confronting the morally uncomplicated problem of de jure segregation to the more difficult issue of de facto segregation; from dealing only with the segregated South to confronting racial disparities in the northern and western states as well; from desegregation to the more ambitious goal of integration; from thinking solely in terms of the Black-white binary to embracing the fully multiracial richness of the American people.[50]

The burden of implementing *Brown* fell on federal district court judges throughout the South. Many of them performed heroically,[51] implementing *Brown II*'s mandate with firmness and tact. But it soon became apparent that changing school policy was going to be a district-by-district slog.[52] While compliance efforts varied among the local districts, the southern states as a whole adopted the Virginia program called "Massive Resistance."[53] The phrase was coined by Senator Harry Byrd of Virginia to describe a program of noncompliance and legal obstruction of the desegregation process.[54] Its constitutional expression was the "Southern Manifesto," formally titled a "Declaration of Constitutional Principles," a screed signed by almost the entire southern congressional delegation in 1956. It was the official constitutional response of the white South to *Brown v. Board of Education*. The Southern Manifesto tried to prop up the cadaver of antebellum pro-slavery constitutional dogma. It provided a constitutional theory and rationalization for Massive Resistance and segregation itself.[55] The manifesto denounced *Brown* and the judges who promulgated it, invoking the Tenth Amendment to protect the South's "habits, customs, tradition and way of life." The southern congressional delegation declared that "The decisions of the Supreme Court in the school cases as a clear abuse of judicial power. It climaxes a trend in the Federal Judiciary undertaking to legislate, in derogation of the authority of Congress, and to encroach upon the reserved rights of the States and the people.... We decry the Supreme Court's encroachment on the rights reserved to the States and to the people, contrary to established law, and to the Constitution."[56] Its call "to resist forced integration by any lawful means" was quickly answered by the Virginia program of Massive Resistance, which led, among other things, to the closure of public schools, founding of segregation academies, and the total denial of public education to African American children in some parts of the commonwealth.

The legislatures of the Deep South (Alabama, Georgia, Mississippi, South Carolina, Louisiana) spouted defiance and exhumed antebellum doctrines of interposition and nullification in fulsome resolutions and noisy posturing. More moderate southern political leaders did not parrot such neo-Calhounian dogmas, but they moved tactically to slow or evade desegregating.[57] White southerners resisted dismantling Jim Crow through the Citizens Councils for the middle classes[58] and the Klan, resurrected again in its third avatar, for the lower orders.[59]

While most southern politicians expressed their resistance in bombast or passive foot-dragging, a few backed up their words with action. In 1957, Governor Orval Faubus of Arkansas deployed his state's National Guard to prevent desegregation of Little Rock High School under a decree of the federal district court. Faubus and the state legislature claimed they were not bound by the Supreme Court's orders in the two *Brown* cases. It took intervention by a reluctant President Dwight Eisenhower, who dispatched paratroopers to enforce the federal decree, to overcome the governor's obstruction.[60] But then the school board sought a postponement of the court's order, in view of the turmoil stirred up by Faubus's fizzled interposition. This forced the Supreme Court to reconsider the meaning of *Brown*, not just for school desegregation, but for the larger project of judicial review as well.

In *Cooper v. Aaron* (1958),[61] the justices began with the unprecedented step of each signing the opinion and taking credit for it,[62] thus signaling to the South that the Court remained unanimous behind the principles of *Brown*. They insisted that the constitutional rights of the Little Rock students "can neither be nullified openly and directly by state legislators or state executive or judicial officers, nor nullified indirectly by them through evasive schemes for segregation." *Cooper v. Aaron* was a resounding reaffirmation of *Brown v. Board of Education,* and, beyond that, of *Marbury v. Madison*.[63] The dramatic display of federal supremacy over state obstruction, with paratroopers of the US Army deployed to ensure integration of a Little Rock, Arkansas high school, was the federal government's necessary censure of a banal attempt by an epigone southern state governor to breathe some life into the corpse of antebellum nullification. But embedded in the *Cooper* opinion was a breathtaking claim: the Court's interpretation of the Constitution was not only final but supreme over all conflicting authorities. That claim could be problematic even in the context of federalism, where it affirmed federal supremacy over the states under the supremacy clause of

Article VI of the Constitution. But if it was improperly extrapolated to define the Court's relationship with other branches of the federal government (an issue of separation of powers), its grandiose vision of judicial authority could prove mischievous, to say the least.

Backing up its stiff warning against state defiance in *Cooper v. Aaron*, the Court reviewed "some basic propositions." Chief Justice John Marshall's ringing declaration in *Marbury v. Madison* (1803)[64] that "it is emphatically the province and duty of the judicial department to say what the law is," potentially implied a claim that judicial authority in constitutional interpretation is superior to that of Congress and the president. Of course, the Court must have the power to say what the law is. But did that imply that neither Congress nor the president had power to interpret the Constitution for itself?[65] Did it mean that congressional interpretation of the Constitution was somehow inappropriate as an intrusion on the Court's authority? Certainly, Congress cannot by statute repudiate a constitutional interpretation rendered by the Court. "Congress may not legislatively supersede our decisions interpreting and applying the Constitution," Chief Justice Rehnquist confirmed in 2000.[66] That is incontestable, and no one challenges it.

But the justices went beyond that in *Cooper* to affirm the "basic principle that the federal judiciary is supreme in the exposition of the law of the Constitution. It follows that the interpretation of the Fourteenth Amendment enunciated by this Court in the Brown case is the supreme law of the land."[67] Here the Court claimed for itself more than the power of judicial review, defined narrowly or broadly. Instead, it proclaimed the principle of judicial supremacy: the Court is "supreme" in interpretation of the Constitution, its views not only binding on the states and other branches of the federal government but superior to them and ultimately controlling. Had this claim been confined to the sphere of federalism—the supremacy of the federal Constitution as interpreted by the Supreme Court over inconsistent interpretations by state officers, confirmed by the supremacy clause of Article VI—it would not have been so provocative, and would merely have reminded everyone of the continuing force of the supremacy clause as originally interpreted in *Martin v. Hunter's Lessee* (1816).[68] But the Court seemed to go beyond that to proclaim that its decisions were "the supreme Law of the Land" on a par with "This Constitution, and the Laws of the United States" and treaties.[69] That claim, if taken literally, is breathtaking.

If (mis)applied in the context of the separation of powers, the Court's assertion of supremacy can be disruptive, demeaning the other branches of the federal government and derogating their authority to construe the Constitution. Carried to an extreme, it implies that the other branches have either no meaningful role in constitutional interpretation or only a preliminary, tentative one, subordinated to the judiciary's and exercised at the sufferance of the Court.[70] That, in turn, enables Congress to abdicate its responsibilities to interpret the Constitution. Stymied by a politically threatening conflict, as it was for example in 1848–1850 and then again in 1854 with the problem of slavery in the territories, Congress has shown itself only too willing to shunt the problem to the Court for resolution, with disastrous results.[71]

Cooper v. Aaron, read in its context, presented an issue of federalism, not separation of powers. The Court was asserting its authority over the states, not over Congress. But the troubling potential of the Court's incautious and unbounded claim of supremacy lay dormant for a generation, until the justices undertook to chastise Congress rather than the states of the old Confederacy.

But after *Cooper v. Aaron*, the Court remained largely outside the fray, abstaining from significant involvement in the ongoing struggles over desegregation for another six years.[72] The southern states tried an array of strategies to avoid desegregating, and for a decade they were successful. By 1964, a decade after *Brown*, only nominal or token desegregation had taken place in the South. A few counties or school districts chose to close their schools altogether rather than integrate, including Prince Edward County, Virginia.[73] (Prince Edward County was the locus of the Virginia case that constituted one of the five companion cases that made up *Brown v. Board of Education*.) County supervisors first closed all public schools; then the county offered tuition vouchers to enable students to attend private schools. Because all private schools were segregated and thus beyond the reach of *Brown*, the African American children of the area got no schooling at all for five years.

Such gross defiance of the desegregation mandate finally provoked the Court to act. It held this arrangement a violation of the equal protection clause in *Griffin v. County School Board of Prince Edward County* (1964) and went so far as to order the county to levy taxes to support the reopened public schools.[74] In response, segregation academies sprung up throughout the South, as white parents shouldered the burden of tuition payments (often state-subsidized by subterfuge).[75] Meanwhile, though segregationists lost the battle in the short term, their ideological innovations prevailed in the longer term. "White supremacist rhetoric was replaced by a 'new conservatism predicated on a language of rights, freedoms, and individualism.'"[76] The shift from naked old-time racism to the more modulated, facially neutral language of rights enabled the Supreme Court to ignore lingering segregation. Appeals to local control, neighborhood schools, taxpayer control of school finance, and parental control of their children's education came to dominate debates over integrating public school education and prevailed in the Supreme Court in less than a decade.

With *Griffin*, it became obvious that the Supreme Court's patience with southern evasion was evaporating. "The time for mere 'deliberate speed' has run out," wrote Justice Black for a unanimous Court. "There has been entirely too much deliberation and not enough speed."[77] But southern school districts continued to concoct ever-more-ingenious ways to nullify *Brown*. Among the more popular were the so-called freedom-of-choice plans, by which children (or rather their parents) in a school district under a desegregation order could choose which of the schools in the district they wanted to attend. Under the actual operation of such plans, no white child ever chose to go to a Black school, and only a small fraction of Black pupils sought admission to the white schools. Freedom of choice put the burden of changing the status quo by enrolling a Black child in a white school on the child's parents, a daunting (and potentially lethal) challenge. It was more than a subterfuge; "freedom of choice" was an effective block to any desegregation at all. It was public education's version of pretextuality. *Green v. County School Board* (1968)[78] took up the challenge posed by freedom-of-choice plans and condemned the South's ploy. Holding that the whole point of *Brown* was to secure admission to public schools on a nonracial basis, the Court unanimously held that the proposed plan failed to effectively desegregate the system, implying that few freedom-of-choice plans were likely to succeed. "The transition to a unitary, nonracial system of public education was and is the ultimate end to be brought about," Justice Brennan reminded the South.

Green marked a momentous change in the Court's and the nation's evolving understanding of *Brown*. *Brown* originally prohibited state-imposed racial segregation that disadvantaged African American children. But the following decade revealed that this original understanding, which we may call "anti-segregation," was inadequate in two respects. *Brown II* (1955) had assigned the responsibility of actually achieving anti-segregation, whatever that might come to mean, to local school boards in the first instance, with follow-up enforcement if necessary by US district courts, the courts of first instance in the federal judicial system. But what was supposed to happen when a school district announced that it would no longer assign pupils by race? That is what freedom-of-choice plans did, but all they delivered was the empty concession of not formally segregating students by race. Segregation continued, enforced not by positive law but by extralegal pressures on Black students' parents (loss of jobs or credit), and by the ever-present threats and actuality of violence. Freedom of choice merely continued the tactic of pretextuality that had worked so effectively for a century. *Green* broadened the stakes by locating school segregation within the larger system of white supremacy and racial caste.[79]

Second, if some kind of further response did prove necessary, what exactly was the school board to do? Americans thus came to realize that the meaning and consequences of anti-segregation were not self-evident. Those meanings and consequences would have to be worked out through lived experience over time. After a decade of passivity and gradualism that produced little desegregation, the Court, backed by public opinion in the North, decided that the white South's do-nothing response would no longer suffice. Something more was needed. Justice Brennan's opinion in *Green* announced the next steps: the school boards had an "affirmative duty" to "convert to a unitary system in which racial discrimination would be eliminated root and branch." Anti-segregation had now morphed into anti-discrimination, a crucial difference, and it was to be pursued in a "unitary school system."[80]

Having moved beyond mere anti-segregation, the Court immediately ran into a challenge that had been lurking, little noticed, since 1955: the so-called *Briggs* dictum. *Briggs v. Elliott* (1952),[81] the South Carolina case that was part of the *Brown* quintet, was the first of those cases to be argued, and its holding, sustaining school segregation, was reversed. Then on remand, the court of appeals in a per curiam opinion that may have been written by Judge John J. Parker[82] accepted the Supreme Court's decision but confined *Brown* to the narrowest possible reading: "The Constitution...does not require integration. It merely forbids discrimination. It does not forbid such segregation as occurs as the result of voluntary action."[83] This idea formed the bedrock of the conservative response to *Brown*, and as such it has endured into the present. It constitutes the basis of the Court's refusal to acknowledge the problem of structural racism. Regrettably, Congress seemed to ratify it in the Civil Rights Act of 1964, defining "desegregation" as assignment of pupils to schools "without regard to their race, color...but shall not mean the assignment of students to public schools in order to overcome racial imbalance."[84] Senator Hubert Humphrey (D.-MN), a liberal Democrat and principal sponsor of the bill, affirmed this understanding: "The bill does not attempt to integrate the schools, but it does attempt to eliminate segregation in the school system."[85] But most federal judges rejected the straitjacket of the *Briggs* dictum, and forged on to realize the implicit affirmative mandate of *Brown I*.

The Court ratcheted up the pressure on de jure segregation in *Alexander v. Holmes County Board of Education* (1969),[86] a per curiam opinion that affirmed "the obligation of every school district is to terminate dual school systems at once and to operate now and hereafter only unitary schools." *Alexander* did not overrule *Brown II*, but it did declare it obsolete: "a standard allowing 'all deliberate speed' for desegregation is no longer constitutionally permissible." *Alexander* was the Court's earliest response to the Nixon administration's go-slow policy concerning school desegregation. Following *Alexander*, "southern schools went through the most audacious social upheaval and prolific change ever required of any educational system in the U.S."[87]

The Burger Court continued *Alexander*'s momentum in a few more cases. In *Coit v. Green* (1971),[88] the Court unanimously affirmed a lower-court decision, *Green v. Connally* (1971),[89] which had held that under the Internal Revenue Code, schools that practiced racial discrimination (i.e., segregation academies, then in a phase of exponential growth) were ineligible for tax-exempt status, a crippling but not fatal blow. It struck a down a state program that furnished textbooks to segregated schools, condemning seg academies as "institutions that practice racial or other invidious discrimination."[90]

Green marked the end of the desegregation phase of the post-*Brown* era, a period of gradualism where the Court tolerated delay and evasion by the white South. The justices shared Frankfurter's misplaced hope that the white South could be counted on for good-faith compliance. The Court's withdrawal from active engagement with desegregation efforts left the lower federal courts and state school boards without guidance, support, or encouragement. "The justices declared what they considered unconstitutional but did not inform Southern officials of what would meet the constitutional test."[91] We cannot know whether more active engagement on the part of the Supreme Court in the critical 1955–1968 period would have made a difference. But it is clear with the benefit of hindsight that the Court's passivity tolerated white resistance while producing no benefit for African American children, the innocent victims of a decade of turmoil.

The drive for integration culminated in *Swann v. Charlotte-Mecklenburg Board of Education* (1971), the last of the major desegregation holdings of the civil rights era.[92] In the wake of *Green v. County Board*, the federal district court supervising desegregation of the combined city-county school system of Charlotte, North Carolina, had ordered the school board to redraw school lines and resort to busing if necessary. The Supreme Court upheld this order. For a unanimous Court, Chief Justice Warren Burger reluctantly held that in school districts with a history of de jure segregation, there will be a presumption that schools "substantially disproportionate in their racial composition" fall within the ban of segregated education. He authorized "frank—and sometimes drastic—gerrymandering of school districts and attendance zones." *Swann* marked "the high-water mark of judicial support for school desegregation remedies."[93]

Swann pushed the remedial envelope in three significant ways. First, it accepted the use of "numerical guidelines" and ratios as criteria for integration. In 1969, the Court had approved a desegregation order affecting public school teachers in Montgomery, Alabama, schools that relied to a loose and limited extent on "numerical ratios."[94] It was apparent from Justice Black's effusive praise for US District Court judge Frank M. Johnson's handling of that case that the justices were willing to place confidence in the equitable discretion of federal trial judges who proved to be of the caliber of Johnson, one of the judicial heroes of the civil rights movement.[95] For a time, this tolerance extended to a carefully qualified and constrained use of quantifiable measures. *Swann* affirmed this, permitting "mathematical ratios" to be used as a "starting point" for desegregation orders.[96]

Second, *Swann* was the Court's first encounter with large, complex urban school systems, as opposed to the uncomplicated unitary rural and small-town districts with which they had been dealing for two decades. The justices at first approved the pairing or grouping of non-contiguous school systems to overcome segregation, an innovation necessary in an urban environment. This worked in an area like Charlotte and surrounding Mecklenburg County, which were already combined in a unified school district. But in a scant three years, the Court was to shut down this possibility when it rejected inter-district remedies if city and county were not already in the same school district.

Finally, and most significant of all, the Court sanctioned busing as a legitimate tool of desegregation, stating that federal judges had power to order it based on their broad equitable discretion emphasized in *Brown II*. Previously, school administrators had used busing to preserve segregation in rural districts like New Kent County, Virginia. (To maintain segregated schools in a rural area, many students had to be bused to the school designated for their race.) But turning busing on its head, to promote *integration*, awakened whites to the merits of neighborhood schools (even if those schools were far off). Busing, as the Court quickly discovered to its chagrin, proved explosively unpopular, especially in the North. It provoked violence throughout the nation as white parents resisted having their children trucked to distant Black schools and, more offensively, having African American children brought into their hitherto-white sanctums. Busing became a principal driver of white flight and, in the South, seg academies.[97]

In reaching the momentous *Swann* result, the Court rejected an overture proposed in an amicus brief by a Richmond, Virginia, attorney then in private practice, Lewis Powell. Powell recommended continued delay in desegregation because busing would diminish the quality of all-white suburban schools, accelerate white flight, and reduce the quality of education provided to whites.[98] He recommended that the Court stop desegregation until residential segregation somehow disappeared. Since that would never occur spontaneously or naturally, Powell was calling on the Court to effectively abandon desegregation. In place of *Brown*'s emphasis on the rights of Black children, Powell's brief in effect urged the Court to give priority to the needs of white children. The passage of time would reveal that a majority of the justices shared this solicitude for the well-being of whites, even if it would override the inconsistent goal of equality for Blacks. Powell would have an opportunity to promote those views after his appointment to the Court three years later. Those three years were pivotal: in that interval, the Court went from insisting on busing to promote equality between the races, to a persistent solicitude for the well-being of whites that eclipsed demands for equality for Blacks.[99]

In *Swann*, Burger made an ominous concession: "once the affirmative duty to desegregate has been accomplished," neither school boards nor courts are under a continuing obligation to tweak the racial ratios annually to maintain the original balance.[100] Within two decades that idea provided the key to stopping desegregation altogether and affirming resegregation.[101]

In a companion decision, *North Carolina State Board of Education v. Swann* (1971), the Court unanimously struck down a state anti-busing statute that prohibited taking race into account or seeking racial balance when making pupil assignment decisions, reasoning that such faux color-blindness interfered with desegregation. Chief Justice Burger wrote that "the statute exploits an apparently neutral form to control school assignment plans by directing that they be 'color blind'; that requirement, against the background of segregation, would render illusory the promise of *Brown v. Board of Education*."[102] Here Burger (of all people) clearly recognized that color-blindness could serve as a mask disguising segregation and enabling discrimination. It had the potential to vitiate *Brown*.

In yet another *Swann* companion, *Davis v. Board of School Commissioners* (1971),[103] Burger again for a unanimous Court bundled together some themes that dominated this sunset moment of the civil rights era. Trial courts could determine specific numerical ratios for teachers and staff for each school that reflected the general demographics of the entire area. (The Supreme Court would soon denounce numerical ratios and specifically quantified remedies.) Courts are not limited to neighborhood schools and may adapt school zoning plans to the unique needs of the district. He demanded "the greatest possible degree of actual desegregation," and admonished lower-court judges that the true "measure of any desegregation plan is its effectiveness."

The desegregative momentum of *Green*, *Griffin*, and *Swann* dwindled after 1971. But before it dissipated completely, it retained enough energy for the Court in 1973 to condemn a Mississippi program of lending textbooks to seg academies. After *Green* in 1968, seg academies became the southern alternative to white flight. White parents did not move out of the school district; they created segregated private schools instead.[104] In *Norwood v. Harrison* (1973),[105] the Court held unanimously that a justifiable educational purpose (improving the education of all Mississippi children) could not overcome the impermissible effect of enabling segregation or racial discrimination even indirectly. "The existence of a permissible purpose cannot sustain an action that has an impermissible effect."[106] Thus the Court was still open to considering the discriminatory effects of actions that were justified by a permissible intent. But the Court would soon snuff out this lingering spirit of the second Reconstruction as the justices, tugged by Rehnquist and Powell, began to withdraw from *Brown I*.

It was inevitable that the Court's holdings striking down segregation in public schools would also apply to all other public facilities, and in a series of decisions over the decade following *Brown*, the Court per curiam eliminated segregation in swimming pools and beaches,[107] golf courses,[108] courtrooms,[109] public libraries,[110] municipal buses,[111] public transportation,[112] and parks.[113] "It is no longer open to question," the Court stated definitively in 1963, "that a State may not constitutionally require segregation of public facilities."[114] And that *was* the final word, bringing to an end a century of official state-imposed de jure segregation of public spaces.

Yet segregation did not collapse overnight throughout the land. It persisted doggedly, even in places where direct federal control and authority might have been sufficient to banish it forthrightly. Public housing provides a striking example. It may not have been surprising that the earliest federally financed public housing projects in the late 1930s were strictly segregated, even outside the South. But federal administrators of all programs relevant to public housing continued to maintain segregation even after *Brown* and its progeny public-facilities cases well into the 1960s. Paradoxically, some liberal federal bureaucrats supported *Plessy*-grounded segregation because they saw it as the only way to preserve racial "equity," that is, some minimal availability of federal bounties like housing to African Americans. Whether bolder approaches might have provided more opportunities is conjectural. What is clear, however, is that as federal courts pursued policies of desegregation in schools and public facilities after 1964, other federal agencies like the Federal Housing Administration and the Public Housing Administration preserved segregation in the spheres they controlled.[115]

A tiny incident in 1963 provides the epigraph for the second Reconstruction. Mary Hamilton, an African American, was being tried for a traffic violation in the circuit court of Etowah County, Alabama. The prosecuting attorney asked her: "What is your name, please?"

A[nswer] Miss Mary Hamilton.
Q[uestion] Mary, I believe—you were arrested—who were you arrested by?
A My name is Miss Hamilton. Please address me correctly.
Q Who were you arrested by, Mary?
A I will not answer a question——
BY ATTORNEY AMAKER: The witness's name is Miss Hamilton.
A—your question until I am addressed correctly.

THE COURT: Answer the question.
THE WITNESS: I will not answer them unless I am addressed correctly.
THE COURT: You are in contempt of court—
ATTORNEY CONLEY: Your Honor—your Honor—
THE COURT: You are in contempt of this court, and you are sentenced to five days in jail and a fifty dollar fine.[116]

The US Supreme Court immediately and summarily reversed, without opinion, simply citing one of the public-facilities desegregation opinions just mentioned, *Johnson v. Virginia*.[117] Without comment, a majority of the Supreme Court swept away over three centuries of social practice that had inscribed white supremacy / Black subordination in the everyday relations of Americans. Mary Hamilton, standing on her dignity in an obscure Alabama courtroom, insisted that she be addressed with the same respect that would have been accorded a white woman, and the US Supreme Court sustained her demand. The law now required that she receive the same formality and respect as whites in a society hitherto dominated by Jim Crow. What the philosopher John Rawls called "the most important primary good," self-respect,[118] was now recognized as the constitutional due of all Americans, Black and white. *Multum in parvo*: slowly the nation was inching toward genuine equality among all its peoples.

The desegregation cases through *Swann* and *Holmes* were the expiring gasp of Warren-era equality as the core meaning of the Fourteenth Amendment. The succeeding Courts would first discount, then abandon altogether, the goal of equality in education, seeming to look back on *Brown* with scarcely concealed unease as a misconceived, regrettable disruption of the social balance between the races. In its place, majorities of the Court would exalt the goals of white innocence and merit.

The First Amendment, Public Demonstrations, and the Sit-In Cases

One of the countless degradations imposed by slavery and servitude had been the unquestioned assumption that African Americans had no First Amendment rights that the white man was bound to respect. Stripped of political agency by Redemption, Black citizens had little hope of claiming protection for rights of speech, press, assembly, and petition through normal political processes. To Redeemers as to their slavocrat forebears, conceding freedom of communication might spread dangerous ideas about equality. *Herndon v. Lowry* (1937) had disturbed these assumptions, but not displaced them.

The second Reconstruction vanquished all those foundational assumptions that undergirded a racist constitutional regime. In their place, the Warren Court affirmed both speech and associational rights derived from First Amendment rights of speech, assembly, and petition; protected the ability of the NAACP to represent clients; and scotched the southern states' use of libel laws to suppress news coverage of civil rights activities. But the Court fractured in the sit-in cases when these First Amendment rights competed with the rights claimed by white property owners who wanted to exclude African Americans.

The southern states responded to *Brown* in numerous ways, one of them being to suppress individuals and organizations who were engaged in civil rights activism. When Alabama's attorney general demanded that the NAACP hand over a list of its members, the organization refused, fearing that the state would then use the list to fire all public employees who were members and induce private employers or creditors to harass Black activists economically. Worse yet, the names could be passed on to Klansmen to identify potential targets for terrorism. In *NAACP v. Alabama ex rel. Patterson* (1958),[119] Justice Harlan for a unanimous Court identified a robust "freedom to engage in association" as indispensable "for the advancement of beliefs and ideas [and] an inseparable aspect of the 'liberty' assured by the due process clause of the Fourteenth Amendment, which embraces freedom of speech." He quashed Alabama's demand for NAACP membership lists. In thus protecting African Americans in the exercise of their First Amendment liberties of speech, press, assembly, and petition, the Court recognized a new, derivative right of association that would soon expand into the right of privacy recognized in *Griswold v. Connecticut* (1965),[120] and from thence into unimaginable new areas. This implicit associational right is broader and vaguer than the express right "to assemble, and to petition" secured by the First Amendment.

Thwarted in its efforts to intimidate African Americans' associational rights, the white South then tried to suppress their ability to litigate. Drawing on centuries-old common-law bans on stirring up or financing litigation, Virginia enacted legislation that penalized ambulance-chasing and other forms of soliciting legal business. It then applied this to the

NAACP's representation of clients in civil rights matters. In *NAACP v. Button* (1963),[121] the Court held that as applied, such a statute "violates the Fourteenth Amendment by unduly inhibiting protected freedoms of expression and association." Litigation was now a form of expression protected by the First Amendment. This relatively obscure case had the effect of upholding public-interest litigation.

Louisiana and Alabama tried a more frontal assault on the NAACP by banning it from conducting business within the state. The Court readily struck down the Louisiana effort in *Louisiana ex rel. Gremillion v. NAACP* (1961),[122] but then found itself balked by the state courts' artful Fabian tactics of delay in dissolving a temporary restraining order, which had the practical effect of shutting down NAACP activities within the state. Finally, after five years the Court blew up this logjam of litigation in *NAACP v. Alabama ex rel. Flowers* (1964),[123] clearing the way for activism throughout the Deep South.

Civil rights organizations won their most far-reaching victory in *New York Times v. Sullivan* (1964).[124] Southern states tried to suppress sympathetic news coverage of civil rights protests by harassing news media. One of the most effective ways of doing so consisted of libel suits, accusing reporters or persons quoted in news coverage of sullying the reputations of individuals who in some ways were opposed to the civil rights cause. A *New York Times* ad that accused the Montgomery, Alabama, police commissioner of harassing Black demonstrators contained several minor factual misstatements. The police commissioner won a half-million-dollar verdict rendered under the state's common law of libel. Had that verdict stood, the *Times* would have been badly damaged financially, and all other news organizations would have been cowed. In overturning the verdict, Justice Brennan articulated a landmark First Amendment principle: "debate on public issues should be uninhibited, robust, and wide-open." He held that in libel cases involving criticism of public officials, the plaintiff must show that the defendant acted with actual malice: either with knowledge that the statement was false or a reckless disregard for whether it was or not. While *New York Times v. Sullivan* is best known as a First Amendment monument, it also helped put an end to harassment of civil rights activists by libel suits.[125]

Sit-ins, boycotts, and other forms of direct-action protests posed more complicated legal issues, often bedeviled by the state action problem.[126] Before enactment of the public accommodations section of the Civil Rights

Act of 1964 (Title II), protest activities on privately owned property became legally a form of criminal and civil trespass once the property owner ordered the participants to leave. If police arrested persons for trespassing in the context of sit-in demonstrations, was state action implicated? *Shelley v. Kraemer* might suggest that it was. But could *Shelley* be extended to prohibit police from interfering with First Amendment activities when those expressive activities conflicted with property interests? Or was law enforcement action merely the neutral duty of the state to keep the peace and protect one of the fundamental rights associated with privately owned property, the right to exclude? This presented a classic clash of two fundamental rights claims: First Amendment rights of communication and association versus the most basic of rights derived from the private ownership of property.[127]

Chief Justice Warren managed to achieve a fleeting unanimity in *Peterson v. Greenville* (1963),[128] where a local ordinance required racial segregation in restaurant seating. In such a case the ultimate decision to discriminate would not be imputed to a private owner (a dime store that operated a lunch counter), where the local government mandated segregation. "When the State has commanded a particular result, it has...'become involved' in it, and, in fact, has removed that decision from the sphere of private choice," Chief Justice Warren concluded. When the demonstration took place on state-owned property, the state's role was similarly obvious. After Black students peacefully protesting racial discrimination were arrested on the grounds of the South Carolina state capitol, the Court overturned their conviction on First Amendment grounds in *Edwards v. South Carolina* (1963).[129] Justice Stewart pointed out that they had been arrested for "an exercise of these basic constitutional rights [of speech and assembly] in their most pristine and classic form."

But where a private property owner chose to discriminate without state compulsion, did its common-law right to exclude rise to constitutional stature and outweigh claims based on human dignity and equality? The Court was unable to achieve consensus or find a doctrinal template to dispose of the numerous sit-in and protest cases that were coming up to it.[130] It resolved each case on an ad hoc, technical, or non-germane basis.[131] The complexities imposed by the state action doctrine fractured the Court and led Justice Hugo Black to voice cranky complaints about violence and disrespect for social order that he attributed to Black protesters. He warned that "force leads to violence, violence to mob conflicts, and these to rule by the strongest groups with control of the most deadly weapons."[132]

After Congress enacted the 1964 Civil Rights Act, legitimizing federal authority to protect freedom from racial discrimination in public venues, the Court managed to come up with a resolution of sorts. In *Hamm v. Rock Hill* (1964),[133] the Court held that enactment of Title II abated all pending prosecutions, even for actions that occurred before the act's passage. After that, prosecutions for sit-in activities dwindled, but that did not allay Justice Black's misgivings about protests on private property. He continued to belabor civil rights protesters. In *Brown v. Louisiana* (1966), he denounced the Court's reliance on First Amendment rights of speech, assembly, and petition: the amendment "does not guarantee to any person the right to use someone else's property, even that owned by government and dedicated to other purposes, as a stage to express dissident ideas."[134] He objected again that year in *Adderly v. Florida* (1966),[135] where students were arrested for protesting on the grounds of a jail. In *Adderly*, a five-to-four majority upheld the convictions after Stewart swung over to the conservatives, marking the first time the Court sustained sit-in convictions.

But once the passions of the 1960s subsided and Black was no longer on the Court, the justices extended the outcome of the First Amendment cases to suits alleging malicious interference with business relationships. The justices applied the leading First Amendment speech precedent, *Brandenburg v. Ohio* (1969),[136] to a civil rights boycott, holding that inflammatory rhetoric denouncing racial discrimination was protected under the First Amendment if it did not incite imminent lawless actions. In *NAACP v. Claiborne Hardware Co.* (1982), the Court upheld a secondary boycott, thereby protecting speech and associational rights of African Americans who challenged racial discrimination.[137] After that, First Amendment litigation in a civil rights context receded in significance.

The Civil Rights Act of 1964

In both the first and the second Reconstructions, progress toward racial equality at the federal level came about because both the Supreme Court and Congress were committed to egalitarian goals. If either of those partners receded from their mutual commitment, progress faltered. If both withdrew, progress ended and then reversed. Each had to support the other, legislation creating substantive rights where judicial fiat alone could not, judicial action filling in the interstices between those rights and enforcing them. Just as the first Reconstruction would have been unfulfilled without the Civil Rights Act of 1866, so the second required the legislative foundation provided by the Civil Rights Act of 1964 and its sibling, the Civil Rights Act of 1965. Without such reciprocal support, equality wanes.

President John F. Kennedy first proposed a civil rights bill in 1963, containing provisions dealing with public accommodations, voting rights, and federal participation in school desegregation suits. The bill stalled in the House, but Kennedy's assassination that November and President Lyndon B. Johnson's strong support pushed it through over a unanimous southern filibuster in the Senate.[138] A year later, in a major commencement address at Howard University that he delivered after Congress had enacted the Voting Rights Act of 1965, the president laid out in limpid terms the rationale for the legislative foundations of the second Reconstruction:

> Freedom is the right to share, share fully and equally, in American society—to vote, to hold a job, to enter a public place, to go to school. It is the right to be treated in every part of our national life as a person equal in dignity and promise to all others.
>
> But freedom is not enough. You do not wipe away the scars of centuries by saying: Now you are free to go where you want, and do as you desire, and choose the leaders you please. You do not take a person who, for years, has been hobbled by chains and liberate him, bring him up to the starting line of a race and then say, "you are free to compete with all the others," and still justly believe that you have been completely fair.
>
> Thus it is not enough just to open the gates of opportunity. All our citizens must have the ability to walk through those gates. This is the next and the more profound stage of the battle for civil rights. We seek not just freedom but opportunity. We seek not just legal equity but human ability, not just equality as a right and a theory but equality as a fact and equality as a result.[139]

In this address, President Johnson eloquently expressed the vision that inspired the civil rights era and anticipated the need to go on to the next stage, the struggle against structural racism. But he also recognized the cost of doing so. After signing the Civil Rights Act of 1964, he supposedly remarked to an aide, "I think we just delivered the South to the Republican Party for a long time to come."[140] The political consequences produced an explosive backlash against progress toward equality in the second Reconstruction.

Having failed to prevent enactment of the Civil Rights Act, the South immediately launched a constitutional assault on Title II, which at the time was the most provocative part of the act to segregationists.[141] The owner of a downtown resort hotel, the Heart of Atlanta Motel, and the proprietor of a neighborhood barbecue restaurant mounted a comprehensive challenge to Title II. Justice Tom Clark wrote for a unanimous court in both cases. In *Heart of Atlanta Motel v. United States* (1964),[142] the more important of the two, Clark held that while Congress could use the commerce clause to protect the "moral" objective of vindicating "personal dignity," its reliance on the clause was amply sustained by the economic impact of discrimination in interstate travel as well. It made no difference that Congress was legislating to right a "moral and social wrong" as well as an economic problem. Clark described the burdens placed on African American travelers in seeking hotel accommodations. He noted the need for the publication called "the Green Book"[143] that provided contact information for motels, boarding houses, and even individual African American householders willing to provide a room for the night to Black travelers, as well as other tourist services. Congress accordingly based its actions on "overwhelming evidence that discrimination by hotels and motels impedes interstate travel." From that factual conclusion, Clark then reviewed prior commerce clauses doctrine, beginning with *Gibbons v. Ogden* (1824),[144] as well as more recent New Deal decisions,[145] Clark held that federal power could reach "local incidents" of economic activity that have a "substantial and harmful effect" on interstate commerce. But the malign influence of the *Civil Rights Cases* of 1883 hovered like a troublesome ghost: the Court could not rely on broader understandings of the equal protection clause because of the state action doctrine. Under later understandings of the Reconstruction Amendments, Congress also derived its authority to enact the 1964 act from the citizenship clause of the Fourteenth Amendment.[146]

In the companion case, *Katzenbach v. McClung* (1964),[147] the Court affirmed the reach of the act to a neighborhood BBQ joint that, unlike the motel, was remote from the arteries of interstate commerce, on the grounds that approximately half its food supplies moved in interstate commerce. From that, the Court found "a close connection to interstate commerce." Congress had "a rational basis for finding that racial discrimination in restaurants had a direct and adverse effect on the free flow of interstate commerce." Important as *Heart of Atlanta* and *McClung* were for sustaining Congress's power to enact public accommodations laws, the cases were even more significant as precedent for broadly expanded congressional power under the commerce clause. They provided something near carte blanche for federal power to regulate the economy.

With the constitutionality of the Civil Rights Act settled, at least as to public accommodations, the justices were free to engage with other issues that came up in dismantling Jim Crow. None proved to be as tenacious as residential segregation and discrimination in access to shelter. Though Congress tried its hand at addressing those problems through the Civil Rights Act of 1968 (later known as the Fair Housing Act), the Supreme Court for its part invoked older and more august sources to deal with them.

The Thirteenth Amendment and the 1866 Civil Rights Act Revived

Redemption had consigned both the Thirteenth Amendment and the 1866 Civil Rights Act to a dungeon of pretextuality and formalism. In theory, African Americans had the same rights of contract and property as white Americans (the pretext), but far from liberating the freedpeople, this contractual capacity only limited their opportunities in a new network of labor-coercion measures (the reality).[148] In the second Reconstruction, the Supreme Court swept away these constraints and resurrected the Reconstruction amendments and statutes, finally giving them full effect.

One of the most far-reaching victories for civil rights causes in the second Reconstruction came in 1968, in the decision that revived the 1866 Civil Rights Act.[149] *Jones v. Alfred H. Mayer Co.* (1968) opened a whole new landscape of opportunity to those who would challenge housing segregation and other forms of discrimination.[150] It shifted attention from the Fourteenth to the Thirteenth Amendment as a source of protection for basic rights founded in property and contractual relationships. An interracial couple trying to buy a home in a St. Louis, Missouri, suburb was rebuffed on the grounds that the developer refused to sell to African Americans, a commonplace occurrence in mid-century America. Suburban housing opportunities were reserved exclusively for whites, in a complex process of federally imposed racial segregation that kept inner cities the only places where African Americans could find urban housing. Federal policies encouraged suburban development but ensured that only whites could access it.[151] The Joneses brought suit under a modern descendant of the 1866 Civil Rights Act, 42 U.S.C. sec. 1982, which guaranteed access to property.[152] In the federal district court, they ran into the stone wall of the state action requirement. Under the *Civil Rights Cases*, plaintiffs had to demonstrate state action in order to protect rights secured by any part of the 1866 Civil Rights Act, and the trial court found none in the purely private discrimination of a real estate developer.[153]

They fared better on appeal to the Eighth Circuit, where Judge Harry Blackmun[154] affirmed, as he had to; the *Civil Rights Cases* were binding precedent that he could not ignore. But he went out of his way to indicate how the Supreme Court could avoid the impasse of the state action doctrine.[155] Instead of relying on the Fourteenth Amendment, he suggested that the petitioners might have more success with the Thirteenth, which Justice Bradley had said in the *Civil Rights Cases* was not bound by any state action requirement.[156] The constitutional foundation of section 1982, after all, had to be the Thirteenth Amendment; the Fourteenth was not ratified until after passage of the 1866 act.

That is exactly what Justice Stewart concluded when the case reached the High Court.[157] He held that section 1982 banned all private racial discrimination in access to housing, whether by purchase or rental. Stewart acknowledged that his opinion had "revolutionary implications": the Thirty-Eighth Congress had meant to "eliminate all racial barriers to the acquisition of real and personal property." The Thirteenth Amendment was an "absolute declaration that slavery shall not exist," and Congress was granted untrammeled enforcement power by section 2 of the amendment. Under this authority, Congress could reach "all badges and incidents of slavery," among which were all "burdens and disabilities…upon those fundamental rights which are the essence of civil freedom." "When racial discrimination herds men into ghettos and makes their ability to buy property turn on the color of their skin, then it too is a relic of slavery." Justice Douglas, concurring, would have gone further, denouncing all forms of racial discrimination as "the spectacle of slavery unwilling to die,"[158] and thus vulnerable to Congress's sweeping remedial power under section 2. The next year Douglas, speaking for the Court, extended the remedies under section 1982 to include damages, in addition to injunctive relief authorized in *Jones*.[159]

Between argument and decision in the Supreme Court, Congress had enacted the Fair Housing Act, which made Stewart's decision to rely on the 1866 act instead even more remarkable. The 1866 statute was comprehensive, applying to all types of housing, whereas the 1968 act contained what was known as the "Mrs. Murphy's boarding house" exception, exempting owner-occupied buildings of four or fewer rental units. The modern act at first had only administrative enforcement mechanisms; the earlier statute implied a private right of action, now vindicated. But the possibilities opened by the Thirteenth Amendment were far more expansive.[160] The Warren Court evinced a realism about racial conditions that all too soon would fade into the arid formalism of the second Redemption.

Court, Congress, and Enforcement of Rights

The Court took up the issue of the congressional enforcement power under the Reconstruction Amendments in the 1966 case of *Katzenbach v. Morgan*,[161] a voting rights case involving a literacy test. There the Court overturned a New York statue mandating English-language literacy to vote. (The measure targeted New York City's large Puerto Rican population.) Justice Brennan for the majority breezily read section 5 expansively as a "positive grant of legislative power" comparable in its scope to the necessary and proper clause of Article I, section 8. It was to be interpreted as generously as Chief Justice Marshall had read that clause in *McCulloch v. Maryland*'s oft-quoted passage (1819): "Let the end be legitimate..."[162] Brennan mandated extreme judicial deference to the powers of Congress: "it is enough that we be able to perceive a basis upon which the Congress might resolve the conflict as it did." The effect of Brennan's opinion was to accord Congress a role in interpreting section 5 equal to the Court's, affirmed by the relaxed scrutiny of the "perceive a basis" standard, and enhanced by his endorsement of judicial deference.

However, Brennan too readily dismissed Justice Harlan's dissent,[163] which identified serious constitutional issues presented by section 5, both of federalism and of separation of powers. What constitute substantive rights are "questions essentially judicial in nature," Harlan wrote.[164] Therefore, whether the state's action violated the Constitution is one for the judicial branch ultimately to determine.[165] Harlan claimed that Brennan's view gave the Court power to decide the substantive meaning of the Constitution. That in turn might enable Congress both to ignore the Supreme Court's interpretation of the Fourteenth Amendment and to bootstrap its own powers to define rights, making it superior to the Constitution.

This was a serious challenge, and it merited more thoughtful consideration than it got from the Warren Court liberal bloc.

Lurking in the problem Harlan identified is a conundrum. Congress legitimately has the power and the duty to interpret the Constitution. As Justice Kennedy put it in *Boerne v. Flores* (1997), "when Congress acts within its sphere of power and responsibilities, it has not just the right but the duty to make its own informed judgment on the meaning and force of the Constitution."[166] It did just that, for example, in the provisions of the 1866 Civil Rights Act guaranteeing a right to own property and enter into contracts. Arguably, that provision created new substantive rights. How else could Congress identify the rights it had to secure if the freedpeople were not to be thrust back into crypto-slavery? Presumably there is a distinction between Congress's power to interpret the Constitution in the first instance and its power to enforce an interpretation already made by the Supreme Court. But how and where draw the line between the exercise of Congress's legitimate powers to enact legislation based on its understanding of the Constitution, and a congressional action that infringes on the Supreme Court's authority as the ultimate interpreter of the Constitution, as proclaimed in *Marbury v. Madison*? That was the conundrum.

The Supreme Court answered those questions restrictively in the first Redemption of the 1870s. Not that it mattered much at the time: after 1876, Congress lost its appetite for protecting the freedpeople in the exercise of their rights. After the 1866 Civil Rights Act, the Thirteenth Amendment as well as the act itself lay dormant and ignored for nearly a century. Thus *Jones v. Alfred H. Mayer Co.* was a constitutional bombshell when it was decided in 1968. In a single stroke, *Jones* brought both the Thirteenth Amendment and the 1966 act back into relevance as part of the living Constitution; showed a way around the state action roadblock; reminded Congress of its expansive powers to promote equality; and re-engaged the nation in the work of ensuring full citizenship deferred through the era of Jim Crow. Section 2 of the Thirteenth Amendment, which Justice Stewart tellingly referred to as "the Enabling Clause" (a phrase broader and more suggestive than "the enforcement clause"), "empowered Congress to do much more. For that clause clothed 'Congress with power to pass *all laws necessary and proper for abolishing all badges and incidents of slavery in the United States*.'"[167] He amplified: "whatever else they may have encompassed, the badges and incidents of slavery—its 'burdens and disabilities'— included restraints upon 'those fundamental rights which are the essence of civil freedom.'" With that, the Court opened its doors to whatever protections Congress chose to legislate to protect freedom under the Thirteenth Amendment. This issue soon returned to the Court.

A provision of the 1871 Ku Klux Klan Act, today codified as 42 U.S.C. sec. 1985(3), imposed civil liability on "two or more persons [who] conspire or go in disguise on the highway" to deprive another of equal protection or equal privileges and immunities. In 1966, white thugs stopped an automobile occupied by some young Black men, who were running errands and visiting friends in Mississippi, and under the mistaken impression that they were civil rights workers, beat and terrorized them. Did section 1985(3) cover this set of facts? In *Griffin v. Breckinridge* (1971),[168] the Court held that it did. Justice Stewart first interpreted the statute to require "invidiously discriminatory motivation" and then upheld its constitutionality, not under section 5 of the Fourteenth Amendment, but under the enforcement clause, section 2, of the Thirteenth Amendment, reflecting the influence of his opinion in *Jones v. Alfred H. Mayer Co.*, decided three years earlier. Congress was empowered to enact laws controlling the behavior of individuals with no connection to the state to stamp out the badges and incidents of slavery, generously defined.

Jones v. Alfred H, Mayer Co. was a section 1982 case: it affirmed the right to acquire property. Presumably the same reasoning would apply to its sibling provision derived from the 1866 Civil Rights Act, section 1981, particularly the right to enter into contracts. This assumption was tested and confirmed in *Runyon v. McCrary* (1976),[169] a case that posed a head-on challenge to seg academies. *Runyon* presented several questions: did the refusal of a white private actor to enter into a contractual relationship with Black parents violate the act? Because those parents might have a statutory right, did that mean that school's proprietors were compelled to enter into a contractual relationship with them? In jurisprudential terms, did the existence of a right of A to enter into a contract imply a corresponding duty in the potential counterparty B to honor that right?[170] Did the schools have a constitutionally protected right to refuse to contract, based on association, privacy, or parents' rights to direct the education of their children?[171] And if section 1981 was found to be dispositive, did Congress have constitutional authority to enact it under section 2 of the Thirteenth Amendment?

Justice Stewart for the majority in *Runyon* found *Jones v. Alfred H. Mayer* controlling, holding that the right to enter into contracts was on a par with the right to own property. This necessarily implied that, whatever the segregationist's rights might be to refuse to enter into contractual relationships, they were subordinated to the Black parents' right to contract. Similarly, though parents may have a right to send their children to racially segregated private schools, "they have no constitutional right to provide their children with private school education unfettered by reasonable government regulation."[172] *Jones* was therefore likewise controlling on Congress's power under the Thirteenth Amendment. Justices White and Rehnquist dissented, maintaining that the 1866 Civil Rights Act and any congressional power under the Thirteenth Amendment could reach only state action. This read into the Thirteenth Amendment a provision that simply was not there.

Runyon v. McCrary reverberated later in several ways. One was ironic. Michael McCrary, the child who was the object of the litigation, grew up and enjoyed a celebrated college and pro football career as a defensive end for the Baltimore Ravens. The NFL Players' Association bestowed its Byron "Whizzer" White Humanitarian Award in 2000 on him, apparently with no sense of the incongruity.[173] White the humanitarian overrode White the jurist.

Of greater significance, when a later employment case, *Patterson v. McLean Credit Union,* was argued in 1988, a five-member conservative majority on its own motion ("sua sponte" as lawyers say) per curiam ordered re-argument on the following question: "Whether or not the interpretation of 42 U.S.C. § 1981 adopted by this Court in *Runyon v. McCrary*... should be reconsidered?"[174] The anonymous opinion that ordered re-argument blandly invoked "the abiding rule that it treat all litigants equally: that is, that the claim of any litigant for the application of a rule to its case should not be influenced by the Court's view of the worthiness of the litigant in terms of extralegal criteria." This was a meaningless truism and non sequitur unless it was intended to demote or disrespect the status of civil rights petitioners generally. Shocked and indignant, Justices Brennan, Marshall, Blackmun, and Stevens wrote blistering dissents denouncing the move. The anonymous author of the per curiam airily shrugged them off, but the gratuitous gambit alarmed the legal community.[175] Ultimately, little came of it: the Court reaffirmed *Runyon* in its *Patterson* opinion, but the unnecessary sua sponte move by the majority justices confirmed the new reality of the second Redemption: anyone who sought to vindicate rights created in the first Reconstruction would now find the Supreme Court an alien, forbidding venue.

The Problem of State Action

Since the *Civil Rights Cases* were decided in 1883, the state action doctrine announced there has hampered congressional efforts to protect the rights of African Americans. But in the second Reconstruction, the Court confined the state action doctrine in two important ways. That development of the doctrine was complex, so a heuristic model of rule-and-exceptions might be helpful to explain its workings.

The US Supreme Court invented the doctrine in the *Civil Rights Cases* of 1883 as the explanation for holding the public accommodations provisions of the 1875 Civil Rights Act unconstitutional.[176] Explaining why Congress lacked power under the Fourteenth Amendment to ban racial discrimination and exclusion in private enterprises like hotels, restaurants, and theaters, Justice Bradley declared that "It is State action of a particular character that is prohibited. Individual invasion of individual rights is not the subject-matter of the amendment."[177] Thus the state action doctrine was born. The doctrine may be restated simply: Congress may exercise its remedial powers under section 5 of the Fourteenth Amendment to protect the privileges or immunities, or the rights of due process or equal protection of persons, only against actions by the state or its agents (including local governments and all agencies of the state). It may not legislate directly upon private individuals who are not acting under the authority of the state.

This nineteenth-century model rests on fundamental though elusive assumptions about American society, the most basic of which is that there is a workable distinction between the public and the private spheres of our individual or collective lives.[178] The public sphere may be regulated by the state; the private sphere (home, family, intimate associations, religious affiliation) is largely insulated from intrusion by public authority. As a crude dichotomy, the public-private distinction is suggestive, but it does not carry us far analytically.[179] Moreover, it is founded on nineteenth-century assumptions about the sanctity of private property, and on racist predilections that make it ill-suited for today's society.[180] The state action doctrine and its embedded assumptions about the public-private distinction constitute the legal underpinning that permits the continuation of de facto discrimination and structural racism in American society.[181] It is, in Charles Black's memorable phrase, " a constitutional disaster area."[182]

Put in these unqualified terms, the state action doctrine, considered as a rule, is too powerful and comprehensive a constraint on Congress's powers.

If not limited by exceptions, it would shrivel the scope of the Fourteenth Amendment to the point where African Americans would find little federal protection for the rights secured by section 1 against wrongs inflicted by nonstate actors. Hence the Court had to carve out exceptions to the doctrine if the amendment is to serve its framers' purposes.

And that is in fact what happened. By the end of the civil rights era, the Court identified four categories of exceptions, which may be called (1) public function; (2) state enforcement; (3) state involvement; and (4) state authorization. The white primary case of *Smith v. Allwright* (1944)[183] illustrates public function: when a nominally private entity like a political party provides a function normally undertaken by the state, like conducting elections, it will be deemed public for purposes of protecting the rights of those whom its actions harm. *Shelley v. Kraemer* (1948)[184] demonstrates the second category, state enforcement. Where the agencies of the state (courts and law enforcement) are involved in a denial of Fourteenth Amendment rights, to the point of becoming the effective means that enforces that denial, the state is considered to have acted, even if the impetus comes in the first instance from private parties. Thus, by the dawn of the second Reconstruction, the Court had created two categorical exceptions. It then created two more before it ran into the roadblock of the second Redemption.

One of the numerous problems with the public-private distinction is its inability to identify a line where state involvement in private activities, like running a restaurant, begins and ends. It was left to the Court to provide guidelines that demarcate the private sphere in *Burton v. Wilmington Parking Authority* (1961).[185] The city of Wilmington, Delaware, constructed and owned a parking garage and then leased space in it to a privately operated restaurant that refused service to Black patrons. Justice Clark found sufficient state involvement in that discrimination to authorize a federal remedy through Title II of the 1964 act. The "peculiar relationship" of private discriminator as lessee and government entity as lessor provided the "degree of state participation and involvement in discriminatory action" "to some significant extent." The state "place[d] its power, prestige, and property behind the admitted discrimination." This did not provide a definitive or universal guideline for measuring the requisite degree of state participation, and the phrase "to some significant extent" left room for less sympathetic courts to ignore state involvement with discriminators, but that is inevitable when legal rules are couched in descriptive language.[186]

Sometimes a state may authorize private discrimination by enabling those who would discriminate to do so under the protection of state law. This proved to be the category that included one of the hottest-button issues of the mid-1960s, fair housing. The state may authorize discrimination by modifying its legal system in ways that either make it easier to discriminate or that deny victims legal redress once discrimination has occurred. The struggles over this issue began in California in 1959, when the legislature enacted three successive public accommodations and fair-housing measures.[187] A coalition of real estate brokers, the state Chamber of Commerce, landlords, neighborhood organizations, and white property owners rode the updrafts of the dynamic conservative activism then upwelling out of Southern California to promote Proposition 14, an initiative measure to amend the state constitution to ban all fair-housing legislation.[188] It prohibited the state and all local governments from restricting "the right of any person...to decline to sell, lease, or rent" real property to anyone "as he, in his absolute discretion, chooses." Ronald Reagan, running successfully for governor, endorsed the idea: "if an individual wants to discriminate against Negroes or others in selling or renting his house, he has a right to do so."[189] In 1964, the people of California endorsed Prop 14 by a two-million vote margin, thereby making the ability to discriminate a fundamental constitutional right, embedded in the state's constitution. (In 1973, the US Supreme Court repudiated that idea, stating in dictum that "invidious private discrimination...has never been accorded affirmative constitutional protection.")[190]

The California Supreme Court held Prop 14 unconstitutional on the grounds that it authorized racial discrimination in violation of the federal equal protection clause. Achieved by popular initiative, such encouragement constituted state action because the people of California were acting directly in their sovereign capacity.[191] But the court did not bother to explain exactly how the state was involved in discriminatory acts in a way that would satisfy the state action requirement.[192] The US Supreme Court affirmed in *Reitman v. Mulkey* (1967)[193] in an opinion by Justice White that did not clarify or add anything to the California decision, thus leaving the core question in the case unanswered. White merely stated that Prop 14 was intended to authorize, and does authorize, racial discrimination in the housing market. "The right to discriminate is now one of the basic policies of the State." The state becomes "involved" in private discrimination if its "permissive statute" (here, the constitutional amendment) could be construed as "authorization" to discriminate.[194]

In a concurring opinion, though, Justice Douglas offered a persuasive rationale for finding state action.[195] Relying on findings by the US Civil Rights Commission, he demonstrated how property changes hands in a typical real estate transaction from owner through the agencies of realtor and title companies to mortgage lender, to purchaser, to demonstrate that the state "harnesses" private actors to do what the state is itself forbidden to do. Then he picked up a point made by the first Justice Harlan in his *Civil Rights Cases* dissent: state action occurs when the state licenses the business of those who discriminate (here, realtors, mortgage brokers, etc.). Such licensing creates an "environment where the whole weight of the system is on the side of discrimination."

The California Supreme Court and the US Supreme Court's majority and concurring opinions did intuit a correct resolution of the issues presented by Prop 14, which was explicitly premised on a racist objective: preserving the power of owners to discriminate in access to shelter. Two years later, the Court extended *Reitman* to cover a city charter amendment requiring that any ordinance regulating the sale or lease of property "on the basis of race, color...or ancestry" be approved by a majority of the city's voters in a referendum. The amendment also suspended all fair-housing legislation until it too was approved by referendum. In *Hunter v. Erickson* (1969),[196] Justice White rejected the amendment as an explicitly racial classification that placed a "special burden on racial minorities."

These two initiative and referendum cases raised the problem anticipated in *Carolene Products*' footnote 4: legislation based on "prejudice against discrete and insular minorities" that "restricts those political processes" that can bring about democratic change. As the California experience has repeatedly proven, modern initiative legislation has an anti-democratic effect that impacts minorities especially hard. In place of legislation refined by the deliberative process, referenda reduce complex issues to a stark binary, take-it-or-leave-it proposition, often drafted in misleading language, unrefined by legislative debate, hearings, and evidence. The vote is insulated from inquiry into the voters' motives, and often racial animosity lurks below the surface of neutral-sounding measures.[197]

These last two categories (state involvement and state authorization) mark the outermost development of exceptions to the state action doctrine to date. When the civil rights climate changed dramatically after 1971, the impetus for creating exceptions to the state action doctrine deflated, while the doctrine itself recruited new supporters on the Court, premier among them Justice William H. Rehnquist. The newly conservative Court refused to find exceptions to the doctrine where the state licensed the business or occupation of the discriminator;[198] where the discriminator is a regulated monopoly;[199] where the state acquiesced in the challenged action;[200] where the state regulated or subsidized the discriminator;[201] and where the state failed to take action to protect the victim.[202] The Court's dwindling interest in finding exceptions to the state action doctrine may be attributable to the fact that in all of these cases but the first (*Moose Lodge*), the complaint was not directly related to racial discrimination. Perhaps in future cases presenting racial issues, the Court may return to the project. But for now, the state action doctrine reigns in nearly the full vigor of its origin in the *Civil Rights Cases*.

Another issue addressed by the state action problem is whether Congress has power to regulate the behavior of private individuals in enforcing the rights recognized by the Reconstruction amendments. This raises issues both of federalism and of separation of powers. In the American federal system, the national government is a government of limited and delegated powers, meaning that it has only those powers granted explicitly in the text of the Constitution or the implied powers that Chief Justice John Marshall described as "incidental to those powers which are expressly given."[203] The states, by contrast, are governments of residuary sovereignty, meaning that they have all powers not explicitly denied them by the state or federal constitutions. So the question becomes: Does a particular implied congressional power exist? That raises the next fundamental question, one of separation of powers: Who decides the answer to that federalism question, Congress or the Supreme Court? Two 1966 companion cases involving terrorist murders by the Ku Klux Klan raised these questions anew in the second Reconstruction.

Lemuel Penn was an Army Reserve officer returning to his home in Washington, DC, from active duty for training when he was murdered in a drive-by shooting by four Klansmen in northeast Georgia in 1964.[204] After the Klansmen were predictably acquitted by an all-white jury in a state prosecution, the US Department of Justice secured an indictment for violation of the federal civil-rights criminal conspiracy statute, 18 U.S.C. sec. 241.[205] Section 241 makes it a federal felony for "any two or more persons [to] conspire to oppress, threaten, or intimidate any inhabitant of any State, Territory, or District in the free exercise or enjoyment of any right or privilege secured to him by the Constitution or laws of the United States." It does not contain a state action requirement; Congress is directly regulating the behavior of private individuals. This raises the question whether Congress had power to enact it under section 5 of the Fourteenth Amendment.[206] In *Guest v. United States* (1966),[207] Justice Stewart, for the Court, avoided answering that difficult constitutional question by discovering a trace of state involvement in the actions of state law enforcement officials who allegedly made false reports about the victim's actions before his death. But *Guest* resulted in a three-three-three split on the Court, with six justices agreeing to dispense with the state action requirement altogether. Justice Clark forthrightly wrote that "there can be no doubt that the specific language of [sec.] 5 empowers Congress to enact laws punishing all conspiracies— with or without state action—that interfere with 14th Amendment rights."[208]

In dictum Justice Brennan repudiated the *Civil Rights Cases'* holding that section 5 was limited to "correcting the effects [of] prohibited State laws" and actions.[209] Section 5 "authorizes Congress to make laws...necessary to protect a right created by [the Fourteenth] Amendment." The combined impact of the Clark and Brennan opinions, who spoke for a total of six justices, was, at a minimum, to open the state action requirement to further challenge, and to restrict its application under statutes enacted under the authority of section 5.[210] Harlan, in a partial dissent in *Guest*, had reached the same conclusion.[211] The companion case of *United States v. Price* (1966),[212] which arose out of the triple murder of civil rights workers Andrew Goodman, James Chaney, and Michael Schwerner in Mississippi during Freedom Summer 1964, did not present a state action problem because three of the eighteen killers were local law enforcement officers. Congress's authority was clear.

An earlier non-related case, *Monroe v. Pape* (1961),[213] created the legal concept known as "constitutional torts,"[214] authorizing a remedy in damages against police officers who committed an unlawful search and seizure during a drug bust. Though the plaintiffs in *Monroe* were African Americans, the case itself did not involve any racial issues. Its larger significance derived from the fact that it opened up the statute known simply as "section 1983"[215] for widespread later use by civil rights plaintiffs. Section 1983 imposes civil liability on "every person who, under color of any statute, ordinance, regulation, custom, or usage," subjects anyone to a loss of rights under the federal Constitution or laws.[216] Section 1983 has become today the most widely used statute of the first Reconstruction for enforcing civil rights. A rough measure of its significance: it requires no fewer than six volumes of the *United States Code Annotated*, approximately forty-five hundred pages, plus pocket parts for each volume, to collect case annotations construing it.

Voting Rights

The restoration of political rights to African Americans was underway by 1964. The Court was fulfilling the promise of *Carolene Products* to scrutinize "legislation which restricts those political processes which can ordinarily be expected to bring about repeal of undesirable legislation [including] restrictions upon the right to vote." The diehard demise of the Texas white primary demonstrated that the Court was determined to demolish much of what remained of the Mississippi Plan. The second Reconstruction saw the Court wage a multifront assault on ballot-box discrimination. Enactment and enforcement of the Voting Rights Act of 1965 assured the Court that the judicial branch did not stand alone in this project: Congress and the executive were equally committed.

Malapportionment presents a subtler form of partial disfranchisement. As the Court later observed in *Allen v. State Board of Elections* (1968),[217] "the right to vote can be affected by a dilution of voting power as well as by an absolute prohibition on casting a ballot." Where legislative districts are grossly unequal in population, the votes of citizens in more populous urban districts will count for less than their rural cousins'. Usually this is seen as a problem of imbalance between urban versus rural political power. That is how the principal case on the topic, *Baker v. Carr* (1962),[218] treated it. Not once in the majority opinion by Brennan or in the two dissents by Frankfurter and Harlan or the concurring opinions of Douglas, Clark, and Stewart, did any of the justices acknowledge the fact that Tennessee's refusal to reapportion its legislature, despite an explicit state constitutional command to do so, reflected the determination by the white out-state regions to retain political dominance while minimizing the voting power of urban African Americans. Frankfurter in fact explicitly denied that race played a role in the malapportionment being challenged.[219] But though the Court declined to broach that delicate topic, the issue lurked unacknowledged. By opening the problem of malapportionment to constitutional challenge, the Court, however inadvertently, began restoring political power to Black citizens. The ensuing reapportionment under the mandate of *Reynolds v. Sims* (1964)[220] helped restore parity and equality to Black voters.

By the mid-1960s, it had become apparent that the judiciary could go only so far in combating discrimination at the ballot box. The Civil Rights Acts of 1957 and 1960 went no further than facilitating case-by-case challenges to the denial of the franchise, a glacial process that quickly consumed financial and personnel resources. A more comprehensive remedy was needed, and Congress stepped in to provide one in the Voting Rights Act of 1965.[221] The statute was aimed primarily at registration of voters. In enumerated areas identified by the US attorney general, section 5 of the statute suspended literacy tests[222] and required that any new "standard, practice, or procedure with respect to voting" be submitted to the Justice Department for clearance before going into effect.[223] The act also authorized the attorney general to deploy federal examiners to register voters.

The Court upheld the constitutionality of the act against the inevitable southern challenge in *South Carolina v. Katzenbach* (1966).[224] After a lengthy review of the history of disfranchisement, Chief Justice Warren for the Court addressed three principal constitutional objections raised by South Carolina. First, Congress had broad discretion under section 2 of the Fifteenth Amendment[225] to identify remedies for voting abuses. Citing *McCulloch v. Maryland* (1819) and *Gibbons v. Ogden* (1824) on the expansive scope of Congress's legislative powers, Warren spurned the state's invitation to construe section 2 power narrowly. Congress may use "any rational means" to eradicate discrimination at the ballot box. Second, identifying only certain states or counties for remedial action did not violate the principle of state equality, which, Warren held, applies only to the admission of new states.[226] Congress had ample grounds to conclude that the areas it identified constituted an "appropriate target" for its remedial powers.

Third, the Court dismissed scattershot separation-of-powers objections that challenged Congress's remedial powers under section 2 of the Fifteenth Amendment, emphasizing the broad scope of legislative authority conferred under section to protect the right to vote against discrimination. More specifically, Congress did not have to wait to exercise its remedial powers until some court had found a denial. It could act preemptively.

As late as 1959, the Supreme Court rejected a facial challenge to the constitutionality of literacy tests.[227] "Literacy and illiteracy are neutral on race," Justice Douglas naively (or obstinately) opined. But he added two qualifications suggesting that that hoary relic of the Mississippi Plan was doomed. The test could not be "merely a device to make racial discrimination easy," and could not "contravene any restriction that Congress acting pursuant to its constitutional powers, has imposed." When some southern states stubbornly clung to the test to suppress the Black vote, Congress took Justice Douglas's hint and enacted a partial ban on use of literacy tests by the Voting Right Act of 1965, and in 1970 banned them outright.[228] A divided

Court upheld abolition of the test in *Oregon v. Mitchell* (1970), but only as to federal elections.[229]

In 1969 the Court struck down the literacy test as applied in *Gaston County v. United States*.[230] Justice Harlan, for once joining the majority in an opinion expanding protections for Black voting rights, rejected North Carolina's application of the test on the grounds that the state had historically provided such an inferior quality of education for its Black citizens in its segregated school system that almost ipso facto they would disproportionately fail any literacy requirement. Owen Fiss refers to the moral and constitutional idea underlying Harlan's opinion as "the theory of cumulative responsibility": no institution, public or private, may "engage in a practice that aggravates, perpetuates, or merely carries over a disadvantage that Blacks had received at the hands of some other institution acting at some other time and in some other domain."[231]

The Court disposed of another vestige of the Mississippi Plan in *Harper v. Virginia State Board of Elections* (1966),[232] striking down a state poll tax in state elections. (The Twenty-Fourth Amendment, ratified in 1964, had abolished the poll tax in federal elections.) In *Harper*, Justice Douglas condemned the poll tax as a violation of the equal protection clause, stating that "voter qualifications have no relation to wealth nor to paying or not paying this or any other tax." He gave the clause a dynamic interpretation: "the Equal Protection Clause is not shackled to the political theory of a particular era. In determining what lines are unconstitutionally discriminatory, we have never been confined to historic notions of equality.... Notions of what constitutes equal treatment for purposes of the Equal Protection Clause do change."

Cohabitation and Marriage

After *Brown*, challenges began coming before the federal courts to state statutes that prohibited interracial sex or marriage.[233] If the meaning of constitutional language in the present is to be resolved at least partly by reference to the traditions of the American people, then we must acknowledge that one of the oldest and most firmly established of those traditions was the taboo on interracial marriage or sexual relations.[234] One of the earliest governmental acts of the mainland English colonies was a judgment of a Virginia court in 1630 ordering a white man to be whipped for "lying with a negro."[235] By 1691, Virginia codified the ban on miscegenation, followed by Maryland the next year,[236] and by all the colonies by Independence. Thus, when individual couples began to challenge anti-miscegenation laws in the 1960s, they confronted the powerful argument that if a practice embodied in statutes and common law is justified by tradition, then surely such laws had the strongest possible claim to legitimacy.

But by that time the second Harlan had reframed the debate on the legitimating force of tradition. In his dissent in *Poe v. Ullman* (1961),[237] Harlan explained that due process

> represented the balance which our Nation, built upon postulates of respect for the liberty of the individual, has struck between that liberty and the demands of organized society.... The balance of which I speak is the balance struck by this country, having regard to what history teaches are the traditions from which it developed as well as the traditions from which it broke. That tradition is a living thing.

The living tradition that Harlan invoked was rapidly mutating in the civil rights era. He accepted the idea that sometimes we must break from tradition, and that when we do, that is just as legitimate as adhering. The issue then is not whether the tradition exists and is well established; it becomes whether the tradition is just.

The Court had affirmed the validity of miscegenation laws in the 1883 case of *Pace v. Alabama*,[238] a prosecution of an interracial couple involved in a long-term affair. After *Pace*, which upheld a tradition by then two centuries old, challenges to miscegenation laws proved futile, a point underscored by the outcome of *Naim v. Naim* (1955).[239] Coming just after *Brown v. Board of Education*, the challenge to white southern sensitivities on the subject of interracial marriage was too much for the Court, which in a desperate gesture of "principled expediency"[240] dismissed the appeal because the action of the Virginia courts "leaves the case devoid of a properly presented federal question."[241] Frankfurter justified this disingenuous result on the grounds that "in the vortex of the present disquietude," any High Court decision on the ultra-touchy subject of race and sex ran the risk of "thwarting or seriously handicapping the enforcement of [*Brown*]."[242]

But though 1955 was not a propitious time for confronting it, the issue was not going away. In 1948, the California Supreme Court, in a plurality opinion by Justice Roger Traynor, had held the state's anti-miscegenation law unconstitutional under the Fourteenth Amendment.[243] Though an overwhelming majority of Americans, over 90 percent, opposed interracial marriage, momentum was building for a decision that would invalidate any state laws that implied racial inferiority. After the furor over *Brown* had quieted somewhat, the issue returned to the US Supreme Court in *McLaughlin v. Florida* (1964),[244] a decision striking down a Florida statute banning interracial cohabitation (not marriage). Justice White for the Court held that any "classification based upon the race of the participants...must be viewed in light of the historical fact that the central purpose of the Fourteenth Amendment was to eliminate racial discrimination emanating from official sources in the States. This strong policy renders racial classifications 'constitutionally suspect,' and 'in most circumstances irrelevant' to any constitutionally acceptable legislative purpose." The state's action "trenches upon the constitutionally protected freedom from invidious official discrimination based on race." This holding enabled the Court to deftly sidestep two issues that it did not want to deal with at that time: bans on interracial marriage, and statutes criminalizing adultery or fornication. It also avoided resolving the ambiguity between anticlassification and antisubordination readings of *Brown*.

Justice Stewart, concurring, added this critical point: "it is simply not possible for a state law to be valid under our Constitution which makes the criminality of an act depend upon the race of the actor. Discrimination of that kind is invidious per se."[245] This was a powerful though underappreciated point. The state may criminalize only actions, not the status or race of the actor. A person may be prosecuted for public intoxication, but not for being an alcoholic; for drug use, but not for addiction. Greater recognition and acceptance of Stewart's point might have resolved many disputes of the era more directly and effectively than the more contorted reasoning sometimes employed.

In 1967, the justices finally grasped the nettle and confronted the bans on interracial marriage in *Loving v. Virginia* (1967),[246] holding them to be unconstitutional as violative of both the due process and equal protection clauses. The Virginia trial court judge who sentenced the Lovings to banishment[247] for violation of "An Act to Preserve Racial Integrity," declared that "Almighty God created the races white, black, yellow, malay and red, and he placed them on separate continents. And but for the interference with his arrangement there would be no cause for such marriages. The fact that he separated the races shows that he did not intend for the races to mix."[248]

The state's Supreme Court of Appeals modified but upheld the sentence. For a unanimous US Supreme Court, Chief Justice Warren held that all racial classifications were to "be subjected to the most rigid scrutiny." He found no valid objective here, seeing miscegenation statutes as nothing more than "measures designed to maintain White Supremacy." After three centuries, the marriage ban was finally laid to rest, and the miscegenation laws were becoming a thing of the past.

The phrase "white supremacy" in this context denotes not primarily a racist ideology but rather a system of totalistic economic, political, and social domination. It is, in Frances Ansley's formulation, "a political, economic, and cultural system in which whites' overwhelming control power and material resources, conscious and unconscious ideas of white superiority and entitlement are widespread, and relations of white dominance and non-white subordination are daily re-enacted across a broad array of institutions and social settings."[249] *Loving* is one of only a handful of instances where the US Supreme Court acknowledged the existence of white supremacy, and the only one in which the Court used the phrase itself. It is as if there is some unspoken verbal taboo that constrains the justices from frankly acknowledging that there is such a thing. If so, such delicacy is sorely misplaced.

Meanwhile, public opinion on the matter continued to evolve toward an indifferent acceptance of marriage between people of different races. The Court implicitly acknowledged this in *Palmore v. Sidoti* (1984).[250] Linda and Anthony Sidoti had a child, Melanie. When Melanie was three, her parents divorced, and Linda was awarded custody. Both parents subsequently remarried; Linda's new husband was African American. Anthony sought custody of Melanie from a Florida trial court, arguing that "changed conditions"—the interracial marriage—required that under the usual test in custody proceedings, the best interests of the child, she be removed from the interracial household. The judge agreed, asserting that Melanie would encounter social opprobrium if she remained in a household composed of her white mother and African American stepfather. Chief Justice Burger, in a vigorous opinion, reversed, holding that while the "Constitution cannot control [racial] prejudices...neither can it tolerate them. Private biases may be outside the reach of the law, but the law cannot, directly or indirectly, give them effect." "The effects of racial prejudice, however real, cannot justify a racial classification removing an infant child from the custody of its natural mother." Burger reiterated the reasons for imposing strict scrutiny on racial classifications: they are "more likely to reflect racial prejudice than legitimate public concerns; the race, not the person, dictates the category."

In the fifteen years of the second Reconstruction, the Court accomplished a great deal. De jure racial discrimination was now everywhere illegitimate. The equal protection clause had been awakened from its eighty-year coma and had begun to reshape the contours of race relations in America. The justices again spurned antebellum theories of state sovereignty ("states' rights") as a mode of understanding and interpreting the American Constitution. The promise of true—as opposed to pretextual—equality was being redeemed. The "new birth of freedom" that Abraham Lincoln had prophesied in the Gettysburg Address seemed at last to be becoming a reality. Public schools, after a glacial start, began to desegregate. African American citizens enjoyed the newly restored protections of the First Amendment for their political activism. Congress played its role in all this, enacting the triad of Civil Rights Acts (1964, 1965, 1968) banning racial discrimination in public accommodations, protecting the right to vote, and passing a federal fair-housing act. More importantly, the justices invoked the 1866 Civil Rights Act, with its sweeping assurances of contractual and property capacity and its guarantee of equal recourse to the laws. The Court identified two new exceptions to the state action limit on congressional authority. It sustained the Voting Rights Act against what at one time not too far in the past might have been a potent challenge. And it swept away the demeaning punishments for love and marriage between people of different races. All in all, for a decade and a half, it was a fair beginning.

But practically unnoticed at the time, a seismic change was occurring in the way that many Americans, both lawyers and laypeople, understood the foundations of their constitutional order. As that change made itself felt in politics and constitutional discourse, the bright promise of the second Reconstruction dimmed, giving way to the dusk of the second Redemption.

The Dark Past: The US Supreme Court and African Americans, 1800–2015. William M. Wiecek, Oxford University Press. © Oxford University Press 2024. DOI: 10.1093/9780197654460.003.0007

8
Right Turn, 1960–1980

The year 1972 marked a major inflection point in American public law.[1] The day of Warren Court liberal activism drew to a close, and with it, the civil rights era itself. The second Reconstruction had come to its end. Within a generation after *Brown*, residential segregation remained entrenched, public schools resegregated, and racial inequality endured, diminished but seemingly ineradicable. All of this was possible because the Supreme Court has refused to acknowledge the reality of structural racism, fearing the threat to white advantage that civil rights challenges pose to the racial status quo.

During October Term 1971,[2] the US Supreme Court began to abandon the second Reconstruction. This turnaround in the Court's decisions would not have occurred without a conservative ideological and political movement that had prepared the ground for it since 1960. Late twentieth-century political conservatism and racial reaction mutually reinforced each other. Both came to dominate the thinking of a majority of justices of the Supreme Court. The conservative majority on the Court was indifferent, if not actually hostile, to the gains of the civil rights era. They showed no interest in addressing the problems of structural racism; indeed, they seemed not to understand it or even realize that it existed. One of them, Justice Clarence Thomas, mocked "the conspiracy theorist's belief that 'institutional racism' is at fault for every racial disparity in our society."[3] As it had done after 1890, the Court seemed to do a U-turn in its reading of the Reconstruction Amendments. This should come as no surprise. The Court has reflected prevalent white racial attitudes and supported the public policies those attitudes produced, throughout its history. As the civil rights era came to an end, white Americans' commitment to racial equality, never ardent to begin with, waned. The sense of urgency that marked the activist sixties deflated in the peculiar cultural potpourri that was the 1970s.[4]

The racial inequality of the first Redemption in the nineteenth century was easy to recognize: it was obvious in physical segregation, the deliberate inferiority of all accommodations available to African Americans, and the regime of white terror inflicted on them to enforce racial subordination. Thus, when the final assault on de jure segregation began in the 1950s, the target was apparent. But as de jure segregation slowly crumbled and overt racism became morally odious to more and more white Americans, structural racism took its place as the anchor of racial inequality, even more potent and entrenched for being invisible, so invisible that the Supreme Court either cannot see it or averts its eyes.

In the turmoil of the 1960s, a powerful conservative movement began to displace New Deal liberalism in American politics. Its counterpart in legal culture produced the Nixon/Burger Court, a string of appointments that were the outcome of the 1968 Nixon presidential campaign's Southern Strategy. A coterie of conservative justices, beginning with Lewis Powell and William H. Rehnquist, and including Antonin Scalia, Sandra Day O'Connor, Anthony Kennedy, and Clarence Thomas, handed down decisions that slowed and then ended the egalitarian trajectory of the Warren Court.

Structural Racism

Structural racism has succeeded slavery and servitude as the basis of enduring racial inequality in our times. Though pervasive throughout American society, it is not widely recognized or understood, because its operation is hidden in plain view. It is like a plague, intangible but lethal. The phrase "structural racism" itself is misleading because we think of racism as an attitude, a malevolent disposition, a deliberate behavior. The concern of structural racism, though, is with effects and outcomes, not states of mind.[5] Traditional racism derives from personal prejudice: dislike, fear, hatred of other people because of their race, a desire to dominate others. Modern racism on the other hand derives from social structures that are embedded in laws, institutions, and practices that are nominally race-neutral. Perhaps "systemic inequality" would be a less misleading way of conveying that idea, but the phrase is wan, passive, and abstract, a milquetoast way of describing the brutal reality of the differing worlds that so many white and Black Americans experience. In a different context, Justice Thurgood Marshall referred to this structural problem as "latent inequality," the hidden-in-plain-sight differences between opportunities open to whites and to Blacks.[6] The inequality is real, impacting the lives of countless

Americans every day. It is latent in the sense of being built into the social structures of American society, operating continuously, like tides or gravity.

To grasp the place of structural racism in our constitutional discourse, it might help to introduce it first as a social scientist thinks of it, deferring legal analysis until we have clearer picture of how it actually works in society.[7] To a social scientist, structural racism is "a complex, dynamic system of conferring social benefits on some groups and imposing burdens on others that results in segregation, poverty, and denial of opportunity for millions of people of color. It comprises cultural beliefs, historical legacies, and institutional policies within and among public and private organizations that interweave to create drastic racial disparities in life outcomes."[8] But however valid such a definition might be, it is abstract and lifeless. It does not begin to convey the human suffering and the widespread injustice of the day-to-day racism experienced by many African Americans.

Rather than parsing scholarly definitions, think of American society as an interconnected complex of

- Institutions, such as schools, universities, public agencies like police departments
- Policies, such as decisions about how to pay for public goods like education or health services
- Routines of conducting both public and private business, such as running fire departments or hiring for jobs in the private sector
- Social practices, such as credit ratings or tests used to select candidates for an opportunity like a job or admission to college
- Customs and norms, such as the expectations we have about what qualifies persons for public service or employment
- Patterns of behavior and human interaction, both public and private.

Structural racism analysis examines how these institutions and processes work together in bestowing benefits or laying burdens on groups of people who are identified by race or ethnicity. It points out that white people enjoy implicit, persisting advantages in access to social goods like jobs, desirable housing, and admission to universities, while people of color run into similarly persistent and implicit barriers to seeking those same benefits. At the same time, law enforcement stop-and-frisk policies or racial profiling target African Americans for violent mistreatment in their ordinary legitimate behaviors like walking or driving. Where two identically situated individuals, who differ only in their race or ethnicity, seek some opportunity (for example, decent housing) and only one of them confronts consistent barriers that cannot be explained by individual merit, structural racism is at work.

More than a half century has passed since *Brown v. Board of Education*, but for many African Americans and other people of color, little has changed since the days of Jim Crow. State and federal laws bar discrimination, but Black Americans still encounter it everywhere in their daily lives, whether in trying to hail a cab, apply for a job, or shop for a home or mortgage. Civil rights efforts have failed to eliminate the impacts of such racism because it is embedded in social systems like law enforcement, the real estate market, or public-school administration, which on the surface supposedly operate in a color-blind manner but in fact reproduce discriminatory outcomes for African Americans.

That is the social reality, verified by hundreds of studies. The question is whether that reality can have any legal or constitutional significance. Since *Brown v. Board of Education*, American society has determined that government may not impose racial barriers or confer racial benefits explicitly and deliberately. But what if those barriers and benefits are not created by law or official action, but rather arise out of the way that the institutions and processes bulleted above go about their daily business? How do we prevent persistent racial outcomes when we cannot prove an explicit, deliberate intent on the part of government officials to create those outcomes? How do we deal with the effects when that intent has been disavowed but its consequences remain? The most oppressive example of that pattern is residential segregation. We have repudiated the public policies that produced it up to the 1970s, but de facto segregation persists.

When sociologists describe structural racism, they focus not on the bigoted attitudes of individuals, but on institutional and structural barriers that people of color encounter in all areas of life.[9] They comprise "an intricate web of laws and norms that maintain disparities of wealth, education, housing, incarceration and access to political power."[10] Structural racism appears in the routine, day-to-day practices of organizations like business firms, banks, police departments, and government agencies. It arises from social policies produced by historical practices and political decisions, such as funding public schools primarily through local property taxes. These policies reduce opportunities and outcomes for people of color, as, for example, by diminishing the quality of education in schools attended by their children. Long-standing, built-in economic advantages enable white people to wield the economic, social, and political power that they have been accumulating for centuries. The policies and procedures that result appear on their face to be race-neutral, but nevertheless consistently reproduce disparate outcomes.

This manifestation of racism is unseen, automatic, iterative, and self-perpetuating. Unacknowledged white self-interest ensures that it remains both effective and elusive. What is sociologically significant here is not anyone's intent to discriminate, but rather the effects of decisions that do not on their face seem to implicate race. The impact of this type of racism is cumulative and is part of a dynamic process that takes place across social domains and over long periods of time.[11] Kimberlé Crenshaw captures its dynamic: "It is a way of seeing, attending to, accounting for, tracing and analyzing the ways that race is produced," "the ways that racial inequality is facilitated, and the ways that our history has created these inequalities that now can be almost effortlessly reproduced unless we attend to the existence of these inequalities."[12]

Racism in our time is therefore a process of traditional, attitude-based malevolence giving way to structural racism based on social and economic impacts that are not directly attributable to states of mind. This is reflected in the dynamism of the English language. The latest edition of the Merriam-Webster *Dictionary* (2021), the oldest American English dictionary, recently changed its definition of "racism." Responding to criticism from a user that its earlier definition referred only to mental states,[13] the editors composed the blended hybrid version that appears today: "a belief that race is a fundamental determinant of human traits and capacities and that racial differences produce an inherent superiority of a particular race" plus "the systemic oppression of a racial group to the social, economic, and political advantage of another."[14] This formula, belief plus systemic oppression, encapsulates the modern understanding of racism.

Our understanding of racism's compounding effect over time and across social domains traces back to Gunnar Myrdal's explanation of the cumulative causation principle,[15] where "there is no single 'cause' [of urban poverty], but rather a web of mutually reinforcing connections in which elements serve both as causes and effects."[16] Whenever we find differential effects, or outcomes repeatedly reflecting disparities by race, structural factors are producing those disparities. African Americans have been injured more in the past three decades by the day-to-day operation of institutions like schools or the housing and job markets than they have been from the deliberate actions of bigoted white individuals.

A principal difference between traditional racism and structural racism is the role of intent. The sociologist Fred Pincus observed that "the key element in structural discrimination is not the intent but the effect of keeping minority groups in a subordinate position."[17] Individual racism is intentional: a bigot means to cause harm and deprivation to another because of skin color or ethnicity.[18] But when sociologists analyze structural racism, intent is irrelevant.[19] Though outbursts of old-style intentional racism flare disturbingly often, "more often racism consists of routine acts of everyday racism that are not viewed as racist by the person performing them and therefore are not intentional. It is this unintentional racism...that produces a good deal of institutional racism and resulting racial inequality."[20] Thus, from a sociologist's perspective, reinforced with findings from psychology, any legal doctrine that requires a showing of intentional discrimination as a sine qua non for a constitutional violation will miss most instances of structural racism.

Structural racism is a sprawling and complex phenomenon, difficult to capture in a few brief pages. But we can note here some of its principal components and characteristics, all of which influence legal reasoning. Together they form a web of ideas and social practices that frustrate Americans' pursuit of racial justice. They include color-blindness, racialization, white normativity and resulting advantage, implicit bias, invisibility, and the dynamic, cumulative effect of racial disparities over time.

Color-Blindness

Color-blindness is structural racism's most effective camouflage. Justice John M. Harlan's dissent in *Plessy v. Ferguson* (1896) declared a noble moral principle: "in view of the constitution, in the eye of the law, there is in this country no superior, dominant, ruling class of citizens. There is no caste here. Our constitution is color-blind, and neither knows nor tolerates classes among citizens. In respect of civil rights, all citizens are equal before the law."[21] But Harlan's valiant statement must be understood, interpreted, and applied in its time and context.[22] He was referring to the laws of his era that deliberately and explicitly arrogated better opportunities to whites, and relegated Blacks to inferior facilities like schools and railroad cars. The modern Court, and particularly Justice Clarence Thomas, rips Harlan's statement about Gilded Age color-blindness out of its context, both textual and social. Thomas's approach raises color-blindness to a level of otherworldly abstraction stripped of time or place, and then reimposes it in the present as a ban on all forms of affirmative action or race-conscious policymaking. Color-blindness would now forbid taking race into account for any purpose, including opening up opportunities to people of color or remediating structural disparities like unequal school funding. "There is a 'moral [and] constitutional equivalence,' between laws designed to subjugate a race and those that distribute benefits on the basis of race in order to foster some current notion of equality," Thomas believes.[23] Such a warped view makes it impossible to recognize the difference between racial oppression and genuine equality among people. Criticizing Justice Stephen Breyer's dissenting view in *Parents Involved in Community Schools v. Seattle School District* (2007),[24] Justice Thomas scorned Breyer's "rejection of the colorblind Constitution." "But I am quite comfortable in the company I keep. My view of the Constitution is Justice Harlan's view in *Plessy*: 'Our Constitution is color-blind.'"[25] This smug, acontextual misreading of color-blindness has been so often and so convincingly refuted that to do so again here would be redundant.[26] It fails to take into account the pervasive impact of implicit bias, that unconscious, unacknowledged tendency in all people to make unthinking assumptions about others based on their race.[27]

Neutrality

An unexamined assumption that social structures and processes are racially neutral in origin and intent runs through the Supreme Court's civil rights opinions. The justices seem to believe that such structures and processes, like the funding of public education or the availability of health care, are blind to the race of those affected. This attitude is a modern relic of nineteenth-century racial formalism. This problem comes up when a civil rights plaintiff challenges some state institution or process, such as public-school funding, that does not seem on its face to have anything to do with race, but that nevertheless affects whites and Blacks differently. The appearance of what lawyers call "facial neutrality" often beguiles them into thinking that if a statute does not explicitly address or mention race, then it does not present an equality problem. Sociologists, unlike lawyers, have long recognized that "ostensibly race-neutral policies can structure and reinforce existing social inequalities."[28] But this obvious insight seems difficult for judges to accept, partly because of their concerns that judicial review of legislative public-policy decisions might disturb the separation of powers. The result is the flaccid standard of review articulated by Justice Byron White in *Washington v. Davis* (1976): "we have not held that a law, neutral on its face and serving ends otherwise within the power of government to pursue, is invalid under the Equal Protection Clause simply because it may affect a greater proportion of one race than of another."[29]

Racialization

American society is thoroughly racialized, and always has been since around 1650. Structural racism would be inoperative if it did not have racial categories to work with. But the supreme irony of racism is that, biologically speaking, when it comes to race, there is no there there, no meaningful genetic basis for racial differentiation. As a matter of genetics, race simply does not exist.[30] It is fictive, not a concept recognized, much less validated, by science.[31] In 2020, the American Medical Association adopted a policy of recognizing race only as a social construct, not a biological category defined by genetic traits.[32] But like a zombie, racism lurches along as an omnipresent social reality in American society. As such, it functions as a metric for sorting and classifying groups of people and then bestowing rewards and imposing disabilities.

For all but an overtly racist fringe, it is a truism today that race is socially constructed. Racial hierarchy is a rationalization created by the dominant white majority to justify its oppression of other groups. Racialization first ascribes racial identities to groups, then, for simplicity's sake, color-codes those identities: white, black, brown, yellow, red.[33] The superordinate race, as social scientists refer to whites, ascribes race to people based on skin pigmentation, physiognomy, and hair characteristics, then implicitly ranks those racial categories on various scales of merit. From there it assigns social benefits and burdens, privileges and deprivations. The dominant group attributes meaning to racial identity as a fundamental principle of social relationships. Whiteness as an idea is a means of political domination. As Benjamin Disraeli, British prime minister from 1874 to 1880, supposedly put it, "race implies difference, difference implies superiority, and superiority leads to predominance."[34] Racism is hegemonic: it provides ideological and political support for the racial status quo, continually thwarting progress toward equality and retarding racial justice.[35] This process becomes taken for granted and remains unexamined unless it is challenged. When it is, the superordinates reactively develop pseudoscientific justifications for its reality.[36]

White Normativity and Advantage

A dominant group in society assumes that its position must be justified by some innate merit or accomplishment.[37] Whatever its defining characteristic—wealth, power, race, religion—the dominant group naturally assumes that that characteristic defines the norm, something that those less favored by fortune might aspire to, if possible. In a society dominated by white people, whiteness defines the norm, and everything else is a deviation from it. White *is* the norm; anything else is "Other." A commonplace example: until recently, the phrases "flesh tone" or "nude" in the United States, whether for crayons or women's fashion, referred to the complexion of people descended from ancestors who came from northern or western Europe and the British Isles.[38] In the United States, whiteness is the norm.

From normativity flows advantage. Racialized domination has its rewards. One of the perquisites of power is the monopoly of social benefits (wealth, political power, social capital). The dominant group justifies this built-in advantage, which accrues automatically at birth, as necessary, if not just.[39] In a kind of reversible feedback loop, domination implies superiority, which justifies racial advantage, which in turn both confirms and legitimizes white supremacy. Justin Mueller aptly defines "Herrenvolk democracy" as a social order where white people are "able to access a slate of benefits...including voting rights, higher wages and two-tiered wage scales, minimal expectations of courtesy and status in the public sphere, more lenient court sentencing, exclusive access to some jobs, privileged access to public services, informal 'first hired last fired' employment insurance, privileged potential access to housing, loans, and capital, a sense of superiority over all non-whites, and (most importantly before the Civil War) the right to avoid enslavement."[40] This advantage accrues automatically, unseen, a part of the routine workings of American society.

Invisibility

Structural racism's invisibility forms its impregnable defense. The familiar becomes the innate, part of the natural order of things. As such, it works best when it is not seen and is taken for granted, like the fish that never thinks to wonder about the medium in which it swims. Invisibility is the feature of structural racism that makes it difficult for whites to recognize that racially differential outcomes are not normal or inevitable. Perversely, Justice Antonin Scalia seized on this unconscious aspect of racism to legitimate implicit bias as part of the routine functioning of the judicial system. In a memorandum to his colleagues justifying the role of racial prejudice in death penalty litigation, Scalia wrote:

> I do not share the view, implicit in [Justice Lewis Powell's 1987 draft opinion in *McCleskey v. Kemp*] that an effect of racial factors upon sentencing...would require reversal. Since it is my view...that the unconscious operation of irrational sympathies and antipathies, including racial, upon jury decisions and (hence) prosecutorial [decisions], is real, acknowledged [in the decisions] of this court and ineradicable, I cannot honestly say that all I need is more proof.[41]

Dynamism

Structural racism is dynamic, not static. Racialization is an ongoing process of "racial formation" in which "racial categories themselves are [constantly] formed, transformed, destroyed, and re-formed."[42] This process is fluid and ongoing, so that new groups can be admitted to the racially dominant class, as successive Irish, Italian, Greek, and Jewish immigrants discovered before World War II.[43] Structural racism automatically actuates and perpetuates itself, insinuating itself imperceptibly like a virus into new or changing social environments, without the stimulus of overt racism. It replicates endlessly unless society determines to recognize its reality and attack it proactively. It is a shape-shifting pathology that adapts fluently to new environments and to challenges to its dominance. It is automatic and self-perpetuating, reproducing itself without outside assistance. In matters of race, causation is not singular, autonomous, and linear, but rather cumulative over time and space, within and across social domains.

All the elements of structural racism are interconnected. Feminist scholars refer to "intersectionality," a "matrix of domination" or a "web of oppression."[44] For example: residential segregation concentrates poverty, which leads to poor health outcomes, cradle to grave. Run-down urban ghettoes reinforce poor health by exposing residents to toxic substances (lead in paint) and other pollutants. Minority neighborhoods are often the unwilling sites of chemical plants, incinerators, toxic waste facilities, sewage treatment plants, and other artifacts of environmental racism.[45] Impoverished neighborhoods have underfunded schools, with dilapidated physical facilities and out-of-date teaching materials. Exposure to street drugs and related violence produces high mortality rates from drive-by shootings. Food deserts result in poor nutrition, especially in children, which leads to obesity caused by eating processed fast foods high in fats, carbohydrates, and chemicals. Reduced or nonexistent employment opportunities caused by disinvestment ensure inescapable poverty. Exploitative financial services like payday loans drain resources and capital out of urban neighborhoods. This depressing catalog could be extended indefinitely, but the point is obvious: each of these racialized outcomes causes, contributes to, and exacerbates the others. They cannot be treated in isolation from each other. Cumulatively, they are overwhelming, passed on across generations. Dealing with only one of these leaves the rest of the matrix of oppression intact. Effects are interconnected and mutually reinforcing: malnutrition leads to poor education, which leads to unemployment, which leads to poverty, in an unbroken circle of Dantean despair.

Claiming that something is invisible yet powerful naturally arouses skepticism. The whiff of crank conspiracy theories attends any explanatory suggestion that hidden forces are at work. So the burden of proving the reality of something intangible rests on anyone promoting such a claim, like social scientists who suggest unconscious racism as an explanation for racially different outcomes in social interactions. Often the most effective way of overcoming such doubts is by examples that demonstrate the invisible forces in action. The tax law scholar Dorothy A. Brown offers one such proof, drawn from an unlikely source, that epitome of statutory obscurantism, the Internal Revenue Code.[46] The IRC is a massive, twenty-six-hundred page, highly technical body of law that on its face bears no trace of deliberate or even implicit racial animus.[47] Yet it repeatedly ignores the reality of societal differences based on race. Black taxpayers consistently pay more in federal income taxes than their similarly situated white counterparts. Seemingly race-neutral tax policies deliver wealth-building benefits to white taxpayers while denying them to Blacks. She demonstrates that the joint return with its marriage bonus, tax subsidies for homeownership like the mortgage interest deduction and the taxation of sales of residences, the tax treatment of student loans, preferential treatment of capital gains, withdrawal penalties for tax-deferred accounts, and tax-free intergenerational wealth transfers all contribute to the racial wealth gap. This is structural racism in operation.

Structural racism is stubbornly resistant to legislative fixes. Attacking it directly seems to produce little in the way of effective results. In testimony before the US Senate Banking Committee in 2021, Lisa Rice, president of the National Fair Housing Alliance, pointed out that the federal government had imposed residential segregation through New Deal housing policies, including the dual credit market and institutionalized redlining. The corrective civil rights legislation of the 1960s left the structures of inequality intact. "Those systemically unfair systems that we left in place are doing their job; they are performing their function. So we should not be surprised at growing inequality and racial disparities."[48]

The Political Origins of Racial Retrenchment

In the 1948 presidential election, Senator Strom Thurmond of South Carolina led a southern rebellion against President Harry Truman's courageous civil rights initiatives.[49] He and his dissident group, known as Dixiecrats, carried four southern states,[50] an ominous portent for the future. Despite this defection, Truman won an unexpected victory. The Dixiecrat run demonstrated that a militant platform of segregation, Jim Crow social policies, and avowed racism had little appeal outside the South at that time. But it also revealed a huge political potential in the white southern vote that could be courted by carefully crafted appeals to their values.

Twelve years after the Dixiecrats' disappointing performance, the languishing segregationist crusade was revived by an unexpected savior. Arizona Republican senator Barry Goldwater reluctantly let himself be put forward as the conservatives' candidate for the GOP presidential nomination in 1960. To launch this effort, Goldwater's speechwriter L. Brent Bozell ghostwrote *Conscience of a Conservative* (1960), laying out a program for conservative and segregationist fusion. Goldwater/Bozell condemned *Brown v. Board of Education I* not on racial grounds but as an illegitimate effort by the US Supreme Court to meddle with an issue, education, where the federal government lacked constitutional authority. He rejected integration, denying that it was a civil right, and endorsed white southern resistance to it.[51] Goldwater urged the GOP to court the southern segregationist vote, recommending that the party abandon its longtime African American clients "to go hunting where the ducks are," the southern white vote.[52] Though Goldwater eventually withdrew from the 1960 race in favor of Richard M. Nixon, his book suggested a way for conservatism to escape the palsied hand of overt racism outside the South.

Goldwater's candidacies in 1960 and 1964 marked the first major step in melding some components of conservatism—business hostility to the regulatory state, traditionalist nostalgia for a homogenous past, ideological anti-statism—with resistance to desegregation. Goldwater pioneered techniques adopted by all later Republican presidential candidates. While denying that he was a racist, he opposed all African Americans' civil rights claims on pretextual non-racist grounds: federalism, limited government, states' rights. His successors grew ever more adept at tweeting the dog whistle, none more so than Nixon, the master of dishonest allusion.[53]

Goldwater's 1960 manifesto electrified conservatives. William Rusher, publisher of the *National Review* and a leader of the conservative movement at the time, urged the Republican Party to abandon the civil rights cause altogether.[54] The influential political pundit Robert Novak noted that by 1963, the GOP was becoming "the White Man's Party."[55] Politicized racial bias was the elephant in the room that Republicans dared not avow openly, but could not afford to ignore. They somehow had to embrace it without seeming to do so; it was the love that dared not speak its name.

Goldwater tried to solve this riddle again in the 1964 election, when he became the Republican presidential candidate. In a speech ghostwritten by William H. Rehnquist, then an Arizona Republican activist lawyer, Goldwater hit on the formula that not only acclimated racism to the conservative agenda but also, more broadly, suggested a way to promote it under the guise of defending lofty constitutional principles. The real issue was not racial animosity, Goldwater/Rehnquist claimed, but rather "freedom of association," now interpreted as the freedom to decide whom you want to be near in schools, in restaurants and businesses, in society generally. "Freedom to associate means the same thing as freedom not to associate," Goldwater explained.[56] This siren lure of false equivalence has exercised a powerful hold on legal minds ever since. It was a mainstay of Herbert Wechsler's infamous criticism of *Brown v. Board of Education* in 1959: the power of majorities to segregate and thereby deny opportunity to Blacks was the legal, logical, and moral equivalent of an oppressed minorities' right to resist exclusion.[57] The Goldwater cover enabled conservatives to acclimate racial discrimination in the guise of an abstract nonracial constitutional principle. Pretextuality was back.

The claim for freedom of association also illustrates the legerdemain quality of conservative thinking on matters of race. At the same time as the Supreme Court was protecting the right of African Americans to protest and demonstrate as an aspect of associational freedom,[58] conservatives like Rehnquist were transforming that same concept to protect segregationists' power to defend white racial monopolies.

In the 1964 presidential campaign, the Republican Party took up the white supremacist program that the Democratic Party had repudiated and made it its own.[59] Goldwater's outreach to the segregationist South had immediate effects: he carried five Deep South states in 1964[60] and provided cover for white voters of all sections to accept a racist platform because it was promoted by a non-southerner in seemingly color-blind terms. Goldwater and the GOP managed to detach racism and opposition to civil rights from its Dixiecrat associations. In so doing, they discovered the power of an appeal to the latent racism prevalent in all parts of the nation, not just the South, and thereby hit on a far more potent anti-egalitarian outreach. Opposition to civil rights as defined by the 1964 Civil Rights Act now became not only morally legitimate but, from one perspective, constitutionally compelling on nonracial grounds.

Goldwater did not spontaneously oppose the Civil Rights Act on his own. That was urged on him by William H. Rehnquist, still a lawyer in private practice in Phoenix, Arizona.[61] Goldwater and Rehnquist rejected the act because they spurned both of its underlying premises: first, that African Americans have distinct constitutional rights, and second, that those rights should be enforced by the federal government. This gave the GOP cover to shed its party-of-Lincoln image and abandon its African American supporters in favor of courting whites north and south. This, together with the national Democratic Party's embrace of the civil rights cause, brought about a racial realignment of the parties. An anecdote recounted by Abraham Lincoln anticipated the moment: "I remember once being much amused at seeing two partially intoxicated men engage in a fight with their greatcoats on, which fight, after a long, and rather harmless contest, ended in each having fought himself out of his own coat, and into that of the other."[62] After 1964, the Republicans ended up donning the Dixiecrats' moth-eaten segregationist coat, while the Democrats absorbed the racial inclusion of northeastern moderate Republicanism, the faded remnant of the party's Lincolnian and antislavery roots.

When President Johnson signed the Civil Rights Act of 1964, he supposedly remarked to an aide, "I think we just delivered the South to the Republican Party for a long time to come."[63] As the Democratic Party after 1964 alienated southern whites who were opposed to desegregation, the GOP sensed its opportunity and welcomed them as refugees, turning the party of Lincoln into a haven for white supremacy and resistance to racial equality. Conservatives originally rejected the egalitarian narrative embodied in *Brown v. Board of Education* as the antithesis of values they cherished. They believed that *Brown* trampled on the basic principle of local autonomy in regulating social relationships. *Brown* negated the states' rights ideal that they thought was enshrined in the Tenth Amendment. To them, *Brown* constituted a judicial veto of the considered judgment of legislatures throughout the South. It disrupted an established, stable social order that had been validated by nearly a century of constitutional judgment. It substituted a radical new vision of racial justice for the existing social order. For conservatives, *Brown* exemplified judicial activism at its worst: judges imposed their personal values on the larger society, ignoring the preferences of the (white) people most directly affected.

But by 1970, segregation had become too déclassé to be defensible by antiquated states' rights dogma. Conservatives had to accept *Brown* as a fait accompli, but they treated it as the ne plus ultra: thus far and no further. Savvy GOP operatives like Richard Nixon recognized that it would be futile to try to breathe life into the cooling corpse of de jure desegregation. But they saw their opportunity in splitting de jure segregation from the de facto kind, conceding the demise of overt Jim Crow while protecting structural racism in all its manifestations: housing, education, employment, wealth accumulation, public health, and criminal justice.

In 1964, segregationist South Carolina senator Strom Thurmond switched his political affiliation to Republican. Now the political Judas goat, he induced countless other white southerners to follow him into his newly adopted party, inaugurating the white South's conversion to the GOP. As the most eminent spokesman of turncoat ex-Democrats, he became a principal architect of the Southern Strategy, second in significance only to Richard Nixon himself. Other Republicans adopted a less crude version of the segregationist appeal. George H. W. Bush, running (unsuccessfully) for the US Senate in the 1964 elections, said, "The new civil rights act was passed to protect 14% of the people. I'm also worried about the other 86%."[64] His party assiduously cultivated that white 86 percent.

The year 1964 also marked the startling debut of George Wallace onto the national stage.[65] In 1963, Wallace had vaulted into national prominence, first with his inaugural address as governor of Alabama vowing "segregation now, segregation tomorrow, segregation forever." He followed that up with his televised melodramatic "stand in the schoolhouse door," when he unsuccessfully tried to stymie the integration of the University of Alabama. In historian Dan Carter's judgment, Wallace was "the alchemist of the new social conservatism as he compounded racial fear, anticommunism, cultural nostalgia, and traditional right wing economics into a movement that laid the foundation for the conservative counterrevolution that reshaped American politics in the 1970s and 1980s."[66] "George Wallace laid the foundation for the dominance of the Republican Party in American society through the manipulation of racial and social issues in the 1960s and 1970s. He was the master teacher, and Richard Nixon and the Republican leadership that followed were his students."[67]

In early 1964, Wallace decided to seek the Democratic nomination for president, running on a platform opposing integration. He thereby unearthed the seething resistance among whites in the North and West to school integration and open-housing legislation. This visceral northern populism revealed many white Democrats to be as crudely negrophobic as traditional southern racists.[68] Wallace's populist demagoguery played on these anxieties. He shocked the nation by polling well in Democratic primaries in Wisconsin, Indiana, and Maryland, capturing a third of the vote. In time, his candidacy faded, though he flirted behind the scenes with the possibility of being Goldwater's running mate. While most political observers were stunned and disbelieving by Wallace's strong showing in northern states, Nixon took note. Wallace had tapped into an unexpected source of energy; the trick was to harness it without the baggage of Wallace's unabashed racism.

In the 1964 election, President Lyndon Johnson trounced Goldwater with a landslide 61 percent of the popular vote.[69] Exultant liberal Democrats complacently assumed that Goldwater-style conservatism was crushed for good, but they overlooked the fact that a viable Republican Party now existed throughout the South. Defectors from the Democratic Party joined suburban transplants throughout the Sunbelt to swell the ranks of GOP voters. As the South was becoming Republican, the GOP itself became more and more "southernized."[70] The parasite not only consumed its host; it *became* the host.

Meanwhile, Goldwater's backers, undaunted by the disappointing 1964 electoral outcome, launched a grass-roots campaign for a conservative takeover of the Republican Party.[71] The Republican Party became a battleground of conflicting views on racial issues and the South. Moderate Republicans tried to bring the GOP around to supporting civil rights issues, but they ultimately failed, were driven out, and became extinct. Conservatives promoted conservative candidates at all levels of government and systematically purged the party of all its moderates.[72] Conservatives opportunistically saw the party's future tied to segregationists.[73] Richard Nixon watched these developments with keen interest.

Richard M. Nixon's Southern Strategy[74] remade the Republican Party. As the GOP targeted its appeals to disaffected white southern voters, the party itself absorbed the values of those it courted. The Republican Party then projected southern white racial politics onto the nation at large. It merged with an appeal to politicized evangelical fundamentalism and antifeminism to constitute the current Republican Party.[75]

The Republican Party had always had a "southern strategy," in the trivial sense that since the Civil War, Republicans had taken the South into consideration in political planning and used the dwindling numbers of party adherents in the region, white and Black, to shore up support for individual candidates at national conventions.[76] But the political strategizing that emerged in 1968 was different. Historians and political commentators have traditionally depicted the Southern Strategy as a political tactic driven by national Republican political leaders, foremost among them Richard Nixon, to entice disaffected white southern Democrats away from their immemorial one-party allegiance into fusion with Republicans to support a traditional nonracial GOP program (low taxes, limited government, social conservatism). This conventional understanding of the Southern Strategy is known as the "top-down" interpretation, in which the strategy was concocted by the highest levels of GOP leadership and based on a direct appeal to white southern racial anxieties.[77] Much of that traditional narrative remains valid and is reflected here because it affirms the centrality of Nixon's political maneuvering that resulted in the making of the conservative Supreme Court after 1972. That Nixonian Court, in turn, is responsible for the judicial doctrines sustaining structural racism. The cases it decided absorbed and reflected the values and racial attitudes of the constituencies courted by Nixon in 1968.

Other historians have challenged the traditional interpretation, contending that it overlooks the spontaneous grass-roots origins of resistance to racial liberalism. This more modulated interpretation of the Southern Strategy downplays the idea of direct racial appeal. It emphasizes instead the suburbanization of the New South based on northern in-migration. The GOP appealed to grassroots, middle-class economic interests, with race playing a more reticent role. Matthew Lassiter contends it was not so much a southern strategy as a "suburban strategy," nationwide in its appeal and oriented more to class than geography.[78] White residents of the burgeoning suburbs surrounding the dynamic cities of the South (Atlanta, Richmond, Raleigh, Charlotte, Dallas) spurned the Massive Resistance of the 1950s with its blatant downscale racism in favor of pursuing straightforward self-interest in such things as quality neighborhood schools, stable residential property values, and local control of taxing and spending.

These middle-class, new Republicans were not diehard Dixiecrat racists, but rather a transplanted bourgeoisie willing to defend residential segregation as the price necessary to preserve their suburban amenities. This complement of Nixon's "silent majority" embraced color-blindness in public policymaking in opposition to what they called "reverse discrimination"; defended residential segregation (white suburbs surrounding Black inner cities) as the innocent and natural product of individual choice and merit (reflected in family wealth); opposed busing for school integration in order to protect their suburban enclaves; tenaciously defended the federal policies and subsidies that made all this possible; rejected race-conscious liberal policies as an unconstitutional exercise in social engineering; justified social and economic privilege as the entitlement of merit and hard work; and exalted individualism over community concerns. The Court's regressive policies found support in this social and political reality in all sections of the country.

As conservatism found its voice in national politics, its expression in grass-roots movements cropped up throughout the United States in suburbs and small towns.[79] In the "suburban strategy" interpretation, the southern version of white flight was the response not of a panicked, white, urban middle class fleeing the encroachments of busing and school desegregation in the cities. Rather, it was a grass-roots mobilization to defend neighborhood schools and de facto residential segregation as the unforced outcome of a social process that rewarded hard work and valorized impersonal market forces. Modern segregationists did not fit the mold of Bull Connor, violent reactionaries who opposed the legitimate rights claims of African Americans, but instead were innocent (if privileged) individuals who were simply defending their own liberties: the ability to choose who they would associate with, where their children would go to school, how their taxes would be spent. They opposed the encroachments of a distant federal government and devoted their energies to immediate concerns and social environment: their town, their schools, their workplace.[80] These suburban interpretations, which were focused on the old Confederacy, melded smoothly with parallel histories of the rise of postwar political conservatism in the West.[81]

Suburban kitchen-table activists demanded low taxation and local control of schools. They extolled individualism, property rights, entrepreneurial opportunity, small government, traditional family values, conventional morality, hostility to regulation, and resistance to the federal government.[82] Residents of cities in the North joined this movement, expanding their repertoire of opposition to residential desegregation and fair-housing legislation to add resistance to school desegregation.[83] Thus the Supreme Court's retreat from the initiatives of the civil rights era resonated with the spontaneous movements among the middle and working classes in both North and South who saw their advantages threatened.

After the 1964 election, events tumbled forward in a flood, opening up the vista of turning the South solidly Republican. The Selma march in the spring of 1965 led President Johnson to recommend a second major piece of civil rights legislation, the Voting Rights Act, which Congress enacted later in the summer, further alienating white southern Democrats. Democrats then proposed an even more provocative piece of legislation, a 1966 civil rights bill that incorporated a federal fair-housing act. This was hugely unpopular in the North. The bill died ignominiously in the Senate, the first clear warning that the civil rights movement was beginning to falter in the face of northern and Republican opposition.[84]

Public schools became another flashpoint of northern resistance. Federal agencies began promoting desegregation in northern schools under authority of the Elementary and Secondary Education Act of 1965,[85] which for the first time provided federal financial aid to pre-college education. The new element of federal funding gave the national government, acting through the Office of Civil Rights (OCR) in the Department of Health, Education, and Welfare, considerable leverage in pushing desegregation in southern school districts.[86] OCR quickly became the focal point of controversy for that reason.[87] In that same year, 1965, after some urban school districts north and south began a cautious program of busing, white neighborhoods exploded into virulent opposition that eventually made its way to the US Supreme Court.[88]

Such northern opposition to desegregation segued into resistance to expansions of federal power more generally. In the politically momentous year of 1966, Ronald Reagan won election as governor of California by leading opposition to open-housing legislation in California. He won handily by a dog-whistling campaign where he slipped racist stereotypes of the "welfare queen" and "big strapping bucks" into American political discourse. Nationally, the GOP picked up a stunning forty-seven seats in the House. If the 1966 midterm elections were, in Rick Perlstein's opinion, a national "referendum on the Negro revolution," white voters emphatically rejected it.[89] The 1966 off-year results were a backlash election, a sudden, dramatic repudiation of what only a year earlier seemed a tsunami of liberal policy.[90]

The embryonic Southern Strategy evolved nimbly in opportunistic response to these fast-moving events. Nixon noted the success of Goldwater's 1964 campaign in the South and Wallace's appeal outside the South, both based on opposition to desegregation and federal disruption of the racial status quo of the 1950s. He crafted a dog-whistle appeal to white racial resentment that incited white racial backlash, based on lofty theories of states' rights, local self-determination, and limited federal authority. Nixon hoped that by stoking white anxieties he could entice a significant southern white Republican vote in 1968, erode the Democratic one-party South, and make a southern GOP a reality at last.[91]

South Carolina GOP operative Harry Dent, a major though now-forgotten architect of the Southern Strategy, brokered a meeting between Strom Thurmond and Nixon in Atlanta in May 1968.[92] One historian called this meeting "probably the single most important event in the election of 1968."[93] No written record exists of what the principals agreed to there, but it seems that Thurmond extracted commitments from Nixon to slow or stop enforcement of the 1964 Civil Rights Act and to appoint only "strict constructionists" to the Supreme Court. So powerful was Thurmond's influence that a disgruntled critic referred to the Nixon White House as "Uncle Strom's Cabin."[94] Nixon thereafter affirmed his opposition to busing and indicated that he would slow-walk desegregation schedules.[95] He did this to mollify southern anxieties aroused by the Supreme Court's recent decision in *Green v. New Kent County School Board* (1968),[96] which portended a speed-up in desegregation. The political scientist Kevin McMahon emphasizes Nixon's "calls for law and order and schools defined by the boundaries of a neighborhood rather than a judge's racially weighted scale." Nixon's 1968 campaign "not only affected the course of constitutional law, but also helped secure an electoral foundation to support a conservative political regime that would eventually dominate the nation's governmental institutions and dictate its public policies."[97]

In the fall campaign, Nixon perfected the dog-whistle. He touted "a new concept of states' rights," not as "an instrument of reaction, but as instruments of progress."[98] Advised by Judge Warren E. Burger of the District of Columbia Circuit, Nixon played on the law-and-order theme to stoke white anxieties about disorder they saw around them.[99] His promise to nominate federal judges who were "strict constructionists" implicitly condemned *Brown v. Board of Education*, assuring whites that no Nixon judge would substitute egalitarian values for the traditional reading of the Constitution that accommodated Jim Crow. "I want men on the Supreme Court who are strict constructionists, men that interpret the law, and don't try to make it."[100] "I think some of our judges have gone too far in assuming unto themselves a mandate which is not there," he assured a southern audience, "and that is, to put their social and economic ideas into their decisions."[101] "It is the judge's responsibility, and the Supreme Court's responsibility," Nixon asserted at a 1969 press conference, "to interpret the Constitution, and interpret the law, and not go beyond that in putting his own socio-economic philosophy and decisions in a way that goes beyond the law, beyond the Constitution."[102]

In the South, Nixon cultivated the politics of regional grievance. He fanned white resentment about "regional discrimination," the annoying tendency of those outside the South to blame whites for creating a society of pronounced racial inequality. By endorsing freedom-of-choice plans for desegregation, he drained off some potential Wallace voters in the South. In the North, Nixon appealed to "Nixiecrats," those Wallace supporters who a dozen years later would be called Reagan Democrats: former blue-collar Democrats who could be lured by a carefully couched appeal to racial anxieties.[103] Nixon conceded that de jure segregation was unconstitutional, but he contended that de facto segregation was not. His judicial nominees reflected that outlook. Throughout, Nixon managed an exquisitely adroit navigation between the Scylla of overt racial appeals that would open him to the charge of being a racist and the Charybdis of political dialogue so sanitized and muted that its intended hearers would not notice the dog whistle. He had a preternatural sense of how far he could go in appealing to racial instincts, tiptoeing up to the edge of racism but never quite overtly stepping into it.

The 1968 presidential election offered American voters a clear referendum on the future of equality in the United States. Vice President Hubert Humphrey and the Democratic Party promised a continuation of the second Reconstruction, with energetic enforcement of the civil rights acts. George Wallace and his vehicle, the American Independent Party, demanded regression to pre-*Brown* levels of segregation, discrimination, and white supremacy. Nixon and the Republican Party cagily positioned themselves between the Democratic and Wallace polar positions. Nixon accomplished this by studied ambiguity and vagueness. His dog whistles invited his listeners to project their own fears and hopes into the hints he threw out. These hints included a halt to judicial activism on behalf of equal rights (the promise of "strict constructionist judges"); suppression of Black protest movements ("law and order"); scaling back school desegregation ("forced integration") or stopping it altogether (leaving such issues to "your local school board"); refusal to support open housing ("to be handled at the state level") or busing (which would "destroy the child"); contempt for the NAACP ("some professional civil rights group"); salving white southern pride and soothing its resentments (do not "use the South as the whipping boy"); rebranding the Civil War for southern audiences as "the War Between the States"; and calming white northern anxieties ("the first civil right of every American is to be free from domestic violence," thereby reframing the very concept of civil rights to be the protection of white interests).[104] Nixon cannily recognized that in order to pull off the Southern Strategy, he did not need to oppose the civil rights movement overtly. All he had to do was to force the Democratic Party to take ownership of it.[105] Disgruntled white voters would take care of the rest.

The 1968 presidential campaign was a pivotal political moment of the twentieth century, second in significance only to 1932.[106] It was another realignment election, fracturing the Democratic Party and delivering the coup de grâce to the New Deal coalition. Moderate and liberal Republicans soon became extinct. Nixon's 1968 campaign was "ideologically ambidextrous," in the apt phrase of the political scientist Ken Kersch, based on a promise of restoring law and order, "strict construction" of the Constitution, and a "new federalism," whatever that might mean.[107] In November, Nixon prevailed, but just barely. He managed to eke out 43 percent of the popular vote, a mere 0.7 percent better than his Democratic rival, Hubert Humphrey. Nixon's nimble equivocations on racial equality siphoned off much of the potential Wallace vote, but the Alabama governor and his explicitly racist platform nevertheless took 13 percent of the vote nationally and carried five states of the Deep South. The 1968 election signaled a dramatic end to the civil rights era. The second Reconstruction began with *Brown v. Board of Education* in 1954; it staggered toward its end fifteen years later with Nixon's inauguration.

Analyzing the results after the 1968 election, Harry Dent advised Nixon that "we must realize that old political loyalties have been dissolved by the racial situation and that we have an unprecedented opportunity to garner votes in large blocks. To capitalize on this opportunity we need a carefully conceived 'master plan' for the Administration to implement."[108] That master plan was the Southern Strategy, already in the works by 1968. At that time, Kevin Phillips, a young political strategist who had worked in the Nixon campaign, published *The Emerging Republican Majority*, a thorough and close-grained analysis of shifts in the American electorate. He pointed out that the partisan and conservative realignment that had been taking place in the 1960s meant that the electoral future of the GOP lay in the Sunbelt, a term that he coined to describe the southern tier of the United States. The party had reoriented its appeal to the South and West, "break[ing] with its formative antecedents and mak[ing] an ideological bid for the anti-civil rights South."[109] (The counterpart development was the Northeast, long a bastion of genteel Republicanism, swinging to the Democrats.) Phillips had not participated in the early development of the Southern Strategy, but his 1969 analysis confirmed its long-term potential as the political foundation of a GOP policy that abandoned the Black vote, relying instead on disaffected southern white Democrats to more than make up the loss. He put the idea incautiously in a 1970 interview: "From now on, Republicans are never going to get more than 10 to 20 percent of the Negro vote, and they don't need any more than that... but Republicans would be shortsighted if they weakened the Voting Rights Act. The more Negroes who register as Democrats in the South, the sooner the Negrophobe whites will quit the Democrats and become Republicans. That's where the votes are":[110] Goldwater's "ducks" a quarter century later.

H. R. Haldeman, Nixon's chief of staff, later recalled that Nixon "emphasized that you have to face the fact that the whole problem is really the blacks. The key is to devise a system that recognizes this while not appearing to."[111] Nixon did a masterly job of appealing to white racial resentments and fears. He found his opportunity in the broad political space between George Wallace's overt racism and the Democratic Party's appeals to its African American constituencies. In the end, his adroit handling of racial issues paid off as the politics of backlash carried him to the White House.

In a 1981 retrospective, a Ronald Reagan campaign staffer, Lee Atwater, later George H. W. Bush's 1988 campaign manager, provided a remarkably frank admission of how dog whistling evolved from the 1968 elections to the 1980 Reagan presidential campaign:

[ATWATER:] As to the whole Southern strategy that Harry Dent and others put together in 1968, opposition to the Voting Rights Act would have been a central part of keeping the South. Now [Reagan] doesn't have to do that. All you have to do to keep the South is for Reagan to run in place on the issues he's campaigned on since 1964...and that's fiscal conservatism, balancing the budget, cut taxes, you know, the whole cluster....

QUESTIONER: But the fact is, isn't it, that Reagan does get to the Wallace voter and to the racist side of the Wallace voter by doing away with legal services, by cutting down on food stamps?

[ATWATER:] You start out in 1954 by saying, "Nigger, nigger, nigger." By 1968 you can't say "nigger"—that hurts you, backfires. So you say stuff like, uh, forced busing, states' rights, and all that stuff, and you're getting so abstract. Now, you're talking about cutting taxes, and all these things you're talking about are totally economic things and a byproduct of them is, blacks get hurt worse than whites.... "We want to cut this," is much more abstract than even the busing thing, uh, and a hell of a lot more abstract than "Nigger, nigger."[112]

Reagan did not need to rely on a Southern Strategy, which by 1980 had already done most of its work. He could veer to a "Sunbelt Strategy" shorn of overt racist appeals, relying instead on racially neutral conservative bromides.[113]

John Ehrlichman, White House counsel and domestic adviser to President Nixon, corroborated the idea that Nixon targeted African Americans in a sub rosa appeal to white prejudices:

> The Nixon campaign in 1968, and the Nixon White House after that, had two enemies: the antiwar left and black people. You understand what I'm saying? We knew we couldn't make it illegal to be either against the war or blacks, but by getting the public to associate the hippies with marijuana and blacks with heroin, and then criminalizing both heavily, we could disrupt those communities. We could arrest their leaders, raid their homes, break up their meetings, and vilify them night after night on the evening news. Did we know we were lying about the drugs? Of course we did.[114]

Stuart Stevens, a veteran Republican campaign strategist and media consultant published a combination tell-all and mea culpa in 2020 that traced his party's devolution into "the de facto White Party of America." As a result, he concludes, "race has defined the modern Republican Party." Stevens admits the party he served mutated into a white-grievance party in the 1960s, abandoning the spirit that had animated it since Lincoln's time, to embrace the racism that pervaded white society, North as well as South.[115] The GOP first absorbed the white South's values; then saw them reaffirmed in the North in struggles over open housing, school integration, and busing; and then translated these into party platforms, executive actions, and legislative proposals. Out of this welter of racial ideas there evolved the constitutional doctrines that defined the second Redemption.

Once in power, though, Nixon pursued a modulated, opportunistic, and inconsistent course on racial issues.[116] He believed that "while legal segregation is totally wrong, forced integration of housing or education is just as wrong." "Legally segregated education, legally segregated housing, legal obstructions to equal employment" might be indefensible, but he was loath to force the issue on reluctant whites, especially in the South.[117] "There are those who want instant integration and those who want segregation forever," he said. "I believe that we need to have a middle course between the two extremes."[118] He found that via media in a strategy of moving desegregation policy out of executive agencies, such as the Department of Education, and foisting responsibility on the federal courts instead.

Nixon was content to leave the actual process of desegregating schools to the federal courts, but he opposed busing as "forced integration." In a similar vein, he refused to support Secretary of Housing and Urban Development George Romney's "Open Communities" program of integrating the suburbs, forcing Romney's resignation in 1972.[119] Nixon believed in equal economic opportunity, and thus supported preferential assistance like set-asides to minority business enterprises. But his backing of the federal government's first affirmative action program, the "Philadelphia Plan," was cynical.[120] He knew that the plan, which would have required contractors on federally funded projects to hire a specified percentage of minority employees, would force a conflict between two core Democratic constituencies, organized labor and African Americans.[121]

The Nixon Court

Watergate brought a premature closure to the racial policies of the Nixon administration in 1974, but the legacy of the Southern Strategy lived on. Its most enduring impact was on the US Supreme Court. In a 1971 memorandum titled "Dividing the Democrats," Nixon advisers Patrick Buchanan and Kevin Phillips advised the president on campaign tactics to consolidate the white vote. They recommended "the Supreme Court nomination of a Southern Strict Constructionist [who] will force Democratic Northern liberals, and major candidates, to anger either the South with a voice vote, or the blacks and labor movement and the Northern liberals. A highly qualified Southern Conservative nominee to the Supreme Court is de facto a divisive issue in the Democratic Party." The Buchanan/Phillips memorandum went on (speaking oddly in the first-person singular), to say, "I understand that the President's [i.e., Nixon's] political and moral position is that it is wrong and contra-productive to forcibly integrate the races." They therefore recommended that Nixon "bring a constitutional end to the national pressure to integrate races in housing and schooling."[122]

Nixon's Supreme Court nominees, particularly William Rehnquist and Lewis Powell, did more than irritate Democrats. They brought to the Court a set of attitudes, beliefs, and policy preferences that set the tone for the

Court on racial issues that persists into our own time.[123] Reflecting the racism that pervaded the Republican Party's changing positions on racial equality through the 1960s, the Nixon Court and its successors shut down the egalitarian impulses of the Warren Court and substituted in their place a judicial mentality that accepted *Brown v. Board of Education*'s repudiation of de jure discrimination but otherwise acclimated de facto inequality to the equal protection clause. The doctrines produced by this conservative outlook protected structural racism and white advantage from constitutional attack.

Nixon was determined to appoint only opponents of busing and school integration to the Supreme Court. He made this a sine qua non for anyone being considered. In discussions with Attorney General John Mitchell about nominations to the Court, Nixon was emphatic: "it would be a slap to the South not to try for a southerner. So I would say that our first requirement is a southerner. The second requirement: He must be a conservative southerner.... Third, within the definition of conservative, he must be... against busing and against forced housing integration. Beyond that, he can do what he pleases." Nixon would not let go of that idea: "I just feel so strongly about that. I mean when I think about what the busing decision has done to this thing in the South and when I think of what it could do if they get into de facto busing and forced integration in housing, I just, I just feel that, I just feel that if it's the last thing we do, we've got to have a conservative." "I want you to have a specific talk with whatever man we consider and I have to have an absolute commitment from him on busing and integration. I really have to. All right? Tell him we totally respect his right to do otherwise, but if he believes otherwise, I will not appoint him to the Court."[124]

Nixon succeeded with two of his nominees. In one of the most significant pivots in the history of the US Supreme Court, William H. Rehnquist was sworn in as an associate justice on December 15, 1971, and Lewis Powell a month on later January 17, 1972. Together, this pair of jurists reversed the jurisprudential momentum of the civil rights era and symbolically ushered in the second Redemption.

Nixon's first nomination to the Court, Warren Burger as chief justice, had little trouble being confirmed, but his second appointment, Judge Harry Blackmun, was confirmed only after his first two nominations, Clement Haynsworth and G. Harrold Carswell, were rejected by the Senate because both were suspected of being segregationists.[125] When Nixon found himself with another two-fer opportunity in 1971 because Justices Black and Harlan resigned for health reasons, he seemed to have learned nothing from the fiasco of the Haynsworth and Carswell nominations. With a careless indifference that is astonishing in retrospect, he proposed two unqualified individuals who had no experience in the kinds of cases coming before the Supreme Court: Herschel Friday, an Arkansas lawyer specializing in municipal bond issues, and Mildred Lillie, a judge on the California Court of Appeals (the intermediate appellate court of the state).[126] William Rehnquist, then assistant attorney general and head of the White House Office of Legal Counsel, was appalled: "Christ, we've got to be able to do better than this."[127] The American Bar Association refused to endorse either. Harlan, though terminally ill, managed to express his opposition.

Determined to avoid a repeat of the Haynsworth/Carswell failure, Attorney General John Mitchell offered the job to a prominent Richmond, Virginia, attorney, Lewis Powell Jr. This was a Hail Mary pass, a last-minute attempt to come up with a plausible nominee who could be confirmed by the Senate. He was quickly confirmed. Powell was sixty-four years old at the time, elderly by modern standards. (It was a measure of the Nixon administration's desperation that they would turn to such a seemingly unpromising candidate.)[128] In private practice in Richmond, Virginia, he served on the board of Philip Morris and other corporations. He was president of the American Bar Association in 1964. Most importantly, he served as chair of the Richmond School Board in the critical decade after 1951. A relative moderate throughout the struggles of the Massive Resistance era, Powell did not promote integration of Richmond's public schools and was unenthusiastic at most about desegregation. But he was successful in keeping the schools open and in resisting more extreme segregationist measures.[129] On the Court, Powell was not modest about invoking his expertise in educational matters. In conference discussion of the 1977 case known as *Milliken II*, which involved court-ordered improvements in educational services in the Detroit schools, Powell reminded his colleagues, "I have sat on a school board and you have not."[130]

Powell's most far-reaching achievement in his pre-Court years was his famous (or infamous, depending on your ideological position) 1971 "Attack of [sic; on] the American Free Enterprise System."[131] This extraordinary document was the blueprint of modern business conservatism, an unabashed call-to-arms for business interests to intervene aggressively in American politics at the federal, state, and local level to promote a conservative economic agenda. A friend of Powell's who was an official of the US Chamber of Commerce asked him for recommendations on ways that the American business community could counteract the creeping influence of "socialist" ideas and push back against government regulation of industry. Powell obliged with a lengthy denunciation of the modern New Deal regulatory state. He recommended a rollback of liberal influence in higher education and the media. He called for lavish funding of conservative think tanks that would produce ideas to rebut dominant liberal thought. The Powell memorandum was the genesis of the conservative institutions that have come to play an outsized role in American society today, like the Heritage Foundation, the American Enterprise Institute, the Cato Institute, and the American Legislative Exchange Council.

The memorandum did not specifically address issues of racial equality, but its conservative agenda would stifle all governmental efforts to reduce inequality. Powell did not denounce judicial activism; instead, he recommended that the Court's activist energies be redirected toward conservative ends. He wrote that "under our constitutional system, especially with an activist-minded Supreme Court, the judiciary may be the most important instrument for social, economic and political change." This proved to be prophetic, as the Rehnquist and particularly the Roberts Courts proved extraordinarily friendly to business interests. The Powell memorandum was the *Carolene Products* of the second Redemption: a proposal for a fundamental ideological reorientation of the Court.

The memorandum was unknown outside business circles at the time Nixon proposed Powell for the Court. (The columnist Jack Anderson ferreted it out and published it a year after Powell had been confirmed.) It probably would not have derailed Powell's confirmation, but it would have given a clear foretaste of the fundamentally conservative orientation of its author. Without trying, Nixon had managed to find an exemplar of conservative constitutional thought who promoted a constitutional regime that boded ill for efforts to make American society more egalitarian. Powell proved to be a noncontroversial choice, and he was easily confirmed eighty-nine to one. Nixon had stumbled upon a jurist who closely matched his own ideology.

Powell's views on racial issues evolved over time, but not in a progressive direction. Before *Brown*, his was the viewpoint of a typical white, middle-class professional in the upper South: he saw nothing wrong with segregation or other aspects of Jim Crow inequality. *Brown* forced him to modify that position, particularly because of the sensitive position he occupied on the Richmond School Board. He was unenthusiastic about desegregation, but as an attorney, he was unwilling to defy *Brown* or the authority of the US Supreme Court. As a conservative, he was leery of sudden disruptions of the social fabric. As a Republican, he was immune from control by the Democratic Byrd machine and its militantly segregationist posture of defiance of *Brown*. Massive Resistance held no appeal for him. He rebuffed modern iterations of the doctrine of interposition peddled by the influential Richmond journalist James J. Kilpatrick.

As an attorney in private practice, Powell submitted an amicus brief on behalf of the Commonwealth of Virginia in the *Swann* case.[132] In it, he extolled the virtues of the neighborhood school, and for that reason opposed busing, which he saw as expensive, disruptive, administratively complex, and not worth the costs. While conceding that busing might result in better education for poor African American students, Powell thought that the quality of education for white students would be diminished. Mandatory busing would encourage white flight, resulting in resegregation. He never evolved beyond that outlook.

Once on the Court, he became confirmed in these views.[133] In his lengthy concurrence/dissent in *Keyes v. School Dist. No. 1 Denver* (1973),[134] he had the opportunity to set forth his thoughts on racial issues more authoritatively. He supported the goals of desegregation (a definite advance from his views of a decade earlier) but rejected busing. Though busing would produce a "greater degree of actual desegregation," it would "infringe on...other important community aspirations and personal rights." Powell critiqued at length the distinction between de jure and de facto segregation, insisting that the legal standards for desegregation be uniform throughout the United States. Potentially, this might have led him to permit governmental action to remedy the effects of structural racism, but that was a point that he did not explore at the time. In the next important desegregation case to come before the Court early in his tenure, *Columbus Board of Education v. Penick* (1979),[135] the logic of his position led him to join Justice Rehnquist in condemning busing in all instances of de facto segregation. Powell's greatest contribution to the issue of racial equality came in the 1978 case of *Regents of the University of California v. Bakke*.[136]

While the Nixon administration was trying to find a suitable replacement for Justice Black, it had simultaneously to fill the seat vacated by the ailing Harlan. The process of doing so was appallingly slipshod.[137] Beyond the general guideline of seeking a "strict constructionist" and an opponent of integration, no one in the administration seems to have given any serious thought about the record or biographies of potential candidates. Vetting by staffers was casual or nonexistent. The president seemed more interested in trolling the political opposition, particularly Democrats and the *New York Times*. Nixon unhelpfully indicated that he wanted "to go for a real rightwinger now," recommending West Virginia's Democratic senator Robert Byrd "because he was a former KKKer."[138] As a political feint, Nixon distributed a list of political nominees, none of whom he was seriously considering: "Oh, God! I don't give a damn who they are. Some Jews and liberals and so forth," he said. Attorney General John Mitchell eventually offered the nomination to Republican senator Howard Baker of Tennessee, but Baker dithered too long.[139] Finally, Nixon imposed on himself a firm two-day deadline for announcing his choices, without any idea at all who the second nominee (besides Powell) would be.

He certainly was not considering William H. Rehnquist, then head of the Office of Legal Counsel in the White House. Nixon at first had a low opinion of him, calling him a "clown" because of his flamboyant taste in office attire. Nixon repeatedly referred to him as "Renchburg."[140] Finally, though, Mitchell sold the president on Rehnquist, persuading the president that Rehnquist was a conservative and a good lawyer. When Nixon at the last moment decided to nominate him, literally at the eleventh hour, he reconciled himself to his choice by instructing Mitchell: "be sure to emphasize to all the southerners that Rehnquist is a reactionary bastard,"[141] then added as an afterthought, "which I hope to Christ he is."[142] (He was.)

Rehnquist was forty-seven years old when he became an associate justice of the US Supreme Court. He had left college to enlist in the US Army Air Forces in 1942.[143] He served stateside until the summer of 1945, when he was deployed to North Africa as a weather observer. Once back in mufti, he graduated from Stanford Phi Beta Kappa, got an MA from Harvard in government, then returned to Stanford for his law degree and finished at the top of his class. He clerked for Justice Jackson for the 1952 Term and then went into private practice in Phoenix, Arizona, where he became active in Republican politics. In that capacity, he emerged as an inveterate opponent of all civil rights legislation. He was quoted as saying at the time, "I am opposed to all civil rights laws."[144] He volunteered as an elections observer and challenged Black and Latino voters, causing some of them to abandon the effort to vote.[145] This behavior was not illegal in Arizona at the time, and

290   THE DARK PAST

Rehnquist denied intimidation in his 1971 nomination hearings. The charges of Black and Latino voter suppression resurfaced with more extensive witness testimony in his 1986 nomination hearings for chief justice, but again did not derail the nomination.[146]

Rehnquist opposed a Phoenix anti-discrimination ordinance, a state civil rights act, and desegregation of Phoenix schools. He persuaded Goldwater to oppose the Civil Rights Act of 1964. In 1970, when Rehnquist was the assistant attorney general in charge of the Office of Legal Counsel in the Nixon White House, he proposed a Twenty-Sixth Amendment to the Constitution. Its section 1 proposed to embed segregated neighborhood schools into the Constitution,[147] and its section 2 provided constitutional protection for freedom-of-choice plans.[148] Nothing ever came of this; the proposal was buried and forgotten. But it provided a clear record of Rehnquist's attachment to de facto segregation.

Rehnquist ran into yet another self-inflicted obstacle in the 1971 confirmation hearings. In the 1950–1954 period, Justice Robert Jackson was deeply conflicted over the challenges to school segregation that coalesced in *Brown v. Board of Education*. In 1952, after the Court had heard the first arguments in the cases, Jackson asked both of his clerks[149] to provide memoranda reviewing possible positions he might take regarding segregation. Rehnquist submitted "A Random Thought on the Segregation Cases," signed "WHR," in which he wrote, "I realize that it is an unpopular and unhumanitarian position, for which I have been excoriated by 'liberal' colleagyes, [sic] but I think *Plessy* v. *Ferguson* was right and should be reaffirmed. If the fourteenth Amendment did not enact Spencer's Social Statics, it just as surely did not enact Myrddahl's [sic] *American Dilemna* [sic]."[150] The memorandum proved to be a bombshell when *Newsweek* disclosed it during the 1971 confirmation hearings. Rehnquist attempted to defend himself by denying that it reflected his own views; rather, he said, he was articulating what he believed Jackson did think, or ought to think, about the issue. The quoted statement "is not an accurate statement of my own views at the time." He claimed that he supported (in 1971, anyway) "the legal reasoning and the rightness from the standpoint of fundamental fairness of the *Brown* decision."[151] Though Jackson's long-term secretary, Elsie Douglas, rejected Rehnquist's claim as a slur on Jackson's memory, the Senate voted to confirm, sixty-eight to twenty-six. By coincidence, he took the seat formerly held by Jackson.

The issue came up again in the 1986 confirmation hearings for Rehnquist's nomination as chief justice. This time the challenges were more extensively documented and debated, and Rehnquist was more tentative in his denials, but now a new issue intruded: whether Rehnquist had been lying in his 1971 hearing. Critics demonstrated that his position was illogical and contradictory; that Jackson was never known to have held the beliefs Rehnquist attributed to him; and that internal evidence pointed to the clerk expressing his own views. To no avail; Rehnquist was again confirmed. Scholars at the time and since have debated whether Rehnquist was being deceptive in his denial that the memorandum expressed his own views rather than Jackson's. The consensus is that he was being untruthful.[152] Truthful or not, however, Rehnquist's grudging affirmation of *Brown*'s rightness as a matter of both law and morality began a pattern whereby later conservative judicial nominees likewise affirmed the correctness of *Brown* and then went on to narrow its force and applicability.[153]

Rehnquist's penchant while a serving as a clerk for attempting to impose his views on Justice Jackson reasserted itself in 1952 as the Court was deliberating *Terry v. Adams* (1953),[154] the Texas Jaybird case challenging a last-ditch attempt to deny African Americans access to the ballot in primary elections. In two memos urging Jackson to reject a challenge to this last of the white primaries, Rehnquist wrote, "I [here unequivocally speaking in his own name, with no pretense that he was speaking for his boss] have a hard time being detached about this case because several of the...clerks began screaming as soon as they saw this that 'Now we can show those damned southerners,' etc. I take a dim view of this pathological search for discrimination." "It is about time," he went on, "that the Court faced the fact that the white people on [*sic*; of] the South don't like the colored people." Any benefits to African Americans from being allowed to vote would be offset by diminished "freedom of association and majority rule" by white people. "The Constitution...most assuredly did not appoint the Court as a sociological watchdog to rear up every time private discrimination rears its admittedly ugly head."[155]

Rehnquist assumed his seat on the Court in 1972, "seemingly dedicated to cleansing, singlehandedly if necessary, the Augean stable that conservative dogma perceives as the Supreme Court of the nineteen-fifties and nineteen-sixties."[156] Throughout his career as associate, then chief, justice, he regarded all race-based classifications, particularly "benign" ones, as innately suspect, subject to the most exacting scrutiny. He required a showing of intentional discrimination; mere de facto discrimination, and with it, structural racism, lay beyond the federal courts' powers. Only official and explicit state involvement could taint racially based discrimination as constitutionally offensive. De jure discrimination was constitutionally vulnerable, but de facto discrimination was beyond the ken of federal judges.[157] Though his handling of other issues softened somewhat after he assumed the responsibilities of the center chair, Rehnquist never relented in his hardline rejection of racial egalitarianism. His grudging affirmation of *Brown I* had to be wrenched out of him by the pressures of the nomination process.

Reagan nominated Rehnquist to the chief justiceship on the retirement of Burger. As chief justice, Rehnquist did not become less conservative, but he sloughed off the inflexible arrogance of his associate years and seemed to mellow somewhat in pushing the conservative agenda. In matters implicating racial inequality, though, Rehnquist voted inerrantly against the egalitarian position every time. His opinions realized the potential implied in his 1952 clerk's memorandum to Justice Jackson.

Four other justices reinforced the conservative bent of Powell and Rehnquist: Sandra Day O'Connor, Antonin Scalia, Anthony Kennedy, and Clarence Thomas. The first three were Reagan nominees; Thomas was nominated by George H. W. Bush. Though all of them were conservative and Republican, except for Scalia their performance let down those who hoped for a decisive repudiation of the Warren Court legacy. But in one respect, they did not fail the man who nominated them: they all retarded the cause of racial equality in American law.

By any measure, Clarence Thomas is one of the most remarkable persons ever to have served on the Supreme Court.[158] Born into poverty in segregated Georgia, by his own account[159] he spoke Gullah (Geechee) in childhood and had to improve his English by diligent application, including majoring in English literature at Holy Cross, where he graduated with honors. At age seven, poverty and homelessness due to a fire forced him to move into his grandfather's home. He was profoundly influenced by the older man's insistence on hard work, discipline, and self-reliance. At that time, again by his own account, he was deeply influenced by the conservative economist Thomas Sowell and Ayn Rand, as well as, from a radically different direction, Richard Wright.

Through the patronage of John Danforth, a rising star in the Republican Party, Thomas rose rapidly in the George H. W. Bush administration. Bush nominated him to a seat on the US Court of Appeals for the DC Circuit, the nation's second most influential federal court. He served on it for less than two years before President Bush nominated him for the Supreme Court seat occupied by retiring justice Thurgood Marshall. Despite a tepid reaction from the American Bar Association, which vetted federal judicial nominees by a painstaking nonpartisan process, Thomas was endorsed by the Senate Judiciary Committee. But when the nomination came before the full Senate, the process was rocked by the allegations of an Equal Employment Opportunity Commission staff attorney who had worked for him, Anita Hill, that Thomas had behaved in a lewd and inappropriate way toward her in a way that amounted to sexual harassment.[160] Despite this shocking disclosure, the Senate voted to confirm him by a fifty-two to forty-eight vote. The experience left Thomas permanently angry and embittered.

Social science analytics confirm the universally held judgment that Thomas is the most conservative justice, not only on the Rehnquist/Roberts Court but of the Court since mid-century.[161] By 2018, he had become the longest-serving justice on the Rehnquist/Roberts Courts, and his influence had grown considerably over the years. Though he seldom wrote for the Court in a major case because his positions were so extreme, his concurrences and dissents have pulled the Court rightward. He carries originalism and textualism to extremes. Justice Thomas disdains precedent and stare decisis, especially for constitutional issues. (Justice Scalia said that Thomas "doesn't believe in stare decisis, period.")[162] With the freedom of maneuver that provides him, Thomas has suggested that all commerce clause precedent since 1937 has been erroneous, hinting that he would return to *Lochner*-era precedents on federal and state regulatory power.[163] He has advanced the preposterous notion that the establishment clause of the First Amendment is not a limit on state power, meaning that the states can establish churches or otherwise exhibit favoritism to religions.[164] He would accord the president virtually unlimited power in the conduct of foreign relations and military engagements, with nearly no judicial oversight.[165] He is the Court's leading death penalty enthusiast, and would shrink the Eighth Amendment's ban on cruel and unusual punishment to permit any form of violence or torture against inmates that is less than "serious injury." Seven of his colleagues felt obliged to point out that Thomas's view in that case violates "the concepts of dignity, civilized standards, humanity, and decency that animate the Eighth Amendment."[166]

With such regressive views, it is strange but not surprising that Thomas has emerged as an inveterate foe of all constitutional gains made by African Americans in the second Reconstruction. His views seem driven by preconceptions and an unquestioned abstract ideology. He rejects the insights of the social sciences: "lower courts should not be swayed by the easy answers of social science, nor should they accept the findings, and the assumptions, of sociology and psychology at the price of constitutional principle."[167] Justice Thomas has criticized some of the key points in *Brown v. Board of Education I*. For Thomas, *Brown I* is nothing more than a simple ban on explicit de jure segregation. He reads out of Warren's opinion everything that constitutes its enduring grandeur, leaving only a bleached skeleton that cannot ever challenge de facto segregation. He was equally critical of *Brown II* on the issue of remedies: "there is no general equitable remedial power expressly granted by the Constitution or by statute [so] we ought to be reluctant to approve its aggressive or extravagant use."[168]

Thomas has always been deeply skeptical of both desegregation and integration, arguing in a concurrence in *Missouri v. Jenkins* (1995) that because "desegregation has not produced the predicted leaps forward in black educational achievement, there is no reason to think that black students cannot learn as well when surrounded by members of their own race as when they are in an integrated environment."[169] The equal protection clause was not meant "to enforce strict race-mixing, but to ensure that blacks and whites are treated equally by the State without regard to their skin color." Thomas went out of his way to affirm the legitimacy of structural racism. In *Grutter v. Bollinger* (2003), he claimed in gratuitous dicta that the equal protection clause "does not prohibit the use of unseemly legacy preferences" at the University of Texas, ignoring the fact that UT did not desegregate until 1957.[170] Under those circumstances, legacy admissions, like grandfather clauses, lock in the benefits of segregation for white students descended from forebears admitted in the Jim Crow era even after formal desegregation had been abandoned. If Thomas were white, he would be pilloried as a reactionary racist.

9

The Resegregation of America's Schools

In the second half of the twentieth century, the American public school system came nearly full circle: until 1954, it was largely segregated; then until 1973, it was becoming desegregated; after 1973, it has been resegregating. More precisely, America's schools went from being fully segregated in 1954;[1] then in the second Reconstruction from 1954 to 1973 to progress in desegregation that aspired to the ultimate goal of fully integrated unitary school systems; then after 1990, a relapse back to (re)segregation.[2] This resulted, in Gary Orfield's words, in the quiet reversal of *Brown v. Board of Education*.[3]

Lest this seem overdrawn, call to mind the words and spirit of Chief Justice Warren's opinion in *Brown*:

> We must look instead to the effect of segregation itself on public education. Today, education is perhaps the most important function of state and local governments. Such an opportunity...is a right which must be made available to all on equal terms. To separate [African American children] from others of similar age and qualifications solely because of their race generates a feeling of inferiority as to their status in the community that may affect their hearts and minds in a way unlikely ever to be undone.
>
> We conclude that in the field of public education the doctrine of "separate but equal" has no place. Separate educational facilities are inherently unequal. [Petitioners are] by reason of the segregation complained of, deprived of the equal protection of the laws guaranteed by the Fourteenth Amendment.[4]

The US Supreme Court does not speak that language today. It has not done so since 1973 and it effectively repudiated it after 1990.

For African American children like those described in Jonathan Kozol's *Savage Inequalities*,[5] *Brown v. Board of Education I* may as well never have been decided. For them and for half the justices of the modern Court, it is still 1896, a world of pretense and pretext, where *Brown* has no more real meaning or impact today than the equal protection clause had after *Plessy*.

For a third, perhaps half, of the African American and Latino children in the United States today, America's public schools are separate and unequal, some as flagrantly inferior as any of the school hovels of 1896. There are multiple causes for this modern Jim Crow education, but the essential one is the US Supreme Court. How did we get here?

After 1976, driven in part by the pernicious intent/effects doctrine of *Washington v. Davis*, the Supreme Court lost sight of the spirit of *Brown I*, and then began to close down desegregation.[6] In doing so, it substituted different values for those of *Brown*, privileging above all the value of "local control," which in time became almost a code phrase for resegregation. The Court followed where Nixon and the Southern Strategy pointed: whites preserved their educational advantages, including a near monopoly on social capital for themselves. Their children's schools would revert to being predominantly white, reproducing the structural inequality of the larger society. A coterie of conservative justices—Rehnquist, Powell, O'Connor, Scalia, Kennedy, Thomas, and then Roberts and Alito—promote doctrines that betray the letter and spirit of *Brown*. In the new dispensation, the equal protection clause, drafted by its framers explicitly to protect and benefit African Americans formerly enslaved, has become a means of preserving white advantage.

Structural racism plays into this process in two ways. First, it is the foundation of residential segregation, which in turn provides the enduring basis for school segregation.[7] The ideal of the neighborhood school appeals to all parents, even to those whose children are harmed by the larger pattern of segregation. The allure of a distant school, no matter how much better, seldom overcomes the convenience of school nearby, where a child can walk to school and socialize with friends she has grown up with in the neighborhood. Residential segregation is the basis of school segregation.

Second, Chief Justice Warren's opinion in *Brown I* contained a latent ambiguity, unnoticed at the time.[8] What exactly was the vice of state-imposed school segregation? Was it that the state impressed on a racial group, African American children, a status of inferiority, and preserved the advantage whites derived from that imputed inferiority? Did *Brown* hold that states may not adopt policies that have the effect of limiting the opportunities of a racially defined group of people?[9] The first Justice Harlan's opinion in *Plessy v. Ferguson* (1896) seemed to suggest that understanding: "in view of the constitution, in the eye of the law, there is in this country no superior, dominant, ruling class of citizens. There is no caste here."[10] This reading, which is known as the antisubordination principle, would prohibit states from adopting policies that have the effect of diminishing the life chances of a racial group or demoting their status in society.[11] This reading would enable the Court to strike down state policies, or even possibly state inaction, that resulted in privileging whites or limiting opportunities of Blacks. Its focus is the impact of state actions (or inactions) on groups.[12] Antisubordination is historically and sociologically contextual, deriving its meaning from the lived experience of African Americans.

Or did *Brown* do no more than declare that a state may not classify people by race? This is known as the anticlassification principle. It simply declares that the state may not adopt racial classifications if doing so disturbs the racial status quo to confer (or deny) a benefit or impose a burden on an individual or a group. It enables judges who are hostile to programs like affirmative action to strike them down if those programs were based on explicit racial categories. Anticlassification, as its principal proponent, Justice Thomas, has insisted, exalts the individual and repudiates group remedies: "government must treat citizens as individuals, and not as members of racial, ethnic, or religious groups."[13] It rests on a formal and ahistorical understanding of race, treating it as an abstract category. Anticlassification has swept the field in judicial interpretation: all the major Roberts Court decisions involving race reaffirm it.[14] A majority of the justices have embraced the anticlassification principle as their definitive understanding of the meaning of equal protection. There is a vast difference between a constitutional universe bounded by the anticlassification principle, where structural racism would continue undisturbed, and an antisubordination constitutional order where courts and legislatures could police the social order energetically to root out the lingering effects of racist agendas.

To impose some order on the narrative that follows, a timeline may be helpful. It identifies periods from *Brown* in 1954 to the present in which the Supreme Court responded (or did not) to the desegregation imperative of the twentieth century's greatest case. The timeline roughly represents the ebb and flow of desegregation and the fate of *Brown*. It also suggests an explanation for why this chronological pattern evolved in the way that it did.

1955–1965: stasis. The decade that began in 1955 inaugurated the stasis phase of desegregation. After the explosive substantive ruling of *Brown I*, the Court withdrew from the field in *Brown II* and for a decade thereafter remained on the sidelines, consigning the struggle to the lower federal courts. With the benefit of hindsight, we see now that this proved to be disastrous. Judge J. Harvie Wilkinson explained why: "the Supreme Court fail[ed] to provide leadership and direction to the southern school controversy. The Court cannot set in motion so complex and multifaceted a process as school desegregation and fail to give it regular attention.... Aloofness, even for our most oracular institution, will not always do.... Particulars did not soil its hands; detail was left to other and lesser folk."[15]

1965–1973: activism. The following eight years constituted the activist period, as the Supreme Court vigorously enforced desegregation and authorized remedies like busing to move the process toward integration. But during this terminal burst of judicial activism, the second Reconstruction came to an end.

1973–1990: faltering. In this faltering phase, the Court stalled out.[16] In multiple ways, it receded from its civil rights-era activist commitments and tamped down lower-court efforts to achieve integration. The justices embraced values that were inconsistent with *Brown I*.

1990–2000: abandonment. In the 1990s, the Court abandoned the desegregation process and voiced impatience with the hope of achieving equality, which it now treated more as a phantasm than a goal. True integration was dead, but even desegregation eluded American public schools like a will-o'-the-wisp. In this period, the Court effectively repudiated *Brown v. Board of Education*.

2000–2020: resegregation. The twenty-first-century Court affirmed resegregation, even as it denied its reality. The Court in this latest era resists integration and complacently accepts the return to inequality, with no apparent regret. It has inverted the foundational values of the equal protection clause to protect white privilege. It ritually acknowledges *Brown v. Board of Education*, then ignores it.

Two dates stand out in this sixty-five-year period: 1972 and 1980. Each began a transition of the Court. 1972 marked the debut of the Nixon Court with the appointment of Justices Rehnquist and Powell. Together with Chief Justice Burger, they coalesced into a cohesive conservative bloc that, with the accession of Justices Stewart and White, provided a new majority that displaced the old liberal wing of the Warren Court, leaving as forlorn holdouts only Justices Brennan and Marshall. In 1980 the conservative consolidation of power accelerated as three Reagan appointees came on board:

Sandra Day O'Connor in 1981, Antonin Scalia and Anthony Kennedy in 1988. The most dramatic shift of all was the replacement of Justice Marshall with the man who was his antithesis, Clarence Thomas, in 1991. With Thomas, the second Redemption became a fait accompli. Old-time Jim Crow and de jure segregation in American public schools gave way to the more modern structural inequality of de facto resegregation.

Desegregation Falters: The Retreat from *Brown I*

A new era began when the Court decided *Keyes v. School District No. 1 Denver* (1973).[17] *Keyes* moved on from the problem of desegregating southern school districts to segregation in the cities of the North and the West; and it shifted from confronting de jure segregation to the thornier issue of de facto segregation. De jure segregation had been morally unambiguous, but the de facto kind lacked the moral clarity that sustained *Brown*. De jure plainly fell on the intent side of the line drawn in *Washington v. Davis* between discriminatory intent and disparate impact, but the ambiguities of de facto segregation were obscured in the fog of causation. Impact might be clear, but proof of intent was difficult.

Petitioners in *Keyes* showed that Denver's school district authorities intentionally segregated Latino and African American students in one core district, but they did not extend that claim to the entire city school system. Nevertheless, Justice Brennan for a six-to-two majority held that a finding of intentional discrimination in one part of a school district would raise a presumption or prima facie case that the remainder of the district was similarly infected with intentional discrimination, thus extending the duty to desegregate to the entire school district (in this case, to the whole city of Denver). This was known at the time as the "*Keyes* presumption." But for the first time in a major desegregation case, the Court was not unanimous. Brennan spoke for a majority of only six. Worse, he made a concession that soon proved damaging to his project of ridding public education of all vestiges of segregation: the "differentiating factor between *de jure* segregation and so-called *de facto* segregation...is *purpose* or *intent* to segregate."[18] De jure segregation is a result of intent, while the de facto kind is found in effects. De facto segregation is the product of structural—that is, non-intentional—inequality. If, as might be implied from Brennan's ill-considered statement, only de jure segregation was constitutionally defective, then the Court could do nothing about the de facto kind.

Justice Powell's dissent/concurrence in *Keyes* presented a much different alternative for desegregation, rejecting the busing authorized by *Swann*.[19] Busing by this time had become widely unpopular and had lost whatever modicum of support it might have had in Congress. Echoing his position as an advocate in *Swann*, Powell promoted an alternative set of values from those that had driven desegregation since 1954. He conceded that de jure segregation was illegitimate but pointed out the difficulties in translating desegregation into integration, defined as the goal of "unitary school districts." He insisted that the distinction between de jure and de facto segregation was illusory, a "constitutional phony" he called it, because it would mandate desegregation only in the South.[20] He demanded that school districts in the North and West not be treated differently from those in the South. As a practical matter, Powell was correct in one respect: there is no meaningful difference between de facto and de jure segregation, particularly from the point of view of someone who is a victim of either. A child stuck in an underperforming, underfunded school does not care whether her fate was by design or by social process. The result is the same: she gets an inferior education.

Powell maintained that the principal cause for segregation in northern cities was "socio-economic influences," including racial covenants, white flight, and Black poverty.[21] (Powell's opinion was refreshingly realistic in its analysis of the causes of segregation, but he did not consider the pervasive effects of structural inequality.) He expressed "profound misgivings" about busing as a remedy for segregation, which was disruptive of the educational experience for everyone involved. He demanded that courts must consider "other, equally important educational interests which a community may legitimately assert": neighborhood schools and local control (which, for all practical purposes, meant segregation).[22] In this, he was reflecting his formative experience as the head of the Richmond, Virginia, school board during the period of post-*Brown* desegregation and Massive Resistance.

By 1973 the moral assault on de jure segregation had done its work and spent its force. It left few guidelines for dealing with the morally ambiguous problems of schooling in the urban North, where structural racism produced outcomes like Jim Crow. Symptomatic of the difficulties posed by this new environment, Coloradans responded to *Keyes* the next year by adopting the "Poundstone amendment" to the state constitution by popular initiative, which prohibited the city of Denver from annexing adjacent areas without the consent of their residents, thus frustrating any attempt by the city to share its burdens of desegregation with its white suburbs. A generation after *Keyes*, the problem of integration still proved intractable.[23] Rehnquist dissented separately from Powell in *Keyes* to criticize *Green v. County School Board* as a "drastic extension of *Brown*" and warned that "the Court has taken a long leap in this area of constitutional law."[24] He confined his comments to questions of fact-finding, but his blunt words were a shot across the bow of the Court's handling of desegregation. Between them, Powell and Rehnquist signaled that the Court was heading in a new direction.

That possibility was confirmed the next year when the Court struck down a school integration plan devised by lower federal courts. *Milliken v. Bradley I* (1974) marked the Court's decisive swerve away from expansive desegregation remedies. For the first time, the Court rejected a desegregation plan, and for the first time, a majority of the Court condemned "racial balancing" as a goal of desegregation. It was the first Supreme Court case after *Brown I* to deny a desegregation remedy. *Milliken* shrunk the constitutional right in question to a pallid substitute for the robust desegregation that was the direction of the *Green*-to-*Swann* trajectory. The Burger Court abandoned both the spirit of *Brown* and the remedies that would have been necessary to realize that spirit. The Court affirmed the constitutional legitimacy of white flight and the creation of the urban "doughnut," an inner city inhabited predominantly by Black and brown people surrounded by a ring of white suburbs. *Milliken I* knowingly rejected the goals of *Brown I* in favor of competing values that secured white advantage and denied Blacks substantive equality.

As the momentum for desegregation in the early 1970s crested, federal judges experimented with what were called "metropolitan consolidation plans" to promote desegregation of inner-city schools. These plans consolidated school districts surrounding a city into a single unified district to counteract white flight out of the cities and into white suburbs. The bellwether case challenging these plans, *Bradley v. School Board* (4th Cir. 1972), involved Richmond, Virginia, and its environs. Judge Robert Merhige, one of the most prominent federal district court judges advancing desegregation, ordered the consolidation of Richmond with surrounding Henrico and Chesterfield Counties.[25] But he was reversed on appeal to the Fourth Circuit, which held that when a school district—here, the city of Richmond—had desegregated to the point of achieving unitary status, a federal district court lacked authority to force further consolidation.[26] The court of appeals' en banc opinion ignored the problem that white flight depleted city schools and created new segregation patterns based on structural racism and residential segregation.[27] The US Supreme Court affirmed without opinion.[28] It was divided four-four after Justice Powell recused himself because of his intimate involvement with Richmond desegregation while in private practice. (Powell would surely have voted to affirm had he sat.) Ominously, the Court was split on the core question of desegregation. The Richmond litigation proved merely to be the warm-up act for the major case in the wings, *Milliken v. Bradley* (1974) (*Milliken I*).[29]

Milliken came to the Court amid Detroit's postwar social crisis. A toxic mix of deindustrialization (Detroit lost three hundred thousand jobs after World War II), disinvestment, devaluation of all forms of real property, global industrial competition, automation, infrastructure decay, shrinkage of the tax base, crime, declining public education, resource hoarding by whites fleeing to the suburbs, and indifference amounting to outright hostility by the state and federal governments left Detroit depopulated and devastated by century's end.[30] White flight and ineradicable racial discrimination left the city segregated and with a rapidly dwindling white population. The Detroit school board had used traditional segregative techniques, including manipulation of school boundaries and attendance zones, and school-siting decisions, to ensure de facto segregated schools.

As this crisis developed, the city's schools grew more and more segregated. After a challenge by the NAACP, the US district court fashioned a remedy that combined the Detroit school district with fifty-three surrounding suburban districts to form a regional busing area. The judge reasoned that, given the increasing Black population, a remedy confined to Detroit alone would result in one-race schools, in effect entrenching segregation, whereas interdistrict busing would ensure a racial mix throughout the region's schools. In *Milliken I*, a five-member majority of the Court, speaking through the chief justice, struck down the plan.

Burger began with a point he had earlier suggested in *Swann*: the scope of the remedy must be limited to the extent of the constitutional violation.[31] "The remedy is necessarily designed, as all remedies are, to restore the victims of discriminatory conduct to the position they would have occupied in the absence of such conduct." "Absent an inter-district violation, there is no basis for an inter-district remedy," Burger held. That enabled him to hold that "the constitutional right of the Negro respondents residing in Detroit is to attend a unitary school system in that district," and only in that district, not in the Detroit metropolitan region as a whole.[32] It was definitely not a right to attend a racially integrated school, in Detroit or elsewhere.[33] The result was, in the words of Justice Douglas dissenting, that "today's decision...means that there is no violation of the Equal Protection Clause though the schools are segregated by race and though the black schools are not only 'separate' but 'inferior.'"[34]

Burger and his majority abandoned the goal of integration, embracing instead the disingenuous alternative of a unitary school system that is confined to a single geographic district. Since those districts are usually defined by attendance zones that coincide with segregated neighborhood residential patterns, Burger was saying that the only right a student could claim was to attend what would in reality be a monoracial school. Racial imbalance alone, even in the extreme of the Detroit school system of the time, where public schools were 75 to 90 percent African American, did not constitute a constitutional violation, he held. The remedy sought by plaintiffs would be a "drastic expansion of the constitutional right itself, an expansion without any support in either constitutional principle or precedent."[35] The state has no duty to bring about racially integrated schools, but only to refrain from deliberately creating segregated ones.

Burger required proof of an intent by the state or its subdivisions (like school districts) to discriminate, which reified the de jure / de facto distinction and made it the bedrock of subsequent desegregation decisions.[36] A mere effect—the existence of de facto segregated schools—did not prove a constitutional violation, even where that segregation was the product of state action like pupil assignment policy or drawing attendance zones. Disparate impact counted for little in the context of school desegregation. Structural racism guaranteed inferior monoracial urban schools.

Burger justified this result by exalting a different set of values, unknown to *Brown*. He extolled local control of schools, the point that Powell had urged first as counsel arguing before the Court, then as associate justice. "No single tradition in public education is more deeply rooted than local control over the operation of schools; local autonomy has long been thought essential both to the maintenance of community concern and support for public schools."[37] Courts could not dismiss local administration or school district boundaries as a "mere administrative convenience." Burger deplored the idea that federal courts might become the "de facto 'legislative authority' to resolve these complex questions, and then the 'school superintendent' for the entire area."[38] He condemned the policy of "racial balancing,"[39] a theme that had particular appeal for conservatives.

Justice Marshall, dissenting, foretold the consequences of this new turn in the court's doctrine. The Court was allowing "our great metropolitan areas to be divided up into two cities—one white, the other black,"[40] "thereby guaranteeing that Negro children in Detroit will receive the same separate and inherently unequal education in the future as they have been unconstitutionally afforded in the past."[41] *Milliken* enabled the development of underfunded Black urban school systems surrounded by an iron ring of white (and exclusive) suburbs, with superior schools for their white children. "Today's holding," Marshall warned, "is more a reflection of a perceived public mood that we have gone far enough in enforcing the Constitution's guarantee of equal justice than it is the product of neutral principles of law."[42]

Milliken and its second round of argument in *Milliken v. Bradley II* (1977)[43] signaled a new attitude on the part of the Court, hostile to expansive remedies for school segregation, reluctant to use federal judicial power to combat inequality. "The nature of the desegregation remedy is to be determined by the nature and scope of the constitutional violation," wrote Burger. Under this formula, the violation was now the measure of the remedy, inviting later courts to confine the scope of their intervention to something that was measured by an increasingly remote past. The commitment to desegregation that drove the line of cases from *Griffin* through *Swann* evaporated. The Court abandoned the struggle. Owen Fiss believes that *Milliken* "repudiated the proudest aspirations of *Brown v. Board of Education* and began the long and extended process of draining that landmark 1954 decision of much of its substantive meaning."[44] As Derrick Bell nicely put it, "the Court allayed [white] middle class fears that the school bus would become the Trojan Horse of their suburban Troys."[45]

However, the Court did confine the impact of *Milliken* when the subject of litigation was housing rather than education. *Hills v. Gautreaux* (1976)[46] grew out of a notorious collusion between the federal Department of Housing and Urban Development (HUD) and the Chicago Housing Authority (CHA) to confine all new public housing projects "within the areas known as the Negro Ghetto."[47] The trial court's remedial order required the CHA to seek sites outside the city of Chicago, but the CHA and HUD resisted, arguing that *Milliken* forbade such trans-jurisdictional remedies. The Supreme Court unanimously rejected that gambit. Justice Stewart stated that *Milliken* "was actually based on fundamental limitations on the remedial powers of the federal courts to restructure the operation of local and state governmental entities," not on some comprehensive opposition to crossing geographic boundaries. "Nothing in the Milliken decision suggests a per se rule that federal courts lack authority to order parties found to have violated the Constitution to undertake remedial efforts beyond the municipal boundaries of the city where the violation occurred," he wrote.[48] Relying on municipal boundaries "would transform Milliken's principled limitation on the exercise of federal judicial authority into an arbitrary and mechanical shield for those found to have engaged in unconstitutional conduct."[49] *Milliken* was far from being declawed, though. Justice O'Connor later declared that Gautreaux was "an affirmation of, not a deviation from, Milliken I."[50] *Gautreaux* had little impact outside the subject of public housing, though there it proved to be a landmark in sociology, demonstrating that an improvement in residential circumstances alone resulted in improvements in employment and educational opportunities.[51]

Keyes and *Milliken* demonstrated that the Court was turning away from the values and goals that underlay its desegregation decisions of 1964–1971 toward some unknown future. Two Ohio desegregation cases of 1979 provided the vehicle for the prophets of the new order, Justices Powell and Rehnquist, to identify what would replace the values of the second Reconstruction.

Columbus Board of Education v. Penick (1979)[52] and *Dayton Board of Education v. Brinkman* (1979)[53] both dealt with a problem that by 1979 was becoming tiresomely familiar: school boards in northern cities engaged in the same sort of desegregation foot-dragging that southern school districts had pioneered two decades earlier. The majority in these two cases, speaking through Justice White, upheld lower-court orders mandating that both school boards implement systemwide desegregation plans based on extensive student transfers among the schools within each system. The lower courts found that the school boards had maintained segregated schools ("dual school systems") at the time *Brown* was decided, and that they had ignored their "continuing affirmative duty" to disestablish those dual systems.

The new element in these 1979 opinions was that three years earlier the Court had injected a major new doctrine into cases involving racial inequality, the discriminatory intent / disparate impact dichotomy. In *Washington v. Davis* (1976), the Court in an opinion by Justice White had held that someone alleging racial discrimination in the workplace must prove that the defendant employer had acted with a racially discriminatory intent.

A mere showing of racially disparate impact would not suffice to prove a constitutional violation. (*Washington v. Davis* is analyzed extensively below in chapter 11.) Now in the Ohio cases, White held that the trial courts had correctly applied the *Davis* formula: by itself, disparate impact, even with foreseeable consequences, was not enough to establish an equal protection violation. But disparate impact could be used to show an improper purpose. By maintaining distinctly Black schools, the school boards had engaged in intentionally segregative practices that had a systemwide impact. This satisfied the *Keyes* requirement that remedies be commensurate with the violation. The Court approved lower-court orders requiring extensive student transfers. In this sense, the Dayton and Columbus cases might be seen as preserving the goals of desegregation while slightly tempering *Davis*. They also subtly shifted the inquiry in desegregation cases from combating racial discrimination to redressing racial imbalances in school systems.[54]

White's opinions correctly applied the Court's desegregation doctrines at the time, conformed to the *Washington v. Davis* discriminatory-intent formula. But Justices Powell and Rehnquist in dissent proposed altogether different approaches to school desegregation. Powell's lengthy opinion in the Columbus case demanded that federal courts reduce their efforts to desegregate public schools. Powell, invoking his pre-Court experience as chair of the Richmond, Virginia, school board, proclaimed himself to be the Court's authority on educational policy, and his conservative views on the subject carried greater weight.[55] He condemned what he called "social engineering" by federal judges. (The real social engineering, however, had been perpetrated earlier by local school boards who manipulated attendance zones to preserve segregation.) There are "limits to effective judicial power," he insisted. "The time has come for a thoughtful re-examination of the proper limits of the role of courts in confronting the intractable problems of public education in our complex society."[56] Responsibility for all educational choices "must be left with school officials and public authorities," not federal judges.[57] Resegregation, he claimed, would result from popular resentment at federal judicial intrusion. White flight will follow, not because of racism, but rather as "a natural reaction to the displacement of professional and local control that occurs when courts go into the business of restructuring and operating school systems."[58] In this new order, resegregation was "natural," while integration was "forced" and thus artificial or unnatural. Segregated housing patterns were "intractable," and judicial efforts to compensate by busing and pupil reassignment would prove futile. Powell was proposing a new—or rather, a retrograde—value system to replace *Brown I*. *Brown* was being overruled *sub silentio*, as lawyers put it, quietly and behind the scenes, under the cover of silence. It would continue to be nominally respected, mostly in performative acts of judicial self-congratulation, but it would be drained both of its values and of practical effect. A new pretextuality was emerging for the era of structural racism: conservative judges proudly condemned de jure discrimination while adopting a regressive value system that sustained the de facto kind.

Rehnquist agreed with Powell's views, but added the new *Davis* requirement of discriminatory purpose, reinterpreted by the nearly insuperable test: "the decisionmaker...selected or reaffirmed a particular course of action at least in part 'because of,' not merely 'in spite of,' its adverse effects upon an identifiable group."[59] This heightened intent requirement would foreclose remedies based on disparate impact, thus closing off the possibility of relying on effects (such as continued de facto segregation or actual resegregation). So even where plaintiffs demonstrated a violation, the Court was beginning to close off effective forms of relief.

A new note was creeping into Supreme Court opinions in the Rehnquist and Powell dissents: the justices seemed to want to be rid of desegregation cases at the earliest opportunity, throwing the problem back to the school boards in the name of "local autonomy" and "neighborhood schools." If this perpetuated single-race schools with inferior facilities, so be it.

The Court Affirms Resegregation

Resegregation began appearing in public schools soon after a trial court finalized its specific remedial program in a desegregation order. Often this occurred at the time the school district gave up on busing and switched to an emphasis on neighborhood schools. Then the problem returned to the Supreme Court in the form of whether the federal district courts had a responsibility to make regular, even annual, revisions in their desegregation order to maintain integration, or whether demographic changes—white flight—that produced increasing segregation were no longer of concern to courts.

The Court first addressed this issue explicitly in *Pasadena City Board of Education v. Spangler* (1976).[60] Like most other American cities going through the turmoil of desegregation and busing in the 1970s, Pasadena, California, was the scene of intense local controversy over how to comply with the evolving understanding of *Brown*. Did *Brown* require only that all traces of de jure segregation be eliminated at one point in time, or did it mandate that all students, particularly African American children, enjoy full, continuing substantive equality in educational opportunity? This was a variant of the *Brown* ambiguity (anticlassification vs. antisubordination).

A federal district court in 1970 ordered the Pasadena school district to arrange attendance zones in such a way that there would be "no school with a majority of minority students." Three years into the process, the school district appealed to the Supreme Court, seeking to enjoin further mandated annual readjustments of attendance zones that were designed to preserve the original racial balance. It also sought to get rid of the ban on majority-minority schools. Rehnquist for the Court readily agreed to the request. White flight was merely "a quite normal pattern of human migration" and not attributable to "any segregative action" by the school board. Implicit in this is an unspoken assumption of what Gary Orfield calls "suburban innocence": white innocence writ large.[61] The historian Kevin Kruse maintains that white flight was also the parent of other mainstays of postwar conservatism, including the so-called tax revolt of the 1970s, the use of tuition vouchers to weaken the public schools, and the privatization of public services more generally.[62] House Speaker Newt Gingrich, purveying a racism that was somehow both crude and yet subtle, warned of "bring[ing] people out [into the suburbs] for public housing who have no middle-class values and whose kids as they become teenagers often are centers of robbery and where the schools collapse because the parents that live in the apartment complexes don't care that the kids don't do well in school and the whole school collapses."[63] As always when structural racism is concerned, Gingrich did not have to specify the race of the people he was talking about. His suburban constituents filled in the blank.

Quoting *Swann*, Rehnquist held that neither school boards nor courts "are constitutionally required to make year-by-year adjustments of the racial composition of student bodies once the affirmative duty to desegregate has been accomplished and racial discrimination through official action is eliminated from the system."[64] It was enough that the court had come up with a "racially neutral attendance pattern" at the outset; ongoing supervision or maintenance of the pattern was not necessary. Under *Washington v. Davis*, actionable racial inequality could only be a product of intent, not of shifting demographics. Once the dual system was dismantled and a unitary system put in its place, judicial involvement should cease, even if the original order immediately proved ineffective. *Pasadena* reflected a Court disillusioned by the futility of attempting to impose integration on communities determined to resist. Only intentional discrimination of the de jure kind would be susceptible of judicial intervention. Structural inequality based on residential patterns was proving beyond the judiciary's reach. The Pasadena case provided the essential prerequisite for resegregation: once a scintilla of de jure desegregation had been attained, even momentarily, any further segregation in the school system was no longer of concern to federal courts.

An oddity of these resegregation cases was that the Supreme Court almost never explicitly considered the crucial issue of the relationship between residential segregation and educational inequality. It confronted the issue only once, obliquely, in a relatively obscure case involving the desegregation of the Austin, Texas, public schools. In *United States v. Texas Education Agency* (1976),[65] Judge John Minor Wisdom of the Fifth Circuit Court of Appeals held that segregative intent could be found from foreseeable consequences, applying the rule derived from tort law that a person intends the natural and foreseeable consequences of his actions.[66] From this he went on to hold that where a school district like Austin is clearly segregated in housing patterns, adoption of a neighborhood-schools policy of pupil assignment will inevitably result in segregated schools. "School authorities may not constitutionally use a neighborhood assignment policy that creates segregated schools in a district with ethnically segregated residential patterns. A segregated school system is the foreseeable and inevitable result of such an assignment policy."[67] He ordered extensive busing to remedy the racial imbalance, particularly as it affected Mexican American students.

The Supreme Court vacated Judge Wisdom's decision in an unsigned opinion, *Austin Independent School District v. United States* (1976), and remanded for reconsideration in light of *Washington v. Davis*, clearly implying that Wisdom's foreseeable consequences test did not meet the *Davis* intent requirement.[68] Justice Powell, joined by Burger and Rehnquist, concurred in a separate opinion to address the residential segregation issue explicitly, rather than leaving it to be inferred from the majority's naked disposition of the certiorari petition. In dicta Powell asserted that "the principal cause of racial and ethnic imbalance in urban public schools across the country North and South is the imbalance in residential patterns. Such residential patterns are typically beyond the control of school authorities. For example, discrimination in housing whether public or private cannot be attributed to school authorities. Economic pressures and voluntary preferences are the primary determinants of residential patterns." The Court has never since reconsidered these assumptions, thereby closing off any possibility of recognizing structural racism, in the form of residential segregation, as being open to constitutional remedy. This, even though the federal government bore a major responsibility for imposing residential segregation on the nation in the first place.[69] Powell's *Austin* dicta continued to be the mostly unacknowledged presumption of the Court. He repeated this point in his 1979 *Dayton* dissent: segregation in contemporary schools "results primarily from familiar segregated housing patterns, which in turn are caused by social, economic, and demographic forces for which no school board is responsible."[70]

The Court continued to undermine its own *Brown I* handiwork in *Freeman v. Pitts* (1992).[71] It there held that a federal court could release a school district from its obligations to desegregate by terminating in a piecemeal manner the court's authority over one aspect of a remedial program, such as teachers' salaries or pupil assignments, while retaining jurisdiction over the rest of the original order. This had the effect of weakening the impact of the court's order by permitting school districts to backslide on the released aspects, thus enfeebling the effect of the overall order. Once a court's authority is relinquished, it is permanently lost unless reinstated by entirely new litigation, which by the time of *Freeman* (1992) was increasingly unlikely to succeed or even be initiated. For those hostile to the desegregation project, partial release was a way of "killing *Brown* softly."[72]

Freeman restated the scope of the court's responsibility narrowly: "whether the vestiges of past discrimination have been eliminated *to the extent practicable*" (italics added). Justice Anthony Kennedy, writing for the majority, did not elaborate on exactly what that fateful italicized qualification meant, but it clearly implied that practical constraints would assume a large role in shaping the scope of future remedies. Kennedy endorsed Powell's severance of the link between residential segregation and school segregation: "where segregation is the product not of state action but of private [housing] choices, it does not have constitutional implications. It is beyond the authority...of the federal courts to try to counteract these kinds of continuous and massive demographic shifts." "Residential housing choices, and their attendant effects on the racial composition of schools, present an ever-changing pattern, one difficult to address through judicial remedies."[73] But to sever the link between residential and school segregation is to unthinkingly ignore or deny the structural foundations of racial inequality.

The problem of remedies continued to plague the desegregation process, as it had since *Brown II* in 1955. It has become apparent in hindsight that the Court's refusal to explicitly define the relation between the substantive right announced in *Brown I* and the remedies necessary to secure that right was a tragic mistake. When the Court did finally address the issue a generation later, it was by an entirely new bench, with a majority of its members deeply unsympathetic to the ideals of *Brown I*, committed to protecting white advantage and indifferent at best to doing anything about the structural racism that produced resegregation.

The Court finally resolved the issue of remedies in *Missouri v. Jenkins*, the protracted litigation over desegregating the Kansas City, Missouri Metropolitan School District (KCMSD). Between them, KCMSD and the state of Missouri made a mess of complying with the *Brown I* command to rid the schools of all vestiges of de jure segregation.[74] The district used school attendance zones and pupil assignment plans to preserve nearly complete racial segregation in the Kansas City schools well into the 1980s. (One example of the lengths to which KCMSD went: "When no further boundary adjustments were possible, black schoolchildren were required to walk to their overcrowded school to be met by a black teacher and a bus. They were then transported to an under-utilized white school where they had their own classroom, cafeteria period, and recess time. They were then bused back to their neighborhood school to walk home. At a time when the district was obligated to reduce racial isolation, it manifestly extended it.")[75]

In litigation that began in 1977, US district court judge Russell Clark lost patience with this kind of behavior, but he recognized the futility of trying to force interdistrict busing after *Milliken*. He therefore resorted to drastic alternative remedies to improve the physical plant and educational opportunities of Kansas City schools by mandating specific expenditures and programs, including creation of magnet schools. (By 2015, the total costs of this improvement, according to critics, amounted to $2 billion.)[76] His orders came before the Supreme Court twice.

In *Missouri v. Jenkins I* (1990),[77] the Court reversed Judge Clark's order that KCMSD raise property taxes to pay for the cost of capital improvements. The conservative bloc of the Court, speaking through Justice

Kennedy, objected to the lower court's order that compelled the school district to raise taxes. He dismissed the distinction between the court itself imposing taxes and requiring the district to do so as a "convenient formalism" that ignored limitations on the power of federal courts. A court that itself imposed taxes directly failed to show a "proper respect for the integrity and function of local government institutions." The majority did, however, permit the lower court to order the district to levy the taxes, even though this ignored state laws imposing limits on the amount of taxes that a school district may raise.

Despite Judge Clark's Sisyphean efforts, the desegregation of Kansas City schools dragged on, seemingly interminably and, to his many critics, without significant results. Not surprisingly, the desegregation struggle ended up back in the Supreme Court again in 1995, and this time the conservative bloc seemed determined to squelch it for good. Judge Clark had ordered across-the-board salary increases for all faculty and staff in the KCMSD as a means of improving the quality of the city's schools to combat white flight. He referred to this goal as "desegregative attractiveness," an unfortunate phrasing that seemed to antagonize the Court's majority. In *Missouri v. Jenkins II* (1995)[78] Chief Justice Rehnquist compiled a catalog of limitations on federal judicial power to manage desegregation. Hearkening back to the narrow scope of remedial authority in the *Swann* and *Milliken II* dicta, Rehnquist repeated what was becoming a mantra taken from the law of remedies: the court's order must serve "as proper means to the end of restoring the victims of discriminatory conduct to the position they would have occupied in the absence of that conduct." Once again, the Court ignored the original aspirational goals of *Brown I* in favor of a more technical, legalistic concept of restoration, quoting *Milliken II*: "The nature of the desegregation remedy is to be determined by the nature and scope of the constitutional violation." The court may not aspire to do more than eliminate "as far as possible the vestiges of de jure segregation." That imposed a double constraint: federal courts could do no more than try to eliminate de jure segregation (implicitly but clearly leaving de facto segregation beyond the scope of judicial power), and they may do so only "as far as possible," an exception that quickly swallowed up the rule.

As *Milliken I* commanded, a federal court may not craft an interdistrict remedy for what was originally an *intradistrict* violation. As anyone who has lived in Missouri knows,[79] separating the segregation that prevailed in Kansas City from the same segregation in neighboring Independence or

Westport is artificial to the point of absurdity. It is not as if segregation existed only within the municipal boundaries of Kansas City while the remainder of the state was a haven of racial equality. Before 1954 (and for a time after), *all* of Missouri was segregated.

"Our cases recognize that local autonomy of school districts is a vital national tradition," Rehnquist intoned, affirming Justice Powell's favorite theme. Therefore an "indefinite extension" of the district court's supervisory authority was unwarranted.[80] The sooner local control of schools was restored, the more the proper constitutional balance of federalism was restored.

In a lengthy and angry concurring opinion, Justice Clarence Thomas seemed to challenge the authority of *Brown I* itself: "the [district] court has read our cases to support the theory that black students suffer an unspecified psychological harm from segregation that retards their mental and educational development.[81] This approach not only relies upon questionable social science research rather than constitutional principle but also rests on an assumption of black inferiority."[82] In this diatribe, Thomas rejected social science itself in unsparing terms; he spurned "the unnecessary and misleading assistance of the social sciences." "The lower courts should not be swayed by the easy answers of social science, nor should they accept the findings, and the assumptions, of sociology and psychology at the price of constitutional principle."[83]

Thomas claimed that "the continuing 'racial isolation' of schools after de jure segregation has ended may well reflect voluntary housing choices or other private decisions."[84] De facto segregation did not trouble him: it "does not constitute a continuing harm after the end of de jure segregation." It is beyond the authority of federal courts to try to counteract "social changes." In these claims, Thomas severed structural racism (even while acknowledging its existence) from constitutional discourse. He imputed to his dissenting colleagues (Souter, Stevens, Ginsburg, and Breyer) "an assumption of black inferiority," a shockingly preposterous claim if meant seriously—and shockingly irresponsible if not.

The justices finally brought the curtain down on further court-ordered desegregation in *Board of Education of Oklahoma City v. Dowell* (1991)[85] by holding that a federal district court could dissolve an injunction imposing a desegregation plan even if schools had resegregated. In 1961, African American parents sought to enjoin the de jure school segregation that had prevailed in Oklahoma ever since statehood in 1907. The Oklahoma City

Board of Education then adopted a neighborhood-schools plan with attendance zones that effectively continued segregation based on residential patterns that themselves were the product of public and private segregationist policies. In 1965 the US district court ordered the Board to "take clear, aggressive, affirmative action" to desegregate.[86] Judge Luther Bohanon held that in framing a desegregation plan, the Board could take race explicitly into account, observing that *Brown* "did not convert Justice Harlan's metaphor ["our Constitution is colorblind," *Plessy v. Ferguson*] into constitutional dogma barring affirmative action to accomplish the purposes of the Fourteenth Amendment." In 1972, the district court entered an injunction mandating busing to comply with a desegregation proposal known as the "Finger Plan." This produced substantial integration, and five years later the court felt confident enough to terminate its jurisdiction in the case. But changing demographic patterns in the city produced enough integration in a few schools that some African American students were being bused lengthy distances to remain in compliance. So the Board adopted what was called the "Student Reassignment Plan" (SRP), which had the effect of resegregating schools in Black neighborhoods. Plaintiffs returned to court, seeking to enjoin the SRP.

In *Dowell*, Chief Justice Rehnquist, writing for the five-member conservative majority, held that lower courts could implement the SRP because the resegregation it produced did not necessarily offend the equal protection clause. Judicial involvement in school desegregation was meant to be a "temporary measure to remedy past discrimination" and its orders were "not intended to operate in perpetuity" to prolong a "judicial tutelage for the indefinite future." Such a judicial role was incompatible with "the important values of local control" of schools.[87] The plaintiff must now prove that the defendant school board either mandated resegregation explicitly or adopted measures to preserve it.

Justice Marshall, joined by Blackmun and Stevens, objected that after sixty-five years of segregation the "majority today suggests that 13 years of desegregation was enough." He found it necessary to remind the majority that one-race schools were a vestige of de jure segregation. The current Court was ignoring the original *Brown* context of stigmatic injury. Momentary compliance with a desegregation order at the time of its issuance was not enough to secure "lasting integration of formerly segregated systems."[88] "The reemergence of racial separation... may revive the message of racial inferiority implicit in the former policy of state-enforced segregation." The correct understanding of *Brown* demands that "the *effects* of past discrimination remain chargeable to the school district regardless of its lack of continued enforcement of segregation."[89] Marshall dismissed the argument that residential segregation was purely an effect of "private decision-making" and "personal preferences" because the majority "pays insufficient attention to the roles of the State, local officials, and the Board in creating what are now self-perpetuating patterns of residential segregation."[90] Events confirmed Marshall's forebodings. A 1996 study of the Oklahoma City school system conducted by the Harvard Graduate School of Education concluded that the neighborhood schools completely resegregated, but the promised benefits (parental involvement, improved test performance) were not realized.[91] The only component of the SRP that was achieved was segregation.

Forty years after *Brown*, the US Supreme Court had forgotten or intentionally abandoned its rationale, what Justice Marshall called the "stigmatic injury" of psychic harm inflicted on African American children by segregation, the inescapable message from the white majority of Americans that they were, in Taney's *Dred Scott* words, "considered as a subordinate and inferior class of beings, who had been subjugated by the dominant race, and…had no rights or privileges but such as those who held the power and the Government might choose to grant them,…beings of an inferior order, and altogether unfit to associate with the white race, either in social or political relations; and so far inferior, that they had no rights which the white man was bound to respect."[92]

The Rehnquist Court treated segregation as something in the past, identified solely by its de jure character, that is, as a problem of discriminatory intent. The modern Court has not only forgotten the substantive basis of *Brown I*; it has discarded *Brown II*'s expansive vision of the equity powers of the federal courts, replacing it with a narrow, grudging insistence on limitations on federal judicial power. The Court shrunk the Fourteenth Amendment first to state action, then to intent rather than effects, then to a shrunken version of intent choked by the tightening *Davis* noose. It foreclosed judicial attempts to suppress de facto segregation that produced the disparate impacts that are the modern foundation of racial inequality in America. Mark Tushnet summarized this half century of the Court's racial jurisprudence memorably: "The Warren Court saw the status of African Americans as *the* central issue in constitutional law; the Burger Court saw it as an important issue; the Rehnquist Court did not see it as an issue at all.

The Rehnquist Court worried not that public policy treated Blacks unconstitutionally, but that it treated whites unconstitutionally. For all practical purposes, concern over the status of African Americans in the law disappeared."[93] Structural racism and segregation in the nation's schools have prevailed, now seemingly beyond the reach of federal judicial power.

School Finance and Fundamental Rights

In 1950, African American parents who sought equality (or at least an improvement) of educational opportunity for their children faced two major challenges: state laws that confined their children to segregated schools, and gross disparities in financial support between whites' schools and Blacks'. De jure segregation was a product of traditional Jim Crow racism, but funding overlaid that with an issue of structural racism. *Brown I* addressed the first of these and, for a time, ignored the second. But as housing segregation ensured continuing segregation in the schools and as whites vociferously fought busing, the problem of school finance came to the fore. By 1970, two realities persisted: schools remained extensively segregated throughout the nation, and schools serving minority populations—African Americans and Latinos—were generally inferior in physical amenities and teacher qualifications. As African American parents' support for busing (never too keen to begin with) waned,[94] they turned to the second issue and sought to equalize funding.

The underlying problem they encountered was structural inequality. In all states, public schools were (and continue to be) funded from a combination of two sources: taxes on real property in the district (an ad valorem tax based on the assessed value of the property), and a contribution from a state fund that was meant to equalize the disparities among the districts to some extent. Since funding for public schools was mostly based on local property taxation, poorer school districts could raise less in taxes than more affluent white districts because the value of real property in their district was lower. This produced ongoing structural disparity. Rebecca Sibilia, an authority on school finance, observes that "the racial and economic segregation created by gerrymandered school district boundaries continues to divide our communities and rob our nation's children of fundamental freedoms and opportunity. Families with money or status can retain both by drawing and upholding invisible lines. This, in conjunction with housing segregation, ensures that—rather than a partial remedy—district geographies serve to further entrench society's deep divisions of opportunity."[95] Due to the class-race nexus, poor districts correlated with minority populations. So would-be plaintiffs at that time assumed that any such challenge would have to come under the equal protection clause of the *federal* Constitution, asserting discrimination based on wealth and its racial correlative. Until the 1970s, the state constitutions had stood aside in the wings, diffident and unnoticed wallflowers. That was about to change.

Equal protection doctrine developed along two lines: suspect classification and fundamental rights. The Burger Court proved hostile to any potential for substantive equal protection based on fundamental rights that might find a constitutionally guaranteed right to the basics of human existence: food, shelter, clothing, and medical care.[96] But advocates for equality hoped that education might prove to be an exception. They took heart from *Brown I*'s promise that "today, education is perhaps the most important function of state and local governments. Compulsory school attendance laws and the great expenditures for education both demonstrate our recognition of the importance of education to our democratic society. It is required in the performance of our most basic public responsibilities.... it is doubtful that any child may reasonably be expected to succeed in life if he is denied the opportunity of an education. Such an opportunity, where the state has undertaken to provide it, is a right which must be made available to all on equal terms."[97] Surely, that canonical text should mean that gross disparities in school funding on racial lines would run afoul of the equal protection clause?

In the late 1960s, Latino parents in Texas and California determined to press this claim in both federal and state courts. These federal and state tracks were intertwined, and it is necessary to follow them both. Latino parents in a San Antonio, Texas, school district brought a class action suit in a federal district court claiming that the state's method of financing schools deprived them of equal protection under the Fourteenth Amendment. They argued that the inequality of funding offended both strands of equal protection.[98] They claimed to be a suspect class: poor people, disadvantaged by the state because of their poverty. They also argued that education was a fundamental right, which was denied them by inferior schools. The three-judge district court agreed on both points, holding that "the current system tends to subsidize the rich at the expense of the poor, rather than the other way around."[99] Because both suspect classifications and fundamental interests were implicated, the court subjected the Texas system to strict scrutiny, and then held that it failed even deferential scrutiny because there was no rational basis for the difference in outcomes—that is, a disparate impact.

The Supreme Court reversed, rejecting both bases, in *San Antonio Independent School District v. Rodriguez* (1973).[100] The Court's self-proclaimed authority on education issues, Justice Powell, writing for a five-member majority, rejected the claim that poverty could constitute a suspect class in a *Carolene Products* sense: plaintiffs and their class "have none of the traditional indicia of suspectness: the class is not saddled with such disabilities, or subjected to such a history of purposeful unequal treatment, or relegated to such a position of political powerlessness as to command extraordinary protection from the majoritarian political process." (Each of those conclusions was obviously wrong and could have been reached only by someone who had never experienced poverty firsthand.) The equal protection clause "does not require absolute equality or precisely equal advantages," he concluded. Powell twice flouted common experience: he doubted that the quality of education depended on how much was spent,[101] and there was no "more than a random chance that racial minorities are concentrated in property-poor districts."[102] The plaintiffs' children were not deprived of *all* education; the state provided a "basic" experience with "an opportunity to acquire the basic minimal skills."[103] There was no "absolute deprivation" of education. "Relative differences in spending" did not amount to the level of gross deprivation that might bring the equal protection clause into play. In any event, "equal quality of education" is a chimera, so it is pointless to try to achieve it.

Rodriguez thus added education to the catalog of "rights" that can claim no protection under the equal protection clause. Powell dismissed *Brown's* insistence on the centrality of education as irrelevant because the right being protected, which he mischaracterized as a "right to an education," was not "fundamental."[104] No fundamental right was implicated: it "is not the province of this Court to create substantive constitutional rights in the name of guaranteeing equal protection of the laws."[105] Education is not explicitly or implicitly protected in the Constitution. It is a matter of "social or economic legislation" that traditionally gets only deferential scrutiny. For authority, Powell invoked *Dandridge v. Williams* (1970) (welfare benefits) and *Lindsey v. Normet* (1972) (housing).[106]

Powell justified these conclusions by considerations of federalism and separation of powers. He cautioned against federal judges making policy decisions assigned by the Constitution to the legislature and to the states. "We have here nothing less than a direct attack on the way in which Texas has chosen to raise and disburse state and local tax revenues."[107] He stressed above all the importance of preserving "local control" over educational policy, including funding: "it would be difficult to imagine a case having a greater potential impact on our federal system than the one now before us, in which we are urged to abrogate systems of financing public education presently in existence in virtually every State."[108] Judicial deference to the judgments of the states and their legislatures is necessary because expertise is presumed to be a matter of legislative judgment. The justices "lack both the expertise and the familiarity with local problems so necessary to the making of wise decisions with respect to the raising and disposition of public revenues."[109]

Rodriguez was another disaster for equality in education. Together with *Milliken v. Bradley*, it drained *Brown I* of much of its egalitarian potential. The ensuing resegregation has demonstrated that Americans can rid their society of official de jure discrimination and still retain the deep enduring inequality that Jim Crow segregation imposed. Erwin Chemerinsky denounced *Rodriguez* as the worst constitutional decision since 1960: "it played a major role in creating the separate and unequal schools that exist today." Steven Shiffrin of Cornell concurred: "it has permitted millions of children to be imprisoned in a system of educational inequality."[110] Rodriguez constituted a triumph for Nixon's program of retreat on educational equality. Four of the five justices in the majority were Nixon's appointees: Powell, Burger, Blackmun, and Rehnquist. (Potter Stewart joined them to make a majority.) If *Brown I* was a victory for educational equality over the first pillar of racial disparity (de jure segregation), *Rodriguez* was a lasting defeat for the second pillar, de facto inequality of resources. But Dean Chemerinsky's judgment is unquestionably valid: *Rodriguez* has played a major role in continuing separate-and-unequal in education. *Brown I* struck down de jure segregation; *Rodriguez* entombed *Brown* in a formalist sarcophagus, affirming the legitimacy of de facto discrimination based on structural racism.[111]

It did not have to be that way. Powell's assumptions and conclusions were nothing more than ipse dixits, reflecting policy choices made by Nixon's new conservative majority. A different court, more attuned to the spirit of *Brown*, operating on different premises, could have reached different conclusions. It might have concluded that school board decisions drawing school boundaries, or state funding schemes, were artifacts of the Jim Crow era, when racial inequality went unchallenged by most white people. *Brown* heralded a new day, when public education was to be the centerpiece of a new civic order in which all people were equal in rights, not in name only, but in substance and reality.

Though plaintiffs failed at the US Supreme Court, they scored greater successes in the state courts. State supreme courts reached strikingly different results and reasoning when petitioners challenged educational inequality under state constitutions. This came about with the encouragement of Justice Brennan, who in his final years on the Court was discouraged by the conservative direction it was taking. Despairing that his colleagues would not continue on the Warren Court liberal path, he urged lawyers to look to state courts and state constitutions to protect civil rights and civil liberties. In two influential law review articles in 1977 and 1986,[112] he urged lawyers to turn to the declarations of rights in the state constitutions and to the state supreme courts as fresh, hitherto overlooked sources of protection for individual liberties. This innovation became known as "the New Judicial Federalism."[113] As the essential conservatism of the Burger Court became apparent and as the climate darkened even more upon Rehnquist's accession to the center seat, state courts began to display a newfound activism in defense of personal freedoms.

California provided the bellwether case for school funding in the recurring litigation known as *Serrano v. Priest*. In *Serrano I*,[114] decided in 1971, the California Supreme Court held that under the equal protection clause of the Fourteenth Amendment, the state constitution's privileges or immunities clause (which differs substantially from its federal counterpart),[115] and the state's equal protection clause, wealth disparities inherent in the state's school finance system constituted discrimination by wealth, a suspect classification under state constitutional law, and violated petitioners' children's fundamental interest in education (citing *Brown I*). It thus disregarded two of the US Supreme Court's reasons for doing nothing about structural inequality. The California judges rejected the de facto / de jure distinction that choked federal judges' opinions, holding that residential patterns were "shaped and hardened" by official actions like zoning.

Then the US Supreme Court handed down its *Rodriguez* decision in 1973, seemingly vitiating much of the California court's reasoning. So the litigation returned to the California Supreme Court, which conceded in *Serrano II*[116] that *Rodriguez* had indeed "undercut" its federal Fourteenth Amendment holding. But it held that the *state's* equal protection clause had an "independent vitality" and on that basis reiterated its suspect-classification and fundamental-rights holdings. It defined the latter as "those individual rights and liberties which lie at the core of our free and representative form of government, [and] are properly considered 'fundamental.'" In both these respects—education as a fundamental right and wealth as a suspect class—the California judges rebuffed the US Supreme Court's *Rodriguez* minimalism and returned to the letter and spirit of *Brown I*.

Serrano v. Priest and comparable litigation in other states have had mixed results. The most untoward came in California, when partly in reaction to the decisions, the people of the state in 1978 adopted a constitutional amendment by an initiative known as Proposition 13, which revised and capped property taxes. One of the consequences of *Serrano* was a modest redistribution of the property tax burden, which, like any equalization measure, had the effect of benefiting poorer school districts at the expense of the more affluent. Middle- and upper-class taxpayers rebelled.[117] Prop 13 was part of the so-called taxpayers' revolt that spread from California throughout the United States and contributed to Ronald Reagan's appeal in national politics. The US Supreme Court upheld the constitutionality of Prop 13 against an equal protection challenge by applying a highly deferential standard of review ("rationally furthers a legitimate state interest").[118] Though African Americans were the only demographic to oppose Prop 13, there was no obvious racial discrimination implied in its adoption.

Prop 13 marked the close of the first phase of school finance litigation, which largely ended unsuccessfully for proponents of an equal protection approach under either the federal or the state constitutions. But the second phase proved more fruitful, where challengers turned to state constitutional provisions that guaranteed something like "equal and adequate" funding for the state's public schools. Here Isaiah Berlin's influential distinction between negative and positive liberty has proven decisive.[119] The equal protection clauses secure a negative liberty: they protect the individual (or groups) against adverse government action. But state constitutions are characterized by much more extensive guarantees of *positive* liberty, such as the right to equal and adequate public education.[120] State supreme courts have been willing to hold that such provisions guarantee a minimal level of support for public education. This in turn has embroiled them in contentious disputes with state legislatures unwilling to pony up the finances mandated by the courts. Nevertheless, under the second-phase strategy, state funding has become more equalized in many states, which has diminished though not eliminated wealth distinctions. To some unmeasurable extent, this softens the negative impact of *Rodriguez*. A strong argument can be made[121] that *Brown I*'s basic equality rationale is better served by reliance on the positive-liberty provisions of the state constitutions and a more extensive resort to state courts to protect those liberties than a recurrent dependence on the US Supreme Court and an increasingly conservative federal judiciary. This may be the ultimate vindication of Justice Brennan's New Judicial Federalism.

Justice Brennan managed to salvage one significant gain for educational equality in the aftermath of *Rodriguez*. *Plyler v. Doe* (1982)[122] recognized a sui generis status for children of undocumented immigrants that enabled them to continue to attend public schools. The state of Texas authorized local school districts to deny such children admission to public schools and denied state financial aid to any district for their education. For the five-to-four majority,[123] Brennan held that the Texas policy bore no rational relation to any "substantial" state policy that might have been served by such denial. He conceded that education was not a fundamental right, and that financial status could not constitute a suspect class, though he did note in dictum that the "Equal Protection Clause was intended to [abolish] all caste-based and invidious class-based legislation."[124] The majority (as well as the dissenters) seem to have been offended by the sheer irrationality of creating a class of uneducated illiterates made up of young innocents who were not responsible for their parents' illegal actions and who had no ability to affect their own status. Though conceding that because of *Rodriguez*, education cannot be claimed as a "right," Brennan reaffirmed the *Brown I* vision of education's centrality to all other rights to "maintaining the fabric of our society."[125]

Busing and Popular Initiatives

By the time the second Reconstruction drew to a close around 1970, busing had become intensely controversial. So it seems odd that the Supreme

Court encountered busing's constitutional dimensions only once, in 1982, and that only on a tangential issue, the use of popular ballot initiatives to stymie desegregation.[126] Otherwise, busing conflicts were addressed and resolved in the streets, in the media, and in national and local politics. Having authorized the practice of busing in *Swann*, the Court then stepped aside while the struggle exploded in the streets (sometimes literally, as terrorists firebombed school buses). The entire episode demonstrated how deeply opposed northern whites were to school integration, if it meant bringing African American kids into their schools, and exponentially more so if it meant sending their kids to Black-majority schools. Opposition to busing was at bottom opposition to school desegregation in the North. As a sardonic slogan among African Americans of the time put it, "It's Not the Bus, It's Us."

Before *Brown*, children were bused to school in rural areas. The yellow school bus did not appear on city streets until the 1950s. Before the automobile came to dominate the American landscape after World War II, most children walked to school, some for remarkably long distances, or rode public transportation. The postwar suburbs, populated by the baby boom generation, made the school bus a fixture of American education. In the postwar period, that kind of busing was not controversial. Throughout the South, busing was popular because it was used to enforce segregation. Linda Brown, the name plaintiff in *Brown v. Board of Education*, recalled riding a school bus past a school two blocks away in her Topeka neighborhood to a segregated school fourteen blocks distant. (And she was one of the fortunate African American kids who was provided any bus transportation at all; many walked, whatever the distance.)

Brown had identified two explicit constitutional rights: African American children have a right to attend public schools that are not segregated by race. And "such an opportunity [education], where the state has undertaken to provide it, is a right which must be made available to all on equal terms." The Court did not identify other potential rights, such as the power of local communities to control public education or its financing. In the interest of avoiding needless controversy, Chief Justice Warren was determined to keep his opinion succinct and to the point, avoiding distracting dicta. But that salutary tactic opened the door to endless debate over details, particularly the minutiae of school attendance zones and student assignment. That was the dog's dinner that the High Court passed on to the lower federal courts in *Brown II*. Busing soon emerged at the center of both, and that transformed what was until then a widely popular practice into a firestorm of controversy. In less than two decades, it enabled the Supreme Court to elevate the interests of white parents and their children over the rights of Black schoolchildren.

Even before *Brown*, busing was becoming unpopular among urban whites.[127] Vocal protests broke out in New York City in 1957 to a Board of Education plan to bus Black kids from Harlem and Bedford-Stuyvesant to white schools elsewhere. This hostility carried over to white New Yorkers' public protests against the civil rights bill in 1964. That fevered opposition led even such dedicated supporters of civil rights as Senator Hubert Humphrey (D.-MN) and Rep. Emmanuel Celler (D.-NY) to promise that the bill would not mandate busing. Section 401(b) of the Civil Rights Act's Title IV accordingly provided that "'Desegregation' means the assignment of students to public schools and within such schools without regard to their race, color, religion, or national origin, but 'desegregation' shall not mean the assignment of students to public schools in order to overcome racial imbalance."[128] ("Racial imbalance" was the preferred northern legislative euphemism for segregation.) Northern supporters of the civil rights bill carefully chose their terminology to confine the problem of desegregation to the South and to avoid any spillover effects on segregation in northern school systems.[129] Justifying the busing ban, Humphrey argued that "this case makes it quite clear that while the Constitution prohibits segregation, it does not require integration."[130] "There is no case in which the thrust of the statute under which the money would be given would be directed toward restoring or bringing about a racial balance in the schools." He too, the most advanced liberal Democrat in the Senate, bought into the de facto / de jure distinction to validate the distinction between desegregation and integration. Arch-segregationist James O. Eastland of Mississippi drolly commented that "the two Senators from New York [Jacob Javits and Kenneth Keating, both liberal Republicans who supported the bill] are, at heart, pretty good segregationists."[131]

Northern anti-busing sentiment enabled President Richard M. Nixon to artfully redefine the desegregation and busing struggles as the search for a golden mean between the two "extremes" of integration versus George Wallace's "segregation forever," creating a false equivalence between a constitutional right and illegal violence. From this he developed his administration's policy on busing, which he announced in a 1972 televised address: a "moratorium" on all future busing. He criticized the disparate treatment of North and South in the matter of pushing integration. Easing up on busing in the North would therefore imply easing up on non-busing integration programs in the South. Nixon's speechwriter Patrick Buchanan expressed the cynical calculation behind this political move: he recommended that the administration try to persuade the federal courts to "back off from compulsory integration to a posture of freedom of choice." He explained: "the second era of Re-Construction is over; the ship of integration is going down.... We ought not to be aboard. For the first time since 1954, the national civil rights community is going to sustain an up-and-down defeat.... For the foreseeable future, it is all over for compulsory social integration." Buchanan recommended that the Nixon administration urge the Court to "back off from compulsory integration to a posture of freedom of choice."[132] But as historian Thomas Sugrue noted, "the language of choice masked white privilege. It rested on the false assumption that blacks and whites were equal players in a market that was deeply constructed by race."[133]

Nixon's policy of receding on integration, first halting and then reversing the progress that had been made from 1968 to 1972, injected another false equivalence into the desegregation debate. Nixon's original point-man on desegregation, HEW secretary Leon Panetta, put it bluntly: "the old bugaboo of keeping federal hands off northern school systems because they are only de facto segregated, instead of de jure segregated as the result of some official act, is a fraud.... There are few if any pure de facto situations. Lift the rock of de facto and something ugly and discriminatory crawls out from under it."[134] (Such candor promptly got him fired.) Or as James Baldwin put it, "De facto segregation means Negroes are segregated, but nobody did it."[135]

Nixon's 1972 initiative formulated the program that underlay the Supreme Court's about-face on integration. He and others who opposed integration built on a valid critique of the de jure / de facto distinction to buttress the assumption that northern "racial imbalance" was the result of natural processes, whether impersonal free-market forces or voluntary housing choices. Therefore, government had not caused racial inequality, and thus bore no responsibility to remedy it, either in education or in housing segregation.[136] In reality, the conjoined twins of residential and school segregation were both products of deliberate human choices meant to exclude African Americans from the benefits of social capital that would be available from integration. By obfuscating deliberate human agency in the creation of apartheid neighborhoods and schools, Nixon enabled those judges reluctant to pursue the *Brown* agenda of true educational equality—that is, the emerging majority of the US Supreme Court—and provided a political backstop for their constitutional doctrine by linking it to northern resistance to busing.

When judges of the federal district courts were at first confronted with the de facto / de jure distinction in the context of school desegregation, they dismissed it as insubstantial. Judge Irving Kaufmann of the Southern District of New York wrote that "it is of no moment whether the segregation is labelled by the defendant as 'de jure' or 'de facto,' as long as the Board, by its conduct, is responsible for its maintenance. Constitutional rights are determined by realities, not by labels or semantics."[137] Judge Damon Keith of the Eastern District of Michigan concluded that "where a Board of Education has...played a major role in the development and growth of a segregated situation, the Board is guilty of de jure segregation. The fact that such came slowly and surreptitiously rather than by legislative pronouncement makes the situation no less evil.... To rationalize thusly is to be blinded to the realities of adult life with its prejudices and opposition to integrated housing."[138] In the Boston busing case,[139] Judge W. Arthur Garrity spurned the Boston School Board's argument that racial differences were attributable only to de facto housing patterns: "when school officials have followed for at least a decade a persistent course of conduct which intentionally incorporated residential segregation into the system's schools, that conduct is unconstitutional." He concluded that the Boston school authorities had "the purpose and intent to segregate the Boston public schools."[140] In this same passage, Judge Garrity rejected the "neighborhood schools" justification as a possible override of plaintiffs' rights to an equal education. Neither extant residential segregation nor the valid rationales favoring neighborhood schools were sufficient to justify segregative policies.

Once the Supreme Court nixed interdistrict busing in *Milliken*, desegregation in the North became a problem only for cities. The suburbs were spared the struggles sparked by busing, and it began to subside as a political issue. Nixon's policy of using federal power only against de jure segregation, followed by Ronald Reagan's refusal to challenge *any* lingering forms of segregation, further reduced the arena of potential political conflict. This encouraged a widespread belief that both busing and racial integration "failed" in some way. That in turn led lawyers, judges, and laypeople to forget "the educational goals that were a pillar of the civil-rights movement and to dismiss the constitutional promise of equality endorsed by *Brown*" and "to accept the continuing racial and socioeconomic segregation of schools in the United States as inevitable and unchangeable."[141]

But the distinctive constitutional culture of California provided one final theater of contestation where the politics and policy of busing could be framed in constitutional terms, and it was from there that the US Supreme Court heard its only significant busing case post-*Milliken*. The two-decades-old background to *Crawford v. Los Angeles Board of Education* (1982) also provides a constitutional understanding by the California Supreme Court that is a welcome alternative to the US Supreme Court's desiccated vision of racial equality.[142]

The nation's first legal blow against de jure school segregation occurred in California in 1946, eight years before *Brown*, when a federal district court held that the policy of segregating Chicano children in some Orange County school districts offended the equal protection clause of the federal Constitution.[143] Despite that holding, California public schools remained pervasively segregated de facto. As elsewhere, school district officials manipulated school district boundaries, student assignment policies, and siting decisions so that school segregation continued to track patterns of residential segregation. As a result, white and Asian American students generally attended better-funded schools, while Latinos and African Americans were stuck in inferior facilities. In the latter group, Latinos outnumbered Blacks, who found themselves a minority within a minority. Moreover, racial segregation was coincident with economic segregation, with each type of segregation mutually reinforcing the other. Segregation was driven by "a self-reinforcing dynamic that treated racially determined attendance and assignment patterns as 'natural' and funneled disproportionate amounts of resources and opportunities to schools serving white students."[144]

In *Jackson v. Pasadena City School District* (1963), the California Supreme Court held that under *Brown I*, "the right to an equal opportunity for education and the harmful consequences of segregation require that school boards take steps, insofar as reasonably feasible, to alleviate racial imbalance in schools *regardless of its cause*."[145] The italicized phrase contained within it the potential, soon realized, that California courts could hold segregation unconstitutional whether de jure or de facto. School boards could not perpetuate inequality by "evasive schemes for segregation," including manipulating school zone boundaries. It was here that the California courts diverged from the US Supreme Court. The California vision of equality opened judicial remedies for de facto segregation, while the US Supreme Court closed them off by retreating to the sterile position of recognizing judicial remedies only for de jure segregation. Federal courts were impotent to deal with structural inequality because the justices clung to their threadbare rationale of residential segregation being caused by "voluntary housing choices."

In that same year (1963), parents brought a class action suit to desegregate the Los Angeles Unified School District, which consisted of the city of Los Angeles and surrounding school districts. The state Superior Court held that segregative patterns in the Los Angeles school system violated the equal protection clauses of both the federal and state constitutions. On appeal, in *Crawford v. Board of Education* (Cal. 1976) (*Crawford I*),[146] the California Supreme Court held that state courts had a duty under the state Constitution to relieve segregation "whether the segregation be de facto or de jure in origin." The California court explicitly rejected the de jure / de facto distinction insofar as it limited judicial power to reach segregation not overtly facial. "In California, all public school districts bear an obligation under the state Constitution to undertake reasonably feasible steps to alleviate school segregation, regardless of the cause of such segregation."[147] "Facial neutrality" was not adequate to sustain a school policy that had damaging practical effects on the education of minority children.

Then at this point in the unfolding struggle over California school segregation, politics intruded. Southern California anti-busing activists organized a group that called itself BUSTOP to mobilize opposition to court-ordered busing. Denouncing what they called "forced integration," BUSTOP members supported Proposition 21, a 1972 initiative measure that provided: "No public school student shall, because of his race, creed, or color, be assigned to or be required to attend a particular school." This was a blunderbuss measure that would have prohibited all forms of student assignment that relied on or even merely adverted to race. The measure was widely popular and was adopted by 63 percent of the electorate. But three years later, the California Supreme Court struck it down. Relying on the US Supreme Court's recent decisions in *Green*, *Keyes*, and *Swann*, the Court held: "To allow school authorities to rest content in the assumption that the pattern of segregation in their district is de facto and therefore to claim that [the initiative measure] prohibits them from eliminating that segregation by pupil assignment on the basis of race implemented through busing, would impermissibly impede the constitutionally mandated task of rooting out de jure segregation." Therefore, the measure "as applied to school districts manifesting either de jure or de facto segregation is unconstitutional."[148]

Prop 21 proved merely to be the warm-up for the main act, another initiative measure known as Proposition 1, in 1979. It was this later initiative that made it to the US Supreme Court and thus gave the High Court its only opportunity to consider issues surrounding busing. On remand of *Crawford I*, the Superior Court ordered busing, and its order went into effect in 1978. Opponents promptly responded with another popular initiative, Prop 1, that would have shrunk the state courts' powers to order busing.[149] The California Court of Appeals (the state's intermediate-level appellate court) upheld the constitutionality of Prop 1 in 1980[150] and banned busing. When the Los Angeles school board then ended busing, the practical effect was to remove students from desegregated schools and send them back to segregated ones: resegregation in its starkest form.

By the time Prop 1 reached the US Supreme Court in 1982, busing had become widely unpopular, not just in California but throughout the nation. Americans were repelled by images of violent protest, bombed-out school buses, and, most horrifyingly, a white busing opponent attempting to impale an African American bystander with a flagpole bearing the American flag.[151] Several states had taken statutory, administrative, or constitutional actions to constrain the power of courts to order busing. Prop 1 was of that ilk. It modified Article I, section 7, of the state constitution, which was its combined due process and equal protection clauses, to add provisions mandating that state courts may not order busing unless a federal court would do so to remedy a violation of the federal equal protection clause.[152] Prop 1 declared its own justifications, as recent California referenda and initiatives tend to do. They were "making the most effective use of the limited financial resources now and prospectively available to support public education, maximizing the educational opportunities and protecting the health and safety of all public-school pupils, enhancing the ability of parents to participate in the educational process, preserving harmony and tranquility in this State and its public schools, preventing the waste of scarce fuel resources, and protecting the environment." Conspicuously (and deliberately) missing from this jumble of rationales was the core value of *Brown I*: the right to equality of educational opportunity for all students.[153]

The US Supreme Court, speaking through Justice Powell, upheld the constitutionality of Prop 1 in *Crawford v. Board of Education* (1982) (*Crawford III*).[154] He maintained that a neighborhood-schools policy was not per se a violation of the equal protection clause. Because Prop 1 was supposedly facially neutral, it was not a racial classification that would have to undergo strict scrutiny.[155] Petitioners failed to prove a discriminatory purpose, and it was doubtful that there was even a discriminatory effect, given the racial makeup of the neighborhoods affected. Finally, Powell held that if a state has gone beyond the minimum required of it under the equal protection clause, it may rescind that overage. Retrogression in remedies is not unconstitutional unless it falls below the floor of the Fourteenth Amendment.

Justice Marshall, the only dissenter, objected that *Crawford*'s holding was inconsistent with a companion case decided that same day, *Washington v. Seattle School District No. 1* (1982).[156] The Seattle case also rose out of an initiative movement and a neighborhood-schools policy. Justice Harry Blackmun, who wrote for the five-member majority, described the case as posing the "extraordinary question" of whether a local school board could claim the Fourteenth Amendment as a shield when challenged by the state over its school attendance policies. ("Extraordinary" because the usual role of the school board up till then had been as the villain in busing suits.) The school district, concerned over racial imbalance in Seattle schools, adopted a student assignment and busing plan to even out racial disparities in the city's schools.[157] Opponents organized an initiative drive that mandated a neighborhood-schools policy but provided numerous exceptions that permitted a more flexible assignment policy, with one exception: it banned busing for desegregation. The majority held this a violation of the Fourteenth Amendment under *Carolene Products* principles: "the State allocates governmental power nonneutrally, by explicitly using the *racial* nature of a decision to determine the decisionmaking process." This "places *special* burdens on racial minorities."[158] This was a "presumptively invalid" racial classification barred by the equal protection clause. The vice lay in putting one political process (here, the initiative) that was used to ameliorate racial problems under a special disadvantage and placing a unique political burden on racial groups who seek to combat prejudice. Justice Powell, for the four dissenters, defended neighborhood-schools policy and insisted that there was no duty to integrate schools absent a showing of unconstitutional segregation. "States are under no constitutional duty to adopt integration programs in their schools."[159]

School District Secession

During the Supreme Court's activist phase of mandating desegregation, from 1965 to 1973, some southern school districts frantically cast about for ways to evade the desegregation-now commands of *Griffin* and *Green*. One of these was school district secession. Where a school district, often a large one encompassing a county-wide area that surrounded an urban core, was under a desegregation decree issued by a federal district court, local municipalities (typically suburbs) would attempt to "secede" or disaggregate themselves by withdrawing from the larger district and forming their own school district. Invariably, these would-be secessionist districts were whiter and wealthier than the district they were trying to secede from. In companion cases decided in 1972, the Supreme Court rebuffed such efforts, but the impulse never died away. In the more auspicious climate of resegregation that began around 2000, secession is enjoying renewed popularity.

Greensville County in Southside Virginia, located on the North Carolina border, surrounds the small city of Emporia. In 1969, a federal district court rejected a freedom-of-choice plan proposed for the consolidated city-county school district. Seeing the handwriting on the wall, Emporia decided to secede to create its own school district. The effect would have been to leave the county schools majority-Black, and the city schools (which enjoyed superior facilities to begin with) with a greater ratio of white students than they would have had under the original decree. In *Wright v. Emporia* (1972),[160] the Court in a five-to-four decision blocked the attempt. The district court had found that race was one of the motives for secession. The court of appeals did not disagree, but held that benign race-neutral purposes (improved quality of education for the seceding district) outweighed the constitutionally objectionable ones. Justice Stewart rejected that rationale. "The effect—not the purpose or motivation—of a school board's action" was decisive. "The existence of a permissible purpose cannot sustain an action that has an impermissible effect." (*Washington v. Davis* was still four years in the future.) The improvement in education afforded the city children would come at the cost of "a substantial adverse effect upon the quality of education available to others." Stewart concluded that secession would hinder the process of desegregation and interfere with dismantling the dual school system. The four recent Nixon appointees dissented. Speaking through Chief Justice Burger, they extolled "local control" as the determinant in a situation where a secession proposal did not create an obviously dual Black-white system. In the companion case of *United*

States v. Scotland Neck Board of Education (1972),[161] the Court enjoined enforcement of a North Carolina statute that authorized secession because the statute would have interfered with dismantling the previous dual system. This time the Nixon justices concurred because secession was "substantially motivated by the desire to create a predominantly white system more acceptable to the white parents of Scotland Neck [and] to minimize the number of Negro children attending school with the white children."

But times changed over the next forty years, and the goal of local control came to eclipse the *Brown I* ideal of educational equality. In this new environment, white parents who wanted to retain the advantages they had enjoyed under previous arrangements, and not have some of their taxes diverted to support poorer schools, turned to secession again. Encouraged by *Milliken*'s and *Rodriguez*'s emphasis on local control, the dominant theme of Justice Powell's school opinions, they pursued secessionist strategies throughout the South and beyond. More than seventy communities seceded by 2020; the North Carolina legislature has considered legislation facilitating secession.[162] Scholars who have followed the recent secessionist efforts in Tennessee have concluded that "a sharply constricted vision of the purpose of education has rationalized the pursuit and accumulation of advantage through local control. The contemporary strength of local control thus is related to both an increasing acceptance of colorblindness—by the courts and by society—and a competitive, individualistic framing of public education." "Local control [is] a means of preserving racial and/or resource advantage."[163]

The secessionist movement hit a roadblock, however, when Gardendale, a city in Jefferson County, Alabama, that is part of the Birmingham metropolitan area, attempted secession in 2015.[164] Birmingham-area secessionist efforts had been blocked by the decision in *Wright v. Emporia* in 1972. But as time passed, the motives for secessionist efforts migrated away from evading *Brown v. Board of Education* outright toward hoarding educational resources by more affluent neighborhoods, which, not coincidentally, were also white. Jefferson County was still under a desegregation order issued in 1971, which made it more necessary for community leaders who advanced secession proposals to couch their demands in terms of local control of community school finances. The US District Court for the Northern District of Alabama found that the Gardendale secession movement was a racially motivated effort to evade the existing desegregation order because it sought to halt the busing of African American students into the district.[165]

Judge Madeline Haikala concluded that "in doing the complicated work of dissolving a desegregation order, a court must ensure that the dying embers of *de jure* segregation aren't once again fanned into flames." She nevertheless permitted partial secession for "practical considerations."

The Eleventh Circuit reversed. In *Stout by Stout v. Jefferson County Board of Education* (2018),[166] it concluded that the school board's decision to secede was racially motivated, and that secession would impede the county's ongoing desegregation efforts. On a note of weary impatience, Judge William Pryor (a prominent judicial conservative) began by observing that "this appeal requires that we revisit the decades-old task of school desegregation." Drawing on *Arlington Heights* criteria, he found improper racial motivation where the school board had "devised secession plans that reflect the same desire to control the racial demographics of the public schools as had been expressed by the secession leaders."[167] Similarly, he recurred to *Wright v. Emporia* to demonstrate that even the carefully circumscribed partial secession prescribed by the district court "would have a substantial adverse effect on the desegregation efforts of the Jefferson County Board." Invoking the familiar words of *Brown*, he stated that the secessionist effort would "generate a feeling of inferiority" by sending a message to African American students that they were unwelcome in Glendale schools. Glendale did not appeal to the Supreme Court, so the most prominent secession effort to date has failed, and the *Wright* standards have survived into the present, but face a dubious future.

Segregation Academies: Racial Discrimination in Private Education

Seg academies, ss they are known throughout the South, were among the countless measures that the white South adopted to avoid desegregation after 1954.[168] The Supreme Court's insistence on eradicating dual systems in *Griffin* and *Green* accelerated the opening of seg academies. At first, they were indirectly subsidized by the states through leases or transfers of public property; scholarships, tuition grants, or vouchers to students; tax credits for tuition paid by parents; or tax-exempt status for the academies themselves. This raised obvious problems of state action: such subsidization suggested either the public function rationale of *Smith v. Allwright* or the state-involvement rationale of *Burton v. Wilmington Parking Authority*.

Such pervasive state encouragement gave the lie to the pretense that seg academies were purely private institutions.

A constitutional challenge was not long in coming. In a broad and comprehensive opinion, *Green v. Connally* (1971),[169] the US District Court for the District of Columbia construed the Internal Revenue Code to deny tax-exempt status to private schools that refuse admission to students on the basis of race. The three-judge court held that federal public policy prohibits racial discrimination in all schools, both public and private. No state law, common or statutory, may contravene that public policy. The court conceded that a parent or child has a constitutionally protected right, derived from the First Amendment right of association,[170] to attend a racially discriminatory school. But there is no right, individual or collective, to have any government support such a school. Even if the associational right to discriminate is seen as fundamental, it may be overridden by a compelling government interest. The governmental interest in stamping out racial discrimination overrides other constitutional rights if there is a direct conflict. The power of federal courts to protect rights against discrimination is based on the role of federal courts as courts of equity, which are required to do "complete justice," including providing "full and equitable relief." Finally, the court held that African American children and their parents have standing "to launch a challenge in case of '*any* amount of state support to help found segregated schools or to help maintain such schools.'"[171] (The Supreme Court would recur to this standing point, with a much different outcome, in *Allen v. Wright* thirteen years later.) The US Supreme Court affirmed the district court's holding unanimously, without opinion.[172] The Court's ready affirmance of *Green v. Connally*'s robust anti-segregationist premises came during the last days of the second Reconstruction. After 1971, such unanimity in the cause of racial equality became a thing of the past.

Green v. Connally was not a direct attack on seg academies, but *Runyon v. McCrary* (1976) was.[173] African American children who were denied admission to a seg academy sought an injunction barring such discrimination, relying on the contract provisions of section 1 of the 1866 Civil Rights Act. In its modern form as section 1981 of Title 42 of the US Code, the act provides that "All persons within the jurisdiction of the United States shall have the same right in every State…to make and enforce contracts…as is enjoyed by white citizens." Five members of the Court, speaking thorough Justice Stewart, upheld the claim, relying on *Jones v. Alfred Mayer*, the 1968 housing case that revived section 1982, the property sibling of section 1981, as authority. The Court had recently held that section 1981 applied to private employment contracts,[174] so *Runyon* merely extended section 1981's reach to other kinds of contracts. Nevertheless, this was a remarkable advance; a federal anti-discrimination statute now potentially covered all private contractual relationships, with no requirement of state action. Justice Stewart reaffirmed the limit on associational freedoms identified in *Green*: racial discrimination in a commercial or educational context "has never been afforded affirmative constitutional protections."[175]

As in *Jones*, Stewart emphasized the Thirteenth Amendment basis of congressional power. Read broadly, Justice Stewart's opinion potentially threatened many discriminatory private associations like social clubs.[176] While this attracted little notice at the time, within a decade it re-emerged explosively. Ominously, Justices Powell and Stevens concurred only reluctantly, stating that they thought that *Jones* had been wrongly decided, but that they felt constrained to follow it because of stare decisis. Justices White and Rehnquist dissented, arguing that section 1981 did no more than confer a right to enter into contracts, with no implied ban on a counterparty refusing to enter into the contract for racist reasons. In this reading, civil rights statutes would have conferred a right on plaintiffs, but no corresponding duty or restraint on defendants.[177] Such a contract would be what is known in law as a *nudum pactum*, a "naked agreement" that is unenforceable because it is not binding on both parties. Fortunately, the Court has not (yet?) adopted such a self-defeating construction of section 1981.

For a time, *Runyon v. McCrary* made life more difficult for seg academies, nudging them toward nominal or pretextual non-discrimination, but the decision was not widely controversial in its time. A decade later, however, the Court retroactively revived the constitutional controversy implicit in *Runyon*. That story took place in a different context, after the Court had moved further along toward its de facto reversal of *Brown*. In the context of educational controversies in the 1970s, *Runyon* built upon *Jones* to realize the potential of the 1866 Civil Rights Act for educational equality, but only for a bare majority on a deeply divided Court.

The problem of tax exemptions for segregated private schools never really went away, but it became complicated by the fact that in the 1970s, evangelical Christian schools had come to outnumber secular seg academies like those run by the Klan, churches, or the White Citizens Council. Some, though not all, of these "Christian schools," as they were commonly known, maintained segregation as a matter of religious belief. This added a complicating overlay of First Amendment free-exercise constitutional issues to the racial equal protection ones litigated in *Green* and *Runyon*. But secular and religious blended to the point where "Christian schools and segregation academies [were] almost synonymous."[178] In 1979, Republican conservatives in Congress tried to force the Internal Revenue Service to amend its guidelines to restore tax exemption for "private, religious, or church-operated schools."[179] After he took office, President Reagan also backed the academies' demands for tax exemption. Two religious entities, a Christian school and Bob Jones University, an evangelical college in South Carolina, sought to enjoin the IRS from denying them tax-exempt status.

The Court in *Bob Jones University v. United States* (1983)[180] upheld the authority of the IRS to deny tax-exempt status to private religious schools that practiced segregation. Chief Justice Burger's majority opinion closely tracked the reasoning of *Green v. Connolly*: the federal "Government has a fundamental, overriding interest in eradicating racial discrimination in education, [which] substantially outweighs whatever burden denial of tax benefits places on petitioners' exercise of their religious beliefs." A charitable status for tax purposes may not contravene public policy, and the powerful interest in suppressing racial discrimination overrides any free-exercise interests of schools (or students and their parents) claiming a biblical mandate for racial segregation. But Burger's opinion in *Bob Jones* soon proved to be anomalous. A ruling threatening the seg academies' legitimacy would have been strongly resisted by southern whites. By 1980, a majority of the justices had no stomach for that kind of confrontation, with the result that the Court enabled their continued existence simply by doing nothing.

Sometimes the Supreme Court pursues a substantive goal by a procedural route.[181] When the problem of seg academies immediately returned to the Court a year after *Bob Jones*, a majority invoked procedural considerations—the vexed doctrine of standing—to duck another head-on challenge to seg academies. A nationwide class of African American parents sought to enjoin the Internal Revenue Service from enforcing guidelines and procedures that they considered inadequate to deal with fraudulent conduct by seg academies. They claimed that the schools promised to comply with IRS non-discrimination policies but then did not actually do so in order to preserve their lily-white character. (Seg academies could still recover their tax-exempt status merely by adopting and certifying a policy of non-discrimination but doing nothing to implement it.) The parents sought to pierce the pretextuality veil behind which segregationist schools carried on a privatized version of Jim Crow.

In *Allen v. Wright* (1984),[182] five justices invoked the constitutional procedural doctrine of standing to evade deciding this issue. Standing is best explored in the context of housing. For our purposes here, it is sufficient to simply state the doctrine as Justice O'Connor expressed it in *Allen*: "The requirement of standing...has a core component derived directly from the Constitution. A plaintiff must allege personal injury fairly traceable to the defendant's allegedly unlawful conduct and likely to be redressed by the requested relief."[183] Plaintiff's injury-in-fact; defendant's causal responsibility; redressability by judicial process: these are the three constitutional components of standing.[184] Who could claim to be injured by seg academies? In what way might seg academies cause an injury and to whom? And even if plaintiff shows injury and causation, is there anything a court can do about it?

O'Connor held that the parents had failed to meet the causation requirement, and hence lacked standing to sue. They had claimed that they suffered two kinds of injuries: first, what O'Connor called the "stigmatic injury" of being "denigrated" by the government's discrimination against them because of its failure to adopt effective anti-segregationist policies; and second, that their children had a diminished opportunity to attend integrated schools because of the competition presented to public schools by the seg academies. The parents did not allege that they had tried to enroll their children in the segregated schools, a tactical decision that may have been fatal to their cause. O'Connor easily brushed off the first claim but labored to dismiss the second. She readily conceded injury to the children: "the injury they identify—their children's diminished ability to receive an education in a racially integrated school—is, beyond any doubt, not only judicially cognizable but, as shown by cases from Brown v. Board of Education to Bob Jones University v. United States, one of the most serious injuries recognized in our legal system."[185] But "the injury alleged is not fairly traceable to the Government conduct." She deployed her favorite dismissive adjectives to describe the weakness of the causal chain: "speculative" and "attenuated." She tried unpersuasively to distinguish *Green v. Connolly* and for good measure gratuitously hinted that it might be vulnerable on the standing issue. Justice Brennan dissented on a point he frequently made: the majority was deploying standing as an under-the-table way of deciding the case on the merits: the "causation component of the

Court's standing inquiry is no more than a poor disguise for the Court's view of the merits of the underlying claims."[186]

Allen v. Wright remains the Court's most explicit discussion of the causation leg of standing doctrine. But together with *Warth v. Seldin* (1975),[187] it erected a formidable procedural barrier to challenging seg academies, which continued to thrive behind the Potemkin village facade of pretextuality.

Parents Involved: The Court Bars States from Preventing Resegregation

Parents Involved in Community Schools (2007) rounded out the trilogy of cases in which Justin Driver traces the way the Supreme Court first abandoned, then immured, *Brown v. Board of Education* in the second Redemption.[188] *Milliken v. Bradley* (1974) validated racial segregation along the urban/suburban axis, and *San Antonio Independent School District v. Rodriguez* (1973) confirmed fiscal (and therefore substantive) inequality along racial lines. By 1974, these two cases erected the remarkably stable system that has nurtured resegregation for over a half century, and bids fair to continue into the indefinite future.

Imagine, however, some malevolent actor who considered this system of resegregation incomplete because it left open the possibility that local authorities such as cities or school boards might try to preserve racial integration or at least forestall one-race schools. What could be done to *prevent* the states from preserving integration? Structural racism provides the answer. Concoct a constitutional doctrine, color-blindness, that blindfolds school boards as they perform their routine tasks of designing school attendance zones or supervising student assignment. Pretend race does not matter. Bar them from taking racial composition into account, even in the most attenuated way, when they compose school populations, in the name of color-blindness. Ignore the intentions of those who framed the Fourteenth Amendment, along with the ideals of *Brown*. Then leave it to the workings of structural racism, grounded in residential segregation (itself imposed by the federal and state governments), to maintain racial inequality invisibly, silently, indefinitely. Ignore or deny this reality, while declaring that its effects are natural and inevitable, beyond judicial control. Cap it all off by boasting that you will now, at last, go beyond race and achieve the egalitarian society where race does not matter because four justices of the Supreme Court declare that it should not. This is the case known as *Parents Involved* (2007).

In an effort to avoid resegregation, some school districts pioneered innovative policies to maintain a racial mix in all public schools that roughly approximates the racial demographics of the city or district. Two of these efforts, involving Seattle, Washington, and Louisville, Kentucky, came before the Court when white parents challenged student placement plans that might deny their children the school of their choice. In *Parents Involved in Community Schools v. Seattle School District No. 1* (2007),[189] the Court struck down both cities' efforts. In the Seattle case, where the school system had never been segregated de jure, school boards tried to resolve the problem of "oversubscription" (too many students choosing a particular school) by adopting a "tiebreaker" solution that relied on three criteria in descending order to control admissions: a sibling already at the school, race ("white" vs. "nonwhite"), and geographic proximity. Louisville and surrounding Jefferson County Kentucky had been de jure segregated, but the desegregation decree had been dissolved in 2000. It adopted a comparable plan.

Parents Involved produced a complicated four-one-four split on the Court. All the justices acknowledged that public policies based on race are subject to strict scrutiny: the government's ends must be "compelling" and the means it adopts to attain those ends must be "narrowly tailored." Chief Justice John Roberts, who wrote the plurality opinion, recognized only two ends as compelling: remedying past intentional discrimination by the government itself, and "diversity" (the *Bakke* standard). He dismissed the former as inapplicable because Seattle had never experienced de jure segregation, and Louisville's desegregation decree had been dissolved seven years earlier. On the first point, Justice Anthony Kennedy agreed, making a majority for part of the compelling-end requirement. Roberts rejected the second criterion, diversity, as inapplicable because it was valid only in the context of higher education. Here Kennedy split from the plurality,[190] harking back to *Brown I*: the chief justice "is too dismissive of the legitimate interest government has in ensuring all people have equal opportunity regardless of their race."[191] Unlike the Roberts bloc, Kennedy recognized that "avoiding racial isolation" is a "compelling interest."[192] He veered from the dissenters[193] in claiming that the school districts should have explored nonracial methods to attain diversity.

In his plurality opinion, Roberts forged ahead to cement the modern conservative reinterpretation of *Brown* that has drained away its force.

He went out of his way to emphasize that "the Constitution is not violated by racial imbalance in the schools."[194] He affirmed the anticlassification reading of *Brown*, spurning the antisubordination alternative.[195] Government must treat citizens as individuals and not as members of a group or class. He condemned all efforts to attain "racial balance," which in this context hinted that trying to achieve realistic integration might be illegitimate if it took race into account in any way. Thus, racial balance or proportionality is off the table, but apparently nothing in the Constitution prohibits racial *im*balance, as long as it is not deliberately imposed. The "ultimate goal" of all equal protection law must be eradicating all considerations of race from government decision-making (which, if realized, would make it impossible to deal with all structural inequality). Roberts concluded his opinion with a grandiloquent, banal peroration: "the way to stop discrimination on the basis of race is to stop discriminating of the basis of race," a bumper sticker masquerading as a constitutional claim.[196]

Roberts inverted standing doctrine to achieve his desired result, which was to block cities or school boards from attempting to prevent resegregation. We might have assumed after *Allen v. Wright* and *Warth v. Seldin* (1975) that all plaintiffs would be bound by the stringent requirements of that doctrine. But not so for white petitioners claiming customary advantage. For them Roberts invented a special stigmatic injury not heretofore allowed for Black petitioners: "being forced to compete in a race-based system that may prejudice the plaintiff."[197] Moreover, Roberts claimed that it was "possible" that plaintiffs might suffer some unspecified injury in the unknown future. For the fortunate white plaintiff, gone was the requirement that he demonstrate actual, present, and non-speculative injury; it is now enough that he fears some future contingency. The Court had earlier rejected fear of potential future injury for claims it disfavors on the merits in *Lujan v. Defenders of Wildlife* (1992),[198] demanding that petitioner prove "actual or imminent" injury." But Roberts waived that demand for white petitioners in the context of school admissions.

The other *Parents Involved* opinions provided a survey of equal protection law. Justice Thomas concurring uttered some of his most egregious dicta: although "racial imbalance," that is, resegregation, "might result from past de jure segregation, racial imbalance can also result from any number of innocent private decisions, including voluntary housing choices." This led him to wave away reality by a bit of magical thinking: "although there is arguably a danger of racial imbalance in schools in Seattle and Louisville, there is no danger of resegregation." (By 2013, resegregation was a fait accompli in most American cities.) He reduced *Brown I* to its narrowest possible reading: only explicit racial discrimination based on law would offend the equal protection clause: "racial imbalance without intentional state action to separate the races does not amount to segregation."[199] He condemned efforts to integrate as "coerced racial mixing," a weird echo of the 1956 Southern Manifesto and other segregationist rhetoric from the time of Jim Crow's death throes. Thomas concluded smugly: the dissenters reject "the color-blind Constitution. But I am quite comfortable in the company I keep," quoting the first Justice Harlan of the *Plessy* dissent.[200]

Justice Kennedy's vote was necessary for the result, but he diverged from the Roberts plurality group in significant ways. They "are too dismissive of the legitimate interest government has in ensuring all people have equal opportunity regardless of their race."[201] He insisted that government be able to take race into account, at least collectively, for purposes of assuring diversity, avoiding racial isolation, and forestalling "de facto resegregation in the schools." While he insisted that schools use race-neutral means[202] wherever possible to achieve these ends, he reminded the Roberts group of something they seemed determined to forget: "This Nation has a moral and ethical obligation to fulfill its historic commitment to creating an integrated society that ensures equal opportunity for all of its children."[203]

Justice John Paul Stevens concurred separately to make a poignant observation: "It is my firm conviction that no Member of the Court that I joined in 1975 would have agreed with today's decision."[204] "The chief justice rewrites the history of one of this court's most important decisions." He was making the same argument that was central to Justice Stephen Breyer's lengthy dissent: the Court was abandoning *Brown*. Breyer devoted his opinion to making an obvious point: there is a vast and decisive difference between taking race into account to oppress a minority, and taking it into account to integrate that minority into the full and equal benefits of the society that for four centuries has oppressed them.[205] "Context matters" was the pervasive theme of the dissenters' opinion: "The context here is one of racial limits that seek, not to keep the races apart, but to bring them together."[206] To no avail: the majority (including Kennedy) remained hostile to the antisubordination reading of *Brown*, and to all efforts to halt resegregation. The impact of this was apparent in viva voce remarks Breyer made while reading parts of his dissent from the bench (an unusual and rare gesture): "It is not often in the law that so few have so quickly changed so much."[207] The great vice of the *Parents Involved* decision was that the Court actively blocked a local effort the achieve racial equality and opportunity in education. In so doing, the justices demonstrated how hollow and opportunistic was their valorization of local control of schools.

The aftermath of *Parents Involved* has been instructive. The Jefferson County, Kentucky, school system accepted the result, as it had to, and eliminated the racial component of its school assignment program. But it doubled down on its commitment to integration, diversity, and busing. In consultation with the scholar-expert on school desegregation, the UCLA political scientist Gary Orfield, it adopted a complex multivariate plan relying on income and educational-attainment levels, without an explicit racial component. Busing remains an essential element of the plan. Consequently, the city and county have managed to retain a high degree of diversity, racial and otherwise, throughout the public schools. Louisville residents have largely (though not universally) embraced the program.[208] Louisville, however, remains the rare exception rather than the rule, both in its commitment to diversity and in the success it has achieved.

By 2000, the Court had reduced *Brown I* to the status of a venerated icon with little practical impact in advancing its essential goal, equality of educational opportunity for all children. From 1964 through 1972, the activist period of *Brown*'s history, the Court had been sternly vigilant over racial distinctions that denied African Americans an education equal to what white children got. But in the second Redemption, a majority of the Court redirected their vigilance to assuring that white plaintiffs were never denied any advantage they claimed, whatever the impact on their black peers might be. In this new regime, "racial imbalance," the Court's euphemism for resegregation, is constitutionally unassailable, its legitimacy beyond challenge. The Court shunted *Brown I* into irrelevance in favor of the *Milliken/Rodriguez* paradigm: "*Milliken* [ensured] racially separate schools, and *Rodriguez* meant they would be unequal." Dean Erwin Chemerinsky concludes: "The promise of *Brown* of equal educational opportunity has been unfulfilled because of the Supreme Court's failures."[209]

10
The Death of Affirmative Action

The public policy that we know as affirmative action has roots going back to the first Reconstruction.[1] Through the Freedmen's Bureau and the 1866 Civil Rights Act, Congress tried to assist the freedpeople in transitioning from enslavement and destitution to some economic and civic status that would enable them to participate as citizens in a market economy. White backlash immediately erupted as President Andrew Johnson in his veto message of the Civil Rights Bill railed that "the distinction of race and color is made by the bill to operate in favor of the colored and against the white race."[2] A white Floridian complained at the time that such measures aimed "to give the nigger more privileges than the white man."[3]

After the demise of Reconstruction, the notion did not recur in public policy debates until the New Deal, when the phrase "affirmative action" first made its appearance—in the Wagner Act of 1935 (though the context had nothing to do with race).[4] But neither there nor in any other New Deal legislation or policy before 1944 did the idea of affirmative action benefit Black citizens. The phrase merely referred to active government involvement to cope with the problems of the Depression. Throughout the New Deal era, affirmative action redounded exclusively to the benefit of white people.[5] But the underlying impetus of modern affirmative action, antipathy to racial discrimination, cropped up occasionally. In *New Negro Alliance v. Sanitary Grocery Co.* (1938), a Black activist group demanded that a corporate predecessor of the Safeway supermarket chain hire African Americans for management positions and picketed to express their demands. The Supreme Court reversed an injunction to halt the picketing, holding that the Norris-LaGuardia Act of 1932 banned federal injunctions against labor picketing. But Justice Owen Roberts made an arresting statement in dicta: "Race discrimination by an employer may reasonably be deemed more unjust and less excusable than discrimination against workers on the ground of union affiliation."[6] Yet twelve years later, the Court, this time speaking through Justice Frankfurter, condemned "proportional employment on ancestral grounds" in another case involving picketing for an increase in Black employment.[7]

Meanwhile, as the Court seemed to waffle in these proto-affirmative action cases, the concept itself began to take more concrete form. President Franklin Roosevelt promulgated Executive Order 8802 in 1941 prohibiting "discrimination in the employment of workers in defense industries or government because of race, creed, color, or national origin," the first explicit adoption of racial affirmative action at the federal level. Some states also enacted legislation banning racial discrimination in employment, the first step in implementing affirmative action. The general idea of racial proportionality was in the air. During most of World War II, the US Army remained segregated, but that did not inhibit it from maintaining an official policy of preserving a racial ratio in its enlisted ranks "on a general basis of the proportion of the Negro population in the country."[8]

As affirmative action began to take shape in the 1960s, it expanded beyond its original anti-discrimination focus to embrace a policy that President John F. Kennedy identified in his Executive Order 10925 (1961): to "encourage by positive measures equal opportunity for all qualified persons" with the federal government. This marked a progression from the negative policy of prohibiting discrimination to the positive goal of opening up opportunities. President Lyndon Johnson's Howard University address of 1965 carried this a step further by demanding "not just equality as a right and a theory but equality as a fact and equality as a result."[9] Johnson's policies pushed affirmative action to its next level: erasing the effects of past discrimination. For the first time the executive branch of the federal government began to grapple with structural racism by realistically emphasizing the systemic difficulties Black Americans faced in education and employment.

Congress, prodded by LBJ, enacted the Civil Rights Act of 1964, with its Title VII provisions banning discrimination in employment. But Title VII explicitly prohibited both "preferential treatment" and taking racial "imbalance" into account in employment policy, thus imposing outer limits on affirmative action. Unlike Title II (the ban on racial discrimination in interstate commerce), Title VII was not immediately challenged as unconstitutional, so the Court did not at first have occasion to define the contours and limits of affirmative action.

Affirmative Action and Higher Education

Affirmative action had been part of the integration debates since the 1960s. May legislatures create special opportunities for African Americans to provide them access to the sorts of social capital that had hitherto been denied them because it was monopolized exclusively by whites? If so, what were the justifications for such opportunity-creating ventures? What were the limitations on it, if any? Would whites be harmed by such innovations? Would affirmative action constitute, in a phrase popular at the time, "reverse discrimination"?[10] Why? Does "disadvantage" in this context simply mean "loss of unearned privilege," and if it does, is that a constitutional wrong? Is "merit" the only legitimate criterion for access to society's benefits? How is "merit" determined? Do traditional measures of merit have an implicit bias in favor of whites? Do these issues have a constitutional dimension, or are they simply matters of policy?

Affirmative action in higher education raised a blizzard of such issues.[11] It was intensely controversial, politically fraught, and constitutionally complex. It just barely survived its first major constitutional challenge in *Regents of the University of California v. Bakke* in 1978. In a peculiar configuration of Supreme Court opinions, Justice Powell's solo opinion spoke ambivalently for the Court by affirming the positions of both supporters and opponents of affirmative action. (With the country as deeply divided on the issue as it has been, perhaps that is why Powell's *Bakke* opinion survived as long as it did.) And then after that initial resolution of the constitutional questions, nothing happened in the Supreme Court for a quarter century. When it did return to the Court, the same exquisitely balanced divisions persisted.

The judicial debates on affirmative action began with a stutter step, reflecting their politically explosive potential. The Supreme Court dismissed the first significant challenge to an affirmative action program in law school admissions on the grounds that the petitioner, who was at the time a third-year student at the law school to which he sought admission,[12] would graduate before the Court could resolve the issue, so the case was moot. But *DeFunis v. Odegaard* (1974)[13] presented a common problem in mootness cases, captured in the formula "capable of repetition yet evading review." (Abortion is the most recurrent example.) Even if this petitioner's case was mooted, hundreds of others would inevitably come before the courts. In addition, the dissenters in this five-to-four decision, particularly Justice Douglas, were insistent on reaching the merits. The issue could not be indefinitely evaded.

So the Court finally grasped the nettle in *Regents of the University of California v. Bakke* (1978).[14] The recently founded medical school of the University of California, Davis, had reserved sixteen places out of an entering class of one hundred for people of color in order to produce more physicians to serve minority communities in the state. The petitioner, who was white, alleged that some of those admitted under the program were less academically qualified than he, so that the program effectively discriminated against him, and in favor of those admitted, on the basis of race.

The Supreme Court held this set-aside unconstitutional on the grounds that it disadvantaged Allan Bakke because of his race. (He was admitted and went on to a successful career as an anesthesiologist.) The liberal bloc—Justices Brennan, White, Marshall, and Blackmun—would have upheld affirmative action programs like those at UC Davis by intermediate (not strict) scrutiny: "important" objectives, "substantially related" means. They would reserve strict scrutiny for only those programs that "stigmatize." Justice Thurgood Marshall, in a separate opinion, wrote that "during most of the past 200 years, the Constitution as interpreted by this Court did not prohibit the most ingenious and pervasive forms of discrimination against the Negro. Now, when a State acts to remedy the effects of that legacy of discrimination, I cannot believe that this same Constitution stands as a barrier."[15] Justice Blackmun forthrightly addressed the paradox of affirmative action: "in order to get beyond racism, we must first take account of race. There is no other way. And in order to treat some persons equally, we must treat them differently. We cannot—we dare not—let the Equal Protection Clause perpetuate racial supremacy."[16] The conservative bloc—Chief Justice Burger and Justices Stevens, Stewart, and Rehnquist—would have resolved the case on statutory grounds: the Davis program violated Title VI of the 1964 Civil Rights Act, which prohibits racial discrimination in the administration of federally funded programs.

Justice Powell, speaking only for himself, agreed with the conservatives' Title VI point, and struck down the Davis program. But he wrote an opinion that, though entirely dicta, has endured until recently as the mainstay of affirmative action programs in higher education.[17] Powell was deeply skeptical of such programs and insisted that they undergo "the most exacting judicial examination." This was later confirmed by the Court in employment discrimination cases as strict scrutiny. All "racial distinctions," benign or malignant, Powell wrote, are "inherently suspect."[18] Powell reinterpreted the nature of whiteness itself, disaggregating people of European descent into various ethnic minorities (Poles, Italians, etc.), each of which, he claimed, had its own history of being victims of discrimination.[19] This had the effect of claiming for whites whatever benefits might be derived from the status of a disadvantaged minority, while implicitly absolving them from the guilt of comprising an undifferentiated majority that had oppressed African Americans.

This move permitted Powell to invoke the theme of white innocence: "forcing innocent persons in respondent's position to bear the burdens of redressing grievances not of their making" was wrong. Powell dismissed concerns about what he called "societal discrimination," by which he seems to have meant what we now call structural racism, "an amorphous concept of injury that may be ageless in its reach into the past."[20] Each of these points remained an element of affirmative action doctrine today: strict scrutiny, the equivalence of benign and malignant racial distinctions, white innocence, the refusal to engage with structural inequality.

However, after erecting this series of daunting barriers to affirmative action programs, Powell abruptly changed course. "A diverse student body...clearly is a constitutionally permissible goal for an institution of higher education."[21] That interest in diversity is "compelling," thus meeting the ends requirement of the strict scrutiny test. Going forward, once a college or university identifies a diversity goal, all it need worry about is showing that its means are narrowly tailored. Powell gave an example of the workings of a legitimate diversity program under these new criteria, that of Harvard College. A school may take race into account, as Harvard did, if it is just one of numerous factors in an individual's profile. Legitimating racial diversity, even if it is only one of the multiple criteria admissions committees may consider, enabled affirmative action programs to survive, but barely. Powell held the UC Davis policy unconstitutional because it was not narrowly tailored to fit within the diversity rationale he articulated.

There is an enduring irony in Powell's *Bakke* opinion. In cases involving primary and secondary education, Powell, in collaboration with Rehnquist, turned American constitutional development away from the ideals and goals of *Brown*, and toward values indifferent to racial justice. No single justice has done more to diminish *Brown v. Board of Education* and to retard integration. Yet his *Bakke* opinion singlehandedly rescued affirmative action in higher education from its many circling enemies, sending it on to its uncertain, clouded future. Powell, the steadfast opponent of everything that would produce meaningful racial integration and educational opportunity for Black and brown students throughout the nation, nevertheless enabled universities to offset the damages wrought by his education opinions.

Powell's *Bakke* opinion has a peculiar quality: it is the Schrödinger's cat of constitutional law.[22] A state university's admissions policy can be constitutional and unconstitutional at the same time when it is adopted, in what physicists might term a state of constitutional "superposition." This seeming paradox is not resolved until it is observed (i.e., evaluated by a court for constitutionality), but then the "observation" resolves the paradox, one way or the other. Affirmative action in higher education after *Bakke* was a duality of complementary (though apparently discordant) principles, either legitimizing or condemning affirmative action, but not until it is resolved by a judicial opinion.[23] Thinking of it this way helps make sense of *Bakke*'s progeny.

After *Bakke*, the focus of debates on the constitutional dimensions of affirmative action shifted to the contexts of employment and public contracts. But the two principal precedents in the public-contracts area, *Richmond v. J. A. Croson Co.* (1989) and *Adarand Constructors v. Pena* (1995), seemed to indicate that the justices were becoming less tolerant of affirmative action than the diversity passages of Powell's *Bakke* opinion would suggest.

Outside the Marble Palace, the tide was running against preferential admissions. In 1996, the people of California adopted Proposition 209, the so-called California Civil Rights Initiative, which amended the state constitution to forbid public institutions from taking race into account for purposes of employment, public contracts, and education.[24] Prop 209 became the bellwether for similar constitutional initiatives in other states. But after *Bakke*, no major issues involving affirmative action in education came before the Supreme Court for the next quarter century. When they did, the Court was no nearer a definitive resolution of the difficult constitutional problems than it had been in 1978.

In a case challenging the admissions policy of the University of Texas at Austin, *Hopwood v. Texas* (1996),[25] a three-judge panel of the US Court of Appeals for the Fifth Circuit declined to follow Powell's *Bakke* opinion, contending that it represented his solo view and never commanded a majority on the Court. (In this, they were wrong: Powell's Bakke opinion did command a majority on the crucial diversity issue.)[26] Two of the judges seemed to think that they had authority to "overrule" Powell's opinion, or at least to refuse to accord it any binding force. (The US Supreme Court later spanked this bit of judicial impudence.)[27] The Supreme Court denied certiorari in *Hopwood* in 1996.[28] That decision forced the Texas legislature to devise the so-called affirmative access or "Top Ten Percent Plan" to salvage something for minority admissions at Texas public universities. All of this would soon return to the Supreme Court. Scholars scrambled to differentiate educational policy in *Bakke* from issues of public contracting in order to save affirmative action in higher education.[29] But after *Bakke*, no major issues involving affirmative action in education came before the Court for the remainder of the twentieth century.

Any lingering doubts about the continued vitality of Powell's *Bakke* dicta were laid to rest, though again just as narrowly, in companion cases from the University of Michigan, *Grutter v. Bollinger* (2003)[30] and *Gratz v. Bollinger* (2003).[31] In both cases, a majority spoke (not a plurality as in nearly all of the *Bakke* case); and again, a majority supported affirmative action (in *Grutter*).

The University of Michigan Law School, one of the nation's most competitive, annually admits about one in ten of those who apply to it. Following the *Bakke*/Harvard criteria, the school pursued diversity in its student body, defined "not solely in terms of racial or ethnic status."[32] The school aimed for "racial and ethnic diversity with special reference to the inclusion of students from groups which have historically been discriminated against, like African Americans, Hispanics, and Native Americans." It sought to create a "critical mass" of such students to avoid racial isolation. In conformity with *Bakke*, race was a "plus factor," but only one of multiple factors included in its "highly individualized, holistic" evaluations. Justice O'Connor, writing for the majority in *Grutter*, held that the law school had demonstrated a compelling interest in pursuing such diversity. To buttress her position, she cited approvingly from several of the flood of amicus briefs submitted before argument, emphasizing points made by retired flag officers of the armed services and corporate executives about the need for racial diversity in military and civilian leadership. She found the application of the law school policies narrowly tailored but cautioned that "we expect that 25 years from now, the use of racial preferences will no longer be necessary."[33] This sunset mandate underscored how obviously O'Connor's majority opinion was an act of legislative will rather than an exercise of judicial reason.[34]

Justices Thomas, Scalia, Rehnquist, and Kennedy dissented in *Grutter*, with each but Kennedy contributing opinions. Justice Thomas's screed denounced the premises of affirmative action, endorsing the "mismatch" theory popular among conservatives,[35] a racist cliché that assumes that most or all minority applicants to elite institutions like the University of Michigan will find themselves in over their heads academically and intellectually. Sounding like a racist bigot, Thomas wrote: "the Law School tantalizes unprepared students with the promise of a University of Michigan degree and all of the opportunities that it offers. These overmatched students take the bait, only to find that they cannot succeed in the cauldron of competition." He declared that such students of color would have been better off if "they had gone to a less 'elite' law school for which they were better prepared."[36] He provided no statistics or other factual data to support these inflammatory assumptions. Nevertheless, he was echoed by Justice Scalia, in *Fisher v. University of Texas* (2013), who claimed in oral argument that "it does not benefit African-Americans to get them into the University of Texas where they do not do well, as opposed to having them go to a less-advanced school, a less—a slower-track school where they do well." He barreled on: "they come from lesser schools where they do not feel that they're being pushed ahead in classes that are too fast for them. I'm just not impressed by the fact that the University of Texas may have fewer [Black students]. Maybe it ought to have fewer."[37]

Gratz v. Bollinger (2003), the companion case to *Grutter*, involved undergraduate admissions at the University of Michigan.[38] Unlike the law school, the College of Literature, Science, and the Arts did not use a *Bakke*-like system of indefinite multiple criteria to create a diverse student body. Rather, it employed a point system in which an applicant needed 100 points for admission on a 150-point scale and awarded an arbitrary 20 points to all applicants of color. Chief Justice Rehnquist readily struck this down as a "quota system," which failed the "narrowly tailored" means part of strict scrutiny. This came as no surprise: the Court had condemned numerically specific and arbitrary criteria since the 1970s, and the Michigan undergraduate system flouted that basic guideline. Justice Souter, joined by Justice Ginsburg, dissented on the merits, and cited the Texas Ten Percent Plan as an acceptable technique of "deliberate obfuscation."[39]

Justice Stevens, joined by Souter, dissented on the question of standing. None of the petitioners in *Gratz* was applying to Michigan (they were students at other institutions during the litigation).[40] They were recruited for the purpose of challenging the Michigan standards by an activist anti-affirmative action group, the Center for Individual Rights. The majority opinion disregarded the fact that the petitioners had no active, personal interest in the outcome of the litigation, and were mere legal mannequins trundled in as vehicles to bring a policy issue before the Court. "Petitioners' own interests must be implicated. Because neither petitioner has a personal stake in this suit for prospective relief, neither has standing," Stevens insisted, to no avail.[41] *Allen v. Wright* stood as a reminder that African American plaintiffs enjoy no comparable ready entrée to the courts. In the twenty-first century, the Supreme Court maintains a racial double standard in its standing doctrine: it slams the courthouse door shut to Black petitioners seeking to challenge racial exclusion, but welcomes white petitioners who complain of often-illusory loss of advantage.

By granting such opportunistic standing to opponents of affirmative action, the Court's majority made it easier for white challengers to civil rights litigation to gain access to the legal process. This position can be justified only if there is an implied assumption that a white applicant's standing is based on some right to compete for admission without a racial filter in place. If this is so, the Court has not yet affirmed it, perhaps because that would constitute a remarkable innovation in equality jurisprudence that blatantly favored whites. Even for the Roberts Court, that might be a step too far. Moreover, there is what Justice Goodwin Liu of the California Supreme Court has identified as the "causation fallacy": at selective elite institutions, all applicants face a highly competitive process in which the applicant pool consists of large numbers of individuals as qualified or more so than they. The competition for admission depends on numerous objective and subjective criteria, some of which, like place of residence, may be arbitrary but not offensive to the Fourteenth Amendment. Others, like legacy admissions, perpetuate structural racism and thus benefit white applicants to the exclusion of applicants of color. In such an environment, a disappointed white applicant may not have done better even if there had been no affirmative action program in place.[42] The causation fallacy rests on an assumption that the admissions process is a zero-sum game, in which if a Black applicant is admitted, it must at the expense of a better-qualified white person.[43] Criteria like legacy admissions benefit white applicants to the exclusion of applicants of color and are thus a glaring example of structural racism. (The University of Texas did not desegregate its undergraduate program until 1957.) Yet Justice Thomas gratuitously defended such legacy admissions in his *Grutter* concurrence/dissent.[44]

The obdurate resistance of the dissenting conservatives, the narrowness of the *Grutter* result, and the unrelentingly controversial character of the affirmative action issue encouraged opponents to persist in challenges. The University of Texas at Austin (UTA), the state's flagship campus, read *Bakke* to permit race-conscious admissions, so it took race into account as one factor in the admissions process. It was this policy that the Fifth Circuit struck down in *Hopwood*. Because the Supreme Court refused certiorari, *Hopwood*, despite its defects, remained controlling law in the Fifth Circuit (which includes Texas). To comply, UTA adopted a two-step revised procedure, with the first step based solely on academic credentials, and the second, known as "holistic" evaluation, based on a wide range of criteria that did not include race. For its part, the Texas legislature enacted the Top Ten Percent Plan, which automatically admitted the top decile of every Texas high school to any state university.[45] Reva Siegal aptly refers to this as "race-conscious in purpose but race-neutral in form."[46] It is race-conscious because of the universally conceded fact that many Texas high schools were de facto segregated because of residential patterns. This provided a crude but effective workaround for the *Hopwood* decision. Then, after the Supreme Court in *Grutter* authorized a qualified consideration of race, UTA added race to the holistic portion of its two-tier plan. It also came up with a complex four-stage process in which race figured in only one preliminary stage, while the ultimate decision was race-blind. That did not satisfy opponents. Amid widespread apprehension that the Texas policy would be the vehicle for the Court's final dismantling of *Bakke*, diversity, and affirmative action, the Supreme Court agreed to review it.[47]

Petitioners in *Fisher v. University of Texas I* (2013)[48] attacked UTA's constricted consideration of race. Justice Kennedy for a seven-member majority sent it back to the trial court for a determination as to whether the program was narrowly tailored, warning that the university's position on this point was not conclusive on the Court. He affirmed the use of race to promote the educational benefits of diversity, but insisted that it be subject to strict scrutiny, with no deference to the university's judgment on the question of means used to reach that goal. As he always did in his affirmative action opinions, Kennedy demanded that the university first seek race-neutral alternatives, but he conceded that "narrow tailoring does not require exhaustion of every *conceivable* race-neutral alternative."[49] Justice Ruth Bader Ginsburg dissented, insisting that the Texas plan was constitutional without further review. She injected this welcome note of realism: "only an ostrich could regard the supposedly neutral alternatives as race unconscious.... Texas' percentage plan was adopted with racially segregated neighborhoods and schools front and center stage.... It is race consciousness, not blindness to race, that drives such plans.... Government actors, including state universities, need not be blind to the lingering effects of 'an overtly discriminatory past,' the legacy of 'centuries of law-sanctioned inequality.'"[50]

On remand, the Fifth Circuit again upheld the UTA process, producing *Fisher II: Fisher v. University of Texas* (2016),[51] which again upheld UTA's actions, this time by a tighter four-to-three margin, with Kennedy again writing for the majority and Justice Alito countering with a lengthy, comprehensive attack on diversity generally and UTA's embrace of it in particular. Kennedy first accepted UTA's statement of its goals as legitimate: destroying racial stereotypes, promoting cross-racial understanding, contributing to a diverse workforce, and sustaining the legitimacy of the nation's leadership. He accepted UTA's claim that race-neutral means had proven insufficient to reach those goals, and that it had done all that it could to achieve those goals without race-conscious measures. He rejected opponents' argument that objective measures like GPA and SAT scores could or should be the sole measures of merit. For the dissenters—himself, Thomas, and Roberts—Alito produced an opinion seething with hostility to affirmative action and to the University of Texas itself. The burden of his critique was that the university's goals were vague and unmeasurable. So once again, affirmative action in higher education limped across the finish line, battered but surviving.

The next line of attack reverted to a technique that had proven successful before: a popular referendum prohibiting affirmative action. After *Grutter/Gratz*, disappointed opponents of affirmative action took a page from California's experience with Proposition 209 and in 2006 promoted a copycat initiative amendment to the Michigan state constitution known as Proposition 2 that banned affirmative action in higher education, public employment, and public contracts. The Supreme Court upheld the constitutionality of this measure in *Schuette v. Coalition to Defend Affirmative Action* (2014),[52] but the justices were divided among themselves.[53] Justice Kennedy for the plurality held that the issue presented was whether the people of the state, acting through the initiative, can instruct their state government "not to follow a course that entails, first, the definition of racial categories and, second, the grant of favored status to persons in some racial categories and not others." He held that this was within the power of the people of a state, and that there is "no authority in the Constitution of the United States or in this Court's precedents for the Judiciary to set aside Michigan laws that commit this policy determination to the voters."

The issue that Kennedy was addressing is known as the "political process" strand of equal protection analysis.[54] This is derived from the second paragraph of footnote 4 of *Carolene Products*. *Washington v. Seattle School District No. 1* (1982) and *Hunter v. Erickson* (1969)[55] struck down initiative or referendum measures that made it more difficult for minority groups to pursue their objectives in the political process, such as measures that required that legislation they support be approved by a special referendum rather than by ordinary legislation. The equal protection clause prohibits burdening groups defined either by race or by sexual orientation from being placed under a special political disability from pursuing their interests or seeking the protection of the laws. As Kennedy put it in *Romer v. Evans* (1996), "a state cannot so deem a class of persons a stranger to its laws" by "singling [them] out for disfavored legal status."[56] Did Prop 2 do that by prohibiting African Americans from seeking enactment of affirmative action programs? The plurality and concurring opinions held that it did not, seeing the issue as merely one of who gets to make policy choices and how. In what appears to be a defect of democracy, it seems easier to enact racist laws by initiative or referenda, where the sovereign people themselves are the source of the laws, than to do so through the filter of republican legislative bodies.

Justice Sonia Sotomayor, joined by Ginsburg, disagreed in an impassioned dissent in which she asserted that the people of Michigan changed the state's political process "in a manner that uniquely disadvantaged racial minorities." In a lengthy review of the history of oppression and discrimination by race, she reminded her colleagues that "race matters. Race matters in part because of the long history of racial minorities' being denied access to the political process.... Race also matters because of persistent racial inequality in society—inequality that cannot be ignored and that has produced stark socioeconomic disparities.... This refusal to accept the stark reality that race matters is regrettable. The way to stop discrimination on the basis of race is to speak openly and candidly on the subject of race, and to apply the Constitution with eyes open to the unfortunate effects of centuries of racial discrimination."[57]

The Supreme Court finally confirmed the inevitable in *Students for Fair Admissions v. Harvard* (2023).[58] A six-member majority speaking through Chief Justice Roberts held that affirmative action in higher education is unconstitutional or illegal because such policies discriminate on the basis of race and fail to meet the "daunting" standards of strict scrutiny.[59]

He claimed that the goals cited by the universities were vague and immeasurable. They supposedly relied on racial stereotyping and used racial classification as a "negative factor" against individual students. They had no logical end point, and they embodied the forbidden policies of racial balancing, quotas, and proportionality. After *Students for Fair Admissions*, it remains unclear how much, if any, of *Bakke*'s diversity rationale survives.

Affirmative Action in the Labor Market

When the Court did engage with workplace affirmative action in the early 1980s, it responded supportively at first. For a decade after 1977, the Court seemed to accept proof of disparate impact as evidence of discriminatory intent; gave its blessing to a voluntary private affirmative action plan; accepted quantitatively defined goals for affirmative action plans, something that seemed to validate numerical quotas or proportionality (both hitherto taboo); upheld numerical set-asides; and approved affirmative action plans under Title VII. By the mid-eighties, the Court seemed to have cleared the way for implementing affirmative action in both the public and private spheres.

The justices first reined in the daunting *Washington v. Davis* requirement that plaintiff demonstrate the employer's discriminatory intent in employment discrimination suits. In two 1977 cases, *Teamsters v. United States* and *Hazelwood School District v. United States*,[60] the Court permitted plaintiffs to offer statistical evidence in pattern-or-practice litigation, rather than requiring conventional proof of a defendant's intent or state of mind.[61] Under the relatively permissive preponderance-of-the-evidence standard, the federal government can rely on statistical evidence to prove that "that racial discrimination was the (employer's) standard operating procedure [and was] the regular rather than the unusual practice." Assuming, without empirical validation, that "it is ordinarily to be expected that nondiscriminatory hiring practices will in time result in a work force more or less representative of the racial and ethnic composition of the population in the community from which employees are hired," the Court declared that "where gross statistical disparities can be shown, they alone may in a proper case constitute prima facie proof of a pattern or practice of discrimination."[62] This eased the *Davis* burden on plaintiffs in employment discrimination cases and took racially disparate impacts into account. This use of statistical evidence to identify and remedy civil rights violations provided a major pillar of the civil rights revolution.[63]

The Court validated a second pillar, the extension of civil rights enforcement into the private sphere, in *United Steelworkers v. Weber* (1979), which upheld a private voluntary affirmative action program.[64] *Weber* was the first Supreme Court case to explicitly address the issue of affirmative action in employment. Under a collective-bargaining agreement, the employer opened an on-the-job training opportunity at one of its plants on a one-to-one racial basis, even though white employees there far outnumbered Blacks. The Court held that this did not violate Title VII's ban on racial discrimination in employment. It affirmed the use of such voluntary race-conscious measures to correct a history of denial of opportunity. The remedy was temporary, to be discontinued when the ratio of Black craft workers approximated the local labor force. But in a long and snarky dissent, Justice William H. Rehnquist insisted that employers should not be "permitted to consider race in making employment decisions." He demanded a strictly color-blind reading of Title VII, under which no one, government or private employer, could consider anyone's race in remedying racial imbalances. If adopted, Rehnquist's position would have made it impossible to formulate remedies that could end racial exclusion.

The next year, a divided Court sustained a requirement that 10 percent of federal funds allocated for public spending programs be reserved for minority business enterprises. Still smarting from the earlier refusal of federal courts to strike down hiring quotas under Nixon's foray into affirmative action, the Philadelphia Plan,[65] Pennsylvania building contractors raised a facial challenge to the set-aside. But in *Fullilove v. Klutznick* (1980),[66] Chief Justice Burger for a plurality upheld the measure, shrugging off claims that it penalized innocent parties and offended the color-blindness principle. He found ample power under the commerce and spending clauses for Congress to use its spending powers to combat the effects of past discrimination and prevent its continuation into the future.

Unions fared no better than corporate employers when they were the discriminators. In a 1986 case involving an obstinately racist trade union local, the New York City Sheetmetal Workers Local 28, the Court condemned the union's "persistent or egregious discrimination" against African Americans for almost two decades in defiance of a federal court order.[67] It approved a court-ordered goal of 29 percent new minority membership (in effect, a numerical quota). The Reagan administration, intervening in the case, argued that only those individuals who were themselves personally victims of discrimination could sue, but the Court's majority rebuffed that challenge. In a companion case, the Court broadened the scope of consent decrees to permit racial preferences where necessary to combat what even the Reagan Justice Department conceded was "contumacious" behavior by the union.[68] The next year, a divided Court upheld an order requiring the Alabama State Police to promote troopers to the rank of corporal on a one-for-one Black-to-white basis to overcome a decade of dogged defiance and foot-dragging.[69] In all these cases, the Supreme Court approved explicitly race-conscious remedies and numerical quotas, but only as a remedy, and only after a showing of persistent defiance of court orders.

The impulse that sustained affirmative action remained strong enough to carry over into a landmark case involving gender, not racial, bias, *Johnson v. Santa Clara County Transportation Agency* (1987).[70] A male employee passed over for promotion to dispatcher in favor of a female claimed that her selection violated Title VII's ban on sex-based discrimination.[71] The Supreme Court upheld the promotion, though, because it conformed to the three Title VII criteria specified eight years earlier in *Steelworkers v. Weber*: it sought to eliminate a "manifest imbalance" that "reflected underrepresentation of women in traditionally segregated job categories"; it did not "unnecessarily trammel" the interests of male workers; and it was temporary. *Johnson* was the first sex-discrimination decision of the Supreme Court. As such, it buttressed the racial discrimination claims of the previous decade, but it proved to be the last victory for workplace affirmative action in the High Court.[72]

The Court's apparent acceptance of affirmative action in employment and public contracts proved illusory, though. In the next decade, the justices attacked congressional affirmative action policy, imposed strict scrutiny on all forms of affirmative action, proclaimed white innocence, protected white advantage, limited Congress's authority, condemned numerical quotas, and displayed an ever-more hostile attitude toward all efforts to rectify the legacy of past discrimination.

The first sign of trouble came, appropriately enough, in *Firefighters v. Stotts* (1984),[73] another in the cavalcade of suits brought by white firefighters contesting layoffs caused by municipal budget cuts. A sharp recession hit the American economy in 1981–1982, with both inflation and unemployment soaring above 10 percent. The recession was then prolonged by the mid-decade savings-and-loan crisis. In such economic headwinds, existing collective-bargaining agreements that structured layoffs pitted different employee groups against each other. If employers followed a last-hired, first-fired policy, Black employees would be the first victims of economic downturns. New minority hires under recently adopted affirmative action programs would be the first to be shoved out, wiping out their tenuous gains.

In *Stotts*, white firefighters who were the beneficiaries of seniority provisions in collective-bargaining agreements objected to enforcement of consent decrees that protected some recently hired Black comrades. The Court sustained the white firefighters' objections. Rejecting group remedies, a majority of the Court insisted on an "individual justice" approach that constituted the greatest setback up to that time in Title VII litigation.[74] Justice White's majority opinion denied relief to the Black newbies (as recently qualified members are known in the fire service), unless they could show that they "have been actual victims of illegal discrimination." White rejected group remedies based on what he dismissively called "mere membership in the disadvantaged class." *Stotts* upheld a Title VII exemption for previously established seniority systems, even though it would disproportionately impact recently hired Black firefighters. *Stotts* also introduced the concept of white innocence into the subject of workplace affirmative action. The majority (White), concurring (O'Connor), and dissenting (Blackmun) opinions all recognized, in Justice Blackmun's words, "the difficulty of reconciling competing claims of innocent employees who themselves are neither the perpetrators of discrimination nor the victims of it," with competing demands of recently hired African American employees when the challenged seniority system had been established under conditions of structural racism.[75]

In a succeeding case a few years later that involved the same mix of economic recession, affirmative action, seniority, and layoffs, the justices again refused to recognize the role that structural racism plays in employment. *Wygant v. Jackson Board of Education* (1986)[76] grew out of a challenge by white public-school teachers to the terms of a contract that protected seniority in layoffs, but with a proviso that minority layoffs would not exceed the ratio of minority employees overall. After a financial retrenchment, some white teachers were laid off while a few of their junior African American peers held on to their jobs. The Court was therefore faced with the choice of affirming either a nominally race-neutral seniority system that would disproportionately lay off Black teachers or a race-conscious, negotiated agreement that would result in the preservation of recent, modest, and hard-won gains in minority hiring.[77] If the burdens of an economic downturn were not proportionately shared by whites and Blacks, the automatic operation of the seniority system (established in an earlier context of racial discrimination) would cause white/Black teacher ratios to revert back toward Jim Crow-era levels, without any need for current racial animus to produce the disparate results. Structural racism blindly, automatically, and invisibly generated racially disparate outcomes that shoved Blacks out of recently gained employment opportunities.

The lower courts had held that it was not necessary for the plaintiffs to show intentional discrimination. They acknowledged the reality of what US district court judge Charles Joiner called "societal discrimination" and acknowledged the value of African American teachers as "role models" for minority students.[78] A majority of the Supreme Court rejected all these points. Writing for a plurality of four, Justice Powell rebuked the lower-court judges: "This Court never has held that societal discrimination alone is sufficient to justify a racial classification."[79] He dismissed the possibility of ever demonstrating structural racism: "Societal discrimination, without more, is too amorphous a basis for imposing a racially classified remedy." (This nod to "societal discrimination" seems to be the closest that Justice Powell and most of his colleagues came to recognizing the reality of structural racism, but even it seems to imply intent rather than effects.) In a concurring opinion, Justice O'Connor piled on: "a governmental agency's interest in remedying 'societal' discrimination, that is, discrimination not traceable to its own actions," can never satisfy the compelling-interest element of the strict scrutiny test.[80] Under *Washington v. Davis*, the sole doctrinal relevance of racially disparate outcomes was to suggest (though not prove) intentional discrimination.

Having dispensed with the need to link legal doctrine to social reality, the Court has never reconsidered its indifference to structural forces. Instead, it withdrew into a fantasy world of wishful or magical thinking: "absent employment discrimination by the school board, 'nondiscriminatory hiring practices will in time result in a work force more or less representative of the racial and ethnic composition of the population in the community from which employees are hired.'"[81] The Court's enthusiasm for this idea has not been diminished by the fact that it has no basis in reality. Such a desirable outcome has never occurred without activist prodding.

The *Wygant* plurality dismissed the justification for affirmative action plans that promoted Black teachers as role models for their students. White normativity made it impossible for the plurality justices to see how vital role models were to people who had previously experienced discrimination and exclusion. It did not seem to occur to the justices that Black teachers would be role models not only for Black students but, just as importantly, for white students as well. Underlying this is an assumption that students can have a whole and complete understanding of the world with only white faculty—an example of the unexamined belief that white advantage is the norm.[82]

Such assumptions are also the basis for claims of the innocence of white "victims" who are disappointed or burdened by race-conscious remedies. Both Powell in his plurality opinion and O'Connor in her separate concurrence emphasized the white-innocence theme. O'Connor wrote that an affirmative action program may not "impose disproportionate harm on the interests, or unnecessarily trammel the rights, of innocent individuals."[83] In this innocence trope, the victims are always white. This is not a matter of overt racism but rather the dominance of white cultural norms: to be white is to be automatically exempt from all burdens of unjust discrimination, intentional or structural.[84] When whites do not receive a hoped-for opportunity that they believe is rightfully theirs (protections for seniority on the job, admission to a public university), then almost by definition they must be victims of unjust and discriminatory policy. If whites and Blacks are seen to be locked in a zero-sum game, where gains for one come at the expense of the other, then it seems intuitive to the disappointed party that whites, individually and collectively presumed to be "innocent" of actions that have contributed to Black oppression, are treated unfairly if they miss an opportunity where an affirmative action program is in place.

Justice Powell took the occasion to reaffirm the individualist bias of the Court's thinking about racial discrimination. To most of the justices, racial inequality is a matter of one individual intentionally denigrating another individual. As the wrong is individual, so must the remedy be. Criticizing Justice Marshall's dissenting position, Justice Powell wrote that Marshall "sees this case not in terms of individual constitutional rights, but as an allocation of burdens 'between two racial groups.'" To this, Powell retorted: "This is really nothing more than group-based analysis." He countered: "the Constitution does not allocate constitutional rights to be distributed like bloc [sic] grants within discrete racial groups." Powell thought that that only individuals may be rights claimants: "the petitioners before us today are not 'the white teachers as a group.' They are Wendy Wygant and other individuals who claim that they were fired from their jobs because of their race."[85]

But that assumes the very point in controversy. To deal with structural racism, the Court must think in group terms because it is groups, not individuals, who have been the principal focus of discrimination by racialized societies. Justice Scalia thus got it exactly wrong when he wrote in 1985 that "the relevant proposition is not that it was blacks, or Jews, or Irish who were discriminated against, but it was individual men and women, 'created equal,' who were discriminated against."[86] Expressing the views of the Reagan administration, Assistant Attorney General William Bradford Reynolds maintained that "our country is not a group of groups; our laws protect individuals, not classes."[87] Similarly, Justice Thomas perverted the meaning of *Brown v. Board of Education I* when he claimed that "at the heart of this interpretation of the Equal Protection Clause lies the principle that the government must treat citizens as individuals, and not as members of racial, ethnic, or religious groups."[88] The hyper-individualism that infects American law generally has a particularly distorting effect here, disabling the Court from seeing the true source of inequality in American life.

The year 1989 was the annus horribilis for workplace and public-contracts affirmative action. In the 1988 Term, three major decisions further embedded structural racism by making it more difficult for plaintiffs to prove it and seek the law's aid in rooting it out.[89] One scholar has referred to these cases collectively as "the civil rights massacre of 1989."[90] They dealt with procedural questions, which are obscure, technical, and difficult for lay readers to follow.[91] They lack drama and interest; they seem colorless and neutral. But for judges determined to scale back civil rights protections, they provide useful cover because their technicalities obscure the consequences of their results. They are a stealthy way to frustrate rights claims that conservative justices opposed, without incurring the odium that open attacks on the rights themselves might invite.[92] These procedural hurdles are examples of the structural arrangements embedded in social and organizational infrastructure that seem to be neutral. Their assumed neutrality makes them almost invulnerable, yet they perpetuate racial disparities.

Through a quarter century of litigation, the federal courts had devised rules for allocating the burdens of proof and persuasion in Title VII cases that made it easier for plaintiffs to prove workplace discrimination. In *McDonnell Douglas v. Green* (1973),[93] the Court held that while the plaintiff bore the initial burden of providing prima facie evidence of discrimination by the employer, he could do so by a simple, straightforward test. The plaintiff merely had to prove that he was a racial minority, he applied for a job for which he was qualified, he was not hired, and the employer continued to try to fill the position. Then the burden shifted onto the employer to demonstrate a legitimate business purpose.

But the 1989 decisions retrenched, making it more difficult for plaintiffs to prove employment discrimination. In *Wards Cove Packing Co. v. Atonio* (1989), a five-justice majority adopted what Justice Stevens's dissent called "changes in [those] elementary and eminently fair rules," making it extremely difficult for plaintiffs to win Title VII disparate impact cases.[94] An Alaska salmon cannery employed two tiers of workers: white-collar and skilled technical workers, who were nearly all white, and unskilled cannery floor workers, who were predominantly Filipino and Alaska Native. Justice White for the majority rejected evidence based on that racial imbalance, mandating instead that plaintiff must prove "a specific or particular employment practice that has created the disparate impact," even though he conceded that this new requirement would be "unduly burdensome."[95]

White's insistence on identifying specific employment practices as the cause of disparate impacts arises from a misunderstanding of racism as existing only in the form of individual bigotry. To conclude that racism was not taking place at the cannery just because overt racism was not in evidence was to ignore the reality that structural racism was silently operating to produce the same disparate outcome. The Court's newly mandated tight linkage between "a particular practice" and results would make proof of discrimination virtually impossible. *Wards Cove* was thus setback for voluntary affirmative action programs.[96] This led Justice Blackmun in dissent to lament the conditions of a "plantation economy" like that of the cannery, with a proven track record of confining nonwhites to lower-paid unskilled positions: "One wonders whether the majority still believes that race discrimination—or, more accurately, race discrimination against nonwhites—is a problem in our society, or even remembers that it ever was."[97] This apparently stung the majority. Justice White in a footnote dismissed Blackmun's critique as "hyperbolic."[98] Merely because "race discrimination" is extensive in the United States, White averred, "does not mean, however, that it exists at the canneries—or more precisely, that it has been proved to exist at the canneries."

Martin v. Wilks (1989), another in the endless procession of white firefighter suits, provided another example of achieving substantive results—here, weakening consent decrees that had settled Title VII actions—through procedural maneuvers that would be opaque or incomprehensible to casual lay observers.[99] In litigation dating back to 1974, African American firefighters in Birmingham, Alabama, reached a consent decree with their municipal employer that mandated remedies for an admitted history of racial discrimination. These provided specific goals for the hiring and promotion of Black firefighters. A group of white firefighters who had declined to participate in the original litigation and hence were not parties to the consent decree then sued to challenge promotions based on the consent decrees as "reverse discrimination" that denied them advancement opportunities because of their race. Normally, a party who chooses not to assert his right in some litigation that might affect his situation is precluded from challenging the result.[100] A majority speaking through Chief Justice Rehnquist nevertheless permitted the white firefighters to challenge the consent decrees by making an exception to the long-standing procedural rules regarding that practice, which is known as impermissible collateral attack. *Martin* cast a long shadow, threatening disruption of existing consent arrangements and discouraging future use of the consent decree by injecting an element of uncertainty and lack of finality into any settlement.

The third of the 1989 cases, *Patterson v. McLean Credit Union* (1989), was both a substantive and a procedural setback for African Americans seeking to challenge workplace discrimination.[101] Brenda Patterson brought an action under 42 U.S.C. sec. 1981 claiming that she had been denied promotion and fired because of her race. Section 1981, descended from section 1 of the 1866 Civil Rights Act, guarantees that "all persons...have the same right...to make and enforce contracts" as whites. The defendant argued, and a five-justice majority agreed, that this language applied only to initial hiring decisions and did not cover subsequent discriminatory acts. Justice Anthony Kennedy soothingly suggested that the plaintiff still had remedies available to her under Title VII because it was a later and more comprehensive regulatory scheme. Thus "we may preserve the integrity of Title VII's procedures without sacrificing any significant coverage of the civil rights laws."[102] But that was cold comfort because section 1981 created an action for damages, thus providing a stronger deterrent to workplace racism, while Title VII authorized only an award of back pay.[103] The kinds of discrimination Patterson alleged could not be rectified by back-pay awards. Moreover, as Justice Brennan argued in dissent, a capacious reading of section 1981 was more consonant with the framers' intentions and the spirit of the first Reconstruction when it was originally enacted.[104]

In these 1989 cases, the Court read expansive and empowering statutes in a crabbed, stingy way, formally and hyper-technically draining off their transformative potential. The justices treated the ideal of equality as a matter of negotiable politics rather than mandated constitutionality, tweaking supposedly neutral procedures to attain outcomes benefiting white plaintiffs but thwarting litigants of color. The effect was to enable whites and white institutions to maintain the racial status quo.[105]

The 1989 decisions were so disruptive that Congress itself intervened to correct the Court's errors. Declaring that the Supreme Court had cut back dramatically on the scope and effectiveness of civil rights protections in these recent cases, the statute known as the Civil Rights Act of 1991 overturned each of the three decisions.[106] Rejecting *Patterson*, it expanded section 1981's "make and enforce contracts" provisions to include performance, modification, termination, and enjoyment of benefits and explicitly stated that the statute applied to private discrimination. It prohibited any "particular employment practice that causes a disparate impact on the basis of race, color, religion, sex, or national origin." The statute explicitly repudiated *Wards Cove* by name, an almost unprecedented rebuke to the Court.[107] It removed the ability of non-parties to upset a consent decree if they were adequately represented by the original parties or knew or should have known of the proceedings, thus rejecting the Court's reading in *Martin*. Finally, and most importantly, it validated a disparate impact reading of Title VII, codifying it in federal law.[108] For good measure, it also authorized punitive damages for malicious discrimination. Seldom has Congress so decisively rebuked the justices' overreaching.

The justices nevertheless seem to have been unabashed by Congress's rebuke. In 2003, the city of New Haven, Connecticut, administered civil service exams for promotion within the fire department. When white applicants outperformed applicants of color on the exam, the city disregarded the results and refused to make any promotions at all. Though it was besieged from both sides, the city claimed that validating the results and promoting some twenty white firefighters (plus one Latino) would expose it to disparate impact liability under the revised Title VII. The disappointed white firefighters sued, alleging disparate treatment. The Supreme Court agreed in a five-to-four decision, *Ricci v. DeStefano* (2009).[109] Justice Kennedy held that the city's decision was based on race, in violation of the 1964 act's goal of basing promotions on merit rather than color. The city failed to show that it had "a strong basis in evidence" that it would be subject to disparate impact liability. Justice Scalia concurred in the result, but with an ominous warning: the Court's disposition "merely postpones the evil day on which the Court will have to confront the question: Whether, or to what extent, are the disparate impact provisions of Title VII of the Civil Rights Act of 1964 consistent with the Constitution's guarantee of equal protection?"[110]

Implicit in Scalia's warning was the threat of a broader attack on the idea of disparate impact itself. That encouraged challenges to disparate impact liability in other areas, such as housing. One such case, *Texas Department of Housing and Community Affairs v. The Inclusive Communities Project* (2015), alleged collusion between local governments and fair housing's opponents (lenders and developers) in siting public and low-income housing. Petitioners claimed that Texas housing agencies allocated low-income housing tax credits in ways that promoted development only in predominantly Black neighborhoods.[111] By the narrowest of margins, the Court upheld the challenged 1991 amendments. Justice Kennedy for the majority even went a bit further by approving efforts to "counteract unconscious prejudices," thereby implicitly recognizing the role of implicit bias in policymaking.[112] But Kennedy's concession to the reality of structural racism was grudging. He warned that analyses based on statistical disparities raise "serious constitutional questions." He specified fifteen doubts, cautions, reservations, qualifications, and warnings that will cramp reliance on disparate impact approaches to statutory interpretation.[113] He made no concessions to the claim that disparate effects ought to determine constitutional analysis. So, little thanks to Justice Kennedy's unenthusiastic affirmation, disparate impact thinking limps along, still a permissible element of statutory (but not constitutional) interpretation. The Court remains reluctant to confront real-life problems that African Americans encounter in the housing market. For the moment, the immediate impact of *Ricci* was confined to its facts: the use of merit-based tests in the employment context. But it posed inescapably the question whether disparate impact liability was incompatible with the equal protection clause or the cluster of values that it represents. The question remains open.[114] After *Texas Inclusive Communities*, it is tenuously permissible for legislative, executive, and administrative bodies to take disparate impact into account, but only under searching judicial oversight.

Affirmative Action in Public Contracts

After *Fullilove v. Klutznick* seemingly settled the matter in 1980, the issue of affirmative action in public contracts lay quiescent before the Supreme Court. Municipalities emulated the federal program and tried in various ways to ensure that some portion of public monies spent for goods or services would go to minority business enterprises (MBEs). The city of Richmond, Virginia, symbolically important as the one-time capital of the Confederacy, confronted the anomaly of having a 50 percent minority population where fewer than 1 percent of public contracts went to MBEs. It followed the congressional program approved in *Fullilove* by a set-aside policy that required the city's prime contractors to direct 30 percent of public contracts to MBE subcontractors.

Six of the justices voted to disallow the Richmond plan in *Richmond v. J. A. Croson Co.* (1989).[115] For the first time, the Court imposed strict scrutiny on an affirmative action program, and then applied it with unyielding rigor. Justice O'Connor for the majority dismissed the history of "past discrimination" against African Americans in employment and business as an "amorphous claim" that relied on "sheer speculation" to create "a patchwork of racial preferences based on statistical generalizations." Such a practice discriminated against whites by preventing them from competing for the set-aside subcontracts. She rejected out of hand the justification that the program was "benign," dismissing a principal justification for affirmative action programs. O'Connor's claim was a classic example of false equivalence: the majority put efforts to open opportunity on the same moral plane as efforts to deny opportunity to African Americans. Justice Marshall refuted this: "a profound difference separates government actions that themselves are racist, and governmental actions that seek to remedy the effects of prior discrimination."[116] But the majority seemed incapable of confronting racism that forthrightly.

O'Connor indulged in tone-deaf speculation about the cause of the gross disparities in Richmond's construction industries, attributing them to "both black and white career and entrepreneurial choices." Those words have a cruel and dismissive quality. Did Justice O'Connor really think that African Americans deliberately passed up opportunities to become electricians and accountants because they preferred to be bellhops and car-wash attendants? O'Connor's unfortunate phrasing ignored three hundred years of enslavement and Jim Crow. As Justice Blackmun laconically observed in dissent:

"this Court, the supposed bastion of equality, strikes down Richmond's efforts as though discrimination had never existed."[117]

The O'Connor majority demanded "identified discrimination in the Richmond construction industry" as the sole basis for relief. The "inherently unmeasurable claim of past wrongs" that constituted "societal discrimination" could never serve to justify "a rigid numerical quota" or "racial balancing."[118] O'Connor seemed particularly indignant that the city identified the groups eligible for the set-asides as "Spanish-speaking, Oriental, Indian, Eskimo, or Aleut persons" (Eskimos in Virginia?), though in doing so the city had simply copied verbatim the congressional categories sustained in *Fullilove*. Three justices distinguished *Fullilove* as based on Congress's extraordinary remedial powers under section 5 of the Fourteenth Amendment. That distinction would not last long.

The *Croson* majority's view was almost entirely backward-looking, permitting local governments to act only against actual past wrongs, and requiring them to be identified with surgical precision. Moreover, these had to be acts of discrimination by the municipality itself. Remedies for discrimination in the private sector must be sought elsewhere. The city could not claim to be acting to prevent discrimination in the future, or to be pursuing distributive justice, that is, wealth redistribution.[119] Manipulating what is known as the "denominator problem" as restrictively as possible, O'Connor defined the relevant criterion for detecting discrimination (the denominator) to be qualified minority subcontractors, not the African American population of Richmond as a whole ("the relevant statistical pool...must be the number of minorities qualified to undertake the particular task").[120] She explained why that denominator was so tiny by speculating about injudicious Black "career choices," as if the skilled trades had ever hitherto been open to African Americans. The narrower the denominator chosen, the more self-defeating it becomes. *Croson* squeezed it to the vanishing point.

Croson "decontextualized" the affirmative action process, abstracting it from the historical reality of pervasive discrimination in Richmond, and reduced it to formulaic abstractions that managed to cobble together a holding out of four widely disparate opinions (O'Connor, Kennedy, Stevens, Scalia).[121] Some of the nation's foremost constitutional authorities tried to salvage something out of the wreckage of "this jurisprudence of dim uncertainties and fragile pluralities"[122] by a joint critique published in the *Yale Law Journal*, but the futility of their effort only underscored how severely *Croson* had set back the cause of racial justice.[123]

With affirmative action at the state and local level effectively quashed, federal power to adopt public-contract set-asides was momentarily sustained by *Metro Broadcasting v. FCC* (1990),[124] which upheld a minority-preference policy for broadcast licensing under an intermediate-scrutiny standard ("closely tailored" to serve an "important governmental objective"). But that proved short-lived. Within five years, the Court overruled it and *Fullilove*, imposing strict scrutiny on the exercise of *federal* power as well, in *Adarand Constructors v. Pena* (1995).[125] Justice O'Connor again wrote for the majority, though what that majority actually held was rendered opaque by the Court Reporter's introduction to her opinion, a note unique in the six hundred volumes of the *United States Reports*:

> Justice O'CONNOR announced the judgment of the Court and delivered an opinion with respect to Parts I, II, III-A, III-B, III-D, and IV, which is for the Court except insofar as it might be inconsistent with the views expressed in Justice SCALIA's concurrence, and an opinion with respect to Part III-C in which Justice KENNEDY joins.[126]

Since Justice Scalia did not then or thereafter deign to explain just which parts of the O'Connor opinion were inconsistent with his views, we do not know what elements of the razor-thin majority were holding and which dicta. (Even that is not the most egregious shortcoming of the *Adarand* judgment, though.)

The federal program in question provided a financial incentive for prime contractors on federally funded highway projects to let out subcontracts to "socially and economically disadvantaged individuals" (itself a constitutionally inoffensive category), but with the further—and fatal—specification that "the contractor shall presume that socially and economically disadvantaged individuals include Black Americans, Hispanic Americans, Native Americans, Asian Pacific Americans, and other minorities, or any other individual found to be disadvantaged by the [Small Business] Administration."[127] To strike that down, O'Connor produced a template of "three general propositions," which were to control all affirmative action programs going forward: "consistency" (strict scrutiny), "skepticism" ("a most searching examination"), and "congruence," the last meaning that federal authority was reduced to the scope of state power. The hitherto-ample grant of constitutional power under section 5 of the Fourteenth Amendment[128] was shrunk to the narrower confines of state authority. O'Connor proffered the wan reassurance that strict scrutiny need not necessarily be "strict in theory but fatal in fact."[129]

The concurring and dissenting opinions traversed the landscape of affirmative action. Justice Scalia, with characteristic brio and excess, trumpeted that in "the eyes of government, we are just one race here. It is American."[130] ("American" is not a race, *pace* Scalia.) Justice Thomas returned to the fray over moral equivalence: "there *is* a moral and constitutional equivalence between laws designed to subjugate a race and those that...foster some current notion of equality."[131] Justice Stevens in dissent flatly rejected that position, condemning the new principle of "consistency." He also upheld a more extensive congressional authority under section 5. Justice Ginsburg gamely tried to salvage something from the wreckage: "today's decision...allows our precedent to evolve, still to be informed by and responsive to changing conditions." The Court continues to recognize "the persistence of racial equality" and government's power "to counteract discrimination's lingering effects." "Congress can surely conclude," she maintained, "that a carefully designed affirmative action may help to realize, finally, the equal protection of the laws."[132] Ginsburg was making the best of a bad thing, but *Adarand* left the future of affirmative action in public contracting precarious.

The Dark Past: The US Supreme Court and African Americans, 1800–2015. William M. Wiecek, Oxford University Press. © Oxford University Press 2024. DOI: 10.1093/9780197654460.003.0010

11
Redemption Redux, 1972–2015

The second Redemption has been a dismaying echo of the first.[1] The Supreme Court hastened the end of the first Reconstruction by its regressive *Slaughterhouse* opinion in 1873, which shrank the potential of the Reconstruction Amendments. It relapsed toward antebellum notions of limited federal power, especially as that power could be used to protect the freedom, dignity, and legal status of the nation's new African American citizens. As the southern states imposed a regime of servitude to oppress those newly enfranchised Americans, the Court turned away, indifferent. Before World War I, the justices repeatedly affirmed Jim Crow, the form of inequality that succeeded slavery.

In the second Redemption, the Court repeated this pattern of behavior by protecting structural racism, the current avatar of racial inequality in America. In 1976 it narrowed federal remedial power by imposing the intent-effects dichotomy of *Washington v. Davis*, the twentieth century's counterpart to *Slaughterhouse*'s constitutional regression in the nineteenth. The de jure / de facto distinction that looms so large in the Court's education cases reflects that intent/effects binary. The Court looked on impassively while public schools resegregated, insisting that such resegregation did not amount to a constitutional violation and was therefore beyond the scope of judicial redress. For higher education, it blunted and eventually terminated affirmative action efforts while preserving white advantage in merit admissions and legacy preferences. The Court confined affirmative action programs in public contracts and employment; enabled voter suppression and disfranchisement of African Americans; and protected exclusionary zoning and popular referenda that stifled fair-housing laws. Well into the twenty-first century, the Supreme Court has shaped our public law in a way that consigns African Americans to a diminished constitutional status, their political power suppressed, and their life opportunities limited. It has declared structural racism invisible to the law and rebuffs legislative efforts to enable genuine equality throughout American society.

Fundamental Rights and State Action

The expansive growth of the equal protection clause in the civil rights era came to an end in the pivotal year of 1972. This deflation was evident in the stillbirth of one doctrine, fundamental rights, and the revival of another, state action.

By the late 1960s, the Court had identified two "strands" or "branches" of equal protection jurisprudence.[2] The first and more familiar strand interrogates all "suspect classifications" made by the other branches of government, principally those based on race or gender. Under this strand, the Court has handed down its most resounding equal protection decisions, beginning with *Brown v. Board of Education*. But there is a second strand, less well known, that relies on the equal protection clause to strike down state attacks on rights deemed "fundamental." Scholars refer to this fundamental-rights strand as "substantive equal protection," the counterpart of substantive due process.[3] The equal protection clause might potentially have become the textual anchor for an expansive reading of substantive standards of equality, especially in two areas of greatest concern to African Americans, education and housing. For a brief moment at the end of the civil rights era, the Court seemed to be on the brink of discovering in the clause a source of the fundamental rights that had been a part of American constitutional discourse since the Revolution.

Before the twentieth century, Americans frequently invoked "fundamental rights" in constitutional discourse, but it was an amorphous concept, not tied specifically to any clause of the Constitution. Then in *Skinner v. Oklahoma* (1942),[4] the Court held that marriage and procreation were a "basic liberty," "one of the basic civil rights of man," and therefore "fundamental," and as such, protected by the equal protection clause. *Skinner* marked the point when the Court began to link fundamental rights to constitutional text.[5] Marriage as a fundamental right protected by the equal protection clause figured in later cases involving various complexities of marriage and family formation.

In 1966, the Court extended the idea of fundamental rights beyond marriage to strike down a poll tax in state elections in *Harper v. Virginia State Board of Elections*,[6] because voting is a fundamental right, and economic discrimination in access to the ballot violates the command of equal protection.[7] Justice Douglas for the majority observed that "notions of what constitutes equal treatment for purposes of the Equal Protection Clause do change," confirming a dynamic understanding of the clause's potential where fundamental values were involved.

In 1969, as the final curtain was falling on the Warren Court, Justice William Brennan wrote for the dwindling liberal bloc in *Shapiro v. Thompson*[8] to invalidate a one-year waiting period for newly arrived migrants into the state before they became eligible for welfare benefits. Brennan held this policy unconstitutional on the grounds that it interfered with an American citizen's right to travel among the states and to be treated like other residents of the destination state, a noncontroversial application of the privileges and immunities clause of Article IV. In reaching this conclusion, though, Justice Brennan referred to "welfare aid upon which may depend the ability of the families to obtain the very means to subsist—food, shelter, and other necessities of life." Whatever Brennan may have meant by this cryptic allusion, alarmed conservatives saw in it the camel's nose of a right to life's necessities poking into the capacious tent of equal protection. Justice Harlan sounded the alarm in dissent, warning against the kind of judicial overreach implied in the "notion that this Court possesses a peculiar wisdom all its own whose capacity to lead this Nation out of its present troubles is contained only by the limits of judicial ingenuity in contriving new constitutional principles to meet each problem as it arises."[9]

For if the Court were to find a broad potential for fundamental rights in the equal protection clause, much else might follow.[10] The Constitution itself might be the source of such rights, with no need for mediation by statute. Statutes can be repealed, modified, interpreted in ways disappointing to their sponsors, or simply ignored (as the experience of the 1866 Civil Rights Act demonstrated for eighty years). A constitutional right rests on a more stable foundation because it is secure from the vagaries of politics. A constitutionally based right to housing, for example, might provide a broad platform for assaults on urban residential segregation patterns. And if the Constitution secures one fundamental human necessity, housing, then why not others? Clothing, nutrition, medical care, and education could be eligible candidates. Beyond sweeping away public and perhaps even private impediments to such access, might such a right include a positive mandate on the state to provide it when an individual could not do so on her own? All this and more could grow out of the seed that Brennan may have been planting in his casual observation. Considering what grew out of *Carolene Products*' footnote 4 after 1938, the possibilities were limited only by a liberal judge's imagination, as Harlan warned in his *Shapiro* dissent.[11]

Thus, it may have reasonably appeared to the emergent conservative bloc on the Court in 1970 that this was indeed in the offing. Harlan moved quickly to tamp down the unwelcome potential for activism growing out of an enlarged sense of equal protection that might extend to housing and "other necessities of life." The opportunity soon appeared in a Maryland case challenging a $250 state-imposed cap on Aid to Families with Dependent Children, *Dandridge v. Williams* (1970).[12] Upholding the limit, Justice Stewart rejected an equal protection challenge to the cap. It would be Lochnerizing for the Court to assume this role, he claimed, but now under the equal protection rather than the due process clause. Two years later, the Court spurned a claim that shelter constituted a fundamental interest protected by the equal protection clause. There is no "constitutional guarantee of access to dwellings," Justice White insisted in *Lindsey v. Normet* (1972).[13] "The Court does not provide judicial remedies for every social and economic ill," he wrote. "The assurance of adequate housing" is a responsibility of legislatures, not courts. This foreclosed the possibility that the Court might take on a proactive role in attacking the bases of residential segregation. With that, the fundamental-rights gambit expired, and with it, the potential for developing an equal protection critique of structural racism. Hopes for a constitutional protection for access to housing faded and struggles over residential segregation moved on to other fronts. The failure of Brennan's initiative was a portent of worse to come.

The worse-to-come soon arrived in the person of William H. Rehnquist, newly minted associate justice. Seven weeks after Rehnquist took his seat, the Court heard arguments in *Moose Lodge v. Irvis* (1972).[14] This case provided the occasion for his debut opinion, in which he tried to stifle any potential for growth in the equal protection clause. *Moose Lodge* raised the problem of state action again. A private fraternal organization refused to serve an African American guest of a member and he sued, alleging racial discrimination by the action of the state. He relied on a theory broached by the first Justice Harlan in the *Civil Rights Cases* of 1873, the original source of the state action doctrine.[15] In his lone dissent, Harlan there advanced two theories that would permit federal anti-discrimination laws to reach the actions of private parties. First, corporations, particularly those like inns that serve the public, are "quasi-public" in nature, and as such have an obligation to serve all members of the public without discrimination. Second, the defendants operated their bar under a license from the state and could not do business without one. Thus, the state was implicated by granting the liquor license that was a sine qua non of doing business. "A license from the public to establish a place of public amusement imports, in law, equality of right, at such places, of all members of the public," Harlan wrote. Discriminatory refusal amounted to the "badges and incidents of slavery" banned by the Thirteenth Amendment. The Court has never accepted these arguments, and the state action doctrine reigned supreme until mid-century.

The state action doctrine has imposed a tight constraint on federal power under the equal protection clause. The clause and the state action doctrine stand in an inverse relationship to each other, as in a zero-sum game. If the state action doctrine expands, the scope of the equal protection clause contracts, and vice versa. If the doctrine itself could be narrowed or confined, federal power to protect against racial discrimination of the sort practiced by the Moose Lodge would expand.

In the twentieth century, the Supreme Court had constricted the state action doctrine in several significant ways. In *Marsh v. Alabama* (1946),[16] it held that when a private entity like a corporation performed "public functions" normally undertaken by the state, state action was involved. In *Shelley v. Kraemer* (1948),[17] the Court found state action when state instrumentalities like courts or police agencies enforced discriminatory private agreements. *Burton v. Wilmington Parking Authority* (1961)[18] found state action when there was "state participation and involvement" in the discriminatory private actor's conduct. *Reitman v. Mulkey* (1967)[19] found such state involvement when the state, acting through its sovereign people, "facilitated" racial discrimination.

Thus by 1972, a momentum seemed to be building over twenty years toward an ever-narrower reading of the state action doctrine. It seemed to be becoming a rule eaten away by exceptions. Rehnquist brought that momentum to an abrupt close. In *Moose Lodge*, he rejected Harlan I's expansive reading, holding that mere licensing did not implicate the state in private discrimination. There being no state action involved in Moose Lodge's discriminatory actions, plaintiff had no remedy. No civil rights statute, either that of 1866 or that of 1964, could be applied. In reaching that conclusion, Rehnquist signaled how narrow was his understanding of the equal protection clause. In a later case, he wrote disparagingly that "except in the area of the law in which the Framers obviously meant [the clause] to apply—classifications based on race or on national origin, the first cousin of race—the Court's decisions can fairly be described as an endless tinkering with legislative judgments, a series of conclusions unsupported by any central guiding principle."[20] Never a friend of racial equality, for the next thirty years Rehnquist would bring his colleagues closer to his view.

Discriminatory Intent versus Disparate Impact: *Washington v. Davis*

American society is perfused by structural racism. The most pressing problem for the social order today is the structural inequality created by social mechanisms that produce Black disadvantage and white benefit. When this problem is translated into constitutional and legal terms, the issue becomes whether the power of government to remedy structural racism requires a challenger to prove that the wrong complained of was created by someone's deliberate intention to discriminate, or whether it would be constitutionally sufficient for the complainant to show significant differential impact.[21]

This issue was not pressing in a society where overt discrimination prevailed, the Jim Crow America of 1872–1954. Then, invidious intent was obvious or could be readily inferred. So when *Brown v. Board of Education* held that overt discrimination was a per se violation of the clause,[22] it settled the issue, at least conceptually. (Eradicating its lingering remnants has proved to be a long and difficult process, though.) But in a society where overt discrimination is at least nominally illegal and unconstitutional when practiced by government, can a claim of disparate impact caused by government action (or inaction), without a showing of discriminatory intent, clear the constitutional hurdle? The Constitution itself does not impose such a bar. The equal protection clause simply states that "No state shall... deny to any person within its jurisdiction the equal protection of the laws." Neither as matter of the plain meaning of words nor of the framers' intent is it obvious that a showing of explicit intent is required.[23] Thus, the intent/impact issue must be resolved by judicial interpretation.

In doing so, the Court must determine the meaning and effect of the equal protection clause itself. Consider a spectrum of possible interpretations of the clause: at one extreme, a strict requirement of intent would force the challenger to prove in every case that federal or state actors made their choices with the deliberate intent of disadvantaging people of color and/or preserving white advantage. Such a requirement would practically render the equal protection clause a dead letter. (Extreme as it is, though, this reading of the clause has come close to being accepted by a majority of the Court.)[24] An individual's intention is difficult or impossible to prove reliably. Where the intent must be attributed to a body of people, like a legislature, the impossibility is compounded by the difficulty of assigning a single intent to a group of divergent individuals, some of whom disagree with the outcome.

Yet at the opposite extreme, a pure disparate impact requirement would invalidate all legislation or policy choices. Any policy decision that affects a large group of people is bound to have different impacts on the individuals and groups affected. A requirement of absolute uniformity of impact would be impossible. The stronger the intent requirement, the less likely it will be that a civil rights claim will succeed. Conversely, if the intent requirement is relaxed, civil right claims stand a better chance of success.

Any workable solution to this seeming dilemma must identify some principled rule between these extremes of intent versus impact, finding a resolution that avoids settling too close to either pole. The rule must meet the legitimate demands of both sides: those who demand some reasonable intentionality and those who want to make policy choices possible at all. If a principled rule proves elusive, then at least we must find a viable, flexible compromise that meets some of objectives of both sides. This roughly describes the Supreme Court's attempt so far to find some solution to the intent/impact dilemma.

The debate over the intent/impact dichotomy is important because it may determine whether structural racism is an actionable evil that the government may address. A strict requirement that a civil rights plaintiff show discriminatory intent in order to obtain relief will effectively shut down most civil rights challenges except those based on de jure discrimination (where intent is obvious on the face of the statute) or those rare unicorn cases where the plaintiff can actually prove intent. Such a holding could be the *Plessy v. Ferguson* for the twenty-first century: a precedent that accepts all forms of racial inequity except those that are overtly and deliberately racist.

This broad problem first came before the Court in a dispute that involved the construction of a statute, not the Constitution itself. *Griggs v. Duke Power Co.* (1971)[25] interpreted Title VII of the Civil Rights Act of 1964, the ban on racial discrimination in employment. After the 1964 statute was enacted, the Court immediately upheld Congress's power to enact Title II, which dealt with public accommodations.[26] It faced no comparable direct challenge to Title VII at that time. Instead, the issues coming before the Court involved the scope and application of Title VII, not its constitutionality. Thus, the justices did not at first have to confront the underlying equal protection constitutional questions.

In its key provisions, Title VII prohibits any employer from limiting an employee's opportunities "because of such individual's race [or] color," and permits the use of "any professionally developed ability test," provided that the test was not "intended or used to discriminate because of race [or] color."[27] The employer in this case, Duke Power Company, had a long history of proven racial discrimination.[28] It required a high school diploma and aptitude tests for advancement out of the lowest ranks (general labor and janitorial). Willie Griggs challenged this requirement on the grounds that North Carolina's history of limiting educational opportunities for African Americans had deprived them of the opportunity to get a high school education. He did not claim intentional discrimination, but only that Title VII had been violated because of a racially disparate impact in the company's promotion policies.

In a remarkably short opinion, considering the stakes involved, Chief Justice Burger wrote for a unanimous Court that "the Act proscribes not only overt discrimination, but also practices that are fair in form, but discriminatory in operation." The company could justify its practice if it was driven by "business necessity," but only if that was "related to job performance." "Good intent or absence of discriminatory intent does not redeem employment procedures or testing mechanisms that operate as 'built-in headwinds' for minority groups," he added. Business practices were illegitimate under the act if they "operate[d] to 'freeze' the status quo of prior discriminatory employment practices."[29]

Griggs was "the most significant employment discrimination case of the civil rights era,"[30] and second only to *Brown* in its sweeping impact on American society generally.[31] It "ushered in one of the greatest social movements in the history of this nation because it opened up jobs...previously limited to white males,...for millions of African Americans, women, Latino/as, Asian Americans, and Native Americans."[32] But it also marked the end of an era, a time when the Court was responsive to the realities that African Americans faced in a segregated society. *Griggs* was one of the last cases when the Supreme Court resolved minority-group claims of disparate effects without requiring some showing of discriminatory intent. When the Court returned to the issue five years later a much different outcome ensued.

Contemporaries recognized that the disparate impact criterion set forth in *Griggs* was far-reaching and assumed that it would apply in constitutional interpretation as well.[33] That assumption was soon tested in a case before the Court of Appeals for the DC Circuit in an appeal in 1975 challenging tests imposed for recruits by the District of Columbia Metropolitan Police Department. The tests gauged reading ability and comprehension, as well as verbal fluency. In practice, the tests filtered out a disproportionate number of Black applicants, and the trial court found that it had not been proven to measure subsequent performance on the job.[34] When the case came before the Supreme Court, the justices at first considered it a relatively unimportant version of the *Griggs* problem. But one of Justice Powell's law clerks alerted him to the distinction between statutory and a constitutional bases for challenges to workplace discrimination. Impact might be enough for a statutory claim, she suggested, but a constitutional challenge required more. At conference, the conservative justices came around to that view.[35]

In *Washington v. Davis* (1976),[36] the Supreme Court speaking through Justice Byron White reversed the lower court, stating that "we have not held that a law, neutral on its face and serving ends otherwise within the power of government to pursue, is invalid under the Equal Protection Clause simply because it may affect a greater proportion of one race than of another." White announced "the basic equal protection principle that the invidious quality of a law claimed to be racially discriminatory must ultimately be traced to a racially discriminatory purpose."[37] "It does not follow that a law or other official act is unconstitutional solely because it has a racially disproportionate impact regardless of whether it reflects a racially discriminatory purpose." A law "neutral on its face" is to be judged by deferential scrutiny: it "rationally may be said to serve a purpose the Government is constitutionally empowered to pursue."[38] White linked the purpose-impact distinction to the anticlassification principle, which would interpret the equal protection clause to forbid any state classification by race unless it meets stringent strict scrutiny requirements: "Disproportionate impact is not irrelevant, but it is not the sole touchstone of an invidious racial discrimination forbidden by the Constitution. Standing alone, it does not trigger the rule that racial classifications are to be subjected to the strictest scrutiny and are justifiable only by the weightiest of considerations."[39]

Justice White admitted that "we have difficulty understanding" how any facially neutral statute could be discriminatory simply because it generated unequal results,[40] thereby explicitly conceding for the first time that the Court did not understand the workings of structural racism. (To be fair, sociologists were only beginning to work out the theory at that time.) He did make one important concession to civil rights plaintiffs though: "Necessarily, an invidious discriminatory purpose may often be inferred from the totality of the relevant facts, including the fact, if it is true, that the law bears more heavily on one race than another."[41] This potentially opened through the back door a limited possibility of showing disparate impact, but only as an auxiliary to the intent requirement.

The triumph of the purpose requirement announced in *Washington v. Davis* solidified the racial stratification of American society.[42] After the end of the first Reconstruction, *Plessy v. Ferguson* confirmed that the equal protection clause would not prohibit Jim Crow; after the end of the second Reconstruction, *Davis* confirmed that the clause would not disturb structural inequality. As the *Slaughterhouse Cases* of 1873 were the pivot from the egalitarianism of the first Reconstruction to the pretextuality of Redemption, so *Washington v. Davis* pivoted from the egalitarianism of the second Reconstruction to sustain structural racism in the second Redemption. In Justin Driver's opinion, it was "the single most influential opinion in shaping the Fourteenth Amendment's racial landscape during the last five decades."[43]

A casual dictum by Justice White toward the end of his opinion revealed that the Court was willing to consider disparate impact, but only when it burdened whites. The rule sought by the respondents "would be far-reaching and would raise serious questions about, and perhaps invalidate, a whole range of tax, welfare, public service, regulatory, and licensing statutes that may be more burdensome to the poor and to the average black than to the more affluent white."[44] So the purpose-impact test was not neutral between the races after all. It sustained social practices like aptitude testing when they disproportionately burdened African Americans, but it used those practices to protect the racial status quo that benefited "the more affluent white." The equal protection clause, which its framers deliberately designed to benefit African Americans, was on its way to becoming a bastion instead that protected white advantage.

The *Davis* intent requirement fails in multiple ways. It is speculative, incoherent, inconsistently applied, and incompatible with prior precedent. Only five years earlier, in *Palmer v. Thompson* (1971),[45] a case involving closure of municipal swimming pools to avoid integration, the Court held that discriminatory intent behind the closure was irrelevant and, in any event, impossible to identify definitively.[46] Individual intent is complex and difficult to discern, and any attempt to do so, even where circumstantial evidence is overwhelming, must remain speculative. Collective intent, as for a legislature, is exponentially more difficult and elusive. Most importantly, the Court has refused to consider the problem of unconscious bias as a component of intent, a critical failing in the era of structural inequality.[47]

The intent requirement embodies an implicit white understanding of color-blindness and ignores the problem that facially neutral norms are based on white presuppositions about such things as merit and neutrality. This has the effect of imposing such white norms, which is itself a form of unconscious and unintended discrimination. This is known as the "transparency phenomenon," an aspect of white normativity that sees white cultural assumptions as neutral, obvious, and normal.[48] This in turn perpetuates white advantage, which whites believe is "neutral, normal, and available to everybody."[49]

Davis "tamed" *Brown v. Board of Education*, in the sense that it shied away from *Brown*'s far-reaching egalitarian implications and possibilities, retreating backward into a narrow and timid reading that left *Brown* declawed when it was needed to deal with issues that go beyond overt, intentional racism.[50] *Davis* has failed to provide a coherent or persuasive guide to resolving issues of veterans' preferences, reduction in welfare benefits, workplace discrimination, and racial harassment. Just as *Slaughterhouse* constrained the Reconstruction Amendments at the end of the first Reconstruction, *Washington v. Davis* brought *Brown* to heel a century later, shutting down the full racial justice potential of the equal protection clause.

Washington v. Davis embedded what the legal scholar Alan Freeman called the perpetrator perspective in the law of equal protection.[51] From the perpetrator perspective, racial discrimination consists only of a willful violation of some extant, legally binding rule. To show an actionable wrong, a civil rights petitioner must prove wrongful intent plus actions by a specific person who committed an identifiable discriminatory act. In analogous criminal law terms, there must be both mens rea and actus reus.[52] The remedy should be limited to punishing the violation and be no broader than that particular violation. This understanding of "discrimination" is based on ideas of causation and fault, derived from tort law. There must be a blameworthy cause of the harm complained of (the discriminatory act), a purpose to discriminate (intent), and a harmful effect (a measurable wrong to the victim). The perpetrator perspective is blind to structural racism because it requires intent, stringently defined. A contrasting victim perspective, on the other hand, would look to the effects of societal structures. It asks whether the conditions complained of (such as workplace disadvantage) are the product of racial oppression, understood both sociologically and historically.

Washington v. Davis has had far-reaching, destructive effects on civil rights litigation. At the doctrinal level, its requirement of proving intent metastasized to frustrate Thirteenth Amendment badges-of-slavery claims of discrimination based on racial animus,[53] and to voting rights claims based on the Fifteenth Amendment.[54] It restrained lower courts from vigorous civil rights enforcement, becoming the foremost setback to the movement since 1954. It "places the nearly impossible burden of proof and persuasion on those who have experienced the exclusion.... it asks the victim to go into the mind of the perpetrator and demonstrate that there exists an unconstitutional motivation."[55]

The *Davis* discriminatory-purpose requirement reduced both the volume and the success rates of constitutionally based civil rights litigation. Fewer claims based on intent were filed thereafter; even fewer were successful; and almost none were awarded damages. At the appellate level virtually no appeals (fewer than 1 percent) were successful, while few trial-court decisions were appealed.[56] The resulting disparity between the volume of potential claims (vast) and the number litigated to a successful conclusion (few) was wide.[57] It produced the paradoxical result that since 1990 an ever-increasing volume of employment discrimination results in fewer awards in individual cases: more litigation, less justice. Plaintiffs typically receive neither their day in court nor a meaningful remedy. It is at best a system of "uncertain justice."[58] The "discriminatory purpose" requirement of *Washington v. Davis* was the object of extensive contemporary criticism,[59] and its reputation has not improved over the years.[60]

One partial solution to the distortions imposed by the *Davis* intent requirement would be a requirement that the legislature consider all impacts of its activities on communities of color. The state of Maine enacted such legislation in 2021. The Maine statute mandates a review process for all legislation being considered "for potential impacts on historically disadvantaged populations. Legislative committees would have the authority to request and receive data needed to assess potential impacts from state departments and agencies."[61] Though this would not eliminate structural racism entirely, it would have the salutary effect of requiring legislators to consider racial impacts as they enact public policies.

The discriminatory-intent requirement of *Davis* was the Burger Court's major contribution to the second Redemption. The Court's growing insistence on intent reflected white backlash against African Americans' claims for equality. As its intent requirement was confirmed and expanded, disparate impact became increasingly irrelevant. The stronger the judicial insistence on a showing of discriminatory intent, the less significant became the social consequences of the policy being challenged. Yet while the Court became ever-more-demanding that Black plaintiffs prove intent, it subjected remedial programs like affirmative action to ever sharper scrutiny, with less deference to legislative authority to determine public policy. Under the regime of *Carolene Products*, the Court had been solicitous of the interests of "discrete and insular minorities." But after *Washington v. Davis* it became vigilant to protect the privileges of the white majority. Judicial doctrine became divorced from the reality of racial disparities. The Burger Court, in tandem with the Reagan administration after 1981, pushed back against claims for racial equality, replacing its former concerns for racial justice with solicitude for white innocence.[62]

After 1972, the Supreme Court's equal protection jurisprudence became "bifurcated," in Reva Siegel's terms. In one branch, where a white plaintiff challenges a racial classification made by the state, the plaintiff need not show a discriminatory purpose; disparate impact is often sufficient to invalidate the regulation. When such impact is proven more merely alleged, the Court subjects what it considers to be racial classifications to the strictest scrutiny. This approach characterized the Court's handling of affirmative action cases.[63] But when a Black plaintiff challenges some state action because of the harmful impact it has on minorities, the Court switches to a mode of extreme deference to legislative judgment. The result has been "a form of judicial review that cares more about protecting members of majority groups from actions of representative government that promote minority opportunities than it cares about protecting 'discrete and insular minorities' from actions of representative government that reflect prejudice."[64]

The second Reconstruction rested on two pillars: the concern for "discrete and insular minorities" identified in *Carolene Products*, and the commitment to equality exemplified in *Brown v. Board of Education*. This produced the judicial component of the second Reconstruction, with its heightened concern for the impact of social policy on African Americans. The struggles of the 1970s over school desegregation, followed by a generation of conflict over affirmative action, clove the equal protection cases coming to the court into two branches, one producing favorable outcomes for whites who challenge programs designed to cope with structural racism, the other generating adverse outcomes for Black parties who complain of the effects of governmental action. There the Court ignores disparate impact. Put bluntly, equal protection law in the twenty-first century has come to protect the interests of the white majority and disfavor the claims of the Black minority.

Despite its intent requirement, *Davis* had nevertheless left open some possibility of introducing evidence of disparate impact.[65] But even this slender concession proved too much for those determined to ignore the significance of disparate effects. In a gender discrimination case decided three years after *Davis, Personnel Administrator v. Feeney* (1979),[66] the Court almost strangled the disparate impact test in the cradle. Massachusetts granted military veterans an arbitrary point preference in civil service exams in hiring over non-veterans, no matter how well the non-vets had performed. At the time, only 2 percent of Massachusetts veterans were women. The trial court found that this had "a devastating impact upon the employment opportunities of women,"[67] relegating them permanently to the lowest-paid rungs of the civil service ladder, the traditionally female occupations of stenographers and clerks. The Court, speaking through Justice Stewart, ratcheted up the *Davis* intent requirement by holding that it "implies more than intent as volition or intent as awareness of consequences. It implies that the decisionmaker, in this case a state legislature, selected or reaffirmed a particular course of action at least in part 'because of,' not merely 'in spite of,' its adverse effects upon an identifiable group."[68] Mere awareness of a possible result, no matter how likely or even certain that result, is insufficient to prove or even infer motivation. Justice Stewart misleadingly declared that "the Fourteenth Amendment guarantees equal laws, not equal results."[69] But of course it does neither; it guarantees the equal *protection* of the laws, and such protection might reasonably be interpreted to prohibit systematically unfavorable outcomes for African American parties.[70]

For constitutional purposes, *Feeney* adopted a standard of intent and foreseeability greater than the usual torts negligence standard, something closer to malice.[71] Tort law draws a distinction between intentional torts, where the plaintiff must prove defendant's intent to commit an act that will have particular consequences, and torts of negligence, where the standard is that "the person acts knowing that the consequence is substantially certain to result."[72] As an example, the latest iteration of the *Torts* Restatement offers an example to illustrate this negligence concept of intent: "The Jones Company runs an aluminum smelter, which emits particulate fluorides as part of the industrial process. Jones knows that these particles, carried by the air, will land on neighboring property, and in doing so will bring about a range of harms. Far from desiring this result, Jones in fact regrets it. Despite its regret, Jones has knowingly, and hence intentionally, caused the resulting harms."[73] Similarly, the Model Penal Code provides that an individual criminal defendant acts "knowingly" where "he is aware that his conduct is of that nature or that such circumstances exist."[74] Why should these standards be inoperable in an equal protection claim?

In a later capital sentencing case, *McCleskey v. Kemp* (1987),[75] the Court went even further in exalting intent. Justice Powell's majority opinion make it virtually impossible for a defendant of color to prove that a legislature acted in a way that made it more likely that he would be sentenced to death because he is not white. Powell held that "to prevail under the Equal Protection Clause, [defendant] must prove that the decisionmakers in his case acted with discriminatory purpose."[76] A person sentenced to death must now "prove that the...Legislature enacted or maintained the death penalty statute because of an anticipated racially discriminatory effect."[77] The Court thus moved the goalposts still further away from civil rights plaintiffs: on top of the *Washington v. Davis* intent requirement, plaintiffs under *Feeney* must show something approaching actual malice and under *McCleskey* that the legislature's malice was directed specifically at them or at least at their class of cases. Once the intent requirement was raised to such alpine heights, the Court ended up with this perverse result: policies that in their effects discriminate against African Americans can be successfully challenged only by proving discriminatory intent by standards almost impossible to satisfy. But programs benefiting Blacks and Latinos are subjected to a scrutiny so strict that almost none can meet it, at least for constitutional equal protection claims.

With these heightened constitutional criteria for intent in place, the Court then retrofitted them for cases involving statutory, not constitutional construction, calling into question the continuing relevance of *Griggs*. A year after *Davis* was decided, in *International Brotherhood of Teamsters v. United States* (1977),[78] the Court took up the recurring problem of Title VII's impact on existing seniority systems. Did it invalidate all seniority systems created before 1964 that were based on then-current discriminatory hiring practices? The problem pitted two legitimate but competing interests against each other: Black employees insisting that such systems were unconstitutional because of the continuing effects of discrimination, versus the interests of white employees covered under the system, who resisted having their seniority reduced. (Seniority can be considered an existing property right, or at least an expectation.) *Teamsters* construed a provision of the 1964 act, section 703(h), which exempted seniority systems established before the effective date of the act,[79] to include seniority systems that perpetuated the effects of prior discrimination. This had the effect of legitimating the locked-in discrimination that was the product of pre-1964 seniority systems, which were based on various widespread discriminatory hiring practices. The Court extended this tendency to denigrate discriminatory impact in *American Tobacco Co. v. Patterson* (1982),[80] which held that section 703(h) exempted seniority systems adopted after 1964, expanding the protection of whites' interests at the expense of more recently hired Black employees.

So enamored was the Court of its discriminatory purpose requirement that it then imposed it requirement on the modern descendants of the 1866 Civil Rights Act. *General Building Contractors Association v. Pennsylvania* (1982)[81] confronted the ineradicable problem of labor union discrimination in the skilled building trades. African American would-be heavy equipment operators sued a contractors' association, employers, and the union, alleging discrimination in hiring practices arising from collusion between the union and contractors. At issue was the reach of section 1981,[82] the modern descendant of section 1 of the 1866 act, which provides that "all persons within the jurisdiction of the United States shall have the same right in every State and Territory to make and enforce contracts." Justice Rehnquist held that "[section] 1981 reaches only purposeful discrimination."[83]

Access to the Ballot

Before 1970, the history of American democracy was a story of the "continuing expansion of the scope of the right of suffrage in this country," as Chief Justice Earl Warren observed in *Reynolds v. Sims* (1964).[84] At the time of American Independence, the number and proportion of enfranchised citizens were small by modern standards. Historians estimate that only about a tenth of the people living in what was then the United States could vote in 1790. In general, that empowered tenth had to be white, male, free, adult, a citizen, literate, property-owning, and Christian. In the antebellum era, the reforms of Jacksonian democracy discarded religious and property qualifications (for white men). The temporary triumph of Reconstruction eliminated racial qualifications (but not sex).[85] Redemption reinstalled the racial barrier throughout the South by the twentieth century. The sex barrier fell with the Nineteenth Amendment in 1920. The civil rights movement attempted to restore political power to African Americans through the Voting Rights Act of 1965. In 1971, the Twenty-Sixth Amendment lowered the definition of adulthood to eighteen years old.[86]

After the *Carolene Products* footnote 4 in 1938 emphasized the importance of political equality,[87] the Court has identified the vote, when given, as a fundamental right. In *Harper v. Virginia State Board of Elections* (1966), Justice Douglas reiterated the principle that "voting [is] a fundamental political right, because preservative of all other rights."[88] The vindication of this right began in earnest with the Warren Court's foundational reapportionment decisions: *Baker v. Carr* (1962),[89] which was implicitly about race (though none of the opinions acknowledged it), and *Reynolds v. Sims* (1964).[90] "The Constitution of the United States protects the right of all qualified citizens to vote, in state as well as in federal elections," Chief Justice Warren there held. In these cases, the fundamental interests strand of the equal protection clause came to the fore. *South Carolina v. Katzenbach* (1966) upheld the constitutionality of the 1965 Voting Rights Act, declaring the Fifteenth Amendment to be self-executing. This meant that of its own force it rendered state discriminatory election practices unconstitutional, without the need for enforcement legislation.[91] At the same time, the Court struck down the poll tax in state elections in *Harper v. Virginia State Board of Elections* (1966).[92] *Harper's* conception of rights as dynamic and expansive was a characteristic of the second Reconstruction. But it has atrophied since 1970, at least when made the basis of claims by African Americans.

A cascade of voting rights decisions followed *Harper*, rounding out the second Reconstruction. *Kramer v. Union Free School District* (1969) inched toward imposing strict scrutiny on any state statute that classified and excluded voters in certain elections,[93] and in *Dunn v. Blumstein* (1972)[94] the Court explicitly adopted strict scrutiny for any restriction on the right to vote (in this case a durational residence requirement of fifteen months). "By denying some citizens the right to vote, such laws deprive them of 'a fundamental political right [that is] preservative of all rights,'" reviving a Reconstruction-era theme that had marshaled support for the Fifteenth Amendment. The Court struck down multimember districting schemes that diluted the minority vote in the district.[95] It was likewise hostile to annexation schemes that added white residents to dilute the minority vote.[96]

Inspiring as that trajectory seemed at the time, it was derailed by the Burger, Rehnquist, and Roberts Courts. The ability to vote has always been contested and precarious. Alexander Keyssar reminds us that universal suffrage is not inevitable, and that an established right to vote can be, and has been, lost in local political struggles.[97] That is occurring in the second Redemption. After 2008, some states reprised the earlier Redemption by again imposing racial barriers to voting by reviving Jim Crow pretextuality. The current proponents of racial disfranchisement avoid doing this overtly, and, unlike the first Redemption, rarely avow their racial intent. But steadily, implacably, Republicans screened out African Americans from the voting booth even before the explosion of vote suppression laws in the aftermath of the 2020 election. Morgan Kousser's meticulous studies have demonstrated that this process is continuous, subtle, adaptable, incessant, deceptive—and successful.[98] Since 1970, the US Supreme Court has consistently supported, legitimized, and even lauded this effort. The Court's opinions, wrote Kousser, "were blatantly contradictory, cynically unprincipled, as full of racial and partisan double standards as they were of inflammatory and misleading logic and based on a bizarre and distorted version of the history of American race relations."[99] The Court's encounters with racial disfranchisement in the second Redemption took place in four areas: felon disfranchisement, racial gerrymandering, vote suppression, and the neutering of the 1965 Voting Rights Act.

The practice of denying the vote to persons who have been convicted of a felony traces back to the early Republic (and before that, to antiquity, in the concept of "civil death").[100] In the modern era, felon disenfranchisement in the United States has become more extreme and extensive than in any other democratic government. Its impact is not limited to the felons themselves. The mere existence of disenfranchisement reduces voter participation by those not immediately involved, with African Americans unsurprisingly being the most severely affected.[101] Because voter qualifications in the American federal system are the sole province of the states, the conditions of felon disenfranchisement vary widely, from lifetime disability to complete restoration upon completion of sentence.[102] (Maine and Vermont even permit convicted felons to vote while still serving their sentences.) In some states, as many as one in four African American males are barred from voting because of a felony conviction. Nationwide, one in thirteen are under this disability.[103]

In the first Redemption, southern whites resorted to felon disenfranchisement as one more weapon in their arsenal to strip newly enfranchised

African Americans of political power.[104] Alabama, for example, in its 1901 constitutional revision expanded the list of felonies that would incur disenfranchisement to include "living in adultery" and vagrancy, behaviors that whites attributed to African Americans. Together with other elements of the Mississippi Plan, including the poll tax, literacy tests, residency requirements, and voter registration, disenfranchisement ensured that by World War I, Black political power had been annihilated in the South.[105]

It is technically correct, but empty to the point of being meaningless, to assert that there is no constitutionally secured general right of any person to vote.[106] Chief Justice Morrison Waite asserted in dictum in 1875 that "the Fifteenth Amendment does not confer the right of suffrage upon any one."[107] Nor, he may as well have added, does any other provision of the Constitution. The states may—indeed, must—determine the qualifications of voters. In doing so, however, they may not make invidious distinctions among those they have qualified. "Our Constitution leaves no room for classification of people in a way that unnecessarily abridges this right," the Court held at the peak of the second Reconstruction.[108] The Supreme Court has repeatedly held in the modern era that the states may not deny or dilute this right once it is accorded. "Once the franchise is granted to the electorate, lines may not be drawn which are inconsistent with the Equal Protection Clause of the Fourteenth Amendment," the Court declared in *Harper v. Virginia State Board of Elections*, (1966).[109] "The Equal Protection Clause confers the substantive right to participate on an equal basis with other qualified voters whenever the State has adopted an electoral process for determining who will represent any segment of the State's population."[110]

Up to 1970, the trajectory of expanding access to be ballot seemed to confirm the historic growth of electoral democracy that had characterized American experience for two centuries. Thus, when this expansion was suddenly stymied in 1974, it came as a shock. In 1973, the California Supreme Court had held that the state's constitutional and statutory felon disfranchisement provisions violated the federal equal protection clause.[111] But the US Supreme Court, speaking through Justice Rehnquist in *Richardson v. Ramirez*,[112] reversed, holding that felon disenfranchisement "has an affirmative sanction in section 2 of the Fourteenth Amendment." Section 2 prohibits the states from denying or abridging "the right to vote" in federal and state elections, "except for participation in rebellion, or other crime." It might be argued[113] that the phrase "or other crime" is textually bounded by "rebellion" and thus refers only to criminal acts committed in the course of rebellion, but most modern authority interprets it to refer to felonies of all sorts. Read in this way, section 2 might provide a constitutional affirmation of the idea that felon disenfranchisement is legitimate, recognized by the supreme law. But whatever the expectations of its framers, section 2 was a dead letter from the outset. Congress never enacted enforcement legislation of any sort, and no court has ever entertained litigation seeking its implementation. Rehnquist argued that the equal protection clause "could not have been meant to bar outright a form of disenfranchisement which was expressly exempted from the less drastic sanction of reduced representation which section 2 imposed for other forms of disenfranchisement."[114]

Justice Marshall, joined by Brennan, dissented in a lengthy opinion that shredded both the procedural ground and the historical justification of Rehnquist's opinion. Marshall insisted that because suffrage was a fundamental right, the equal protection clause required that denials of it be subjected to strict scrutiny. It failed both prongs of that test. But he argued in vain. In the modern Redemption, the Supreme Court has been cool, if not hostile, to the interests of African Americans in securing access to political power, and tolerant of most Republican efforts to restrict that access.

Richardson presents a tragic irony. Congress adopted section 2 specifically with the aim of protecting Black suffrage. But Rehnquist's opinion instead interpreted it to disenfranchise a class of persons disproportionately African American. This has become especially true in the era of mass incarceration that began at the same time.[115] Under Rehnquist's interpretation, as a component of Jim Crow, felon disenfranchisement is uniquely insulated from equal protection challenges, unlike literacy tests and other suffrage-related components of the Mississippi Plan. In this, it is emblematic of how the modern Court has inverted the values of the first Reconstruction. A provision meant to empower African Americans has instead become a means of stripping away their power and agency.

Felon disenfranchisement and its justification in Rehnquist's *Richardson* majority opinion have been universally condemned.[116] Most critiques rely on either the equal protection clause or section 2 of the Voting Rights Act, but Gabriel Chin contends that section 2 of the Fourteenth Amendment was implicitly nullified if not repealed by the Fifteenth Amendment.[117] He suggests that "Section 2 [of the Fourteenth Amendment] is not a venerated part of the current Constitution, but instead part of a brief political experiment quickly recognized as a mistake and then abandoned." That historical judgment seems exactly right, but the modern Court has shown no disposition to revisit Rehnquist's shallow judgment. In the meantime, some states are attempting piecemeal reform through the political process. Florida, for example, by a popular referendum in 2018, abolished lifetime disfranchisement for most felonies. But they were thwarted by a Republican legislature hostile to the reform, which enacted legislation requiring payment of all associated fees and costs (for most affected persons, an effective practical bar). A federal district court held the legislation unconstitutional,[118] but the US Supreme Court refused to stay a court of appeals order vacating that decision. In dissent, Justice Sonia Sotomayor condemned "Florida's voter paywall" and "pay-to-vote scheme."[119] The political struggle continues, while felon disfranchisement continues to prevail in most jurisdictions.

Some states have restricted the Black vote by gerrymandering—drawing the boundaries of political districts in ways that benefit a party in power or a particular demographic group. The term itself derives from one of the earliest gerrymanders, pulled off in 1812 by the Revolutionary-era figure Massachusetts governor Elbridge Gerry, who gave the practice its eponymous name thanks to a critical editorial and one of the most influential political cartoons in American history.[120] But gerrymandering is not just a historical curiosity; it is rife and recurrent today. Even when race is not directly implicated, the Supreme Court has been flummoxed by challenges to it.

Litigation challenging the constitutionality of gerrymanders (both partisan and racial) raises the problem of justiciability, a vague but indispensable quality of a lawsuit that qualifies it as suitable for being resolved by a court. Can and should a court "intrude on this most political of legislative functions?" asked Justice White in a plurality opinion in *Davis v. Bandemer* (1986),[121] a decision that set up this critical question but did not answer it. Eventually, the Court gave up on the project. In *Rucho v. Common Cause* (2019), it held that political gerrymandering cases, untainted by racial issues, are non-justiciable.[122]

The Court thereby withdrew from the problem of partisan gerrymanders, but the issue of racial gerrymanders persists. Overlaying a racial component makes the problem of gerrymandering vastly more complicated, both as a matter of constitutional doctrine and as a problem of feasibility. The original racial gerrymander involved white communities redrawing district bounds or annexing surrounding territory to preserve a white majority as the African American community grew. This is known as a "negative racial gerrymander." The Court had little trouble striking that practice down in the second Reconstruction. In *Gomillion v. Lightfoot* (1960),[123] the Court was confronted with a glaring example: the white majority population of Tuskegee, Alabama, redrew their city's boundaries from a square to what Justice Felix Frankfurter described as an "uncouth twenty-eight sided figure" that managed to oust the entire Black population (including the community affiliated with the Tuskegee Institute, one of the nation's foremost Black centers of higher education.) "Even within familiar abuses of gerrymandering," Frankfurter confidently asserted, "the legislation is solely concerned with segregating white and colored voters by fencing Negro citizens out of town so as to deprive them of their pre-existing municipal vote." Frankfurter brushed aside the problem of inferring intent: a map reprinted with the opinion showed how blatant the exclusionary move was. But later courts would not find it so easy to ascribe malign intent even when it was as obvious. Perhaps the pictorial proof provided by the map was indeed worth a thousand words. Frankfurter had to rely solely on the Fifteenth Amendment because the Voting Rights Act was five years in the future. Justice Charles Whittaker, in one of his rare opinions, concurred to suggest that the equal protection clause was a superior candidate for the job.

In *Gaffney v. Cummings* (1973),[124] the Court observed that nonracial political or partisan gerrymandering is inevitable and constitutionally unobjectionable if it seeks to "provide a rough sort of proportional representation" in the legislature. However, proportional representation has never been fully acclimated to the American political scene; it seems like a European exotic to many. The winner-take-all nature of most elections in the United States makes proportional representation seem alien and suspicious, especially if it were used to correct two centuries of racial exclusion. So toxic was the idea of proportional representation that it nearly torpedoed enactment of the 1965 Voting Rights Act, which was passed only because the Senate injected a provision explicitly disclaiming any intent to impose proportional representation.

The problem of affirmative racial gerrymanders originated with the 1965 Voting Rights Act.[125] In that legislation Congress addressed two distinct but intermingled problems. First, it attempted to block all ongoing efforts to suppress African American voting. Second, it tried to overcome the effects of two centuries of Black exclusion from political power by affirmatively enabling African Americans to vote as equal citizens. These linked and overlapping goals were reflected in the core of the statute, sections 2 and 5. Section 2 is the substantive heart of the act: "No voting qualification or prerequisite to voting, or standard, practice, or procedure shall be imposed or applied by any State" that, in the words of the Fifteenth Amendment, denied or abridged the right to vote. Section 2 bans both vote denial and vote dilution.

Its auxiliary, section 5, became known as the preclearance provision. It mandated that either the US District Court for the District of Columbia or the US attorney general approve any changes in "standard, practice, or procedure" to ensure that the innovation did not trench on the right to vote. Section 4(a) permits a showing of either purpose or effect to prove abridgment of the right to vote.[126] Finally, section 4(b) authorizes the attorney general to draw up a list of states or their subdivisions that had maintained a forbidden "test or device" and where less than 50 percent of the eligible population had been registered or voted in the 1964 presidential election. These states or subdivisions would be subject to section 5 preclearance. They included Alabama, Georgia, Louisiana, Mississippi, South Carolina, Virginia, and some counties in North Carolina and Arizona. For a half century, section 5 was effective in rooting out discriminatory practices in voting. Congress reauthorized section 5 in 1970, 1975, 1982, and 2006, extending it for another quarter century, but it did not update the 1975 coverage formula of section 4(b).[127] In *Mobile v. Bolden* (1980),[128] the Court held that a plaintiff suing under section 2 had to prove invidious intent behind the challenged practice. Congress responded in 1982 by amending section 2 to impose a "totality of the circumstances" test, which permitted plaintiffs to prove discriminatory effects.

The Voting Rights Act introduced new complications in restoring political agency to a people that had been disfranchised for nearly all of the nation's history.[129] Nevertheless, it has been hailed as the single most effective piece of civil rights legislation ever produced in the United States.[130] The background demographic problem it addressed was that in most areas, the Black population was sufficiently dispersed among the white that natural minority-majorities seldom existed above the narrowly local level.[131] This resulted in usually submerging minority voters into the white majority.[132] As long as whites vote, deliberately or subconsciously, in ways that preserve exclusive white representation, African Americans could seldom if ever elect a delegate who would represent their interests. To remedy this, section 2 of the Voting Rights Act bans "practices and procedures," including redistricting, that discriminate on the basis of race.[133] The act reaches both intentional discriminatory practices and, as amended in 1982, those that have a discriminatory effect, including dilution of the minority vote. In 1986, the Supreme Court in *Thornburgh v. Gingles* upheld section 2's effects test: "Plaintiffs need not prove causation or intent in order to prove a prima facie case of racial bloc voting," the amended statutory standard under section 2. Such white bloc voting frustrated the ability of "politically cohesive groups of black voters to participate equally in the political process and to elect candidates of their choice."[134]

The problem of redistricting with racial overtones first came to the Court in the case of *United Jewish Organizations v. Carey* (1977).[135] A plurality there held that a state may consider racial factors in redistricting. Fostering a Black-majority district does not stigmatize white voters "as long as whites...as a group, are provided with fair representation." Representation is not a zero-sum game, and whites lose no rights when African Americans become empowered. Nor do they suffer any sort of discrimination or other infringement of rights if through redistricting they find themselves in a district predominantly composed of people of color. White challengers to the Voting Rights Act persistently refuse to recognize this obvious point.

After the 1990 census, the US Department of Justice, proceeding under the authority of *Thornburgh v. Gingles*, promoted creation of majority-minority districts in states that had a history of racial discrimination in voting under section 5. This is the practice known as the "affirmative racial gerrymander." A succession of Supreme Court confrontations with such racial gerrymandering ensued. Could the federal government encourage creation of a congressional district designed to produce a racially defined majority-minority voting population? The dilemma was acute: on one hand, could the federal and state governments acting together deliberately compose a voting population on racial lines? Was this essentially different from a state doing the same thing in order to exclude Blacks from political power by creating a majority-white district? Did this not impose proportional representation of the minority population, supposedly so incompatible with American political traditions that it was expressly prohibited by the very act itself? Was this not also incompatible with the tradition, or at least ideal, of compact and contiguous district shapes if it resulted in a district of unusual or contorted shape?

On the other hand, if the state and federal governments did not manipulate congressional districts in this way, African Americans who constituted between 20 and 40 percent of a state's population in some southern states might perpetually be submerged politically if their population was dispersed in majority-white districts. A further complication is that if African Americans demands were somehow met, it would amount to an endorsement of group rights, something anathema to the individualistic orientation of American constitutionalism (at least for conservatives). As Justice Powell (one of those conservatives) noted, any relief in the area of gerrymandering implicates "the concept of representation [because representation] necessarily applies to groups; groups of voters elect representatives, individual voters do not."[136]

For a decade in the 1990s, the Supreme Court wrestled with this dilemma and its multiple complications. This produced a series of four major cases before the Court seemingly abandoned the struggle from exhaustion.[137] The series began with *Shaw v. Reno* (1993) (*Shaw I*),[138] after the Justice Department required creation of a second majority-minority district in North Carolina. The state Republican Party and some white voters objected, claiming that the "deliberate segregation of voters into separate districts on the basis of race violated their [the objecting voters] constitutional right to participate in a 'color-blind' electoral process."[139] Petitioners, however, misstated the character of the redistricting. The revised redistricting did not segregate voters into separate districts, as if the legislature had created an all-white Eleventh District and an all-Black Twelfth. Rather, it altered boundaries to rebalance the population ratios in the Eleventh and Twelfth in a way that could result in African Americans gaining numerical voting majorities in both. But there is no such thing as a "right to participate in a color-blind electoral process," in part because such a claim would raise insuperable standing problems. Petitioners did not claim that their vote was denied or diluted. Moreover, as Justice O'Connor conceded, legislatures always, and legitimately, take race into account in drawing legislative districts, as they consider religious affiliation, ethnicity, economics, and everything else that goes into creating political interests and identity. The district court upheld the redistricting.

A five-member majority of the Court nevertheless reversed the holding below in an opinion by O'Connor that bristled with suspicion and hostility toward the kind of racial gerrymandering that attempted to provide African Americans with some effective voice in a political process that had hitherto been single-mindedly dedicated to excluding them. She agglomerated a collection of restrictive principles. Foremost among them was that "odd" or "irregular"-shaped districts that were "unexplainable on grounds other than race" were subject to strict scrutiny. They had to be measured against traditional districting principles, including compactness, contiguity, and integrity of political subdivisions (like counties or townships). The danger they posed was of a new "political apartheid [that would] balkanize competing racial factions." The core of her position was that a bizarre shape of a congressional district rendered it constitutionally suspect and potentially a violation of the equal protection rights of the (invariably white) complainants.

Throughout her opinion, O'Connor repurposed constitutional ideas that were meant to protect African Americans into constitutional barriers against efforts to restore their rights. She deployed constitutional ideals that once condemned Jim Crow to resist African Americans' emergent political agency. She also made a concession that benefited Republican efforts to pack, crack, and stack African American voters:[140] "a reapportionment plan that concentrates members of a racial group in one district and excludes them from others may reflect wholly legitimate purposes." Though this was only dictum, it provided a handy fig leaf to cover GOP racial gamesmanship that, not coincidentally, diminished Democratic political power in North Carolina. In the period concurrent with the *Shaw* line of cases after 1990, political affiliation in the South became increasingly racially polarized, as African Americans voted Democratic, and the Republican Party careened ever more dangerously toward becoming the white man's party of the Southern Strategy. In that environment, *Shaw* could provide little protection against political—not explicitly racial—gerrymandering that would exclude a multiracial Democratic Party from power.

A fundamental principle of standing doctrine holds that citizens and taxpayers may not use the federal courts to air generalized grievances about the conduct of government.[141] Appellants seemed to argue that their rights were diminished because they found themselves voting in a district that had a majority of African American voters. In what possible way could that have been an injury? As Justice White put it in dissent, "appellants have not presented a cognizable claim, because they have not alleged a cognizable injury."[142] Justice David Souter, dissenting, reminded the majority that "in districting,...the mere placement of an individual in one district instead of another denies no one a right or benefit provided to others."[143] In a congressional delegation like North Carolina's that consisted of ten white and two African American members, white voters could hardly complain that their votes were submerged.

Justice White's dissent pointed out that the majority opinion "imagined a heretofore unknown type of constitutional claim," the plaintiffs' "neo-segregation" idea that O'Connor seemingly endorsed.[144] "Remedying a Voting Rights Act violation does not involve preferential treatment," White explained. "It involves, instead, an attempt to equalize treatment, and to provide minority voters with an effective voice in the political process."[145] But to no avail: *Shaw* raised more questions than it answered, so the problem of racial gerrymanders kept recurring to the Court in subsequent terms.

Despite O'Connor's concern about bizarre district configurations, *Shaw I* did not resolve the question whether an odd shape was necessary to find the redistricting unconstitutional. *Miller v. Johnson* (1995)[146] held that it was not. The Georgia district in question was of a more conventional shape, so Kennedy for the five-to-four majority deflected attention away from shape and to a new criterion that "race for its own sake...was the legislature's dominant and controlling rationale." This brought the problem of legislative intent, that perennial apple of discord, back into the picture. The majority held the districting unconstitutional because it suspected a predominant racial motive behind the new district. Kennedy softened that point a bit in a passing moment of judicial reticence and deference to legislative prerogative when he conceded that "the good faith of the legislature must be presumed." Legislatures will "almost always be aware of racial demographics," but that alone does not prove that racial considerations were dominant. But Kennedy also threw in a gratuitous warning that the Justice Department's authority to require majority-minority districts brings the Voting Rights Act itself, "once upheld as a proper exercise of Congress' authority under § 2 of the Fifteenth Amendment, into tension with the Fourteenth Amendment."[147] The conservatives on the Court apparently were beginning to grow uneasy about the Voting Rights Act.

Justice Stevens in dissent again demonstrated that white petitioners in redistricting cases suffer no denial or dilution of their vote and thus no cognizable injury, and therefore have no standing. Justice Ginsburg, dissenting, reminded the majority that federal courts and the Justice Department had to intervene in the redistricting process because of the state legislatures' resistance to programs that protected the rights of African Americans.

Miller redirected the Court's attention to the issue of legislative purpose or motive, and that in turn required scrutiny of the reasons for the particular form that redistricting took. *Hunt v. Shaw* (1996) (*Shaw II*)[148] raised the question whether compliance with the Voting Rights Act would of itself constitute the compelling state interest mandated by strict scrutiny, but then left it unanswered. At the same time, Justice O'Connor upped the ante on the issue of motivation, holding in *Bush v. Vera* (1996)[149] that those who challenged redistricting had to prove that nonracial considerations were "subordinated" to race. "Race must be 'the predominant factor motivating the legislature's [redistricting] decision.'" But the Court faced stubbornly resistant difficulties in coming up with a coherent redistricting rule. O'Connor managed to gather only a plurality for the Court's result. She was reduced to writing a separate concurrence to her own plurality opinion to defend her position at a greater depth than her colleagues in the plurality (Rehnquist and Kennedy) were willing to support (and Kennedy too wrote a concurrence). The Court seemed to be dissolving into incoherence on the subject.

Finally, however, the Court managed closure of a sort on the vexed problem of judicial supervision of racially inflected redistricting in *Easley v. Cromartie* (2001),[150] a case that marked the fourth time that the *Shaw* district itself came before the High Court in less than a decade.[151] Justice Breyer wrote for a majority that now consisted of the liberal bloc augmented by Justice O'Connor. He reprised a decade of litigation over this one North Carolina district and applied the tests from O'Connor's opinions but concluded that redistricting is a matter that ordinarily "falls within a legislature's sphere of competence." A legislative judgment on something as political as redistricting is entitled to judicial deference. "Courts must exercise extraordinary caution in adjudicating claims that a State has drawn district lines on the basis of race." He declined to overturn the latest iteration of North Carolina's Twelfth Congressional District.

With that, the Supreme Court's involvement with racial redistricting limped to a conclusion that in retrospect should have been evident from the beginning: redistricting involves political judgments with which courts intermeddle at their peril. To finally recognize this, the Court had to thaw the rigidity of its *Adarand* strict scrutiny formulation. The constitutional authority Pamela Karlan thinks this was done to "mitigate the impact of racially polarized voting that involves otherwise constitutionally protected private choice."[152]

One of the core components of the first Redemption was disfranchisement of African American voters. Inspired by Mississippi's 1890 constitution, white southerners accomplished this over a generation at the turn of the century by a variety of devices embedded in their constitutions and codes: poll taxes, literacy and understanding tests, residency requirements, good-character testimonials, the white primary, felon disfranchisement, grandfather clauses, and voter registration.[153] Collectively, these devices became known as the Mississippi Plan. In addition to these legal and above-the-board moves (nearly all ratified by the US Supreme Court), whites resorted to intimidation, violence, and the rest of the Jim Crow extralegal agenda in its social, cultural, and economic aspects.

A major component of the southern states' efforts to reprise the Mississippi Plan was renewed suppression of Black voters. Congress and the Lyndon Johnson administration made it plain that old overt obstructions would no longer work a century later. So those who would stifle the Black vote, including leading figures in the Reagan administration, turned their ingenuity to crafting more subtle successor schemes. These included at-large voting and multimember districts, the original racial gerrymanders, and felon disfranchisement. But the most effective schemes were Republican efforts to implement a comprehensive catalog of substantive and procedural measures that would inhibit, reduce, or eliminate electorates that voted Democratic: racial minorities, young people, disabled persons, and the poor.

The centerpiece of these latter-day Mississippi Plan measures consists of onerous voter ID requirements. In addition, state legislatures have changed times and places of voting, sometimes notifying the public of these changes late or in inconspicuous venues. They cut back on same-day registration, early voting, and absentee ballots. Some legislatures regulated organizations that registered voters, such as the League of Women Voters, so heavy-handedly that these groups withdrew from the field for fear of prosecution. State secretaries of state purged voter rolls, ostensibly to weed out registered voters who had moved or died.[154] Republican "poll monitors"—informal, self-appointed pseudo-officials who hang around polling stations and harass those they suspect of being ineligible to vote[155]—inject an element of fear and intimidation into the act of in-person voting.

Republicans pushed these throughout the new century, but the Supreme Court's decision in *Shelby County v. Holder* (2013) had the effect of the starting bell at Churchill Downs: the southern states stampeded out of the starting gate to enact new or expanded restrictions, freed from the onus of section 5 preclearance under the Voting Rights Act. This produced a gusher of voter-suppression measures in red states throughout the next decade that had a long history of Mississippi Plan–type discrimination against Black voters.[156] The most significant of these barriers to date have been the voter ID requirements.[157] These must be issued by an agency of government and contain a photo of the holder. In some states, people can register to vote only by presenting birth certificates, naturalization papers, or a passport, which are difficult and costly to obtain for many people.[158] Some states fine-tune these ID requirements to winnow out a disfavored constituency by rejecting university student IDs, while accepting hunting licenses and gun registration. Supporters defend them on the grounds that they are necessary to suppress "voter fraud," but the only fraud that they could potentially reach is voter impersonation at the polls, a vanishingly rare and insignificant occurrence. The real problem with voter fraud occurs at other stages of the voting process, which are not affected by ID requirements. Opponents maintain that both the purpose and the effect of such laws is to suppress voting by constituencies that vote Democratic: racial minorities (particularly African American and Latino), the poor (especially the elderly poor), disabled persons, and all those who for whatever reason suffer impaired mobility or access.

In 2006, Indiana became the first state to mandate a photo ID for prospective voters. The state Democratic Party and organizations representing poor, old, disabled, and racial-minority voters promptly filed a facial challenge, alleging an equal protection violation comparable to the poll tax struck down in *Harper v. Virginia Board of Elections* (1966). The Supreme Court upheld the scheme in *Crawford v. Marion County Election Board* (2008),[159] but only in a fractured response.[160] Speaking for a plurality of three, Justice Stevens rejected both the strict-scrutiny criterion and *Harper* as the relevant precedent. Instead, he substituted a test that balanced the state's interests against the burdens imposed on affected voters. The Stevens balancing test has become the principal criterion for resolving cases involving the administration of elections.[161]

Justice Stevens's test identified three state interests, each of which he found sufficient: "deterring...voter fraud," "orderly administration and accurate record-keeping," and "protecting public confidence" in the integrity of elections. He conceded that there was no evidence that impersonation at the polls had ever occurred in Indiana, but it was enough for him that it had happened in the past elsewhere (he was able to cite only nineteenth-century New York Tammany corruption) and might possibly recur someplace in the future. He dismissed "the inconvenience of making a trip to the BMV,[162] gathering the required documents, and posing for a photograph" as insubstantial. As for the elderly, the poor, and "homeless persons," they were just "a few voters" whose interests were not enough to tip the scales. (He did not mention African Americans or other people of color in his burdened category. He seems to have taken no notice of the elephant in the room.) Stevens conceded that if there were an expense involved, *Harper* (the poll tax case) might be relevant, but he took comfort in the thought that the state offered to provide alternative special-purpose ID cards at no cost. Finally, he shrugged off the fact that every vote in the legislature for the statute was cast by a Republican, and every opposing vote by Democrats. If the law had "valid neutral justifications," partisan motivation would not invalidate it. He did hint, though, that an as-applied challenge was still open.

That last concession was too much for the conservative bloc (Scalia, Thomas, and Alito), who concurred in the result. They insisted that if the statute was "non-discriminatory," even as-applied challenges were barred. Scalia went out of his way to reject any structural racist critique of state voter suppression. "Individual impacts are [not] relevant to determining the severity of the burden it imposes." If a law is neutral (meaning not explicitly targeted at one specific group), then it cannot be "invidious" under the Fourteenth Amendment, "*even when their burdens purportedly fall disproportionately on a protected class.*"[163] (The italics were Scalia's, presumably to emphasize his point and perhaps to rub the dissenters' noses in it.) Under this view, only statutes that explicitly burden protected groups could be open to an equal protection challenge. The conservatives' approach would force the equal protection clause back into its nineteenth-century crypt.

Justices Souter and Ginsburg refuted each of the plurality's points in their joint dissent. *Harper* should be controlling, because the state's ID requirement did in fact impose significant financial burdens on the poor and elderly: the travel costs of getting to a Department of Motor Vehicles office or other state office, plus the expenses of obtaining a birth certificate or passport. The Indiana statute "targets the poor and the weak."[164] Because these costs burdened a "fundamental right," the right to vote, the statute should be subjected to strict scrutiny. Souter insisted that no legitimate state interest could be served by a statute that purported to resolve a problem that did not exist. "The State has not come across a single instance of in-person voter impersonation fraud in all of Indiana's history." The only interest Indiana had shown was "the object of deterring poorer residents from exercising the franchise," an obviously illegitimate goal.

The *Crawford* case had been heard on appeal by a three-judge panel of the US Court of Appeals for the Seventh Circuit. Judge Richard Posner wrote the majority opinion upholding the Indiana law in that case,[165] and it was his opinion that was affirmed by the US Supreme Court. Both he and Justice Stevens later had second thoughts about their handiwork. In his reminiscences, *Reflections on Judging* (2013), Chief Judge Posner expressed regret for his decision. The Indiana statute was "a type of law now widely regarded as a means of voter suppression rather than of fraud prevention."[166] Explaining his change of heart, he said, "we weren't given the information that would enable that balance to be struck between preventing fraud and protecting voters' rights."[167] In a public discussion of *Crawford*, Justice Stevens characterized it as a "fairly unfortunate decision." He stated that he had doubts about the bona fides of the statute based on information "outside the record" but did not think it was appropriate to rely on such information, even though it led to what he regarded as a regrettable outcome. He complimented the Souter dissent as "one of his best opinions."[168]

The *Crawford* decision imposed a particular view of what constitutes the essence of democracy, much as *Baker v. Carr* (1962) had done a half century earlier. Both the Stevens plurality and the Scalia concurrence assumed that the core of democracy was the legitimacy of outcomes, with either the elite of elected officials (Stevens) or the self-constituted majority of voters (Scalia) as the focus of concern and legitimacy. To the *Crawford* majority, "all the Constitution requires is the protection of voter outcomes even if a significant number of voters are excluded."[169] Souter and Ginsburg, by contrast, saw the sine qua non of democracy as the participation by every citizen in voting.

But maximizing individual voter participation in self-government should be the whole point of democracy. Democratic government is corrupted when existing majorities entrench themselves, and doubly so when the basis of this entrenchment is racial, as it is in the modern voter ID cases. The Mississippi Plan in its latter-day reincarnations enables rule by a racial master class, the Herrenvolk, resulting in what the historian David Roediger calls "herrenvolk republicanism," where the white freedom and independence necessary to self-government (of, by, and for whites) rest on the disfranchisement of people of color.[170] In a society as racialized as the United States (circa 1890 or 2008), anything less than Souter's vision of universal voter participation enables a racially corrupted form of republicanism, a de facto white hegemony. As it is, voter ID laws currently in effect depress turnout among people of color in all elections, and, not coincidentally, shift American politics to the right.[171]

The foundation of voting rights cases is the Fifteenth Amendment, which prohibits the states from denying or abridging "the right of citizens of the United States to vote...on account of race, color, or previous condition of servitude." Its enforcement clause, section 2, empowers Congress "to enforce this article by appropriate legislation." Before 1965, such legislation as Congress had enacted, like the Enforcement Act of 1870, was remedial and retrospective; that is, it provided a corrective for wrongs that had occurred in the past. Enforcement was by litigation, on a case-by-case basis. Confronted with the white South's dogged resistance to Black voting through the twentieth century, Congress enacted the Voting Rights Act in 1965, following earlier, less ambitious civil rights legislation, to provide prophylactic, rather than simply remedial, enforcement, looking to prevent wrongs in the future. The Voting Rights Act was not an ordinary statute. Like the Civil Rights Act of 1964, it has a kind of quasi-constitutional status, inscribing a fundamental constitutional settlement: African American people have full political agency, expressed through the right to vote and to hold public office. They are fully participating, fully empowered citizens of the Republic.

The Supreme Court promptly upheld the constitutionality of the act in *South Carolina v. Katzenbach* (1966).[172] Chief Justice Warren's majority opinion readily sustained the prophylactic role of section 5 congressional authority under the enforcement clause of the Fifteenth Amendment. "Congress might well decide to shift the advantage of time and inertia from the perpetrators of the evil to its victims."[173] He reinforced the sweep of congressional power by invoking Chief Justice John Marshall's magisterial defense of it in *McCulloch v. Maryland* (1819), quoting Marshall's resounding passage: "Let the end be legitimate, let it be within the scope of the constitution, and all means which are appropriate, which are plainly adapted to that end, which are not prohibited, but consist with the letter and spirit of the constitution, are constitutional."[174]

The Voting Rights Act of 1965 has been an irritant to many southern whites ever since its enactment. When that voting bloc abandoned the Democratic Party for the Republicans in response to the siren call of the Southern Strategy, the GOP, formerly the home of African American voters in the South, flipped its concern and espoused the grievances of the white bloc.[175] As the post-Warren Court inexorably became more conservative with the appointment of Republican nominees, it became more responsive to GOP and southern white concerns. In a 2009 case, *Northwest Austin Municipal Utility District v. Holder*,[176] Chief Justice John Roberts sent a shot across the bow of Congress with a warning that the Voting Rights Act raised serious "constitutional concerns." Whether "conditions continue to justify such legislation is a difficult constitutional question." His opinion was a clear hint to Congress that it must update at least section 4(b).[177] Congress failed to act on such a touchy issue, not surprisingly, given the high degree of partisanship and the Republican Party's resistance to all measures that would expand the ballot, especially when that expansion would increase the number of African American voters.

Roberts resolved the problem four years later by declaring that the unrevised section 4(b) was unconstitutional, or, more accurately, had become so through legislative inertia and inaction. *Shelby County v. Holder* (2013)[178] was the most serious setback to African Americans' voting rights since *Giles v. Harris* in 1903. Roberts concluded his majority opinion on a note of I-told-you-so: "Congress could have updated the coverage formula at that time [2009], but did not do so. Its failure to act leaves us today with no choice but to declare § 4(b) unconstitutional."[179] His basis for doing so was more threatening to African Americans' rights than the result itself. Roberts invoked the "fundamental principle of equal sovereignty" to buttress his conclusion that Congress in exercising its enumerated powers must respect the states' "residual sovereignty" supposedly enshrined in the Tenth Amendment.[180] That statement was doubly radical. First, it seemed to announce a sweeping new principle of federalism: that the Court would balance explicit powers of Congress, such as the enforcement clauses of the Fourteenth and Fifteenth Amendments, against reserved states' powers, including their authority to regulate elections. This would seem to place the equal protection clause on a plane with a state's power to determine the sites of polling places, surely a distorted imbalance of the federal system. Even if states retain "broad powers to determine the conditions under which the right of suffrage may be exercised,"[181] they cannot exercise it in a way that would discriminate against African Americans in either purpose or effect. The majesty of federal authority under the equal protection clause should overwhelm the lesser state authority over times and places of elections under Article I, section 2.

Second, Roberts's supposed "fundamental principle" was actually quite limited, almost trivial, in its origin: it applied only to the equal status of states at the time of their admission to the Union.[182] (It derived from a clumsy attempt by Congress in 1910 to dictate to the aborning state of Oklahoma where its new capital was to be located.)[183] Going further back in time, the state-equality idea traces its origins to Chief Justice Taney's insistence in *Dred Scott* that the states were equal among themselves in their authority over slavery, so that any restriction on slavery amounted to an assault on the equal sovereignty of the states. Roberts's gambit, if it proves permanent, will mark a severe limitation on Congress's power to curb illegal state actions, with its feet of clay in *Dred Scott*. *Shelby County* is both a descendant and an echo of that odious decision.

But since 1975 (the date of the last revision of section 4(b)), "things have changed dramatically," Roberts claimed.[184] He cited rosy statistics about voter registration and election of Black public officials. (Apparently the glow of a supposed post-racial America lingered on longer on First Street than elsewhere in the nation.) Thus section 4(b) "coverage today is based on decades-old data and eradicated practices."[185] Congress may not shirk its responsibilities for aligning regulation of the states with current conditions.

Roberts insisted that the Court was not calling into question the constitutionality of section 2's substantive provisions, though he was less reassuring about section 5. (Justice Thomas suffered no such inhibition: in a brief concurrence, he insisted that section 5 was unconstitutional, too.) During oral argument, Justice Scalia piled on. He shocked observers by claiming that the Voting Rights Act was nothing more than a claim for a "perpetuation of racial entitlement" for the Black community.[186] In any event, section 5 remains a dead letter without the coverage formula of 4(b), and Congress's stasis, brought on by the Republican Party's dysfunctionality, ensures that the Voting Rights Act will remain what earlier lawyers called *brutum fulmen*, an empty noise, posing no threat to racial disfranchisement.[187]

In her dissent for the liberal wing of the Court, Justice Ginsburg pinioned Roberts's reasoning with a metaphor: "Throwing out preclearance when it has worked and is continuing to work to stop discriminatory changes is like throwing away your umbrella in a rainstorm because you are not getting wet."[188] The real issue, she pointed out, is "who decides whether [section 5] remains justifiable, this Court, or a Congress charged with the obligation to enforce the post–Civil War Amendments 'by appropriate legislation.'"[189] She insisted that the issue in 2013 was not the old Jim Crow voter-suppression practices that preceded the civil rights era, but rather what she called the "second-generation barriers to minority voting":

gerrymandering, at-large voting, annexation, and other modern vote-dilution moves.[190] She reminded the Court that "racially polarized voting" was the new reality that Roberts's formalistic approach ignored.

The most eloquent comment on the consequences of *Shelby County* came from a panel of the US Court of Appeals for the Fourth Circuit in 2016, commenting on yet another North Carolina attempt to disfranchise its Black citizens. Judge Diana Gribbon Motz wrote:

> After years of preclearance and expansion of voting access, by 2013 African American registration and turnout rates had finally reached near-parity with white registration and turnout rates. African Americans were poised to act as a major electoral force. But, on the day after the Supreme Court issued *Shelby County v. Holder* (2013), eliminating preclearance obligations, a leader of the party that newly dominated the legislature [the Republican Party] (and the party that rarely enjoyed African American support) announced an intention to enact what he characterized as an "omnibus" election law. Before enacting that law, the legislature requested data on the use, by race, of a number of voting practices. Upon receipt of the race data, the General Assembly enacted legislation that restricted voting and registration in five different ways, all of which disproportionately affected African Americans.... In response to claims that intentional racial discrimination animated its action, the State offered only meager justifications. Although the new provisions target African Americans with almost surgical precision, they constitute inapt remedies for the problems assertedly justifying them and, in fact, impose cures for problems that did not exist.[191]

Scholarly research confirms Judge Motz's conclusions. After enactment of the Voting Rights Act, its section 5 preclearance mechanism produced an increase of 30 percent in voting by people of color, and an overall gain in voter participation among people of all races of 4 to 8 percent. Moreover, that gain was not a temporary blip: the advance in minority participation persisted right up to *Shelby County*.[192] Voting discrimination persists in all the states and areas covered by section 4(b). Traditional vote-suppression techniques like literacy tests have become obsolete, but new, more sophisticated measures like voter ID laws, plus constant fiddling with details like location or times of voting, work effectively to exclude African Americans from the ballot. Chief Justice Roberts was simply wrong in assuming that section 4's coverage was no longer congruent with racial exclusion.[193] As if to confirm this finding, in the 2016 presidential election, the first national vote to be affected by the neutering of section 4(b), minority voting fell off sharply in counties subject to preclearance. Further, Republican enthusiasm for vote-suppression measures was not confined to the covered jurisdictions or even to the South as a whole. Red states throughout the nation displayed a newfound zeal for what their sponsors termed "the integrity of the ballot" and for measures that supposedly ensured "the purity of the ballot box," both Jim Crow–era euphemisms for Black disfranchisement.

Housing and Residential Segregation

The Supreme Court's decisions that involve residential segregation and housing discrimination provide no clear, unitary narrative throughline.[194] In the second Reconstruction, the Court had at first produced two landmark decisions that helped crack open the housing market for African Americans, *Shelley v. Kraemer* (1948) (holding racial covenants unenforceable) and *Jones v. Alfred Mayer Co.* (1968) (resurrecting the 1866 Civil Rights Act and the Thirteenth Amendment for the housing market). But later decisions in the second Redemption reveal no particular pattern. *Evans v. Abney* (1970) and *Palmer v. Thompson* (1971), both involving urban amenities (parks and swimming pools), were disappointments to those who sought equality of opportunity in city living. *Arlington Heights v. Metropolitan Housing Authority* (1977) (exclusionary zoning) salvaged something from the setback of *Washington v. Davis* (1976). On the other hand, *Memphis v. Green* (1981) (closing off a neighborhood) revealed a Court blind or indifferent to structural racism in urban residential patterns.

The same mixed outcomes mark later cases. The Court has approached the problems of residential segregation and housing discrimination piecemeal, with no comprehensive understanding of structural racism's impact on people of color who are simply looking for a decent place to live. The justices have mistaken racial exclusion by popular referenda as a praiseworthy expression of popular democracy. They have fumbled exclusionary zoning cases, seemingly clueless or indifferent about the non-obvious ways that prosperous white suburbs can exclude poorer people of other races. They lost sight of the problem of blockbusting and white flight in a contest over First Amendment liberties. They did not recognize structural forces at work when a city excluded Black traffic from a white neighborhood. And they expanded the procedural issues of standing as a way of ducking exclusionary zoning issues that they preferred not to tackle head-on. Yet despite the variety of contexts in which the problem of segregation appears, one constant endures: urban residential segregation lingers on. Multigenerational transmission of poverty and disadvantage persists due to the silent, unseen operation of structural racism.[195]

Racial inequality and discrimination are endemic in the American law of property. Seemingly neutral rules governing the control and distribution of material resources camouflage pervasive, deep, and long-lasting ways in which white Americans have suppressed Black access to those resources and hoarded advantages for themselves. The property scholar Bethany Berger concludes that "racial relationships shaped property law for all in the United States. From the power to foreclose for debts, to the power of local governments to zone, to the scope of the welfare state's 'new property,' efforts to control, exclude, and take from racialized groups changed what property means today."[196] Residential segregation is one consequence of that comprehensive racial bias in property law.

By the late twentieth century, American cities had become hypersegregated.[197] This residential segregation is the principal cause of the urban poverty and racial inequality in the United States today.[198] It "remains the 'lynchpin'—the deep root cause—that sustains systemic racial inequality." Access to adequate, non-segregated housing "connects (or fails to connect) residents to good schools, nutritious foods, healthy environments, good paying jobs, and access to health care, clinics, critical amenities and services. leaving crumbling infrastructure, poisonous water, predatory financial institutions, and food deserts behind." Moreover, this segregation is not declining; it is getting worse. Stephen Menendian and his collaborators have found that "81 percent of American cities and metropolitan regions are more segregated today than they were in 1990."[199]

Racial residential segregation did not occur by accident, happenstance, or a preference of African Americans to immure themselves in racial ghettoes. It came about through collective action on the part of whites in both the public and private sectors. Government at all levels—federal, state, and local—imposed segregation on America's cities throughout the twentieth century. Richard Rothstein demonstrates that segregation "is not the unintended consequence of individual choices and of otherwise well-meaning law or regulation but of unhidden public policy that explicitly segregated every metropolitan area in the United States."[200] Such segregation is de jure, not de facto, imposed deliberately through law and regulation by government actors who knew what they were doing and intended its consequences. Private for-profit entities such as banks and real estate brokers partnered with government agencies to inhibit Black homeownership and constrain Black mobility. (And then, perversely, when forced to abandon Black exclusion in the 1970s, these institutions adopted policies that the historian Keeanga-Yamahtta Taylor aptly calls "predatory inclusion," sucking capital out of the Black community by subprime mortgages.)[201] Sadly, the Fair Housing Act of 1968, the weakest of the civil rights acts trilogy of the 1960s at the time of its enactment, has been underenforced and has proved disappointingly inadequate to the massive challenges it was meant to address. Racism has overwhelmed fair housing.[202]

Collusion between public agencies and the private sector to impose segregation was not limited to housing. In multiple domains—particularly health and education—Congress authorized spending on construction of deliberately segregated facilities, in effect subsidizing racial discrimination by subventions derived from all who paid federal taxes. The effects of this spending lasted through the late twentieth century.[203]

The Supreme Court refuses to acknowledge this historico-sociological reality and has colluded in perpetuating it. For example, Justice Clarence Thomas maintained in his concurrence in *Missouri v. Jenkins* (1995) that "the continuing 'racial isolation' of schools after de jure segregation has ended may well reflect voluntary housing choices or other private decisions."[204] He repeated this point in his concurrence in *Parents Involved*: "Although presently observed racial imbalance might result from past de jure segregation, racial imbalance can also result from any number of innocent private decisions, including voluntary housing choices."[205] As Justice Ruth Bader Ginsburg observed in another context, only an ostrich could reach such a myopic conclusion.[206] When it comes to urban segregation, sociologists like Nancy Denton dismiss such notions of individual choice as a fallacy. "Focusing on the individual characteristics [and choices] of the poor rather than the structural effects of segregation and discrimination too often enables politicians and the public to assume that little can or should be done."[207] Space itself, as George Lipsitz has demonstrated, has been "racialized" by the web of practices that comprise structural racism.[208] Racially identified space "results from public policy and legal sanctions—in short, from state action—rather than being the unfortunate but irremediable consequence of purely private or individual choices." In these circumstances, neutrality is illusory. The Stanford legal scholar Richard Thompson Ford concludes that "race-neutral policies, set against an historical backdrop of state action in the service of racial segregation and thus against a contemporary backdrop of racially identified space—physical space primarily associated with and occupied by a particular racial group—predictably reproduce and entrench racial segregation and the racial-caste system that accompanies it."[209]

After having imposed residential segregation on both cities and suburbs from 1934 through 1970, the federal government in collusion with states and cities embarked on programs of slum clearance, urban renewal, public housing, and highway construction. These programs lightly regulated private enterprise through decentralized public planning (zoning, building codes, and other land-use controls) under amorphous policy guidelines. Follow-up and enforcement seldom occurred. The process was supercharged and financed by convoluted funding schemes authorized under the Housing Acts of 1949 and 1954.[210] Urban renewal policies that relied on zoning and redlining practices established before and during the New Deal forced African American residents to relocate in rental or public housing while promoting fee-simple homeownership by whites.[211] The urban planning documents of the postwar era are irradiated with implicit, and occasionally explicit, racism. Sometimes participants in urban renewal planning indiscreetly admitted that the displacement of Black communities was intentional. Chancellor Lawrence Kimpton of the University of Chicago proposed solving what he called the "racial problem" of Black neighborhoods near his institution in the 1950s by simply "cutting down [the] number of Negroes" living there, using slum clearance programs to do so.[212] The people directly affected—chiefly African American residents of the neighborhoods razed by slum clearance or highway construction projects—were not consulted on any of this. But the consequences were disastrous for them.

Urban renewal destroyed functioning city neighborhoods, scattering the communities that lived there. Interstate highways cut through the heart of cities, which simultaneously obliterated vibrant Black and white neighborhoods while enabling the suburban sprawl to which displaced whites could flee. Racialized poverty became concentrated in the Projects, which all too frequently became high-rise slums that housed the urban pathology they were supposed to displace: drugs, crime, vandalism, despair. The sociologist Xavier de Souza Briggs refers to these policies as "containment plus sprawl."[213] "This is the sacking of cities," Jane Jacobs mourned in her classic *The Death and Life of Great American Cities*.[214] James Baldwin spoke for the Black community when he condemned such urban renewal policies as "Negro removal."[215]

The US Supreme Court gave its blessing to these urban renewal processes in *Berman v. Parker* (1954),[216] shutting its eyes to the racial implications and the structural consequences of slum clearance programs. Justice Douglas, for a unanimous bench, accorded abjectly low deference to all legislative judgments involving urban renewal, even though he conceded that the affected property, a profitable department store, was not a slum dwelling. "We do not sit to determine whether a particular housing project is or is not desirable. The concept of the public welfare is broad and inclusive." He broadened the constitutional term "public use"[217] to embrace any "public purpose," as determined by the legislature, a reading that has had expansive consequences, including seizure of residential property by eminent domain.[218] *Berman v. Parker* gave free rein to the notorious planning policies of the 1950s and 1960s that dispersed and destroyed Black communities with no concern for the well-being of those displaced. In its rush to endorse urban planning, the Court gave no thought to the primary victims of such mass vandalism and ignored the racial effects plainly playing out before them, literally just a few miles from where they sat. Justice Thomas later noted in his dissent in *Kelo v. New London* that 97 percent of the people removed by the *Berman* project were African American.[219] The Court's willful unconcern helped insulate housing-related structural racism from judicial scrutiny.

Popular referenda reinforced racial exclusion. When the US Supreme Court first encountered the problem of white voter majorities using popular initiatives and referenda to authorize or protect racial discrimination, the Court's responded in an opinion that was correct but analytically thin. *Reitman v. Mulkey* (1967) condemned California's Proposition 14, but neither Justice White's majority opinion nor the prior opinion of the California Supreme Court satisfactorily explained exactly why.[220] Both were conclusory, though indisputably correct: the white majority of the people of California had written into the state constitution a right to discriminate that offended state and federal constitutional and statutory protections for equality. Only Justice Douglas's concurring opinion provided a satisfactory explanation for why they were so offensive. He demonstrated the state's complicity in the discriminatory practices of private actors, including licensing some of those actors. But the Supreme Court did at least condemn the notion that there was a "right to discriminate," implicitly in *Reitman*, then explicitly in *Norwood v. Harrison* (1973), where it declared in dictum that "invidious private discrimination...has never been accorded affirmative constitutional protection."[221]

After *Reitman*, it took only two years for the next generation of popular-democracy measures protecting racial discrimination to reach the Court. The city of Akron, Ohio, amended its municipal charter to require that any ordinance regulating the sale or lease of property "on the basis of race, color...or ancestry" be approved by a majority of the city's voters in a referendum. It also suspended all existing fair-housing legislation until that too was approved by popular vote. In *Hunter v. Erickson* (1969),[222] Justice White, for the Court's majority, held the charter provision unconstitutional because it "discriminates against minorities, and constitutes a real, substantial, and invidious denial of the equal protection of the laws."

The Court understood the discriminatory impact of these racial referenda, but its decision came at an inauspicious moment. Fair housing was deeply contentious at that time, comparable to school integration and busing in its power to bring submerged racism to the surface. So after *Reitman* and *Hunter* struck down racially specific referenda, opponents of fair housing came up with a third-generation assault on fair housing, via exclusionary zoning schemes that did not refer to race. In 1970, they promoted an amendment to the California Constitution, Article 34, that prohibited construction of low-income housing without approval in a local election. The provision avoided mention of race or ethnicity, referring only to a "low rent housing project." A federal court held the provision unconstitutional on the authority of *Hunter v. Erickson*, because it placed a special burden on both the poor and racial minorities (which the three-judge panel recognized as largely overlapping categories) who were seeking better housing.[223]

But the Supreme Court reversed that decision in *James v. Valtierra* (1971).[224] Justice Hugo Black for the majority summarily rejected the possibility that the referendum requirement might have anything at all to do with race; it was "a law seemingly neutral on its face," and that feeble standard was good enough. He declined to go behind the record to investigate further.[225] He extolled the supposedly democratic nature of a referendum. He refused to extend *Hunter* and dismissed any possibility of an equal protection challenge merely because a statute "disadvantages" some group. Black stretched to find race-neutral bases for urban residential segregation that gave local communities veto power over proposed low-income housing options. Increased expenditures for public services to occupants of low-income housing, as well as declining tax revenues, were justification enough to slide by the obvious racial impacts of the referendum veto. In the light of subsequent California experience with initiatives, Black's encomium to direct democracy seems either naive (not a failing often attributed to Black) or a fig leaf for a constitutional posture that amounted to letting white majorities exclude racial or economic minorities from their suburbs.

In *James*, Black imposed a daunting standard that anyone challenging a referendum must meet: they must prove "that a law seemingly neutral on its face is in fact aimed at a racial minority."[226] It did not trouble Black that this position was inconsistent with his professed skepticism about proving motivation, which he expressed that same year in *Palmer v. Thompson* (1971), where he doubted that it was possible to attribute racist motives to a decision to close city swimming pools in Jackson, Mississippi, rather than integrate, even after the city's mayor explicitly avowed racist motives. Yet here he demanded that Black petitioners prove that a referendum was "aimed at" African Americans. The Court reaffirmed its approval of the referendum as a popular-democracy device for forestalling construction of low-income housing in *Eastlake v. Forest City Enterprises* (1976) five years later. "As a basic instrument of democratic government, the referendum process does not, in itself, violate the Due Process Clause of the Fourteenth Amendment when applied to a rezoning ordinance."[227]

The full significance of *James v. Valtierra* became apparent in a 2003 case that is an epitome of the way in which the modern Court ignores the workings of structural racism even when the sociological reality of the referendum process is laid out for them. In 1995, the residents of Cuyahoga Falls, an exurb of Akron, Ohio, some fifty miles south of Cleveland,[228] vetoed a low-income housing project by referendum. Judge Nathaniel R. Jones of the Sixth Circuit Court of Appeals, one of the nation's most distinguished African American jurists, reviewed the public debates that preceded the referendum under *Arlington Heights* criteria.[229] He found ample evidence of racial bias driving the referendum vote: white residents said "they know what kind of element is going to move in there"; "the Mayor also linked the project to the same type of 'social engineering that brought us busing,'" and so on.[230] This ought to have met Black's *Valtierra* standard of showing that a facially neutral statute was "aimed at a racial minority." He accordingly reversed a summary judgment for the city.[231]

But when the city appealed, the Supreme Court, speaking through Justice Sandra Day O'Connor in *Cuyahoga Falls v. Buckeye Community Hope Foundation* (2003),[232] refused to accord the thinly veiled racist sentiments behind the referendum any dispositive weight. Instead, she claimed that the petitioners were challenging the referendum process itself, not its substantive outcome. Racist comments by private citizens and even the city's mayor did not constitute state action, the only role for them that the Court recognized. (O'Connor even went out of her way to insist that such remarks enjoyed First Amendment protection.) Thus, for the present, it is seemingly impossible to raise the question of whether anti-public-housing referenda are a way of preventing the development of low-income housing and thereby serve as a proxy for de facto segregation. Direct democracy sometimes facilitates structural racism.[233]

The problems associated with residential segregation were not limited to housing, narrowly conceived. They spilled over into the provision of public services and other amenities of urban living such as parks and public swimming pools, which affected the quality of life in cities and neighborhoods. After the Court condemned de jure segregation of such facilities in the wake of *Brown v. Board of Education I*, it backslid in the second Redemption to sustain segregation by public authorities so long as the segregative intent was not avowed openly (or even when it was). It upheld a segregationist-motivated closure of public facilities in *Palmer v. Thompson*, decided in 1971.[234] Public recreational facilities involve residential segregation issues because they are a component of the physical space in which we live our lives. Jackson, Mississippi, had segregated the four pools that it maintained for whites and the one pool it provided for Blacks. When a federal court ordered the pools desegregated, the city determined to close all of them, claiming that it could not safely and economically operate them as integrated facilities. Its mayor proclaimed that "if these agitators keep up their pressure, we would have five colored swimming pools because we are not going to have any intermingling." Thereupon, "Governor Ross Barnett commended Mayor Thompson for his pledge to maintain Jackson's present separation of the races."[235] The city government refused to abandon segregation, even if it meant closing its pools.

A governmental action that closes swimming pools rather than integrate them reinforces other forms of spatial segregation, above all, housing. Notionally, shuttering a swimming pool in Jackson, Mississippi, or a leafy park in Macon, Georgia, deprived whites as well as Blacks of relief from the oppressive southern summer heat.[236] But the impact was more severe on African Americans because it denied them one of the few available escapes from the segregated spaces in the South that confined their bodies as much as their aspirations. Some whites could find relief in private pools or other recreational sites off-limits to African Americans, but Black residents were left to swelter in non-air-conditioned housing.

This presented the Supreme Court with the problem of legislative motivation, always a perplexing challenge for the justices.[237] Did the government of the city of Jackson close its pools to avoid racial integration, or as a neutral municipal cost-savings measure with no racist taint? Some of the Court's leading precedents from John Marshall's day to Earl Warren's cautioned against any inquiry at all into the motives of legislators.[238] Yet during the second Reconstruction, the Court would sometimes jettison its reserve when racist motivation was obvious, as in *Gomillion v. Lightfoot* (1960),[239] where whites gerrymandered African American residents of Tuskegee, Alabama, out of the city's governance, or *Griffin v. County School Board of Prince Edward County* (1964),[240] where a Virginia county closed its public schools rather than integrate, while providing public tuition support for white children to attend seg academies. But in *Palmer*, Justice Black, speaking for the majority, blocked any inquiry into even blatant racist intent, observing that "it is difficult or impossible for any court to determine the 'sole' or 'dominant' motivation behind the choices of a group of legislators."[241] Thus the majority refused to question even an openly racist decision "solely because of the motivations of the men who voted for it." Read in tandem with *Washington v. Davis*, decided five years later, *Palmer* might foreclose all judicial review of state actions disadvantaging African Americans: *Davis* required proof of malign legislative intent, but *Palmer* suggested that even such intention, standing alone, was insufficient to prove a constitutional violation. Together, they could potentially insulate all state-promoted housing segregation from the equal protection clause.

Cases involving issues of residential segregation are often frustratingly ambiguous, a characteristic inherent in the problem of structural racism. Are racially disparate outcomes caused by actionable discriminatory intent, or do they have a racially neutral justification? This often leads the Court into the cul-de-sac of motive: What did official decision-makers intend by their policy choice? Was there a discriminatory purpose? What if there were multiple motivations, some legitimate, some not? Is it even possible for a court to draw reliable inferences about something as amorphous as human motivation? These issues came up when the city council of Memphis, Tennessee, ordered a street to be closed.

Hein Park is a white neighborhood in Memphis, located in a quadrangle formed by Rhodes College to the west; a large public space, Overton Park, to the south; a residential area buffering a commercial district to the east; and, to the north, the predominantly Black community of Hollywood/Chelsea.[242] A street known as West Drive runs north–south thorough Hein Park, providing Hollywood residents direct access to Overton Park and downtown Memphis. Two years after Memphis was roiled by the sanitation workers' strike and the assassination of Martin Luther King, Hein Park residents asked the city council to close West Drive to "undesirable traffic" coming from Hollywood. But the city's traffic engineer denied that West Drive carried a heavy or dangerous flow of vehicular traffic. The police, fire, and sanitation departments all opposed the closing.

What did that ambiguous phase "undesirable traffic" signify? Could it convey legitimate as well as racist meanings? If it did, could the Court unpack the ambivalent meanings and strike down the closure because of its racist component? Throughout the 1950s, the word "undesirable" had served as a dog-whistle euphemism for people of color. In a class action suit, Hollywood residents challenged the closure decision on two grounds. First, they claimed that the city's action violated section 1982, a descendant of the 1866 Civil Rights Act that secured the right to acquire and use property.[243] They argued that the proposed closure would diminish the value of their property and inconvenience them in a way that did not affect white residents in surrounding neighborhoods. Second, they contended that their exclusion from West Drive constituted one of the badges of slavery forbidden by the Thirteenth Amendment.

Justice John Paul Stevens's opinion for the Court in *Memphis v. Greene* dismissed the section 1982 claim, holding that the "slight inconvenience to black motorists" caused by the closing did not affect the value of their properties in the Hollywood area or severely restrict access to their homes.[244] The badges-of-slavery argument was weighty in light of *Jones v. Alfred Mayer*, but it too proved unavailing. Even assuming some disparate impact on Black residents caused by the city's decision, the displacement they experienced did not amount to a relic of slavery. Conceding that the traffic diversion did discomfit Black residents, Stevens thought that harm nevertheless was too slight to invoke the majestic interdict of the Thirteenth Amendment.

Structural racism was operating invisibly in the background: an all-white neighborhood sought and got an amenity at the expense of its Black neighbors. Had he been more sensitized to the sociological pattern, Stevens might have noted that the events leading up to the closing of West Drive met most of the *Arlington Heights* criteria for finding discriminatory purpose: negative impact on petitioners, historical background of the decision, and departures from normal procedures. (Until then, Memphis had never closed a road to alleviate routine traffic.) Stevens evaded the implications of the closure by circular reasoning: because urban neighborhoods are often characterized by a "common ethnic or racial heritage," a decision that affects a neighborhood can also affect a distinct racial group but is not on that count unconstitutional. He emphasized the need for courts to accord broad discretion to land-use planning made by local governments. Given this generic principle of judicial deference, those who challenged zoning decisions that were not overtly and explicitly racially motivated would face a daunting challenge.

In *Evans v. Abney* (1970)[245] the struggle over residential segregation spilled over into trust law. The problem began in 1911 when a US senator and Confederate veteran from Georgia, Augustus O. Bacon, devised land in trust for use as a public park by "the white women, white girls, white boys and white children of the City of Macon."[246] The park was managed by a board of managers ("all seven to be white persons" under terms of the will), with the city of Macon as trustee. When the city as trustee determined in 1963 that it could no longer maintain a segregated public park,[247] the (white) managers asked that the city be removed as trustee and be replaced with private trustees who would continue to operate the park on a segregated basis, a request granted by Georgia courts.[248] The US Supreme Court struck down this move in *Evans v. Newton* (1966),[249] holding that the park was a "public institution," whatever the legal title might be under Georgia trust law and that therefore segregation was banned.

The litigation then returned to the Georgia Supreme Court as segregationists tenaciously continued to fight the park's integration. The Georgia judges obliged, holding that the trust had failed, and the property should therefore revert to Bacon's heirs.[250] But that result was not inevitable: the Georgia court actually had two options before it in construing the trust to effect the settlor's intent.[251] The Georgia judges might have asked, which did Bacon want more, a park or segregation? The judges assumed that it was the latter, but they might have as easily found the former. Had they decided that Bacon was more interested in creating a park for the people of Macon, whatever the later changes in the social climate, they could have reached that result simply by applying a trust doctrine known as cy pres.[252] The Georgia judges considered that idea, and explicitly rejected it.

The effect of that decision was thus to place the case squarely within the scope of *Shelley v. Kraemer*, which ought to have been controlling. A state court, construing state substantive law, interpreted legal instruments (the devise and trust) in such a way as to frustrate racial integration in the interests of preserving what all conceded to be unconstitutional racial discrimination. State action was involved because Georgia courts were enforcing a racial restriction that, as in *Shelley*, prevented potentially willing parties from revising park policies to conform to constitutional understandings not prevalent when the testator Bacon wrote his will. Justice Brennan in dissent cogently pointed out that "a public park [is] being closed for a discriminatory reason...and it is a state court that is enforcing the racial restriction."[253]

But to no avail: Macon lost a park, Bacon's remote heirs reaped a windfall they never anticipated, and both white and Black residents of Macon suffered diminished recreational opportunities, all in the service of honoring a paternalistically racist dead hand. *Evans v. Abney* did not overrule *Shelley v. Kraemer*, but it diminished its authority as precedent for finding impermissible state action in the doings of state courts. In place of *Shelley's* realism, *Evans* substituted an empty formalism and reinvigorated the state action doctrine as a looming roadblock in the way of racial justice.

Despite federal policies that imposed segregation, enabled white flight, and denied Blacks the opportunity to reap the benefits of homeownership, many African Americans sought to move out of urban ghettoes and into adjacent neighborhoods or suburbs after World War II. This in turn produced the practice known as blockbusting, which flourished into the 1980s. Real estate agents and speculators would identify a neighborhood that might be attractive to Black would-be home buyers. They would then approach white residents, telling them that Blacks would soon be moving into the neighborhood, causing real estate values to plummet. This induced panic selling, sometimes lubricated by cash offers (often at a steep discount to market value). The blockbuster would then sell the property, sometimes reinflated above its original value, to a Black buyer, validating a self-fulfilling prophecy. Soon the neighborhood would be "turned," in the parlance of the times. The realtors involved would profit from the commissions churned by this activity.[254] Blockbusting was viciously exploitative, both of its primary Black victims and of the white communities and homeowners on which the blockbusters were parasites. At the time, though, it was the white victims and communities who were the principal objects of the law's solicitude. The Fair Housing Act of 1968 attempted to throttle this practice by banning blockbusting.[255]

People of goodwill also tried to suppress blockbusting. One stratagem had municipalities ban the use of "For Sale" yard signs to advertise houses on the market. One such community was New Jersey's original Levittown, located within commuting distance of Philadelphia and Camden, New Jersey. Originally segregated by corporate policy, the township experienced rapid growth and abandoned its whites-only business plan under integrationist pressure.[256] In the early 1970s, Levittown/Willingboro saw a dramatic decline in its white population, accompanied by a corresponding rise in African American residents. Local real estate firms attributed that to blockbusting, with ensuing panic selling. In 1974 the township responded with an ordinance banning "For Sale" signs to stem the apparent white flight.

The Supreme Court unanimously held the ordinance unconstitutional in *Linmark Associates v. Willingboro* (1977).[257] Though Justice Marshall reviewed the anti-blockbusting origin of the ordinance and the racial composition of the community in detail, he did not rely on the town's racial population dynamics in the substance of his opinion, except to note that the evidence at trial failed to establish that panic selling had actually taken place. Instead, he relied entirely on First Amendment doctrine regulating commercial speech. He concluded that the ordinance was a blanket ban on the content of communication (advertising residential real estate) and thus could not be prohibited by a paternalistic local government trying to prevent people from making bad decisions about their economic interests. The result was in accord with commercial-speech doctrine up to that point, but it had the unfortunate effect of scuttling efforts to control the flow of information as a way of protecting the public-policy goal of integration.

Exclusionary zoning is another suburban technique of controlling the racial composition of local communities. By 1970, the federal government had mandated segregation, discrimination, and exclusion in housing since the thirties. Suburbs mushroomed around all American cities after World War II, and suburban population growth outpaced urban. Suburban growth was promoted by federal discrimination directives, supplemented by federal highway policy. Urban renewal and highway policy in tandem promoted segregation by reorganizing and redistributing urban land on the basis of race.[258] In this environment, earlier segregationist techniques like segregation ordinances and racial covenants, which had been suited to the process of urbanization, proved inadequate to extend housing segregation into the new postwar suburbs. Something new in public policy was needed. That something was exclusionary zoning.

Exclusionary zoning is the structural racist refinement of more traditional forms of residential segregation, adapted to the suburbs. If a suburban community wants to exclude newcomers who are poor and people of color, it can keep them out by the simple and seemingly color-blind, facially neutral expedient of tweaking its zoning ordinances, and perhaps its building code as well, to prohibit mobile homes or apartment buildings, and to mandate single-family housing, large lot sizes, generous setback requirements, square footage minimums, and other amenities that make housing more attractive but also more expensive. Proponents of these measures defend them on the grounds that they keep up property values, sustain the tax base, and encourage occupancy by older and wealthier people, who make fewer demands on public services (schools, police) than poorer, younger families with many children.[259] But they also fence out people of color, just not as crudely and overtly as the earlier forms of racial exclusion. Exclusionary zoning offers the advantage of not being overtly racialized, while it achieves the same objective: retaining white privilege and excluding African Americans from opportunity.[260] Since its inception in the United States after World War 1, zoning had always had a potential for racial exclusion and confinement.[261] Exclusionary zoning realized that potential.

During the civil rights era, legal commentators and state courts began to apply equal protection principles to exclusionary zoning practices.[262] When issues of exclusionary zoning reached the Supreme Court, the justices responded with opinions that were murky on the substantive issues presented,[263] but clear and forceful on the procedural issues. Those procedural cases restricted federal judicial oversight of exclusionary zoning, leaving the practice difficult to challenge in federal courts.

At first, though, the Court read the Fair Housing Act of 1968 broadly to allow standing for plaintiffs in a pattern-or-practice suit who alleged discrimination in rental housing. In *Trafficante v. Metropolitan Life Insurance Co.* (1972), the plaintiffs, who were tenants in a large apartment complex, complained that the landlord's discriminatory practices in excluding people of color caused them to lose the social benefits and business opportunities that came from living in an integrated community. They were stigmatized as residents of a "white ghetto."[264] The Court upheld their standing. A "generous construction" of the act was needed to permit standing, Justice Douglas claimed, to achieve the purposes of the legislation. The Court valorized such "private attorneys general" who brought suits to protect the public interest. But after that victory, the climate chilled for those who would challenge exclusionary zoning. The Court interposed standing as a bar to public-interest groups who would challenge exclusionary zoning.

Standing consists of three constitutional components and three sub-constitutional, "prudential" ones. Plaintiffs must show that they have sustained an injury that is personal to them, that it was caused by the defendant, and that a court can provide some sort of relief for that injury. Each of these is mandated by the case or controversy requirements of Article III, section 2 of the federal Constitution, and may not be waived by courts, Congress, or the parties.[265] The non-constitutional prudential requirements forbid plaintiffs' proffering a claim of some third party not before the court, rather than their own, or presenting a "generalized grievance" that they share with most other people, and require that the claim be within the "zone of interests" protected by the Constitution or statute under which plaintiffs claim.

Standing is indispensable to constitutional adjudication, but it has an opportunistic potential that sometimes enables judges to reach the merits of a case through a pretext, deciding it based on their unstated policy or ideological preferences. Abused in this way, it lends itself to unprincipled judging. Standing is inherently indeterminate, which makes it useful for judges who want to protect the status quo of white advantage and its auxiliary values of white innocence and individualism.[266] This sinister quality pervades the exclusionary zoning cases.

In *Warth v. Seldin* (1975),[267] an array of low-income housing advocates challenged the zoning ordinance and practices of Penfield, New York, a well-to-do suburb of Rochester that was 98 percent white at the time.[268] Petitioners included four individuals who were poor and either Black or Puerto Rican who wanted to move to Penfield but could not find housing there within their means; four other individuals who were Rochester residents and taxpayers, who alleged that their taxes were higher than they might have been if Penfield had not closed itself off to affordable housing; two activist nonprofits dedicated to creating affordable housing; and two associations that wanted to build low-income housing in Penfield. They alleged that Penfield's zoning ordinance was exclusionary, and that Penfield officials had resisted all their efforts to obtain permits and variances.

Justice Powell, writing for the conservative majority of the Burger Court, systematically denied the standing of each of the petitioners, relying on both constitutional and prudential grounds. He claimed that the poor/minority plaintiffs failed to satisfy all the constitutional bases: they did not show actual injury to themselves, because they failed to show at least a "substantial probability" that they had been or would be frustrated in their attempts to find a place to live in Penfield. They did not prove that their plight was the result of defendant town's actions or that that they would be able to buy or rent housing in Penfield if courts granted the injunction. To reach this result, Powell had to resort to catch-22 reasoning: petitioners did not have a "present interest" in any Penfield property, so they were not harmed by Penfield's actions. He was saying in effect: you cannot challenge Penfield's zoning unless you acquire property (by purchase or lease) in Penfield, which Penfield's zoning makes it impossible for you to do. Or as Justice Brennan put it in dissent, petitioners are thrown out "because they have not succeeded in breaching, before the suit was filed, the very barriers which are the subject of the suit."[269] As for the Rochester taxpayers, their injury was "conjectural," and they were in reality trying to enforce the rights of third parties. The activist groups failed to show injury to their members and thus were also in the position of representing the interests of third parties. The builders failed to demonstrate that they had any current projects underway in Penfield that would be thwarted by restrictive zoning, and a failed effort three years earlier was water over the dam by then.

A frustrated Justice Brennan could only splutter in dissent that the majority "tosses out of court almost every conceivable kind of plaintiff who could be injured by the activity claimed to be unconstitutional," a result that can "be explained only by an indefensible hostility to the claim on the merits."[270] "Today's decision will be read as revealing hostility to breaking down even unconstitutional zoning barriers," he warned.[271] Events proved Brennan correct. Standing doctrine in the context of housing is inherently indeterminate, which means that it can be opportunistically invoked, as it was by Powell, to rid the Court of unwelcome challenges to the racial status quo. Reinforced by other pillars of inequality, including the pervasive trait of individualism and the dogma of white innocence, standing is a stealth way of protecting extant privilege.[272] Standing doctrine enables the Court to rationalize racial inequality as a natural, apolitical phenomenon not caused by legal actors and therefore not amenable to redress by legal institutions. It is just "out there," impervious to judicial writs. Standing's application in racial cases resembles a game of "Calvinball," where preexisting rules either do not exist or can be changed at will during the game by the players to promote their own advantage.[273] Specifically, as in *Warth v. Seldin* or *Allen v. Wright*,[274] the Court defined injury narrowly, to the vanishing point, to deny racial minorities access to relief. In contrast, in cases like *Regents v. Bakke* or *Parents Involved*, the Court generously interpreted injury or causation to grant white plaintiffs entrée to courts even when their injuries were purely conjectural, immeasurable, or lying only in the future.[275]

There was another source for the conservatives' reluctance to permit challenges to exclusionary zoning: a strongly felt need for federal courts to defer to local governments in all matters pertaining to zoning. Powell noted in a *Warth* footnote that "zoning laws...are peculiarly within the province of state and local legislative authorities."[276] Dissatisfied petitioners "need not overlook the availability of the normal democratic process," which was another catch-22 since none of the petitioners lived in Penfield and were therefore in no position to influence the actions of local officials. Moreover, the "normal democratic process" included popular referenda that squelched affordable housing in the suburbs. But this judicial hands-off attitude left zoning decisions, including those that manifestly excluded the poor and minorities (and were meant to do so), beyond the ken of the federal courts.[277]

The standing cases were procedural: they aborted litigation before the Court even approached the substantive issues. The Court's principal substantive encounters with issues of exclusionary zoning came in cases that involved questions not of physical spaces like square-footage minimums, but of family composition. Some municipalities filtered out undesirable prospective residents not by pricing them out of the market, as zoning or building codes did, but by controlling their living arrangements in ways that disfavored family structures of African American and Latino populations.

The first of these cases, *Belle Terre v. Boraas* (1974),[278] challenged a local ordinance that restricted occupancy of dwellings to a "single family," defined as "one or more persons related by blood, adoption, or marriage." This ordinance was not directed explicitly at a racial group, but it had a broad potential impact on African American families trying to move out of the inner cities, who relied on fictive kin family structures for survival and childcare.[279] Once again, structural racism intruded in civic governance, disguised as it often is in seemingly non-related costume. The village of Belle Terre, a well-to-do Long Island community near the State University of New York at Stony Brook, was trying to preclude student slums that grow up in or near college towns. The Court readily upheld the ordinance, giving it only deferential scrutiny as "social and economic legislation." The case did not present obvious racial implications, but its deferential posture toward local zoning and related municipal decisions boded ill for cases that did. Justice Marshall dissented in vain, failing to persuade his colleagues that "the choice of household companions—of whether a person's "intellectual and emotional needs are best met by living with family, friends, professional associates, or others—involves deeply personal considerations as to the kind and quality of intimate relationships within the home." They should be protected from governmental interference with rights of association and privacy.[280] Marshall was alluding to alternative kinship relations formed in African American households to cope with the countless impediments of discrimination and poverty they faced.

Moreover, had the justices cared to dig more deeply, they would have found ample evidence of the discriminatory effects of such seemingly facially neutral zoning. The federal Department of Commerce concluded in 1992 that "zoning is consistently used to prevent the spatial extension of people of color into white, middle-class America. Stereotypes influence zoning regulations that attempt to keep alternative living arrangements out of neighborhoods called 'single-family,' where the mythical nuclear family resides."[281] Progressive state supreme courts found in their state constitutions protections for the rights of unrelated persons to live together. The New Jersey Supreme Court stated that a "municipality may not, for example, zone so as to exclude from its borders the poor or other unwanted minorities."[282] In 1977, Justice Stevens identified seven states that had already overridden similar unrelated-persons ordinances.[283]

Though *Belle Terre* lacked obvious racial overtones, *Moore v. East Cleveland* (1977)[284] was saturated with them. The facts of the case were peculiar. Inez Moore lived in a home she owned with her son, his son, and the son of her deceased daughter. The boys were therefore cousins, not brothers, a degree of consanguinity excluded by the city's zoning ordinance. The town prosecuted Mrs. Moore when she refused to evict her grandson. Like Belle Terre, the suburb of East Cleveland, Ohio, limited residential occupancy to "members of a single family" but defined that phrase in a complex ordinance that had both the intent and the effect of excluding extended families. The racial dynamics behind the ordinance were confounding: African Americans were migrating out of the eastside ghetto of Cleveland into its eastern suburbs in search of better schools and other amenities of suburban life long enjoyed by whites. At the time the ordinance was adopted, the mayor and a majority of the city council were African Americans,[285] and they seem to have been determined to preserve the middle-class character of the city by excluding the extended families that were more characteristic of poor Black than of affluent white households, and that they feared would be infiltrating the suburbs as they escaped the inner city.

Reflecting these complexities, the Court, in no fewer than six separate opinions, split four-one-four on the result, which was to hold the ordinance unconstitutional. Justice Powell for a plurality held it invalid on privacy and substantive due process grounds, apparently offended by the city's heartless determination to separate a grandmother from her orphaned grandson. He insisted that the American constitutional tradition made room for extended as well as traditional nuclear families, though he did not allude to racial disparities in family composition.[286] Justices Brennan and Marshall, in a sociologically informed concurrence, condemned the implicit racial bias in favor of white family composition (even if those preferences were expressed by Black political leaders). A city government may not impose "upon the rest of us of white suburbia's preference in patterns of family living." "The 'extended' form is especially familiar among Black families," Brennan wrote. "Black citizens, like generations of white immigrants before them, have been victims of economic and other disadvantages that would worsen if they were compelled to abandon extended, for nuclear, living patterns."[287] Ironically, though the case was so heavily freighted with racial consequences, *Moore* provided neither precedent nor guidance for the Court in confronting other substantive issues of exclusionary zoning.

Issues of family composition and integrity, difficult enough in themselves, become more tangled when racial considerations influence judicial choices. *Palmore v. Sidoti* (1984)[288] illustrates how race complicates judges' reasoning in what should otherwise not be problematic cases. Linda Palmore, who was white, was awarded custody of her three-year-old daughter when she was divorced from Anthony Sidoti. When she subsequently married Clarence Palmore, who was African American, Sidoti sought to have custody of the child transferred to himself. A Florida court agreed, contending that the prevalence of racial prejudice in American society would cause difficulties for a child of biracial parents. The US Supreme Court unanimously reversed the ruling. Chief Justice Burger declared that "classifying persons according to their race is more likely to reflect racial prejudice than legitimate public concerns; the race, not the person, dictates the category" (thereby affirming the anticlassification principle). He imposed strict scrutiny and reversed because social stigma based on racist reactions was an insufficient basis for taking a child from her mother. "Private biases may be outside the reach of the law, but the law cannot, directly or indirectly, give them effect." But the Court did not prohibit all consideration of race in other cases involving child custody, particularly adoption,[289] which provided no guidance or clarification for other judges and administrators in interracial adoption cases today.

Epilogue

"The Gloomy Past"

For two centuries, the US Supreme Court has usually been on the wrong side in the struggle for racial justice. It has sustained the successive dominant regimes of racial oppression: slavery, Jim Crow, and structural racism. The justices have never transcended the prevailing white racial attitudes of their times. In periods when racial inequality has been ascendant, the Court has accepted or even supported it. In those few brief times when Congress has tried to ensure greater equality for Black Americans, the justices have been laggard in supporting the effort, if they supported it at all. (Perhaps we should not expect the justices of the Supreme Court to be more virtuous than the American people at large, or at least not be disappointed when we find that they are not.) The civil rights era of the 1960s was the unique exception to the Court's sorry record because then all three branches of the federal government—the president, Congress, and the federal courts—mutually sustained the egalitarian program of the 1964 and 1965 Civil Rights Acts. But when that cooperation weakened, racial progress stalled. The Court abandoned its commitment to racial justice after its conservative about-face in 1972, personified in the appointment of William Rehnquist and Lewis Powell to the Court. Aside from the second Reconstruction of the 1960s, the Court has disappointed the hopes of Black Americans. It has been unable to disenthrall itself from its tendency to sustain prevalent forms of racism.

Before 1850, the justices sensed that they could do nothing to suppress the disruptive potential of slavery, and so they refrained from meddling with it. They wisely avoided provocative decisions involving fugitives or the western territories. But the overwhelming pressures imposed by the successive crises of the Union broke that resolve. When the struggle over slavery intensified after 1846, the justices abandoned their prudence. Tensions driven by territorial expansion encouraged the foolhardy conceit that judges could finally resolve the exigent constitutional issues posed by slavery. Flinging away caution, the Court plunged first into problems involving fugitives from slavery, then fatally took on slavery's expansion into the West. The Court's majority capitulated to its own worst instincts. It attempted to impose a judicial settlement on issues that had proven insoluble for normal politics and produced what all acknowledge today to be its worst decision ever, *Dred Scott v. Sandford,* in 1857. That ghoul of a case still haunts us from its unhallowed grave. To promote slavery's unfettered expansion into the West, and to secure the internal security of slavery where it existed in the South, the Court repudiated democracy in favor of the brittle originalism of Taney's opinion. The decision prostrated the free states of the North before the slavocracy. It would have enabled the slaveholding South's sectional minority to control the nation's future. In doing so, the justices endorsed the most extreme expression of racism that had ever been broached in constitutional discourse in the United States.

After that short-lived, Pyrrhic victory for the Slave Power, Congress tried to replace the constitution of the slaveholders' republic with a racially egalitarian legal order in Reconstruction. Republicans sought to vanquish the lethal ideology of "states' rights," replacing it with a regime of national supremacy that secured the equal protection of the laws for all people. Congress founded this new constitutional order on national citizenship and an equality of privileges, immunities, and protection of the law for all Americans, guaranteed by the federal government and its courts. The modern Supreme Court has belatedly recognized that this constituted the nation's "Second Founding."[1]

But the Court, vacillating and uncertain, failed to sustain that nationalizing vision. It fell back on antebellum notions of state power and limited national authority when it anesthetized Reconstruction in its *Slaughterhouse* decision of 1873. The justices then acquiesced in the constitutional equivalent of a medically induced coma for Reconstruction that was imposed by the political settlement of 1877. The Court and nation both abandoned African Americans to the resurgent racist Redeemers then coming into power throughout the South. Political reaction and counterrevolutionary violence snuffed the beginnings of a more egalitarian, democratic society. Through pretense and pretext, the Court reconciled the formal equality guaranteed by the Reconstruction Amendments with the social reality of forced labor and political disfranchisement. The backlash mentality that dominated Redemption—never learn, never forget—exhumed much of the social and economic order of unfreedom in the southern states. Public law became its compliant servant in sustaining segregationist legal regimes in the South, and in tolerating discrimination prevalent elsewhere. Throughout

Redemption, the Supreme Court consistently upheld regressive initiatives in the former slave states, beginning with the *Civil Rights Cases* of 1883. After Congress abandoned Reconstruction altogether in 1890, the Court readily accommodated Jim Crow and upheld the white South's revival of slavery under different forms. By 1910, the fortunes of African American people sank to the Nadir of their experience.

But after that, Jim Crow began to totter. Through mid-century the Court made modest efforts to abate the worst inequalities in the status of African Americans in criminal prosecutions and in access to the ballot. By the 1940s, the justices began to adopt egalitarian readings of the Reconstruction Amendments and considered constitutional interpretations that might realize the promise of equality.

The Supreme Court began the second Reconstruction in 1954 with *Brown v. Board of Education*, where the Court began eradicating de jure discrimination. After a decade of inaction, Congress resumed leadership of constitutional restoration through the Civil Rights Acts of the 1960s. For a decade, the Court and the executive and legislative branches joined forces supportively. In the civil rights era of 1954–1972 it seemed that the American people might at last usher in a constitutional regime based on racial justice and the authentic equality promised in the Declaration of Independence. The equal protection clause came into its own; the Thirteenth Amendment took on new substantive significance; the state action requirement abated somewhat. For a brief time, the justices found themselves in the vanguard of racial justice.

But the moment passed, and the Court led the way into a second era of Redemption after 1972. Equality again proved elusive, especially as it became apparent that racial justice would come with costs that would be borne by whites, through the loss of customary advantages they had hitherto taken for granted. By a seeming paradox, racial disparity has been reinforced, not reduced, by being decoupled from the overt discrimination of the Jim Crow era. Inequality is still potent even if no longer overtly imposed by state action. Thanks to structural racism, this latest iteration of inequality today flourishes in plain view, though its countless mechanisms are often not visible.

The Court's response to these trends since 1972 has been disheartening. It once again accepted policies that produce adverse outcomes for African Americans. The justices rejected efforts to interpret the equal protection clause as a source of unenumerated fundamental rights. After first permitting Congress to remedy racially disparate impacts in employment, in *Washington v. Davis* (1976) the justices backtracked by requiring proof of discriminatory intent to document complaints that were constitutionally grounded. The Court abandoned *Brown v. Board of Education*'s vision of educational equality, substituting in its place local control of schools as the core value of school policy. This affirmed the apartheid in the schools caused by the structural disparities that characterize city neighborhoods defined by residential segregation. Underfunded, monoracial urban public schools have been the unsurprising result. Having accepted resegregation, the Court then guaranteed inequality by sustaining unequal funding levels for public schools. It invoked the doctrine of standing to disable Black parents from challenging segregation academies and discriminatory admissions. The justices prohibited local school districts from trying to prevent resegregation through admissions and transportation policies. Though the Court has reluctantly recognized diversity as a legitimate goal in higher education, it first narrowed the scope of affirmative action there, then finally killed it altogether, as it had already done for primary and secondary education. Only the narrowest scope remains for affirmative action in awarding public contracts and in assuring workplace opportunity.

The Supreme Court has permitted Republican legislatures in many states to impose constraints on voting that restrict the political power of African Americans. Modern vote-suppression techniques approach Redemption-era levels. The Court has upheld felon disfranchisement, a device that was first used in Redemption to suppress the Black vote and continues to do so today. *Shelby County v. Holder* has disabled the Voting Rights Act. The Court's decisions in racial matters are more exercises of legislative will than of impartial judicial judgment.

The residue of two centuries of slavery followed by eight decades of Jim Crow servitude, permeated by pervasive racism (both overt and unconscious), has created a condition of intrinsic inequality for African Americans today. This reality has been disguised in part by the genuine (though insufficient) progress toward racial justice has been made in the last half century. Some of the justices believe that America today offers authentic equality and opportunity for all who wish to seize it. Such wishful thinking assumes that the current status quo of racial relations constitutes a just baseline from which any change that disturbs the existing distribution of racial advantage is constitutionally suspect. These basic assumptions defend the current racial status quo as legitimate and equitable. Any disturbance of it threatens its presumed fair allocation of rights, privileges, and opportunities among all Americans.

The constitutional expression of these complacent assumptions about status quo equality is found in the doctrines that dominate the Supreme Court's treatment of race-inflected cases today. The justices insist that that these assumptions are compatible with the Fourteenth Amendment's guarantee of the equal protection of the laws. Foremost is color-blindness, which was an honorable ideal when John Marshall Harlan uttered it in 1896 to condemn demeaning discrimination against African Americans. But that ideal is drained of moral force when used by Justice Thomas to block efforts to create genuine equality in life chances for African Americans today. Context is all. Invoking color-blindness to overthrow inequality based on structural racism is altogether different from, and antithetical to, using it to protect white advantage.

Color-blindness, seemingly impartial, in fact frustrates egalitarian efforts to provide true equality when it prevents us from seeing and dealing with racial realities. Facial neutrality revives the pretextuality of Jim Crow and dresses it up in modern garb, holding out an illusory promise of faux equality that disables our ability to identify and correct genuine inequality. The intent/disparate effects distinction condemns Black litigants to an impossible Sisyphean challenge, the juristic equivalent of proving a negative. At the same time, the Court waives the intent requirement for white complainants who want to protect programs that protect white advantage. The illusion that residential segregation with its attendant educational inequality is the product of free individual choice elides the massed efforts of the federal government, the states, private associations, the nation's banks, and night-riding violence to deny decent housing to countless Black Americans throughout the twentieth century. Under these assumptions, formal equality is adequate, or at least good enough for the Supreme Court. Actual reality be damned.

These labored pretenses tricked out as legal dogma ignore a wisdom that traces back to Hippocrates, Plato, and Aristotle: inequality results when we treat unequals alike. Justice Felix Frankfurter cited it in *Dennis v. United States* (1950): "there is no greater inequality than the equal treatment of unequals."[2] President Lyndon B. Johnson affirmed its wisdom in his 1965 Howard University address: "Freedom is not enough....You do not take a person who, for years, has been hobbled by chains and liberate him, bring him up to the starting line of a race and then say 'you are free to compete with all the others.'...We seek not just legal equity but human ability, not just equality as a right and a theory but equality as a fact and equality as a result."[3]

Instead, the Court has decreed that racism's structural causes are constitutionally inoffensive and their effects beyond legal remedy. Colorblindness, facial neutrality, the intent/effects distinction, anticlassification, and sanitized de facto segregation decide the Court's approach to questions of racial inequality today. The Fourteenth Amendment, originally meant to secure for African Americans the equality envisioned by the Declaration of Independence, has become a shield of white advantage justified by presumed racial innocence. By 2015, the Court had reinstated a racial legal order that protects white preference in access to social capital, abandons the egalitarian command of *Brown*, and ignores structural inequality. Racial disparities again endure today behind a Potemkin-village facade of nominal equality. Most of the justices seem content with that.

The conflict between Congress and the Supreme Court over the enforcement clauses of the Reconstruction Amendments has gone dormant for the time being. Congress has been unable to act on racial justice issues since 1992 because the Republican Party remains in thrall to the Southern Strategy, still going strong a half century later. The GOP has internalized the racial mindset that riles its base, roiling it in a churning state of racial resentment.

The Court has refused to confront racism in American society and its manifestations in the practices of white supremacy. Throughout the six hundred volumes of the *United States Reports* the justices have almost never alluded to the reality of racism or used words that denote it. Only once has the phrase "White Supremacy" appeared in an opinion of the Court;[4] only thirty or so times has a member of the Court referred to "racism." The justices have never referred to "structural racism" or cognates like "systemic racism" or "institutional racism." Such a persistent silence suggests that they refuse or are unable to recognize this reality. But a body of judicial doctrine that cannot acknowledge a massive underlying reality, the proverbial elephant in the room, is doomed to produce unforeseeable trouble and eventually fail.[5]

Imagine this counterfactual as a thought experiment: suppose that Congress might somehow again become committed to the cause of racial justice, as it was in the civil rights era when it enacted the civil rights trilogy of the 1960s. Instead of attacking the overtly racist proscriptions of the Jim

Crow era, suppose that a modern Congress understood the problems of structural racism in all their complexity and was determined to root them out. Try to picture a Congress dedicated to genuine equality for all, having in mind the three centuries of wrongs inflicted on African Americans. Then imagine the many initiatives it might undertake to eradicate the structural racist effects of slavery and Jim Crow, such as affirmative action, or fair-housing legislation that eliminates exclusionary zoning.

Given the performance the of the Court since 1972, how might it be expected to react to such egalitarian activism? If the Court were to behave as it did in the years from 1800 to 1862, and then from 1873 to 1923, and from 1972 to the present, it would stifle all efforts by Congress, the states, other public entities like school boards, as well as private organizations to create true equality. It would be persistently obstructive. Sometimes it might do this in decisions that shock the conscience, modern repeats of *Dred Scott*, *Plessy v. Ferguson*, *Shelby County v. Holder*, and *Parents Involved*. It would block egalitarian initiatives, eradicating all remnants of affirmative action, closing its eyes to resegregation in the schools, winking at denial and dilution of the Black vote. It would reaffirm doctrines such as state action, the discriminatory intent/disparate effects dichotomy, and anticlassification that confine the equal protection clause in a straitjacket of judicial negativism. It would sustain all effects of racism that could not be traced to explicit racist intent on the part of public agencies. It would disable public activism generally, weakening and narrowing government's ability to respond to racial injustice. It would ignore de facto residential segregation, the root of all racial inequality evils that bedevil American society today.

It would do all this because that is what it has done for most of its history. Why should we hope that it would behave differently in the future from the ways it has behaved for most of its past and is behaving in the present? Rare jurists like the first John Marshall Harlan (on his better days), Charles Evans Hughes, Frank Murphy, Wiley Rutledge, William Brennan, Thurgood Marshall, Ruth Bader Ginsburg, or Sonia Sotomayor might be a beacon of light in dark times, but such individuals would be overwhelmed by modern counterparts of Roger Taney, Peter Daniel, James McReynolds, William Rehnquist, Lewis Powell, Clarence Thomas, Antonin Scalia, John Roberts, and Samuel Alito, who were determined to squelch every initiative for racial justice that comes before them. In doing so, the justices could be confident that they will be backed by the Republican Party and by that segment of the electorate that has convinced itself that it is white people who are the real victims of racial injustice and inequality.

The confident optimism of "Lift Every Voice and Sing" is premature. Expecting support from the Supreme Court for racial justice is misplaced for now. We are still in "the gloomy past" recalled in the Black National Anthem: "Stony the road we trod, bitter the chastening rod, Felt in the days when hope unborn had died."

The justices have not been candid about the consequences of their decisions that have had a racial impact. They have not considered how their decisions will affect the lives, opportunities, and dignity of African Americans. *Plessy v. Ferguson* should have taught us that abstract speculation about racial relations, divorced from a clear-headed and candid observation of social realities, will have disastrous consequences for all Americans. The social sciences, or simply the day's news, can provide a corrective to the kind of unfounded speculation and theorizing about racial and social realities that condemns the *Plessy* majority opinion. Justice Harlan's dissent in *Plessy* showed us how to face up to the consequences of the Court's decisions. He correctly foretold that "the judgment this day rendered will, in time, prove to be quite as pernicious as the decision made by this tribunal in the Dred Scott Case" because it will "only stimulate aggressions, more or less brutal and irritating, upon the admitted rights of colored citizens." Instead, he called for "the clear, distinct, unconditional recognition by our governments, national and state, of every right that inheres in civil freedom, and of the equality before the law of all citizens of the United States, without regard to race."[6] The rest of the Court refused to acknowledge that reality then and continues to do so today.

Despite its disappointing performances so far, the Court can align its decisions and doctrine with the egalitarian potential of the Declaration of Independence and the Reconstruction Amendments. Justice Thurgood Marshall taught us that "the Constitution [is] a living document, including the Bill of Rights and the other amendments protecting individual freedoms and human rights."[7] That is the heart of the American constitutional experience, and our best hope for breaking free from four centuries of racial injustice. Only then will "We the People of the United States...form a more perfect Union, establish Justice, insure domestic Tranquility...and secure the Blessings of Liberty to ourselves and our Posterity."

The Dark Past: The US Supreme Court and African Americans, 1800–2015. William M. Wiecek, Oxford University Press. © Oxford University Press 2024. DOI: 10.1093/9780197654460.003.0012

Notes

Prologue

1. Michelle Alexander, *The New Jim Crow*, 10th anniversary ed. (New York: New Press, 2020), x, xviii. Michael J. Klarman in *Unfinished Business: Racial Equality in American History* (New York: Oxford University Press, 2007) similarly characterizes inequality as fitting an ebb-and-flow pattern.
2. *American Heritage Dictionary of the English Language*, 5th ed. (New York: Dell, 2011): "servitude: a state of subjection to an owner or master; lack of personal freedom, as to act as one chooses."
3. On the beginnings of the legal status of slavery in America, see Winthrop Jordan, *White over Black: American Attitudes toward the Negro, 1550–1812* (Chapel Hill: University of North Carolina Press, 1968), 71–83, 168; and in greater detail, Edmund S. Morgan, *American Slavery, American Freedom* (New York: Norton, 1975).
4. Dred Scott v. Sandford, 60 U.S. (19 How.) 393, 407 (1857).
5. The conventional term for emancipated African Americans after 1865 is "freedmen," as in Freedmen's Bureau. I prefer the word *freedpeople* to reincorporate half of the Black population into the discussion. The neologism may be clunkier, but it is more accurate and comprehensive.
6. Military Reconstruction Acts: Act of March 2, 1867, ch. 153, 14 Stat. 428; Act of March 23, 1867, ch. 6, 15 Stat. 2; Act of July 19, 1867, ch. 30, 15 Stat. 14; and Act of March 11, 1868, ch. 25, 15 Stat. 41.
7. Enforcement Acts: Act of May 31, 1870, ch. 114, 16 Stat. 140; Act of Feb. 28, 1871, ch. 99, 16 Stat. 433; Act of April 20, 1871, ch. 22, 17 Stat. 13.
8. Eric Foner, *Reconstruction: America's Unfinished Revolution, 1863–1877*, rev. ed. (New York: Harper, 2014), 564–601; Michael Perman, *The Road to Redemption: Southern Politics, 1869–1879* (Chapel Hill: University of North Carolina Press, 1984); James T. Moore, "Redeemers Reconsidered: Change and Continuity in the Democratic South, 1870–1900," 44 *Journal of Southern History* 357 (1978).
9. The eminent historian C. Vann Woodward coined the phrase "Second Reconstruction" in a 1957 essay, "The Political Legacy of Reconstruction," 26 *Journal of Negro Education* 231 (1957). Since then it has attained canonical status. Its foremost modern exponent is Eric Foner. See Foner, *The Second Founding: How the Civil War and Reconstruction Remade the American Constitution* (New York: Norton, 2019); Foner, "Reconstruction Revisited," 10 *Reviews in American History* 82 (1982); Manning Marable, *Race, Reform, and Rebellion: The Second Reconstruction and Beyond in Black America*, 3rd. ed. (Jackson: University Press of Mississippi, 2007).
10. Gary Orfield, "Plessy Parallels: Back to Traditional Assumptions," in Gary Orfield and Susan Eaton, eds., *Dismantling Desegregation: The Quiet Reversal of Brown v. Board of Education* (New York: New Press, 1996), 23–52; Adam Serwer, "Is This the Second Redemption?," *The Atlantic*, November 10, 2016, at https://www.theatlantic.com/politics/archive/2016/11/welcome-to-the-second-redemption/507317/.
11. George Lipsitz, *The Possessive Investment in Whiteness: How White People Profit from Identity Politics*, rev. ed. (Philadelphia: Temple University Press, 2006); Peggy McIntosh, "White Privilege: Unpacking the Invisible Knapsack," 49 *Independent School* 31 (1988).
12. With one major exception, *Prigg v. Pennsylvania* (1842), discussed in chapter 1 below.
13. Don Fehrenbacher, *The Slaveholding Republic: An Account of the United States Government's Relations to Slavery* (New York: Oxford University Press, 2001), 219–241, 280–289; George W. Van Cleve, *A Slaveholders' Union: Slavery, Politics, and the Constitution in the Early American Republic* (Chicago: University Chicago Press, 2010). They built upon [Wendell

Phillips], *The Constitution a Pro-slavery Compact: or, Selections from the Madison Papers* 2nd ed. (New York: American Anti-Slavery Society, 1845).

14. Reprinted in Imani Perry, *May We Forever Stand: A History of the Black National Anthem* (Chapel Hill: University of North Carolina Press, 2018).

15. Orville V. Burton and Armand Derfner attempt this in *Justice Deferred: Race and the Supreme Court* (Cambridge: Harvard University Press, 2021).

16. On which, see Nell Irvin Painter, *The History of White People* (New York: Norton, 2010); Nancy Isenberg, *White Trash: The 400-Year Untold History of Class in America* (New York: Viking, 2016).

17. Alexander, *The New Jim Crow*.

Chapter 1

1. Michael R. Haines, "Population, by Sex and Race: 1790–1990," Table Aa145-149, in *Historical Statistics of the United States, Earliest Times to the Present: Millennial Edition* (Washington, DC: U.S. Department of Commerce, 2006). The figure is for 1790.

2. Article I of the 1780 Massachusetts Constitution provided: "All men are born free and equal, and have certain natural, essential, and unalienable rights; among which may be reckoned the right of enjoying and defending their lives and liberties; that of acquiring, possessing, and protecting property; in fine, that of seeking and obtaining their safety and happiness."

3. Arthur Zilversmit, *The First Emancipation: The Abolition of Slavery in the North* (Chicago: University of Chicago Press, 1967).

4. But the ban on slavery in the Northwest Territory was ambiguous, and pockets of slavery persisted in Indiana and Illinois into the 1840s. Paul Finkelman, *Slavery and the Founders: Race and Liberty in the Age of Jefferson*, 3rd ed. (New York: Routledge, 2014), 34–79.

5. Don Fehrenbacher, *The Slaveholding Republic: An Account of the United States Government's Relations to Slavery* (New York: Oxford University Press, 2001). Professor Fehrenbacher there insisted that the United States was not a slaveholding republic at the beginning but degenerated into one as the nineteenth century wore on, due to the persistence of slave-state political leaders.

6. George W. Van Cleve, *A Slaveholders' Union: Slavery, Politics, and the Constitution in the Early American Republic* (Chicago: University of Chicago Press, 2010).

7. A. Leon Higginbotham, *In the Matter of Color: Race and the American Legal Process: The Colonial Period* (New York: Oxford University Press, 1980); William M. Wiecek, "The Statutory Law of Slavery and Race in Thirteen Mainland Colonies of British America," 34 *William and Mary Quarterly* 258–280 (1977); Wiecek, "The Origins of the Law of Slavery in British North America," 17 *Cardozo Law Review* 1711–1792 (1996).

8. Thomas D. Morris explores this body of law in detail in *Southern Slavery and the Law, 1619–1860* (Chapel Hill: University of North Carolina Press, 1996).

9. Art. I, sec. 2, apportioning members of the House of Representatives according to population but counting only 60 percent of enslaved African Americans in those populations.

10. Art. IV, sec. 2, the fugitive slave clause.

11. Art. I, sec. 9, restraining Congress from abolishing the international slave trade before 1808.

12. Paul Finkelman enumerates fifteen clauses of the Constitution that directly or indirectly protect slavery: "Slavery and the Constitutional Convention: Making a Covenant with Death," in Richard Beeman et al., eds., *Beyond Confederation: Origins of the Constitution and American National Identity* (Chapel Hill: University of North Carolina Press, 1987), 188–225. William M. Wiecek, *The Sources of Antislavery Constitutionalism in America, 1760–1848* (Ithaca: Cornell University Press, 1977) 228–248, counts ten.

13. Paul Finkelman, "Garrison's Constitution: The Covenant with Death and How it Was Made," 34.2 *Prologue* (2000), https://www.archives.gov/publications/prologue/2000/winter/garrisons-constitution-1.html. The biblical source for Garrison's image was Isaiah 28:18: "And your covenant with death shall be disannulled and your agreement with hell shall not stand." All Bible quotations in this study are from the King James Version.

14. [Wendell Phillips], *The Constitution a Pro-slavery Compact: or, Selections from the Madison Papers* 2nd ed. (New York: American Anti-Slavery Society, 1845).

15. Professor Paul Finkelman is the one-man cottage industry of the neo-Garrisonian school. In addition to "Slavery and the Constitutional Convention," see his *Supreme Injustice: Slavery in the Nation's Highest Court* (Cambridge: Harvard University Press, 2018), 11–25; "Garrison's Constitution: The Covenant with Death and How It Was Made," in Finkelman, *Slavery and the Founders: Race and Liberty in the Age of Jefferson*, 2nd ed. (Armonk: M. E. Sharp, 2001), 3–45; "Affirmative Action for the Master Class: The Creation of the Proslavery Constitution," 32 *Akron Law Review* 423 (1999); "The Cost of Compromise and the Covenant with Death," 38 *Pepperdine Law Review* 845 (2011); "The Root of the Problem: How the Proslavery Constitution Shaped American Race Relations," 4 *Barry Law Review* 1 (2003); "The Proslavery Origins of the Electoral College," 23 *Cardozo Law Review* 1145 (2002); *Slavery and the Law* (Madison, WI: Madison House, 1996). Joining Finkelman and Wiecek in the neo-Garrisonian camp are the original neo-Garrisonian Staughton Lynd, "The Abolitionist Critique of the Constitution," in Lynd, *Class Conflict, Slavery, and the United States Constitution* (Westport: Greenwood Press, 1980), 153–184; David Waldstreicher, *Slavery's Constitution: From Revolution to Ratification* (New York: Farrar, Strauss and Giroux, 2009); James Oakes, "'The Compromising Expedient': Justifying a Proslavery Constitution," 17 *Cardozo Law Review* 2023 (1996); and Van Cleve, *A Slaveholders' Union*. Justice Thurgood Marshall distilled the proslavery Constitution thesis in his "Bicentennial Speech" (1987), at Thurgood Marshall, "The Constitution's Bicentennial: Commemorating the Wrong Document?", 40 *Vanderbilt Law Review* 1337, 1342 (1987) (discussed below in chapter 11).
16. Fehrenbacher, *Slaveholding Republic*; Earl M. Maltz, "The Idea of a Proslavery Constitution," 17 *Journal of the Early Republic* 37–59 (1997); William W. Freehling, "The Founding Fathers and American Slavery," 77 *American Historical Review* 81–93 (1972); Patrick Rael, *Eighty-Eight Years: The Long Death of Slavery in the United States, 1777–1965* (Athens: University of Georgia Press, 2015); and Sean Wilentz, *No Property in Man: Slavery and Antislavery at the Nation's Founding* (Cambridge: Harvard University Press, 2018).
17. Wilentz, *No Property in Man*, 113, 2.
18. *Oxford English Dictionary*, 2nd ed. (Oxford: Oxford University Press, 2000–), "genius": "the tutelary and controlling spirit…[appointed] to govern [its] fortunes and determine [its] character." Simon J. Gilhooley's *The Antebellum Origins of the Modern Constitution: Slavery and the Spirit of the American Founding* (New York: Cambridge University Press, 2022), describes the spirit at the time of the founding.
19. Harold M. Hyman and William M. Wiecek, *Equal Justice under Law: Constitutional Development, 1835–1875* (New York: Harper & Row, 1982), 86. In ancient Greek religion, Nemesis was the goddess of retribution, exacting punishment for crime or hubris.
20. William M. Wiecek, "The Witch at the Christening: Slavery and the Constitution's Origins," in Leonard W. Levy and Dennis J. Mahoney, eds., *The Framing and Ratification of the Constitution* (New York: Macmillan, 1987), 167–184.
21. On the Marshall Court generally, the principal modern studies are George Lee Haskins and Herbert A. Johnson, *Foundations of Power: John Marshall, 1801–1815* (vol. 2 of the Holmes Devise History of the Supreme Court of the United States) (New York: Cambridge University Press, 1981); G. Edward White, *The Marshall Court and Cultural Change, 1815–35* (Cambridge: Cambridge University Press, 1988) (vols. 3–4 of the *Holmes Devise History of the Supreme Court of the United States*); and Herbert A. Johnson, *The Chief Justiceship of John Marshall, 1801–1835* (Columbia: University of South Carolina Press, 1997). The imperturbable conservatism of Charles Warren, *The Supreme Court in United States History*, rev. ed., 2 vols. (Boston: Little, Brown, 1926), 1:231–814 endures as a challenge to modern liberal interpretations.
22. South Carolinians and Georgians, and later Alabamians and Mississippians, were a partial exception to this generalization. Though many whites in the Deep South shared the general attitudes enumerated in text above, the official political posture of their representatives was consistently one of avid support of slavery and a determination to acquire and employ as many slaves as possible to advance their economies. William M. Freehling, *The Road to Disunion: Secessionists at Bay, 1776–1854* (New York: Oxford University Press, 1990), 213–252.
23. The necessary-evil thesis has experienced a strange and startling resurrection in our own times. Sen. Tom Cotton (R.-AR), speaking in support of a bill he introduced to prohibit the use of federal funds for teaching the *New York Times*' "1619 Project" in grades K–12, contended that "As the Founding Fathers said, [slavery] was the necessary evil upon which the union was

built, but the union was built in a way, as [Abraham] Lincoln said, to put slavery on the course to its ultimate extinction." *The Guardian*, July 27, 2020, at https://www.theguardian.com/world/2020/jul/26/tom-cotton-slavery-necessary-evil-1619-project-new-york-times.

24. Historians with a sociological bent distinguish between "slave societies" and "societies having slaves." Quantitatively, the tipping point is around 20 percent; that is, a slave society is one in which a fifth of the population or more was held in slavery. In such societies, all other institutions and social relationships—labor, the family, politics, the churches—were shaped by slavery, by the incessant need to control the enslaved people, force their labor, and keep them in absolute subordination at all times. Their politics were single-mindedly devoted to preserving slavery. Georgia, South Carolina, Alabama, and Mississippi were slave societies. Ira Berlin, *Many Thousands Gone: The First Two Centuries of Slavery in North America* (Cambridge: Harvard University Press, 1998), 8–12. In "societies with slaves" (less than 20 percent enslaved), on the other hand, slavery was not *the* dominant social, economic, and political institution, and its disappearance would not have changed their fundamentals.

25. Edward E. Baptist, *The Half Has Never Been Told: Slavery and the Making of American Capitalism* (New York: Basic Books, 2014).

26. Act of March 2, 1807, ch. 22, 2 Stat. 426.

27. Donald L. Canney, *Africa Squadron: The U.S. Navy and the Slave Trade, 1842–1861* (Washington, DC: Potomac Books, 2006).

28. I avoid the word "slave" when it refers to a person unless the context requires otherwise (as in "fugitive slave clause"). To say that a person is a slave implies that there is some innate quality about him or her that makes him a slave, that renders her unfit to be free, an owned thing rather than a human like us. "Slave": the word itself carries an unmistakable frisson of contempt. My preferred usage, "enslaved person," is a clumsy alternative—four syllables in place of one—but it offers the advantage of emphasizing the humanity of the individual, a human being who was unlucky enough to be held in the unnatural condition of slavery. "Enslaved person" recognizes that enslavement is merely a contingent condition, the result of misfortune, but that the person's essence is his humanity, not his temporary status. The framers of the US Constitution may have agreed when they adopted the phrase "Person held to Service or Labour in one State, under the Laws thereof." That wordy circumlocution has at least the merit of being accurate and, in that sense, true.

29. Steven Deyle, *Carry Me Back: The Domestic Slave Trade in American Life* (New York: Oxford University Press, 2005), 40–62.

30. "Postnati" comes from the Latin: "after-born," that is, people born after a certain date, usually the Fourth of July.

31. Leon F. Litwack, *North of Slavery: The Negro in the Free States, 1790–1860* (Chicago: University of Chicago Press, 1961). Litwack's emphasis on the oppressive conditions African Americans endured in the free states has been challenged by Paul Finkelman, who points out that despite racially discriminatory laws and decisions in the northern states, African Americans in the free states actually enjoyed extensive liberties and protections through the antebellum period. See Finkelman, "Prelude to the Fourteenth Amendment: Black Legal Rights in the Antebellum North," 17 *Rutgers Law Journal* 415 (1985); Finkelman, "The Protection of Black Rights in Seward's New York," 34.3 *Civil War History* 213 (1988), 213.

32. Sven Beckert, *Empire of Cotton: A Global History* (New York: Vintage, 2014).

33. Henry Sumner Maine, *Ancient Law* (London: John Murray, 1861), 182.

34. Christopher Tomlins, *Freedom Bound: Law, Labor, and Civic Identity in Colonizing English America, 1580–1865* (Cambridge: Cambridge University Press, 2010), 29–31, 80–81, 242–243, 286.

35. Jeremiah 13:23.

36. Genesis 9:25. This was known as "the curse of Ham."

37. Joshua 9:23. In neither Genesis nor Jeremiah nor Joshua were the accursed people identified as African. That attribution came later, a product of myth. David M. Goldenberg, *Black and Slave: The Origins and History of the Curse of Ham* (Berlin: De Gruyter, 2017).

38. These paragraphs do not purport to describe reality, but rather whites' perceptions. See generally George M. Fredrickson, *The Black Image in the White Mind: The Debate on Afro-American Character and Destiny, 1817–1914* (New York: Harper & Row, 1971).

39. On Garrison and his thought, see Henry Mayer, *All on Fire: William Lloyd Garrison and the Abolition of Slavery* (New York: Norton, 1998), 300–331.

40. On these sects, see Wiecek, *Sources of Antislavery Constitutionalism*, 227–248 (Garrisonians), 249–275 (radical abolitionists).
41. 13 N. C. 263, 265 (1829).
42. On colonizationists and the American Colonization Society, see Eric Burin, *Slavery and the Peculiar Solution: A History of the American Colonization Society* (Gainesville: University Press of Florida, 2005) and the older P. J. Staudenraus, *The African Colonization Movement, 1816–1865* (New York: Columbia University Press, 1961).
43. Ousmane K. Power-Greene, *Against Wind and Tide: The African American Struggle against the Colonization Movement* (New York: New York University Press, 2014).
44. Finkelman, *Slavery and the Founders*, 80–104.
45. Wiecek, *Sources of Antislavery Constitutionalism*, 16 and passim.
46. These sources include Leon Friedman and Fred L. Israel, eds., *The Justices of the United States Supreme Court: Their Lives and Major Opinions* (New York: Chelsea House, 1997); Henry J. Abraham, *Justices and Presidents: A Political History of Appointments to the Supreme Court*, 3rd. ed. (New York: Oxford University Press, 1992); Clare Cushman, *The Supreme Court Justices: Illustrated Biographies, 1789–1995*, 2nd ed. (Washington, DC: Congressional Quarterly, 2001); Kermit L. Hall et al., eds., *The Oxford Companion to the Supreme Court of the United States*, 2nd ed. (New York: Oxford University Press, 2005); Melvin I., Urofsky, *The Supreme Court Justices: A Biographical Dictionary* (New York: Garland, 1994); Melvin I. Urofsky, ed., *Biographical Encyclopedia of the Supreme Court: The Lives and Legal Philosophies of the Justices* (Washington, DC: CQ Press, 2006); Allison Dunham and Philip B. Kurland, eds., *Mr. Justice* (Chicago: University of Chicago Press, 1956) (dated, but valuable individual entries); G. Edward White, *The American Judicial Tradition: Profiles of Leading American Judges*, 3rd. ed. (New York: Oxford University Press, 2007) (selective, noting only the greats, but insightful as to them).
47. The principal recent interpretive study of Marshall is R. Kent Newmyer, *John Marshall and the Heroic Age of the Supreme Court* (Baton Rouge: Louisiana State University Press, 2001) (quotations from pp. 414–434). Newmyer's earlier *The Supreme Court under Marshall and Taney*, 2nd ed. (Arlington Hts.: Harlan Davidson, 2005) remains useful. Charles Hobson, *The Great Chief Justice: John Marshall and the Rule of Law* (Lawrence: University Press of Kansas, 1996) is an accessible biography.
48. Paul Finkelman implacably recounts the details of Marshall's extensive personal involvement with slaveholding in *Supreme Injustice*, 36–54, and in Finkelman, "Master John Marshall and the Problem of Slavery," *University of Chicago Law Review Online* (2020) at https://lawrckaeviewblog.uchicago.edu/2020/08/31/marshall-slavery-pt1/ and "John Marshall's Proslavery Jurisprudence: Racism, Property, and the 'Great' Chief Justice," *University of Chicago Law Review Online* (2020) at https://lawreviewblog.uchicago.edu/2020/08/31/marshall-slavery-pt2/.
49. In 1821, Washington sold fifty-four of his slaves to a Louisiana slaveholder because they had been insubordinate. He engaged in a fierce public defense of the legality of slavery, and of his actions, in response to criticism that he had broken up families. He also sold off slaves to provide for the upkeep of Mount Vernon, which he inherited from this uncle, the late president. From 1798 to his death in 1829, Washington served on the Court, where he consistently voted with Marshall.
50. Annette Gordon-Reed, *The Hemingses of Monticello: An American Family* (New York: Norton, 2008).
51. With one exception, a house servant named Robin Spurlock, who chose to remain in slavery, because the price of accepting emancipation under Virginia law at the time was expulsion from the commonwealth. Finkelman, *Supreme Injustice*, 43.
52. 27 U.S. (2 Pet.) 150, 154 (1829).
53. Frances Rudko, "Pause at the Rubicon: John Marshall and Emancipation: Reparations in the Early National Period," 35 *John Marshall Law Review* 75 (2001).
54. John Marshall, *The Life of George Washington*, 2 vols., 2nd ed. (Philadelphia: James Crissy, 1832), 2:239.
55. Finkelman, *Supreme Injustice*, 76–111; quotation at p. 111.
56. Donald M. Roper, "In Quest of Judicial Objectivity: The Marshall Court and the Legitimation of Slavery," 21 *Stanford Law Review* 532 (1969).
57. Marshall to Lafayette, May 2, 1827, quoted in Newmyer, *John Marshall*, 421, 423.

58. Marshall to Lafayette, August 26, 1827, quoted in Newmyer, *John Marshall*, 422.
59. Donald G. Morgan, *Justice William Johnson: The First Dissenter* (Columbia: University of South Carolina Press, 1954), 101–103, 135–139.
60. Michael A. Schoeppner estimates that more than ten thousand Black seamen were arrested under the Negro Seamen Acts, which were enacted in all the coastal slave states south of Virginia: Schoeppner, *Moral Contagion: Black Atlantic Sailors, Citizenship, and Diplomacy in Antebellum America* (New York: Cambridge University Press, 2019), 221–230.
61. 8 F. Cas. 493 (C.C.D.S.C. 1823) (No. 4366). On the case and its significance, see Scott W. Stucky, "Elkison v. Deliesseline: Race and the Constitution in South Carolina, 1823," 14 *North Carolina Central Law Journal* 361 (1983). "On circuit" means that Johnson was sitting in the case not as a justice of the US Supreme Court, but as the presiding judge of an intermediate federal court, known at the time as a US circuit court.
62. Act of Feb. 28, 1803, ch. 10, 2 Stat. 205.
63. The Brig Wilson, 30 F. Cas. 239 (C.C.D.Va. 1820) (No. 17,846). Admiralty cases are often in rem proceedings (a suit against a thing rather than a person), in which the action is nominally against the vessel itself. Thus, as here, the full case title is simply the ship's name.
64. Almost half the seamen of the American merchant marine in the 1850s were men of color. Richard N. Current et al., *The Essentials of American History*, 2nd ed. (New York: Knopf, 1976), 116. On those Black sailors, see W. Jeffrey Bolster, *Black Jacks: African American Seamen in the Age of Sail* (Cambridge: Harvard University Press, 1998).
65. 17 U.S. (4 Wheat.) 316 (1819).
66. Marshall to Story, letter of September 26, 1823, in Joseph Story Papers, Massachusetts Historical Society, quoted in Warren, *Supreme Court in United States History*, 2:626.
67. Leonard L. Richards, *The Slave Power: The Free North and Southern Domination, 1780–1860* (Baton Rouge: Louisiana State University Press, 2000).
68. R. Kent Newmyer, *Supreme Court Justice Joseph Story: Statesman of the Old Republic* (Chapel Hill: University of North Carolina Press, 1968) is comprehensive and appreciative. Paul Finkelman is acerbic in *Supreme Injustice*, 112–171, and in *An Imperfect Union: Slavery, Federalism, and Comity* (Chapel; Hill: University of North Carolina Press, 1981). Gerald T. Dunne, *Justice Joseph Story and the Rise of the Supreme Court* (New York: Simon and Schuster, 1970) is an older but still useful work.
69. Thompson, a justice and then chief justice of the New York Supreme Court, served on the US Supreme Court from 1823 to 1843. Donald M. Roper, *Mr. Justice Thompson and the Constitution* (New York: Garland, 1987).
70. On McLean's views, see Paul Finkelman, "John McLean: Moderate Abolitionist and Supreme Court Politician," 62 *Vanderbilt Law Review* 519–565 (2009).
71. Alfred Moore (1799–1804), Henry Brockholst Livingston (1806–1823), Thomas Todd (1807–1826), Gabriel Duvall (1811–1835), and Robert Trimble (1826–1828). (All parenthetical dates are years of service on the Court.) The (non-)achievements of these jurists are celebrated in David P. Currie, "The Most Insignificant Justice: A Preliminary Inquiry," 50 *University of Chicago Law Review* 466 (1983) and Frank H. Easterbrook, "The Most Insignificant Justice: Further Evidence," 50 *University of Chicago Law Review* 481 (1983). However, Andrew T. Fede rescued Duvall from obscurity in "Not the Most Insignificant: Reconsidering Justice Gabriel Duvall's Slavery Law Opinions Favoring Liberty," 42 *Journal of Supreme Court History* 7 (2017) (contending that Duvall, a Marylander, was sympathetic to individual freedom suits).
72. There was no written opinion or official report of the decision. Numerous versions of Mansfield's words exist. I have relied on the version reprinted as Somerset v. Stewart, Lofft 1, 98 Eng. Rep. 499 (K.B. 1772).
73. "Reception" refers to the process by which the colonies accepted and adapted the common law of the metropolis as law in their jurisdictions as the basis for decisions in their courts. William B. Stoebuck, "Reception of English Common Law in the American Colonies," 10 *William & Mary Law Review* 393 (1968).
74. Frederick Pollock and Frederic William Maitland, *The History of English Law before the Time of Edward I*, 2 vols. (Cambridge: Cambridge University Press, 1895), 2:674.
75. Most of the colonial charters granted lawmaking authority to the government of the colony, with the qualification that all colonial laws must conform to the law of the metropolis or at least not be repugnant to it.
76. Mary Sarah Bilder, *The Transatlantic Constitution: Colonial Legal Culture and the Empire* (Cambridge: Harvard University Press, 2004), 1–14.

77. Quoted in William Wetmore Story, ed., *The Life and Letters of Joseph Story* (Boston: Little, Brown, 1851), I, 361.
78. Grand jury charges reprinted in William Wetmore Story, ed., *The Miscellaneous Writings of Joseph Story* (Boston: Little, Brown, 1852), 136–147.
79. An action in admiralty against a vessel is begun by filing a document known as a libel, the counterpart of a petition in equity. The party filing it is known as the libellant. A libel typically seeks recovery of the vessel and/or its cargo.
80. Including admiralty cases in both instance and prize jurisdiction. Prize jurisdiction encompassed capture of enemy vessels in time of war; instance jurisdiction includes all other cases in admiralty.
81. 26 F. Cas. 832, 846–848 (C.C.D. Mass. 1822) (No. 15,551).
82. Privately, however, he rejected such an interpretation. Writing to his colleague Justice Bushrod Washington in 1821 about his *Jeune Eugenie* opinion, Story stated, "I have not meddled at all with the question of the right of slavery in general, nor could I with any decent respect for the institutions of my country deem it proper to engage in such speculation." Letter of December 21, 1821, quoted in White, *Marshall Court and Cultural Change*, 696.
83. McLean to "Mr. Mathews," 1847 but otherwise undated, quoted in Warren, *Supreme Court in United States History*, 2:157.
84. Leslie Friedman Goldstein, "Slavery and the Marshall Court: Preventing 'Oppressions of the Minor Party'?," 67 *Maryland Law Review* 166 (2007), elaborated in Goldstein, *The U.S. Supreme Court and Racial Minorities: Two Centuries of Judicial Review on Trial* (Cheltenham: Edward Elgar, 2017), 13–31.
85. The Latin phrase *in favorem libertatis* appeared routinely in contemporary English and American judicial opinions relating to slavery and reflected a sometime judicial preference for outcomes resulting in personal liberty.
86. Mima Queen v. Hepburn, 11 U.S. (7 Cranch) 290, 292–293, 299 (1813).
87. 23 U.S. (10 Wheat.) 66, 114, 120–121 (1825). See the discussion in White, *Marshall Court*, 693–703.
88. A predecessor of the US Coast Guard.
89. John T. Noonan, *The Antelope: The Ordeal of the Recaptured Africans in the Administrations of James Monroe and John Quincy Adams* (Berkeley: University of California Press, 1977), provides not only a detailed recounting of the litigation, but a rumination on the role of lawyers in securing or thwarting human freedom. Earl M. Maltz reviews the arguments of those lawyers in *Slavery and the Supreme Court, 1825–1861* (Lawrence: University Press of Kansas, 2009), 6–10.
90. Act of March 3, 1819, ch. 101, 3 Stat. 532.
91. The Antelope, 23 U.S. (10 Wheat.) 66, 115, 120–122 (1825).
92. Story to Ezekiel Bacon, November 19, 1842, quoted in White, *Marshall Court*, 700.
93. The Taney Court was of course involved with issues of great moment besides slavery. It deserves a comprehensive modern study worthy of the subject. Carl Brent Swisher's *The Taney Period, 1836–1864* (New York: Macmillan, 1974), the fifth volume of the *Holmes Devise History of the Supreme Court of the United States*, is dated, particularly in its treatment of slavery issues, which reflect the views of a political scientist whose vision of the world was formed in the 1930s. Harold M. Hyman and William M. Wiecek offered a more modern reinterpretation in *Equal Justice under Law: Constitutional Development, 1835–1875* (New York: Harper and Row, 1982), 1–202, but that study is now some forty years old. Timothy Huebner, *The Taney Court: Justices, Rulings, and Legacy* (Santa Barbara: ABC-CLIO, 2003), provides a brief overview with documents. But the subject cries out for the extensive treatment that its importance merits. Daniel Walker Howe's *What Hath God Wrought: The Transformation of America, 1815–1848* (Cambridge: Cambridge University Press, 2007), winner of the 2008 Pulitzer Prize in History, provides a valuable overview of the earlier part of the antebellum era.
94. Austin Allen, *Origins of the Dred Scott Case: Jacksonian Jurisprudence and the Supreme Court 1837–1857* (Athens: Ohio University Press, 2006), 6–7, 227.
95. Maltz, *Slavery and the Supreme Court*, is the first monograph to analyze in depth the Taney Court's slavery cases. It was preceded by a brief overview a generation earlier: William M. Wiecek, "Slavery and Abolition before the United States Supreme Court, 1820–1860," 65 *Journal of American History* 34 (1978). G. Edward White considers the slavery decisions of the Taney Court in *Law in American History*, vol. 1: *From the Colonial Years through the Civil War* (New York: Oxford University Press, 2012), 338–381. Goldstein, *U.S. Supreme Court and Racial Minorities*, 52–79, is a concise review.

96. Taney badly needs a modern biographer. Carl B. Swisher's *Roger B. Taney* (New York: Macmillan, 1935) is woefully inadequate, mired in the racist worldview of the Dunning school. H. H. Walker Lewis, *Without Fear or Favor: A Biography of Chief Justice Roger Brooke Taney* (Boston: Houghton Mifflin, 1965) is not much better.
97. Unpublished opinion as US attorney general, 1832, quoted in Don E. Fehrenbacher, *The Dred Scott Case: Its Significance in American Law and Politics* (New York: Oxford University Press, 1978), 70.
98. John P. Frank, *Justice Daniel Dissenting: A Biography of Peter V. Daniel, 1784–1860* (Cambridge: Harvard University Press, 1964), viii.
99. John P. Frank titled his biography *Justice Daniel Dissenting.*
100. Dred Scott v. Sandford, 60 U.S. (19 How.) 393, 475 (1857) (Daniel, J. concurring).
101. Robert Saunders, *John Archibald Campbell: Southern Moderate, 1811–1889* (Tuscaloosa: University of Alabama Press, 1997). His role in Reconstruction is discussed below in chapter. 2.
102. U.S. v. Hanway, 26 F. Cas. 105, 122–123 (C.C.E.D. Pa. 1851) (No. 15,299).
103. This is a version of the thesis propounded in Wiecek, *Sources of Antislavery Constitutionalism*, and Hyman and Wiecek, *Equal Justice under Law*, 160–202.
104. On the collision of slavery and westward expansion, see Michael A. Morrison, *Slavery and the American West: The Eclipse of Manifest Destiny and the Coming of the Civil War* (Chapel Hill: University of North Carolina Press, 1997).
105. Donald L. Robinson discussed these settlements in *Slavery in the Structure of American Politics, 1765–1820* (New York: Norton, 1971), 177–247, and the causes for their ultimate failure, 378–423.
106. On the Missouri Compromises generally, see Robert P. Forbes, *The Missouri Compromise and Its Aftermath: Slavery and the Meaning of America* (Chapel Hill: University of North Carolina Press, 2007), 33–120. On its constitutional implications, see Wiecek, *Sources of Antislavery Constitutionalism*, 106–125.
107. William W. Freehling, *Prelude to Civil War: The Nullification Controversy in South Carolina, 1816–1836* (New York: Oxford University Press, 1966). Manisha Sinha evaluates the influence of immediatist abolitionists in her comprehensive *The Slave's Cause: A History of Abolition* (New Haven: Yale University Press, 2017), 215–223, 586–591.
108. These early antislavery constitutional theories are discussed in Randy Barnett, "Whence Comes Section 1? The Abolitionist Origins of the Fourteenth Amendment," 3 *Journal of Legal Analysis* 165 (2011), and in Wiecek, *Sources of Antislavery Constitutionalism*, 92–105, 150–248.
109. Art. IV, sec. 2: "The Citizens of each State shall be entitled to all Privileges and Immunities of Citizens in the several States."
110. State v. Crandall, 10 Conn. 339 (1834); Edmund Fuller, *Prudence Crandall: An Incident of Racism in Nineteenth-Century Connecticut* (Middletown: Wesleyan University Press, 1971).
111. Under the territories clause of Art. IV, sec. 3.
112. *The Declaration of Sentiments and Constitution of the American Anti-Slavery Society* . . . (New York: American Anti-Slavery Society, 1835).
113. 35 Mass. (18 Pick.) 193 (1836). Cf. a similar result in Jackson v. Bulloch, 12 Conn. 38 (1837).
114. Leonard W. Levy, *The Law of the Commonwealth and Chief Justice Shaw: The Evolution of American Law, 1830–1860* (Cambridge: Harvard University Press, 1957), 62–69.
115. State v. Post and State v. Van Buren, 20 N.J. Law 368 (1845).
116. Hobbs v. Fogg, 6 Watts 553 (Pa. 1837).
117. Maltz, *Slavery and the Supreme Court*, 52–116.
118. Maltz, *Slavery and the Supreme Court*, xx, 51.
119. Art. I, sec. 8, cl. 3: "The Congress shall have Power . . . To regulate Commerce with foreign Nations, and among the several States, and with the Indian Tribes."
120. Art. I. sec. 9. Cl. 1: "The Migration or Importation of such Persons as any of the states now existing shall think proper to admit, shall not be prohibited by the Congress prior to the Year one thousand eight hundred and eight."
121. "It cannot be presumed that any clause in the constitution is intended to be without effect, and therefore, such a construction is inadmissible." *Marbury v. Madison*, 5 U.S. (1 Cranch) 137, 174 (1803).
122. Walter Berns made this argument in "The Constitution and the Migration of Slaves," 78 *Yale Law Journal* 198 (1968).

123. David L. Lightner, *Slavery and the Commerce Power: How the Struggle against the Interstate Slave Trade Led to the Civil War* (New Haven: Yale University Press, 2006), 37–64.
124. Quoted in Maltz, *Slavery and the Supreme Court*, 69.
125. Gilhooley, *Antebellum Origins of the Modern Constitution*, 125–157.
126. Mayor of New York v. Miln, 36 U.S. (11 Pet.) 102, 136 (1837).
127. 40 U.S. (15 Pet.) 449 (1841).
128. The various opinions are discussed in greater detail in Maltz, *Slavery and the Supreme Court*, 68–82, and Lightner, *Slavery and the Commerce Power*, 71–78.
129. The dramatic potential of the incident was later exploited in the 1997 film *Amistad*, which featured Justice Harry Blackmun of the US Supreme Court in a cameo role as Justice Joseph Story.
130. The facts of the case are detailed in Howard Jones, *Mutiny on the Amistad: The Saga of a Slave Revolt and Its Impact on American Abolition, Law, and Diplomacy* (New York: Oxford University Press, 1987); Marcus Rediker, *The Amistad Rebellion: An Atlantic Odyssey of Slavery and Freedom* (New York: Penguin, 2012); William A. Owens, *Black Mutiny: The Revolt on the Schooner Amistad* (1953; rpt. New York: Penguin, 1997); Maltz, *Slavery and the Supreme Court*, 52–67; Finkelman, *Supreme Injustice*, 133–139.
131. United States v. The Amistad, 40 U.S. (15 Pet.) 518, 595 (1841).
132. Stanley Campbell, *The Slave Catchers: Enforcement of the Fugitive Slave Law, 1850–1860* (Chapel Hill: University of North Carolina Press, 1970).
133. Eugene H. Berwanger, *The Frontier against Slavery: Western Anti-Negro Prejudice and the Slavery Extension Controversy* (Urbana: University of Illinois Press, 1967).
134. Art. IV, sec. 2, cl. 3. On these statutes generally, see Thomas D. Morris, *Free Men All: The Personal Liberty Laws of the North, 1780–1861* (Baltimore: Johns Hopkins University Press, 1974).
135. On the challenges facing free African Americans, see Ira Berlin, *Slaves without Masters: The Free Negro in the Antebellum North*, rev. ed. (New York: Vintage, 1981); Litwack, *North of Slavery*.
136. Rogers M. Smith, *Civic Ideals: Conflicting Visions of American Citizenship in U.S. History* (New Haven: Yale University Press, 1997), 132–134, 174–181; James H. Kettner, *The Development of American Citizenship, 1608–1870* (Chapel Hill: University of North Carolina Press, 1978).
137. Carol Wilson, *Freedom at Risk: The Kidnapping of Free Blacks in America, 1780–1865* (Lexington: University Press of Kentucky, 1994), 67–82.
138. On comity and most of the cases discussed in this chapter, see Finkelman, *Imperfect Union*.
139. *Black's Law Dictionary*, 11th ed. (St. Paul: Thomson Reuters, 2019): "Recaption: ... 2. Peaceful retaking, without legal process, of one's own property that has been wrongfully taken."
140. An Act respecting fugitives from justice, and persons escaping from the service of their masters, ch. 7, 1 Stat. 302.
141. Sustaining the act's constitutionality: Wright v. Deacon, 5 Serg. & Rawle 63 (Pa. 1819); Commonwealth v. Griffith, 14 Mass. (2 Pick.) 11 (1823). Questioning it: the opinion of Chancellor Reuben Walworth in Jack v. Martin, 14 Wend. 507, 528 (N.Y. 1835); and an unreported case from New Jersey, State v. Sheriff of Burlington.
142. Morris, *Free Men All*, 23–58.
143. 41 U.S. (16 Pet.) 539, 611, 613 (1842). Litigation is collusive when there is no actual dispute between the parties, but they nevertheless seek a judicial opinion on some matter in dispute. The US Supreme Court has often and rightly condemned collusive suits ever since 1850 (Lord v. Veazie, 49 U.S. [8 How.] 251), in part because such suits have often produced disastrous results. But the justices have also opportunistically taken such cases when they felt that they should resolve some constitutional question. *Prigg* is a compelling example of why this is always a bad idea.
144. Maltz, *Slavery and the Supreme Court*, 104.
145. The literature on *Prigg* is extensive. Among the most important items are Paul Finkelman, "Storytelling on the Supreme Court: Prigg v. Pennsylvania and Justice Joseph Story's Judicial Nationalism," 1994 *Supreme Court Review* 247 (1994); Finkelman, "Sorting Out Prigg v. Pennsylvania," 24 *Rutgers Law Journal* 605 (1993); Finkelman, *Supreme Injustice*, 140–171; H. Robert Baker, *Prigg v. Pennsylvania: Slavery, the Supreme Court, and the Ambivalent Constitution* (Lawrence: University Press of Kansas, 2012). Leslie Friedman Goldstein maintains that Story's opinion was more of a concession to northern antislavery sentiment than

such critical opinion admits: "A 'Triumph of Freedom' after All? Prigg v. Pennsylvania Reexamined," 29 *Law & History Review* 763 (2011).
146. 41 U.S. 612–613.
147. Paul Finkelman, "Prigg v. Pennsylvania and Northern State Courts: Anti-slavery Use of a Proslavery Decision," 25 *Civil War History* 5 (1979); Morris, *Free Men All*, 109–129.
148. Charles Sumner, who was Story's protégé and confidant, quotes Story to this effect in a letter to Salmon P. Chase, dated March 12, 1847, in the Salmon P. Chase Papers, Manuscripts Division, Library of Congress. He was seconded by William Wetmore Story, Story's filiopietistic son, who claimed that this part of Story's opinion encouraged other states to emulate Pennsylvania's personal liberty laws: Story, *Life and Letters of Joseph Story*, 2:392–395.
149. Story to John M. Berrien, April 29, 1842, in John M. Berrien Papers, microfilm roll 1, Southern Historical Collection, University of North Carolina–Chapel Hill.
150. Leonard L. Richards, *The Slave Power: The Free North and Southern Domination, 1780–1860* (Baton Rouge: Louisiana State University Press, 2000); contemporary views were John E. Cairnes, *The Slave Power: Its Character, Career, and Probable Designs* . . . (London: Macmillan, 1862), and Henry Wilson, *The History of the Rise and Fall of the Slave Power in America* (Boston: J.R. Osgood, 1872).
151. 46 U.S. (5 How.) 215, 231 (1847).
152. S. P. Chase, *Reclamation of Fugitives from Service: An Argument for the Defendant...* (Cincinnati: R.P. Donogh & Co., 1847), 77.
153. Robert M. Cover critiqued such formalism in *Justice Accused: Antislavery and the Judicial Process* (New Haven: Yale University Press, 1975).
154. Chase to Sumner, 1847, reprinted in *Diary and Correspondence of Salmon P. Chase* (Washington, DC: GPO, 1902), 2:114.
155. See generally Joel H. Silbey, *Storm over Texas: The Annexation Controversy and the Road to Civil War* (New York: Oxford University Press, 2005); Frederick Merk, *Slavery and the Annexation of Texas* (New York: Knopf, 1972). For broad overviews of the entire process encapsulated in the next few pages, David M. Potter's magisterial *The Impending Crisis, 1848–1861* (New York: Harper and Row, 1976) has been supplemented (but not superseded) by Sean Wilentz, *The Rise of American Democracy: Jefferson to Lincoln* (New York: Norton, 2005), and Howe, *What Hath God Wrought*.
156. On the impact of the Proviso and its aftermath, see Michael F. Holt, *The Political Crisis of the 1850s* (New York: Norton, 1978); Potter, *Impending Crisis*, 112 ff.; Chaplain W. Morrison, *Democratic Politics and Sectionalism: The Wilmot Proviso Controversy* (Chapel Hill: University of North Carolina Press, 1967); Allan Nevins, *Ordeal of the Union: Fruits of Manifest Destiny, 1847–1852* (New York: Charles Scribner's Sons, 1947).
157. Holman Hamilton, *Prologue to Conflict: The Crisis and Compromise of 1850* (New York: Norton, 1964); Michael F. Holt, *The Fate of Their Country: Politicians, Slavery Extension, and the Coming of the Civil War* (New York: Farrar, Strauss and Giroux, 2005), 50–92; and Freehling, *Road to Disunion*, 489–510.
158. On the impact of the act, see R. J. M. Blackett, *Making Freedom: The Underground Railroad and the Politics of Slavery* (Chapel Hill: University of North Carolina Press, 2013).
159. Quoted in Potter, *Impending Crisis*, 116.
160. 51U.S. (10 How.) 82, 92, 96 (1851).
161. Anne Twitty, *Before Dred Scott: Slavery and Legal Culture in the American Confluence, 1787–1857* (Cambridge: Cambridge University Press, 2019).
162. The Slave, Grace (Rex v. Allan), 2 Haggard 94, 166 Eng. Rep. 179 (Adm. 1827).
163. These dicta were the remote ancestor of the equality-of-the-states notion that held a pernicious appeal for Chief Justice John Roberts in *Shelby County v. Holder* (2013), discussed below in chapter 11.
164. James Gillespie Birney, *Examination of the Decision of the Supreme Court of the United States, in the Case of Strader*... (Cincinnati: Truman and Spofford, 1852).
165. The italics signal that in context this phrase refers not to the basic underlying principle of republican government, but rather to the specific northern Democratic political program of the 1850s that would turn control over slavery in the territories to the territorial settlers themselves. Christopher Childers, *The Failure of Popular Sovereignty: Slavery, Manifest Destiny, and the Radicalization of Southern Politics* (Lawrence: University Press of Kansas, 2012).

166. To declutter the narrative, I omit discussion of the legal status of Dred Scott's wife Harriet and their two daughters, but theirs is an important story in its own right. Lea VanderVelde discusses its significance in *Mrs. Dred Scott: A Life on Slavery's Frontier* (New York: Oxford University Press, 2009).
167. Scott v. Emerson, 15 Mo. 576, 586 (Mo. 1852).
168. I omit the complex narrative of litigation of these freedom suits in lower state and federal courts because that story is not directly germane to the focus of this study. The literature on the *Dred Scott* case is vast and contentious; interest in the subject is apparently inexhaustible. Full treatments may be found in Don E. Fehrenbacher's magisterial *The Dred Scott Case: Its Significance in American Law and Politics* (New York: Oxford University Press, 1978) (Pulitzer Prize in History, 1979); Walter Ehrlich, *They Have No Rights: Dred Scott's Struggle for Freedom* (Westport: Greenwood, 1979); Maltz, *Slavery and the Supreme Court*, 210–226, 235–277; Finkelman, *Supreme Injustice*, 172–210; Allen, *Origins of the Dred Scott Case*; and Earl M. Maltz, *Dred Scott and the Politics of Slavery* (Lawrence: University Press of Kansas, 2007). Mark Graber considers the case in the larger context of constitutionalism and the values that it serves: *Dred Scott and the Problem of Constitutional Evil* (New York: Cambridge University Press, 2006).
169. Fehrenbacher, *Dred Scott Case*, 322–388; Maltz, *Slavery and the Supreme Court*, 245–267.
170. Sanford's name was misspelled by the Reporter of Decisions.
171. "Thus the rights of property are united with the rights of person, and placed on the same ground by the fifth amendment to the Constitution, which provides that no person shall be deprived of life, liberty, and property, without due process of law. And an act of Congress which deprives a citizen of the United States of his liberty or property, merely because he came himself or brought his property into a particular Territory of the United States, and who had committed no offence against the laws, could hardly be dignified with the name of due process of law." 60 U.S. 450.
172. 60 U.S. 426.
173. Specifically, Dred Scott, "a negro of African descent, whose ancestors were of pure African blood, and who were brought into this country and sold as slaves"; 60 U.S. 400.
174. 60 U.S. 404–405.
175. Fehrenbacher, *Dred Scott Case*, 341.
176. Fehrenbacher, *Dred Scott Case*, 335–364.
177. 60 U.S. 407. Daniel in his concurrence supported this view of African Americans: "the African negro race never have been acknowledged as belonging to the family of nations; that as amongst them there never has been known or recognized by the inhabitants of other countries anything partaking of the character of nationality, or civil or political polity; that this race has been by all the nations of Europe regarded as subjects of capture or purchase; as subjects of commerce or traffic; and that the introduction of that race into every section of this country was not as members of civil or political society, but as slaves, as *property* in the strictest sense of the term." 60 U.S. 475.
178. 60 U.S. 410.
179. Daniel concurred: in constructing the constitutional order, "the African was not deemed politically a person." 60 U.S. 481.
180. Fehrenbacher, *Dred Scott Case*, 349.
181. Art. IV, sec. 3, paragraph 2: "The Congress shall have Power to dispose of and make all needful Rules and Regulations respecting the Territory or other Property belonging to the United States."
182. 60 U.S. at 450.
183. 60 U.S. 452.
184. Melvin I. Urofsky and Paul Finkelman, *A March of Liberty: A Constitutional History of the United States: From the Founding to 1900*, 3rd ed. (New York: Oxford University Press, 2011), I, 436.
185. William Faulkner, *Requiem for a Nun* (1951; London: Vintage, 2015).
186. In re Booth, 3 Wis. 134 (1854). On the Booth cases, see H. Robert Baker, *The Rescue of Joshua Glover: A Fugitive Slave, the Constitution, and the Coming of the Civil War* (Athens: Ohio University Press, 2006).
187. *New York Times*, February 2, 1855, quoted in Maltz, *Slavery and the Supreme Court*, 204.
188. In re Booth and Rycraft, 3 Wis. 157 (1855).

189. Wisconsin was not alone in its defiance of *Dred Scott*. The Ohio Supreme Court rejected its doctrines in Anderson v. Poindexter, 6 Ohio 622 (1857), as did the Maine Supreme Judicial Court in Opinion of the Justices, 44 Maine 505 (1857).
190. 14 U.S. (1 Wheat.) 304 (1816).
191. 62 U.S. 506 (21 How.) 506, 526 (1858). On the Ableman case, see Maltz, *Slavery and the Supreme Court*, 278–286.
192. Warren, *Supreme Court in United States History*, 2:336.
193. Henry Adams, *John Randolph* (Boston: Houghton Mifflin, 1898), 178.
194. 60 U.S. 459 (Nelson, J. concurring) (ital. added).
195. Commonwealth v. Aves, 35 Mass. (18 Pick.) 193 (1836). On the significance of this precedent, see Levy, *Law of the Commonwealth and Chief Justice Shaw*, 62–71.
196. *New York Times*, September 27, 1856. Toombs denied having made the statement, but contemporaries disbelieved him.
197. Robert W. Johannsen, ed., *The Lincoln-Douglas Debates of 1858* (New York: Oxford University Press, 1965), 19.
198. Quoted and discussed in Noah Feldman, *The Broken Constitution: Lincoln, Slavery, and the Refounding of America* (New York: Farrar, Strauss and Giroux, 2022), 113–115.
199. Quoted in Wiecek, "Slavery and Abolition," 56–57.
200. Samuel A. Foot, *An Examination of the Case of Dred Scott . . .* (Geneva: Geneva Literary and Scientific Institution, 1859), 19.
201. Quoted in Marie Tyler-McGraw and Dwight T. Pitcaithley, "The Lemmon Slave Case," 14 *Common-Place* (2013), http://www.common-place-archives.org/vol-14/no-01/mcgraw/#.XVxFGlB7k1.
202. Quoted and discussed in Wiecek, "Slavery and Abolition," 57.
203. Tyler-McGraw and Pitcaithley, "Lemmon Slave Case," provide full details. Lemon's name was consistently misspelled in all reports of the case. Paul Finkelman explores the legal proceedings in *An Imperfect Union*, 296–312.
204. In 1841 the state had repealed a statute permitting sojourners to retain rights in enslaved people up to nine months.
205. Then and now New York's highest court.
206. Respectively: Fifth Amendment, Art. IV, sec. 1; Art. IV, sec. 2.
207. Lemmon v. People ex rel. Napoleon, 26 Barb. 270 (N.Y. Sup. Ct. 1857).
208. Quoted in Tyler-McGraw and Pitcaithley, "Lemmon Slave Case."
209. Quoted in Finkelman, *Imperfect Union*, 301.
210. Lemmon v. The People, 20 N.Y. 562 (1860).
211. 505 U.S. 833, 1001 (1992).
212. Reprinted in Samuel Tyler, *Memoir of Roger Brooke Taney* (Baltimore: John Murphey, 1872), 578–605.
213. Swisher, *Roger B. Taney*, 570–572; unpublished draft memorandum, 1860–1863?, in "Oddments" file, Roger B. Taney Papers, Mss. Div., Library of Congress.

Chapter 2

1. Recounted in detail by James Oakes, *Freedom National: The Destruction of Slavery in the United States, 1861–1865* (New York: Norton, 2013).
2. Harold M. Hyman, *A More Perfect Union: The Impact of the Civil War and Reconstruction on the Constitution* (Boston: Houghton Mifflin, 1973); Eric Foner, *The Second Founding: How the Civil War and Reconstruction Remade the American Constitution* (New York: Oxford University Press, 2019); and Timothy S. Huebner, *Liberty and Union: The Civil War Era and American Constitutionalism* (Lawrence: University Press of Kansas, 2016) survey of the constitutional impact of Reconstruction. The classic studies of Reconstruction itself are W. E. B. Du Bois, *Black Reconstruction in America, 1860–1880* (New York: Harcourt, Brace, 1935); Eric Foner, *Reconstruction: America's Unfinished Revolution, 1863–1877*, rev. ed. (New York: Oxford University Press, 2014); John Hope Franklin, *Reconstruction after the Civil War* (Chicago: University of Chicago Press, 1961); Kenneth M. Stampp, *The Era of Reconstruction* (New York Vintage, 1964). On the demise of Reconstruction and the ensuing period of

Redemption, see C. Vann Woodward, *Origins of the New South, 1877–1913* (Baton Rouge: Louisiana State University Press, 1951). For an overview of the entire period of Reconstruction and Redemption, see Richard White, *The Republic for Which It Stands: The United States during Reconstruction and the Gilded Age, 1865–1896* (New York: Oxford University Press, 2017).
3. Ira Berlin, *The Long Emancipation: The Demise of Slavery in the United States* (Cambridge: Harvard University Press, 2018).
4. James Oakes, *The Crooked Path to Abolition: Abraham Lincoln and the Antislavery Constitution* (New York: Norton, 2021).
5. Robert J. Kaczorowski, "Revolutionary Constitutionalism in the Era of the Civil War and Reconstruction," 61 *NYU Law Review* 863, 869 (1986).
6. David Williams, *I Freed Myself: African American Self-Emancipation in the Civil War Era* (Cambridge: Cambridge University Press, 2014); Ira Berlin, "Who Freed the Slaves? Emancipation and Its Meaning," in David W. Blight and Brooks D. Simpson, eds., *Union and Emancipation: Essays on Politics and Race in the Civil War Era* (Kent: Kent State University Press, 1997), 105; Vincent Harding, *There Is a River: The Black Struggle for Freedom in America* (New York: Vintage, 1981); Guyora Binder, "Did the Slaves Author the Thirteenth Amendment? An Essay on Redemptive History," 5 *Yale Journal of Law & the Humanities* 471 (1993).
7. Leon F. Litwack, *Been in the Storm So Long: The Aftermath of Slavery* (New York: Knopf, 1980), 64–166; Oakes, *Freedom National*, 192–223; Laura F. Edwards, *A Legal History of the Civil War and Reconstruction: A Nation of Rights* (Cambridge: Cambridge University Press, 2015), 65–66; Michael Vorenberg, *Final Freedom: The Civil War, the Abolition of Slavery, and the Thirteenth Amendment* (Cambridge: Cambridge University Press, 2001), 23–25, 79–80; Ira Berlin et al., eds., *Freedom: A Documentary History of Emancipation*, ser. 1, vol. 1: *The Destruction of Slavery* (Cambridge: Cambridge University Press, 1985), 1–56.
8. Stephen Hahn, *A Nation under Our Feet: Black Political Struggles in the Rural South from Slavery to the Great Migration* (Cambridge: Harvard University Press, 2005), 7.
9. Kate Masur, *Until Justice Be Done: America's First Civil Rights Movement, from Revolution to Reconstruction* (New York: Norton, 2021).
10. See the Colored Conventions Project at the University of Delaware and more recently at Penn State, at coloredconventions.org; P. Gabrielle Foreman et al., eds., *The Colored Conventions Movement: Black Organizing in the Nineteenth Century* (Chapel Hill: University of North Carolina Press, 2021).
11. Those laws are collected in Stephen Middleton, *The Black Laws in the Old Northwest: A Documentary History* (New York: Praeger, 1993).
12. Masur, *Until Justice Be Done*, 1–41; Paul Finkelman, "The Strange Career of Race Discrimination in Antebellum Ohio," 55 *Case Western Reserve Law Review* 371 (2004).
13. "The Citizens of each State shall be entitled to all Privileges and Immunities of Citizens of the several States."
14. Masur, *Until Justice Be Done*, 42–82, 303–341.
15. Lincoln to A. G. Hodges, April 4, 1864, in Roy P. Basler, ed., *Collected Works of Abraham Lincoln* (New Brunswick: Rutgers University Press, 1953), 7:281.
16. [First] Confiscation Act, ch. 60, 12 Stat. 319 (1861); [Second] Confiscation Act, ch. 195, 12 Stat. 589 (1862). Silvana R. Siddali, *From Property to Person: Slavery and the Confiscation Acts, 1861–1862* (Baton Rouge: Louisiana State University Press, 2005), 70–94, 120–144; John Syrett, *Civil War Confiscation Acts: Failing to Reconstruct the South* (New York: Fordham University Press, 2005), 1–72.
17. Act of April 16, 1862, ch. 54, 12 Stat. 376; Kate Masur, *An Example for All the Land: Emancipation and the Struggle over Equality in Washington, D.C.* (Chapel Hill: University of North Carolina Press, 2010), 1–31.
18. An Act to Secure Freedom to All Persons within the Territories of the United States, ch. 111, 12 Stat. 432 (1862).
19. Eric Foner, *The Fiery Trial: Abraham Lincoln and American Slavery* (New York: Norton, 2010), 240–249, 268–271, 307–308, 312; Louis P. Masur, *Lincoln's Hundred Days: The Emancipation Proclamation and the War for the Union* (Cambridge: Harvard University Press, 2012); Allen C. Guelzo, *Lincoln's Emancipation Proclamation: The End of Slavery in America* (New York: Simon & Schuster, 2006).

20. Missouri, Tennessee, West Virginia (having been cleaved from Virginia in 1863), Maryland, Arkansas, and Louisiana.
21. Alexander Tsesis, *The Thirteenth Amendment and American Freedom: A Legal History* (New York: New York University Press, 2004), 34–58, covers its adoption and ratification.
22. On evolving meanings of "freedom" in antebellum and Reconstruction America, see Eric Foner, "The Meaning of Freedom in the Age of Emancipation," 81 *Journal of American History* 435 (1994).
23. Jacobus tenBroek, "Thirteenth Amendment to the Constitution of the United States: Consummation to Abolition and Key to the Fourteenth Amendment," 39 *California Law Review* 171 (1951). On the Reconstruction amendments generally, see Eric Foner, *The Second Founding: How the Civil War and Reconstruction Remade the Constitution* (New York: Norton, 2019).
24. Alexander Tsesis, "The Thirteenth Amendment's Revolutionary Aims," in Tsesis, ed., *The Promises of Liberty*, 1, 10–12 (quoting Reps. Isaac Arnold, Russell Thayer, and Sen. James Harlan respectively from floor debates on the amendment).
25. Darrell A. H. Miller, "The Janus of Civil Rights Law," in Christian G. Samito, ed., *The Greatest and the Grandest Act: The Civil Rights Act of 1866 from Reconstruction to Today* (Carbondale: Southern Illinois University Press, 2018), 245.
26. McDonald v. Santa Fe Trail Transp. Co., 427 U.S. 273 (1976).
27. George A. Rutherglen, "The Badges and Incidents of Slavery and the Power of Congress to Enforce the Thirteenth Amendment," in Alexander Tsesis, ed., *The Promises of Liberty: The History and Contemporary Relevance of the Thirteenth Amendment* (New York: Columbia University Press, 2010), 163–181.
28. James Gray Pope, "Section 1 of the Thirteenth Amendment and the Badges and Incidents of Slavery," 65 *UCLA Law Review* 426 (2018); William M. Carter Jr., "Race, Rights, and the Thirteenth Amendment: Defining the Badges and Incidents of Slavery," 40 *UC Davis Law Review* 13121, 1342–1346 (2007).
29. Mark DeWolfe Howe, "Federalism and Civil Rights," in Archibald Cox et al., *Civil Rights, the Constitution, and the Courts* (Cambridge: Harvard University Press, 1967), 30–51.
30. tenBroek, "Thirteenth Amendment to the Constitution."
31. David A. J. Richards, *Conscience and the Constitution: History, Theory, and Law of the Reconstruction Amendments* (Princeton: Princeton University Press, 1993), 3.
32. Edwards, *Legal History of the Civil War*, 88.
33. Sometimes called the exceptions clause.
34. In 2020, some Democratic members of Congress tried again, introducing a constitutional amendment, known as the "Abolition Amendment," that would delete the criminal exemption clause. Eric Foner, "Abolition Is Not Complete," *New York Times*, December 15, 2020.
35. Bryan v. Walton, 14 Ga. 185 (1853). See the fuller discussion of the freedpeople's evolving civic status in William M. Wiecek, "Emancipation and Civic Status: The American Experience, 1865–1915," in Tsesis, ed., *The Promises of Liberty*, 78–99.
36. Theodore B. Wilson, *The Black Codes of the South* (University: University of Alabama Press, 1965); William Cohen, *At Freedom's Edge: Black Mobility and the Southern White Quest for Racial Control, 1861–1915* (Baton Rouge: Louisiana State University Press, 1991); Pete Daniel, "The Metamorphosis of Slavery, 1865–1900," 66 *Journal of American History* 88 (1979); Daniel A. Novak, *The Wheel of Servitude: Black Forced Labor after Slavery* (Lexington: University Press of Kentucky, 1978); William Cohen, "Negro Involuntary Servitude in the South, 1865–1940: A Preliminary Analysis," 42 *Journal of Southern History* 31 (1976).
37. Quoted in Du Bois, *Black Reconstruction in America*, 178.
38. Papachristou v. Jacksonville, 405 U.S. 156 (1972).
39. Ch. 31, 14 Stat. 27. George Rutherglen discusses the origins, content, and development of the act in *Civil Rights in the Shadow of Slavery: The Constitution, Common Law, and the Civil Rights Act of 1866* (Oxford: Oxford University Press, 2013), 3–92. Christopher W. Schmidt provides a valuable study of the evolving, contested meanings of the phrase "civil rights" in *Civil Rights in America: A History* (Cambridge: Cambridge University Press, 2021); see pp. 11–31 on its emergence in Reconstruction debates.
40. *Cong. Globe*, 39th Cong., 1st sess. 471 (1866).
41. *Cong. Globe*, 39th Cong., 1st sess. 1152 (1866).
42. Section 1 of the statue, quoted in text, has been codified today almost verbatim as 42 U.S.C. § 1982 (the property provisions) and 42 U.S.C. § 1981 (everything else). The criminal enforcement provisions of section 2 are found in 18 U.S.C. § 242.

43. Rutherglen, *Civil Rights in the Shadow*, 40–42.
44. Garfield quoted in Herman Belz, *A New Birth of Freedom: The Republican Party and Freedmen's Rights, 1861–1866* (New York: Fordham University Press, 1976), 160.
45. Rebecca E. Zietlow, "Slavery, Liberty, and the Right to Contract," 19 *Nevada Law Journal* 447, 462–465, 473–475 (2019).
46. Section 2 is currently codified as 18 U.S.C. § 242.
47. *Cong. Globe*, 39th Cong. 1st sess., 566 (1866).
48. Fergus M. Bordewich, *Congress at War: How Republican Reformers Fought the Civil War, Defied Lincoln, Ended Slavery, and Remade America* (New York: Anchor Books, 2020).
49. Robert J. Kaczorowski, *The Nationalization of Civil Rights: Constitutional Theory and Practice in a Racist Society, 1866–1883* (1971; New York: Garland, 1987).
50. Earl Maltz, *Civil Rights, the Constitution, and Congress, 1863–1869* (Lawrence: University Press of Kansas, 1990) (an originalist perspective); Michael Les Benedict, *A Compromise of Principle: Congressional Republicans and Reconstruction, 1863–1869* (New York: Norton, 1974), 134–187; and Benedict, "Preserving the Constitution: The Conservative Basis of Radical Reconstruction," 61 *Journal of American History*, 65 (1974), offer a more conservative interpretation of Reconstruction, stressing a more limited scope for congressional power.
51. Richard M. Valelly, *The Two Reconstructions: The Struggle for Black Enfranchisement* (Chicago: University of Chicago Press, 2004), 105.
52. These doubts were put to rest by re-enactment of the 1866 act in 1870, as section 18 of the Enforcement Act of 1870, ch. 114, 16 Stat. 140. The 1870 Enforcement Act was enacted under the authority of the Fourteenth as well as the Thirteenth Amendment.
53. On Bingham's role, see Gerald N. Magliocca, *American Founding Son: John Bingham and the Invention of the Fourteenth Amendment* (New York: New York University Press, 2013), ch. 7, "The Fourteenth Amendment."
54. William E. Nelson, *The Fourteenth Amendment: From Political Principle to Judicial Doctrine* (Cambridge: Harvard University Press, 1988); Rutherglen, *Civil Rights in the Shadow*, 70–83. Ilan Wurman provides a brief introduction to the purposes and framing of section 1 of the Fourteenth Amendment in *The Second Founding: An Introduction to the Fourteenth Amendment* (Cambridge: Cambridge University Press, 2020).
55. I defer consideration of a sixth, section 2 dealing with the franchise, to a discussion of the Fifteenth Amendment, below.
56. US Const. Amend. XIV, sec. 1: "All persons born or naturalized in the United States, and subject to the jurisdiction thereof, are citizens of the United States and of the state wherein they reside. No state shall make or enforce any law which shall abridge the privileges or immunities of citizens of the United States; nor shall any state deprive any person of life, liberty, or property, without due process of law; nor deny to any person within its jurisdiction the equal protection of the laws."
57. "Citizenship," Opinion of US Attorney General Edward Bates, November 29, 1862, at https://quod.lib.umich.edu/m/moa/AEW6575.0001.001?rgn=main;view=fulltext.
58. James H. Kettner, *The Development of American Citizenship, 1608–1870* (Chapel Hill: University of North Carolina Press, 1978), 300–332.
59. The first was the Eleventh Amendment, correcting the holding of Chisholm v. Georgia, 2 U.S. (2 Dall.) 419 (1973), involving suits against a state by citizens of another state.
60. Randy Barnett, "Whence Comes Section 1? The Abolitionist Origins of the Fourteenth Amendment," 3 *Journal of Legal Analysis* 165 (2011), contends that the abolitionist constitutional theories should be read as *legal* arguments, not mere antislavery rhetoric, and seen in that light were remarkably sophisticated.
61. Timothy S. Huebner, "'In Defiance of Judge Taney': Black Constitutionalism and Resistance to Dred Scott," 45 *Journal of Supreme Court History* 215 (2020).
62. Martha S. Jones, *Birthright Citizens: A History of Race and Rights in Antebellum America* (Cambridge: Cambridge University Press, 2018); Christopher J. Bonner, *Remaking the Republic: Black Politics and the Creation of American Citizenship* (Philadelphia: University of Pennsylvania Press, 2020); Masur, *Until Justice Be Done*, 303–341.
63. Jack M. Balkin, "The Reconstruction Power," 85 *NYU Law Review* 1801 (2010).
64. Civil Rights Cases, 103 U.S. 3, 46 (1883) (Harlan, J. dissenting) (ital. in orig.).
65. Balkin, "Reconstruction Power," 1856.
66. Rogers M. Smith, *Civic Ideals: Conflicting Visions of Citizenship in U.S. History* (New Haven: Yale University Press, 1997), ch. 10, "The America That Never Was: The Radical Hour, 1866–1876."

67. Smith, *Civic Ideals*, 3.
68. Balkin, "Reconstruction Power."
69. Art. I, sec. 8: "The Congress shall have Power To…"
70. 17 U.S. (4 Wheat.) 316, 421 (1819).
71. Balkin, "Reconstruction Power," 1807.
72. 5 U.S. (1 Cranch) 137, 163 (1803).
73. On this concept of "state neglect," see Pamela Brandwein, *Rethinking the Judicial Settlement of Reconstruction* (Cambridge: Cambridge University Press, 2011), 161–183. However, the Supreme Court has been hostile to this idea: DeShaney v. Winnebago County Social Services Department, 489 U.S. 189 (1989).
74. Corfield v. Coryell, 6 F. Cas. 546, 551 (C.C.E.D. Pa. 1823), No. 3230.
75. Which provided: "The Citizens of each State shall be entitled to all Privileges and Immunities of Citizens in the several States." The original Article IV clause spoke of the "Privileges *and* Immunities"; the Fourteenth Amendment's version is "privileges *or* immunities," necessitated by the fact that the later clause commands that "No State shall…" Fortunately, the framers were scrupulous about grammar and syntax.
76. *The Federalist*, No. 80, at https://avalon.law.yale.edu/18th_century/fed80.asp.
77. Kurt T. Lash, *The Fourteenth Amendment and the Privileges and Immunities of American Citizenship* (New York: Cambridge University Press, 2014) provides an exhaustive review of the creation of the Fourteenth Amendment privileges or immunities clause. There he contends that the clause incorporates all "enumerated rights" in the Constitution, including but not limited to those specified in the Bill of Rights.
78. *Cong. Globe*, 39 Cong. 1 sess., 2519 (1866).
79. Christopher R. Green, *Equal Citizenship, Civil Rights, and the Constitution: The Original Sense of the Privileges or Immunities Clause* (New York: Routledge, 2015).
80. Green, *Equal Citizenship*; Randy E. Barnett and Evan D. Bernick, "The Privileges or Immunities Clause, Abridged: A Critique of Kurt Lash on the Fourteenth Amendment," 95 *Notre Dame Law Review* 499 (2019); Akhil Reed Amar, "The Bill of Rights and the Fourteenth Amendment," 101 *Yale Law Journal* 1193, 1233–1238 (1998); Curtis, *No State Shall Abridge*, 58–91 and *passim*; Maltz, *Civil Rights, the Constitution, and Congress*, 113–118; John Hart Ely, *Democracy and Distrust: A Theory of Judicial Review* (Cambridge: Harvard University Press, 1980), 22–30; Philip B. Kurland, "The Privileges and Immunities Clause: 'Its Hour Come Round At Last'?," 1972 *Washington University Law Quarterly* 405, 419–420 (1972); Richard Aynes, "On Misreading John Bingham and the Fourteenth Amendment," 103 *Yale Law Journal* 57, 74 (1993); Kurt Lash, "The Origins of the Privileges or Immunities Clause, Part II: John Bingham and the Second Draft of the Fourteenth Amendment," 99 *Georgetown Law Journal* 329, 432 (2011). Phillip Hamburger disagrees in "Privileges or Immunities," 105 *Northwestern University Law Review* 61 (2011).
81. "…nor shall any State deprive any person of life, liberty, or property, without due process of law."
82. Murray's Lessee v. Hoboken Land & Improvement Co., 59 U.S. (18 How.) 272, 276 (1856). This was historically inaccurate: Magna Carta's phrase *per legem terrae* was not identical or equivalent to the phrase "par due proces de lei" found in the legislation of 28 Edw. 3, c. 3 (1354). But as with so many others of the Court's ipse dixits, when the Court declares something to be so, that fixes its meaning for legal purposes, whatever the quibbles of historians.
83. Michael K. Curtis, *The Fourteenth Amendment and the Bill of Rights* (Durham: Duke University Press, 1986).
84. Akhil R. Amar provides a useful brief introduction to the problem of incorporation in *The Bill of Rights: Creation and Recreation* (New Haven: Yale University Press, 1998), 215–231.
85. Barron v. Mayor and City Council of Baltimore, 32 U.S. (7 Pet.) 243 (1833).
86. 3 U.S. (3 Dall.) 386, 388 (1798).
87. Corfield v. Coryell, 6 Fed. Cas. 546, 551–553 (C.C.E.D.Pa. 1823) (No. 3,230).
88. Missouri Pacific Ry. v. Nebraska, 164 U.S. 403 (1896) (public use); Chicago, Burlington & Quincy Ry. v. Chicago, 166 U.S. 226 (1897) (just compensation).
89. "…nor deny to any person within its jurisdiction the equal protection of the laws."
90. The only reference to equality in the 1787 Constitution was the guarantee of equal voting weight for the states in the Senate, guaranteed by Article V: "…no State, without its Consent, shall be deprived of its equal Suffrage in the Senate."
91. *Cong. Globe*, 38th Cong. 1st sess., 1488 (1864).

92. Jeremy Waldron, *One Another's Equals: The Basis of Human Equality* (Cambridge: Harvard University Press, 2019).
93. Jacobus tenBroek, *Equal under Law*, 2nd ed (New York: Collier, 1965) (the title of the first edition better expresses its author's principal thesis: *The Antislavery Origins of the Fourteenth Amendment* [1951]); Michael Kent Curtis, *No State Shall Abridge: The Fourteenth Amendment and the Bill of Rights* (Durham: Duke University Press, 1986); Robert J. Kaczorowski, *The Politics of Judicial Interpretation: The Federal Courts, Department of Justice, and Civil Rights, 1866–1876* (New York: Fordham University Press, 1985); Howard Jay Graham, "The Early Antislavery Background of the Fourteenth Amendment," reprinted in Graham, *Everyman's Constitution: Historical Essays on the Fourteenth Amendment, the "Conspiracy Theory," and American Constitutionalism* (Madison: State Historical Society of Wisconsin, 1968), 152–241; Jack M. Balkin, *Living Originalism* (Cambridge: Harvard University Press, 2011), 222, drawing on Nelson, *Fourteenth Amendment*, 115–147.
94. William Blackstone, *Commentaries on the Laws of England* (1765), 1:*354; Christopher R. Green, "The Original Sense of the (Equal) Protection Clause: Pre-enactment History," 19 *George Mason University Civil Rights Law Journal* 44 (2008).
95. 5 U.S. (1 Cranch) 137, 163 (1803).
96. Robert J. Kaczorowski, "To Begin Anew: Congress, Citizenship, and Civil Rights after the Civil War," 92 *American Historical Review* 45 (1987).
97. Judith N. Shklar, *American Citizenship: The Quest for Inclusion* (Cambridge: Harvard University Press, 1991), 27–57.
98. Stephen Kantrowitz, *More Than Freedom: Fighting for Black Citizenship in a White Republic, 1829–1889* (New York: Penguin, 2012).
99. Bonner, *Remaking the Republic*, 11–37, 149–179.
100. Edwards, *Legal History of the Civil War*, 14, 71, 176.
101. This discussion follows Hyman and Wiecek, *Equal Justice under Law*, 395–398; see esp. diagram p. 396.
102. Wiecek, "Emancipation and Civic Status."
103. The use of this term is deliberate: not until 1869 did a state (or, in this case, a territory, Wyoming) enfranchise women. Nor until 1898 did a state—Utah—permit women to serve on juries, and by the middle of the twentieth century almost half the states still prohibited them from doing so. Carol Weisbrod, "Images of the Woman Juror," 9 *Harvard Women's Law Journal* 59, 61 (1986).
104. Because African Americans would now be counted as full human beings for purposes of determining population, rather than the three-fifths of a person they had been under the Constitution of 1787.
105. Gabriel J. Chin, "Reconstruction, Felon Disenfranchisement, and the Right to Vote: Did the Fifteenth Amendment Repeal Section 2 of the Fourteenth Amendment?," 92 *Georgetown Law Journal* 259, 264 (2004), and Richard W. Bourne, "Richardson v. Ramirez: A Motion to Reconsider," 42 *Valparaiso University Law Review* 1 (2000), provide historical overviews of the origins of section 2. On Black voting in the North, see William Gillette, *The Right to Vote: Politics and the Passage of the Fifteenth Amendment* (Baltimore: Johns Hopkins University Press, 1969), 25.
106. The phrase "section 2" as used in this subchapter refers to the second sentence of section 2 of the Fourteenth Amendment.
107. By "counting the whole number of persons in each State." The entire section reads: "Representatives shall be apportioned among the several States according to their respective numbers, counting the whole number of persons in each State, excluding Indians not taxed. But when the right to vote at any election for the choice of electors for President and Vice President of the United States, Representatives in Congress, the Executive and Judicial officers of a State, or the members of the Legislature thereof, is denied to any of the male inhabitants of such State, being twenty-one years of age, and citizens of the United States, or in any way abridged, except for participation in rebellion, or other crime, the basis of representation therein shall be reduced in the proportion which the number of such male citizens shall bear to the whole number of male citizens twenty-one years of age in such State."
108. Richardson v. Ramirez, 418 U.S. 24, 74 (1974) (Marshall, J. dissenting).
109. And has been: Abigail M. Hinchcliff, "The 'Other' Side of Richardson v. Ramirez: A Textual Challenge to Felon Disenfranchisement," 121 *Yale Law Journal* 194 (2011).

110. Under the clause (Art. I, sec. 2, ¶ 3), only 60 percent of enslaved southern Blacks were counted as part of the state's population for purposes of assigning seats in the House. With the clause abrogated by emancipation, 100 percent of the Black population would be counted, thereby increasing the number of Representatives returned by the former slave states. This would have given the southern delegation in the House of Representatives an increment of thirteen seats, ensuring their control of at least one half of Congress, plus an advantage in the electoral college. Lawrence Goldstone, *On Account of Race: The Supreme Court, White Supremacy, and the Ravaging of African American Voting Rights* (Berkeley: Counterpoint, 2020), 31.
111. Xi Wang, *The Trial of Democracy: Black Suffrage and Northern Republicans, 1860–1910* (Athens: University of Georgia Press, 1997), 1–53.
112. On debates in Congress, see Gillette, *The Right to Vote*, 46–78.
113. Susan B. Anthony and Elizabeth Cady Stanton of the successor National Woman Suffrage Association opposed ratification of the amendment without women's suffrage, while Lucy Stone and Julia Ward Howe of the American Woman Suffrage Association supported it.
114. Michael P. Zuckert, "Congressional Power under the Fourteenth Amendment: The Original Understanding of Section 5," 3 *Constitutional Commentary* 123 (1986).
115. Art. I, sec. 8: "The Congress shall have Power To lay and collect Taxes…" etc. Balkin, "Reconstruction Power," 1809.
116. *Black's Law Dictionary*, 11th ed. (St. Paul: Thomson Reuters, 2019): "In pari materia: It is a canon of construction that statutes that are *in pari materia* may be construed together, so that inconsistencies in one statute may be resolved by looking at another statute on the same subject." This is a canon of statutory construction, but it should be equally applicable to construing the text of the Constitution unless some clear indication of framers' intent to the contrary counsels otherwise.
117. US Const. Art. I, sec. 8, cl. 18: "To make all Laws which shall be necessary and proper for carrying into Execution the foregoing Powers and all other Powers vested by the Constitution in the Government of the United States, or in any Department or Officer thereof."
118. 17 U.S. (4 Wheat.) 316, 421 (1819).
119. 100 U.S. 339, 345–346 (1879).
120. Hepburn v. Griswold, 75 U.S. (8 Wall.) 603, 614–615 (1870), overruled in part on other grounds, Legal Tender Cases, 79 U.S. 457 (1871).
121. Carole Emberton, *Beyond Redemption: Race, Violence and the American South after the Civil War* (Chicago: University of Chicago Press, 2013), 168–216; George C. Rable, *But There Was No Peace: The Role of Violence in the Politics of Reconstruction* (Athens: University of Georgia Press, 1984); Michael Perman, "Counter Reconstruction: The Role of Violence in Southern Redemption," in Eric Anderson and Alfred A. Moss, eds., *The Facts of Reconstruction* (Baton Rouge: Louisiana State University Press, 1991), 121–140; Foner, *Reconstruction*, 246–247; *Report of the Joint Committee on Reconstruction*, 39th Cong., 1st sess., vii–xxi (1866). The Joint Committee drafted the Fourteenth Amendment, which distilled the conclusions reached by the twelve majority (Republican) members of the committee.
122. Carl Schurz, "Report on the Condition of the South," S. Exec. Doc., No. 2, 39th Cong., 1st sess., 17–25 (1865).
123. C. Vann Woodward's classic *Reunion and Reaction: The Compromise of 1877 and the End of Reconstruction* (1951, rev. ed. New York: Oxford University Press, 1991) details the political and economic explanations for Reconstruction's end. The principal recent studies are William Gillette, *Retreat from Reconstruction, 1869–1879* (Baton Rouge: Louisiana State University Press, 1979); Michael Perman, *The Road to Redemption: Southern Politics, 1869–1879* (Chapel Hill: University of North Carolina Press, 1984), 135–280; and, from a northern perspective, Heather Cox Richardson, *The Death of Reconstruction: Race, Labor, and Politics in the Post–Civil War North, 1865–1901* (Cambridge: Harvard University Press, 2004). Charles Fairman compiled the exhaustive (and exhausting), pointlessly detailed *Reconstruction and Reunion, 1864–1888* (New York: Macmillan, 1971) (vols. 6–7 of the *Holmes Devise History of the Supreme Court of the United States*). Fairman's work reflected an outdated, hostile view of Republican Reconstruction and lost sight of the forest because of its numbing attention to the minutiae of the trees. It was further warped by the crabbed views of Reconstruction entertained by Fairman's patron Felix Frankfurter, which Fairman shared or absorbed. On the malignant impact of this racist historiography in influencing the thinking of the justices about Reconstruction see Eric Foner, *The Second Founding: How the Civil War and Reconstruction*

Made the Constitution (New York: Norton, 2019), xxi-xxix; Foner, "The Supreme Court and the History of Reconstruction—and Vice Versa," 112 *Columbia Law Review* 1585, 1585-1590 (2012); and the essays collected in John D. Smith and J. Vincent Lowery, eds., *The Dunning School: Historians, Race, and the Meaning of Reconstruction* (Lexington: University Press of Kentucky, 2013), esp. Smith, "Introduction," 1-48.

124. Barry Friedman, *The Will of the People: How Public Opinion Has Influenced the Supreme Court and Shaped the Meaning of the Constitution* (Farrar, Strauss and Giroux, 2009), 14-16, 146-149.
125. See the cases cited in Nelson, *The Fourteenth Amendment*, 148-155.
126. 27 F. Cas. 785, 794 (C.C.D. Ky. 1866) (No. 16,151).
127. The facts of the case are explored in depth in Harold M. Hyman, *The Reconstruction Justice of Salmon P. Chase: In re Turner and Texas v. White* (Lawrence: University Press of Kansas, 2001), 123-139, and White, "Reconstructing the Constitutional Jurisprudence of Chase," 74-78.
128. In re Turner, 24 F. Cas. 337, 339 (C.C.D. Md. 1867) (No. 14,247).
129. He presided over the circuit court hearings in the *Slaughterhouse Cases* and in *United States v. Cruikshank*, both discussed below. He was nominated to the Supreme Court in 1880 and served until his death in 1887.
130. 26 F. Cas. 79, 81 (C.C.S.D. Ala. 1871) (No. 15,282).
131. The state action problem introduced here is discussed at length in the next chapter.
132. US Const. Amend. XIV, sec. 1: "All persons born or naturalized in the United States and subject to the jurisdiction thereof, are citizens of the United States and of the State wherein they reside."
133. 74 U.S. (7 Wall.) 700, 725, 728 (1869). On this case, see Hyman, *Reconstruction Justice*, 140-150.
134. Art. III, sec. 2: "In all Cases...in which a State shall be a Party, the supreme Court shall have original Jurisdiction."
135. On the applicability of this seldom-cited clause to Texas, see William M. Wiecek, *The Guarantee Clause of the U.S. Constitution* (Ithaca: Cornell University Press, 1972), 235-236.
136. Slaughterhouse Cases, 83 U.S. (16 Wall.) 36 (1873).
137. The Court split five to four on the result, with Field, Chase, Swayne, and Bradley dissenting. The *Slaughterhouse Cases* remain controversial among historians. The case has most recently been analyzed by Ronald M. Labbe and Jonathan Lurie, *The Slaughterhouse Cases: Regulation, Reconstruction, and the Fourteenth Amendment* (Lawrence: University Press of Kansas, 2003), 208-222, 244-251, and in Michael A. Ross, *Justice of Shattered Dreams: Samuel Freeman Miller and the Supreme Court of the Civil War Era* (Baton Rouge: Louisiana State University Press, 2003), 189-210. Most scholarly evaluations are unsparingly critical of Miller's majority opinion: inter alia, Richard L. Aynes, "Constricting the Law of Freedom: Justice Miller, the Fourteenth Amendment, and the Slaughter-House Cases," 70 *Chicago-Kent Law Review* 627 (1994); Richard L. Aynes, "On Misreading John Bingham and the Fourteenth Amendment," 103 *Yale Law Journal* 57 (1993); Laurence Tribe, *American Constitutional Law*, 3rd ed. (New York: Foundation, 2000), 1:1321; Akhil Amar, "The Bill of Rights and the Fourteenth Amendment," 101 *Yale Law Journal* 1193 (1992); Michael Kent Curtis, "Resurrecting the Privileges and Immunities Clause and Revising the Slaughter-House Cases without Exhuming Lochner: Individual Rights and the Fourteenth Amendment," 38 *Boston College Law Review* 1, 2 (1996); Wilson R; Huhn, "The Legacy of Slaughterhouse, Bradwell, and Cruikshank in Constitutional Interpretation." 42 *Akron Law Review* 1051 (2009); William M. Wiecek, "The Emergence of Equality as a Constitutional Value: The First Century," 82 *Chicago-Kent Law Review* 233 (2007); James W. Fox, "Re-readings and Misreadings: Slaughter-House, Privileges or Immunities, and Section Five Enforcement Powers," 91 *Kentucky Law Journal* 67 (2002). But Lurie, Ross, and G. Edward White (White, *Law in American History*, vol. 2: *From Reconstruction through the 1920s* (New York: Oxford University Press, 2016), 32-38, present strong defenses of Miller's opinion.
138. Michael Kent Curtis, "Resurrecting the Privileges or Immunities Clause," 2.
139. 83 U.S. 67, 71.
140. Michael A. Ross, "Obstructing Reconstruction: John A. Campbell and the Legal Campaign against Louisiana's Republican Government, 1868-1873," 49 *Civil War History*, 235-253 (2003); Robert Saunders, *John Archibald Campbell: Southern Moderate, 1811-1889* (Tuscaloosa: University of Alabama Press, 1997), 214-228.

141. *Black's Law Dictionary*: Police power: "The inherent and plenary power of a sovereign to make all laws necessary and proper to preserve the public security, order, health, morality, and justice. It is a fundamental power essential to government."

142. William J. Novak, *The People's Welfare: Law and Regulation in Nineteenth Century America* (Chapel Hill: University of North Carolina Press, 1996).

143. 83 U.S. 69.

144. Pamela Brandwein, *Reconstructing Reconstruction: The Supreme Court and the Production of Historical Truth* (Durham: Duke University Press, 1999), 38–41, 61–95; Brandwein, *Rethinking the Judicial Settlement of Reconstruction* (Cambridge: Cambridge University Press, 2011); Brandwein, "Slavery as an Interpretive Issue in the Reconstruction Congresses," 34 *Law & Society Review* 315 (2000).

145. US Const. Amend. XIV, sec. 1, first sentence: "All persons born or naturalized in the United States and subject to the jurisdiction thereof, are citizens of the United States and of the State wherein they reside."

146. White, *Law in American History*, 2:24–26, 32–36.

147. Had antebellum pro-slavery thought not polluted public discourse, it would have been convenient to refer to these as "state rights" or more accurately, "state-derived rights." But pro-slavery invocation of "states' rights" hopelessly confused our vocabulary. (States do not possess rights; only humans do. States have *powers*; *people* have rights.) So we will have to stick with phrases like "natural rights," though that too introduces its own source of confusion.

148. Aynes, "Constricting the Law of Freedom," 627, 646–649.

149. Green, *Equal Citizenship*.

150. Curtis, "Resurrecting the Privileges or Immunities Clause," 2. Curtis contends that this more expansive reading is justified by the original meaning of the phrase "privileges and immunities": Michael Kent Curtis, "Historical Linguistics, Inkblots, and Life after Death: The Privileges or Immunities of Citizens of the United States," 78 *North Carolina Law Review* 1071 (2000). See also Kevin C. Newsom, "Setting Incorporationism Straight: A Reinterpretation of the Slaughterhouse Cases," 109 *Yale Law Journal* 739 (2000). Robert C. Palmer contended that Miller's opinion rightly read actually *did* rely on the privileges or immunities clause to incorporate not only the first eight amendments, but also much of Article I, section 8 as well: "The Parameters of Constitutional Reconstruction: Slaughterhouse, Cruikshank, and the Fourteenth Amendment," 1984 *University of Illinois Law Review* 739.

151. Laurent B. Frantz, "The New Supreme Court Decisions on the Federal Civil Rights Statutes," 11 *Lawyers' Guild Law Review* 142, 145 (1951).

152. 83U.S. 80.

153. 83 U.S. 76, quoting Corfield v. Coryell, 6 F.Cas. 546 (C.C.E.D. Pa. 1823) (No. 3,230) (ital. in orig.).

154. The phrase is Pamela Brandwein's: *Reconstructing Reconstruction*, 92.

155. McDonald v. City of Chicago, 561 U.S. 742, 807–858 (2010) (Thomas, J. concurring in part, dissenting in part); Saenz v. Roe, 526 U.S. 489 (1999); Laurence Tribe, "Saenz Sans Prophecy: Does the Privileges or Immunities Revival Portend the Future—or Reveal the Structure of the Present?," 113 *Harvard Law Review* 110, 181–182 (1999); Clarence Thomas, "The Higher Law Background of the Privileges or Immunities Clause of the Fourteenth Amendment," 12 *Harvard Journal of Law & Public Policy* 63 (1989); Philip Kurland, "The Privileges or Immunities Clause: Its Hour Come Round at Last?," 1972 *Washington University Law Quarterly* 405 (1972).

156. 83 U.S. 81.

157. 83 U.S. 81.

158. 83 U.S. 82. White, *Law in American History, Volume 2*, 6–42 offers an interpretation of Reconstruction generally and Slaughterhouse specifically that is critical of the "conventional historiography" of the topics that is presented here, seeing Miller's position as more authentically reflecting the constitutional understandings of the time.

159. 83 U.S. 82.

160. Robert J. Kaczorowski, "The Chase Court and Fundamental Rights," 21 *Northern Kentucky Law Review* 151 (1993).

161. Michael Les Benedict, "Preserving Federalism: Reconstruction and the Waite Court," 1978 *Supreme Court Review* 39 (1978).

162. Michael Les Benedict, "Preserving the Constitution: The Conservative Basis of Radical Reconstruction," in Benedict, comp., *Preserving the Constitution: Essays and Politics and the*

Constitution in the Reconstruction Era (New York: Fordham University Press, 2006), 4–5 (originally published in the *Journal of American History* in 1974).
163. Cynthia Nicoletti, "The Rise and Fall of Transcendent Constitutionalism in the Civil War Era," 106 *Virginia Law Review* 1631 (2020).
164. Michael A. Ross, "Justice Miller's Reconstruction: The Slaughter-House Cases, Health Codes, and Civil Rights in New Orleans, 1861–1873," 64 *Journal of Southern History* 649 (1998).
165. Ross, *Justice of Shattered Dreams*, 200; Labbe and Lurie, *Slaughterhouse Cases*, 108.
166. Leslie F. Goldstein, "The Specter of the Second Amendment: Rereading Slaughterhouse and Cruikshank," 21 *Studies in American Political Development* 131 (2007).
167. David S. Bogen, "Rebuilding the Slaughterhouse: The Cases' Support for Civil Rights," 42 *Akron Law Review* 1129 (2006).
168. United States v. Guest, 383 U.S. 745 (1966) (discussed at greater length below in chapter 11); Heart of Atlanta Motel v. United States, 379 U.S. 241 (1964) (discussed below in chapter 7).
169. See the discussions of *Ex parte Seibold* and *Ex parte Yarbrough* below in this chapter.
170. Hague v. CIO, 307 U.S. 496 (1939).
171. William M. Wiecek, "The Great Writ and Reconstruction: The Habeas Corpus Act of 1867," 36 *Journal of Southern History* 530 (1970).
172. Alito, J.: "We therefore decline to disturb the *Slaughter-House* holding." McDonald v. City of Chicago, 561 U.S. 742, 758 (2010).
173. Twining v. New Jersey, 211 U.S. 78, 96 (1908).
174. Daniel S. Stowell, "Why 'Redemption'? Religion and the End of Reconstruction, 1869–1877," in Edward J. Blum and W. Scott Poole, eds., *Vale of Tears: New Essays on Religion and Reconstruction* (Macon: Mercer University Press, 2005), 132–146.
175. Michael Perman, *Road to Redemption*; Foner, *Reconstruction*, 412–459, 587–601.
176. 80 U.S. (13 Wall.) 581 (1872).
177. The Kentucky Supreme Court had held the act unconstitutional in Bowlin v. Commonwealth, 65 Ky. (2 Bush) 5 (1867).
178. Or parties in interest in civil litigation.
179. 80 U.S. 599. Swayne joined Bradley in dissent.
180. Robert D. Goldstein, "Blyew: Variations on a Jurisdictional Theme," 41 *Stanford Law Review* 469, 477, 526 (1989). *Accord*, Douglas L. Colbert, "Liberating the Thirteenth Amendment," 30 *Harvard Civil Rights–Civil Liberties Law Review* 1, 18–19 (1995).
181. Robert M. Goldman, *Reconstruction and Black Suffrage: Losing the Vote in Reese and Cruikshank* (Lawrence: University Press of Kansas, 2001); Goldstone, *On Account of Race*, 79–90.
182. 92 U.S. 542 (1876).
183. Estimates vary so widely because many of the victims' bodies were buried in mass graves, hauled off, or dumped in the nearby Red River. The story is told in Charles Lane, *The Day Freedom Died: The Colfax Massacre, the Supreme Court, and the Betrayal of Reconstruction* (New York: Henry Holt, 2008); LeeAnna Keith, *The Colfax Massacre: The Untold Story of Black Power, White Terror, and the Death of Reconstruction* (New York: Oxford University Press, 2007); and Nicholas Lemann, *Redemption: The Last Battle of the Civil War* (New York: Farrar, Strauss and Giroux, 2006).
184. Quoted in Paul Kens, *The Supreme Court under Morrison R. Waite, 1874–1888* (Columbia: University of South Carolina Press, 2012), 16.
185. Quoted in Ross, *Justice of Shattered Dreams*, 215.
186. Robert J. Kaczorowski offers a traditional and critical interpretation of Bradley's opinion in *The Politics of Judicial Interpretation: The Federal Courts, Department of Justice and Civil Rights, 1866–1876* (New York: Fordham University Press, 1985), 179–184.
187. James Gray Pope, "Snubbed Landmark: Why United States v. Cruikshank (1876) Belongs at the Heart of the American Constitutional Canon," 49 *Harvard Civil Rights–Civil Liberties Law Review* 385, 388 (2014).
188. *Washington v. Davis* is discussed below in chapter 8 and *Boerne v. Flores* in chapter 11.
189. Pope, "Snubbed Landmark," 447. Pamela Brandwein, *Rethinking Reconstruction*, 87–183, attributes to Bradley's opinion the origin of both the state action doctrine and the idea that a state's neglect to act in the face of private deprivation of rights constitutes a form of state action. See also White, *Law in American History*, 2:23–27.
190. McDonald v. City of Chicago, 561 U.S. 742, 855 (2010) (Thomas, J. concurring). Justice Thomas's view is driven by his belief that the privileges or immunities clause has been ignored and by his avid enthusiasm for expansive readings of the Second Amendment.

191. 92 U.S. 214 (1876).
192. Here Waite was drawing on the holding of Minor v. Happersett, 88 U.S. 162 (1874), which held that the Fourteenth Amendment did not confer a right to vote on women.
193. 92 U.S. 219, 217.
194. United States v. Raines, 362 U.S. 17, 24 (1960).
195. 92 U.S. 243. This was Hunt's only significant contribution in his otherwise short and unremarkable service on the Court, 1872–1882. It provides cause for regret that he did not enjoy better health and greater longevity. Goldman, *Reconstruction and Black Suffrage*, 95–100, offers an appreciation of the Hunt dissent.
196. Rutherglen, *Civil Rights in the Shadow*, 94.
197. Foner, *Reconstruction*, 529.

Chapter 3

1. In a new and enlarged edition, Logan retitled this book *The Betrayal of the Negro: From Rutherford B. Hayes to Woodrow Wilson* (New York: Collier, 1965).
2. Henry Louis Gates provides an overview of the history and culture of Reconstruction and Redemption in *Stony the Road: Reconstruction, White Supremacy, and the Rise of Jim Crow* (New York: Penguin, 2019).
3. Ulrich B. Phillips, "The Central Theme of Southern History," 30 *American Historical Review* 30, 31 (1925).
4. David W. Blight, *Race and Reunion: The Civil War in American Memory* (Cambridge: Harvard University Press, 2001); Alan T. Nolan, "The Anatomy of the Myth," in Gary W. Gallagher and Alan T. Nolan, eds., *The Myth of the Lost Cause and Civil War History* (Bloomington: Indiana University Press, 2000); Nina Silber, *Romance of Reunion: Northerners and the South, 1865–1900* (Chapel Hill: University of North Carolina Press, 1993); Gaines M. Foster, *Ghosts of the Confederacy: Defeat, the Lost Cause and the Emergence of the New South, 1865–1913* (New York: Oxford University Press, 1988).
5. The Fuller Court is defined chronologically as the Court of 1888 to 1910, the years when Melville Weston Fuller served as chief justice. The convention of identifying periods in the Court's history by the chief justice who presided at the time can be unhelpful, misleading, or merely a shorthand convenience. For once, though, Fuller's occupancy of the center seat happens to provide a periodization that nicely bookends the coherence of the Court of that period. He wholeheartedly supported the Court's embrace of Redemption and joined in all its most regrettable decisions of those years.
6. Owen Fiss surveys the Fuller Court in *Troubled Beginnings of the Modern State, 1888–1910* (New York: Macmillan, 1993) (vol. 8 of the *Holmes Devise History of the Supreme Court of the United States*); James W. Ely's *The Chief Justiceship of Melville W. Fuller, 1888–1910* (Columbia: University of South Carolina Press, 1995) is appreciative. Three studies cover the Supreme Court in the period of Reconstruction and Redemption: Lawrence Goldstone, *Inherently Unequal: The Betrayal of Equal Rights by the Supreme Court, 1865–1903* (New York: Walker, 2011); Frank J. Scaturro, *The Supreme Court's Retreat from Reconstruction: A Distortion of Constitutional Jurisprudence* (Westport: Greenwood, 2000); John R. Howard, *The Shifting Wind: The Supreme Court and Civil Rights from Reconstruction to Brown* (Albany: State University of New York Press, 1999).
7. George M. Frederickson, *The Black Image in the White Mind: The Debate on Afro-American Character and Destiny, 1817–1914* (New York: Harper & Row, 1971); Thomas F. Gossett, *Race: The History of an Idea in America* (New York: Oxford University Press, 1997); Joel Williamson, *The Crucible of Race: Black/White Relations in the American South since Emancipation* (New York: Oxford University Press, 1984).
8. Except in the *Siebold* and *Yarbrough* cases.
9. 17 U.S. (4 Wheat.) 316, 423, 387 (1819).
10. Department of Commerce v. New York, 139 S.Ct. 2551, 2579 (2019) (Thomas, J. concurring and dissenting).
11. 517 U.S. 806 (1996).
12. M. K. B. Darmer, "Teaching Whren to White Kids," 15 *Michigan Journal of Race & Law* 109, 110–120 (2009).

NOTES TO PAGES 89-96   457

13. David A. Harris, "Addressing Racial Profiling in the States: A Case Study of the 'New Federalism' in Constitutional Criminal Procedure," 3 *University of Pennsylvania Journal of Constitutional Law* 367 (2001).
14. On this topic generally, see Leon Festinger, *A Theory of Cognitive Dissonance* (New York: Harper & Row, 1957).
15. James W. Fox, "Doctrinal Myths and the Management of Cognitive Dissonance: Race, Law, and the Supreme Court's Support of Jim Crow," 34 *Stetson Law Review* 293 (2005).
16. Benno C. Schmidt Jr., "Juries, Jurisdiction, and Race Discrimination: The Lost Promise of Strauder v. West Virginia," 61 *Texas Law Review* 1401 (1983).
17. 100 U.S. 303 (1880).
18. *Strauder* did not address the other basis of a constitutional challenge to racial exclusion, namely, that the right to serve on a jury was an aspect of citizenship, like voting, that was comprehended in the concept of political rights. This would have been a weaker claim for the appellant, because of the controverted status of political rights.
19. Justices Field and Clifford dissented. They were the only two Democrats on the Court and reflected their party's views on race and federalism.
20. Moreover, Congress had specifically forbidden racial discrimination in jury selection for both federal and state juries by section 4 of the 1875 Civil Rights Act: Act of March 1, 1875, ch. 114, 18 Stat. 336, a part of the 1875 statute that was not held unconstitutional in the *Civil Rights Cases*.
21. 100 U.S. 306–308.
22. James M. DeLise, "Racial Impermissibility under the Equal Protection Clause from Strauder v. West Virginia to Ricci v. Destefano," 17 *Rutgers Race & Law Review* 179, 179–180 (2016).
23. Smith v. Mississippi, 162 U.S. 592 (1896); Murray v. Louisiana, 163 U.S. 101 (1896); Martin v. Texas, 200 U.S. 316 (1906).
24. Thomas v. Texas, 212 U.S. 278, 282 (1909).
25. 100 U.S. 339 (1880).
26. 100 U.S. 313 (1880).
27. Act of April 9, 1866, ch. 30, § 3, 14 Stat. 27.
28. Schmidt, "Juries, Jurisdiction, and Race Discrimination," 1433–1435.
29. 103 U.S. 370 (1881).
30. 100 U.S. 310.
31. A reminder: "Reconstruction's constitutional triad" consists of (1) federalism: the relations between the states and the national government; (2) the status and rights of African Americans; and (3) federal judicial power. On the third leg of this triad, see William M. Wiecek, "The Reconstruction of Federal Judicial Power, 1863–1875," 13 *American Journal of Legal History* 333 (1969).
32. Jud Mathews provides a useful overview of the subject in "State Action Doctrine and the Logic of Constitutional Containment," 2017 *University of Illinois Law Review* 655, 655–667 (2017).
33. Lugar v. Edmondson Oil Co., 457 U.S. 922, 936 (1982); Blum v. Yaretsky, 457 U.S. 991 (1982).
34. United States v. Cruikshank, 92 U.S. 542, 554–555 (1875).
35. 100 U.S. 313, 318 (1880). Strong was referring to the privileges or immunities, due process, and equal protection clauses.
36. Civil Rights Act of 1875, ch. 114, § 1, 18 Stat. 335. Section 2 made it a misdemeanor to deny such access and imposed a fine and imprisonment for less than a year, or in the alternative, permitted the aggrieved party to collect the penalty.
37. 109 U.S. 3 (1883).
38. "The Congress shall have power to enforce, by appropriate legislation, the provisions of this article."
39. G. Edward White, *Law in American History*, vol. 2: *From Reconstruction through the 1920s* (New York: Oxford University Press, 2016), 42–49, contends that Bradley's opinion correctly reflected the understanding of American federalism in the postwar period.
40. Eugene Gressman, "The Unhappy History of Civil Rights Legislation," 50 *Michigan Law Review* 1323 (1952).
41. William M. Carter, "Race, Rights, and the Thirteenth Amendment: Defining the Badges and Incidents of Slavery," 40 *University of California Davis Law Review* 1311 (2007).
42. Jennifer M. McAward, "Defining the Badges and Incidents of Slavery," 14 *Journal of Constitutional Law* 561 (2012).
43. 109 U.S. 21.

44. 109 U.S. 24-25.
45. Linda Przybyszewski, *The Republic according to John Marshall Harlan* (Chapel Hill: University of North Carolina Press, 1999); Loren P. Beth: *John Marshall Harlan: The Last Whig Justice* (Lexington: University Press of Kentucky, 1992); Tinsley E. Yarbrough, *Judicial Enigma: The First Justice Harlan* (New York: Oxford University Press, 1995); and G. Edward White, "John Marshall Harlan I: The Precursor," in White, ed., *The American Judicial Tradition*, 3rd ed. (New York: Oxford University Press, 2007), 105-120, are the leading modern studies of this jurist. He should not be confused with his grandson and namesake John Marshall Harlan II, who served on the Supreme Court from 1955 to 1971.
46. All ensuing quotes from Harlan's dissent are at 109 U.S. 33-34, 38, 41-42, 48, 58-59, 62.
47. However, in response to the *Civil Rights Cases*, eighteen states adopted public accommodations statutes after 1883: Duane Lockard, *Toward Equal Opportunity: A Study of State and Local Anti-discrimination Laws* (New York: Macmillan, 1968), 16.
48. Moose Lodge v. Irvis, 407 U.S. 163 (1972); Jackson v. Metropolitan Edison Co., 419 U.S. 345 (1974); Flagg Bros. v. Brooks, 436 U.S. 149 (1978); U.S. v. Morrison, 529 U.S. 598 (2000).
49. 106 U.S. 629 (1883).
50. Act of April 20, 1871, ch. 31, § 2, 17 Stat. 13.
51. United States v. Hall, 26 F.Cas. 79 (D.C.S.D.Ala. 1871) (No. 15,2820).
52. 403 U.S. 88, 104-105 (1971): "there has never been any doubt of the power of Congress to impose liability on private persons under sec. 2 of that [Thirteenth] amendment, 'for the amendment is not a mere prohibition of state laws establishing or upholding slavery, but an absolute declaration that slavery or involuntary servitude shall not exist in any part of the United States,'" citing, ironically, the *Civil Rights Cases*.
53. In Baldwin v. Franks, 120 U.S. 678 (1887), the Court extended Harris to exonerate whites in California who expelled Chinese resident aliens from their homes and workplaces.
54. 100 U.S. 371 (1880). Field and Clifford dissented. Both were Democrats.
55. 110 U.S. 651, 665 (1884). Bancroft Davis, the Supreme Court reporter, officially styled this "The Ku-Klux Cases," but it is known today as *Ex parte Yarbrough*.
56. *Proprio vigore* is a law Latin phrase meaning "by its own force."
57. The term "miscegenation" was a neologism coined ca. 1864 to replace the less-jarring "amalgamation" in an effort to delegitimate interracial unions. Peggy Pascoe, *What Comes Naturally: Miscegenation Law and the Making of Race in America* (New York: Oxford University Press, 2009), 4. The usage today has become pejorative.
58. Joel Williamson, *New People: Miscegenation and Mulattoes in the United States* (Baton Rouge: Louisiana State University Press, 1980), 6-24.
59. Winthrop D. Jordan, *White over Black: American Attitudes toward the Negro, 1550-1812* (Chapel Hill: University of North Carolina Press, 1968), 78.
60. Burns v. State, 48 Ala. 196 (1872).
61. Green v. State, 58 Ala. 190 (1878).
62. Julie Novkov, *Racial Union: Law, Intimacy, and the White State in Alabama, 1865-1954* (Ann Arbor: University of Michigan Press, 2008); Pascoe, *What Comes Naturally*.
63. Pace and Cox v. State, 69 Ala. 231, 232 (1881).
64. 106 U.S. 583 (1883).
65. 388 U.S. 1, 11 (1967).
66. 350 U.S. 891 (1955), 350 U.S. 985 (1956). The evasion was driven by Justice Frankfurter's concern that the topic was too incendiary and endangered whites' acceptance of *Brown v. Board of Education*. Michael J. Klarman, *From Jim Crow to Civil Rights: The Supreme Court and the Struggle for Racial Equality* (New York: Oxford University Press, 2004), 322.
67. 379 U.S. 184 (1964).
68. 388 U.S. 1 (1967).
69. Alabama did not repeal its miscegenation statute until 2000.
70. Mia Bay tells the story of travel segregation comprehensively in *Traveling Black: A Story of Race and Resistance* (Cambridge: Harvard University Press, 2021). See also Barbara Y. Welke, *Recasting American Liberty: Gender, Race, Law, and the Railroad Revolution, 1865-1920* (Cambridge: Cambridge University Press, 2001), 249-375; Welke, "When All the Women Were White, and All the Blacks Were Men: Gender, Class, Race, and the Road to Plessy, 1855-1914," 13 *Law & History Review* 261 (1995).
71. White, *Law in American History*, 2:424-445, treats the transportation cases, including *Plessy*, as being consistent with the era's understandings of police powers, due process, and civil rights.

72. Earl M. Maltz, "Separate but Equal and the Law of Common Carriers in the Era of the Fourteenth Amendment," 17 *Rutgers Law Journal* 553 (1984).
73. Kenneth W. Mack, "Law, Society, Identity, and the Making of the Jim Crow South: Travel and Segregation on Tennessee Railroads, 1875–1905," 24 *Law & Social Inquiry* 377 (1999).
74. Stephen J. Riegel, "The Persistent Career of Jim Crow: Lower Federal Courts and the 'Separate but Equal' Doctrine," 20 *American Journal of Legal History* 22 (1984).
75. US Const. Art. I, sec. 8: "The Congress shall have Power . . . To regulate Commerce with foreign Nations, and among the several States, and with the Indian Tribes."
76. 22 U.S. (9 Wheat.) 1, 196–197 (1824).
77. 27 U.S. (2 Pet.) 245 (1829).
78. 84 U.S. 445 (1873).
79. However, Justice David Davis did not specify the source of congressional power and did not allude to the commerce clause.
80. Patricia H. Minter, "The Failure of Freedom: Class, Gender, and the Evolution of Segregated Transit in the Nineteenth-Century South," 70 *Chicago-Kent Law Review* 993 (1995); J. David Hoeveler, "Reconstruction and the Federal Courts: The Civil Rights Act of 1875," 31 *Historian* 604 (1969).
81. 95 U.S. 485, 487–489 (1878); Jack M. Beermann, *The Journey to Separate but Equal: Madame DeCuir's Quest for Racial Justice in the Reconstruction Era* (Lawrence: University Press of Kansas, 2021).
82. In *Gibbons*, Chief Justice Marshall had not held that Congress's power was exclusive, though he toyed with the idea: 22 U.S. at 209. Justice William Johnson, concurring, insisted that it was.
83. This is one early version of what has come to be known as the "dormant commerce clause," a doctrine derived remotely from Willson v. Black Bird Creek Marsh Co., 27 U.S. (2 Pet.) 245 (1829).
84. On the role of logic and formalism in judicial thought of the era, see William M. Wiecek, *The Lost World of Classical Legal Thought: Law and Ideology in America, 1886–1937* (New York: Oxford University Press, 1998), 79–93.
85. 133 U.S. 587, 591, 594 (1890).
86. The cases are Bob-lo Excursion Co. v. Michigan (1948) and Morgan v. Virginia 328 U.S. 373 (1946).
87. Owen Fiss surveys these and related cases of the Fuller Court in *Troubled Beginnings*, 352–385.
88. The statute excluded street railways from its coverage because they were more thoroughly integrated at the time and segregating them would have proved impractical.
89. Mark Elliott, *Color-Blind Justice: Albion Tourgée and the Quest for Racial Equality from the Civil War to Plessy v. Ferguson* (New York: Oxford University Press, 2006), 262–295; Carolyn L. Karcher, *A Refugee from His Race: Albion W. Tourgée and His Fight against White Supremacy* (Chapel Hill: University of North Carolina Press, 2016), 253–293.
90. 163 U.S. 537 (1896). Justice Brewer did not participate because of the death of his daughter.
91. The literature on *Plessy* is extensive: Charles A. Lofgren, *The Plessy Case: A Legal-Historical Interpretation* (New York: Oxford University Press, 1987); Williamjames H. Hoffer, *Plessy v. Ferguson: Race and Inequality in Jim Crow America* (Lawrence: University Press of Kansas, 2012); Harvey Fireside, *Separate and Unequal: Homer Plessy and the Supreme Court Decision That Legalized Racism* (New York: Carroll & Graf, 2004); Klarman, *From Jim Crow to Civil Rights*, 8–25 (condensing his article "The Plessy Era," 1998 *Supreme Court Review* 303 [1998]). Steve Luxenberg tells the story of the case through the participants' biographies in *Separate: The Story of Plessy v. Ferguson, and America's Journey from Slavery to Segregation* (New York: Norton, 2019).
92. 163 U.S. 543.
93. 163 U.S. 544.
94. 163 U.S. 550.
95. 59 Mass. (5 Cush.) 198 (1850). On this case, see Leonard M. Levy, *The Law of the Commonwealth and Chief Justice Shaw* (Cambridge: Harvard University Press, 1957), 109–117.
96. 163 U.S. 551.
97. 163 U.S. 544.
98. 163 U.S. 544.
99. 163 U.S. 551.

100. Rebecca J. Scott, "Public Rights, Social Equality, and the Conceptual Roots of the Plessy Challenge," 106 *Michigan Law Review* 777, 800 (2008).
101. Cheryl I. Harris, "The Story of Plessy v. Ferguson: The Death and Resurrection of Racial Formalism," in Michael C. Dorf, ed., *Constitutional Law Stories* (St. Paul: Foundation, 2004), 218–222.
102. 163 U.S. 555.
103. 163 U.S. 560.
104. 163 U.S. 558.
105. For that context and its historical development, see Andrew Kull, *The Color-Blind Constitution* (Cambridge: Harvard University Press, 1992); on *Plessy*, see pp. 113–132.
106. On caste systems, see Isabel Wilkerson, *Caste: The Origins of Our Discontents* (New York: Random House, 2020).
107. 163 U.S. 558. Sixteen years later, Justice Brown conceded that Harlan had been right on this point. In an obituary tribute to his colleague Harlan, Brown wrote that "it was probably the fact that" Louisiana did intend to exclude Blacks from white cars. The equality announced in *Plessy* was in fact false equivalence. Expressing the idea in a double negative, he asked "whether the spirit of the Amendments was not sacrificed to the letter, and whether the Constitution was not intended to secure the equality of the two races in all places affected with a public interest." Henry B. Brown, "The Dissenting Opinions of Mr. Justice Harlan," 46 *American Law Review* 321, 336 (1912).
108. 163 U.S. 559.
109. The passage reads in full: "The white race deems itself to be the dominant race in this country. And so it is, in prestige, in achievements, in education, in wealth, and in power. So, I doubt not, it will continue to be for all time, if it remains true to its great heritage, and holds fast to the principles of constitutional liberty. But in view of the constitution, in the eye of the law, there is in this country no superior, dominant, ruling class of citizens. There is no caste here. Our constitution is color-blind, and neither knows nor tolerates classes among citizens. In respect of civil rights, all citizens are equal before the law."
110. 163 U.S. 557.
111. 163 U.S. 553–554.
112. 326 U.S. 501 (1946).
113. Smith v. Allwright, 321 U.S. 649 (1944).
114. See, e.g., Jackson v. Metropolitan Edison Co., 419 U.S. 345 (1974).
115. 163 U.S. 560.
116. 163 U.S. 562–563.
117. 163 U.S. 560.
118. 163 U.S. 563.
119. 163 U.S. 560.
120. J. R. Pole, *The Pursuit of Equality in American History*, 2nd ed. (New York: Oxford University Press, 1993), 222.
121. Enforcement Act of 1870, ch. 114, §§ 6, 7, 14, 16 Stat. 140; [the third] Enforcement Act of 1871, ch. 22, 17 Stat. 13; Civil Rights Act of 1875, ch. 114, secs. 3 & 4, 18 Stat. 335.
122. Benno C. Schmidt, "Principle and Prejudice: The Supreme Court and Race in the Progressive Era, Part 3: Black Disfranchisement from the KKK to the Grandfather Clause," 82 *Columbia Law Review* 835 (1982).
123. 92 U.S. 214 (1876).
124. 92 U.S. 542 (1876).
125. Senator Oliver P. Morton, *Cong. Globe*, 40 Cong., 3rd sess. 863 (1869).
126. The story is told in Michael Perman, *Struggle for Mastery: Disfranchisement in the South, 1888–1908* (Chapel Hill: University of North Carolina Press, 2001), and J. Morgan Kousser, *The Shaping of Southern Politics: Suffrage Restriction and the Establishment of the One-Party South, 1880–1910* (New Haven: Yale University Press, 1974).
127. Robert M. Goldman, *"A Free Ballot and a Fair Count": The Department of Justice and the Enforcement of Voting Rights in the South, 1877–1893* (New York: Fordham University Press, 1990), 109–162.
128. J. Morgan Kousser enumerates over a dozen different devices by which white Democrats stripped Blacks of the vote: *Shaping of Southern Politics*, 45–62; Kousser, *Colorblind Injustice: Minority Voting Rights and the Undoing of the Second Reconstruction* (Chapel Hill: University of North Carolina Press,1999), 25–26, 35. Some of these measures have reappeared in the

Republican vote-suppression measures adopted in the wake of *Shelby County v. Holder* (2013), particularly since 2020.
129. Not to be confused with his better-known grandson Henry Cabot Lodge Jr., Republican senator from Massachusetts, who served in 1937–1944 and 1947–1953.
130. Alexander Keyssar, *The Right to Vote: The Contested History of Democracy in the United States* (New York: Basic Books, 2000), 86.
131. Thomas A. Upchurch, *Legislating Racism: The Billion-Dollar Congress and the Birth of Jim Crow* (Lexington: University Press of Kentucky, 2004), 85–166.
132. On the effect of racist beliefs on disfranchisement, see Stanley Hirshson, *Farewell to the Bloody Shirt: Northern Republicans and the Southern Negro, 1877–93* (Bloomington: Indiana University Press, 1962); Paul Lewinson, *Race Class, and Party: A History of Negro Suffrage and White Politics in the South* (New York: Grossett & Dunlap, 1932); Richard M. Valelly, *The Two Reconstructions: The Struggle for Black Enfranchisement* (Chicago: University of Chicago Press, 2004), 47–146.
133. R. Volney Riser, *Defying Disfranchisement: Black Voting Rights Activism in the Jim Crow South, 1890–1908* (Baton Rouge: Louisiana State University Press, 2010), 36–73.
134. Quoted in Neil R. McMillen, *Dark Journey: Black Mississippians in the Age of Jim Crow* (Urbana: University of Illinois Press, 1989), 44.
135. Ratliffe v. Beale, 74 Miss. 247, 20 So. 865, 868 (1896).
136. Quoted in Ward E. Y. Elliott, *The Rise of Guardian Democracy: The Supreme Court's Role in Voting Rights Disputes, 1845–1969* (Cambridge: Harvard University Press, 1974), 69.
137. Gabriel J. Chin and Randy Wagner, "The Tyranny of the Minority: Jim Crow and the Countermajoritarian Difficulty," 43 *Harvard Civil Rights–Civil Liberties Law Review* 65 (2008).
138. 20 So. 867.
139. Act of Feb. 8, 1894, ch. 25, 28 Stat. 36.
140. 170 U.S. 213, 222 (1898).
141. Quoted in Morton Stavis, "A Century of Struggle for Black Enfranchisement in Mississippi: From the Civil War to the Congressional Challenge of 1965—and Beyond," 57 *Mississippi Law Journal* 603, 604 (1987).
142. Stavis, "Century of Struggle," 603–605.
143. Kousser, *Shaping of Southern Politics*, 262, 264.
144. 118 U.S. 356, 373–374 (1886).
145. 170 U.S. 225.
146. 175 U.S. 528 (1899).
147. The facts of the case are discussed in J. Morgan Kousser, "Separate but Not Equal: The Supreme Court's First Decision on Racial Discrimination in Schools," 46 *Journal of Southern History*17 (1980), and C. Ellen Connally, "Justice Harlan's 'Great Betrayal'? A Reconsideration of Cumming v. Richmond County Board of Education," 25 *Journal of Supreme Court History* 72 (2000).
148. 175 U.S. 200.
149. 175 U.S. 201.
150. Molly T. O'Brien, "Justice John Marshall Harlan as Prophet: The Plessy Dissenter's Color-Blind Constitution," 6 *William & Mary Bill of Rights Journal* 753 (1998).
151. Buck v. Bell, 274 U.S. 200, 208 (1927). Stephen A. Siegel contests this evaluation: "Justice Holmes, Buck v. Bell, and the History of Equal Protection," 90 *Minnesota Law Review* 106 (2005) but concedes its validity in matters of race.

Chapter 4

1. Pamela Brandwein, *Rethinking the Judicial Settlement of Reconstruction* (Cambridge: Cambridge University Press, 2011), 184–192.
2. Quoted in Hunter v. Underwood, 471 U.S. 222, 229 (1985). On this struggle, see R. Volney Riser, *Defying Disfranchisement: Black Voting Rights Activism in the Jim Crow South, 1890–1908* (Baton Rouge: Louisiana State University Press, 2010), 112–225.
3. 189 U.S. 475, 486, 488 (1903). On this case, see Samuel Brenner, "'Airbrushed Out of the Constitutional Canon': The Evolving Understanding of Giles v. Harris, 1903–1925," 107 *Michigan Law Review* 853 (2009), and Richard H. Pildes, "Democracy, Anti-democracy, and the Canon," 17 *Constitutional Commentary* 295, 303 (2000).

4. Holmes was wounded three times in combat, once almost fatally, and resigned his commission in 1864, emotionally burned out.
5. Holmes admitted as much in a 1926 letter to Harold Laski: Holmes to Laski, November 5, 1926, in Mark De Wolfe Howe, ed., *The Holmes-Laski Letters: The Correspondence of Mr. Justice Holmes and Harold J. Laski, 1915–1935*, 2 vols. (Cambridge: Harvard University Press, 1926), 2:893.
6. Mark De Wolfe Howe, *Justice Oliver Wendell Holmes: The Shaping Years* (Cambridge: Harvard University Press, 1957), 137–153.
7. Albert W. Alschuler, *Law without Values: The Life, Work, and Legacy of Justice Holmes* (Chicago: University of Chicago Press, 2000); Yosal Rogat, "Mr. Justice Holmes: A Dissenting Opinion (Part 2)," 15 *Stanford Law Review* 254–275 (1963).
8. E.g., Buck v. Bell, 274 U.S. 200 (1927) (upholding involuntary sterilization of people with intellectual disabilities). Grant Gilmore, who worked on a biography of Holmes for fifteen years before giving up, summed up his character: "Put out of your minds the picture of the tolerant aristocrat, the great liberal, the eloquent defender of our liberties, the Yankee from Olympus. All that was a myth, concocted principally by Harold Laski and Felix Frankfurter, about the time of World War I. The real Holmes was savage, harsh, and cruel, a bitter and lifelong pessimist who saw in the course of human life nothing but a continuing struggle in which the rich and powerful impose their will on the poor and weak." And, it might be added, who saw nothing wrong with that. Grant Gilmore, *The Ages of American Law* (New Haven: Yale University Press, 1977), 44.
9. G. Edward White, *Justice Oliver Wendell Holmes: Law and the Inner Self* (New York: Oxford University Press, 2011), 333–334.
10. 193 U.S. 146, 164 (1904).
11. Jamal Greene, "The Anticanon," 125 *Harvard Law Review* 379, 383 (2011).
12. Brad Snyder, *The House of Truth: A Washington Political Salon and the Foundations of American Liberalism* (New York: Oxford University Press, 2017), 614 n. 131; Pildes, "Democracy, Anti-democracy, and the Canon," 317 ("the most legally disingenuous analysis in the pages of the U. S. Reports").
13. 190 U.S. 127 (1903).
14. 203 U.S. 1, 20 (1906); overruled by Jones v. Alfred H. Mayer Co., 392 U.S. 409, 442–443 n. 78 (1968).
15. The phrase "White Court" refers to the Supreme Court during the chief justiceship of Edward Douglass White, 1910–1921.
16. William F. Holmes, "Whitecapping: Agrarian Violence in Mississippi, 1902–1906," 35 *Journal of Southern History* 165 (1969).
17. Pamela S. Karlan, "Contracting the Thirteenth Amendment: Hodges v. United States," 85 *Boston University Law Review* 783 (2005).
18. United States v. Morris, 125 F. 322, 325 (E.D. Ark. 1903).
19. 202 U.S. 19, 18, 16.
20. Civil Rights Cases, 109 U.S. 3, 20 (1883).
21. 202 U.S. 37.
22. Jones v. Alfred H. Mayer Co., 392 U.S. 409, 441 n. 78 (1968).
23. 198 U.S. 45 (1905).
24. Female employees were another matter: Muller v. Oregon, 208 U.S. 412 (12908); Bunting v. Oregon, 243 U.S. 426 (1917).
25. Karlan, "Contracting the Thirteenth Amendment," 784.
26. Benno C. Schmidt, "Principle and Prejudice: The Supreme Court and Race in the Progressive Era. Part I: The Heyday of Jim Crow," 82 *Columbia Law Review* 444, 446 (1982) (hereafter cited as Schmidt, "Heyday of Jim Crow"). This was the first of three similarly titled articles in vol. 82 of the *Columbia Law Review* that were published in modified form as the author's contribution to Alexander N. Bickel and Benno C. Schmidt, *The Judiciary and Responsible Government, 1910–1921* (New York: Macmillan, 1984) (vol. 9 of the *Holmes Devise History of the Supreme Court of the United States*).
27. 211 U.S. 45 (1908). On this case, see David E. Bernstein, "Plessy vs. Lochner: The Berea College Case," 25 *Journal of Supreme Court History* 93 (2000).
28. Berea College v. Commonwealth, 123 Ky. 209, 94 S.W. 623, 626 (1906).
29. 165 U.S. 578 (1897) and 198 U.S. 45 (1905) respectively. The Kentucky court cited *Allgeyer* but not *Lochner*.

30. Brewer wrote for the majority, joined by Fuller, Peckham, White, and McKenna. Holmes and Moody concurred in the judgment, without opinion. Harlan and Day dissented, the latter without an opinion.
31. 211 U.S. 54, quoting from Home Ins. Co. v. New York, 134 U.S. 594 (1890).
32. Andrew Kull, *The Color-Blind Constitution* (Cambridge: Harvard University Press, 1992), 134; Ronald S. Rauchberg, "Berea College v. Kentucky: Scientific Racism in the Supreme Court," 45 *Journal of Supreme Court History* 262, 281–282 (2020).
33. 211 U.S. 67.
34. Meyer v. Nebraska, 262 U.S. 390 (1923) and Pierce v. Society of Sisters, 268 U.S. 510 (1925), both pillars of modern non-economic substantive due process.
35. Linda Przybyszewski, *The Republic according to John Marshall Harlan* (Chapel Hill: University of North Carolina Press, 1999), 107.
36. 211 U.S. 68.
37. Benno C. Schmidt, "Principle and Prejudice: The Supreme Court and Race in the Progressive Era: Part 2: The Peonage Cases," 82 *Columbia Law Review* 646, 646–656 (1982) (hereafter cited as Schmidt, "Peonage Cases"). This article was the second in a series that was collated into Dean Schmidt's contribution to Bickel and Schmidt, *The Judiciary and Responsible Government, 1910–21*, 725–990.
38. Charles W. Russell, *Report on Peonage* (Washington, DC: GPO, 1908).
39. Harold D. Woodman, "Economic Reconstruction and the Rise of the New South, 1865–1900," in John B. Boles and Evelyn T. Nolen, eds., *Interpreting Southern History* (Baton Rouge: Louisiana State University Press, 1987), 254.
40. William Cohen, "Negro Involuntary Servitude in the South, 1865–1940: A Preliminary Analysis," 42 *Journal of Southern History* 31 (1976); Pete Daniel, *The Shadow of Slavery: Peonage in the South, 1901–1969* (Urbana: University of Illinois Press, 1972); Daniel A. Novak, *The Wheel of Servitude: Black Forced Labor after Slavery* (Lexington: University Press of Kentucky, 1978); William Cohen, *At Freedom's Edge: Black Mobility and the Southern White Quest for Racial Control, 1861–1915* (Baton Rouge: Louisiana State University Press, 1991); Douglas Blackmon, *Slavery by Another Name: The Re-enslavement of African Americans from the Civil War to World War II* (New York: Random House, 2008).
41. Robert Higgs, *Competition and Coercion: Blacks in the American Economy, 1865–1914* (New York: Cambridge University Press, 1977), 38–59, 77–80.
42. Russell, *Report on Peonage*, 31.
43. Blackmon, *Slavery by Another Name*, 7.
44. Blackmon, *Slavery by Another Name*.
45. Matthew J. Mancini, *"One Dies, Get Another": Convict Leasing in the American South, 1866–1928* (Columbia: University of South Carolina Press, 1996).
46. William S. Kiser, *Borderlands of Slavery: The Struggle over Captivity and Peonage in the American Southwest* (Philadelphia: University of Pennsylvania Press, 2017), 100.
47. Slaughter-House Cases, 83 U.S. (16 Wall.) 36, 90, 72 (1872).
48. Peonage Act of 1867, ch. 187, 14 Stat. 546.
49. 18 U.S.C. sec. 1581.
50. 197 U.S. 207 (1905).
51. Daniel, *Shadow of Slavery*, 9.
52. Quoted in Schmidt, "Peonage Cases," 660.
53. 197 U.S. 218.
54. 197 U.S. 215.
55. Schmidt, "Peonage Cases," 663–674.
56. 219 U.S. 219 (1911).
57. Bailey v. Alabama, 211 U.S. 452 (1908).
58. 219 U.S. 219 (1911).
59. 219 U.S. 241.
60. 219 U.S. 244, 245.
61. 219 U.S. 231. Holmes in dissent agreed: "We all agree that this case is to be considered and decided in the same way as if it arose in Idaho or New York. The fact that in Alabama it mainly concerns the blacks does not matter." 219 U.S. 245–246.
62. Risa L. Goluboff, "The Thirteenth Amendment and the Lost Origins of Civil Rights," 50 *Duke Law Journal* 1609, 1650 (2001).

464   NOTES TO PAGES 134–42

63. Holmes, with Lurton joining him, dissented in an opinion that was an exercise in pure logic, abstracted from any sociological reality of the case. The seats of the recently deceased Fuller and Brewer remained vacant.
64. 235 U.S. 133, 146 (1914).
65. 235 U.S. 150.
66. Michael J. Klarman, *From Jim Crow to Civil Rights: The Supreme Court and the Struggle for Racial Equality* (New York: Oxford University Press, 2004), 73–76, 86–88.
67. John M. Barry, *Rising Tide: The Great Mississippi Flood of 1927 and How It Changed America* (New York: Simon & Schuster, 1997).
68. 315 U.S. 25 (1942).
69. 322 U.S. 4, 11 (1944); James Gray Pope, "Contract, Race, and Freedom of Labor in the Constitutional Law of 'Involuntary Servitude,'" 119 *Yale Law Journal* 1474 (2010).
70. Schmidt, "Peonage Cases," 718.
71. 235 U.S. 151, 161–162 (1914). See Schmidt, "Heyday of Jim Crow," 485–499.
72. Catherine Barnes, *Journey from Jim Crow: The Desegregation of Southern Transit* (New York: Columbia University Press, 1983), 10, 13.
73. A fundamental principle of equity jurisprudence holds that petitioner must show that he lacks an adequate remedy at law, i.e., monetary damages.
74. 235 U.S. 161–162.
75. Rev. 6:1–8.
76. Quoted in Schmidt, "Heyday of Jim Crow," 489.
77. 305 U.S. 337, 344 (1938).
78. Anonymous, "Statutory Discrimination against Negroes with Reference to Pullman Cars," 28 *Harvard Law Review* 417 (1915); *The Nation*, December 3, 1914, 99.
79. See generally Benno C. Schmidt, "Principle and Prejudice: The Supreme Court and Race in the Progressive Era: Part 3: Black Disfranchisement from the KKK to the Grandfather Clause," 88 *Columbia Law Review* 835 (1982) (hereafter cited as Schmidt, "Black Disfranchisement"), the third article of Schmidt's trilogy incorporated into Bickel and Schmidt, *The Judiciary and Responsible Government*.
80. Alexander Keyssar, *The Right to Vote: The Contested History of Democracy in the United States*, rev. ed. (New York: Basic Books, 2009); Michael Perman, *The Struggle for Mastery: Disfranchisement in the South, 1888–1908* (Chapel Hill: University of North Carolina Press, 2001); Richard M. Valelly, *Two Reconstructions: The Struggle for Black Enfranchisement* (Chicago: University of Chicago Press, 2004).
81. E.g., the percentage reduction in estimated African American voter turnout between the 1880s and ca. 1900–1904 varied from 96 percent (Alabama) to 69 percent (Mississippi) to 68 percent (Tennessee); see table 9.2 in J. Morgan Kousser, *The Shaping of Southern Politics: Suffrage Restriction and the Establishment of the One-Party South, 1880–1910* (New Haven: Yale University Press, 1974), 241.
82. The veterans' provisions seemed to overlook the fact that 180,000 African Americans had served in "the sable arm" of Union forces during the war. Many of these Black veterans resided in southern states. Dudley T. Cornish, *The Sable Arm: Black Troops in the Union Army, 1861–1865* (Lawrence: University Press of Kansas, 1987). Presumably, though, the intended beneficiaries of the grandfather clauses were exclusively Confederate veterans.
83. David Zucchino, *Wilmington's Lie: The Murderous Coup of 1898 and the Rise of White Supremacy* (New York: Grove, 2020).
84. 92 U.S. 214 (1876).
85. 92 U.S. 542 (1876).
86. Posse Comitatus Act, ch. 264, 20 Stat. 152.
87. "Repeal of Federal Election Laws," House Report (1893), quoted in Schmidt, "Black Disfranchisement," 841.
88. Quoted in Klarman, *From Jim Crow to Civil Rights*, 33.
89. Giles v. Harris (1903) and Giles v. Teasley (1904).
90. 238 U.S. 347 (1915).
91. 238 U.S. 363. Judged by criteria of clarity and simplicity, White's is by far the murkiest prose in the United States Reports.
92. In a companion case, *Myers v. Anderson*, 238 U.S. 368 (1915), White again for a unanimous Court struck down a Maryland property qualification on the same grounds.
93. 238 U.S. 383, 386 (1915).

94. 307 U.S. 268, 275 (1939).
95. Klarman, *From Jim Crow to Civil Rights*, 97.
96. Storey to Oswald G. Villard (1917), quoted in Schmidt, "Heyday of Jim Crow," 521. Storey, who was white, was the first president of the NAACP.
97. Garrett Power, "Apartheid Baltimore Style: The Residential Segregation Ordinances of 1910–1913," 42 *Maryland Law Review* 289 (1982); Roger L. Rice, "Residential Segregation by Law, 1910–1917," 34 *Journal of Southern History* 179 (1968).
98. Richard Rothstein, *The Color of Law: A Forgotten History of How Our Government Segregated America* (New York: Norton, 2017), ch. 2, "Racial Zoning," reviews the history of how municipalities experimented with zoning and other forms of land use control (including siting of toxic waste sites) to impose segregation.
99. On the Louisville ordinance and the formation of the local chapter of the NAACP there, see George C. Wright, "The NAACP and Residential Segregation in Louisville, Kentucky, 1914–1917," *Register of the Kentucky Historical Society* 78 (1980), 39.
100. A long line of precedent going back to 1850 holds that federal courts lack jurisdiction of collusive litigation because of Article III's cases-or-controversies requirement: Lord v. Veazie, 49 U.S. (8 How.) 251 (1850). The parties here made no effort to conceal the feigned nature of the suit. That the Supreme Court would wink at this egregious move suggests that the justices were reaching out to decide an issue that for whatever reason had such a powerful appeal for them that they were willing to condone such in-your-face evasion of a wise principle of judicial self-restraint.
101. It upheld this exercise of the police power even if that diminished property rights, claiming that "the jus disponendi [the power to dispose of property] has but little place in modern jurisprudence"! Harris v. City of Louisville, 165 Ky. 559, 177 S.W. 472, 476 (1915). That claim about *jus disponendi* was nonsense: the power to alienate was and remains one of the fundamental attributes of ownership identified in the law of property.
102. 177 S.W. at 478.
103. 245 U.S. 60 (1917).
104. Thoughtful evaluations of the case include Schmidt, "Heyday of Jim Crow," 498–523; Patricia H. Minter, "Race, Property, and Negotiated Space in the American South: A Reconsideration of Buchanan v. Warley," in Sally E. Hadden and Patricia H. Minter, eds., *Signposts: New Directions in Southern Legal History* (Athens: University of Georgia Press, 2013), 345–368; Klarman, *From Jim Crow to Civil* Rights, 79–85; David Bernstein, "Philip Sober Controlling Philip Drunk: Buchanan v. Warley in Historical Perspective," 51 *Vanderbilt Law Review* 798, 839–872 (1998); David Delaney, *Race, Place, and the Law, 1836–1948* (Austin: University of Texas Press, 1998), 98–147.
105. 245 U.S. 74, 81.
106. 245 U.S. 78, 82.
107. For a different evaluation of Buchanan reflecting an "alternative civil rights vision to the progressive vision," but which also emphasizes the importance of property rights for Black equality, see David E. Bernstein, "Reflections on the 100th Anniversary of Buchanan v. Warley: Recent Revisionist History," 48 *Cumberland Law Review* 101 (2018).
108. See, e.g., Justice Brandeis dissenting in Pennsylvania Coal Co. v. Mahon, 260 U.S. 393 (1922).
109. Note, "Constitutional Law—Due Process—Segregation Ordinance," 15 *Columbia Law Review* 545 (1915) (contending that segregation ordinances were a variety of the regulation of nuisances); Rachel D. Godsil, "Race Nuisance: The Politics of Law in the Jim Crow Era," 105 *Michigan Law Review* 505 (2016).
110. Hadacheck v. Sebastian, 239 U.S. 394 (1915).
111. Euclid v. Ambler Realty Co., 272 U.S. 365 (1926).
112. 245 U.S. 77, 79.
113. The sole exception was *Giles v. Teasley*.
114. Christopher W. Schmidt, "Buchanan v. Warley and the Changing Meaning of Civil Rights," 48 *Cumberland Law Review* 463 (2018).
115. Schmidt, "Heyday of Jim Crow," 524.
116. Harmon v. Tyler, 273 U.S. 668 (1927) (New Orleans segregation ordinance) and Richmond v. Deans, 281 U.S. 704 (1930) (Richmond, Va. ordinance). When the Court renders an opinion per curiam, it summarily disposes of the appeal by handing down a judgment resolving the dispute, cutting off further argument. The court acts as a body (Latin *per curiam*: "by the court"). The unsigned opinion is not attributable to any single justice, though individual

justices may concur or dissent by name and in separate opinions. The decision is usually based on a determination that the outcome is so obvious and compelling that further argument would be a pointless waste of time. However, occasionally major constitutional landmarks are decided per curiam, in relatively brief opinions that nevertheless make important constitutional statements: e.g., Brandenburg v. Ohio, 395 U.S. 444 (1969) (defining the principles controlling the power of states to regulate political speech).

Chapter 5

1. "Taft Court": 1921–1930; "Hughes Court": 1930–1941. On the Court in this period, see Jonathan Lurie, *The Chief Justiceship of William Howard Taft, 1921–1930* (Columbia: University of South Carolina Press, 2019); Mark V. Tushnet, *The Hughes Court: From Progressivism to Pluralism, 1930–1941* (vol. 11 of the Holmes Devise History of the Supreme Court of the United States) (New York: Cambridge University Press, 2021), 610–678, on cases affecting African Americans; William G. Ross, *The Chief Justiceship of Charles Evans Hughes, 1930–1941* (Columbia: University of South Carolina Press, 2007).
2. 21 U.S. (8 Wheat.) 543, 590 (1823) ("the tribes of Indians inhabiting this country were fierce savages...as brave and as high spirited as they were fierce, and were ready to repel by arms every attempt on their independence").
3. Justin Desautels-Stein, "Race as a Legal Concept," 2 *Columbia Journal of Race & Law* 1 (2012).
4. Ian Haney-Lopez, *White by Law: The Legal Construction of Race*, rev. ed. (New York: New York University Press, 2006), 14, 10; on the legal construction of race, see pp. 7–14, 78–108.
5. In re Halladjian, 174 F. 834 (C.C.D. Mass. 1909).
6. Keith Aoki, "No Right to Own: The Early Twentieth-Century Alien Land Laws as a Prelude to Internment." 19 *Boston College Third World Law Journal* 37 (1998).
7. On such access to property as constitutive of race, see Bethany R. Berger, "Property to Race/Race to Property" (2021) at Social Science Research Network, Downloads/SSRN-id3825124.pdf, 27–29.
8. Noel Ignatiev, *How the Irish Became White* (New York: Routledge, 1995); Theodore W. Allen, *The Invention of the White Race*, 2 vols. (London: Verso, 1994, 1997).
9. Matthew Frye Jacobson, *Whiteness of a Different Color: European Immigrants and the Alchemy of Race* (Cambridge: Harvard University Press, 1998).
10. Michael Omi and Howard Winant, *Racial Formation in the United States*, 3rd ed. (New York: Routledge, 2015).
11. See the critique of the binary in Juan F. Perea, "The Black-White Binary Paradigm of Race: The 'Normal Science' of American Legal Thought,'" 85 *California Law Review* 1213 (1997).
12. For overviews and critique, see Dorothy Roberts, *Fatal Invention: How Science, Politics, and Big Business Recreate Race in the Twenty-First Century* (New York: New Press, 2011); Stephen J. Gould, *The Mismeasure of Man* (New York: Norton, 1981); Audrey Smedley, *Race in North America: The Origin and Evolution of a World View*, 4th ed. (New York: Perseus, 2011); Thomas F. Gossett, *Race: The History of an Idea in America*, new ed. (New York: Oxford University Press, 1997); George M. Fredrickson, *Racism: A Short History* (Princeton: Princeton University Press, 2002); and Fredrickson, *The Black Image in the White Mind: The Debate on Afro-American Character and Destiny, 1817–1914* (New York: Harper & Row, 1971). A prevalent diktat of scientific racism in the 1920s proclaimed that Europeans were divided into three races, Nordic, Alpine, and Mediterranean: Madison Grant, *The Passing of the Great Race; or, The Racial Basis of European History* (New York: Scribner, 1916); William Z. Ripley, *The Races of Europe: A Sociological Study* (New York: D. Appleton, 1899).
13. On scientific racism in the nineteenth century, see William R. Stanton, *The Leopard's Spots: Scientific Attitudes toward Race in America, 1815–1859* (Chicago: University of Chicago Press, 1960), and John S. Haller, *Outcasts from Evolution: Scientific Attitudes of Racial Inferiority, 1859–1900* (Carbondale: Southern Illinois University Press, 1971).
14. Naturalization Act of 1790, ch. 3, 1 Stat. 103.
15. Naturalization Act of 1870, ch. 254, sec. 7, 16 Stat. 254.
16. Ch. 126, 22 Stat. 58.
17. Chae Chan Ping v. United States, 130 U.S. 581 (1889).
18. Act of Feb. 5, 1917, ch. 29, 39 Stat. 874.

19. Ch. 190, 43 Stat. 153. The exclusion was achieved by denying visas to any "alien ineligible to citizenship."
20. Buck v. Bell, 274 U.S. 200 (1926). On the impact of eugenics, see Daniel J. Kevles, *In the Name of Eugenics: Genetics and the Uses of Human Heredity* (New York: Knopf, 1985), on the Buck case specifically, 110–111; Daniel Okrent, *The Guarded Gate: Bigotry, Eugenics, and the Law That Kept Jews, Italians, and Other European Immigrants Out of America* (New York: Scribner, 2019).
21. David W. Southern, *The Progressive Era and Race: Reaction and Reform, 1900–1917* (Wheeling: Harlan Davidson, 2005); Herbert Hovenkamp, "The Progressives: Racism and Public Law," 59 *Arizona Law Review* 947 (2017).
22. John Calmore, "Critical Race Theory, Archie Shepp, and Fire Music: Securing an Authentic Intellectual Life in a Multicultural World," 65 *Southern California Law Review* 2129, 2160 (1992).
23. Ian Haney-Lopez refers to fifty-some state and federal precedents as "racial prerequisite cases" preceding *Thind* that provided the matrix within which judges addressed questions of status based on race: *White by Law*, 2 and *passim*. He lists and categorizes those cases on pp. 162–167.
24. In re Ah Yup, 1 Fed. Cas. 223 (C.C.D. Cal. 1878) (No. 104).
25. In re Najour, 174 F. 735 (N.D. Ga. 1909); Haney-Lopez, *White by Law*, 47–55.
26. Nell Irvin Painter, "Collective Degradation: Slavery and the Construction of Race," unpublished paper 2003, https://glc.yale.edu/sites/default/files/files/events/race/Painter.pdf.
27. 260 U.S. 178 (1922). On the Ozawa case, see Devon W. Carbado, "Yellow by Law," 97 *California Law Review* 633 (2009); Mark S. Weiner, *Americans without Law: The Racial Boundaries of Citizenship* (New York: New York University Press, 2006), 97–105; and Doug Coulson, *Race, Nation, and Refuge: The Rhetoric of Race in Asian American Citizenship* (Albany: State University of New York Press, 2017), 1–44 (Ozawa), 45–88 (Thind), 89–114 (Armenians).
28. 260 U.S. 196–197.
29. *Black's Law Dictionary*, 11th ed. (St. Paul: Thomson, 2019): "ipse dixit" [Latin "he himself said it"]: Something asserted but not proved."
30. 260 U.S. 197.
31. John Henry Wigmore, "American Naturalization and the Japanese," 28 *American Law Review* 818 (1894).
32. Gossett, *Race*, 36–37.
33. 260 U.S. 198.
34. See generally Roger Daniels, *The Politics of Prejudice: The Anti-Japanese Movement in California and the Struggle for Japanese Exclusion* (Berkeley: University of California Press, 1962); Rose Cuison Villazor, "Rediscovering Oyama v. California: At the Intersection of Property, Race, and Citizenship," 87 *Washington University Law Review* 979 (2010).
35. United States v. Thind, 261 U.S. 204 (1923). On this case and its repudiation of Ozawa, see Haney-Lopez, *White by Law*, 61–76; Doug Coulson, "British Imperialism, the Indian Independence Movement, and the Racial Eligibility Provisions of the Naturalization Act: U.S. v. Thind Revisited," 7 *Georgetown Journal of Law & Modern Critical Race Perspectives* 1 (2015).
36. 261 U.S. 209–210.
37. In contemporary usage, "Hindu" referred to racial characteristics, not religion. Only a minority of immigrants from the Indian subcontinent were religiously Hindu, the majority being Sikhs. Sutherland and his contemporaries considered these religious distinctions irrelevant.
38. 261 U.S. 215.
39. 261 U.S. 215.
40. Morrison v. California, 291 U.S. 82, 94 (1934).
41. 275 U.S. 78 (1927). On the social and cultural background of the case, see James W. Loewen, *The Mississippi Chinese: Between Black and White* (Cambridge: Harvard University Press, 1988), 58–72; on Gong Lum, 66–68.
42. Rice v. Gong Lum, 139 Miss. 760, 104 So. 105, 108 (1925).
43. 5 Cush. (59 Mass.) 198 (1849).
44. Charles King, *Gods of the Upper Air: How a Circle of Renegade Anthropologists Reinvented Race, Sex, and Gender in the Twentieth Century* (New York: Doubleday, 2019).
45. Elazar Barkan, *The Retreat of Scientific Racism: Changing Concepts of Race in Britain and the United States Between the World Wars* (Cambridge: Cambridge University Press, 1992), 76–134.

46. 42 U.S.C. secs. 1981, 1982.
47. The opposing parties argued that both Jews and Arabs are "Caucasians" and hence cannot complain of discrimination visited upon them by fellow Caucasians.
48. Saint Francis College v. Al-Khazraji, 481 U.S. 604, 610 (1987) (respondent was an Arab). Its companion case was Shaare Tefila Congregation v. Cobb, 481 U.S. 615 (1987) (petitioners were Jews).
49. Angela Saini, *Superior: The Return of Race Science* (New York: HarperCollins, 2019).
50. Tushnet, *Hughes Court*, 610–647, reviews these cases.
51. Michael J. Klarman reviews this social context in *From Jim Crow to Civil Rights: The Supreme Court and the Struggle for Racial Equality* (New York: Oxford University Press, 2004), 100–116.
52. Neil R. McMillen, *Dark Journey: Black Mississippians in the Age of Jim Crow* (Urbana: University of Illinois Press, 1989), ch. 6, "Jim Crow's Courts." This description of Mississippi courts applies generally to the court systems of all the Deep South states.
53. Melanie S. Morrison provides a detailed study of one such trial: *Murder on Shades Mountain: The Legal Lynching of Willie Peterson and the Struggle for Justice in Jim Crow Birmingham* (Durham: Duke University Press, 2019).
54. Quoted in McMillen, *Dark Journey*, 195.
55. Finch was the protagonist in Harper Lee's *To Kill a Mockingbird* (1960, film adaptation 1962).
56. Quoted in McMillen, *Dark Journey*, 202.
57. On incorporation, see generally Richard C. Cortner, *The Supreme Court and the Second Bill of Rights: The Fourteenth Amendment and the Nationalization of Civil Liberties* (Madison: University of Wisconsin Press, 1981).
58. Missouri Pacific Ry. v. Neb., 164 U.S. 403 (1896) ("public use" under the takings clause); Chicago, B. &. Q. Ry. v. Chicago, 166 U.S. 226 (1897) ("just compensation" under the takings clause), followed by Gitlow v. New York, 268 U.S. 652 (1925) (incorporating the First Amendment freedom of speech and press).
59. McNabb v. United States, 318 U.S. 332, 347 (1943).
60. Chicago, Milwaukee & St. Paul Railway v. Minnesota, 134 U.S. 418 (1890), culminating in Lochner v. New York, 198 U.S. 45 (1905) and Adkins v. Childrens Hospital, 261 U.S. 525 (1923).
61. 232 U.S. 383 (1914).
62. 211 U.S. 78 (1908).
63. Daniel J. Flanigan, "Criminal Procedure in Slave Trials in the Antebellum South," 40 *Journal of Southern History* 537 (1974); A. E. Keir Nash, "Fairness and Formalism in the Trials of Blacks in the State Supreme Courts of the Antebellum South," 56 *Virginia Law Review* 64 (1970).
64. McMillen *Dark Journey*, 197–223.
65. Linda Gordon, *The Second Coming of the KKK: The Ku Klux Klan of the 1920s and the American Political Tradition* (New York: Liveright, 2018); Kenneth T. Jackson, *The Ku Klux Klan in the City, 1915–1930*, rev. ed. (Chicago: I. R. Dee, 1992).
66. National Commission on Law Observance and Enforcement, *Lawlessness in Law Enforcement* (Report No. 11 of the Wickersham Commission reports), p. 153 (1931). The commission was appointed to investigate law enforcement activities in the Prohibition era.
67. 110 U.S. 516, 535 (1884).
68. 211 U.S. 78, 99 (1908).
69. Cameron McWhirter, *Red Summer: The Summer of 1919 and the Awakening of Black America* (New York: Henry Holt, 2012); Robert Whitaker, *On the Laps of Gods: The Red Summer of 1919 and the Struggle for Justice That Remade a Nation* (New York: Three Rivers, 2008); David Krugler, *1919: The Year of Racial Violence: How African Americans Fought Back* (New York: Cambridge University Press, 2014).
70. What is commonly known as the Elaine Race Riot has been extensively studied: Whitaker, *On the Laps of Gods*; Richard Cortner, *A Mob Intent on Death: The NAACP and the Arkansas Riot Cases* (Middletown: Wesleyan University Press, 1988); Grif Stockley, *Blood in Their Eyes: The Elaine Race Massacres of 1919* (Fayetteville: University of Arkansas Press, 2001).
71. Whitaker, *On the Laps of Gods*, 131.
72. 261 U.S. 86, 88–89, 91 (1923); Megan Ming Francis, *Civil Rights and the Making of the Modern American State* (Cambridge: Cambridge University Press, 2014), 127–163.
73. For a detailed review of all legal proceedings in the *Moore* case, see Eric M. Freedman, "Milestones in Habeas Corpus Part II: Leo Frank Lives. Untangling the Historical Roots of Meaningful Federal Habeas Corpus Review of State Convictions," 51 *Alabama Law Review* 1467, 1497–1535 (2000).

74. *Hicks v. State*, 143 Ark. 158, 220 S.W. 308 (1920).
75. 237 U.S. 309, 326, 346, 348 (1915).
76. Leo Frank was Jewish, and thus the object of religious rather than racial prejudice, but the animosity of the lynch mob was no less fierce. After his sentence had been commuted because of improprieties at trial, a mob lynched him anyway. Leonard Dinnerstein, *The Leo Frank Case* (New York: Columbia University Press, 1968).
77. Justice McReynolds, joined by Justice Sutherland, dissented, insisting that the Supreme Court should not interfere with the "solemn adjudications by courts of a great state" that appeared on the surface to be formally adequate. 261 U.S. 102.
78. Klarman, *From Jim Crow to Civil Rights*, 117.
79. The story of the Scottsboro Boys is told in Dan T. Carter, *Scottsboro: A Tragedy of the American South*, rev. ed. (Chapel Hill: University of North Carolina Press, 1979); James E. Goodman, *Stories of Scottsboro* (New York: Pantheon, 1994); and James R. Acker, *Scottsboro and Its Legacy: The Cases That Challenged American Legal and Social Justice* (Westport: Greenwood, 2008).
80. Quoted in Carter, *Scottsboro*, 18.
81. Glenda E. Gilmore, *Defying Dixie: The Radical Roots of Civil Rights, 1919–1950* (New York: Norton, 2009), 118–137; James A. Miller, Susan Pennypacker, and Eve Rosenhaft, "Mother Ada Wright and the International Campaign to Free the Scottsboro Boys," 106 *American Historical Review* 387–430 (2001), situates ILD's involvement in an international context.
82. Weems v. State, 224 Ala. 524, 141 So. 215 (1932); Patterson v. State, 224 Ala. 531, 141 So. 195 (1932); Powell v. State, 224 Ala. 540, 141 So. 201 (1932).
83. 287 U.S. 45, 52 (1932).
84. The Court did not begin the process of incorporating the Sixth Amendment until Johnson v. Zerbst, 304 U.S. 458 (1938), holding that the amendment guaranteed the right of representation in federal courts, and then, in Gideon v. Wainwright, 372 U.S. 335 (1963), that the right extended to state court trials as well.
85. Those cases included Hurtado v. California, 110 U.S. 516 (1884); Ex parte Spies (popularly known at the time as "The Anarchists' Case," by which name it appears in the United States Reports), 123 U.S. 131 (1887); Brown v. New Jersey, 175 U.S. 172 (1899); Maxwell v. Dow, 176 U.S. 581 (1900).
86. Justices Butler and McReynolds dissented, insisting that the trials had been fair and counsel adequate to the task. Butler complained that this marked "an extension of the Federal authority into a field hitherto occupied exclusively by the several states," correctly sensing the long-term significance of the Court's holding.
87. 110 U.S. 516, 535 (1884) (holding that the right to be indicted by a grand jury, rather than by information, was not such a right).
88. 287 U.S. 71.
89. *New York Times*, November 13, 1932, III, E1.
90. 372 U.S. 335 (1963).
91. Michael J. Klarman, "The Racial Origins of Modern Criminal Procedure," 99 *Michigan Law Review* 48 (2000).
92. Douglas O. Linder, "Without Fear or Favor: Judge James Edwin Horton and the Trial of the 'Scottsboro Boys,'" 68 *University of Missouri Kansas City Law Review* 549 (2000).
93. The person bringing a complaint of rape is referred to as the prosecutrix (Latin feminine plural: prosecutrices).
94. Norris v. State, 229 Ala. 226, 156 So. 556 (1934).
95. 294 U.S. 587 (1935).
96. Neal v. Delaware, 103 U.S. 370 (1880).
97. In a companion case, *Patterson v Alabama*, 294 U.S. 600 (1935), the Court reversed the conviction of another of the defendants on the grounds that the procedural basis of the Alabama Supreme Court's rule would have had the anomalous result that one of the defendants would have been executed despite the same flaws for which his fellow defendants had had their convictions reversed.
98. 311 U.S. 128 (1940).
99. 297 U.S. 278 (1936). See Richard C. Cortner, *A "Scottsboro" Case in Mississippi: The Supreme Court and Brown v. Mississippi* (Jackson: University Press of Mississippi, 1986); McMillen, *Dark Journey*, 197–206.

100. Quoted in the dissenting opinion of Judge Virgil Griffith of the Mississippi Supreme Court in Brown v. State, 173 Miss. 542, 161 So. 465, 471 (1935).
101. Brown v. State, 173 Miss. 542, 161 So. 465, 469 (1935).
102. 309 U.S. 227 (1940).
103. Chambers v. State, 123 Fla. 734, 741, 167 So. 697 (1936).
104. 309 U.S. 237–238 (citing the Wickersham Commission report).
105. 309 U.S. 241. For the rest of his life, Black cherished this passage, regarding it as an epitome of his judicial values. Professor Floyd Feeney, who clerked for Black in the 1961–1962 Term, personal communication to author, February 19, 2015.
106. Klarman, *From Jim Crow to Civil Rights*, 282–283. See also Klarman, "Is the Supreme Court Irrelevant? Race and the Southern Criminal Justice System in the 1940s," 89 *Journal of American History* 119 (2003).
107. J. Morgan Kousser, *The Shaping of Southern Politics: Suffrage Restriction and the One-Party South, 1880–1910* (New Haven: Yale University Press, 1974); Michael Perman, *Struggle for Mastery: Disfranchisement in the South, 1888–1908* (Chapel Hill: University of North Carolina Press, 2001); Richard Vallely, *The Two Reconstructions: The Struggle for Black Enfranchisement* (Chicago: University of Chicago Press, 2004), 23–148; Alexander Keyssar, *The Right to Vote: The Contested History of Democracy in the United States* (New York: Basic Books, 2009), 105–116. Disfranchisement of Blacks often had the effect of disfranchising a number of whites as well: Glenn Feldman, *The Disfranchisement Myth: Poor Whites and Suffrage Restriction in Alabama* (Athens: University of Georgia Press, 2004). Disfranchisement also meant automatic exclusion from eligibility for jury service.
108. 107 U.S. 213 (1898) and 189 U.S. 475 (1903) respectively.
109. David A. Bateman, Ira Katznelson, and John S. Lapinski, *Southern Nation: Congress and White Supremacy after Reconstruction* (Princeton: Princeton University Press, 2020).
110. 273 U.S. 536, 541 (1927). On these cases, see Darlene Clark Hine, *Black Victory: The Rise and Fall of the White Primary in Texas* (Columbia: University of Missouri Press, 1979), 51–209; Tushnet, *Hughes Court*, 648–666.
111. Ward E. Y. Elliott criticized the Court's reliance on the Fourteenth Amendment as the basis of voting rights decisions in *The Rise of Guardian Democracy: The Supreme Court's Role in Voting Rights Disputes, 1845–1969* (Cambridge: Harvard University Press, 1974), 55–88.
112. Brad Snyder, *The House of Truth: A Washington Political Salon and the Foundations of American Liberalism* (New York: Oxford University Press, 2017), 453–454.
113. Newberry v. United States, 256 U.S. 232 (1921), implicitly overruled by United States v. Classic (1941).
114. 286 U.S. 73, 89 (1932). The Four Horsemen, speaking through McReynolds, dissented, maintaining that the power of a political party to exclude members (and therefore voters) based on race or sex "is essential to free government." 286 U.S. at 104.
115. 295 U.S. 45 (1935).
116. Smith v. Allwright, striking down the white primary, was decided in 1944. It will be discussed in the next chapter.
117. 302 U.S. 277 (1937).
118. Harper v. Virginia State Board of Elections, 383 U.S. 663 (1966).
119. 238 U.S. 347 (1915).
120. 307 U.S. 268, 274 (1939). McReynolds and Butler dissented.
121. Even so, Frankfurter could not escape the racist preconceptions of his class and time: "It must be remembered that we are dealing with a body of citizens lacking the habits and traditions of political independence and otherwise living in circumstances which do not encourage initiative and enterprise." 307 U.S. at 276.
122. "This case is very different from Giles v. Harris,—the difference having been explicitly foreshadowed by Giles v. Harris itself. In that case this Court declared 'we are not prepared to say that an action at law could not be maintained on the facts alleged in the bill.' That is precisely the basis of the present action, brought under the following 'appropriate legislation' of Congress to enforce the Fifteenth Amendment." 307 U.S. 273.
123. 313 U.S. 299, 317 (1941).
124. Douglas, joined by Black and Murphy, dissented on a question of statutory construction.
125. "The Times, Places and Manner of holding Elections for Senators and Representatives, shall be prescribed in each State by the Legislature thereof; but the Congress may at any time by Law make or alter such Regulations, except as to the Places of chusing Senators."

126. And in doing so, overruled *Newberry v. United States*, though not explicitly. Later courts recognized the overruling: McConnell v. Federal Election Commission, 251 F.Supp.2d 176, 191 (D.D.C. 2003); Buckley v. Valeo, 519 F.2d 821 (D.C. Cir. 1975).
127. Stone was here referring to Art. I, sec. 2: "The House of Representatives shall be composed of Members chosen every second Year by the People of the several States."
128. Mason, *Harlan Fiske Stone*, 617.
129. Charles H. Martin, *The Angelo Herndon Case and Southern Justice* (Baton Rouge: Louisiana State University Press, 1976).
130. Act of Dec. 22, 1829, "An Act to…prevent the circulation of written or printed papers within this State calculated to excite disaffection among the colored people of this State," in *Digest of the Laws of the State of Georgia* (1837), 804. It was enacted in response to David Walker's incendiary *Appeal to the Coloured Citizens of the World* (1829).
131. Acts of 1866, in *The Code of the State of Georgia* (1867), sec. 4252, p. 852.
132. Quoted in Martin, *Angelo Herndon Case*, 57–58.
133. 268 U.S. 652 (1925). Gitlow affirmed the conviction of a Communist for violation of a criminal anarchy statute. It is notable for incorporating the First Amendment as a limitation on the states.
134. Zechariah Chafee Jr., *Free Speech in the United States* (Cambridge: Harvard University Press, 1941), 392.
135. Seymour was a prominent New York City attorney with Simpson Thatcher & Bartlett, and later president of the American Bar Association. Gellhorn and Wechsler were legal academics, both at Columbia Law School. Tuttle was an Atlanta attorney and later chief judge of the United States Court of Appeals for the Fifth Circuit. All were eminent civil libertarians.
136. The Supreme Court dismissed Herndon's first appeal because it did not seasonably raise the issue of the constitutionality of the insurrection statute. Herndon v. Georgia, 295 U.S. 441 (1935). Cardozo, Brandeis, and Stone dissented.
137. 301 U.S. 242 (1937). The Four Horsemen (Van Devanter, Sutherland, Butler, and McReynolds) dissented.
138. Kendall Thomas, "Rouge et Noir Reread: A Popular Constitutional History of the Angelo Herndon Case," 65 *Southern California Law Review* 2599 (1992).
139. Fiske v. Kansas, 274 U.S. 380 (1927) (reversing a criminal syndicalism prosecution on tightened clear-and-present-danger standards); Stromberg v. California, 283 U.S. 359 (1931) (striking down a statute forbidding display of a red flag on overbreadth grounds); Near v. Minnesota, 283 U.S. 697 (1931) (holding a statute that shut down "malicious, scandalous, and defamatory newspapers" void as a prior restraint). All were based on the Fourteenth, not the First, Amendment.
140. The First Amendment provides, after the religion clauses: "Congress shall make no law…abridging the freedom of speech, or of the press, or the right of the people peaceably to assemble, and to petition the government for a redress of grievances."
141. 303 U.S. 552 (1938).
142. 299 U.S. 353, 365 (1937). For a comparison on other grounds, see Mark Tushnet, "The Hughes Court and Radical Political Dissent: The Case of Dirk De Jonge and Angelo Herndon," 28 *Georgia State University Law Review* 333 (2011), incorporated into Tushnet, *Hughes Court*, 702–716.
143. Justice Stone did not participate in argument, so De Jonge was an eight-to-zero decision.
144. See his mug shots at https://www.google.com/search?q=de+jonge+v.+oregon&tbm=isch&so urce=iu&ictx=1&fir=wdZVYBmueTn1IM%253A%252CQa1sIYX4z2tmHM%252C_&vet=1 &usg=AI4_-kSoZj9RUc4UbUiR_vKm-gF0MfB_cA&sa=X&ved=2ahUKEwjUzam7pJzmAhX RmuAKHYr-BewQ_h0wDHoECAwQBQ#imgrc=wdZVYBmueTn1IM.
145. Mark V. Tushnet, *The NAACP's Strategy Against Segregated Education, 1925–1950* (Chapel Hill: University of North Carolina Press, 1987), 30–77.
146. Historically Black college or university.
147. Murray v. Pearson, 169 Md. 478, 182 A. 590 (1936).
148. Richard Kluger, *Simple Justice: The History of Brown v. Board of Education and Black America's Struggle for Equality* (New York: Knopf, 2011), 186–193.
149. 305 U.S. 337, 354, 344, 350 (1938).
150. James W. Endersby and William T. Horner provide a detailed study of the case in *Lloyd Gaines and the Fight to End Segregation* (Columbia: University of Missouri Press, 2016); Tushnet, *Hughes Court*, 666–670.

151. McReynolds and Butler dissented, in an opinion sneering at the majority's insistence on equality as "theorization inadequately restrained by experience."
152. Kevin M. Kruse, "Personal Rights, Public Wrongs: The Gaines Case and the Beginning of the End of Segregation," 22 *Journal of Supreme Court History* 113 (1997).
153. This approach to law, also referred to as legal classicism, is described and critiqued in Duncan Kennedy, *The Rise & Fall of Classical Legal Thought* (Washington, DC: Beard Books, 2006), the published version of a manuscript that had been privately circulated since 1975), and in William M. Wiecek, *The Lost World of Classical Legal Thought: Law and Ideology in America, 1886–1937* (New York: Oxford University Press, 1998).
154. 304 U.S. 144 (1938).
155. The secondary literature on *Carolene Products* is vast and, lately, contentious. It is discussed in William M. Wiecek, *The Birth of the Modern Constitution: The United States Supreme Court, 1941–1953* (New York: Cambridge University Press, 2006) (vol. 12 of the *Holmes Devise History of the Supreme Court of the United States*), ch. 3, "Carolene Products (1938): Prism of the Stone Court," and in David A. Strauss, "Is Carolene Products Obsolete?," 2010 *University of Illinois Law Review* 1251 (2010).
156. Lewis Powell, "Carolene Products Revisited," 82 *Columbia Law Review* 1087 (1982).
157. Substantive due process is a vast and contested topic. For a brief, lucid, and balanced introduction, see Melvin I. Urofsky and Paul Finkelman, *A March of Liberty: A Constitutional History of the United States*, 3rd ed. (New York: Oxford University Press, 2011), 569–590, 615–642, 697–716.
158. Milnot (the product's commercial name) consisted of milk from which all butterfat had been removed and replaced by vegetable oils.
159. 304 U.S. 152.
160. Carolene Products Co. v. United States, 323 U.S. 18, 31 (1944) (opinion by Reed, J.).
161. Lusky (1915–2001) graduated from Columbia Law School in 1937, clerked for Stone 1937–38, and later served as Betts Professor at his alma mater for twenty-three years, writing extensively about constitutional law. He discussed his work on *Carolene Products* in "Footnote Redux: A Carolene Products Reminiscence," 82 *Columbia Law Review* 1093 (1982) and in *Our Nine Tribunes: The Supreme Court in Modern America* (Westport: Praeger, 1993), 119–132.
162. 304 U.S. 152.
163. John Hart Ely, *Democracy and Distrust: A Theory of Judicial Review* (Cambridge: Harvard University Press, 1980) (propounding what is widely known as the "political process theory" of judicial review).

Chapter 6

1. For an overview of equal protection in its first half century: Michael J. Klarman, "An Interpretive History of Modern Equal Protection," 90 *Michigan Law Review* 213 (1991).
2. Stone Court: 1941–1946; Vinson Court: 1946–1953. Two histories of the Stone and Vinson Courts discuss these developments in greater depth: William M. Wiecek, *The Birth of the Modern Constitution: The United States Supreme Court, 1941–1953* (New York: Cambridge University Press, 2006) (vol. 12 of the *Holmes Devise History of the Supreme Court of the United States*), 621–706, and Melvin I. Urofsky, *Division and Discord: The Supreme Court under Stone and Vinson, 1941–1953* (Columbia: University of South Carolina Press, 1997).
3. Risa L. Goluboff, *The Lost Promise of Civil Rights* (Cambridge: Harvard University Press, 2007).
4. Kevin J. McMahon, *Reconsidering Roosevelt on Race: How the Presidency Paved the Road to Brown* (Chicago: University of Chicago Press, 2004).
5. Two other FDR appointees, James F. Byrnes and Stanley Reed, had no impact on the Court's decisions involving African Americans. In his eight months of service on the Court, and in his post-Court career as governor of South Carolina, Byrnes proved to be an outright segregationist and racist. Reed, though longer serving than Byrnes, contributed nothing to the story told here except negatively, indirectly, or passively.
6. "[Japanese] exclusion goes over 'the very brink of constitutional power' and falls into the ugly abyss of racism." *Korematsu v. United States*, 323 U.S. 214, 233 (1944).

7. On the nature and impact of a paradigm shift: Thomas Kuhn, *The Structure of Scientific Revolutions* (Chicago: University of Chicago Press, 1962).
8. See generally John Dower, *War without Mercy: Race and Power in the Pacific War* (1986; New York: Pantheon, 1993), 160–164; Roger Daniels, *The Politics of Prejudice, the Anti-Japanese Movement in California, and the Struggle for Japanese Exclusion* (Berkeley: University of California Press, 1962).
9. A total of sixteen states enacted some sort of legislation around the turn of the century that banned alien landownership with an eye to excluding Japanese and other Asians.
10. The literature on Japanese internment is extensive. The semi-official account, published under congressional auspices, was Commission on Wartime Relocation and Internment of Civilians, *Personal Justice Denied* (Washington, DC: GPO, 1982). Peter Irons, *Justice at War* (Berkeley: University of California Press, 1983), reviews legal and constitutional issues of internment. Erik K. Yamamoto et al., *Race, Rights and Reparation: Law and the Japanese American Internment* (Gaithersburg: Aspen Law & Business, 2001) is a casebook consisting of all relevant legal materials pertaining to internment. See also Greg Robinson, *A Tragedy of Democracy: Japanese Confinement in North America* (New York: Columbia University Press, 2009); Neil Gotanda, "The Story of Korematsu: The Japanese-American Cases," in Michael C. Dorf, ed., *Constitutional Law Stories*, 2nd ed. (St. Paul: Foundation, 2009), 231–270; and Richard Reeves, *Infamy: The Shocking Story of the Japanese-American Internment in World War* (New York: Henry Holt, 2015). Small numbers of German Americans and Italian Americans were briefly interned as well.
11. Act of March 21, 1942, ch. 191, 56 Stat. 173.
12. 320 U.S. 81, 100, 111 (1943).
13. Korematsu v. United States, 323 U.S. 214, 216 (1944).
14. Eugene Rostow, "The Japanese American Cases—a Disaster," 54 *Yale Law Journal* 489 (1945).
15. 138 S.Ct. 2392 (2018).
16. 323 U.S. 223, 243.
17. A Westlaw search for the term "racism" on December 13, 2019, turned up only 108 hits in Supreme Court opinions. Those 108 hits would be reduced to approximately 30 if citations to the Supreme Court case Ward v. Rock Against Racism, 491 U.S. 781 (1989) were excluded. By contrast, for secondary sources the algorithm stopped counting at 10,000. A similar search for the term "racist" turned up only 55 hits. There too hits in secondary sources promptly exceeded 10,000.
18. 323 U.S. 246.
19. Keith Aoki, "No Right to Own? The Early Twentieth Century 'Alien Land Laws' as a Prelude to Internment," 40 *Boston College Law Review* 37 (1998); Dudley O. McGovney, "The Anti-Japanese Land Laws of California and Ten Other States," 35 *California Law Review* 7 (1947); Allison B. Tirres, "Property Outliers: Non-citizens, Property Rights and State Power," 27 *Georgetown Immigration Law Journal* 77, 94–95, 101–106 (2012).
20. 332 U.S. 633, 673 (1948). See Rose Cuison Villazor, "Rediscovering Oyama v. California: At the Intersection of Property, Race, and Citizenship," 87 *Washington University Law Review* 979 (2010).
21. Sei Fujii v. State, 38 Cal.2d 718, 242 P.2d 617 (1952).
22. 334 U.S. 410 (1948).
23. 325 U.S. 91 (1945), discussed in greater detail in Wiecek, *Birth of the Modern Constitution*, 650–657.
24. The legislative history of these and related provisions can be confusing. In summary: section 2 of the 1866 Civil Rights Act is today 18 U.S.C. sec. 242. Section 6 of the 1870 act is 18 U.S.C. sec. 241. See the overview of this enforcement legislation in Noah Feldman and Kathleen M. Sullivan, eds., *Constitutional Law*, 21st ed. (St. Paul: Foundation, 2022), 889–892.
25. This understanding derived both from popular culture, especially the nostalgia-infused invention of the Lost Cause: David Blight, *Race and Reunion: The Civil War in American Memory* (Cambridge: Harvard University Press, 2001), 138–139, 258–299; and from the scholarly publications collectively known as the Dunning school, a series of state histories of Reconstruction directed by the Columbia University historian William A. Dunning. On the Dunning school and its long shadow, see John D. Smith and J. Vincent Lowery, eds., *The Dunning School: Historians, Race, and the Meaning of Reconstruction* (Lexington: University Press of Kentucky, 2013).
26. Respectively *Brown v. Board of Education* (1954), *Gomillion v. Lightfoot* (1960), *Naim v. Naim* (1956), and *Colegrove v. Green* (1946).

27. *Black's Law Dictionary*, 11th ed. (St. Paul: Thomson, 2019): "Scienter: A degree of knowledge that makes a person legally responsible for the consequences of his or her act or omission."
28. Robert K. Carr, "Screws v. United States: The Georgia Police Brutality Case," 31 *Cornell Law Quarterly* 48 (1945).
29. Paul J. Watford, "Screws v. United States and the Birth of Federal Civil Rights Enforcement," 98 *Marquette Law Review* 465 (2014).
30. Douglas S. Massey and Nancy A. Denton, *American Apartheid: Segregation and the Making of the Underclass* (Cambridge: Harvard University Press, 1993), viii.
31. For an introduction to the web of oppression, see Pierre W. Orelus, "Unveiling the Web of Race, Class, Language, and Gender Oppression: Challenges for Social Justice Educators," 19 *Race, Gender and Class* 35–51 (2012).
32. Both Richard Rothstein, *The Color of Law: A Forgotten History of How Our Government Segregated America* (New York: Liveright, 2017), and William M. Wiecek, "The United States Supreme Court and Residential Segregation: 'Slavery Unwilling to Die,'" 3 *Journal of Law, Property, and Society* 35 (2017), survey the role of law and structural racism in maintaining segregated housing throughout the twentieth century.
33. Missouri v. Jenkins, 515 U.S. 70, 116 (1995) (Thomas, J. concurring).
34. The Great Migration is conventionally understood as the relocation of some six million African Americans out of the South and into the cities of the North in the first half of the twentieth century. See Elizabeth Wilkerson, *The Warmth of Other Suns: The Epic Story of America's Great Migration* (New York: Random House, 2010), and Nicholas Lemann, *The Promised Land: The Great Black Migration and How It Changed America* (New York: Vintage, 1991).
35. Christopher Silver, "The Racial Origins of Zoning in American Cities," and Marsha Ritzdorf, "Family Values, Municipal Zoning, and African American Family Life," in June M. Thomas and Marsha Ritzdorf, eds., *Urban Planning and the African American Community: In the Shadows* (Thousand Oaks: Sage, 1997), 23–42, 75–89; Richard H. Chused, "Euclid's Historical Imagery," 51 *Case Western Reserve Law Review* 597 (2001).
36. 245 U.S. 60 (1917).
37. Harmon v. Taylor, 273 U.S. 668 (1927); Richmond v. Deans, 281 U.S. 704 (1930).
38. James W. Loewen, *Sundown Towns: A Hidden Dimension of American Racism* (New York: New Press, 2005).
39. Leonard S. Rubinowitz and Imani Perry, "Crimes without Punishment: White Neighbors' Resistance to Black Entry," 92 *Journal of Criminal Law & Criminology* 335 (2002).
40. Ironically, the acronym NAREB has today been appropriated by the National Association of Real Estate *Brokers*, an association of minority real estate professionals.
41. The history of real covenants, their rise and fall, is reviewed by Richard R. W. Brooks and Carol M. Rose, *Saving the Neighborhood: Racially Restrictive Covenants, Laws, and Social Norms* (Cambridge: Harvard University Press, 2013). See also Carol M. Rose, "Property Law and the Rise, Life, and Demise of Racially Restrictive Covenants," in *Powell on Real Property*, vol. 11, WFL 13-1 (2013).
42. Gandolfo v. Hartman, 49 F. 181, 182 (C.C.S.D. Cal. 1892) (covenant barring conveyance to "Chinamen" stricken because "any result inhibited by the constitution can no more be accomplished by contract of individual citizens than by legislation"); Title Guaranty & Trust Co. v. Garrott, 42 Cal.App. 152, 183 P. 470 (1919) (expressing hostility to restraints on alienation as contrary to public policy).
43. Koehler v. Rowland, 205 S.W. 217 (Mo. 1918); Parmalee v. Morris, 188 N.W. 330 (Mich. 1922) (sustaining racially restrictive covenants).
44. Brooks and Rose, *Saving the Neighborhood*, 47–70.
45. The Fifth Amendment was implicated because the jurisdiction was not a state (covered by the Fourteenth Amendment ["No State shall…"]) but rather the District of Columbia, a federal enclave over which Congress could exercise "exclusive Legislation" authority under Art. I, sec. 8, cl. 17.
46. 271 U.S. 323, 329 (1926).
47. *Restatement of Property*, sec. 406, comment 1. The drafters included the elite of the American property bar at the time: Richard Powell, A. James Casner, Harry Bigelow, Lewis Simes, and William Draper Lewis.
48. Rothstein, *The Color of Law*, 77–92.

49. Price Fishback et al., *Well Worth Saving: How the New Deal Safeguarded Home Ownership* (Chicago: University of Chicago Press, 2013).
50. Adam Gordon, "The Creation of Homeownership: How New Deal Changes in Banking Regulation Simultaneously Made Homeownership Accessible to Whites and Out of Reach for Blacks," 115 *Yale Law Journal* 186 (2005). See generally Kenneth T. Jackson, *Crabgrass Frontier: The Suburbanization of the United States* (New York: Oxford University Press, 1985).
51. John Kimble, "Insuring Inequality: The Role of the Federal Housing Administration in the Urban Ghettoization of African Americans," 32 *Law & Social Inquiry* 399 (2007).
52. On this giant of American jurisprudence in the twentieth century and his influence, see G. Edward White, *The American Judicial Tradition: Profiles of Leading American Judges*, rev. ed. (New York: Oxford University Press, 2007), 243–266; Henry J. Friendly, "Ablest Judge of His Generation," 71 *California Law Review* 1039 (1983).
53. Fairchild v. Raines, 24 Cal.2d 818, 151 P.2d 260 (1944).
54. Dudley O. McGovney, "Racial Residential Segregation by State Court Enforcement of Restrictive Agreements, Covenants, or Conditions in Deeds Is Unconstitutional," 33 *California Law Review* 5 (1945); Harold I. Kahen, "Validity of Anti-Negro Restrictive Covenants: A Reconsideration of the Problem," 12 *University of Chicago Law Review* 198 (1945).
55. 334 U.S. 1, 22–23 (1948). Justices Reed, Jackson, and Rutledge recused themselves in these cases. Contemporary observers speculated that they did so because they owned properties covered by such covenants.
56. Jeffrey D. Gonda, *Unjust Deeds: The Restrictive Covenant Cases and the Making of the Civil Rights Movement* (Chapel Hill: University of North Carolina Press, 2015). Clement Vose's study *Caucasians Only: The Supreme Court, the NAACP, and the Restrictive Covenant Cases* (Berkeley: University of California Press, 1959) remains essential. Carol M. Rose tells the story of the case in "Property Stories: Shelley v. Kraemer," in Gerald Korngold and Andrew P. Morris, eds., *Property Stories*, 2nd ed. (St. Paul: Foundation, 2009), 189–220. A 1988 symposium explored other issues raised by the case: "Symposium on the State Action Doctrine of Shelley v. Kraemer," 67 *Washington University Law Quarterly* 673 (1989).
57. I recall my dismay as a young attorney doing title searches in New Hampshire registries of deeds in the early 1960s when I kept running across post-1948 racial covenants in chains of title. At a distance of sixty years, my naivete seems quaint.
58. 334 U.S. 14, 19–20.
59. 334 U.S. 11.
60. 334 U.S. 22.
61. Mark D. Rosen, "Was Shelley v. Kraemer Incorrectly Decided? Some New Answers," 95 *California Law Review* 451 (2007).
62. Amend. XIII, sec. 2: "Congress shall have power to enforce this article by appropriate legislation."
63. 334 U.S. 34 (1948).
64. Vinson did not rely on the equal protection clause because the Court had not yet "reverse-incorporated" it via the due process clause of the Fifth Amendment as a constraint on federal power. That was to come in Bolling v. Sharpe, 347 U.S. 497 (1954).
65. This is known as "liquidated damages" in the law of remedies.
66. 346 U.S. 249 (1953).
67. For overviews of Vinson's contributions, see Frances H. Rudko, *Truman's Court: A Study in Judicial Restraint* (New York: Greenwood, 1988), and Michal Belknap, *The Vinson Court: Justices, Rulings, and Legacy* (Santa Barbara: ABC-CLIO, 2004).
68. William Domnarski, *The Great Justices, 1941–1954: Black, Douglas, Frankfurter, and Jackson in Chambers* (Ann Arbor: University of Michigan Press, 2002).
69. Irving Lefberg, "Chief Justice Vinson and the Politics of Desegregation," 24 *Emory Law Journal* 243 (1975).
70. Herbert Wechsler, "Toward Neutral Principles of Constitutional Law," 73 *Harvard Law Review* 1, 29–31 (1959); Louis Henkin, "Shelley v. Kraemer: Notes for a Revised Opinion," 110 *University of Pennsylvania Law Review* 473 (1962); Lawrence Tribe, *American Constitutional Law*, 2nd ed. (New York: Foundation, 1988), 1698. Philip B. Kurland, "Foreword: Equal in Origin and Equal in Title to the Legislative and Executive Branches of the Government," 78 *Harvard Law Review* 143, 148 (1964), referred to *Shelley* as "constitutional law's *Finnegan's Wake*" (not meant in any complimentary way).

71. Bray v. Alexandria Women's Health Clinic, 506 U.S. 263, 282 n. 14 (1993).
72. The succeeding passage is taken from a more extensive defense of Vinson's opinion in *Shelley* in Wiecek, *Birth of the Modern Constitution*, 672–681.
73. *Black's Law Dictionary*: "precatory *adj.* (Of words) requesting, recommending, or expressing a desire rather than a command."
74. Burton to Vinson, handwritten note, April 25, 1948, quoted in Wiecek, *Birth of the Modern Constitution*, 678.
75. On the 1940s Court's voting rights cases generally, see Michael J. Klarman, *From Jim Crow to Civil Rights: The Supreme Court and the Struggle for Racial Equality* (New York: Oxford University Press, 2004), 196–204.
76. United States v. Carolene Products, 304 U.S. 144, 152 (1938).
77. United States v. Classic, 313 U.S. 299, 315–316 (1941).
78. David M. Bixby, "The Roosevelt Court, Democracy, Ideology, and Minority Rights: Another Look at United States v. Classic," 90 *Yale Law Journal* 741 (1981).
79. 321 U.S. 649, 664 (1944). Justice Roberts was the lone dissenter. On this case, see Darlene C. Hine, *Black Victory: The Rise and Fall of the White Primary in Texas*, new ed. (Columbia: University of Missouri Press, 2003), 231–257, and Charles E. Zelden, *Battle for the Black Ballot: Smith v. Allwright and the Defeat of the Texas All-White Primary* (Lawrence: University Press of Kansas, 2004).
80. 336 U.S. 933 (1949).
81. Quoted in *Davis v. Schnell*, 81 F. Supp. 872, 879, 880 (S.D. Ala.), aff'd, 336 U.S. 933 (1949).
82. 345 U.S. 461, 468 (1953).
83. Black wrote the plurality opinion, joined by Douglas and Burton; Clark, Vinson, Reed, and Jackson concurred on other grounds. Frankfurter concurred solo and Minton dissented.
84. Rehnquist memorandum in Robert H. Jackson Papers, Library of Congress Manuscripts Division, quoted in Wiecek, *Birth of the Modern Constitution*, 639.
85. 328 U.S. 549 (1946).
86. The judgment of the Court was delivered by Frankfurter, who was joined by Reed and Burton. Black, Douglas, and Murphy dissented. On the core issue of justiciability, the dissenters were joined by Rutledge, so, on the merits, four members of the Court actually supported the power of the Court to entertain challenges to malapportionment. Only seven justices participated in the decision. Chief Justice Stone had died, and Justice Jackson was in Nuremberg as chief prosecutor at the war crimes trials.
87. 369 U.S. 186 (1962).
88. 339 U.S. 276, 280 (1950).
89. See generally Catherine A. Barnes, *Journey from Jim Crow: The Desegregation of Southern Transit* (New York: Columbia University Press, 1983).
90. The inconveniences to Black travelers were dramatically demonstrated by the "Green Books," annual paperbound publications in green covers that provided addresses and phone numbers of individuals and businesses who would accommodate them. Candacy Taylor, *Overground Railroad: The Green Book and the Roots of Black Travel in America* (New York: Abrams, 2019).
91. 313 U.S. 80, 97 (1941). *Mitchell* was the last decision of the Hughes Court that involved civil rights issues.
92. Interstate Commerce Act of 1887, ch. 104, sec. 3, 24 Stat. 379.
93. 339 U.S. 816 (1950).
94. Henderson v. United States, 80 F.Supp. 32 (D. Md. 1948).
95. If the Supreme Court agrees, it then vacates the lower court's judgment and remands the decision.
96. Quoted in Dennis Hutchinson, "Unanimity and Desegregation: Decisionmaking in the Supreme Court, 1948–1958," 68 *Georgetown Law Journal* 1, 19 (1979).
97. A misnomer: the commerce clause of Article I, section 8 never sleeps. But Congress may slumber on its regulatory power under the clause by declining to act. "Dormant commerce power" would be a more accurate way of characterizing the doctrine, but it seems impossible to banish the phrase "dormant commerce clause" from lawyers' common usage, inaccurate though it is.
98. Willson v. Blackbird Creek Marsh Co., 27 U.S. (2 Pet.) 245, 252 (1829), where Marshall referred to the congressional "power to regulate commerce in its dormant state."
99. Cooley v. Board of Wardens of the Port of Philadelphia, 53 U.S. (12 How.) 299, 319 (1851).

100. 95 U.S. 485 (1878).
101. 131 U.S. 587 (1890).
102. Joseph R. Palmore, "The Not-So-Strange Career of Interstate Jim Crow: Race, Transportation, and the Dormant Commerce Clause," 83 *Virginia Law Review* 1773 (1997).
103. 328 U.S. 323 (1946).
104. 364 U.S. 454 (1960).
105. Raymond Arsenault, *Freedom Riders: 1961 and the Struggle for Racial Justice* (New York: Oxford University Press, 2006), 93, 97, 121.
106. 333 U.S. 28 (1948).
107. Railway labor unions have referred to themselves as "brotherhoods" since their founding in the post–Civil War era. They comprise craft unions of engineers, firemen, conductors, clerks, telegraphers, trainmen, yardmasters, dispatchers, and porters. The one conspicuous exception to the all-white brotherhoods was the all-Black Brotherhood of Sleeping Car Porters. All the others were exclusively white and determined to stay that way.
108. Eric Arnesen, *Brotherhoods of Color: Black Railroad Workers and the Struggle for Equality* (Cambridge: Harvard University Press, 2001); Arnesen, "'Like Banquo's Ghost, It Will Not Down': The Race Question and the American Railroad Brotherhoods, 1880–1920," 99 *American History Review* 1601 (1994); David E. Bernstein, "Racism, Railroad Unions, and Labor Regulation," 5 *Independent Review* 237 (2000); Herbert Hill, *Black Labor and the American Legal System* (Madison: University of Wisconsin Press, 1985), 334–372.
109. 323 U.S. 192 (1944). In Railway Mail Ass'n v. Corsi, 326 U.S. 88 (1945), the Court upheld a state statute banning union discrimination against African Americans.
110. 343 U.S. 768 (1952).
111. Missouri ex rel. Gaines v. Canada, 305 U.S. 337 (1938).
112. On the school desegregation litigation preceding *Brown v. Board of Education*, see Mark V. Tushnet, *The NAACP's Legal Strategy against Segregated Education, 1925–1950* (Chapel Hill: University of North Carolina Press, 1987); Tushnet, *Making Civil Rights Law: Thurgood Marshall and the Supreme Court, 1936–1961* (New York: Oxford University Press, 1994); and Dennis Hutchinson, "Unanimity and Desegregation: Decision-Making in the Supreme Court, 1948–1958," 68 *Georgetown Law Journal* 1 (1979).
113. The Court assumed, without explicitly so holding, that *Plessy's* separate-but-equal doctrine, developed in the context of transportation, applied to education as well: Cumming v. Richmond County Board of Education (1899) and *Gong Lum v. Rice*, 275 U.S. 78 (1927).
114. Brief for appellant, quoted in Richard Kluger, *Simple Justice: The History of Brown v. Board of Education and Black America's Struggle for Equality* (1975; New York: Knopf, 2004), 258.
115. Sipuel v. Oklahoma State Board of Regents, 332 U.S. 631, 633 (1948).
116. Fisher v. Hurst, 333 U.S. 147 (1948).
117. The three cases are *Henderson v. United States*, *Sweatt v. Painter*, and *McLaurin v. Regents*.
118. 339 U.S. 629 (1950). On this case, see Gary M. Lavergne, *Before Brown: Heman Marion Sweatt, Thurgood Marshall, and the Long Road to Justice* (Austin: University of Texas Press, 2010); Jonathan L. Entin, "Sweatt v. Painter, the End of Segregation, and the Transformation of Education Law," 5 *Review of Litigation* 3 (1986); Paul Finkelman, "Breaking the Back of Segregation: Why Sweatt Matters," 36 *Thurgood Marshall Law Review* 7 (2010).
119. This entity evolved into the Texas State University for Negroes, which in time became the Thurgood Marshall School of Law of Texas Southern University, an HBCU.
120. The brief was published as Thomas I. Emerson et al., "Segregation and the Equal Protection Clause: Brief for the Committee of Law Teachers against Segregation in Legal Education," 34 *Minnesota Law Review* 284 (1950).
121. Wiecek, *Birth of the Modern Constitution*, 685–692, reviews the attitudes of all the justices.
122. Jackson quoted in Wiecek, *Birth of the Modern Constitution*, 689. See his letter to Charles Fairman, March 13, 1950, reprinted as an appendix in Wiecek, 713–715, for the full expression of his anxious ambivalence.
123. Quoted in Wiecek, *Birth of the Modern Constitution*, 692.
124. 339 U.S. 633–634.
125. 339 U.S. 637 (1950).
126. Kluger, *Simple Justice*, 267.
127. 339 U.S. 641–642.

Chapter 7

1. See generally Hugh D. Graham, *The Civil Rights Era: Origins and Development of National Policy, 1960–1972* (New York: Oxford University Press, 1990), a superb account of federal civil rights programs in the second Reconstruction.
2. On the degradations of Jim Crow: Leon F. Litwack, *Been in the Storm So Long: The Aftermath of Slavery* (New York: Knopf, 1979); Litwack, *Trouble in Mind: Black Southerners in the Age of Jim Crow* (New York: Vintage, 1998).
3. See Geoffrey R. Stone and David A. Strauss, *Democracy and Equality: The Enduring Constitutional Vision of the Warren Court* (New York: Oxford University Press, 2020), an appreciation of the Warren Court a half century after its demise; Morton J. Horwitz, *The Warren Court and the Pursuit of Justice* (New York: Hill and Wang, 1998); Michal Belknap, *The Supreme Court under Earl Warren, 1953–1969* (Columbia: University of South Carolina Press, 2004); Melvin I. Urofsky, *The Warren Court: Justices, Rulings, Legacy* (Oxford: ABC-CLIO, 2001).
4. The biographical literature on Warren is extensive: G. Edward White, *Earl Warren: A Public Life* (New York: Oxford University Press, 1982) (the author clerked for Warren in the 1971–72 Term); Bernard Schwartz, *Superchief: Earl Warren and His Supreme Court: A Judicial Biography* (New York: New York University Press, 1983); Ed Cray, *Chief Justice: A Biography of Earl Warren* (New York: Simon & Schuster, 1997).
5. Producing the leading First Amendment precedent, Whitney v. California, 274 U.S. 357, 376 (1927), with Justice Brandeis's imperishable dissent ("Men feared witches and burned women. It is the function of speech to fee men from the bondage of irrational fears").
6. 332 U.S. 633 (1948).
7. He later expressed regret for his actions in his *Memoirs* (Garden City: Doubleday, 1977).
8. James F. Simon, *Eisenhower vs. Warren: The Battle for Civil Rights and Liberties* (New York: Liveright, 2018).
9. The principal biography is by Tinsley E. Yarbrough: *John Marshall Harlan: Great Dissenter of the Warren Court* (New York: Oxford University Press, 1992). The ironic allusion is to his grandfather's nickname.
10. On this concept of equality, see Kenneth L. Karst, "Equal Citizenship under the Fourteenth Amendment," 91 *Harvard Law Review* 1, 66–67 (1976); Karst, *Belonging to America: Equal Citizenship and the Constitution* (New Haven: Yale University Press, 1989).
11. Seth Stern and Stephen Wermiel, *Justice Brennan: Liberal Champion* (Lawrence: University Press of Kansas, 2010); Kim I. Eisler, *A Justice for All: William J. Brennan Jr. and the Decisions That Transformed America* (New York: Simon and Schuster, 1993).
12. Quoted in Garrett Epps, "Justice Scalia's Outsized Legacy," *The Atlantic*, February 13, 2016, https://www.theatlantic.com/politics/archive/2016/02/justice-scalias-outsized-legacy/462756/.
13. Dennis J. Hutchinson, *The Man Who Once Was Whizzer White: A Portrait of Justice Byron R. White* (New York: Free Press, 1998). The author clerked for Justice White in the 1975 Term.
14. Dennis Hutchinson, "Two Cheers for Judicial Restraint: Justice White and the Role of the Supreme Court," 74 *University of Colorado Law Review* 1409 (2003).
15. 431 U.S. 494, 544 (1977) (White, J. dissenting).
16. 418 U.S. 717 (1974).
17. 426 U.S. 229 (1976).
18. 488 U.S. 469 (1989).
19. 427 U.S. 160 (1976).
20. Mark Tushnet, who clerked for Marshall in the 1972–73 Term, has written a two-volume appreciation: *Making Civil Rights Law: Thurgood Marshall and the Supreme Court, 1936–1961* (New York: Oxford University Press, 1994), and *Making Constitutional Law: Thurgood Marshall and the Supreme Court, 1961–1991* (New York: Oxford University Press, 1997). The latter volume is limited in its reach by the author's reticence to rely on the views of former clerks (including his own) and by Marshall's reluctance to discuss his service on the Court (p. viii). Howard Ball provides a more conventional scholarly treatment in *A Defiant Life: Thurgood Marshall and the Persistence of Racism in America* (New York: Crown, 1998). Charles Zelden's *Thurgood Marshall: Race, Rights, and the Struggle for a More Perfect Union* (London: Routledge, 2013) is an accessible brief introduction.

21. 169 Md. 468, 182 A. 590 (1936).
22. "The Bicentennial Speech" (1987) at "The Constitution's Bicentennial: Commemorating the Wrong Document?" 40 *Vanderbilt Law Review* 1337 (1987).
23. Mark V. Tushnet, *The NAACP's Legal Strategy against Segregated Education, 1925–1950* (Chapel Hill: University of North Carolina Press, 2005), 105–166.
24. The literature on *Brown v. Board of Education* is immense. The best accounts include Richard Kluger, *Simple Justice: The History of Brown v. Board of Education and Black America's Struggle for Equality* (New York: Knopf, 1975), 545–717; Michael J. Klarman, *From Jim Crow to Civil Rights: The Supreme Court and the Struggle for Racial Equality* (New York: Oxford University Press, 2004), 290–343; Tushnet, *Making Civil Rights Law*, 150–216; Mark Tushnet and Katya Lezin, "What Really Happened in Brown v. Board of Education," 91 *Columbia Law Review* 1867 (1991). Klarman compressed *From Jim Crow to Civil Rights* into a brief volume focused on *Brown*: *Brown v. Board of Education and the Civil Rights Movement* (New York: Oxford University Press, 2007).
25. Douglas, "Memorandum for the File," May 17, 1954, reprinted in Del Dickson, ed., *The Supreme Court in Conference (1940–1985)* (New York: Oxford University Press, 2001), 660–662.
26. This brief account omits all nuance. Each of the nine had more extensive and complicated views on the various issues presented than can be conveyed by a simple binary sort. Klarman, *From Jim Crow*, 293–301, traces these with sensitive attention to context.
27. Frankfurter, an agnostic, famously quipped to a former clerk that Vinson's providential demise was "the first indication I have ever had that there is a God." Carlton F. W. Larson provides a thoughtful reconsideration of Frankfurter's bon mot and of Vinson's role in "What if Chief Justice Fred Vinson Had Not Died of a Heart Attack in 1953? Implications for Brown and Beyond," 45 *Indiana Law Review* 131 (2011).
28. Alexander M. Bickel, "The Original Understanding and the Segregation Decision," 69 *Harvard Law Review* 1 (1955) provides an insight into the evolution of Frankfurter's thinking.
29. On Jackson's agonizing over Brown, see David M. O'Brien, *Justice Robert H. Jackson's Unpublished Opinion in Brown v. Board: Conflict, Compromise, and Constitutional Interpretation* (Lawrence: University Press of Kansas, 2017), 81–121.
30. Dennis J. Hutchinson, "Unanimity and Desegregation: Decision-Making in the Supreme Court, 1948–1958," 68 *Georgetown Law Journal* 1, 33–50 (1979); Kluger, *Simple Justice*, 543–747.
31. 347 U.S. 483, 489, 492–495 (1954). On the question of the framers' intent conceived of as a problem of originalism, see Michael McConnell, "Originalism and the Desegregation Decisions," 81 *Virginia Law Review* 947 (1995), and Michael J. Klarman, "Brown, Originalism, and Constitutional Theory: A Response to Professor McConnell," 81 *Virginia Law Review* 1881 (1995).
32. Reliance on social science has proved to be the Achilles' heel of *Brown*; its methods and conclusions seem primitive to later scholars. Mark G. Yudof, "School Desegregation: Legal Realism, Reasoned Elaboration, and Social Science Research in the Supreme Court," 42 *Law & Contemporary Problems* 57, 70–74 (1978).
33. 347 U.S. 494.
34. 347 U.S. 497 (1954). *Brown I* was a congeries of four cases from Kansas, South Carolina, Delaware, and Virginia. Bolling was the fifth.
35. For this purpose, the District of Columbia is not considered a state, though it is for other jurisdictional issues.
36. Plessy v. Ferguson, 163 U.S. 537, 559 (1896).
37. On the role of caste, as distinct from race, in American society, see Isabel Wilkerson's brief introduction, *Caste: The Origins of Our Discontents* (New York: Random House, 2020). The idea is not new: W. Lloyd Warner, "American Caste and Class," 42 *American Journal of Sociology* 237 (1936).
38. This distinction is explored in Reva B. Siegel, "Equality Talk: Antisubordination and Anticlassification Values in Constitutional Struggles over Brown," 117 *Harvard Law Review* 1470 (2004), and Jack M. Balkin and Reva B. Siegel, "The American Civil Rights Tradition: Anticlassification or Antisubordination," 58 *University of Miami Law Review* 9 (2004).
39. Justice Thomas concurring in Missouri v. Jenkins, 515 U.S. 70, 121 (1995).
40. Cheryl I. Harris, "Whiteness as Property," 106 *Harvard Law Review* 1709, 1762 (1993).
41. Robert Carter, "The Warren Court and Desegregation," 67 *Michigan Law Review* 237, 247 (1968). Judge Carter played a role second only to Thurgood Marshall in the NAACP's struggles against segregation, and presented part of the oral argument in Brown I.

42. Owen Fiss, "Groups and the Equal Protection Clause," *Philosophy and Public Affairs*, 5 (1976), 107; Alan D. Freeman, "Legitimizing Racial Discrimination through Antidiscrimination Law: A Critical Review of Supreme Court Doctrine," 62 *Minnesota Law Review* 1049 (1978); Reva Siegel, "Discrimination in the Eyes of the Law: How 'Color Blindness' Discourse Disrupts and Rationalizes Social Stratification," 88 *California Law Review* 77 (2000); Paul Brest, "Foreword: In Defense of the Antidiscrimination Principle," 90 *Harvard Law Review* 1, 2 (1976) (presenting a hybrid version of anticlassification: legislative classifications based on race are to be disfavored, but only those "that disadvantage members of minority groups").
43. Kenneth L. Karst, "Foreword: Equal Citizenship under the Fourteenth Amendment," 91 *Harvard Law Review* 1 (1977).
44. Jack M. Balkin, ed., *What Brown v. Board of Education Should Have Said* (New York: New York University Press, 2002).
45. Stephen N. Subrin, "How Equity Conquered Common Law: The Federal Rules of Civil Procedure in Historical Perspective," 135 *University of Pennsylvania Law Review* 909 (1987).
46. Abram Chayes, "The Role of the Judge in Public Law Litigation," 89 *Harvard Law Review* 1281 (1976); Owen Fiss, "The Supreme Court, 1978 Term—Foreword: Forms of Justice," 93 *Harvard Law Review* 1 (1979).
47. Frankfurter quoted in Dickson, ed., *The Supreme Court in Conference*, 651; Black quoted in Klarman, *From Jim Crow to Civil Rights*, 294.
48. Miscellaneous Orders, Brown v. Board of Education, 345 U.S. 972 (1953).
49. 349 U.S. 294, 300 (1955).
50. Both the short-range and the longer-term impact of *Brown* are considered by James T. Patterson, *Brown v. Board of Education: A Civil Rights Milestone and Its Troubled Legacy* (New York: Oxford University Press, 2001); Justin Driver, *The Schoolhouse Gate: Public Education, the Supreme Court, and the Battle for the American Mind* (New York: Vintage, 2018), 247–293; Taylor Branch, *Parting the Waters: America in the King Years, 1954–1963* (New York: Macmillan, 1988); J. Harvie Wilkinson, *From Brown to Bakke: The Supreme Court and School Integration, 1954–1978* (New York: Harvard University Press, 1979); Klarman, *From Jim Crow to Civil Rights*, 321–468; and Harvard Sitkoff, *The Struggle for Black Equality, 1954–1992*, 3rd ed. (New York: Hill & Wang, 2008).
51. Their story is told by Jack Bass in *Unlikely Heroes: The Dramatic Story of the Southern Judges of the Fifth Circuit Who Translated the Supreme Court's Brown Decision into a Revolution for Equality* (New York: Simon and Schuster, 1981), and Jack W. Peltason in *Fifty-Eight Lonely Men: Southern Federal Judges and School Desegregation* (New York: Harcourt, 1961) ("lonely" refers to the social ostracism that most of them experienced because of their desegregation rulings). Joel W. Friedman recounts the experiences of one of these district court judges in *Champion of Civil Rights: Judge John Minor Wisdom* (Baton Rouge: Louisiana State University Press, 2009).
52. Benjamin Muse, *Ten Years of Prelude: The Story of Integration Since the Supreme Court's 1954 Decision* (New York: Viking, 1964).
53. Gabriel J. Chin catalogs the techniques and strategies of resistance in "Jim Crow's Long Goodbye," 21 *Constitutional Commentary* 107, 111–121 (2004).
54. Numan V. Bartley, *The Rise of Massive Resistance: Race and Politics in the South during the 1950s* (Baton Rouge: Louisiana State University Press, 1969); Benjamin Muse, *Virginia's Massive Resistance* (Bloomington: Indiana University Press, 1961); James W. Ely Jr., *The Crisis of Conservative Virginia: The Byrd Organization and the Politics of Massive Resistance* (Knoxville: University of Tennessee Press, 1976).
55. John K. Day, *The Southern Manifesto: Massive Resistance and the Fight to Preserve Segregation* (Jackson: University Press of Mississippi, 2014). While not endorsing its substantive content, Justin Driver attributes greater legal acumen to its authors than is usually accorded: "Supremacies and the Southern Manifesto," 92 *Texas Law Review* 1053 (2013).
56. "The Declaration of Constitutional Principles," 102 *Cong. Rec.* 4459–4460 (March 12, 1956). Only a handful of southern congressmen, including Lyndon B. Johnson of Texas, refused to sign it; Day, *Southern Manifesto*, 148–153.
57. Anders Walker, *The Ghost of Jim Crow: How Southern Moderates Used Brown v. Board of Education to Stall Civil Rights* (New York: Oxford University Press, 2009) (discussing the roles played by Governors J. P. Coleman of Mississippi, LeRoy Collins of Florida, and Luther Hodges of North Carolina in preserving segregation and dampening the impact of *Brown*).

58. Stephanie Rolph, *Resisting Equality: The Citizens' Council, 1954–1989* (Baton Rouge: Louisiana State University Press, 2019); Neil R. McMillen, *The Citizens Council: Organized Resistance to the Second Reconstruction, 1954–64* (Urbana: University of Illinois Press, 1994).
59. David M. Chalmers, *Hooded Americanism: The History of the Ku Klux Klan*, 3rd ed. (Durham: Duke University Press, 1981), 28–318.
60. David A. Nichols, *A Matter of Justice: Eisenhower and the Beginnings of the Civil Rights Revolution* (New York: Simon & Schuster, 2007), 169–213.
61. 358 U.S. 1, 17–18 (1958). See Tony A. Freyer, *Little Rock on Trial: Cooper v. Aaron and School Desegregation* (Lawrence: University Press of Kansas, 2007); Freyer, *The Little Rock Crisis: A Constitutional Interpretation* (Westport: Greenwood Press, 1984); and Freyer, "Cooper v. Aaron (1958): A Hidden Story of Unanimity and Division," 33 *Journal of Supreme Court History* 89 (2008).
62. Thus: "Opinion of the Court by The CHIEF JUSTICE, Mr. Justice BLACK, Mr. Justice FRANKFURTER, Mr. Justice DOUGLAS, Mr. Justice BURTON, Mr. Justice CLARK, Mr. Justice HARLAN, Mr. Justice BRENNAN, and Mr. Justice WHITTAKER." Ordinarily, a majority opinion, even a unanimous one, simply begins: "Opinion of the Court by Mr. Justice X." Justice Brennan was supposedly the principal author of the opinion.
63. Daniel A. Farber, "The Supreme Court and the Rule of Law: Cooper v. Aaron Revisited," 1982 *University of Illinois Law Review* 387, 396–403, 409–411 (1982).
64. 5 U.S. (1 Cranch) 137, 177 (1803).
65. Gerald Gunther, "The Subtle Vices of the 'Passive Virtues'—a Comment on Principle and Expediency in Judicial Review," 64 *Columbia Law Review* 1 (1964).
66. Dickerson v. United States, 530 U.S. 428, 437 (2000). The constitutional ruling Rehnquist referred to was the *Miranda* rule: Miranda v. Arizona, 384 U.S. 436 (1966).
67. 358 U.S. 1, 18 (1958).
68. 14 U.S. (1 Wheat.) 304 (1816).
69. U.S. Const. Art. VI.
70. See the critique of judicial supremacy in Richard H. Fallon, "Judicial Supremacy, Departmentalism, and the Rule of Law in a Populist Age," 96 *Texas Law Review* 487 (2018).
71. Neal Devins, "Why Congress Does Not Challenge Judicial Supremacy," 58 *William & Mary Law Review* 1495 (2017).
72. On desegregation efforts in this period, see Wilkinson, *From Brown to Bakke*, 61–127 (critical of the Court's inaction); Stephen Wasby et al., *Desegregation from Brown to Alexander: An Exploration of Supreme Court Strategies* (Carbondale: Southern Illinois University Press, 1977), 162–222.
73. Christopher Bonastia, *Southern Stalemate: Five Years without Public Education in Prince Edward County, Virginia* (Chicago: University of Chicago Press, 2012); Jill O. Titus, *Brown's Battleground: Students, Segregationists, and the Struggle for Justice In Prince Edward County, Virginia* (Chapel Hill: University of North Carolina Press, 2011); Amy E. Murrell, "The Impossible Prince Edward Case: The Endurance of Resistance in a Southside Community," in Matthew Lassiter and Andrew B. Lewis, eds., *The Moderates' Dilemma: Massive Resistance to School Desegregation in Virginia* (Charlottesville: University Press of Virginia, 1998), 134–167; Bob Smith, *They Closed Their Schools: Prince Edward County, Virginia, 1951–1964* (Chapel Hill: University of North Carolina Press, 1965), 151–266; Kristen Green, *Something Must Be Done about Prince Edward County: A Family, a Virginia Town, a Civil Rights Battle* (New York: Harper, 2015).
74. 377 U.S. 218 (1964).
75. Segregation academies, called "seg academies" in the South, were private schools organized by parents and sometimes sponsored at first by the Klan and then shortly after by churches, that provided schooling comparable to that offered by the public schools, but that were ostensibly privately financed and controlled, and thus beyond the pale of state action. They accepted only white students. Note, "Segregation Academies and State Action," 82 *Yale Law Journal* 1436 (1973).
76. Bonastia, *Southern Stalemate*, 163.
77. 377 U.S. 234, 229. The justices reiterated the point the next year in Bradley v. School Board of Richmond, 382 U.S. 103, 105 (1965): "Delays in integrating school systems are no longer tolerable."
78. Green v. County School Board of New Kent County, 391 U.S. 430, 435–436 (1968).

79. Will Stancil, "The Radical Supreme Court Decision That America Forgot," *The Atlantic*, May 28, 2018.
80. 391 U.S. 437–438.
81. 103 F.Supp. 920 (D.S.C. 1952).
82. Parker was a controversial judge, seemingly a closet segregationist, who figured prominently (though unsuccessfully) in President Richard Nixon's effort to create a more conservative Supreme Court.
83. Briggs v. Elliott, 132 F.Supp. 776, 777 (1955). Judge Parker's words merit quotation in full: "it is important that we point out exactly what the Supreme Court has decided and what it has not decided in this case. It has not decided that the federal courts are to take over or regulate the public schools of the states. It has not decided that the states must mix persons of different races in the schools or must require them to attend schools or must deprive them of the right of choosing the schools they attend. What it has decided, and all that it has decided, is that a state may not deny to any person on account of race the right to attend any school that it maintains.... Nothing in the Constitution or in the decision of the Supreme Court takes away from the people freedom to choose the schools they attend. The Constitution, in other words, does not require integration. It merely forbids discrimination. It does not forbid such segregation as occurs as the result of voluntary action. It merely forbids the use of governmental power to enforce segregation."
84. Civil Rights Act of 1964, 78 Stat. 241, sec. 401(b).
85. 110 *Cong. Rec.* 12717 (1964).
86. 396 U.S. 19, 20 (1969).
87. William P. Hustwit, *Integration Now: Alexander v. Holmes and the End of Jim Crow Education* (Chapel Hill: University of North Carolina Press, 2019), 2.
88. 404 U.S. 997 (1971).
89. 330 F.Supp. 1150 (D.D.C. 1971).
90. Norwood v. Harrison, 413 U.S. 455, 467 (1973).
91. Melvin I. Urofsky and Paul Finkelman, *A March of Liberty: A Constitutional History of the United States*, vol. 2: *From 1989 to the Present*, 3rd ed. (New York: Oxford University Press, 2011), 880–881; Wilkinson, *From Brown to Bakke*.
92. 402 U.S. 1 (1971). Bernard Schwartz, *Swann's Way: The School Busing Case and the Supreme Court* (New York: Oxford University Press, 1986), 88–193; Davison Douglas, *Reading, Writing, and Race: The Desegregation of the Charlotte Schools* (Chapel Hill: University of North Carolina Press, 1999), 107–214.
93. Derrick Bell, *Race, Racism, and American Law*, 5th ed. (Boston: Little, Brown, 2004), 153.
94. United States v. Montgomery County Board of Education, 395 U.S. 225, 234 (1969).
95. Reflecting his contemporary eminence and moral stature, Judge Johnson is memorialized in no fewer than *four* book-length biographies: Tinsley E. Yarbrough, *Judge Frank Johnson and Human Rights in Alabama* (University: University of Alabama Press, 1981); Jack Bass, *Taming the Storm: The Life and Times of Judge Frank M. Johnson and the South's Fight over Civil Rights* (New York: Doubleday, 1992); Robert F. Kennedy Jr., *Judge Frank M. Johnson Jr.: A Biography* (New York: Putnam, 1978); and Frank Sikora, *The Judge: The Life and Opinions of Alabama's Frank M. Johnson* (Montgomery: New South Books, 2007).
96. 401 U.S. 1, 25 (1971). The ratio in Swann was 71 percent white to 29 percent Black.
97. On the failure of busing, see Matthew F. Delmont, *Why Busing Failed: Race, Media, and the National Resistance to School Desegregation* (Oakland: University of California Press, 2016).
98. The Powell amicus is discussed in John C. Jeffries Jr., *Justice Lewis F. Powell* (New York: Scribner's, 2001), 284–287.
99. On this retreat from equality, see Michael J. Graetz and Linda Greenhouse, *The Burger Court and the Rise of the Judicial Right* (New York: Simon & Schuster, 2016), 79–102.
100. 401 U.S. at 30–31.
101. Pasadena City Board of Education v. Spangler, 427 U.S. 424 (1976).
102. 402 U.S. 43, 45–46 (1971).
103. 402 U.S. 33, 37 (1971).
104. On the role and financing of seg academies, see Noliwe Rooks, "Cindy Hyde-Smith Is Teaching Us What Segregation Academies Taught Her," *New York Times*, November 28, 2018.
105. 413 U.S. 455 (1973).
106. Quoting from a case decided the previous year, Wright v. City Council of Emporia, 407 U.S. 451, 462 (1972).

107. Mayor of Baltimore v. Dawson, 350 U.S. 877 (1955). Dawson was the bellwether case, controlling the result in all subsequent public-facilities cases.
108. Holmes v. Atlanta, 350 U.S. 879 (1955).
109. Johnson v. Virginia, 373 U.S. 61 (1963) (reversing conviction of contempt for refusal to comply with judicial order to take a seat in segregated seating in municipal traffic court).
110. Brown v. Louisiana, 383 U.S. 131 (1966).
111. Gayle v. Browder, 352 U.S. 903 (1956). This was the decision that resolved the Montgomery, Alabama, bus boycott initiated by Rosa Parks in 1955.
112. Boynton v. Virginia, 364 U.S. 454 (1960).
113. New Orleans City Park Improvement Ass'n. v. Detiege, 358 U.S. 54 (1958). However, see the inconsistent outcome and reasoning in Evans v. Abney, 396 U.S. 435 (1970) (complex and extensive litigation resulting in a public park reverting to private ownership rather than be subjected to desegregation). The details of this decision are explored at greater length, and the Court's reasoning critiqued, in William M. Wiecek, "The United States Supreme Court and Residential Segregation: 'Slavery Unwilling to Die,'" 3 *Journal of Law, Property and Society* 35, 88–90 (2017).
114. Johnson v. Virginia, 373 U.S. at 62.
115. Joy Milligan, "Plessy Preserved: Agencies and the Effective Constitution," 129 *Yale Law Journal* 924 (2020). See also Milligan, "Remembering: The Constitution and Federally Funded Apartheid," 89 *University of Chicago Law Review* 65 (2022).
116. Ex parte Hamilton, 275 Ala. 574 (1963).
117. Hamilton v. Alabama, 376 U.S. 650 (1964). Justices Clark, Harlan, and White would have denied cert., in effect dissenting.
118. John Rawls, *A Theory of Justice*, rev. ed. (Oxford: Oxford University Press, 1999), 386.
119. 357 U.S. 449. 460 (1958). The Court reaffirmed the NAACP's associational rights in *Bates v. Little Rock* (1961) as now "beyond dispute": 361 U.S. 516, 523 (1961).
120. 381 U.S. 479 (1965).
121. 371 U.S. 415, 437 (1963).
122. 366 U.S. 293 (1961).
123. 377 U.S. 288 (1964).
124. 376 U.S. 254, 270 (1964).
125. Anthony Lewis, *Make No Law: The Sullivan Case and the First Amendment* (New York: Vintage, 1991); Christopher Schmidt, "New York Times v. Sullivan and the Legal Attack on the Civil Rights Movement," 66 *Alabama Law Review* 293 (2014).
126. On the constitutional significance of the sit-in cases, see Christopher W. Schmidt, *The Sit-Ins: Protest and Legal Change in the Civil Rights Era* (Chicago: University of Chicago Press, 2018).
127. Chief Justice Rehnquist later repeatedly recurred to "one of the most essential sticks in the bundle of rights that are commonly characterized as property—the right to exclude others." Kaiser Aetna v. United States, 444 U.S. 164, 176 (1979). Accord, Thomas W. Merrill, "Property and the Right to Exclude," 77 *Nebraska Law Review* 730 (1998).
128. 373 U.S. 244, 248 (1963).
129. 372 U.S. 229, 235 (1963).
130. Monrad G. Paulson, "The Sit-In Cases of 1964: 'But Answer There Came None,'" 1964 *Supreme Court Review* 137 (1964).
131. Garner v. Louisiana, 368 U.S. 157 (1961) (insufficiency of evidence); Taylor v. Louisiana, 370 U.S. 154 (1962) (local custom violated federal law).
132. Bell v. Maryland, 378 U.S. at 346 (1964).
133. 379 U.S. 226, 306 (1964).
134. 383 U.S. 131, 166–168 (1966).
135. 385 U.S. 39 (1966).
136. 395 U.S. 444 (1969).
137. 458 U.S. 866 (1982).
138. Clay Risen, *The Bill of the Century: The Epic Battle for the Civil Rights Act* (New York: Bloomsbury, 2014); Todd S. Purdum, *An Idea Whose Time Has Come: Two Presidents, Two Parties, and the Civil Rights Act of 1964* (New York: Henry Holt, 2014); Nick Kotz, *Judgment Days: Lyndon Baines Johnson, Martin Luther King, Jr., and the Laws That Changed America* (Boston: Houghton Mifflin, 2005), 87–152.
139. *Public Papers of the Presidents of the United States: Lyndon B. Johnson, 1965*, vol. 1 (Washington, DC: GPO, 1966), 636.

140. There is some controversy as to whether Johnson actually said this, to whom, and when. Bill Moyers, in *Moyers on America: A Journalist and His Times* (New York: New Press, 2011), 167, states that he was the aide, and that Johnson made the comment to him on the night of the bill-signing. See also Michael Oreskes, "Civil Rights Act Leaves Deep Mark on American Political Landscape," *New York Times*, July 2, 1989; Nick Kotz, *Judgment Days*, 61 (LBJ to Ted Sorensen: "I know the risks are great and we might lose the South, but those sorts of states may be lost anyway"); Rick Perlstein, *Before the Storm: Barry Goldwater and the Unmaking of the American Consensus* (New York: Hill and Wang, 2001), 365.
141. Civil Rights Act of 1964, 78 Stat. 241, 42 U.S.C. sec. 2000a.
142. 379 U.S. 241, 253, 258 (1964). Justices Black, Douglas, and Goldberg concurred in separate opinions. Black injected the necessary and proper clause as an additional buttress for the commerce clause holding; Douglas added section 5 of the Fourteenth Amendment; and Goldberg emphasized the right to be treated as equal members of the community.
143. From the color of its paper cover (and its publisher was named Victor Green). *The Negro Motorist Green Book* was published between 1936 and 1964 and was known as "the AAA guide for black people." Candacy A. Taylor, *Overground Railroad: The Green Book and the Roots of Black Travel in America* (New York: Abrams, 2020).
144. 22 U.S. (9 Wheat.) 1 (1824).
145. NLRB v. Jones & Laughlin Steel Corp., 301 U.S. 1 (1937); United States v. Darby, 312 U.S. 100 (1941); Wickard v. Filburn, 317 U.S. 111 (1942).
146. Jack Balkin, "The Reconstruction Power," 85 *NYU Law Review* 1801 (2010).
147. 379 U.S. 294, 304 (1964).
148. Douglas A. Blackmon, Slavery by Another Name: The Re-enslavement of Black Americans from the Civil War to World War II (New York: Anchor, 2008); William Cohen, At Freedom's Edge: Black Mobility and the Southern White Quest for Racial Control, 1861–1915 (Baton Rouge: Louisiana State University Press, 1991).
149. Jones revived the Civil Rights Act in part by explicitly overruling Hodges v. United States, 203 U.S. 1 (1906), which had denied congressional power under the Thirteenth Amendment to reach private behavior.
150. Lengthier treatments of this case may be found at Darrell A. H. Miller, "White Cartels, the Civil Rights Act of 1866, and the History of Jones v. Alfred H. Mayer Co.," 77 *Fordham Law Review* 999 (2008) and Wiecek, "Supreme Court and Residential Segregation," 72–77.
151. Richard Rothstein, *The Color of Law: A Forgotten History of How Our Government Segregated America* (New York: Liveright, 2017); Kenneth T. Jackson, *Crabgrass Frontier: The Suburbanization of the United States* (New York: Oxford University Press, 1985); Ira Katznelson, *When Affirmative Action Was White: An Untold History of Racial Inequality in Twentieth Century America* (New York: Oxford University Press, 2005), 113–114, 163–164.
152. "All citizens of the United States shall have the same right, in every State and Territory, as is enjoyed by white citizens thereof to inherit, purchase, lease, sell, hold, and convey real and personal property."
153. Jones v. Alfred H. Mayer Co., 255 F.Supp. 115 (E.D. Mo. 1966).
154. Who was elevated to the Supreme Court three years later.
155. Jones v. Alfred H. Mayer Co., 379 F.2d 33 (8th Cir. 1967); Linda Greenhouse, *Becoming Justice Blackmun: Harry Blackmun's Supreme Court Journey* (New York: New York Times Books, 2005), 30.
156. *Bradley*: "legislation [under the Thirteenth Amendment] may be primary and direct in its character; for the amendment is not a mere prohibition of State laws establishing or upholding slavery, but an absolute declaration that slavery or involuntary servitude shall not exist in any part of the United States." 109 U.S. 3 at 20. In that character, the Thirteenth Amendment banned the badges and incidents of slavery, one of which was contractual incapacity.
157. Jones v. Alfred H. Mayer Co., 392 U.S. 409, 438–442 (1968). Justice Harlan, joined by White, dissented in a lengthy opinion.
158. 392 U.S. 446.
159. Sullivan v. Little Hunting Park, 396 U.S. 229 (1969).
160. However, the contemporary academic reception of Jones was cool. Gerhard Casper went so far as to claim that the 1968 Fair Housing Act limited the 1866 act: "Jones v. Mayer: Clio, Bemused and Confused Muse," 1968 *Supreme Court Review* 89. Fortunately, Casper's view found no takers.

161. 384 U.S. 641, 653 (1966). See generally William D. Araiza, *Enforcing the Equal Protection Clause: Congressional Power, Judicial Doctrine, and Constitutional Law* (New York: New York University Press, 2015); on the Morgan case specifically, 94–97.
162. 17 U.S. at 421: "Let the end be legitimate, let it be within the scope of the constitution, and all means which are appropriate, which are plainly adapted to that end, which are not prohibited, but consist with the letter and spirit of the constitution, are constitutional."
163. Harlan was joined in this dissent by Justice Stewart. The Harlan/Stewart dissenting opinion was published separately as a memorandum opinion in the Morgan case and its companion, Cardona v. Power, 384 U.S. 672 (1966) at 384 U.S. 659.
164. 384 U.S. 666.
165. 384 U.S. 667–668.
166. 521 U.S. 535.
167. Jones v. Alfred H. Mayer Co., 392 U.S. 409, 439, 441 (1968).
168. 403 U.S. 88, 102 (1971).
169. 427 U.S. 160 (1976).
170. On rights and duties as "jural correlatives," see Wesley Hohfeld, "Some Fundamental Legal Conceptions as Applied in Judicial Reasoning," 23 *Yale Law Journal* 16 (1913).
171. The parental right to control the upbringing and education of their children dates back to Meyer v. Nebraska, 262 U.S. 390 (1923) and Pierce v. Society of Sisters, 268 U.S. 510 (1925).
172. Runyon, 427 U.S. at 178.
173. Michael Ollove, "Up in Arms," *Baltimore Sun*, June 3, 2001, at https://www.orlandosentinel.com/news/os-xpm-2001-06-03-0106030282-story.html.
174. Patterson v. McLean Credit Union, 485 U.S. 617, 619 (1988).
175. E.g.: Peter B. Bayer, "Patterson and Civil Rights: What Rough Beast Slouches towards Bethlehem to Be Born?," 21 *Columbia Human Rights Law Review* 401 (1990); Camille Townsend, "Stare Decisis and the Supreme Court's Decision to Reconsider Runyon v. McCrary," 20 *Loyola University of Chicago Law Journal* 197 (1988); 'Play It Again, Says the Court," *Time*, May 9, 1988, 73.
176. 109 U.S. 3 (1883).
177. 109 U.S. 3, 11 (1883). Bradley elaborated: "Civil rights, such as are guaranteed by the Constitution against State aggression, cannot be impaired by the wrongful acts of individuals, unsupported by State authority in the shape of laws, customs, or judicial or executive proceedings. The wrongful act of an individual, unsupported by any such authority, is simply a private wrong, or a crime of that individual; an invasion of the rights of the injured party, it is true, whether they affect his person, his property, or his reputation; but if not sanctioned in some way by the State, or not done under State authority, his rights remain in full force, and may presumably be vindicated by resort to the laws of the State for redress."
178. Anon., "Developments in the Law: State Action and the Public/Private Distinction," 123 *Harvard Law Review* 1248–1266 (2010).
179. Alan Freeman and Elizabeth Mensch provided a trenchant critique in "The Public-Private Distinction in American Law and Life," 36 *Buffalo Law Review* 237 (1987).
180. Francisco M. Ugarte, "Reconstruction Redux: Rehnquist, Morrison, and the Civil Rights Cases," 41 *Harvard Civil Rights–Civil Liberties Law Review* 481 (2006); Ira Nerkin, "A New Deal for the Protection of Fourteenth Amendment Rights: Challenging the Doctrinal Bases of the Civil Rights Cases and State Action Theory," 12 *Harvard Civil Rights–Civil Liberties Law Review* 297 (1977).
181. Charles L. Black Jr., "Foreword: 'State Action,' Equal Protection, and California's Proposition 14," 81 *Harvard Law Review* 69, 70 (1967); Erwin Chemerinsky, "Rethinking State Action," 80 *Northwestern University Law Review* 503 (1985).
182. Black, "Foreword: 'State Action,'" 95. Accord, Henry J. Friendly "The Public-Private Penumbra, Fourteen Years Later," 130 *University of Pennsylvania Law Review* 1289, 1290 (1982).
183. 321 U.S. 649 (1944).
184. 344 U.S. 1 (1948).
185. 365 U.S. 715, 724, 722 (1961).
186. Thomas P. Lewis, "Burton v. Wilmington Parking Authority—a Case without Precedent," 61 *Columbia Law Review* 1458 (1961).
187. Daniel M. HoSang, *Racial Propositions: Ballot Initiatives and the Making of Postwar California* (Berkeley: University of California Press, 2010), ch. 3, "Get Back Your Rights: Fair Housing

and the Right to Discriminate, 1960-1972"; Lisa McGirr, *Suburban Warriors: The Origins of the New American Right* (Princeton: Princeton University Press, 2001), 133, 182-185; Wiecek, "Supreme Court and Residential Segregation," 64-69.
188. The people of California can amend their constitution by initiative, which needs only a simple majority to take effect.
189. Quoted in Christopher W. Schmidt, "Defending the Right to Discriminate: The Libertarian Challenge to the Civil Rights Movement," in Sally E. Hadden and Patricia H. Minter, eds., *Signposts: New Directions in Southern Legal History* (Athens: University of Georgia Press, 2013), 438.
190. Norwood v. Harrison, 413 U.S. 455, 470 (1973).
191. Mulkey v. Reitman, 64 Cal.2d 529, 413 P.2d 825 (1966).
192. See the critiques in Harold W. Horowitz and Kenneth L. Karst, "The Proposition Fourteen Cases: Justice in Search of a Justification," 14 *UCLA Law Review* 37 (1966); Karst and Horowitz, "Reitman v. Mulkey: A Telophase of Equal Protection," 1967 *Supreme Court Review* 39.
193. 387 U.S. 369, 379, 381 (1967). Justices Harlan, Black, Clark, and Stewart dissented in a persuasive critique by Harlan, which however was weakened by his disingenuous claim that the plaintiffs had not shown discriminatory purpose or effect behind Prop 14.
194. For a defense of White's opinion in Reitman v. Mulkey and a thoroughgoing critique of the state action doctrine, see Charles L. Black, "Foreword: 'State Action,' Equal Protection, and California's Proposition 14," 81 *Harvard Law Review* 69 (1967).
195. 387 U.S. 381-387.
196. 393 U.S. 385, 391 (1969).
197. Derrick Bell, "The Referendum: Democracy's Barrier to Racial Equality," 60 *Ohio State Law Journal* 399 (1999).
198. Moose Lodge No. 107 v. Irvis, 407 U.S. 163 (1972).
199. Jackson v. Metropolitan Edison Co., 419 U.S. 315 (1974).
200. Flagg Bros. Inc. v. Brooks, 436 U.S. 149 (1978).
201. Blum v. Yaretsky, 457 U.S. 991 (1982); Rendell-Baker v. Kohn, 457 U.S. 830 (1982).
202. DeShaney v. Winnebago County Social Services Dept., 489 U.S. 189 (1989).
203. McCulloch v. Maryland, 17 U.S. (4 Wheat.) 316, 411.
204. Michal R. Belknap, "The Legal Legacy of Lemuel Penn," 25 *Howard Law Journal* 467 (1982).
205. Section 241 is derived from section 6 of the 1870 Enforcement Act.
206. "The Congress shall have power to enforce, by appropriate legislation, the provisions of this article."
207. 383 U.S. 745 (1966).
208. 383 U.S. at 762. Clark was joined by Black and Abe Fortas.
209. 383 U.S. at 783. Brennan was joined by Warren and Douglas.
210. However, a generation later in United States v. Morrison, 529 U.S. 598, 623 (2000) Chief Justice Rehnquist explicitly rejected any reading of the Brennan or Clark opinions in *Guest* that might call the *Civil Rights Cases* into question.
211. 383 U.S. 763.
212. 383 U.S. 787 (1966).
213. 365 U.S. 167 (1961).
214. *Black's Law Dictionary*, 11th ed. (St. Paul: Thomson, 2019): "constitutional tort: A violation of one's constitutional rights by a government officer, redressable by a civil action filed directly against the officer."
215. 42 U.S.C. sec. 1983 is derived from sec. 1 of the 1871 Ku Klux Klan Act.
216. Section 1983's criminal counterpart, 18 U.S.C. sec. 242, derived from section 2 of 1866 Civil Rights Act, imposes *criminal* liability for deprivation of rights done under color of state authority.
217. 393 U.S. 544, 569 (1969).
218. 369 U.S. 186, 300 (1962).
219. 369 U.S. 300: "This is not a case in which a State has, through a device however oblique and sophisticated, denied Negroes or Jews or redheaded persons a vote, or given them only a third or a sixth of a vote."
220. 377 U.S. 533 (1964).
221. Voting Rights Act of 1965, Pub. L. No. 89-110, 79 Stat. 437, also known at the time as the Civil Rights Act of 1965. On enforcement of the statute, see Ari Berman, *Give Us the Ballot: The Modern Struggle for Voting Rights in America* (New York: Farrar, Strauss and Giroux, 2015).

222. In Lassiter v. Northampton County Election Board, 360 U.S. 45, 53 (1959), the Court had upheld the constitutionality of literacy tests, but added a cautionary note: "a literacy test, fair on its face, may be employed to perpetuate that discrimination which the Fifteenth Amendment was designed to uproot. No such influence is charged here."
223. Christopher W. Schmidt reviews constitutional development on the subject of Congress's authority in "Section 5's Forgotten Years: Congressional Power to Enforce the Fourteenth Amendment before Katzenbach v. Morgan," 113 *Northwestern University Law Review* 47 (2018). See William D. Araiza, *Enforcing the Equal Protection Clause: Congressional Power, Judicial Doctrine, and Constitutional Law* (New York: New York University Press, 2015), 94–97.
224. 383 U.S. 301, 324, 328 (1966). See Richard M. Valelly, ed., *The Voting Rights Act: Securing the Ballot* (Washington, DC: CQ Press, 2006).
225. "Section 2. The Congress shall have power to enforce this article by appropriate legislation."
226. The leading case on point is Coyle v. Smith, 221 U.S. 559 (1911). The Roberts Court disregarded that interpretation in *Shelby County v. Holder* (2013).
227. Lassiter v. Northampton County Board of Elections, 360 U.S. 45, 53, 51 (1959).
228. Voting Rights Amendments Act of 1970, Pub. L. No. 91-285, 84 Stat. 314, 315 (1970).
229. 400 U.S. 112 (1970).
230. 395 U.S. 285 (1969).
231. Owen Fiss, "The Accumulation of Disadvantages," 106 *California Law Review* 1945, 1946 (2018).
232. 383 U.S. 663, 665, 669, 685–686 (1966).
233. Peggy Pascoe, *What Comes Naturally: Miscegenation and the Making of Race in America* (New York: Oxford University Press, 2009), 224–284; Peter Wallenstein, *Tell the Court I Love My Wife: Race, Marriage, and Law. An American History* (New York: St. Martin's, 2002), 189–231; Fay Botham, *Almighty God Created the Races: Christianity, Interracial Marriage, and American Law* (Chapel Hill: University of North Carolina Press, 2009).
234. Charles F. Robinson, *Dangerous Liaisons: Sex and Love in the Segregated South* (Fayetteville: University of Arkansas Press, 2003).
235. Winthrop D. Jordan, *White over Black: American Attitudes toward the Negro, 1550–1812* (Chapel Hill: University of North Carolina Press, 1968), 78.
236. William M. Wiecek, "The Statutory Law of Slavery and Race in Thirteen Mainland Colonies of British America," 34 *William and Mary Quarterly* 258–280 (1977).
237. 367 U.S. 497, 542 (1961).
238. 106 U.S. 583 (1883). See Julie Novkov, *Racial Union: Law, Intimacy, and the White State in Alabama, 1865–1954* (Ann Arbor: University of Michigan Press, 2009), on the long shadow of the miscegenation laws in confirming white supremacy and constituting the state.
239. 350 U.S. 985 (1956).
240. Gregory M. Dorr, "Principled Expediency: Eugenics, Naim v. Naim, and the Supreme Court," 42 *American Journal of Legal History* 119 (1998).
241. The Virginia Court of Appeals, the state's highest court, refused to comply with the Supreme Court's instructions on remand to return the case to lower courts for clarification of a technical point of state law. This bordered on insolence and in the heated climate of the times was interpreted as judicial nullification.
242. Extrajudicial comment quoted in Klarman, *From Jim Crow to Civil Rights*, 322.
243. Perez v. Sharp, 32 Cal.2d 711, 198 P.2d 17 (1948).
244. 379 U.S. 184, 191–192, 196, 198 (1964). See Ariela R. Dubler, "From McLaughlin v. Florida to Lawrence v. Texas: Sexual Freedom and the Road to Marriage," 106 *Columbia Law Review* 1165 (2006).
245. He would repeat this point in a concurring opinion in *Loving v. Virginia*.
246. 388 U.S. 1, 11 (1967). See Rose Cuison Villazor and Kevin N. Maillard, eds. *Loving v. Virginia in a Post-racial World: Rethinking Race, Sex, and Marriage* (New York: Cambridge University Press, 2012); Dorothy E. Roberts, "Loving v. Virginia as a Civil Rights Decision," 59 *New York Law School Law Review* 175 (2014).
247. Their one-year sentence to prison was suspended on condition that they leave the commonwealth and not return for twenty-five years.
248. Quoted at 388 U.S. 3.
249. Frances I. Ansley, "Stirring the Ashes, "Race, Class, and the Future of Civil Rights Scholarship," 74 *Cornell Law Review* 993, 1024 (1989).
250. 466 U.S. 429, 433–434 (1984).

Chapter 8

1. Earl M. Maltz, *The Coming of the Nixon Court: The 1972 Term and the Transformation of American Law* (Lawrence: University Press of Kansas, 2016).
2. October Term 1971 ran from October 1971 through June 1972.
3. *Grutter v. Bollinger*, 539 U.S. 306, 377 (2003). This statement demonstrates that Justice Thomas does not understand either what institutional racism is or what conspiracy theories are.
4. David Frum, *How We Got Here: The 70s. The Decade that Brought You Modern Life (for Better or Worse)* (New York: Basic Books, 2000).
5. The linguist John McWhorter persuasively draws this distinction between racism as state of mind and racism as manifested in its second-order effects in "'Racism' Has Too Many Definitions. We Need Another Term," *New York Times*, May 17, 2022.
6. Clark v. Community for Creative Non-violence, 468 U.S. 288, 314 n. 14 (1984) (Marshall, J. dissenting).
7. This introduction to structural racism draws on ideas sketched in William M. Wiecek, "Structural Racism and the Law in America Today: An Introduction," 100 *Kentucky Law Journal* 1, 6–19 (2011), and in Wiecek and Judy L. Hamilton, "Beyond the Civil Rights Act of 1964: Confronting Structural Racism in the Workplace," 74 *Louisiana Law Review* 1095, 1111–1125 (2014). This introduction selectively cites only a few of the most important secondary social-science sources compiled in those two articles.
8. Wiecek, "Structural Racism and the Law," 5 (paraphrasing various social science authorities quoted in that article).
9. Eduardo Bonilla-Silva, "Rethinking Racism: Toward a Structural Interpretation," 62 *American Sociological Review* 465–480 (June 1997); Lawrence Bobo et al., "From Jim Crow Racism to Laissez-Faire Racism: An Essay on the Transformation of Racial Attitudes in America," in Wendy F. Katkin et al., eds., *Beyond Pluralism: The Conception of Groups and Group Identities in America* (Urbana: University of Illinois Press, 1998), 182–220; Devah Pager and Hana Shepherd, "The Sociology of Discrimination: Racial Discrimination in Employment, Housing, Credit, and Consumer Markets," 34 *Annual Review of Sociology* 198 (2008); Fred L. Pincus, "Discrimination Comes in Many Forms—Individual, Institutional, and Structural," 40 *American Behavioral Scientist* 186–194 (1996).
10. Robert P. Baird, "The Invention of Whiteness: The Long History of a Dangerous Idea," *The Guardian*, April 20, 2021.
11. Rebecca M. Blank, Marilyn Dabady, and Constance F. Citro, "Measuring Racial Discrimination: Panel on Methods for Assessing Discrimination," Washington, DC, National Research Council, 2004, 4–5, 11, http://books.nap.edu/catalog.php?record_id=10887; john a. powell, "Structural Racism: Building Upon the Insights of John Calmore," 86 *North Carolina Law Review* 791 (2008).
12. Kimberlé Crenshaw quoted in Jacey Fortin, "Critical Race Theory: A Brief History," *New York Times*, July 27, 2021.
13. Christine Hauser, "Merriam-Webster Revises 'Racism' Entry after Missouri Woman Asks for Changes," *New York Times*, November 1, 2021.
14. https://www.merriam-webster.com/dictionary/racism#usage-1.
15. Gunnar Myrdal, *An American Dilemma: The Negro Problem and Modern Democracy* (New York: Harper, 1944), 75–77.
16. George C. Galster, "A Cumulative Causation Model of the Underclass: Implications for Urban Economic Development Policy," in George C. Galster and Edward W. Hill, eds., *The Metropolis in Black and White* (New Brunswick: Center for Urban Policy Research, 1992), 190–215.
17. Fred L. Pincus, "From Individual to Structural Discrimination," in Fred L. Pincus and Howard J. Ehrlich, eds., *Race and Ethnic Conflict: Contending Views on Prejudice, Discrimination and Ethnoviolence* (London: Routledge, 1994), 120–124.
18. On the impact of such traditional racism, see Eduardo Porter, *American Poison: How Racial Hostility Destroyed Our Promise* (New York: Knopf, 2020).
19. David Wellman, "Unconscious Racism, Social Cognition Theory, and the Legal Intent Doctrine: The Neuron Fires Next Time," in Hernan Vera and Joe R. Feagin, eds., *Handbook of the Sociology of Racial and Ethnic Relations* (Cham: Springer, 2007), 39–65.
20. Barbara Trepagnier, *Silent Racism: How Well-Meaning White People Perpetuate the Racial Divide* (London: Routledge, 2006), 3–4. "Institutional racism" often appears as a synonym for structural racism.

21. 163 U.S. 537, 559 (1896).
22. This color-blindness segment is drawn from William M. Wiecek, "The United States Supreme Court and Residential Segregation: 'Slavery Unwilling to Die,'" 3 *Journal of Law, Property & Society* 36, 120 (2017).
23. Adarand Constructors v. Pena, 515 U.S. 200, 240 (1995) (Thomas, J. concurring).
24. 551 U.S. 701 (2007).
25. 551 U.S. at 772.
26. To cite only a few of these refutations: Kimberlé W. Crenshaw, "Unmasking Colorblindness in the Law: Lessons from the Formation of Critical Race Theory," and George Lipsitz, "The Sounds of Silence: How Race Neutrality Preserves White Supremacy," in Kimberlé W. Crenshaw et al., eds. *Seeing Race Again: Countering Colorblindness Across the Disciplines* (Berkeley: University of California Press, 2019), 52–84, 23–51; David A. Strauss, "The Myth of Colorblindness," 1986 *Supreme Court Review* 99 (1986); Neal Gotanda, "Our Constitution Is Color-Blind: A Critique," 44 *Stanford Law Review* 1 (1991); J. Morgan Kousser, *Colorblind Injustice: Minority Voting Rights and the Undoing of the Second Reconstruction* (Chapel Hill: University of North Carolina Press, 1999); Michael K. Brown et al., *Whitewashing Race: The Myth of a Colorblind Society* (Berkeley: University of California Press, 2003); Jerry Kang and Kristin Lane, "Seeing through Colorblindness: Implicit Bias and the Law," 58 *UCLA Law Review* 465 (2010).
27. Anthony G. Greenwald and Linda Hamilton Krieger, "Implicit Bias: Scientific Foundations," 94 *California Law Review* 945 (2006).
28. Devah Pager and Hana Shepherd, "The Sociology of Discrimination: Racial Discrimination in Employment, Housing, Credit, and Consumer Markets," 34 *Annual Review of Sociology* 181, 198 (2008).
29. 426 U.S. 229, 242 (1976).
30. Stephen J. Gould, *The Mismeasure of Man*, 2nd ed. (New York: Norton, 1996).
31. However, there are troubling signs that scientific racism is currently being reinvented through genomics to reaffirm racial classifications. This new genetic understanding of race focuses on molecular biology and biotechnology but obscures the impact of racism on American society. Dorothy E. Roberts, *Fatal Invention: How Science, Politics, and Big Business Re-create Race in the Twenty-First Century* (New York: New Press, 2011); Rob DeSalle and Ian Tattersall, *Troublesome Science: The Misuse of Genetics and Genomics in Understanding Race* (New York: Columbia University Press, 2018); Megan Gannon, "Race Is a Social Construct, Scientists Argue," *Scientific American*, February 4, 2016, discussing Michael Yudell et al., "Taking Race Out of Human Genetics," *Science*, February 5, 2016, 564–565.
32. "New AMA Policies Recognize Race as a Social, Not Biological, Construct" (AMA press release November 16, 2020), https://www.ama-assn.org/press-center/press-releases/new-ama-policies-recognize-race-social-not-biological-construct. Accord, American Anthropological Association, "AAA Statement on Race" (1998): "Historical research has shown that the idea of 'race' has always carried more meanings than mere physical differences; indeed, physical variations in the human species have no meaning except the social ones that humans put on them" at https://www.americananthro.org/ConnectWithAAA/Content.aspx?ItemNumber=2583.
33. Michael Omi and Howard Winant, *Racial Formation in the United States: From the 1960s to the 1980s*, 3rd ed. (New York: Routledge, 2015).
34. Quoted in Baird, "The Invention of Whiteness."
35. Kimberlé W. Crenshaw, "Race, Reform, and Retrenchment: Transformation and Legitimation in Antidiscrimination Law," 101 *Harvard Law Review* 1331, 1335, 1385 (1988).
36. George M. Frederickson, *The Arrogance of Race: Historical Perspectives on Slavery, Racism and Social Inequality* (Middletown: Wesleyan University Press, 1988). For one example of such reactive pseudoscience: Richard Herrnstein and Charles Murray, *The Bell Curve: Intelligence and Class Structure in American Life* (New York: Simon & Schuster, 1994).
37. I use the term "advantage" in preference to "privilege." The term "privilege" often provokes defensive emotional reactions on the part of those to whom it is imputed, which interferes with productive discourse. "Advantage" seems for some reason to be more emollient.
38. In May 2020, Crayola, the world's leading crayon-maker, announced release of a twenty-four-unit box of crayons representing all the skin tones of humanity. "Crayola Unveils New Packs of Crayons to Reflect World's Skin Tones," https://www.cnn.com/2020/05/22/us/crayola-skin-tone-crayons-trnd/index.html. The pinkish crayon called "flesh" is no more.
39. The classic legal statement of this idea was Chief Justice John Marshall's justification of the appropriation of Indian lands in *Johnson v. M'Intosh*, 21 U.S. (8 Wheat.) 543, 590–592 (1823).

Rationalizing the appropriation after the conquest, Marshall conceded that though the land theft of an entire continent "may be opposed to natural right and to the usage of civilized nations," "it may perhaps be supported by reason, and certainly cannot be rejected by Courts of justice." "It becomes the law of the land, and cannot be questioned." The "reason" he offered was that the native peoples were "fierce savages."

40. Justin C. Mueller, "America's Herrenvolk Democracy Is a Social Democracy for the White Majority," http://www.milwaukeeindependent.com/articles/americas-herrenvolk-democracy-social-democracy-white-majority/+. The term "Herrenvolk democracy" seems to have been coined by Pierre L. Van Den Berghe, *Race and Racism: A Comparative Perspective* (New York: Wiley, 1967), 18, 77, 88.
41. Scalia memorandum quoted in Dennis D. Dorin, "Far Right of the Mainstream: Racism, Rights and Remedies from the Perspective of Justice Antonin Scalia's McCleskey Memorandum," 45 *Mercer Law Review* 1035, 1038 (1994).
42. Paula S. Rothenberg, *Race, Class and Gender in the United States: An Integrated Study* (New York: Worth, 1998), 15; Omi and Winant, *Racial Formation in the United States*.
43. David R. Roediger, *Working toward Whiteness: How America's Immigrants Became White: The Strange Journey from Ellis Island to the Suburbs* (New York: Basic Books, 2005), 124.
44. Kimberlé Crenshaw, "Mapping the Margins: Intersectionality, Identity Politics, and Violence against Women of Color," 43 *Stanford Law Review* 1241 (1993); Crenshaw, *On Intersectionality: Essential Writings* (New York: New Press, 2019); Jerome McCristal Culp, "Colorblind Remedies and the Intersectionality of Oppression: Policy Arguments Masquerading as Moral Claims," 69 *NYU Law Review* 162 (1994).
45. Robert D. Bullard, "Environmental Justice in the 21st Century: Race Still Matters," 49.3–4 *Phylon* 151–171 (2001).
46. Dorothy A. Brown, *The Whiteness of Wealth: How the Tax System Impoverishes Black Americans—and How We Can Fix It* (New York: Crown, 2021), 20–22, 29–63, 218–220; see esp. the illustration on p. 45.
47. The number of pages in the Internal Revenue Code is disputed and strangely difficult to resolve definitively. See the discussion in Dylan Mathews, "The Myth of the 70,000-Page Federal Tax Code" (2017) at https://www.vox.com/policy-and-politics/2017/3/29/15109214/tax-code-page-count-complexity-simplification-reform-ways-means from which the number twenty-six hundred is taken.
48. https://www.banking.senate.gov/imo/media/doc/Rice%20Testimony%204-13-21.pdf.
49. *"To Secure These Rights": The Report of the President's Committee on Civil Rights* (Washington: GPO, 1947). See generally Michael R. Gardner, *Harry Truman and Civil Rights: Moral Courage and Political Risks* (Carbondale: Southern Illinois University Press, 2002).
50. Louisiana, Mississippi, Alabama, and South Carolina, plus one Tennessee electoral vote.
51. Barry Goldwater, *The Conscience of a Conservative* (New York: Hillman, 1960), 32, 37–38; Rick Perlstein, *Before the Storm: Barry Goldwater and the Unmaking of the American Consensus* (New York: Basic Books, 2001), 43–68.
52. Goldwater quoted in Dan T. Carter, *The Politics of Rage: George Wallace, the Origins of the New Conservatism, and the Transformation of Southern Politics*, 2nd ed. (Baton Rouge: Louisiana State University Press, 2000), 218.
53. Ian Haney-Lopez, *Dog Whistle Politics: How Coded Racial Appeals Have Reinvented Racism and Wrecked the Middle Class* (New York: Oxford University Press, 2014), 13–34.
54. William Rusher, "Crossroads for the GOP," *National Review*, February 12, 1963.
55. Robert D. Novak, *The Agony of the GOP* (New York: Macmillan, 1965), 179.
56. Goldwater speech 1964, quoted in Theodore H. White, *The Making of the President 1964* (New York: Atheneum, 1965), 349.
57. Herbert Wechsler, "Toward Neutral Principles of Constitutional Law," 73 *Harvard Law Review* 1, 34 (1959).
58. NAACP v. Alabama ex rel. Patterson, 357 U.S. 449 (1958); Bates v. Little Rock, 361 U.S. 516 (1961); NAACP v. Claiborne Hardware Co., 458 U.S. 886 (1982).
59. On the Republican espousal of racial anti-egalitarianism, see Eric Schickler, *Racial Realignment: The Transformation of American Liberalism, 1932–1965* (Princeton: Princeton University Press, 2016), 237–270. This transformation is a leitmotif in Rick Perlstein's four-volume study of modern conservatism: *Before the Storm*; *Nixonland: The Rise of a President and the Fracturing of America* (New York: Simon & Schuster, 2008); *The Invisible Bridge: The Fall of Nixon and the Rise of Reagan* (New York: Scribner, 2014); and *Reaganland: America's Right Turn 1976–1980* (New York: Simon & Schuster, 2020).

60. Louisiana, Mississippi, Alabama, South Carolina (the Dixiecrats' 1948 states), and Georgia, plus, of course, Arizona.
61. John A. Jenkins, *The Partisan: A Life of William Rehnquist* (New York: Public Affairs, 2012), 72–74. Rehnquist was seconded by Robert Bork, then at Yale Law School, who contributed a seventy-five-page "brief" to Goldwater arguing that the Civil Rights Bill was unconstitutional. See Perlstein, *Before the Storm*, 363–364. Goldwater's attitude was grounded in a generalized western Jeffersonian hostility to federal power. Christopher Shepard, "A True Jeffersonian: The Western Conservative Principles of Barry Goldwater and His Vote against the Civil Rights Act of 1964," 49.1 *Journal of the West* 34–40 (2010).
62. Lincoln to Henry L. Pierce, April 6, 1859, in Roy P. Basler, ed., *The Collected Works of Abraham Lincoln* (New Brunswick: Rutgers University Press, 1959), 3:375.
63. Discussed above in chapter 7.
64. Quoted in Dan T. Carter, *From George Wallace to Newt Gingrich: Race in the Conservative Counterrevolution, 1963–1994* (Baton Rouge: Louisiana State University Press, 1996), xiii.
65. Dan T. Carter, *The Politics of Rage: George Wallace, the Origins of the New Conservatism, and the Transformation of Southern Politics*, 2nd ed. (Baton Rouge: Louisiana State University Press, 2000), 195–225. See also Carter, *From George Wallace to Newt Gingrich*, 1–23.
66. Carter, *Politics of Rage*, 21.
67. John Anderson, "Former Governor Shaped Politics of Alabama, Nation," *Huntsville* [Alabama] *Times*, September 14, 1998, A8.
68. Thomas J. Sugrue, *The Origins of the Urban Crisis: Race and Inequality in Postwar Detroit* (Princeton: Princeton University Press, 1993); Stephen G. Meyer, *As Long as They Don't Move Next Door: Segregation and Racial Conflict in American Neighborhoods* (Lanham: Rowman & Littlefield, 2000).
69. On the long-term significance of the 1964 election for both parties, see Gary A, Donaldson, *Liberalism's Last Hurrah: The Presidential Campaign of 1964* (New York: Routledge, 2002).
70. Michael Lind, *Made in Texas: George W. Bush and the Southern Takeover of American Politics* (New York: Basic Books, 2003); Carter, *Politics of Rage*, 16, 324–370; Peter Applebome, *Dixie Rising: How the South Is Shaping American Values, Politics, and Culture* (San Diego: Harcourt Brace, 1997).
71. Mary C. Brennan, *Turning Right in the Sixties: The Conservative Capture of the GOP* (Chapel Hill: University of North Carolina Press, 1995); William C. Berman, *America's Right Turn from Nixon to Clinton*, 2nd ed. (Baltimore: Johns Hopkins University Press, 1998). On the rise of conservativism through the last century, see Matthew Continetti, *The Right: The Hundred-Year War for American Conservatism* (New York: Basic Books, 2022).
72. Geoffrey Kabaservice, *Rule and Ruin: The Downfall of Moderation and the Destruction of the Republican Party, from Eisenhower to the Tea Party* (New York: Oxford University Press, 2012).
73. Timothy N. Thurber, "Goldwaterism Triumphant? Race and the Republican Party, 1965–1968," 7 *Journal of the Historical Society* 349 (2007).
74. The phrase "Southern Strategy" is a misnomer. The strategy had a nationwide appeal, not just sectional, and was not confined to the single issue of public-school desegregation. Haney-Lopez, *Dog Whistle Politics*, 26–33, demonstrates the inadequacy of the phrase. "Racial strategy" might have been more accurate. But the phrase "Southern Strategy" does have the virtue of locating its origins in the relationship between the GOP and the white southern electorate in the 1960s.
75. Angie Maxwell and Todd Shields, *The Long Southern Strategy: How Chasing White Voters in the South Changed American Politics* (New York: Oxford University Press, 2019).
76. George B. Tindall, "Southern Strategy: A Historical Perspective," 48 *North Carolina History Review* 126 (1971); Vincent P. De Santis, *Republicans Face the Southern Question: The New Departure Years, 1877–1897* (Baltimore: Johns Hopkins University Press, 1959); Edward O. Frantz, *The Door of Hope: Republican Presidents and the First Southern Strategy, 1877–1933* (Gainesville: University Press of Florida, 2011); Bruce H. Kalk, *The Origins of the Southern Strategy: Two-Party Competition in South Carolina, 1950–1972* (Lanham: Lexington Books, 2001).
77. Joseph A. Aistrup, *The Southern Strategy Revisited: Republican Top-Down Advancement in the South* (Lexington: University Press of Kentucky, 2015).
78. Matthew D. Lassiter, *The Silent Majority: Suburban Politics in the Sunbelt South* (Princeton: Princeton University Press, 2006); Lassiter and Kevin Kruse, "The Bulldozer Revolution: Suburbs and Southern History since World War II," *Journal of Southern History* 75 (2009), 699;

Glenn Feldman, *Painting Dixie Red: When, Where, Why, and How the South Became Republican* (Gainesville: University Press of Florida, 2011).
79. Donald T. Critchlow, *Phyllis Schlafly and Grassroots Conservatism: A Woman's Crusade* (Princeton: Princeton University Press, 2005).
80. Kevin Kruse, *White Flight: Atlanta and the Making of Modern Conservatism* (Princeton: Princeton University Press, 2005).
81. Lisa McGirr, *Suburban Warriors: The Origins of the New American Right* (Princeton: Princeton University Press, 2001). Heather Cox Richardson emphasizes the connections between the Old South and the frontier West in *How the South Won the Civil War: Oligarchy, Democracy, and the Continuing Fight for the Soul of America* (New York: Oxford University Press, 2020).
82. Jefferson Cowie, *Freedom's Dominion: A Saga of Resistance to Federal Power* (New York: Basic Books, 2022) (winner of the Pulitzer Prize in History 2023).
83. On northern resistance to school integration, long antedating *Brown v. Board of Education*, see Davison M. Douglas, *Jim Crow Moves North: The Battle over Northern School Segregation, 1865–1954* (Cambridge: Cambridge University Press, 2005), 123–166; Sugrue, *Origins of the Urban Crisis*, 209–258.
84. "1966 Civil Rights Act dies in Senate," *CQ Almanac 1966*, https://library.cqpress.com/cqalmanac/document.php?id=cqal66-1301767.
85. Pub.L. 89-10, 79 Stat. 27.
86. This marked a turnabout in federal education policy. Until explicitly countermanded under the authority of the 1964 Civil Rights Act, federal bureaucrats in the Office of Education (subcabinet predecessor to the Department of Education) spent federal funds to *maintain* segregation in schools and resisted efforts to change that policy. Joy Milligan, "Subsidizing Segregation," 104 *Virginia Law Review* 847 (2018).
87. Chronicled by a chastened Office of Civil Rights head Leon Panetta and Peter Gall in *Bring Us Together: The Nixon Team and the Civil Rights Retreat* (Philadelphia: Lippincott, 1971). Nixon fired Panetta within a year.
88. Crawford v. Los Angeles Board of Education, 458 U.S. 527 (1982). Matthew F. Delmont, *Why Busing Failed: Race, Media, and the National Resistance to School Desegregation* (Oakland: University of California Press, 2016).
89. Perlstein, *Nixonland*, 166.
90. Julian Zelizer, "50 Years Ago, Americans Fired Their Dysfunctional Congress," *The Atlantic*, January 21, 2015.
91. Nixon, however, denied that he ever had a Southern Strategy based on a sectional appeal to white racist sentiment. Joan Hoff, *Nixon Reconsidered* (New York: Basic Books, 1995), 79. That self-serving claim is refuted by the record of both his administrations.
92. Rick Perlstein evaluated the significance of this underappreciated figure in "The Southern Strategist," *New York Times*, December 30, 2007.
93. Perlstein, *Nixonland*, 283; Stanley I. Kutler, *The Wars of Watergate: The Last Crisis of Richard Nixon* (New York: Norton, 1990), 64.
94. Quoted in Bruce H. Kalk, "The Machiavellian Nominations: Richard Nixon's Southern Strategy and the Struggle for the Supreme Court, 1968–1970," PhD dissertation, University of North Carolina at Chapel Hill (1992), 58.
95. Perlstein, *Nixonland*, 283. Harry S. Dent, *The Prodigal South Returns to Power* (New York: Wiley, 1978), 82.
96. Green v. County School Board of New Kent County, 391 U.S. 430 (1968).
97. Kevin J. McMahon, *Nixon's Court: His Challenge to Judicial Liberalism and Its Political Consequences* (Chicago: University of Chicago Press, 2011), 13.
98. Quoted in Perlstein, *Nixonland*, 148.
99. Chris Hickman, "Courting the Right: Richard Nixon's 1968 Campaign against the Warren Court," 36 *Journal of Supreme Court History* 287 (2011).
100. Nixon speech to southern delegates to 1968 GOP convention, quoted in McMahon, *Nixon's Court*, 30.
101. Quoted in Michael J. Graetz and Linda Greenhouse, *The Burger Court and the Rise of the Judicial Right* (New York: Simon & Schuster, 2016), 4.
102. Quoted in McMahon, *Nixon's Court*, 120.
103. Don Oberdorfer, "Ex-Democrat, Ex-Dixiecrat, Today's Nixiecrat," *New York Times Magazine*, October 6, 1968.

104. All Nixon quotes from Perlstein, *Nixonland*, 300, 306.
105. Louis Menand, "Been There," *New Yorker*, January 8, 2018, 73.
106. The literature confirming this point is voluminous: Lawrence O'Donnell, *Playing with Fire: The 1968 Election and the Transformation of American Politics* (New York: Penguin, 2017); Michael A. Cohen, *American Maelstrom: The 1968 Election and the Politics of Division* (New York: Oxford University Press, 2016); Michael Nelson, *Resilient America: Electing Nixon in 1968, Channeling Dissent, and Dividing Government* (Lawrence: University Press of Kansas, 2014); Robert C. Cottrell and Blaine T. Browne, *1968: The Rise and Fall of the New American Revolution* (Lanham: Rowman & Littlefield, 2018); Theodore H. White, *The Making of the President 1968* (New York: Atheneum, 1969); Lewis L. Gould, *1968: The Election That Changed America* (Chicago: Ivan R. Dee, 1993); Lewis Chester et al., *An American Melodrama: The Presidential Campaign of 1968* (New York: Dell, 1969).
107. Kersch, *Conservatives and the Constitution*, vii; Jeremy D. Mayer, "Nixon Rides the Backlash to Victory: Racial Politics in the 1968 Campaign," 64 *The Historian* 351 (2002).
108. Harry Dent to Richard M. Nixon, October 13. 1969, quoted in Mayer, "Nixon Rides the Backlash to Victory," 365–366.
109. Kevin Phillips, *The Emerging Republican Majority* (New York: Doubleday, 1969), 9.
110. James Boyd, "Nixon's Southern Strategy: It's All in the Charts," *New York Times*, May 17, 1970.
111. H. R. Haldeman, *The Haldeman Diaries: Inside the Nixon White House* (New York: Berkley, 1994), 53. Nixon went on: he "pointed out that there has never in history been an adequate black nation, and they are the only race of which this is true. [Nixon] Says Africa is hopeless."
112. Quoted in Alexander P. Lamis, *The Two-Party South* (New York: Oxford University Press, 1988), 26. Republicans long denied the validity of the quotation, but it was authenticated later by publication of the recorded interview where it first appeared. See the discussion of this controversy in Rick Perlstein, *The Nation*, November 13, 2012, at https://www.thenation.com/article/archive/exclusive-lee-atwaters-infamous-1981-interview-southern-strategy/.
113. David Farber, *The Rise and Fall of Modern Conservatism: A Short History* (Princeton: Princeton University Press, 2010), 181.
114. Dan Baum, "Legalize It All," *Harpers Magazine*, April 2016, at https://harpers.org/archive/2016/04/legalize-it-all. Ehrlichman's surviving family members (he died in 1999; the quotation is from a reminiscence seventeen years earlier) vehemently denied its accuracy: J. Wheaton, "Richard Nixon Drug Wars Quote Rears Its Ugly Head.—Again," *Newsmax*, March 14, 1016, at https://www.newsmax.com/TheWire/richard-mixon-drugs-war-quote/2016/03/24/id/720681/.
115. Stuart Stevens, *It Was All a Lie: How the Republican Party Became Donald Trump* (New York: Knopf, 2020), 7–36. Stevens drew on Haney Lopez, *Dog Whistle Politics*, ch. 1, "The GOP's Rise as 'the White Man's Party,'" esp. pp. 17–22.
116. Dean J. Kotlowski, "Nixon's Southern Strategy Revisited," 10 *Journal of Policy History* 207 (1998).
117. Quoted in Dean J. Kotlowski, *Nixon's Civil Rights: Politics, Principle, and Policy* (Cambridge: Harvard University Press, 2001), 8, 16.
118. Rowland Evans Jr. and Robert D. Novak, *Nixon in the White House: The Frustration of Power* (New York: Vintage, 1971), 156.
119. Kotlowski, *Nixon's Civil Rights*, 55–57; Chris Bonastia, "Hedging His Bets: Why Nixon Killed HUD's Desegregation Efforts," 28 *Social Science History* 19–52 (2004).
120. On the Philadelphia Plan, see Melvin I. Urofsky, *The Affirmative Action Puzzle: A Living History from Reconstruction to Today* (New York: Pantheon, 2020), 84–102.
121. Perlstein, *Nixonland*, 515.
122. Quoted in George Packer, "Dividing the Democrats," *New Yorker*, August 12, 2008.
123. Thomas M. Keck, *The Most Activist Supreme Court in History: The Road to Modern Judicial Conservatism* (Chicago: University of Chicago Press, 2010).
124. Audio tape of conversation between Nixon and John Mitchell, Oval Office of the White House, Washington, DC (September 18, 1971) (National Archives Nixon White House Tape Conversation 576-6), quoted in David S. Tatel, "Judicial Methodology, Southern School Desegregation, and the Rule of Law," 79 *NYU Law Review* 1071, 1098 (2004).
125. Carswell undoubtedly was; in 1948, he had affirmed his "firm, vigorous belief in the principles of white supremacy" and the "segregation of the races." Haynsworth, a more competent jurist, was merely conservative on racial issues. On the failed Haynsworth and Carswell nominations,

see Kalk, "The Machiavellian Nominations"; McMahon, *Nixon's Court*, 113–145; Laura Kalman, *The Long Reach of the Sixties: LBJ, Nixon, and the Making of the Contemporary Supreme Court* (New York: Oxford University Press, 2017), 198–251.
126. Kalman, *Long Reach of the Sixties*, 252–306.
127. Quoted in Bob Woodward and Scott Armstrong, *The Brethren: Inside the Supreme Court* (New York: Avon, 1979), 159. All quotations in *The Brethren* are unattributed. Nevertheless, this particular quotation seems entirely in character.
128. Woodward and Armstrong, *The Brethren*, 162, relate this anecdote about Mississippi senator James Eastland, chair of the Judiciary Committee, when Powell came by for the usual courtesy visit: "Eastland sat behind his desk, silently puffing his cigar. 'You're going to be confirmed,' he told Powell. Powell thanked him. 'Do you know why you're going to be confirmed?' Eastland asked. "No," he replied. "Because,' Eastland drawled, 'they think you're going to die.'"
129. John C. Jeffries Jr., *Justice Lewis F. Powell, Jr.* (New York: Scribners, 1994), 131–137. The author clerked for Justice Powell in the 1972 Term.
130. Milliken v. Bradley, 433 U.S. 267 (1977) (Milliken II); Powell's comments in conference quoted in Del Dickson, ed., *The Supreme Court in Conference (1940–1985)* (New York: Oxford University Press, 2001), 686.
131. Reproduced at https://www.webcitation.org/64jAmJkKB?url=http://www.pbs.org/wnet/supremecourt/personality/sources_document13.html. On the impact of this memorandum, see Jane Mayer, *Dark Money: The Hidden History of the Rise of the Billionaires behind the Rise of the Radical Right* (New York: Doubleday, 2016), 72–81; Kim Phillips-Fein, *Invisible Hands: The Making of the Conservative Movement from the New Deal to Reagan* (New York: Norton, 2009), 156–165.
132. Jeffries, *Justice Lewis F. Powell*, 285–287.
133. Earl M. Maltz, "The Triumph of the Southern Man: Dowell, Shelby County, and the Jurisprudence of Justice Lewis F. Powell, Jr.," 14 *Duke Journal of Constitutional Law & Public Policy* 169 (2019).
134. 413 U.S. 189, 217–253 at 242, discussed below in chapter 9.
135. 443 U.S. 449 (1979).
136. 438 U.S. 265 (1978).
137. The process is described in detail in John W. Dean, *The Rehnquist Choice: The Untold Story of the Nixon Appointment That Redefined the Supreme Court* (New York: Free Press, 2001) (a book-length narrative of the subject by a key inside player), and Jenkins, *The Partisan*, 111–130.
138. All quotations in this paragraph from Jenkins, *The Partisan*, 113, 116.
139. George Lardner, "Rehnquist Got Call That Baker Missed for Nixon Court Nomination," *Washington Post*, December 18, 1998.
140. Jenkins, *The Partisan*, 108–109. On "Renchburg": Jeffrey Rosen, "Renchburg's the One," *New York Times*, November 4, 2001.
141. Nixon finally got the name right.
142. Jenkins, *The Partisan*, 130.
143. Rehnquist was only the second justice of the US Supreme Court with prior military experience to have served as an enlisted man rather than an officer (the other being Horace Lurton).
144. Quoted in Sue Davis, *Justice Rehnquist and the Constitution* (Princeton: Princeton University Press, 1989), 6.
145. Tova A. Wang, *The Politics of Voter Suppression: Defending and Expanding Americans' Right to Vote* (Ithaca: Cornell University Press, 2012), 44–48.
146. The challenges to minority voters are discussed in Dean, *Rehnquist Choice*, 270–273.
147. The proposed amendment read: "No provision of the Constitution shall be construed to prohibit the United States, any State, or any subdivision of either, from assigning persons to its educational facilities on the basis of geographic boundaries, provided only that such boundaries are reasonably related to school capacity, availability of transportation, safety or other similar considerations." The Rehnquist memorandum containing his proposed constitutional amendment is at 132 *Cong. Rec.* 12,068.
148. "No provision of the Constitution shall be construed to prohibit the United States, or any State, or any subdivision of either, from permitting persons to choose or transfer voluntarily among its educational facilities, provided only that the opportunity to choose or transfer is

available either to all persons within its jurisdiction or to any eligible person, when standards of eligibility are reasonably related to school capacity, availability of transportation, availability of curriculum, safety or other similar considerations."
149. At that time, associate justices were assigned two clerks.
150. The memorandum may be found at https://www.gpo.gov/fdsys/pkg/GPO-CHRG-REHNQUIST/pdf/GPO-CHRG-REHNQUIST-4-16-6.pdf. Orthography was not Rehnquist's strong suit.
151. Letter of Rehnquist to Sen. James O. Eastland (D.-MS), quoted in Dean, *Rehnquist Choice*, 276.
152. The debates are reviewed in Dean, *Rehnquist Choice*, 272–284; Bernard Schwartz, "Chief Justice Rehnquist, Justice Jackson, and the Brown Case," 1988 *Supreme Court Review* 245 (1988); and in footnote *, pp. 609–615, of Richard Kluger, *Simple Justice: The History of Brown v. Board of Education and Black America's Struggle for Equality* (New York: Knopf, 2004). See also Brad Snyder and John Q. Barrett, "Rehnquist's Missing Letter: A Former Law Clerk's 1955 Thoughts on Justice Jackson and Brown," 53 *Boston College Law Review* 631 (2012). Jackson's view, rather than Rehnquist's, is considered at William M. Wiecek, *The Birth of the Modern Constitution: The United States Supreme Court, 1941–1953* (New York: Cambridge University Press, 2006), 700–704, and esp. 713–715 (letter of Jackson to Charles Fairman, March 13, 1950, expressing at length the justice's views, which were hopelessly ambivalent).
153. Brad Snyder, "How the Conservatives Canonized Brown v. Board of Education," 52 *Rutgers Law Review* 383 (2000).
154. 345 U.S. 461 (1953).
155. Quoted and discussed in Jenkins, *The Partisan*, 40–41.
156. Warren Weaver, "Mr. Justice Rehnquist Dissenting," *New York Times Magazine*, October 13, 1974, 36.
157. Davis, *Justice Rehnquist and the Constitution*, 56–62.
158. Book-length studies devoted exclusively to Thomas include Ken Foskett, *Judging Thomas: The Life and Times of Clarence Thomas* (New York: Morrow, 2003); Kevin Merida and Michael Fletcher, *Supreme Discomfort: The Divided Soul of Clarence Thomas* (New York: Doubleday, 2007); Corey Robin, *The Enigma of Clarence Thomas* (New York: Henry Holt, 2019); Ralph A. Rossum, *Understanding Clarence Thomas: The Jurisprudence of Constitutional Restoration* (Lawrence: University Press of Kansas, 2014); Scott D. Gerber, *First Principles: The Jurisprudence of Clarence Thomas* (New York: New York University Press, 1999), 69–112.
159. "In His Own Words: Justice Clarence Thomas," *New York Times*, December 14, 2000; Clarence Thomas, *My Grandfather's Son: A Memoir* (New York: Harper, 2007), 29–30.
160. See the exhaustive study by Jane Mayer and Jill Abramson, *Strange Justice: The Selling of Clarence Thomas* (Boston: Houghton Mifflin, 1995). An opposing view, with religious overtones (fittingly, since its author was an Episcopal priest), is John A. Danforth, *Resurrection: The Confirmation of Clarence Thomas* (New York: Viking, 1994). Danforth has been Thomas's sponsor throughout his career.
161. Based on Martin/Quinn scores at https://mqscores.lsa.umich.edu/measures.php; see the invaluable color-coded graph that provides a summary visualization of this data at https://en.wikipedia.org/wiki/Ideological_leanings_of_United_States_Supreme_Court_justices#cite_ref-Bailey2012_16-1.
162. Quoted in Lincoln Caplan, "Justice Thomas's Brand of Judicial Logic," *New York Times*, October 22, 2011.
163. United States v. Lopez, 514 U.S. 549, 584–602 (1995) (Thomas, J. concurring); United States v. Morrison, 529 U.S. 598, 627 (2000) (Thomas, J. concurring); Gonzalez v. Raich, 545 U.S. 1, 57–66 (2005) (Thomas, J. dissenting).
164. "The text and history of [the Establishment] Clause suggest that it should not be incorporated against the States." American Legion v. American Humanist Ass'n, 139 S. Ct. 2067, 2095 (2019).
165. Hamdi v. Rumsfeld, 542 U.S. 507 (2004) (Thomas, J. dissenting); Hamdan v. Rumsfeld, 548 U.S. 557 (20060 (Thomas, J. dissenting).
166. Hudson v. McMillian, 503 U.S. 1, 11 (1992).
167. 515 U.S. 122–123.
168. 515 U.S. 124.
169. 515 U.S. 70, 121–122 (1995) (Thomas, J. concurring).
170. Grutter v. Bollinger, 539 U.S. 306, 368 (2003) (Thomas, J. concurring and dissenting)).

Chapter 9

1. In the South; some northern school systems were nominally integrated.
2. Erwin Chemerinsky, "The Segregation and Resegregation of American Public Education: The Courts' Role," 81 *North Carolina Law Review* 1597 (2003); Jonathan Kozol, *The Shame of the Nation: The Restoration of Apartheid Schools in America* (New York: Crown, 2005); Gary Orfield and Chungmei Lee, "Historical Reversals, Accelerating Resegregation, and the Need for New Integration Strategies," a report of the Civil Rights Project, UCLA, 2007, https://escholarship.org/uc/item/8h02n114; Gary Orfield, "Schools More Separate: Consequences of a Decade of Resegregation" (2001), https://civilrightsproject.ucla.edu/research/k-12-education/integration-and-diversity/schools-more-separate-consequences-of-a-decade-of-resegregation/orfield-schools-more-separate-2001.pdf.
3. Gary Orfield et al., *Dismantling Desegregation: The Quiet Overruling of Brown v. Board of Education* (New York: Norton, 1996), 1–114, 291–330; Orfield, "Schools More Separate."
4. Brown v. Board. of Education, 347 U.S. 483, 492–495 (1954).
5. Jonathan Kozol, *Savage Inequalities: Children in America's Schools* (New York: Broadway Books, 2012), 9–50.
6. Myron Orfield, "Milliken, Meredith, and Metropolitan Segregation," 62 *UCLA Law Review* 364 (2015); David S. Tatel, "Judicial Methodology, Southern School Desegregation, and the Rule of Law," 79 *NYU Law Review* 1071, 1098 (2004).
7. Nancy A. Denton, "The Persistence of Segregation: Links between Residential Segregation and School Segregation," 80 *Minnesota Law Review* 795 (1996).
8. The following paragraphs are taken from William M. Wiecek, "The United States Supreme Court and Residential Segregation: 'Slavery Unwilling to Die,'" 3 *Journal of Law, Property, and Society* 35, 115–117 (2017).
9. Owen Fiss, "Groups and the Equal Protection Clause," 5 *Philosophy and Public Affairs* 107 (1976).
10. Plessy v. Ferguson, 163 U.S. 537, 559 (1896) (Harlan, J. dissenting).
11. Reva B. Siegel, "Equality Talk: Antisubordination and Anticlassification Values in Constitutional Struggles over Brown," 117 *Harvard Law Review* 1470 (2004); Jack M. Balkin and Reva B. Siegel, "The American Civil Rights Tradition: Anticlassification or Antisubordination?," 58 *University of Miami Law Review* 8 (2004).
12. Alan D. Freeman, "Legitimizing Racial Discrimination through Antidiscrimination Law: A Critical Review of Supreme Court Doctrine," 62 *Minnesota Law Review* 1049 (1978); Reva Siegel, "Discrimination in the Eyes of the Law: How 'Color Blindness' Discourse Disrupts and Rationalizes Social Stratification," 88 *California Law Review* 77 (2000).
13. Missouri v. Jenkins, 515 U.S. 70, 121 (1995) (Thomas, J. concurring).
14. Culminating in Parents Involved in Community Schools v. Seattle School District, 551 U.S. 701 (2007).
15. J. Harvie Wilkinson, *From Brown to Bakke: The Supreme Court and School Integration, 1945–1978* (New York: Oxford University Press, 1979), 126–127.
16. On this phase, see Michael J. Graetz and Linda Greenhouse, *The Burger Court and the Rise of the Judicial Right* (New York: Simon & Schuster, 2016), 79–102.
17. 413 U.S. 189, 203 (1973). See John C. Jeffries, *Justice Lewis F. Powell, Jr.* (New York: Scribners, 1994), ch. 10, "Race and the Public Schools."
18. 413 U.S. 208 (ital. in orig.).
19. On Powell's Keyes opinion, see Jeffries, *Justice Lewis F. Powell*, 294–305.
20. Powell to J. Harvie Wilkinson, September 28, 1972, quoted in Jeffries, *Justice Lewis F. Powell*, 299.
21. 413 U.S. 236.
22. 413 U.S. 238.
23. Rachel F. Moran, "Untoward Consequences: The Ironic Legacy of Keyes v. School District. No. 1," 90 *Denver University Law Review* 1209 (2013).
24. 413 U.S. 258, 265 (Rehnquist, J. dissenting).
25. Bradley v. School Board, 338 F.Supp. 67 (E.D. Va. 1972).
26. Bradley v. School Board, 462 F.2d 1058 (4th Cir. 1972).
27. On the reality of white flight following Milliken, see Charles T. Clotfelter, "Are Whites Still Fleeing? Racial Patterns and Enrollment Shifts in Urban Public Schools, 1987–1996," 20 *Journal of Policy Analysis and Management* 199 (2001).
28. School Board v. State Board of Education, 412 U.S. 92 (1973).

29. 418 U.S. 717 (1974). Joyce A. Baugh, *The Detroit School Busing Case: Milliken v. Bradley and the Controversy over Desegregation* (Lawrence: University Press of Kansas, 2011), 1–137, reviews the background of the case.
30. Thomas J. Sugrue, *The Origins of the Urban Crisis: Race and Inequality in Postwar Detroit*, updated ed. (Princeton: Princeton University Press, 2014).
31. Burger there wrote: "As with any equity case, the nature of the violation determines the scope of the remedy." *Swann*, 402 U.S. 16.
32. 418 U.S. 746.
33. Robert A. Sedler, "The Profound Impact of Milliken v. Bradley," 33 *Wayne Law Review* 1693 (1986).
34. 418 U.S. 767 (Douglas, J. dissenting).
35. 418 U.S. 717.
36. Recall that Justice Brennan had earlier stated in Keyes that "the differentiating factor between *de jure* segregation and so-called *de facto* segregation…is *purpose* or *intent* to segregate." Keyes, 413 U.S. at 208 (ital. in orig.).
37. 418 U.S. 741–742.
38. 418 U.S. 744.
39. 418 U.S. 749.
40. 418 U.S. 814.
41. 418 U.S. 782.
42. 418 U.S. 814.
43. 433 U.S. 267 (1977).
44. Owen Fiss, quoted in Andrea Sachs, "The Worst Supreme Court Decisions since 1960," *Time*, October 6, 2015, at http://time.com/4056051/worst-supreme-court-decisions/.
45. Derrick Bell, *Race, Racism, and American Law*, 5th ed. (Boston: Little, Brown, 2004), 155.
46. 425 U.S. 284 (1976). The attorney who argued *Gautreaux* before the Supreme Court provided a comprehensive review of the case: Alexander Polikoff, *Waiting for Gautreaux: A Story of Segregation, Housing, and the Black Ghetto* (Evanston: Northwestern University Press, 2006).
47. 425 U.S. 286.
48. 425 U.S. 293.
49. 425 U.S. 300.
50. Missouri v. Jenkins, 515 U.S. 70, 108 (1995) (O'Connor, J. concurring).
51. James E. Rosenbaum, "Changing the Geography of Opportunity by Expanding Residential Choice: Lessons from the Gautreaux Program," 6.1 *Housing Policy Debate* 231 (1995), https://doi.org/10.1080/10511482.1995.9521186; Leonard S. Rubinowitz and James E. Rosenbaum, *Crossing the Class and Color Lines: From Public Housing to White Suburbia* (Chicago: University of Chicago Press, 2000).
52. 443 U.S. 449 (1979).
53. 443 U.S. 526 (1979). The Powell dissent is at 99 S.Ct. 2988.
54. Edmund W. Kitch, "The Return of Color-Consciousness to the Constitution: Weber, Dayton, and Columbus," 1979 *Supreme Court Review* 1 (1979).
55. Justin Driver refers to him as "the patron saint of local control within the field of education law." *The Schoolhouse Gate: Public Education, the Supreme Court, and the Battle for the American Mind* (New York: Pantheon, 2018), 18.
56. 443 U.S. 487.
57. 443 U.S. 489.
58. 443 U.S. 487.
59. 443 U.S. 510.
60. 427 U.S. 424 (1976).
61. Orfield, *Dismantling Desegregation*, 293.
62. Kevin M. Kruse. *White Flight: Atlanta and the Making of Modern Conservatism* (Princeton: Princeton University Press, 2005), 105–130, 259–265.
63. Quoted in Kruse, *White Flight*, 261.
64. 427 U.S. 436.
65. 532 F.2d 380 (5th Cir. 1976).
66. 532 F.2d 388.
67. 532 F.2d 392.
68. Austin Independent School District v. United States, 429 U.S. 990, 994 (1976). Justices Brennan and Marshall dissented without opinion.

69. Richard Rothstein, *The Color of Law: A Forgotten History of How Our Government Segregated America* (New York Liveright, 2018), 153–175; David M. P. Freund, *Colored Property: State Policy and White Racial Politics in Suburban America* (Chicago: University of Chicago Press, 2007), 99–241.
70. Dayton Board of Education, 443 U.S. at 480.
71. 503 U.S. 467 (1992).
72. Bradley W. Joondeph, "Killing Brown Softly: The Subtle Undermining of Effective Desegregation," 47 *Stanford Law Review* 147 (1993).
73. Freeman v. Pitts, 503 U.S. 467, 495 (1992).
74. A Kansas City attorney prominent in the push for desegregation, Arthur Benson, provided a history of the effort in "School Segregation and Desegregation in Kansas City" (undated, but from internal evidence probably published around 1995) at http://www.bensonlaw.com/kcmsd/deseg_history.htm.
75. Benson, "School Segregation and Desegregation."
76. Paul Ciotti, "America's Most Costly Educational Failure" (undated), at https://www.cato.org/publications/commentary/americas-most-costly-educational-failure. Preston C. Green III and Bruce D. Baker challenge the conservative complaint: "Urban Legends, Desegregation, and School Finance: Did Kansas City Really Prove That Money Doesn't Matter?," 12 *Michigan Journal of Race & Law* 57, 90–95 (2006).
77. 495 U.S. 33, 51, 64 (1990).
78. 515 U.S. 70, 89 (1995).
79. The author taught from 1968 to 1985 at the University of Missouri–Columbia.
80. 515 U.S. 99.
81. Chief Justice Warren's opinion in Brown stated: "To separate [African American students] from others of similar age and qualifications solely because of their race generates a feeling of inferiority as to their status in the community that may affect their hearts and minds in a way unlikely ever to be undone." Brown v. Board of Education, 347 U.S. 483, 494 (1954).
82. 515 U.S. 114 (Thomas, J. concurring).
83. 515 U.S. 121, 123 (Thomas, J. concurring).
84. 515 U.S. 116 (Thomas, J. concurring).
85. 498 U.S. 237 (1991).
86. Dowell v. School Board, 244 F.Supp. 971, 981 (W.D. Okla. 1965).
87. 498 U.S. 247–249.
88. 498 U.S. 251, 259 (Marshall, J. dissenting).
89. 498 U.S. 262 (ital. in orig.).
90. 498 U.S. 265.
91. Jennifer Jellison, "Resegregation and Equity in Oklahoma City" (1996), summarized in "Study Finds Resegregated Neighborhood Schools in Oklahoma City Fail to Meet District Promises of Achievement and Equity," September 16, 1996, https://www.gse.harvard.edu/news/96/09/study-finds-resegregated-neighborhood-schools-oklahoma-city-fail-meet-district-promises.
92. Dred Scott v. Sandford, 60 U.S. (19 How.) 393, 407 (1857).
93. Mark Tushnet, *A Court Divided: The Rehnquist Court and the Future of Constitutional Law* (New York: Norton, 2005), 223.
94. Jennifer Woodward, "How Busing Burdened Blacks: Critical Race Theory and Busing for Desegregation in Nashville-Davidson County," 80 *Journal of Negro Education* 22–32 (2011).
95. Quoted in Clare Lombardo, "Why White School Districts Have So Much More Money," NPR, February 26, 2019, at https://www.npr.org/2019/02/26/696794821/why-white-school-districts-have-so-much-more-money. See the related report written by Sibilia, at https://edbuild.org/content/23-billion.
96. Shapiro v. Thompson, 394 U.S. 618 (1969).
97. Brown v. Board of Education I, 347 U.S. 483. 493 (1954).
98. Their claim was based on these statistics: because of low property values ($5,960 per student), their district (Edgerton) raised $21 per student, in comparison with Alamo Heights, a wealthy district (property value: $49,000 per student), which raised $307. Yet perversely, Edgewood had the highest property taxes as a percentage of property value, while Alamo Heights had the lowest, because poor parents did their best to support their schools with scant resources in the tax base. Texas contributed $231 per student to Edgewood, $543 per student to Alamo Heights. The total spending (local + state) per pupil was Edgewood $356, Alamo Heights $594, a 60 percent disparity.

99. Rodriguez v. San Antonio Independent School District, 337 F.Supp. 280, 282–283 (W.D. Texas 1971).
100. 411 U.S. 128 (1973). On this case, see Michael Heise, "The Story of San Antonio Indep. School Dist. v. Rodriguez: School Finance, Local Control, and Constitutional Limits," in Michael A. Olivas and Ronna G. Schneider, eds., *Education Law Stories* (St. Paul: Foundation, 2008), 51–82; Richard Schragger, "San Antonio v. Rodriguez and the Legal Geography of School Finance Reform," in Myriam E. Gilles and Risa Goluboff, eds., *Civil Rights Stories* (St. Paul: Foundation, 2008), 85–109; Graetz and Greenhouse, *Burger Court*, 90–94.
101. Green and Baker, "Urban Legends."
102. 411 U.S. 57. Justice Powell had to shut his eyes to reality to reach the conclusion he did. The population of the Edgewood school district, the focus of Rodriguez, was 90 percent Latino plus 6 percent African American.
103. 411 U.S. 37.
104. 411 U.S. 33–34.
105. 411 U.S. 30.
106. 397 U.S. 471 (1970) and 405 U.S. 56 (1972) respectively.
107. 411 U.S. 40.
108. 411 U.S. 57.
109. 411 U.S. 41.
110. Both quoted in Sachs, "Worst Supreme Court Decisions."
111. Judge Jeffrey Sutton offers a more hopeful evaluation of the aftermath of *Rodriguez* in his thoughtful reconsideration of the case and its consequences, "San Antonio Independent School District v. Rodriguez and Its Aftermath," 94 *Virginia Law Review* 1963 (2008).
112. William J. Brennan, "State Constitutions and the Protection of Individual Rights," 90 *Harvard Law Review* 493 (1977); Brennan, "The Bill of Rights: The Revival of State Constitutions as Guardians of Individual Rights," 59 *NYU Law Review* 535 (1986).
113. G. Alan Tarr, "The New Judicial Federalism in Perspective," 72 *Notre Dame Law Review* 1097 (1999).
114. Serrano v. Priest (I), 5 Cal.3d 584 (1971).
115. California Constitution, Art. I, Declaration of Rights, sec. 7 (b): "(b) A citizen or class of citizens may not be granted privileges or immunities not granted on the same terms to all citizens. Privileges or immunities granted by the Legislature may be altered or revoked."
116. Serrano v. Priest (II), 18 Cal.3d 728, 763–764, 767–768 (1976). *Serrano III* (Serrano v. Priest, 20 Cal.3d 25 [1977]) involved the unrelated problem of attorneys' fees, but the Court there emphasized that its prior *Serrano II* decision was "final."
117. The evidence of this is admittedly uncertain and conflicting. See Isaac Martin, "Does School Finance Litigation Cause Taxpayer Revolt? Serrano and Proposition 13," 40 *Law & Soc. Review* 525 (2006). Causal explanations should be tentative for this complex phenomenon, but the results are not: Prop 13 has become the third rail of California politics. It has distorted both local and state finance and the real estate market and has diminished state funding for public-school education.
118. Nordlinger v. Hahn, 505 U.S. 1, 11 (1992).
119. Isaiah Berlin, "Two Concepts of Liberty" (1958), inaugural lecture reprinted in Berlin, *Four Essays on Liberty* (Oxford: Oxford University Press, 1969).
120. Emily Zackin, *Looking for Rights in All the Wrong Places: Why State Constitutions Contain America's Positive Rights* (Princeton: Princeton University Press, 2013), ch. 5, "Education: A Long Tradition of Positive Rights in America."
121. And has been made by Judge Jeffrey S. Sutton in *51 Imperfect Solutions: States and the Making of American Constitutional Law* (New York: Oxford University Press, 2018), 22–41, which is a revised and extended version of his article "San Antonio Independent School District and Its Aftermath," 94 *Virginia Law Review* 1963 (2008). Judge Sutton clerked for Justices Powell and Scalia.
122. 457 U.S. 202 (1982). On this case, see Michael Oliveras, "*Plyler v. Doe*, the Education of Undocumented Children, and the Polity," in David A. Martin and Peter H. Schuck, *Immigration Stories* (St. Paul: Foundation, 2005), 197–220.
123. Justice Powell, the author of the *Rodriguez* majority opinion, joined the majority here. He explained his seeming change of heart: "a legislative classification that threatens the creation of an underclass of future citizens and residents cannot be reconciled with one of the fundamental purposes of the Fourteenth Amendment." 457 U.S. at 239.

124. 457 U.S. 213.
125. 457 U.S. 221; Derrick Bell, *Race, Racism, and American Law*, 5th ed. (New York: Aspen, 2004), 301–308.
126. Bell, *Race, Racism*, 301–308.
127. Matthew F. Delmont, *Why Busing Failed: Race, Media, and the National Resistance to School Desegregation* (Oakland: University of California Press, 2016). See also Thomas Sugrue, *Sweet Land of Liberty: The Forgotten Struggle for Civil Rights in the North* (New York: Random House, 2008), 479–487.
128. Civil Rights Act of 1964, Pub. L. 88–352, 78 Stat. 241, Tit. IV, sec. 401(b).
129. Matthew Delmont, "The Lasting Legacy of the Busing Crisis," *The Atlantic*, March 29, 2016, https://www.theatlantic.com/politics/archive/2016/03/the-boston-busing-crisis-was-never-intended-to-work/474264/.
130. *Cong. Rec.*, 88th Cong., 2nd sess., June 4, 1964, 12,717. The case Humphrey referred to was Bell v. School City of Gary, 213 F.Supp. 819 (1963).
131. *Cong. Rec.*, 88th Cong., 2nd sess., March 21, 1964, 5861.
132. Buchanan memorandum to Nixon quoted in Paul R. Dimond, *Beyond Busing: Reflections on Urban Segregation, the Courts, and Equal Opportunity* (Ann Arbor: University of Michigan Press, 1985), 58.
133. Sugrue, *Sweet Land of Liberty*, 484.
134. Leon Panetta, *Bring Us Together: The Nixon Team and the Civil Rights Retreat* (Philadelphia: Lippincott, 1971), 312.
135. Quoted in Delmont, *Why Busing Failed*, 6.
136. Matthew D. Lassiter, "De Jure / De Facto Segregation: The Long Shadow of a National Myth," in Lassiter and Joseph Crespino, eds., *The Myth of Southern Exceptionalism* (New York: Oxford University Press, 2010), 27; Lassiter, *The Silent Majority: Suburban Politics in the Sunbelt South* (Princeton: Princeton University Press, 2007), 4–17, 305–310; George Lipsitz, *How Racism Takes Place* (Philadelphia: Temple University Press, 2011).
137. Taylor v. Board of Education ... of New Rochelle, 191 F.Supp. 181, 194 (S.D.N.Y. 1961).
138. Davis v. School District of City of Pontiac, 309 F.Supp. 734, 742 (E.D. Mich. 1970).
139. On the Boston turmoil, which became the focal point of opposition to busing and desegregation in the North, see Ronald P. Formisano, *Boston against Busing: Race, Class, and Ethnicity in the 1960s and 1970s* (Chapel Hill: University of North Carolina Press, 2012).
140. Morgan v. Hennigan, 379 F.Supp. 410, 470 (D.Mass. 1974).
141. Delmont, "Lasting Legacy."
142. On Crawford and associated struggles over anti-busing initiatives, see Daniel M. HoSang, *Racial Propositions: Ballot Initiatives and the Making of Postwar California* (Berkeley: University of California Press, 2011), ch. 4, "'We Love All Kids': School Desegregation, Busing, and the Triumph of Racial Innocence, 1972–1982."
143. Mendez v. Westminster School District, 64 F.Supp. 544 (S.D. Cal. 1946), aff'd on other grounds by 161 F.2d 774 (9th Cir. 1947). See Philippa Strum, *Mendez v. Westminster: School Desegregation and Mexican-American Rights* (Lawrence: University Press of Kansas, 2010). In 1890, the California Supreme Court had held that school boards could not establish de jure segregation: Wysinger v. Crookshank, 82 Cal. 588 (1890). This holding was based on state statutes, not the state constitution.
144. HoSang, *Racial Propositions*, 95.
145. Jackson v. Pasadena City School District, 59 Cal.2d 876, 881 (1963) (ital. added).
146. Crawford v. Board of Education, 17 Cal. 3d 280, 290 (1976). This decision is commonly referred to as *Crawford I*.
147. *Crawford I*, 17 Cal. 3d at 301–302.
148. Santa Barbara School District v. Superior Court, 13 Cal. 3d 315, 327–328 (1975).
149. In California, the people may alter their state constitution by initiative. Such a measure requires only a majority for passage. (In this respect, California is unique.) As a result, the California Constitution, particularly its Declaration of Rights, is cluttered with quasi-statutory provisions, some of bloated length and/or verbose prose, that reflect passions of the moment. Prop 1 was just such a specimen.
150. Crawford v. Board of Education, 113 Cal.App.3d 633 (1980). This was known as *Crawford II*.
151. The iconic 1976 image, titled "The Soiling of Old Glory," may be found at https://www.npr.org/2016/09/18/494442131/life-after-iconic-photo-todays-parallels-of-american-flags-role-in-racial-protest.

152. The full text of the operative addition to Article I, section 7 reads: "nothing contained herein or elsewhere in this Constitution imposes upon the State of California or any public entity, board, or official any obligations or responsibilities which exceed those imposed by the Equal Protection Clause of the 14th Amendment to the United States Constitution with respect to the use of pupil school assignment or pupil transportation. In enforcing this subdivision or any other provision of this Constitution, no court of this State may impose upon the State of California or any public entity, board, or official any obligation or responsibility with respect to the use of pupil school assignment or pupil transportation, (1) except to remedy a specific violation by such party that would also constitute a violation of the Equal Protection Clause of the 14th Amendment to the United States Constitution, and (2) unless a federal court would be permitted under federal decisional law to impose that obligation or responsibility upon such party to remedy the specific violation of the Equal Protection Clause of the 14th Amendment of the United States Constitution." This is followed by even wordier provisions regulating minutiae of busing orders.
153. "Where the state has undertaken to provide [public education], it is a right which must be made available to all on equal terms." Brown v. Board of Education, 347 U.S. 483, 493 (1954).
154. 458 U.S. 527 (1982).
155. Strict scrutiny would require the state to prove that its policy goals were "compelling" and the means to attain those goals "narrowly tailored."
156. 458 U.S. 457 (1982).
157. The Seattle School Board's concern about racial imbalance in the city schools prefigured its role in the case known as *Parents Involved in Community Schools* (2007).
158. 458 U.S. 470 (ital. in orig.). In reaching this conclusion, Blackmun relied on Hunter v. Erickson, 393 U.S. 385 (1969), another initiative case but one that involved the siting of low-income housing projects. Though *Hunter* was central to the Court's reasoning here, discussion of it will be deferred until chapter 11, which takes up the problem of housing referenda.
159. 458 U.S. 493.
160. Wright v. Council of the City of Emporia, 407 U.S. 451, 462–463 (1972).
161. 407 U.S. 484, 492 (1972).
162. Lauren Camera, "The Quiet Wave of School District Secessions," *U.S. News & World Report*, May 5, 2017, https://www.usnews.com/news/education-news/articles/2017-05-05/the-quiet-wave-of-school-district-secessions; Margaret Newkirk, "The South's Push to Resegregate Its Schools," *Bloomberg Businessweek*, April 10, 2018, https://www.bloomberg.com/news/articles/2018-04-10/the-south-s-push-to-resegregate-its-schools. For a graphic presentation of secessionist efforts, current as of 2019, see https://edbuild.org/content/fractured#intro.
163. Genevieve Siegel-Hawley, Erica Frankenberg, and Sarah Diem, quoted in Valerie Strauss, "Back to the Future: A New School District Secession Movement Is Gaining Steam," *Washington Post*, May 2, 2018, https://www.washingtonpost.com/news/answer-sheet/wp/2018/05/02/back-to-the-future-a-new-school-district-secession-movement-is-gaining-steam/?utm_term=.9e19d1368394. For a detailed scholarly study of school district secession, see Richard V. Reeves and Nathan Joo, "Do School Secessions Worsen Racial Segregation? It's Complicated," 2018, at https://www.brookings.edu/research/do-school-secessions-worsen-racial-segregation-its-complicated/.
164. Nikole Hannah-Jones, "The Resegregation of Jefferson County," *New York Times*, September 6, 2017, https://www.nytimes.com/2017/09/06/magazine/the-resegregation-of-jefferson-county.html, recounts the Gardendale secession effort in detail.
165. Stout v. Jefferson County Board of Education, 250 F.Supp.3d 1092, 1181 (N.D. Ala. 2017).
166. 882 F.3d 988, 991, 1007, 1011 (11th Cir. 2018).
167. Arlington Heights v. Metropolitan Housing Corp., 429 U.S. 252 (1977).
168. See Note, "Segregation Academies and State Action," 82 *Yale Law Journal* 1436 (1973), for a valuable early overview of seg academies and their history. See also David Nevin and Robert E. Bills, *The Schools That Fear Built: Segregationist Academies in the South* (Washington, DC: Acropolis, 1976).
169. 330 F.Supp. 1150, 1163–1164 (D.D.C. 1971).
170. The Supreme Court identified a First Amendment right of association in, inter alia, N.A.A.C.P. v. Alabama (1958). This implied associational right is derived from the explicitly mentioned rights of speech, assembly, and petition.
171. Ital. in orig.

172. Coit v. Green, 404 U.S. 997 (1971).
173. 427 U.S. 160, 176 (1976). See George Rutherglen, "Civil Rights in Private Schools: The Surprising Story of Runyon v. McCrary," in Myriam E. Gilles and Risa L. Goluboff, eds., *Civil Rights Stories* (St. Paul: Foundation, 2008), 111–130.
174. Johnson v. Railway Express Agency, 421 U.S. 454, 460 (1975): section 1981 "affords a federal remedy against discrimination in private employment on the basis of race."
175. Citing Norwood v. Harrison, 413 U.S. 455, 470 (1973). *Norwood* affirms the proposition that there is no affirmative constitutional "right" to discriminate, and therefore no constitutional protection for such a (non-)right.
176. Theodore Eisenberg and Stewart J. Schwab, "The Importance of Section 1981," 73 *Cornell Law Review* 596 (1988).
177. In jurisprudential terms, the existence of a right in A (e.g., to enter into a contract) implies or mandates a "correlative" duty in B not to refuse to enter into the contract for illicit reasons. This is known as a "jural correlative." See Wesley Hohfeld, "Some Fundamental Legal Conceptions as Applied in Judicial Reasoning," 23 *Yale Law Journal* 16 (1913). Joseph W. Singer elaborates on this concept in "The Legal Rights Debate in Analytical Jurisprudence: From Bentham to Hohfeld," 1982 *Wisconsin Law Review* 975 (1982).
178. Joseph Crespino, "Civil Rights and the Religious Right," in Bruce J. Schulman and Julian E. Zelizer, eds., *Rightward Bound: Making America Conservative in the 1970s* (Cambridge: Harvard University Press, 2008), 96 (quoting Southern Regional Council).
179. Olati Johnson, "The Story of Bob Jones University v. United States: Race, Religion, and Congress' Extraordinary Acquiescence," 2010, Columbia Public Law & Legal Theory Working Papers, Paper 9184, https://lsr.nellco.org/cgi/viewcontent.cgi?article=1076&context=columbia_pllt.
180. 461 U.S. 574, 604 (1983).
181. On constitutional procedure as a determinant of substantive outcomes, see William M. Wiecek, "The Debut of Modern Constitutional Procedure," 26 *Review Litigation* 641 (2007).
182. 468 U.S. 737 (1984).
183. 468 U.S. 751.
184. Standing also has three non-constitutional prudential components not relevant here.
185. 468 U.S. 756; citations omitted.
186. 468 U.S. 782.
187. 422 U.S. 490 (1975).
188. Driver, *Schoolhouse Gate*, 242–329.
189. 551 U.S. 701 (2007).
190. Consisting of Roberts, Scalia, Thomas, and Alito.
191. 551 U.S. 787.
192. 551 U.S. 783.
193. Consisting of Breyer, Stevens, Souter, and Ginsburg.
194. 551 U.S. 721, quoting from *Milliken*.
195. Joel K. Goldstein, "Not Hearing History: A Critique of Chief Justice Roberts's Reinterpretation of Brown," 69 *Ohio State Law Journal* 791 (2008).
196. 551 U.S. 748.
197. 551 U.S. 719.
198. 504 U.S. 555 (1992).
199. 551 U.S. 750.
200. 551 U.S. 772.
201. 551 U.S. 787–788.
202. Including "strategic site selection of new schools; drawing attendance zones with general recognition of neighborhood demographics; allocating resources for special programs; recruiting students and faculty in a targeted fashion; and tracking enrollments, performance, and other statistics by race." 551 U.S. 707.
203. 551 U.S. 797.
204. 551 U.S. at 803. Justice Stevens's colleagues in 1975 were Chief Justice Burger and Justices Brennan, Stewart, White, Marshall, Blackmun, Powell, and Rehnquist.
205. On this point, Kennedy agreed with the dissenters. He wrote that the result "undermines *Brown*'s promise of integrated primary and secondary education that local communities have sought to make a reality." 551 U.S. 803.

NOTES TO PAGES 341–8   503

206. 551 U.S. 835.
207. Quoted in Linda Greenhouse, "Justices Limit the Use of Race in School Plans for Integration," *New York Times*, June 29, 2007. These oral remarks were not part of Breyer's written opinion.
208. Alana Semuels, "The City That Believed in Desegregation," *The Atlantic*, March 27, 2015.
209. Erwin Chemerinsky, "Making Schools More Separate and Unequal: Parents Involved in Community Schools v. Seattle School District No. 1," 2014 *Michigan State Law Review* 633, 634.

Chapter 10

1. On the origins of affirmative action, see Melvin I. Urofsky, *The Affirmative Action Puzzle: A Living History from Reconstruction to Today* (New York: Pantheon, 2020), 3–56, and Terry Anderson, *The Pursuit of Fairness: A History of Affirmative Action* (New York: Oxford University Press, 2004).
2. Andrew Johnson, veto of Civil Rights Bill, March 27, 1866, https://millercenter.org/the-presidency/presidential-speeches/march-27-1866-veto-message-civil-rights-legislation.
3. Quoted in Urofsky, *Affirmative Action Puzzle*, 4.
4. Wagner Act of 1935, Pub. L. No. 74–198, 49 Stat. 449.
5. Ira Katznelson, *When Affirmative Action Was White: An Untold History of Racial Inequality in Twentieth-Century America* (New York: Norton, 2005).
6. New Negro Alliance v. Sanitary Grocery Co., 303 U.S. 552, 561 (1938).
7. Hughes v. Superior Court, 339 U.S. 460, 464 (1950).
8. Quoted in Urofsky, *Affirmative Action Puzzle*, 22.
9. President Lyndon B. Johnson, "Howard University Commencement Address," 1965, https://www.presidency.ucsb.edu/documents/commencement-address-howard-university-fulfill-these-rights.
10. Nathan Glazer, *Affirmative Discrimination: Ethnic Inequality and Public Policy* (1975; Cambridge: Harvard University Press, 1987); John Hart Ely referred to it as "The Constitutionality of Reverse Racial Discrimination," 41 *University of Chicago Law Review* 723 (1974). Glazer was critical, Ely supportive.
11. Michael Graetz and Linda Greenhouse provide a brief overview of affirmative action in higher education in *The Burger Court and the Rise of the Judicial Right* (New York: Simon & Schuster, 2016), 103–128.
12. He had been admitted by order of a state trial court, which upheld his claim that he had been unconstitutionally discriminated against by admissions policies that, he alleged, accepted minority students less qualified than he. The Washington Supreme Court reversed, and he appealed to the US Supreme Court.
13. 416 U.S. 312 (1974).
14. 438 U.S. 265 (1978). See Howard Ball, *The Bakke Case: Race, Education, and Affirmative Action* (Lawrence: University Press of Kansas, 2000); Bernard Schwartz, *Behind Bakke: Affirmative Action and the Supreme Court* (New York: New York University Press, 1988); Urofsky, *Affirmative Action Puzzle*, 140–154.
15. 438 U.S. 387.
16. 438 U.S. 407.
17. On Powell's *Bakke* opinion, see John C. Jeffries, *Justice Lewis F. Powell, Jr.* (New York: Scribners, 1994), ch. 14, "Bakke and Beyond."
18. 438 U.S. 290.
19. 438 U.S. 292.
20. 438 U.S. at 291, 298, 307.
21. 438 U.S. 311.
22. In 1935, the physicist Erwin Schrodinger critiqued Albert Einstein's interpretation of quantum mechanics by arguing that under Einstein's theory, a notional cat in an experiment might be both alive and dead at the same time, depending on the release (or not) of a radioactive particle that activates a mechanism that would kill the cat.
23. To extend the analogy: in physics, an observer may identify a subatomic particle's position or speed, but not both at the same time (as Werner Heisenberg noted in formulating his uncertainty principle). Such observations are not incompatible, but cannot be both simultaneous and accurate.

24. In 2020, the people of California, in another initiative measure, declined to repeal this constitutional provision.
25. 78 F.3d 932 (5th Cir. 1996).
26. John Hart Ely, "Foreword: On Discovering Fundamental Values," 92 *Harvard Law Review* 5, 9 (1978).
27. Grutter v. Bollinger 539 U.S. 306, 325 (2003), which affirmed the diversity point.
28. Texas v. Hopwood, 518 U.S. 1033 (1996).
29. Akhil Reed Amar and Neal Kumar Katyal, "Bakke's Fate," 43 *UCLA Law Review* 1745 (1996).
30. 539 U.S. 306 (2003). On Grutter and Gratz, see Barbara A. Perry, *The Michigan Affirmative Action Cases* (Lawrence: University Press of Kansas, 2007); Urofsky, *Affirmative Action Puzzle*, 346–374.
31. 539 U.S. 244 (2003).
32. Quoted from the law school's official statement of admissions policy in Grutter v. Bollinger, 539 U.S. at 316.
33. 539 U.S. at 343. Justices Ginsburg and Breyer concurring rejected this time limitation.
34. Cf. Alexander Hamilton in *Federalist* No. 78: "The legislature not only commands the purse, but prescribes the rules by which the duties and rights of every citizen are to be regulated. The judiciary, on the contrary, has no influence over either the sword or the purse; no direction either of the strength or of the wealth of the society; and can take no active resolution whatever. It may truly be said to have neither FORCE nor WILL, but merely judgment; and must ultimately depend upon the aid of the executive arm even for the efficacy of its judgments." *The Federalist*, reproduced in https://avalon.law.yale.edu/18th_century/fed78.asp.
35. Richard H. Sander and Stuart Taylor, *Mismatch: How Affirmative Action Hurts Students It's Intended to Help, and Why Universities Won't Admit It* (New York: Basic Books, 2012).
36. 539 U.S. 372.
37. Quoted in Tal Koppen, "Scalia Questions Place of Some Black Students in Elite Colleges," *CNN Politics*, December 9, 2015, https://www.cnn.com/2015/12/09/politics/scalia-black-scientists-scotus/index.html.
38. 539 U.S. 244 (2003).
39. 539 U.S. 298.
40. The two petitioners, Jennifer Gratz and Patrick Hamacher, had applied to Michigan, were put on wait lists, then applied elsewhere and were accepted. Both had graduated by the time the Supreme Court agreed to hear their case.
41. 539 U.S. 289].
42. Gordon Liu, "The Causation Fallacy: Bakke and the Basic Arithmetic of Selective Admissions," 100 *Michigan Law Review* 1045 (2002).
43. Both Chief Justice Roberts and Justice Thomas insist that college admissions are a zero-sum game: Students for Fair Admissions v. Harvard, 600 U.S. 181, 218, 272 (2023).
44. 539 U.S. at 368: "The Equal Protection Clause does not, however, prohibit the use of unseemly legacy preferences."
45. Later reduced by the legislature to 7 percent.
46. Reva Siegel, "Race-Conscious but Race-Neutral: The Constitutionality of Disparate Impact in the Roberts Court," 66 *Alabama Law Review* 653 (2015).
47. Adam Liptak, "College Diversity Nears Its Last Stand," *New York Times*, October 15, 2011; Jeffrey Toobin, "The Other Big Supreme Court Case," *New Yorker*, April 30, 2012.
48. 570 U.S. 297 (2013).
49. 570 U.S. 312 (ital. in orig.)
50. 570 U.S. 335.
51. 136 S.Ct. 2198 (2016).
52. 572 U.S. 291, 314 (2014).
53. Justice Kennedy, joined by Roberts and Alito, wrote the plurality opinion; Justices Scalia and Thomas concurred (they would overrule *Grutter*); Justice Breyer concurred, supporting both affirmative action and the referendum as a way to resolve the dispute; and Justices Sotomayor and Ginsburg dissented. Justice Kagan recused.
54. On political process analysis in constitutional law, see John Hart Ely, *Democracy and Distrust: A Theory of Judicial Review* (Cambridge: Harvard University Press, 1980).
55. 393 U.S. 385 (1969).
56. 517 U.S. 620, 635 (1996).

57. 572 U.S. 380–381. Roberts was apparently irked by Sotomayor twitting him about his *Parents Involved* tagline. He concluded his concurring opinion with an irritated complaint: "People can disagree in good faith on this issue, but it similarly does more harm than good to question the openness and candor of those on either side of the debate." 572 U.S. 315.
58. 600 U.S. 181 (2023).
59. If a state institution like the University of North Carolina is involved, it offends the equal protection clause. If a private institution like Harvard College is involved, it violates Title VI of the 1964 Civil Rights Act.
60. International Brotherhood of Teamsters v. United States, 431 U.S. 324, 336, 340 (1977); Hazelwood School District v. United States, 433 U.S. 299 (1977).
61. The U.S. Department of Justice describes pattern-or-practice litigation as cases where "courts have found a 'pattern or practice' when the evidence establishes that the discriminatory actions were the defendant's regular practice, rather than an isolated instance. A 'pattern or practice' means that the defendant has a policy of discriminating, even if the policy is not always followed." US Department of Justice, "A Pattern or Practice of Discrimination," 2015, https://www.justice.gov/crt/pattern-or-practice-discrimination.
62. International Brotherhood of Teamsters, 431 U.S. 339 n. 20.
63. Bruce Ackerman, *We the People: The Civil Rights Revolution* (Cambridge: Harvard University Press, 2014), 14.
64. 443 U.S. 193, 222 (1979).
65. Contractors Ass'n of Eastern Pennsylvania v. Secretary of Labor, 442 F.2d 159 (3rd Cir. 1971), cert. denied, 404 U.S. 854 (1971). On the Philadelphia Plan, see Urofsky, *Affirmative Action Puzzle*, 84–102.
66. 448 U.S. 448 (1980). The Court overruled *Fullilove* fifteen years later in *Adarand Constructors v. Pena* (1985), after the political climate turned inhospitable to affirmative action.
67. Local 28 of Sheetmetal Workers [Union] v. E.E.O.C., 478 U.S. 421 (1986).
68. Local 93, I.A.F.F. v. Cleveland, 478 U.S. 501 (1986). The International Association of Fire Fighters is the firefighters' union.
69. United States v. Paradise, 480 U.S. 149 (1987).
70. 480 U.S. 616, 631–632 (1987). Melvin I. Urofsky examines the case in *A Conflict of Rights: The Supreme Court and Affirmative Action* (New York: Scribner's, 1991) and in Urofsky, *Affirmative Action on Trial: Sex Discrimination in Johnson v. Santa Clara* (Lawrence: University Press of Kansas, 1997).
71. Johnson was a statutory claim and did not rest on the equal protection clause itself.
72. Except for the short-lived *Metro Broadcasting* decision (1990).
73. Firefighters Local Union No. 1764 v. Stotts, 467 U.S. 561, 580 (1984).
74. Richard H. Fallon and Paul C. Weiler, "Firefighters v. Stotts: Conflicting Models of Racial Justice," 1984 *Supreme Court Review* 1, 2, 68 (1984).
75. 467 U.S. 621 (Blackmun, J. dissenting).
76. 476 U.S. 267 (1986).
77. This discussion of *Wygant* is taken from William M. Wiecek and Judy L. Hamilton, "Beyond the Civil Rights Act of 1964: Confronting Structural Racism in the Workplace," 74 *Louisiana Law Review* 1095, 1143–1149 (2014).
78. Wygant v. Jackson Board of Education, 546 F. Supp. 1195, 1201 (E. D. Mich. 1982), aff'd. 746 F.2d 1152 (6th Cir. 1984).
79. 476 U.S. 274.
80. 476 U.S. 288 (O'Connor, J. concurring).
81. 276 U.S. 274–275 (quoting Teamsters v. United States, 431 U.S. 324, 340 (1977)). The justices seem enamored of this quotation; they also used it in *Hazelwood School District v. United States* (1977).
82. Robert St. Martin Westley, "White Normativity and the Rhetoric of Equal Protection," in Lewis R. Gordon, ed., *Existence in Black: An Anthology of Black Existential Philosophy* (New York: Routledge, 1997), 97–98.
83. 476 U.S. 287.
84. Compare Kathleen Sullivan's contrasting analysis of the innocence trope, which treats it in quasi-religious terms, emphasizing themes of sin, penance, suffering, sacrifice, and redemption: "Sins of Discrimination: Last Term's Affirmative Action Cases," 100 *Harvard Law Review* 78 (1986).

85. 476 U.S. 281 n. 8.
86. Richmond v. J.A. Croson Co., 488 U.S. 469, 528 (1989) (Scalia, J., concurring).
87. Quoted in Urofsky, *Affirmative Action Puzzle*, 249. Reynolds expounded this view at length in "Individualism vs. Group Rights: The Legacy of Brown," 93 *Yale Law Journal* 995 (1984). See James M. DeLise, "Racial Impermissibility under the Equal Protection Clause from Strauder v. West Virginia to Ricci v. Destefano," 17 *Rutgers Race & Law Review* 179, 181 (2016).
88. Missouri v. Jenkins, 515 U.S. 70, 120-121 (1995) (Thomas, J., concurring).
89. The four cases are Wards Cove Packing Co., Inc. v. Atonio, 490 U.S. 642 (1989); Martin v. Wilks, 490 U.S. 755 (1989); Patterson v. McLean Credit Union, 491 U.S. 164 (1989); Price Waterhouse v. Hopkins, 490 U.S. 228 (1989). The significance of this quartet was obscured by the blockbuster affirmative action case of that term, Richmond v. J.A. Croson Co., 488 U.S. 468 (1989).
90. Belton, *Crusade for Equality in the Workplace*, 268.
91. This material on the 1989 cases draws on Wiecek and Hamilton, "Beyond the Civil Rights Act," 1149-1154.
92. Melissa Hart, "Procedural Extremism: The Supreme Court's 2008-2009 Labor and Employment Cases," 13 *Employer Rights and Employment Policy Journal* 253, 253-256 (2009). See also Catherine R. Albiston and Laura Beth Nielsen, "The Procedural Attack on Civil Rights: The Empirical Reality of Buckhannon for the Private Attorney General," 54 *UCLA Law Review* 1087 (2007).
93. 411 U.S. 792 (1973).
94. 490 U.S. 642, 679 (1989) (Stevens, Brennan, Marshall, and Blackmun, J., dissented).
95. 490 U.S. 657.
96. Michael Braswell et al., "Disparate Impact Theory in the Aftermath of Wards Cove Packing Co. v. Atonio: Burdens of Proof, Statistical Evidence, and Affirmative Action," 54 *Albany Law Review* 1, 2 (1989).
97. 490 U.S. at 662 (Blackmun, J., dissenting).
98. 490 U.S. 649, n. 4.
99. 490 U.S. 755 (1989).
100. This is known as "impermissible collateral attack." The non-participating parties are said to be "sitting on the sidelines" and are precluded from getting into the game after it is over.
101. 491 U.S. 164 (1989). The Court had earlier alarmed civil rights advocates by *sua sponte* ordering re-argument on the question of whether it should reverse its earlier decision in Runyon v. McCrary, 427 U.S. 160 (1976), which held that section 1981 covered private conduct. *Patterson*, 485 U.S. at 617. Justices Stevens, Brennan, Marshall, and Blackmun dissented from the order for re-arguments in opinions by Stevens and Blackmun, criticizing the majority's unfounded and capricious determination to reopen a settled issue in such a fraught area. 485 U.S. 619-623. The reargument attracted eminent counsel on both sides of that issue on brief and as amici. The Court prudently decided to decline that radical move. See "Symposium on the Reconsideration of Runyon v. McCrary," 67 *Washington University Law Quarterly* 1 (1989).
102. 491 U.S. 181-182.
103. 42 U.S.C. § 1981(a)(1) (1989) (damages); 42 U.S.C. § 2000e(5) (back pay).
104. 491 U.S. at 191-200 (Brennan, J., dissenting).
105. Linda S. Greene, "Race in the 21st Century: Equality through Law?," 64 *Tulane Law Review* 1515, 1517 (1990).
106. Civil Rights Act of 1991, Publ. Law No. 102-166, 105 Stat. 1071.
107. 105 Stat. 1071: "(2) the decision of the Supreme Court in Wards Cove Packing Co. v. Atonio, 490 U.S. 642 (1989) has weakened the scope and effectiveness of Federal civil rights protections."
108. 42 U.S.C., sec. 2000e-2(k). However, Justice Scalia later suggested that the disparate impact standard, codified or not, may be unconstitutional: Ricci v. DeStefano, 557 U.S. 557, 594-595 (2009) (Scalia, J. concurring).
109. 557 U.S. 557 (2009).
110. 557 U.S. 594.
111. Texas Department of Housing and Community Affairs v. The Inclusive Communities Project, 576 U.S. 519 (2015).
112. Here the Court for the first time acknowledged the insights of Charles R. Lawrence's pathbreaking "The Id, the Ego, and Equal Protection: Reckoning with Unconscious Racism," 39

Stanford Law Review 317 (1987). See Lawrence, "Unconscious Racism Revisited: Reflections on the Impact and Origins of 'The Id, the Ego, and Equal Protection,'" 40 *Connecticut Law Review* 931 (2008).
113. These are itemized in Wiecek, "Supreme Court and Residential Segregation," 115–116.
114. Richard Primus, "The Future of Disparate Impact," 108 *Michigan Law Review* 1341 (2010); Primus, "Equal Protection and Disparate Impact: Round Three," 117 *Harvard Law Review* 493 (2003).
115. 488 U.S. 469, 499, 503, 506–507, 561 (1989).
116. 488 U.S. 469, 551–551 (Marshall, J. dissenting).
117. 488 U.S. 561 (Blackmun, J. dissenting).
118. 488 U.S. 508.
119. Kathleen M. Sullivan, "City of Richmond v. J. A. Croson Co.: The Backlash against Affirmative Action," 64 *Tulane Law Review* 1609 (1989).
120. 488 U.S. 501.
121. Michel Rosenfeld, "Decoding Richmond: Affirmative Action and the Elusive Meaning of Constitutional Equality," 87 *Michigan Law Review* 1729 (1989).
122. Rosenfeld, "Decoding Richmond," 1731.
123. "Constitutional Scholars' Statement on Affirmative Action after City of Richmond v. J. A. Croson Co.," 98 *Yale Law Journal* 1711 (1989).
124. 497 U.S. 547 (1990).
125. 515 U.S. 200 (1995).
126. 515 U.S. at 204.
127. 515 U.S. 205.
128. "The Congress shall have power to enforce, by appropriate legislation, the provisions of this article."
129. This was the influential thesis propounded by Gerald Gunther in "The Supreme Court 1971 Term—Foreword: In Search of Evolving Doctrine on a Changing Court: A Model for a Newer Equal Protection," 86 *Harvard Law Review* 1 (1972). Adam Winkler concludes, however, that O'Connor has been proven correct: "Fatal in Theory and Strict in Fact: An Empirical Analysis of Strict Scrutiny in the Federal Courts," 59 *Vanderbilt Law Review* 793 (2006).
130. 515 U.S. 239. This was an unfortunate rhetorical flourish by Scalia. "One nation, one race" evokes memories of the Nazi slogan of the 1930s: *Ein Volk, ein Reich, Ein Fuhrer.*
131. 515 U.S. 240 (ital. added).
132. 515 U.S. 274.

Chapter 11

1. Richard A. Primus, "Second Redemption, Third Reconstruction," 106 *California Law Review* 1987 (2018).
2. The metaphor of strands or branches of equal protection was suggested by the late Gerald Gunther in his enduring casebook *Constitutional Law*. Its current iteration is Noah Feldman and Kathleen M. Sullivan, *Constitutional Law*, 21st ed. (St. Paul: Foundation, 2022), 836–837. This section on fundamental-rights analysis is taken from William M. Wiecek, "The United States Supreme Court and Residential Segregation: 'Slavery Unwilling to Die,'" 3 *Journal of Law, Property & Society* 36, 80–86 (2017).
3. Wallace Mendelson, "From Warren to Burger: The Rise and Decline of Substantive Equal Protection," 66 *American Political Science Review* 1226 (1972).
4. 316 U.S. 535, 541 (1942) (holding that an arbitrary decision to impose sterilization on one class of repeat offenders [grand larceny] but not on a comparable group [embezzlers] violated the equal protection clause). There was, unsurprisingly, a racial motif behind such legislation: the more drastic penalty was reserved for categories of crimes that white legislators thought were likely to be committed by African Americans, such as chicken-stealing. Just as unsurprisingly, the Court did not advert to this racial subtext.
5. Jud Campbell, "Fundamental Rights before Realism," 2020 *University of Illinois Law Review* 1433 (2020).
6. The Twenty-Fourth Amendment, ratified in 1964, had abolished the poll tax in *federal* elections.

7. Harper v. Virginia State Board of Elections, 383 U.S. 663, 669 (1966). However, the Court has declined to apply fundamental-rights analysis to racially tinged voting rights cases.
8. 394 U.S. 618, 627 (1969).
9. 394 U.S. at 677.
10. Academic commentators pounced on this possibility immediately: Frank I. Michelman, "Foreword: On Protecting the Poor through the Fourteenth Amendment," 83 *Harvard Law Review* 7 (1969).
11. "Rights such as these are in principle indistinguishable from those involved here, and to extend the 'compelling interest' rule to all cases in which such rights are affected would go far toward making this Court a super-legislature." Harlan J. dissenting at 394 U.S. 661.
12. 397 U.S. 471 (1970). AFDC (Aid to Families with Dependent Children) was replaced in 1997 by TANF (Temporary Assistance to Needy Families).
13. 405 U.S. 56, 74 (1972) (upholding a state procedure that barred the defense of warranty of habitability in proceedings for evicting holdover tenants who are behind in rent payments).
14. 407 U.S. 163 (1972).
15. Civil Rights Cases, 109 U.S. 3, 42 (1873).
16. 326 U.S. 501 (1946). The "white primary" cases, culminating in Smith v. Allwright, 321 U.S. 649 (1944), also attributed a public function to a nominally private actor (a subset of a political party).
17. 334 U.S. 1 (1948).
18. 365 U.S. 715 (1961).
19. 387 U.S. 369 (1967).
20. Trimble v. Gordon, 430 U.S. 762, 777 (1977) (Rehnquist, J. dissenting).
21. J. Morgan Kousser provides a valuable historical introduction to the problem of discriminatory intent / disparate impact in *Colorblind Injustice: Minority Voting Rights and the Undoing of the Second Reconstruction* (Chapel Hill: University of North Carolina Press, 1999), 317–365.
22. *Black's Law Dictionary*, 11th ed. (St. Paul: Thomson, 2019): "per se": "Of, in, or by itself; standing alone, without reference to additional facts."
23. However, the intent of the framers in drafting the Fourteenth Amendment is difficult to resolve with certainty. See Paul Finkelman, "Original Intent and the Fourteenth Amendment: Into the Black Hole of Constitutional Law," 89 *Chicago-Kent Law Review* 1019 (2014); William E. Nelson, *The Fourteenth Amendment: From Political Principle to Judicial Doctrine* (Cambridge: Harvard University Press, 1988), 1–147; Robert J. Kaczorowski, "Searching for the Intent of the Framers of the Fourteenth Amendment," 5 *Connecticut Law Review* 368 (1972).
24. McCleskey v. Kemp, 481 U.S. 289 (1987).
25. 401 U.S. 424 (1971).
26. Heart of Atlanta Motel v. United States, 379 U.S. 241 (1964), and Katzenbach v. McClung, 379 U.S. 294 (1964).
27. Civil Rights Act of 1964, sec. 703, 78 Stat. 255, codified at 42 U.S.C. sec. 2000e-2 (a)(h).
28. The foremost authority on Griggs is Robert Belton, *The Crusade for Equality in the Workplace: The Griggs v. Duke Power Story* (Lawrence: University Press of Kansas, 2014). Belton was one of the attorneys who participated in the case before the Supreme Court. Robert S. Smith provided a detailed history of the Griggs litigation in *Race, Labor & Civil Rights: Griggs v. Duke Power and the Struggle for Equal Employment Opportunity* (Baton Rouge: Louisiana State University Press, 2008). See too David J. Garrow, "Toward a Definitive History of Griggs v. Duke Power Co.," 67 *Vanderbilt Law Review* 197 (2014); Samuel Estreicher, "The Story of Griggs v. Duke Power Co.," in Joel W. Friedman, ed., *Employment Discrimination Stories* (New York: Foundation, 2006), 153–172.
29. 401 U.S. 431–432. In *McDonnell Douglas v. Green*, 411 U.S. 792 (1973), the Court specified the procedures under this new standard. The plaintiff bore the initial burden of providing prima facie evidence of discrimination by the employer, but could do so by a simple, straightforward test. The plaintiff merely had to prove that he was a racial minority, he applied for a job for which he was qualified, he was not hired, and the employer continued to try to fill the position. Then the burden shifted onto the employer to demonstrate a legitimate business purpose.
30. Smith, *Race, Labor & Civil Rights*, 174.
31. Alfred W. Blumrosen, "The Legacy of Griggs: Social Progress and Subjective Judgment," 63 *Chicago-Kent Law Review* 1 (1987); Blumrosen, "Strangers in Paradise: Griggs v. Duke Power and the Concept of Employment Discrimination," 71 *Michigan Law Review* 59 (1972).

32. Belton, *Crusade for Equality in the Workplace*, 3.
33. For example: among lower federal courts: Castro v. Beecher, 459 F.2d 725 (1st Cir. 1971); among academic commentators: Owen Fiss, "The Charlotte-Mecklenburg Case—Its Significance for Northern School Desegregation," 38 *University of Chicago Law Review* 697 (1971) (in the context of school desegregation, not employment).
34. Davis v. Washington, 512 F.2d 956 (D.C. Cir. 1975).
35. Michael J. Graetz and Linda Greenhouse, The *Burger Court and the Rise of the Judicial Right* (New York: Simon and Schuster, 2016), 287–293.
36. 426 U.S. 229, 242 (1976). This material on *Washington v. Davis* is drawn from William M. Wiecek and Judy L. Hamilton, "Beyond the Civil Rights Act of 1964: Confronting Structural Racism in the Workplace," 74 *Louisiana Law Review* 1095, 1137–1140 (2014).
37. 426 U.S. 239, 240.
38. 426 U.S. 246.
39. 426 U.S. 242.
40. 426 U.S. 245.
41. 426 U.S. 242.
42. Reva Siegel, "Why Equal Protection No Longer Protects: The Evolving Forms of Status Enforcing State Action," 49 *Stanford Law Review* 1111 (1997).
43. Justin Driver, *The School House Gate: Public Education, the Supreme Court, and the Battle for the American Mind* (New York: Random House, 2018), 281.
44. 426 U.S. 248.
45. 403 U.S. 217 (1971).
46. For purposes of discussion here, I treat the concepts of intent, purpose, and motive as rough equivalents.
47. Charles R. Lawrence, "The Id, the Ego, and Equal Protection: Reckoning with Unconscious Racism," 39 *Stanford Law Review* 317 (1987). See the discussion of unconscious bias in Wiecek and Hamilton, "Beyond the Civil Rights Act," 1114–1118 and sources cited there, particularly those in note 82. However, in *Texas Dept. of Community Affairs v. Inclusive Communities Project* (2015), Justice Anthony Kennedy conceded that "recognition of disparate-impact liability under the [Fair Housing Act] also plays a role in uncovering discriminatory intent: It permits plaintiffs to counteract unconscious prejudices and disguised animus that escape easy classification as disparate treatment." 576 U.S. 519, 540 (2015). The Court has not otherwise acknowledged the pervasive role of unconscious bias in human decision-making, and the *Inclusive Communities* case may prove to be a wobbly precedent in the future.
48. Barbara J. Flagg, "'Was Blind, but Now I See': White Race Consciousness and the Requirement of Discriminatory Intent," 91 *Michigan Law Review* 953, 957 (1993).
49. John O. Calmore, "Close Encounters of the Racial Kind: Pedagogical Reflections and Seminar Conversations," 31 *University of San Francisco Law Review* 903, 917 (1997).
50. David A. Strauss, "Discriminatory Intent and the Taming of Brown," 56 *University of Chicago Law Review* 935 (1989).
51. Alan D. Freeman, "Legitimizing Racial Discrimination through Antidiscrimination Law: A Critical Review of Supreme Court Doctrine," 62 *Minnesota Law Review* 1049 (1978).
52. Pamela Karlan, "Discriminatory Purpose and Mens Rea: The Tortured Argument of Invidious Intent," 93 *Yale Law Journal* 111 (1989) (comparing the Davis purpose requirement with the criminal standard of mens rea). *Mens rea* refers to a criminal state of mind, inferring intent, while *actus reus* means the criminal act itself.
53. City of Memphis v. Greene, 451 U.S. 100 (1981).
54. City of Mobile v. Bolden, 446 U.S. 55 (1980).
55. Margaret Richardson and Todd L. Pittinsky, "The Mistaken Assumption of Intentionality in Equal Protection Law: Psychological Science and the Interpretation of the Fourteenth Amendment," John F. Kennedy School of Government, Faculty Research Working Papers Series, May 12, 2005.
56. Theodore Eisenberg and Sheri Lynn Johnston, "The Effect of Intent: Do We Know How Legal Standards Work?," 76 *Cornell Law Review* 1151 (1991).
57. Laura Beth Nielsen and Robert L. Nelson, "Scaling the Pyramid: A Sociolegal Model of Employment Discrimination Litigation," in Laura Beth Nielsen and Robert L. Nelson, eds. *Handbook of Employment Discrimination Research: Rights and Realities* (New York: Springer, 2005), 3–34.

510   NOTES TO PAGES 381–6

58. Laura Beth Nielsen and Robert L. Nelson, "Uncertain Justice: Litigating Claims of Employment Discrimination in the Contemporary U.S.," 19 *Researching Law* No. 2, https://www.americanbarfoundation.org/resources/uncertain-justice-litigating-claims-of-employment-discrimination-in-the-contemporary-u-s/.
59. Paul Brest, "Foreword: In Defense of the Antidiscrimination Principle," 90 *Harvard Law Review* 1 (1976); Theodore Eisenberg, "Disproportionate Impact and Illicit Motive: Theories of Constitutional Adjudication," 52 *NYU Law Review* 36 (1977); Michael J. Perry, "The Disproportionate Impact Theory of Racial Discrimination," 125 *University of Pennsylvania Law Review* 540 (1977); Robert Schwemm, "From Washington to Arlington Heights and Beyond: Discriminatory Purpose in Equal Protection Litigation," *University of Illinois Law Forum* 961 (1977); Kenneth L. Karst, "The Costs of Motive-Centered Inquiry," 15 *San Diego Law Review* 1163 (1978); Freeman, "Legitimizing Racial Discrimination."
60. Gayle Binion, "Intent and Equal Protection: A Reconsideration," 1983 *Supreme Court Review* 397 (1983); David A. Strauss, "Discriminatory Intent and the Taming of Brown," 56 *University of Chicago Law Review* 935 (1989).
61. "Governor Signs Bill Requiring Reviews of All Legislation for Legislative Impacts," *Portland* [Maine] *Press Herald*, March 19, 2021, at https://www.pressherald.com/2021/03/19/mills-signs-into-law-bill-requiring-racial-impact-statements-on-new-legislation/.
62. Graetz and Greenhouse, *Burger Court*, 79–102.
63. Reva B. Siegel, "Foreword: Equality Divided," 127 *Harvard Law Review* 1 (2013).
64. Siegel, "Foreword: Equality Divided," 7 (2013).
65. Justice White wrote: "Necessarily, an invidious discriminatory purpose may often be inferred from the totality of the relevant facts, including the fact, if it is true, that the law bears more heavily on one race than another." 426 U.S. 242.
66. 442 U.S. 256 (1979).
67. Quoted at 442 U.S. 260.
68. 442 U.S. at 279.
69. 442 U.S. 273.
70. The following paragraphs are taken from Wiecek and Hamilton, "Beyond the Civil Rights Act," 1141–1142.
71. Reva Siegal, "Why Equal Protection No Longer Protects: The Evolving Forms of Status Enforcing State Action," 49 *Stanford Law Review* 1111, 1135 (1997); Ian Haney-Lopez, "Intentional Blindness," 87 *NYU Law Review* 1781, 1833–1877 (2012).
72. *Restatement (Third) of Torts: Liability for Physical and Emotional Harm* (2010), sec. 1.
73. *Restatement (Third) of Torts: : Liability for Physical and Emotional Harm*, sec. 1, comment c, illustration 3.
74. *Model Penal Code*, sec. 2.02.
75. 481 U.S. 279, 281, 292 (1987).
76. 481 U.S. 292 (ital. in orig.).
77. 481 U.S. 298 (ital. in orig.).
78. 431 U.S. 324 (1977).
79. Section 703(h) provided that "it shall not be an unlawful employment practice for an employer to apply different standards of compensation [etc.]...pursuant to a bona fide seniority or merit system...provided that such differences are not the result of an intent to discriminate because of race, color..."
80. 456 U.S. 63 (1982). See Note, "American Tobacco Company v. Patterson: The Supreme Court Clarifies the Scope of Title VII's Section 703(h) Seniority System Exception," 14 *University of Toledo Law Review* 433 (1982).
81. 458 U.S. 375 (1982).
82. 42 U.S.C. sec. 1981.
83. 458 U.S. 389.
84. 377 U.S. 533, 555 (1964).
85. Bradwell v. Illinois, 83 U.S. (16 Wall.) 130 (1873); Minor v. Happersett, 88 U.S. (21 Wall.) 162 (1874).
86. In addition, the Seventeenth Amendment made the US Senate elected by the people; the Twenty-Third granted residents of the District of Columbia a vote in the electoral college; the Twenty-Fourth abolished the poll tax in federal elections.
87. "It is unnecessary to consider now whether legislation which restricts those political processes which can ordinarily be expected to bring about repeal of undesirable legislation, is to be

subjected to more exacting judicial scrutiny under the general prohibitions of the Fourteenth Amendment than are most other types of legislation [such as] restrictions upon the right to vote." *United States v. Carolene Products Co.*, 304 U.S. 144, 153 (1938).
88. 383 U.S. 663, 667 (1966) quoting *Yick Wo v. Hopkins*, 118 U.S. 356, 370 (1886) and citing *Reynolds v. Sims*, 377 U.S. 533, 561 (1964).
89. 369 U.S. 186 (1962).
90. 377 U.S. 533, 554 (1964).
91. 383 U.S. 301, 325 (1966). On the history of implementation of the Voting Rights Act, see Ari Berman, *Give Us the Ballot: The Modern Struggle for Voting Rights in America* (New York: Farrar, Strauss and Giroux, 2015).
92. 383 U.S. 633, 669 (1966).
93. 395 U.S. 621 (1969) (school board elections).
94. 405 U.S. 330, 336 (1972).
95. White v. Regester, 412 U.S. 755 (1973); Thornburg v. Gingles, 478 U.S. 30 (1986).
96. City of Petersburg v. United States, 410 U.S. 962 (1973), affirming 353 F.Supp. 1021 (1972).
97. Alexander Keyssar, *The Right to Vote: The Contested History of Democracy in the United States* (New York: Basic Books, 2000), 318.
98. J. Morgan Kousser, *Colorblind Injustice: Minority Voting Rights and the Undoing of the Second Reconstruction* (Chapel Hill: University of North Carolina Press, 1999); Kousser, *The Shaping of Southern Politics: Suffrage Restriction and the Establishment of the One-Party South, 1880–1910* (New Haven: Yale University Press, 1974).
99. J. Morgan Kousser, "The Supreme Court and the Undoing of the Second Reconstruction," 80.2 *Phi Kappa Phi Journal* 28 (2000), http://www.its.caltech.edu/~kousser/racial%20discrimination/The%20Supreme%20Court%20and%20the%20Undoing%20of%20the%20Second%20Reconstruction.pdf.
100. Alec C. Ewald, "'Civil Death': The Ideological Paradox of Criminal Disenfranchisement Law in the United States," 2002 *Wisconsin Law Review* 1045 (2002); Pippa Holloway recounts the history of felon disfranchisement before World War I in *Living in Infamy: Felon Disfranchisement and the History of American Citizenship* (New York: Oxford University Press, 2014).
101. Melanie Bowers and Robert R. Preuhs, "Collateral Consequences of a Collateral Penalty: The Negative Effect of Felon Disenfranchisement Laws on the Political Participation of Nonfelons," 90 *Social Science Quarterly* 722–743 (2009); Bridgett A. King and Laura Erickson, "Disenfranchising the Enfranchised: Exploring the Relationship between Felony Disenfranchisement and African American Voter Turnout," 47 *Journal of Black Studies* 799–821 (2016).
102. Angela Behrens, "Voting—Not Quite a Fundamental Right? A Look at Legal and Legislative Challenges to Felon Disfranchisement Laws," 89 *Minnesota Law Review* 231, 236–240 (2004).
103. Jamie Fellner and Marc Mauer of Human Rights Watch and the Sentencing Project, *Losing the Vote: The Impact of Felony Disenfranchisement Laws in the United States* (New York: Human Rights Watch, 1998).
104. Angela Behrens et al., "Ballot Manipulation and the 'Menace of Negro Domination': Racial Threat and Felon Disfranchisement in the United States, 1850–2002," 109 *American Journal of Sociology* 559 (2003).
105. "The Mississippi Plan" refers to a strategy white Democrats adopted in that state to deprive African Americans of the vote by a combination of overt legal techniques like the literacy test plus extralegal violence like nightriding. It culminated in the 1890 Mississippi constitutional convention and the revised state constitution that it produced, which rolled back nearly all aspects of Reconstruction in that state. It provided a blueprint for similar efforts in the other ex-Confederate states.
106. The argument contra: the phrase "the right to vote" in section 2 explicitly recognizes that there *is* a right to vote, and that it enjoys constitutional protection. A right to vote is implicitly recognized by the guarantee clause of Article IV, second 4: "The United States shall guarantee to every State in this Union a Republican Form of Government." But that is an argument for another time. See Gabriel J. Chin, "Justifying a Revised Voting Rights Act: The Guarantee Clause and the Problem of Minority Rule," 94 *Boston University Law Review* 1551 (2014).
107. *United States v. Reese*, 92 U.S. 214, 217 (1875).
108. *Wesberry v. Sanders*, 376 U.S. 1, 17 (1964).
109. 383 U.S. 663, 665 (1966).
110. Lubin v. Panish, 415 U.S. 709, 714 (1974).

111. Ramirez v. Brown, 9 Cal.3d 199, 507 P.2d 1345 (1973).
112. 418 U.S. 24, 54–55 (1974).
113. And has been: Abigail M. Hinchcliff, "The 'Other' Side of Richardson v. Ramirez: A Textual Challenge to Felon Disenfranchisement," 121 *Yale Law Journal* 194 (2011).
114. 418 U.S. 55.
115. Michelle Alexander, *The New Jim Crow: Mass Incarceration in the Age of Colorblindness*, rev. ed. (New York: New Press, 2020), 158–161.
116. In addition to the works by Kousser and Keyssar, see Ewald, "Civil Death"; Andrew L. Shapiro, "Challenging Criminal Disenfranchisement under the Voting Rights Act: A New Strategy," 103 *Yale Law Journal* 537, 543 (1993); Fellner and Maurer, *Losing the Vote*; Patricia Allard and Marc Mauer, *Regaining the Vote: An Assessment of Activity Relating to Felon Disenfranchisement Laws* (Washington, DC: Sentencing Project, 2001); Note, "One Person, No Vote: The Laws of Felon Disenfranchisement," 115 *Harvard Law Review* 1939 (2002); Pamela S. Karlan, "Convictions and Doubts: Retribution, Representation, and the Debate over Felon Disenfranchisement," 56 *Stanford Law Review* 1147 (2004); Jeff Manza, Christopher Uggen, and Angela Behrens, "The Racial Origins of Felon Disenfranchisement," in Manza and Uggen, *Locked Out: Felon Disenfranchisement and American Democracy* (New York: Oxford University Press, 2006), 41–68; Katherine Pettus, *Felony Disenfranchisement in America: Historical Origins, Institutional Racism, and Modern Consequences* (Albany: State University of New York Press, 2013); Jean Chung, Felony Disenfranchisement: A Primer (2018), https://www.sentencingproject.org/publications/felony-disenfranchisement-a-primer.
117. Chin, "Reconstruction, Felon Disenfranchisement," 264.
118. Jones v. DeSantis, U.S.D.C. Northern District of Fla., 2020; opinion reprinted at https://www.miamiherald.com/latest-news/article242972806.ece/BINARY/Amendment%204%20ruling.pdf#storylink=readmore_inline.
119. Raysor v. DeSantis, U.S. Supreme Court No. 19A1071 at https://www.supremecourt.gov/opinions/19pdf/19a1071_4h25.pdf.
120. The original gerrymander cartoon is reproduced at https://theoligarchkings.files.wordpress.com/2011/02/gerrymander.jpg.
121. 478 U.S. 109, 143 (1986).
122. 139 S.Ct. 2484 (2019), abrogating *Davis v. Bandemer*.
123. 364 U.S. 339, 341 (1960).
124. 412 U.S. 735, 754 (1973).
125. Pub. L. 89-110, 79 Stat. 437.
126. "[F]or the purpose or with the effect of denying or abridging the right to vote on account of race or color": 79 Stat. 438.
127. On the tangled history of enactment of the Voting Rights Act, see J. Morgan Kousser, "The Strange, Ironic Career of Section 5 of the Voting Rights Act, 1965–2007," 86 *Texas Law Review* 667 (2008).
128. 446 U.S. 55 (1980).
129. On the Voting Rights Act history, see Berman, *Give Us the Ballot*. Christopher M. Burke examines theories of representation that inform the debates on the Voting Rights Act in *The Appearance of Equality: Racial Gerrymandering, Redistricting, and the Supreme Court* (Westport: Greenwood, 1999).
130. Lawrence Goldstone, *On Account of Race: The Supreme Court, White Supremacy, and the Ravaging of African American Voting Rights* (Berkeley: Counterpoint, 2020), 5.
131. To cite just one representative example: Justice O'Connor noted that in North Carolina, "the black population is relatively dispersed; blacks constitute a majority of the general population in only 5 of the State's 100 counties." Shaw v. Reno, 509 U.S. 630, 634 (1993). In that same case, Justice White referred to North Carolina's "voluntary effort to endure a modicum of voluntary representation [where] a minority population is geographically dispersed." 509 U.S. at 673.
132. L. Paige Whitaker, "Congressional Redistricting and the Voting Rights Act: A Legal Overview," Congressional Research Service, April 13, 2015, https://fas.org/sgp/crs/misc/R42482.pdf.
133. Redistricting consists of redrawing the boundaries of federal and state legislative districts in response to shifts in population. It follows the decennial US census.
134. 478 U.S. 30, 31, 74, 80 (1986).
135. 430 U.S. 144, 161 (1977).
136. Davis v. Bandemer, 478 U.S. 109, 167 (1986) (Powell, J. concurring).

137. On these cases, see Tinsley E. Yarbrough, *Race and Redistricting: The Shaw-Cromartie Cases* (Lawrence: University Press of Kansas, 2002), and Nancy L. Maveety, *Representation Rights and the Burger Years* (Ann Arbor: University of Michigan Press, 1991).
138. 509 U.S. 630 (1993).
139. 509 U.S. 641–642.
140. In gerrymandering terminology, "pack" means to concentrate a racial bloc like African Americans or Latinx into one district, where their votes will be "wasted"; "crack" means to split such blocs into different districts to reduce or eliminate their voting effectiveness; and "stack" means to place that bloc in a district where its size will be overshadowed by an even larger opposing bloc. "Waste" refers to the votes above the minimum (50 percent plus one in a two-way race) needed to elect a candidate.
141. Flast v. Cohen, 392 U.S. 83, 106 (1968).
142. 509 U.S. 659.
143. 509 U.S. 681–682.
144. 509 U.S. 667.
145. 509 U.S. 675 (ital. in orig.).
146. 515 U.S. 900, 913–916 (1995).
147. 515 U.S. 927.
148. 517 U.S. 899 (1996).
149. 517 U.S. 952, 959 (1996).
150. 532 U.S. 234, 242 (2001).
151. The third, Hunt v. Cromartie, 526 U.S. 541 (1999), simply reversed a summary judgment.
152. Pamela S. Karlan, "Easing the Spring: Strict Scrutiny and Affirmative Action after the Redistricting Cases," 43 *William & Mary Law Review* 1569, 1572–1573, 1603 (2002).
153. Kousser, *Shaping of Southern Politics*, 45–63; Keyssar, *The Right to Vote*, 87–116 generally; 108–116 on disfranchisement.
154. See in general Richard L. Hasen, *Election Meltdown: Dirty Tricks, Distrust, and the Threat to American Democracy* (New Haven: Yale University Press, 2020), 15–46.
155. William H. Rehnquist got his start in Arizona Republican politics this way. Tova A. Wang, *The Politics of Voter Suppression: Defending and Expanding Americans' Right to Vote* (Ithaca: Cornell University Press, 2012), 42–60.
156. Carol Anderson, *One Person, No Vote: How Voter Suppression Is Destroying Our Democracy* (New York: Bloomsbury, 2019); Allan J. Lichtman, *The Embattled Vote in America: From the Founding to the Present* (Cambridge: Harvard University Press, 2018).
157. A thorough, dispassionate, and nonpartisan review of these laws (a rare achievement) and the controversies surrounding them is Eric A. Fischer et al. of the Congressional Research Service, *State Voter Identification Requirements: Analysis, Legal Issues, and Policy Considerations*, October 21, 2016, https://fas.org/sgp/crs/misc/R42806.pdf.
158. A new adult passport cost $140 in 2020, not a trivial sum for poor people.
159. 553 U.S. 181, 191, 196–197, 194, 198, 204 (2008). See Joshua A. Douglas, "The History of Voter ID Laws and the Story of Marion County Election Board," in Douglas and Eugene D. Mazo, eds., *Election Law Stories* (St. Paul: Foundation, 2016), 453–504.
160. Three justices supported the plurality opinion: Stevens, Rehnquist, Kennedy; three others concurred in the result: Scalia, Thomas, Alito; three dissented: Souter, Ginsburg, Breyer. The Court considered only the equal protection issue; it did not take up section 2 of the Voting Rights Act.
161. Cody S. Barnett and Joshua A. Douglas, "A Voice in the Wilderness: John Paul Stevens, Election Law, and a Theory of Impartial Governance," 60 *William & Mary Law Review* 335 (2018).
162. Bureau of Motor Vehicles.
163. 553 U.S. 205, 207 (ital. in orig.)
164. 553 U.S. 236–237, 226.
165. Crawford v. Marion County Election Board, 472 F.3d 949 (7th Cir. 2007).
166. Richard A. Posner, *Reflections on Judging* (Cambridge: Harvard University Press, 2013), 85.
167. John Schwartz, "Judge in Landmark Case Disavows Support for Voter ID," *New York Times*, October 15, 2013, at https://www.nytimes.com/2013/10/16/us/politics/judge-in-landmark-case-disavows-support-for-voter-id.html.
168. Robert Barnes, "Stevens Says Supreme Court Decision on Voter ID Was Correct, but Maybe Not Right," *Washington Post*, May 15, 2016, https://www.washingtonpost.com/politics/

169. courts_law/stevens-says-supreme-court-decision-on-voter-id-was-correct-but-maybe-not-right/2016/05/15/9683c51c-193f-11e6-9e16-2e5a123aac62_story.html?utm_term=.536daee64132.
169. "Comment: The Supreme Court—Leading Cases," 122 *Harvard Law Review* 355, 364 (2008).
170. David R. Roediger, *The Wages of Whiteness: Race and the Making of the American Working Class* (New York: Verso, 1997), 59–60, 172.
171. Anderson, *One Person, No Vote*; Zoltan Hajnal et al., "Voter Identification Laws and the Suppression of Minority Votes," 79 *Journal of Politics* 363 (2017).
172. South Carolina v. Katzenbach, 383 U.S. 301, 328 (1966).
173. 383 U.S. 328.
174. 17 U.S. (4 Wheat.) 316, 326 (1819).
175. Jaime Fuller, "Republicans Used to Unanimously Back the Voting Rights Act. Not Any More," *Washington Post*, June 26, 2014, https://www.washingtonpost.com/news/the-fix/wp/2014/06/26/republicans-used-to-unanimously-back-voting-rights-act-not-any-more/?utm_term=.dccaf4b461d3.
176. 557 U.S. 193, 207, 211 (2009).
177. Section 4(b) is the "coverage provision" of the statute, defining which jurisdictions fell under its preclearance requirement. 4(b) covered all jurisdictions (states and counties) that imposed a "test or device" (such as a literacy test) for voting and had less than 50 percent voter registration or turnout in the 1964 presidential election.
178. 570 U.S. 529, 557 (2013). On Shelby, see Berman, *Give Us the Vote*, 270–285.
179. 570 U.S. 557.
180. 570 U.S. 543 (ital. in orig.).
181. Citing Carrington v. Rash, 380 U.S. 89, 91 (1965).
182. As Justice Ginsburg emphasized in her dissent, 570 U.S. 587.
183. Coyle v. Smith, 221 U.S. 559 (1911).
184. 570 U.S. 547.
185. 570 U.S. 551.
186. Amy Davidson Sorkin, "In Voting Rights, Scalia Sees a 'Racial Entitlement,'" *New Yorker*, February 28, 2013.
187. *Black's Law Dictionary*: "brutum fulmen": "An empty noise; an empty threat; something ineffectual. 2. A judgment void on its face; one that is, in legal effect, no judgment at all."
188. 570 U.S. 590.
189. 570 U.S. 559.
190. 570 U.S. 563.
191. North Carolina State Conference of NAACP v. McCrory, 831 F.3d 204, 214 (4th Cir. 2016).
192. Desmond Ang, "Do 40-Year-Old Facts Still Matter? Long-Run Effects of Federal Oversight under the Voting Rights Act," 11 *American Economic Journal: Applied Economics* 1 (2019).
193. Morgan Kousser, "Do the Facts of Voting Rights Support Chief Justice Roberts's Opinion in Shelby County?," 1 *Transatlantica* (2015), http://journals.openedition.org/transatlantica/7462.
194. Most of this subchapter is taken from William M. Wiecek, "The United States Supreme Court and Residential Segregation: 'Slavery Unwilling to Die,'" 3 *Journal of Law, Property, and Society* 35–124 (2017).
195. Patrick Sharkey, *Stuck in Place: Urban Neighborhoods and the End of Progress toward Racial Equality* (Chicago: University of Chicago Press, 2013).
196. Bethany R. Berger, "Property to Race / Race to Property," April 12, 2021, https://dx.doi.org/10.2139/ssrn.3825124; quotation at p. 2.
197. Douglas S. Massey and Nancy A. Denton, "Hypersegregation in U.S. Metropolitan Areas: Black and Hispanic Segregation along Five Dimensions," 26.3 *Demography* 373–391 (1989).
198. Douglas S. Massey and Nancy A. Denton, *American Apartheid: Segregation and the Making of the Underclass* (Cambridge: Harvard University Press, 1993), viii.
199. Stephen Menendian, Arthur Gailes, and Samir Gambhir, "The Roots of Structural Racism: Twenty-First Century Racial Residential Segregation in the United States," June 1, 2021, https://www.councilforthehomeless.org/wp-content/uploads/2021/07/the_roots_of_structural_racism_report_and_appendix.pdf.
200. Richard Rothstein, *The Color of Law: A Forgotten History of How Our Government Segregated America* (New York: Liveright, 2017), vii–viii; Deborah Kenn, "Institutionalized Legal Racism: Housing Segregation and Beyond," 11 *Boston University Public Interest Law Journal* 35 (2001).

201. Keeanga-Yamahtta Taylor, *Race for Profit: How Banks and the Real Estate Industry Undermined Black Homeownership* (Chapel Hill: University of North Carolina Press, 2019), 5, 17–19, and *passim*.
202. John O. Calmore, "Race/ism Lost and Found: The Fair Housing Act at Thirty," 52 *University of Miami Law Review* 1067, 1071 (1998); John Yinger, *Closed Doors, Opportunities Lost: The Continuing Costs of Housing Discrimination* (New York: Russell Sage Foundation, 1995); James Kushner, "The Fair Housing Amendments Act of 1988: The Second Generation of Fair Housing," 42 *Vanderbilt Law Review* 1049, 1050 (1989); Margery Austin Turner, "Limits on Housing and Neighborhood Choice: Discrimination and Segregation in U.S. Housing Markets," 41 *Indiana Law Review* 797 (2008).
203. Joy Milligan, "Remembering: The Constitution and Federally Funded Apartheid," 89 *University of Chicago Law Review* 65 (2022).
204. Missouri v. Jenkins, 515 U.S. 70, 116 (1995) (Thomas, J. concurring).
205. Parents Involved in Community Schools. v. Seattle Sch. Dist. No. 1, 551 U.S. 701, 750 (2007) (Thomas, J. concurring).
206. Ginsburg, J. dissenting in Fisher v. University of Texas, 133 S.Ct. 2411 (2010).
207. Nancy A. Denton, "Segregation and Discrimination in Housing," in Rachel Bratt et al., *A Right to Housing: Foundation for a New Social Agenda* (Philadelphia: Temple University Press, 2006), 62.
208. George Lipsitz, *How Racism Takes Place* (Philadelphia: Temple University Press, 2011), 1–70.
209. Richard Thompson Ford, "The Boundaries of Race: Political Geography in Legal Analysis," 107 *Harvard Law Review* 1841, 1845 (1994).
210. Publ. L. 81-171, 63 Stat. 413; Publ. L. 83-560, 68 Stat. 590.
211. Robert Nelson, "Renewing Inequality," data visualization project at https://dsl.richmond.edu/panorama/renewal/#view=0/0/1&viz=cartogram.
212. Arnold R. Hirsch, *Making the Second Ghetto: Race and Housing in Chicago, 1940–1960* (Chicago: University of Chicago Press, 1998), 153.
213. Xavier de Souza Briggs, "Politics and Policy: Changing the Geography of Opportunity," in Briggs, ed., *The Geography of Opportunity: Race and Housing Choice in Metropolitan America* (Washington, DC: Brookings Institution, 2005), 311.
214. Jane Jacobs, *The Death and Life of Great American Cities* (New York: Random House, 1961), 4.
215. James Baldwin, "Urban Renewal…Means Negro Removal," interview, 1963, https://www.youtube.com/watch?v=T8Abhj17kYU; Brent Cebul, "Tearing Down Black America," *Boston Review*, July 22, 2020, http://bostonreview.net/race/brent-cebul-tearing-down-black-america.
216. 348 U.S. 26, 33 (1954); Amy Lavine, "Urban Renewal and the Story of Berman v. Parker," 42 *Urban Lawyer* 423 (2010).
217. US Const. Amend. V: "nor shall private property be taken for public use, without just compensation."
218. Hawaii Housing Authority v. Midkiff, 467 U.S. 229 (1984); Kelo v. New London, 545 U.S. 469 (2005).
219. 545 U.S. at 522 (Thomas, J. dissenting).
220. Reitman v. Mulkey, 387 U.S. 369 (1967).
221. 413 U.S. 455, 470 (1973).
222. 393 U.S. 385, 393 (1969).
223. Valtierra v. Housing Authority, 313 F. Supp. 1 (1970).
224. 402 U.S. 137 (1971). Justices Marshall, Brennan, and Blackmun, dissenting, treated the issue as one of poverty, not race, and attempted to have poverty given suspect-classification status, a doomed effort at the time.
225. 402 U.S. 141–142.
226. 402 U.S. at 141.
227. 426 U.S. 668, 679 (1976).
228. Approximately 95 percent of the residents of Cuyahoga Falls at the time were white. Twenty-five percent of the residents of Akron were Black, while approximately 45 percent of Cleveland's population were Black.
229. Arlington Heights v. Metropolitan Housing Corp., 429 U.S. 252, 266–268 (1977).
230. Buckeye Community Hope Foundation v. Cuyahoga Falls, 262 F.3d 627, 636 (6th Cir. 2001). Judge Jones also required that petitioners be given an opportunity to demonstrate a violation of the Fair Housing Act of 1968.

231. Reversal of a summary judgment does not result in a judgment for either party or a decision on the merits. It merely restores the litigation, sending it back to the trial court to be tried.
232. 538 U.S. 188 (2003).
233. On the discriminatory use of referenda generally, see Derrick Bell, "The Referendum: Democracy's Barrier to Racial Equality," 54 *Washington Law Review* 1 (1974).
234. 403 U.S. 217 (1971).
235. Quoted in Justice White's dissent, 403 U.S. 250.
236. In reality, of course, it did not. Jackson merely privatized some of the pools, which then continued to operate on a segregated basis.
237. I treat motive, intent, and purpose as equivalents.
238. Fletcher v. Peck, 10 U.S. (6 Cranch) 87 (1810); United States v. O'Brien, 391 U.S. 367 (1968).
239. 364 U.S. 339 (1960).
240. 377 U.S. 218 (1964).
241. Palmer v. Thompson, 403 U.S. 217, 224–225 (1971). See Paul Brest, "Palmer v. Thompson: An Approach to the Problem of Legislative Motive," 1971 *Supreme Court Review* 95 (1971). Black had been the author of the Griffin opinion, which he distinguished by claiming that that decision had actually been based on the effects of the closure, not the legislators' state of mind. White's dissent in Palmer provided ample proof of explicit segregationist intent at 403 U.S. 249–262.
242. David Tyler, "Traffic Regulation or Racial Segregation? The Closing of West Drive and Memphis v. Greene," 66 *Tennessee History Quarterly* 56 (2007).
243. Codified as 42 U.S.C. sec. 1982, affirming the right of "all citizens of the United States" "to inherit, purchase, lease, sell, hold, and convey real and personal property."
244. 451 U.S. 100, 119 (1981).
245. 396 U.S. 435 (1970). The following materials are drawn from Wiecek, "Supreme Court and Residential Segregation," 88–95.
246. Quoted in Evans v. Newton, 220 Ga. 280, 281, 138 S.E.2d 573 (1964).
247. In conformity with the holding in New Orleans City Park Improvement Ass'n. v. Detiege, 358 U.S. 54 (1958).
248. Evans v. Newton, 220 Ga. 280 (1964).
249. 382 U.S. 296 (1966).
250. Evans v. Newton, 221 Ga. 870 (1966); 224 Ga. 826 (1968).
251. I.e., Bacon. In trust law, the settlor is the person who creates the trust; the trustee is the person, body, or institution that holds legal title to the property given in trust and administers it; and the beneficiary is the person who benefits from it and holds what is called equitable title. In this case, that could be the residents of Macon, irrespective of race.
252. *Cy pres* is a Law rench term meaning an "equitable doctrine under which a court reforms a written instrument with a gift to charity as closely to the donor's intention as possible, so that the gift does not fail." *Black's Law Dictionary*, "cy pres."
253. 396 U.S. 454–455, 457.
254. On blockbusting, see Dmitri Mehlhorn, "A Requiem for Blockbusting: Law, Economics, and Race-Based Real Estate Speculation," 67 *Fordham Law Review* 1145 (1998); Gregory Sharp and Matthew Hall, "Emerging Forms of Racial Inequality in Homeownership Exit, 1968–2009," 61 *Social Problems* 427–447 (2014); Keeanga-Yamahtta Taylor, *Race for Profit*, 48–49.
255. Fair Housing Act of 1968, P.L. 90-284, 82 Stat. 73, sec. 804 (e), prohibiting "for profit, to induce or attempt to induce any person to sell or rent any dwelling by representations regarding the entry or prospective entry into the neighborhood of a person or persons of a particular race, color, religion, sex, handicap, familial status, or national origin."
256. Local residents then changed the township's name from Levittown to Willingboro, harking back to the area's original seventeenth-century name.
257. 431 U.S. 85 (1977).
258. Raymond A. Mohl, "Race and Space in a Modern City: Interstate 95 and the Black Community in Miami," in Mohl and Arnold R. Hirsch, *Urban Policy in Twentieth-Century America* (New Brunswick: Rutgers University Press, 1993), 102–103; Mark A. Rose and Raymond A. Mohl, *Interstate: Highway Politics and Policy since 1939* (Knoxville: University of Tennessee Press, 2012); Ronald H. Bayor, "Roads to Racial Segregation: Atlanta in the Twentieth Century," 15.1 *Journal of Urban History* 3–21 (1988).
259. William Bogart, "'What Big Teeth You Have!': Identifying the Motivations for Exclusionary Zoning," 30 *Urban Studies* 1669–1681 (1993).

260. On exclusionary zoning, see David M. Freund, *Colored Property: State Policy and White Racial Politics in Suburban America* (Chicago: University of Chicago Press, 2007); Marsha Ritzdorf, "Locked Out of Paradise: Contemporary Exclusionary Zoning, the Supreme Court, and African Americans, 1970 to the Present," in June M. Thomas and Marsha Ritzdorf, eds. *Urban Planning and the African American Community* (Thousand Oaks: Sage, 1996), 43–57; Kenneth Pearlman, "The Closing Door: The Supreme Court and Residential Segregation," 44 *Journal of the American Institute of Planners* 160–169 (1978); Paul King, "Exclusionary Zoning and Open Housing: A Brief Judicial History," 68 *Geographical Review* 460 (1978).
261. Christopher Silver, "The Racial Origins of Zoning in American Cities," in Thomas and Ritzdorf, eds., *Urban Planning*, 23–42.
262. Lawrence G. Sager, "Tight Little Islands: Exclusionary Zoning, Equal Protection, and the Indigent," 21 *Stanford Law Review* 767 (1969).
263. Lawrence G. Sager, "Questions I Wish I Had Never Asked: The Burger Court and Exclusionary Zoning," 11 *Southwestern University Law Review* 509 (1979).
264. 409 U.S. 205, 208, 212 (1972).
265. Allen v. Wright, 468 U.S. 737 (1984). Article III, section 2 of the Constitution limits "the judicial Power" of the federal courts to "Cases" and "Controversies."
266. Christian B. Sundquist, "The First Principles of Standing: Privilege, System Justification, and the Predictable Incoherence of Article III," 1 *Columbia Journal of Race & Law* 120 (2011).
267. 422 U.S. 490 (1975).
268. Note, "Standing to Challenge Exclusionary Zoning Ordinances," 89 *Harvard Law Review* 189 (1975).
269. 422 U.S. at 523.
270. 422 U.S. 520.
271. 422 U.S. 528.
272. Sundquist, "First Principles of Standing"; Gene R. Nichol, "Standing for Privilege: The Failure of Injury Analysis," 82 *Boston University Law Review* 301, 309–316 (2002).
273. "Calvinball," https://calvinandhobbes.fandom.com/wiki/Calvinball. The second Justice Harlan precociously noticed this capricious characteristic in Flast v. Cohen, 392 U.S. 83, 129 (1967).
274. Warth v. Seldin, 422 U.S. 490 (1975); Allen v. Wright, 468 U.S. 737 (1984).
275. Sundquist, "First Principles of Standing," 134–148.
276. 422 U.S. 508 n. 18.
277. Lawrence G. Sager, "Insular Majorities Unabated: Warth v. Seldin and Eastlake v. Forest City Enterprises Inc.," 91 *Harvard Law Review* 1373 (1978). However, the Court was receptive to standing for "testers," individuals who sought housing in an attempt to sniff out discriminatory practices: Gladstone Realtors v. Bellwood, 441 U.S. 91 (1979) and Havens Realty Corp. v. Coleman, 455 U.S. 363 (1982).
278. 416 U.S. 1, 16–17 (1974).
279. The literature on extended families and fictive kin relationships in families of color is rich, but the Supreme Court has resolutely ignored it. See, e.g., Robert J. Taylor et al., "Racial and Ethnic Differences in Extended Family, Friendship, Fictive Kin, and Congregational Informal Support Networks," 62 *Family Relations* 609–624 (2013); Marsha Ritzdorf, "Family Values, Municipal Zoning, and African American Family Life," in Thomas and Ritzdorf, eds., *Urban Planning*, 75–89; Joyce Aschenbrenner, "Extended Families among Black Americans," 4.2 *Journal of Comparative Family Studies* 266 (1973); Linda M. Chatters et al., "Fictive Kinship Relations in Black Extended Families," 25.3 *Journal of Comparative Family Studies* 297 (1994); Carol Stack, *All Our Kin* (New York: Basic Books, 1974), 58–61.
280. See Kenneth Karst, "The Freedom of Intimate Association," 89 *Yale Law Journal* 624 (1980), a critique of *Belle Terre* supporting Marshall's position.
281. US Commerce Department, *The Diverse Living Arrangements of Children*, Report No. P70-38 (Washington, DC: GPO, 1992), 83.
282. State v. Baker, 81 N.J. 99, 405 A.2d 368, 371 (1979), citing Oakwood at Madison, Inc. v. Township of Madison, 72 N.J. 481, 371 A.2d 1192 [1977]) (1977); McMinn v. Town of Oyster Bay, 66 N.Y.2d 544, 488 N.E.2d 1240 (1985).
283. Stevens, J. concurring in Moore v. East Cleveland, 431 U.S. 494, 517 (1977) (the states were Illinois, New York, New Jersey, California, Connecticut, Wisconsin, Ohio).
284. 431 U.S. 494, 508–509 (1977).
285. A point Justice Stewart made in dissent: 431 U.S. 537 n. 7.

286. Justice Stevens concurred to make a majority for the result, but only on substantive due process property grounds, condemning the ordinance as an interference with an owner's freedom to use and occupy her property as she saw fit. He did not mention the racial implications.
287. Angela Onwuachi-Willig, "Extending the Normativity of the Extended Family: Reflections on Moore v. City of East Cleveland," 85 *Fordham Law Review* 2655 (2017).
288. 466 U.S. 429, 432–433 (1984).
289. Dorothy E. Roberts, "Reconciling Equal Protection Law in the Public and in the Family: The Role of Racial Politics," 62 *University of Pennsylvania Law Review Online* 283 (2014).

Epilogue

1. Students for Fair Admissions v. Harvard, 600 U.S. 181, 230 (2023) (Roberts, C.J.); 232, 234 (Thomas, J. concurring); 320 (Sotomayor, J. dissenting) (drawing on the work of Eric Foner, *The Second Founding: How the Civil War and Reconstruction Remade the Constitution* [New York: Norton, 2019]).
2. *Dennis v. United States*, 339 U.S. 162, 184 (1950) (Frankfurter, J. concurring).
3. *Public Papers of the Presidents of the United States: Lyndon B. Johnson, 1965* (Washington, DC: GPO, 1966), 2:636.
4. Loving v. Virginia, 388 U.S. 1, 7 (1967).
5. But that may be changing. Justice Ketanji Brown Jackson's dissenting opinion (joined by Justices Kagan and Sotomayor) in *Students for Fair Admissions v. Harvard* (600 U.S. 181, 383–412) is based on an extensive review of the many realities of racial inequality in the United States. She did not discuss structural racism in those terms, but her analysis was informed throughout by a deep understanding of how both deliberate and structural racism hold African Americans back in all sectors of American life. That is the first glimmer of hope that the Court might recognize the reality of structural racism.
6. Plessy v. Ferguson, 163 U.S. 537, 559–560 (1896).
7. Thurgood Marshall, "The Constitution's Bicentennial: Commemorating the Wrong Document?," 40 *Vanderbilt Law Review* 1337, 1342 (1987).

Suggested Reading

Judicial doctrine embodies our formal understanding of what the US Constitution means and commands. *The Dark Past* tells the story of how one tranche of that doctrine—the way our public law has treated Americans of African ancestry—has developed through the nation's struggles over race and racism. Law, including the law of the Constitution, does not have some innate and autonomous teleological end or driving principle—not democracy, not liberty, not even the "Republican Form of Government" that the Constitution itself mandates in Article IV. It is driven, rather, by values and public policy that develop outside the law itself. I call these values and policies "metadoctrine" (from the Greek *meta*, "outside" or "beyond"). So, to understand our Constitution, you must look beyond judicial doctrine to these values and policies, to what happened in American society—in other words, to our history. Public law can be understood only against this background of historical context, where law emerges from the struggles of the entire society, sometimes outside conventional legal venues like courts and legislatures.

You will find a thorough narrative of that history in the series Oxford History of the United States. The relevant volumes are Gordon S. Wood, *Empire of Liberty: A History of the Early Republic, 1789–1815* (New York: Oxford University Press, 2009); Daniel Walker Howe, *What Hath God Wrought: The Transformation of America, 1815–1848* (New York: Oxford University Press, 2007); James M. McPherson, *Battle Cry of Freedom: The Civil War Era* (New York: Oxford University Press, 1988); Richard White, *The Republic for Which It Stands: The United States during Reconstruction and the Gilded Age, 1865–1896* (New York: Oxford University Press, 2017); David M. Kennedy, *Freedom from Fear: The American People in Depression and War, 1929–1945* (New York: Oxford University Press, 1999); James T. Patterson, *Great Expectations: The United States, 1945–1974* (New York: Oxford University Press, 1974); and James T. Patterson, *Restless Giant: The United States from Watergate to Bush v. Gore* (New York: Oxford University Press, 2005).

As the subtitle of Patterson's *Restless Giant* suggests, some of that history has been made by the US Supreme Court. To start your exploration of that history, Melvin I. Urofsky and Paul Finkelman provide an excellent textbook overview of our constitutional past in *A March of Liberty: A Constitutional History of the United States* (New York: Oxford University Press, 2011), in two volumes. If you seek a deeper and more extensive analysis of the Court's work, the *Holmes Devise History of the Supreme Court of the United States* offers a multivolume scholarly history of the Court. The relevant volumes are George Lee Haskins and Herbert A. Johnson, *Foundations of Power: John Marshall, 1801–15* (New York: Macmillan, 1981); G. Edward White, *The Marshall Court and Cultural Change, 1815–1835* (New York: Macmillan, 1988); Owen M. Fiss, *Troubled Beginnings of the Modern State, 1888–1910* (New York: Macmillan, 1993); Alexander M. Bickel and Benno C. Schmidt, *The Judiciary and Responsible Government, 1910–1921* (New York: Macmillan, 1984) (pp. 725–990 cover issues affecting African Americans); Robert C. Post, *The Taft Court: Making Law for a Divided Nation, 1921–1930* (Cambridge: Cambridge University Press, 2023); Mark V. Tushnet, *The Hughes Court: From Progressivism to Pluralism, 1930 to 1941* (Cambridge: Cambridge University Press, 2022); and William M. Wiecek, *The Birth of the Modern Constitution: The United States Supreme Court, 1941–1953* (New York: Cambridge University Press, 2006) (pp. 621–706 deal with civil rights issues). Laura Kalman is preparing the volume on the Warren Court, 1953–1969. (Unfortunately, the extant volumes on the Court covering the period before 1800 and between 1835 and 1888 are dated and unsatisfactory. They badly need revising.) You will find in Charles Warren's magisterial study of a century ago, *The Supreme Court in United States History*, rev. ed. (Boston: Little, Brown, 1937), 1:231–814 a stimulating challenge to modern liberal interpretations. His implacable conservatism reminds us that the way we understand the Constitution is deeply traditional.

G. Edward White offers a history of American law in his panoramic trilogy: *Law in American History*, vol. 1: *From the Colonial Years through the Civil War* (New York: Oxford University Press, 2012), vol. 2: *From Reconstruction through the 1920s* (New York: Oxford University Press, 2016), and vol. 3: *1930–2000* (New York: Oxford University Press, 2019). The University Press of Kansas publishes the Landmark Law Cases and American Society series: some eighty relatively brief volumes (~ two hundred pages) meant for classroom use on selected major cases, most decided by the Supreme Court. Books in the series lack notes but contain extensive bibliographies. To date, sixteen of its volumes cover cases discussed in *The Dark Past*, including *Slaughterhouse, Plessy,* and *Brown*. Myriam E. Gilles and Risa L. Goluboff, eds., *Civil Rights Stories* (St. Paul: Foundation, 2008), contains perceptive accounts of some of the cases recounted here, including *Brown v. Board of Education, San Antonio v. Rodriguez, Runyon v. McCrary*, and others.

Because the focus of *The Dark Past* is judicial doctrine, its biographical notices of the individual justices are scant. For such information, you can turn to biographical encyclopedias. These include Leon Friedman and Fred L. Israel, eds., *The Justices of the United States Supreme Court: Their Lives and Major Opinions*, 2nd ed., 5 vols. (New York: Chelsea House, 1997); Melvin I. Urofsky, *The Supreme Court Justices: A Biographical Dictionary* (New York: Garland, 1994); and G. Edward White, *The American Judicial Tradition: Profiles of Leading American Judges*, 3rd ed. (New York: Oxford University Press, 2007) (selective but insightful). Two encyclopedias are devoted to the Court: Leonard W. Levy and Kenneth Karst, eds., *Encyclopedia of the American Constitution*, 2nd ed., 6 vols. (New York: Macmillan, 2000), and Kermit L. Hall et al., eds, *The Oxford Companion to the Supreme Court of the United States*, 2nd ed. (New York: Oxford University Press, 2005).

Finally, three books cover approximately the same subject as *The Dark Past*: Orville V. Burton and Armand Derfner, *Justice Deferred: Race and the Supreme Court* (Cambridge: Harvard University Press, 2021); Donald G. Nieman, *Promises to Keep: African Americans and the Constitutional Order, 1776 to the Present* (New York: Oxford University Press, 1991); and Loren Miller, *The Petitioners: The Story of the Supreme Court of the United States and the Negro* (New York: Pantheon, 1966) (pathbreaking but now dated).

For the era of slavery (ca. 1650 to 1865), you will find valuable studies in Paul Finkelman, *Slavery and the Founders: Race and Liberty in the Age of Jefferson* (New York: Routledge, 1996) (slavery in the early Republic), and Cheryl I. Harris, "'Too Pure an Air': Somerset's Legacy from Anti-slavery to Colorblindness," 13 *Texas Wesleyan Law Review* 439 (2007) (an overview of the impact of *Somerset's Case* on American constitutional law). William M. Wiecek explored abolitionist constitutional thought in *Sources of Antislavery Constitutionalism in America, 1760–1848* (Ithaca: Cornell University Press, 1977). Numerous studies have explored the way that slavery influenced the thinking of judges: Paul Finkelman, *Supreme Injustice: Slavery in the Nation's Highest Court* (Cambridge: Harvard University Press, 2018) (emphasizing John Marshall's shortcomings); Finkelman, *An Imperfect Union: Slavery, Federalism, and Comity* (Chapel Hill: University of North Carolina Press, 1981); Earl M. Maltz, *Slavery and the Supreme Court, 1825–1861* (Lawrence: University Press of Kansas, 2009) (the first book devoted almost entirely to the Taney Court's slavery cases); Harold M. Hyman and William M. Wiecek, *Equal Justice under Law: Constitutional Development, 1835–1875* (New York: Harper & Row, 1982), 1–202 (an earlier overview); Don Fehrenbacher, *The Slaveholding Republic: An Account of the United States Government's Relations to Slavery* (New York: Oxford University Press, 2001); Fehrenbacher, *The Dred Scott Case: Its Significance in American Law and Politics* (New York: Oxford University Press,1978) (as definitive as any single volume is likely to be on that mausoleum of judicial failure); and James Oakes, *The Scorpion's Sting: Antislavery and the Coming of the Civil War* (New York: Norton, 2014).

The first Reconstruction (1862 to 1873) attempted to bury antebellum pro-slavery constitutional theories that sustained slavery and, in their place, establish an egalitarian social order that transcended racism. All work in this area is grounded in W. E. B. Du Bois's pioneering *Black Reconstruction in America: An Essay toward a History of the Part Which Black Folk Played in the Attempt to Reconstruct Democracy in America, 1860–1880* (New York: Harcourt, Brace, 1935). A generation later, historians reclaimed the egalitarian legacy of Reconstruction, led by Harold M. Hyman, *A More Perfect Union: The Impact of the Civil War and Reconstruction on the Constitution* (Boston: Houghton Mifflin, 1973), and pp. 203–515 of Hyman and Wiecek, *Equal Justice under Law*. This rethinking culminated in Eric Foner's monumental *Reconstruction: America's Unfinished Revolution, 1863–1877*, rev. ed. (New York: Harper & Row, 2014) and his more synoptic Foner, *The Second Founding: How the Civil War and Reconstruction Remade the American Constitution* (New York: Norton, 2019). Recent surveys concentrating on the constitutional aspects of Reconstruction include Laura F. Edwards, *A Legal History of the Civil War and Reconstruction: A Nation of Rights* (Cambridge: Cambridge University Press, 2015), and Timothy S. Huebner, *Liberty and Union: The Civil War Era and American Constitutionalism* (Lawrence: University Press of Kansas, 2016).

Constitutional issues affecting African Americans have become the focus of Reconstruction studies, following Du Bois's lead: Alexander Tsesis, *The Thirteenth Amendment and American Freedom: A Legal History* (New York: Columbia University Press, 2004); William E. Nelson, *The Fourteenth Amendment: From Political Principle to Judicial Doctrine* (Cambridge: Harvard University Press, 1988); Jack M. Balkin, "The Reconstruction Power," 85 *NYU Law Review* 1801 (2010); David A. J. Richards, *Conscience and the Constitution: History, Theory, and Law of the Reconstruction Amendments* (Princeton: Princeton University Press, 1993); George Rutherglen, *Civil Rights in the Shadow of Slavery: The Constitution, Common Law, and the Civil Rights Act of 1866* (New York: Oxford University Press, 2013); and Robert J. Kaczorowski, *The Nationalization of Civil Rights: Constitutional Theory and Practice in a Racist Society, 1866–1883* (1971, New York: Garland, 1987). J. Morgan Kousser covers Black disfranchisement comprehensively in *The Shaping of Southern Politics: Suffrage Restriction and the Establishment of the One-Party South, 1880–1910* (New Haven: Yale University Press, 1924) and *Colorblind Injustice: Minority Voting Rights and the Undoing of the Second Reconstruction* (Chapel Hill: University of North Carolina Press, 1999). Works focusing on the Supreme Court include Pamela Brandwein, *Rethinking the Judicial Settlement of Reconstruction* (Cambridge: Cambridge University Press, 2011); Ronald M. Labbe and Jonathan Lurie, *The Slaughterhouse Cases: Regulation, Reconstruction, and the Fourteenth Amendment* (Lawrence: University Press of Kansas, 2003); Robert M. Goldman, *Reconstruction and Black Suffrage: Losing the Vote in Reese and Cruikshank* (Lawrence: University Press of Kansas, 2001); and Charles A. Lofgren, *The Plessy Case: A Legal-Historical Interpretation* (New York: Oxford University Press, 1987).

From the Nadir to *Brown v. Board of Education I* (1954) the Court began to move away from supporting Jim Crow in all its legal and constitutional manifestations to a greater awareness of the injustices inflicted on Black Americans by segregation. Michael J. Klarman, *From Jim Crow to Civil Rights: The Supreme Court and the Struggle for Racial Equality* (New York: Oxford University Press, 2004), 3–289, covers the period in detail. See also Klarman, *Unfinished Business: Racial Equality in American History* (New York: Oxford University Press, 2007) for a synoptic view. John Hart Ely, *Democracy and Distrust: A Theory of Judicial Review* (Cambridge: Harvard University Press, 1980) extols one impact of *Carolene Products'* footnote 4. Ira Katznelson, *When Affirmative Action Was White: An Untold History of Racial Inequality in Twentieth-century America* (New York: Norton, 2005); Ian Haney-Lopez, *White by Law: The Legal Construction of Race*, rev. ed. (New York: New York University Press, 2006); Richard Rothstein, *The Color of Law: A Forgotten History of How Our Government*

Segregated America (New York: Liveright, 2018); and David M. P. Freund, *Colored Property: State Policy and White Racial Politics in Suburban America* (Chicago: University of Chicago Press, 2007), explain the enduring power of white advantage. Dan T. Carter, *Scottsboro: A Tragedy of the American South*, rev. ed. (Baton Rouge: Louisiana State University Press, 1979) revealed the working of southern criminal justice.

Numerous studies discuss the impact of the second Reconstruction: Geoffrey R. Stone and David A. Strauss, *Democracy and Equality: The Enduring Constitutional Vision of the Warren Court* (New York: Oxford University Press, 2020); G. Edward White, *Earl Warren: A Public Life* (New York: Oxford University Press, 1982); Bernard Schwartz, *Superchief: Earl Warren and His Supreme Court: A Judicial Biography* (New York: New York University Press, 1983); Noah Feldman, *Scorpions: The Battles and Triumphs of FDR's Great Supreme Court Justices* (New York: Twelve, 2010); and Charles Zelden, *Thurgood Marshall: Race, Rights, and the Struggle for a More Perfect Union* (London: Routledge, 2013) consider the Warren Court and some of its individual members. *Brown* itself is the subject of Richard Kluger, *Simple Justice: The History of Brown v. Board of Education and Black America's Struggle for Equality* (New York: Knopf, 2004); Klarman, *From Jim Crow to Civil Rights*, 290–468; Alexander M. Bickel, "The Original Understanding and the Segregation Decision," 69 *Harvard Law Review* 1 (1955); Mark Tushnet, *Making Civil Rights Law: Thurgood Marshall and the Supreme Court, 1936–1961* (New York: Oxford University Press, 1994). *Brown*'s aftermath is the subject of J. Harvie Wilkinson, *From Brown to Bakke: The Supreme Court and School Integration, 1954–1978* (New York: Oxford University Press, 1979); James T. Patterson, *Brown v. Board of Education: A Civil Right Milestone and Its Troubled Legacy* (New York: Oxford University Press, 2001); Justin Driver, *The Schoolhouse Gate: Public Education, the Supreme Court, and the Battle for the American Mind* (New York: Vintage, 2018); Erwin Chemerinsky, "The Segregation and Resegregation of American Public Education: The Courts' Role," 81 *North Carolina Law Review* 1597 (2003); and Gary Orfield et al., *Dismantling Desegregation: The Quiet Overruling of Brown v. Board of Education* (New York: New Press, 1996).

The judicial response to structural racism has been intensively analyzed. Owen Fiss, "Groups and the Equal Protection Clause," 5 *Philosophy and Public Affairs* 107–177 (1976), and Alan D. Freeman, "Legitimizing Racial Discrimination through Antidiscrimination Law: A Critical Review of Supreme Court Doctrine," 62 *Minnesota Law Review* 1049 (1978) were the earliest studies. For recent work see Eduardo Bonilla-Silva, "Rethinking Racism: Toward a Structural Interpretation," 62.3 *American Sociological Review* 465–480 (1997); Reva Siegel, "Why Equal Protection No Longer Protects: The Evolving Forms of Status-Enforcing State Action," 49 *Stanford Law Review* 1111 (1997); David A. Strauss, "The Constitution Is Color-Blind: A Critique," 44 *Stanford Law Review* 1 (1991); Reva Siegel, "Discrimination in the Eyes of the Law: How 'Color Blindness' Discourse Disrupts and Rationalizes Social Stratification," 88 *California Law Review* 77 (2000); Reva B. Siegel, "Equality Talk: Antisubordination and Anticlassification Values in Constitutional Struggles over Brown," 117 *Harvard Law Review* 1470 (2004); Jack M. Balkin and Reva B. Siegel, "The American Civil Rights Tradition: Anticlassification or Antisubordination," 58 *University of Miami Law Review* 9 (2004); Richard Primus, "Equal Protection and Disparate Impact: Round Three," 117 *Harvard Law Review* 493 (2003); Primus, "The Future of Disparate Impact," 108 *Michigan Law Review* 1341 (2010); Reva Siegel, "Race-Conscious but Race-Neutral: The Constitutionality of Disparate Impact in the Roberts Court," 66 *Alabama Law Review* 653 (2015).

Index

Since the index has been created to work across multiple formats, indexed terms for which a page range is given (e.g., 52–53, 66–70, etc.) may occasionally appear only on some, but not all of the pages within the range.

Ableman v. Booth 40–1
Abolitionists 4, 19–20, 39, 45–6, 49, 53, 58
Adarand Constructors v. Pena 368–9, 489 n.23, 505 n.66
Adderly v. Florida 237
Adkins v. Childrens Hospital 468 n.60
Affirmative action 343–69
Ah Yup, In re 467 n.24
Alexander v. Holmes County Board of Education 228
Alien Land Laws 150, 185–6
Alito, Samuel 353
Allen v. State Board of Elections 252
Allen v. Wright 337–8, 517 n.265
Allgeyer v. Louisiana 462 n.29
American Antislavery Society 20
American Colonization Society 6
American Legion v. American Humanist Assn. 495 n.164
American Medical Association 266
American Tobacco Co. v. Patterson 384–5
Amistad, The see: *United States v. The Amistad*
Anderson, John C. 163–4
Anderson v. Poindexter 446 n.189
Antelope, The 15
Anthropology 156–7
Anticlassification principle 218–19, 297, 339–40
Antisubordination principle 219–20, 296–7
Arlington Heights v. Metropolitan Housing Corp. 501 n.167, 515 n.229
Armenians 150
Association, right of 234, 271–2
Atwater, Lee 282
Austin Independent School District v. United States 309–10

Badges and incidents of slavery 96, 110–11, 241, 243–4, 415
Bailey v. Alabama 132–5

Baker v. Carr 200–1, 252, 386
Bakke case: *see*: *Regents of the University of California v. Bakke*
Baldwin v. Franks 458 n.53
Barron v. Baltimore 450 n.85
Barrows v. Jackson 196
Bates v. Little Rock 483 n.119, 490 n.58
Bell v. Maryland 483 n.132
Belle Terre v. Boraas 422–3
Berea College v. Commonwealth 462 n.28
Berea College v. Kentucky 126–7
Berman v. Parker 410
Bingham, John A. 53, 56
Birthright citizenship 53
Black Codes 45–6, 50
Black National Anthem xvi, 433
Black, Hugo 167–8, 184–5, 226, 236
Blackmun, Harry 241, 285–6, 346
"Bleeding Kansas" 19–20, 34
Blockbusting 417–18
Blum v. Yaretsky 457 n.33, 486 n.201
Blyew v. United States 80–1
Board of Education of Oklahoma City v. Dowell 313–15
Bob Jones University v. United States 336
Bob-Lo Excursion Co. v. Michigan 204–5
Boerne v. Flores 243
Bohanon, Luther 313–14
Bolling v. Sharpe 218, 475 n.64
Booth, In re 39
Booth and Rycraft, In re 40
Boyce v. Anderson 7–8
Boynton v. Virginia 204, 483 n.112
Bozell, Brent 270–1
Bradley, Joseph 81, 95
Bradley v. School Board 301–2
Bradwell v. Illinois 510 n.85
Brandenburg v. Ohio 237
Breedlove v. Suttles 172
Brennan, William J. 213, 235, 242, 250–1, 320

524 INDEX

Brewer, David J. 105, 125, 132
Brig Wilson 9–10
Briggs v. Elliott 227–8
Brotherhood of Railway Trainmen v. Howard 205
Brown, Henry B. 107–8
Brown v. Board of Education I 210, 216, 273, 295, 306–7, 323–4
Brown v. Board of Education II 220–1, 226–7
Brown v. Louisiana 237
Brown v. Mississippi 166–7
Brown v. New Jersey 469 n.85
Brown v. State 470 nn.100–101
Bryan v. Walton 49–50
Buchanan, Patrick 284, 324–5
Buchanan v. Warley 143–7, 191
Buck v. Bell 119, 123, 467 n.20
Buckley v. Valeo 471 n.126
Bunting v. Oregon 462 n.24
Burger, Warren 229, 231, 285–6
Burns v. State 458 n.60
Burton, Harold 198, 202
Burton v. Wilmington Parking Authority 247, 374
Bush, George H. W. 273–4
Bush v. Vera 396–7
Business necessity 377
Busing 230, 288, 322–30

Calder v. Bull 57–8
California 150, 320–2, 327–30
Campbell, John A. 18, 73–4, 79
Cardona v. Power 485 n.163
Cardozo, Benjamin N. 156, 171
Carolene Products v. United States 177–9
Carswell, G. Harrold 285–6
Carter, Robert 219
Caste 110, 218–19
Castro v. Beecher 509 n.33
Catron, John 24
Chae Chan Ping 466 n.17
Chambers v. Florida 167–8
Chambers v. State 167–8
Chase, Salmon P. 28–9, 31, 69–71
Chicago, Burlington & Quincy Ry. v. Chicago 450 n.88, 468 n.58
Chicago, Milwaukee & St. Paul Ry. v. Minnesota 468 n.60
Chisholm v. Georgia 53
Citizenship 25–6, 35–6, 53, 59–60
Citizenship Clause 98
Civil Rights Act (1866) 50–2, 60, 69, 80–1, 240–3

Civil Rights Act (1875) 95
Civil Rights Act (1964) 227–8, 237–40, 324, 344
Civil Rights Act (1965): *see*: Voting Rights Act
Civil Rights Act (1968) 241–2
Civil Rights Act (1991) 364
Civil Rights Cases xv, 54, 95–9, 239, 246, 373–4, 462 n.20
Clark, Russell 311
Clark, Thomas 207–8, 250–1
Clark v. Community for Creative Non-violence 488 n.6
Clayton Compromise 30–1
Clyatt v. United States 132
Coit v. Green 228, 502 n.172
Colegrove v. Green 200–1
Colfax Massacre 82
Collusive litigation 26, 143–4
Colonization 6, 8, 14
Colorblindness 110, 231, 264–5
Columbus Board of Education v. Penick 288, 305–7
Commerce Clause 21, 103, 239
Common carriers 102
Commonwealth v. Aves 20–1, 41–2
Commonwealth v. Griffith 443 n.141
Compromise of 1850 19, 31
Confiscation Acts 47–8
Constitution, US, as pro-slavery 1–2, 5–6
Contractors Ass'n of Eastern Pennsylvania v. Secretary of Labor 505 n.65
Cooley v. Board of Wardens 476 n.99
Cooper v. Aaron 223–4
Corfield v. Coryell 55–8
Corrigan v. Buckley 192
Counsel, right to 164
Covenants, racial 190–3
Coyle v. Smith 514 n.183
Crawford v. Los Angeles Board of Education 328–30, 492 n.88
Crawford v. Marion County Election Board 399–401
Crises of the union 19–20
Cruikshank v. United States 81–4, 94–5, 113, 140–1
Cumming v. Richmond County Board of Education 117–19
Curtis, Benjamin R. 57
Custom 13, 16, 100
Cuyahoga Falls v. Buckeye Community Hope Foundation 412

Dandridge v. Williams 318, 373
Daniel, Peter V. 18

INDEX   525

Davis v. Bandemer   390, 512 n.136
Davis v. Board of School Commissioners   231
Davis v. Schnell   476 n.81
Davis v. School District of Pontiac   500 n.138
Davis v. Washington   509 n.34
Day, William   123, 144–6
Dayton Board of Education v. Brinkman   305–7, 309–10
De Jonge v. Oregon   175
De jure/de facto distinction   299–300, 303, 320, 326
Declaration of Independence   45
DeFunis v. Odegaard   345
Democracy   17, 36, 39
Dennis v. United States   430–1
Dent, Harry   277–9
Department of Commerce v. New York   456 n.10
DeShaney v. Winnebago County Social Services Dept.   450 n.73, 486 n.202
Dowell v. School Board   313–14
Desegregation   222–9
Discriminatory purpose / disparate impact   377–83
Disfranchisement: *see*: Voting rights
Disparate impact   303
District of Columbia   22, 47–8, 217–18
Diversity   347–55
Dixiecrats   270
Dog-whistle politics   278–80
Dormant commerce clause   203
Douglas, Stephen A.   33
Douglas, William O.   188, 241, 249
Dred Scott v. Sanford   xii, 12, 19–20, 34–40, 403–4
Due process, substantive   35–6, 39, 56, 76–7, 127, 144, 177
Due process, procedural   90, 157–69
Due process clause (Fourteenth Amendment)   57, 76–7
Dunn v. Blumstein   386
Duvall, Gabriel   14

Easley v. Cromartie   397
Eastlake v. Forest City Enterprises   412
Edwards v. South Carolina   236
Ehrlichman, John   283
Elkison v. Deliesseline   8–9
Emancipation Proclamation   48
Enforcement clauses (Reconstruction Amendments)   64–5, 242–5
Equal Protection Clause   58, 77, 91, 145, 375
Equity   220–1, 293–4

Euclid v. Ambler Realty   465 n.111
Eugenics   152
Evans v. Abney   416–17
Evans v. Newton   416
Exclusionary zoning   190, 418–24

Fair Housing Act: *see*: Civil Rights Act (1968)
Fairchild v. Raines   475 n.53
Families   101, 422–5
Faubus, Orval   223
"Federal consensus"   5–6, 20, 28–9
Federal Housing Administration   194, 232
Federalism   20–1, 27, 77–8, 93–4, 158–9, 224, 250, 403
Felon disfranchisement   387–90
Fictive kin   423
Field, Stephen   101
Fifteenth Amendment   63, 84, 389–91, 402
Fifth Amendment   218
Finance, school   316–22
Firefighters v. Stotz   357–8
First Amendment   174–5, 233–7
Fisher v. Hurst   477 n.116
Fisher v. University of Texas   349–50, 352–3, 515 n.206
Fiske v. Kansas   471 n.139
Flagg Bros. v. Brooks   458 n.48, 486 n.200
Flast v. Cohen   513 n.141, 517 n.273
Fletcher v. Peck   516 n.238
Formalism   145, 162
"Four Horsemen"   138–9
Fourteenth Amendment   53–4, 75, 146, 217
   Section 2   61–2, 112–13, 388–9
Framers' intent   217
Franchise *See*: voting rights
Frank v. Mangum   161–2
Frankfurter, Felix   142–3, 164–5, 172–3, 187–8, 207–8, 390–1
"Freedom of choice"   226
Freeman v. Pitts   310
Friday, Herschel   285–6
Fugitive Slave Act (1793)   26–7
Fugitive Slave Act (1850)   28, 31, 41
Fugitive Slave Clause   1–2, 27
Fugitive slaves   25–6
Fuller Court   88
Fuller, Melville Weston   91–2
Fullilove v. Klutznick   356
Fundamental rights   317–22, 371–4, 389

Gaffney v. Cummings   391
Gandolfo v. Hartman   474 n.37
Garner v. Louisiana   483 n.130

Garrity, Arthur 326
Gaston County v. United States 254
Gayle v. Browder 483 n.111
General Building Contractors Association v. Pennsylvania 385
Gerrymandering 390
  Racial gerrymandering 390–7
Gibbons v. Ogden 103, 239
Gideon v. Wainwright 164, 469 n.84
Giles v. Harris 122, 470 n.108
Giles v. Teasley 123, 465 n.113
Gitlow v. New York 174
Gladstone Realtors v. Bellwood 517 n.277
Glass, Carter 115, 141
Goldwater, Barry 270–3
Gomillion v. Lightfoot 390–1, 414
Gong Lum v. Rice 156
Gonzalez v. Raich 495 n.163
Grandfather clause 140–1
Gratz v. Bollinger 349–50
"Green Book" 239
Green v. Connally 228, 334
Green v. New Kent County School Board 226, 492 n.96
Green v. State 458 n.61
Grier, Robert 18
Griffin v. Breckinridge 99, 244
Griffin v. County School Board of Prince Edward County 225–6, 414
Griggs v. Duke Power Co. 376–8
Griswold v. Connecticut 234
Groves v. Slaughter 23
Grovey v. Townsend 171–2
Grutter v. Bollinger 294, 349–50, 488 n.3
Guarantee Clause 57–8, 71
Guest v. United States 250–1
Guinn v. United States 141–3, 172–3

Hadacheck v. Sebastian 465 n.110
Hague v. CIO 455 n.170
Haldeman, H. R. 282
Hall v. DeCuir 104, 203
Halladjian, In re 466 n.5
Hamdan v. Rumsfeld 495 n.165
Hamdi v. Rumsfeld 495 n.165
Hamilton, Mary 232
Hamilton, Ex parte 483 n.116
Hamilton v. Alabama 483 n.117
Hamm v. Rock Hill 237
Harlan, John Marshall I 54, 97–8, 105, 109–12, 117–19, 125–6, 128, 264–5
Harlan, John Marshall II 212–13, 242–3, 255
Harmon v. Tyler 465 n.116, 474 n.37

Harper v. Virginia State Board of Elections 254, 371–2, 386, 388, 399, 470 n.118
Harris v. Louisville 465 n.101
Havens Realty Corp. v. Coleman 517 n.277
Hawaii Housing Authority v. Midkiff 515 n.218
Haynsworth, Clement 285–6
Hazelwood School District v. United States 355–6
Heart of Atlanta Motel v. United States 239, 455 n.168, 508 n.26
Hepburn v. Griswold 452 n.119
Henderson v. United States 202
Herndon v. Georgia 471 n.135
Herndon v. Lowry 174–5, 235
Hicks v. State 469 n.74
Higher education 205–9, 344–55
Highways: *see*: Urban renewal
Hill, Anita 292–3
Hills v. Gautreaux 304–5
Hobbs v. Fogg 20–1
Hodges v. United States 124–6, 484 n.149
Holmes. Oliver Wendell, Jr. 122–3, 135–6, 162, 170
Holmes v. Atlanta 483 n.108
Home Owners Loan Corporation 193–4
Hopwood v. Texas 348–9, 351–2
Housing: *see*: Residential segregation
Hudson v. McMillian 495 n.166
Hughes, Charles Evans 133, 137–9, 167, 176
Hughes v. Superior Court 503 n.7
Humphrey, Hubert 227–8, 280, 324
Hunt, Ward 84–5
Hunt v. Cromartie 513 n.151
Hunt v. Shaw 396–7
Hunter v. Erickson 249, 354, 411, 501 n.158
Hurd v. Hodge 196
Hurtado v. California 160–1, 164–5, 469 n.85

Incorporation 56–8, 158–9
Initiative and referendum 249, 322–30, 410–13
Innkeepers 88, 97–8
Intent 264, 303
Intent/impact distinction 305–6, 375–85
International Brotherhood of Teamsters v. United States 384–5
Intersectionality 269
Interstate Commerce Act (1887) 201–2

Jack v. Martin 16–17
Jackson, Robert H. 136, 185, 199–200, 207–8
Jackson v. Metropolitan Edison Co. 458 n.48, 486 n.199
Jackson v. Pasadena School District 327–8
James v. Bowman 123–4

James v. Valtierra 411–12
Japanese persons 153
Jeune Eugenie, La 13, 57–8
Johnson, Andrew 343
Johnson, Frank M. 229
Johnson, Lyndon B. 238, 273, 344
  Howard Univ. commencement
    address 238, 430–1
Johnson, William 8–10, 15
Johnson v. M'Intosh 149, 489 n.39
Johnson v. Railway Express Agency 502 n.174
Johnson v. Santa Clara County Transportation Agency 357
Johnson v. Virginia 233, 483 nn.109, 114
Johnson v. Zerbst 469 n.84
Jones v. Alfred H. Mayer Co. 240–4, 334–5, 462 nn.14, 22
Jones v. DeSantis 512 n.118
Jones v. Van Zandt 28–9
Judicial supremacy 223–4
Juries 90, 166
Justiciability 390

Kaiser Aetna v. United States 483 n.127
Kansas-Nebraska Act 19–20, 25, 33–4
Katzenbach v. McClung 239–40, 508 n.26
Katzenbach v. Morgan 242
Kaufman, Irving 326
Keith, Damon 326
Kelo v. New London 410
Kennedy, Anthony 213, 344, 365
Keyes v. School District No.1 288, 299–301
Kidnapping 25–7
Koehler v. Rowland 474 n.42
Korematsu v. United States 183–5
Kramer v. Union Free School District 386
Ku Klux Klan 160, 250–1
Ku Klux Klan Act 99, 244

Labor coercion 130
Labor unions 205
Lane v. Wilson 142–3, 172–3
Lassiter v. Northampton County Election Board 487 n.222
Legacy admissions 351
Legal Tender Cases 452 n.120
Legislative intent 396, 414
Lemmon v. The People ex rel. Napoleon 42–3
Lemmon v. The People 42–3
Licensing 373–4
"Lift Every Voice and Sing": see: Black National Anthem
Lillie, Mildred 285–6

Lincoln, Abraham 42, 47
Lindsey v. Normet 318, 373
Linmark Associates v. Willingboro 418
Litigation as a right 234–5
Little Rock crisis 223
Local control 296, 300, 303, 319, 331–2, 422
Local 28 of Sheetmetal Workers v. EEOC 505 n.67
Local 93, I.A.F.F. v. Cleveland 505 n.68
Lochner v. New York 126, 462 n.29, 468 n.60
Lodge Force Bill 114
Logan, Rayford 87
Lord v. Veazie 443 n.143, 465 n.100
Louisiana ex rel. Gremillion v. NAACP 235
Louisville, Ky. 143–4, 339
Louisville, New Orleans and Texas Railway Co. v. Mississippi 105, 203
Loving v. Virginia 101, 256–7
Lubin v. Panish 511 n.110
Lugar v. Edmondson Oil Co. 457 n.33
Lujan v. Defenders of Wildlife 340
Lumpkin, Joseph 49–50
Lusky, Louis 178

Maine 381
Malapportionment 252
Mansfield, Baron (William Murray) 1
Marbury v. Madison 55–6, 58–9, 223–4, 243
Marriage 101, 254–8, 371
Marsh v. Alabama 113, 374
Marshall, John 2–3, 7–10, 58–9
Marshall, Thurgood 176, 207, 214–16, 304, 314–15, 346, 433
Martin v. Hunter's Lessee 40, 224
Martin v. Texas 91
Martin v. Wilks 362–3
Massive Resistance 222
Mayor of Baltimore v. Dawson 483 n.107
Mayor of New York v. Miln 3
McCabe v. Atchison, Topeka, & Santa Fe Ry. 137–9, 201–2
McCleskey v. Kemp 268, 384, 508 n.24
McConnell v. FEC 471 n.126
McCulloch v. Maryland 9–10, 55–6, 88–9, 242, 402, 486 n.203
McDonald v. Chicago 454 n.155, 455 nn.172, 190
McDonald v. Santa Fe Trail Transp. Co. 48–9
McDonnell Douglas v. Green 361–2, 508 n.29
McGhee v. Sipes 197
McKenna, Joseph 116
McLaughlin v. Florida 102, 255–6
McLaurin v. Oklahoma State Regents 208–9

McLean, John 10, 13–14
McMinn v. Oyster Bay 517 n.282
McNabb v. United States 468 n.59
McReynolds, James 138–9
Med's Case see: Commonwealth v. Aves
Memphis v. Greene 415–16, 509 n.53
Mendez v. Westminster School District 327
Metro Broadcasting Co, v. FCC 368
Meyer v. Nebraska 463 n.34, 485 n.171
Miller, Samuel Freeman 72, 76–8
Miller v. Johnson 396
Milliken v. Bradley I 301–5, 494 n.130
Milliken v. Bradley II 304
Mima Queen v. Hepburn 14
Minor v. Happersett 456 n.192, 510 n.85
Miscegenation 100, 258
Mississippi Plan 114–15
Missouri crises 19, 22
Missouri Compromises 25, 33–6, 38–9
Missouri ex rel. Gaines v. Canada 176, 205, 464 n.77
Missouri v. Jenkins I 311
Missouri v. Jenkins II 311–13, 335, 408–9, 474 n.33, 479 n.39, 495 nn.167–169, 496 n.13, 497 n.50, 506 n.88
Missouri Pacific Ry. v. Nebraska 450 n.88, 468 n.57
Missouri v. Jenkins 311–13, 408–9
Mitchell v. United States 201–2
Mobile v. Bolden 392, 509 n.54
Monroe v. Pape 251
Moody, William 80
Moore v. Dempsey 161–3
Moore v. East Cleveland 213, 423–4
Moose Lodge v. Irvis 373–4, 458 n.48, 486 n.198
Morgan v. Hennigan 500 n.140
Morgan v. Virginia 204
Morrison v. California 467 n.40
Motz, Diana Gribbin 405
Mulkey v. Reitman 486 n.191
Muller v. Oregon 462 n.24
Murphy, Frank 185–6
Murray v. Louisiana 457 n.23
Murray v. Pearson 214, 471 n.147
Murray's Lessee v. Hoboken Land & Improvement Co. 450 n.82
Myrdal, Gunnar 205, 217–18, 263–4
Myers v. Anderson 464 n.92

NAACP v. Alabama ex rel. Patterson 234, 490 n.58, 501 n.170
NAACP ex rel. Alabama v. Flowers 235

NAACP v. Button 234–5
NAACP v. Claiborne Hardware Co. 237, 490 n.58
Nadir, the xv, 87, 121–8
Naim v. Naim 102, 255
Najour, In re 152–3
Natural law 13, 23–4, 27
Neal v. Delaware 92–3, 469 n.96
Near v. Minnesota 471 n.139
"Necessary evil" thesis 3
Negro Seamen' Acts 8–9, 17, 22
Neutrality, in sociology 265–6
"New Judicial Federalism" 320
New Negro Alliance v. Sanitary Grocery Co. 175, 343
New Orleans City Park Improvement Assn. v. Detiege 483 n.113, 516 n.247
New York Times v. Sullivan 235
Newberry v. United States 170–1, 471 n.126
Nixon, Richard M. 271–86, 324–5
Nixon Court 275–6, 284–94
Nixon v. Condon 171
Nixon v. Herndon 170
NLRB v. Jones & Laughlin Steel Corp. 484 n.145
Nordlinger v. Hahn 499 n.118
Norris v. Alabama 165–6
Norris v. State 469 n.94
North Carolina State Board of Education v. Swann 231
North Carolina State Conference of NAACP v. McCrory 514 n.191
Northwest Austin Municipal Utility District v. Holder 402–3
Northwest Ordinance 1, 4, 19, 30
Norwood v. Harrison 231, 410–11, 482 n.90, 486 n.190, 502 n.175
Nuisance 145–6
Nullification crisis 19

Oakwood v. Madison 517 n.282
O'Connor, Sandra Day 337, 366
Opinion of the Justices 446 n.189
Oregon v. Mitchell 253–4
Originalism 36
Oyama v. California 185–6, 478 n.6
Ozawa v. United States 153

Pace v. Alabama 101, 255
Pace and Cox v. State 458 n.63
Palmer v. Thompson 379, 412–14
Palmore v. Sidoti 257–8, 424–5
Papachristou v. Jacksonville 448 n.38

INDEX 529

Parents Involved in Community Schools v. Seattle School District 264–5, 338–42, 515 n.205
Parker, John J. 211
Pasadena City Board of Education v. Spangler 307–9, 482 n.101
Patterson v. Alabama 469 n.97
Patterson v. McLean Credit Union 245, 363–5
Patterson v. State 469 n.82
Pennsylvania Coal Co. v. Mahon 465 n.108
Peonage 129–34
Perez v. Sharp 487 n.244
Perlman, Philip 202
Personal Liberty Laws 25–8
Personnel Administrator v. Feeney 383
Petersburg v. United States 511 n.96
Peterson v. Greenville 236
Philadelphia Plan 284, 356
Phillips, Kevin 281–2, 284
Phillips, Ulrich B. 87
Phillips, Wendell 2
Pierce v. Society of Sisters 244, 463 n.34, n.171
Pitney, Mahlon 162, 296–7
Plessy v. Ferguson 108–12, 262–3, 296, 518 n.6
Plyler v. Doe 322
Poe v. Ullman 255
Police power 74, 108
Pollock v. Williams 136
Popular sovereignty 30–1, 33–4, 36
"Positive good" thesis 3
Positive law 11–14
Posner, Richard 401
Powell, Lewis 230, 284–8, 300, 306–7, 309–10, 318–19, 346–8, 359–61
Powell v. Alabama 164–5
Powell v. State 469 n.82
Preclearance provision 392, 405–6
Pretense and pretext 88–90, 93, 164
Prigg v. Pennsylvania 17, 26–8, 31–2
Privileges and Immunities Clause (Art. IV) 20, 47
Privileges or Immunities Clause (Fourteenth Amendment) 56, 75–6, 83
Progressives 129–30, 141
Proportional representation 391
Public contracts 366–9
Public facilities 232, 413
Public function doctrine 110–11, 199–200, 247
Public housing 232, 304–5
Public-private distinction 247
Punishment Clause 45
Purpose-effect distinction 231, 300

Race 4–5, 107–8, 148–57, 268
 Racialization 266
 Racism 5–6, 37–8, 108, 185, 263
  Scientific racism 150–1, 154
  Social construction of race 266–7
  See also: Structural racism
Railroads 103–6
Railroad Co. v. Brown 103–4
Ramirez v. Brown 512 n.111
Randolph, John 22
Ratliffe v. Beale 115
Raysor v. DeSantis 512 n.119
Reapportionment 200–1
Reattachment principle 32
Recaption 25–7
Reception of English law 440 n.73
Reconstruction (first) xii, xiv–xv
Reconstruction (second) xv
Redemption (first) xii–xiii, xv, 80, 87–120
Redemption (second) xiii–xvi
Redistricting 200–1
Regents of the University of California v. Bakke 288, 345–8
Rehnquist, William H. 200, 244–5, 271–3, 284–6, 289–92, 300–1, 307, 373–4
Reitman v. Mulkey 248, 374, 410–11
Remedies, law of 220–1, 312
Republican Party 35–6
Residential segregation 143–7, 189–98, 240, 296, 309–11, 373, 406–25
Restatement of Property 192
Reynolds v. Sims 252, 385–6
Ricci v. DeStefano 364–5
Rice v. Gong Lum 467 n.42
Richardson v. Ramirez 388–9, 451 n.108
Richmond v. Deans 465 n.116, 474 n.37
Richmond v. J. A. Croson 214, 366–7, 506 n.86
Roberts, John 339–40
Roberts, Owen 174–5
Roberts v. City of Boston 108, 467 n.43
Rodriguez v. San Antonio Independent School District 317–18
Romer v. Evans 354
Romney, George 284
Roosevelt, Franklin D 344
Roosevelt Court 180–2
Rucho v. Common Cause 390
Runyon v. McCrary 214, 244, 334–5, 506 n.101
Russell, Charles 129–31
Rutledge, Wiley 188–9

530 INDEX

Saint Francis College v. Al-Khazraji 468 n.48
San Antonio Independent School District v. Rodriguez 318–20
Santa Barbara v. Superior Court 500 n.148
Scalia, Antonin 43–4, 196, 268, 349–50, 364–5, 369
Schnell v. Davis 199
School Board v. State Board of Education 496 n.28
Schuette v. Coalition to Defend Affirmative Action 353
Scott v. Emerson 34–5
Scottsboro Boys Cases 163–5
Screws v. United States 186–9
Secession (school districts) 331–3
Secession (states) 20
Second Amendment 79
Segregation academies 225–6, 228, 333–8
Sei Fujii v. State 473 n.21
Seniority systems 384–5
Separate-but-equal 103–4
Separation of powers 224–5, 250
Serrano v. Priest 320
"Servitude" 67–8
Shaare Tefila Congregation v. Cobb 468 n.48
Shapiro v. Thompson 317, 372
Shaw, Lemuel 20–1, 41–2, 108
Shaw v. Reno 394–6, 512 n.131
Shelby County v. Holder xv–xvi, 398–9, 403–6
Shelley v. Kraemer 194–8, 235–6, 247, 374, 417
Siebold, Ex parte 99–100
Sipuel v. Oklahoma Board of Regents 206–7
Sit-in Cases 235–7
Skinner v. Oklahoma 371
Slaughterhouse Cases xiv–xv, 72–80, 94–5, 463 n.47
Slave Grace, The 32
Slave Power, the 28
Slave trade, international 3–4, 12–13, 15–16
Slave trade, interstate 3–4, 20–3
Slave trade clause 1–2, 21
Slavecatchers 25, 28
"Slaveholders' constitution" xiv, 29–44
Slum clearance: *see*: Urban renewal
Smith v. Allwright 199, 247, 460 n.113, 508 n.16
Smith v. Mississippi 457 n.23
Smith v. Texas 166
"Societal discrimination" 347, 359
Sojourners, enslaved 20–2
Somerset v. Stewart 10–11, 15, 21, 23–4, 27–9, 31–2, 34

Sotomayor, Sonia 354
South Carolina v. Katzenbach 253, 386, 402
South v. Peters 201
Southern Manifesto 222
Southern Strategy 275–7
Speech, freedom of 175
Spies, Ex parte 469 n.85
Standing 337, 340, 350–1, 395, 420–2
State action 55, 70, 83, 94–100, 195, 197, 235–6, 246–51, 373–4
State constitutions 320
State equality principle 33, 403
State v. Baker 517 n.282
State v. Crandall 20
State v. Mann 6
State v. Post 20–1
Steele v. Louisville & Nashville Rr. 205
Stevens, John Paul 399–401
Stewart, Potter 241, 244, 256
Stone, Harlan Fiske 173, 178, 205
Story, Joseph 10, 12–14, 16, 23–4, 26–8
Stout v. Jefferson County Board of Education 333
Strader v. Graham 31–3
Strauder v. New York 90, 93
Strict scrutiny 183–5
Stromberg v. New York 471 n.139
Strong, William 80–1, 90, 92–3
Structural racism 260–70, 296
Students for Fair Admissions v. Harvard 354–5, 518 nn.1, 5
Sullivan v. Little Hunting Park 484 n.159
Sundown towns 191
Suspect classification 317, 371
Sutherland, George 153, 164
Swann v. Charlotte-Mecklenburg Board of Education 229, 288
Swayne, Noah 69
Sweatt v. Painter 207–8

Takahashi v. Fish and Game Commission 185–6
Taney, Roger B. xii, 17, 24, 31–44
Taxation 269–70, 311–12, 316–17, 336
Taylor v. Board of Education…New Rochelle 500 n.137
Taylor v. Georgia 136
Taylor v. Louisiana 483 n.131
Teamsters v. United States 355–6
Territories, slavery in 19, 24, 29–30, 39, 47–8
Terrorism, white 81–4, 140, 160, 191, 322–3
Terry v. Adams 199–200, 291

Texas 29–30, 45, 170–2, 348–9
Texas Department of Housing and Community Affairs v. Inclusive Communities Project 365, 509 n.47
Texas v. Hopwood 504 n.28
Texas v. White 71
Thayer, Martin 51
Thirteenth Amendment 48–50, 69–70, 74, 96, 107–8, 125, 133–4, 195, 240–2
Thomas, Clarence 83–4, 259, 264–5, 292–4, 313, 340–1, 349–50
Thomas v. Texas 457 n.24
Thompson, Smith 10, 23
Thornburg v. Gingles 392–3, 511 n.95
Three-fifths Clause 1–2, 61
Thurmond, Strom 270, 273–4, 278–9
Times, Places and Manner Clause 173, 199
Title Guarantee & Trust. Co. v. Garrott 474 n.37
Trafficante v. Metropolitan Life Insurance 419–20
Transportation, interstate 201–5
Traynor, Roger 194, 255–6
Trimble v. Gordon 508 n.20
Trumbull, Lyman 51
Trump v. Hawaii 184
Trust law 416
Turner, In re 69–70
Twining v. New Jersey 159–61

United Jewish Organizations v. Carey 393
United States v. Amistad 23
United States v. Carolene Products xv, 177–9, 198, 252, 354
United States v. Classic 173, 199
United States v. Cruikshank 81–4, 457 n.34, 464 n.85
United States v. Darby 484 n.145
United States v. Guest 78, 250–1
United States v. Hall 70, 458 n.51
United States v. Harris 99
United States v. Lopez 495 n.163
United States v. Mitchell 201–2
United States v. Montgomery County Board of Education 482 n.94
United States v. Morris 462 n.18
United States v. Morrison 458 n.48, 495 n.163
United States v. Mosley 142
United States v. O'Brien 516 n.238
United States v. Paradise 505 n.69
United States v. Price 250–1
United States v. Raines 456 n.194
United States v. Reese 81–5, 113, 140–1, 511 n.107
United States v. Reynolds 135
United States v. Rhodes 69
United States v. Scotland Neck Board of Education 331–2
United States v. Texas Education Agency 309
United States v. Thind 154–6
United Steelworkers v. Weber 356
Urban renewal 409–10

Valtierra v. Housing Authority 515 n.223
Vardaman, James 114–15
Veterans Administration 193–4
Vinson, Fred 194–8, 208–9, 216–17
Violence: *see*: Terrorism, white
Virginia, Ex parte 64, 92
Virginia v. Rives 92–3, 95
Voter ID requirements 398–9
Voter suppression 398–402
Voting rights 61–2, 82–5, 112–17, 121–4, 139–43, 169–73, 198–201, 252–4, 371–2, 385–406
Voting Rights Act 253, 391–2, 396

Waite, Morrison 82–3, 104, 388
Wallace, George 274, 280
Ward v. Rock Against Racism 473 n.17
Wards Cove Packing Co. v. Atonio 362, 364
Warren Court 232
Warren, Earl 212–13, 217–18
Warth v. Seldin 420–2
Washington, Bushrod 55–8
Washington v. Davis xv–xvi, 83, 214, 265–6, 305–6, 377–83
Washington v. Seattle School District 330
Wayne, James Moore 24
Weeks v. United States 159
Weems v. State 469 n.82
Wesberry v. Sanders 511 n.108
White, Byron 157, 214, 244–5, 378–83
White, Edward Douglass 141
White flight 230, 307–8
White innocence 347, 360
White normativity 267
White privilege 267
White supremacy 101, 109–10, 199, 257
White v. Regester 511 n.95
Whitecapping 124
Whren v. United States 89

Wickard v. Filburn 484 n.145
Wickersham Commission 160
Wigmore, John Henry 153–4
Wilkinson, J. Harvie 297–8
Williams v. Mississippi 116, 470 n.108
Willson v. Black Bird Creek Marsh Co. 103, 476 n.98
Wilmot Proviso 19, 30
Wisdom, John Minor 309
Woodbury, Levi 29

Woods, William B. 70, 99
Wright v. Deacon 16–17
Wright v. Emporia 331–2
Wygant v. Jackson Board of Education 358–61
Wysinger v. Crookshank 500 n.143

Yarbrough, Ex parte 99–100
Yick Wo v. Hopkins 117

Zoning 145–6, 419